Letters
of the
Century

America
1900–1999

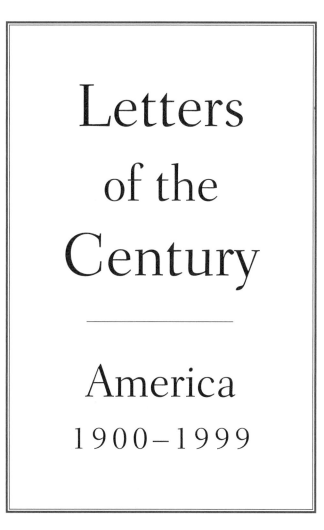

Letters
of the
Century

America

1900–1999

EDITED BY

Lisa Grunwald & Stephen J. Adler

THE DIAL PRESS

Published by
The Dial Press
Random House, Inc.
1540 Broadway
New York, New York 10036

Sources and permissions are located on page 677 and
constitute an extension of the copyright page.

Library of Congress Cataloging in Publication Data
Letters of the century : America 1900–1999 / edited by Lisa Grunwald and Stephen J. Adler.
p.   cm.
ISBN 0-385-31590-2
1. United States—Civilization—20th century Sources.   2. United States Biography.
3. American letters.   I. Grunwald, Lisa.   II. Adler, Stephen J.
E740.5.L48   1999
973.9—dc21   99-16808
CIP

Book design by Brian Mulligan
Photo editor: Vincent Virga

Manufactured in the United States of America
Published simultaneously in Canada

October 1999

10   9   8   7

For Elizabeth and Jonathan

Letters
of the
Century

America
1900–1999

Introduction

In 1955, the day after Jonas Salk announced that he had found a vaccine for polio, an expectant mother in Nyack, New York, sat down to write him a letter. The gratitude she expressed in this letter still mingles, on its pages, with a note of relief and longing, and an echo of recent pain.

The difference between knowing that Americans were grateful to Jonas Salk and reading this letter to him is like the difference between knowing the words of a song and hearing it sung. Letters give history a voice.

This book celebrates that voice, as it has changed and deepened, whispered and shouted, wept and teased, laughed and pleaded, throughout the letters written during the last hundred years in America. Yet this is not a book about letters. It is a book about the twentieth century, as told in letters. The 412 letters printed in this volume are arranged chronologically—with the hope that as you read them, you will feel as if you are hearing successive verses in a national ballad.

Throughout the last hundred years—beginning, in fact, with the very first letter in this book—observers have lamented the fact that people don't write letters anymore. Yet letters have described most of the century's major events, have reflected or reflected upon most of its social and cultural trends, have captured most of its political passions, and have been written by most of its principal figures. We may think we've heard the whole story, but that story resonates more deeply when we read the century's letters.

Part of the reason for that resonance is the immediacy of letters. Letters are what history sounds like when it is still part of everyday life. While aftershocks from the San Francisco earthquake continue, a man who owns a clothing store recounts the terror of watching it burn. A teacher who doesn't yet know how many friends of hers have been killed describes being forced to leave her home during the St. Louis race riots of 1919. A nurse living in Honolulu tells her brother in Ohio how the smoke looks over Pearl Harbor just a few hours after the bombing. Immediate and evocative, letters witness and fasten history, catching events as they happen. Sometimes letters even shape those events: the order to drop the bomb on Hiroshima; the Lindbergh baby ransom note; Nixon's letter of resignation.

History resonates, too, because of the intimacy of letters. Lord Byron wrote: "Letter writing is the only device for combining solitude and good company," and the safety of that combination seems to inspire the courage to be honest. Dreams are confided in letters—both the nightmares and the hopes. Love is confided in letters—without fear of hearing laughter. Sex and jealousy, money and drugs: all of these are subjects that the intimacy of letters allows. A young man dying of AIDS describes to his parents how he wants to be buried. A woman tells her mother about having an abortion. An illegal immigrant reveals for his family the details of his journey across the border.

A lot of the joy of reading letters comes from hearing the ring of unaffected truth. People describe things in letters, in passing, that they take for granted but we need not. The pack of wolves passing the schoolhouse near the shack of a lone woman homesteader. The code words for ordering liquor during the dry days of Prohibition. The overcrowded schedule of a doctor's loyal secretary during the 1950s. The Kennedy calendars adorning the walls of ramshackle houses in Mississippi during the summer of 1964. These are the little details that refresh even the most familiar events.

The same thing happens with the most familiar people. When Charlie Chaplin was offered his first film contract and sat down to write an ecstatic letter to his brother, he could not have known that that letter would survive him: as a consequence, we get to hear all his youthful, unsophisticated enthusiasm— misspellings and all. When Janis Joplin went to San Francisco to try out for Big Brother and the Holding Company, she wrote home to her parents in a tone of girl-down-the-block contrition that completely defies her Woodstock image. Rock Hudson and Bill Gates, Frank Lloyd Wright and Lady Bird Johnson, Elvis Presley and Groucho Marx: in their letters in this volume, they all reveal unexpected sides of themselves. Henry James burned most of the letters he received precisely because he feared for the privacy of the letter writers. E. B. White once lamented: "A man who publishes his letters becomes a nudist—nothing shields him from the world's gaze except his bare skin." But fortunately, he wrote that lament in a letter, and the letter was saved.

There was a surprising familiarity in the voices of these letters, despite all the dizzying changes of the twentieth century. A fledgling journalist writing home from New York City in 1916 to explain her antiwar protests could be any young woman of any decade reveling in her independence. Likewise, the slightly self-pitying college musings of Carl Van Doren may have been written in 1909, but in spirit they are no different from any number of soul-searching letters, and they are a touching reminder that even great men have to search for their beginnings. War letters, apart from references to specific battles, are remarkably similar in tone. So are letters of bigotry, and letters of love. Through all the advances and setbacks, people, it turns out, didn't change all that much. We kept finding men and women we thought we knew—including ourselves—in the letters we read. The thrill of voyeurism mingled with the wonder of recognition. We hope you will feel this too.

Because this is not a book about letters, you will not find a lot of speculation about how letter writing has changed over the century. Obviously, there's less of it now, at least of an intimate sort. (The post office reports that, while the volume of letters has increased, less than 2 percent of it is now personal mail.) Obviously, too, e-mail has taken over, with its oft-lamented knack for scattering ideas, observations, and potential memories to the wind. And it's true that e-mail lacks a lot, at least in romance. Reading a typewritten John Reed letter at Columbia University, you can see that he pounded the period key so hard that every sentence ends with a tiny hole. You can sense the force of his feelings in a way that e-mail may never allow. (You can also see that this champion of the masses used dollar signs to cross out his mistakes.) But if e-mail is a threat to real letters, it is nonetheless reviving certain skills of communicating that became rusty with the telephone, and it is giving anyone open-minded enough to try it the joy of putting thoughts into words that they can see. (There are also more similarities than one might suspect between mail and e-mail. At the turn of the century, hundreds of books were written on the etiquette of correspondence, and in tone and content they are remarkably similar to the Internet's "netiquette" tips today.)

We come to the question of e-mail with a special bias. This book could not have been completed without the Internet, or at least not completed on time. From virtual exhibitions (such as those on the invaluable Library of Congress site) to on-line library catalogs to e-mail exchanges with experts in various fields, we found the Web an indispensable—and ever-growing—resource. In the last months of our research, we found some wonderful documents on the Web that had simply not been there when this project began.

The research for this book took nearly four years and provided us with the joy of a scavenger hunt and the edification of a college course. It gave us something to look for in flea markets, at bookstores, and on our friends' bookshelves, and, incidentally, a topic of conversation to last a lifetime. Our rough estimate is that we read about a half a million letters to choose the 412 that are here. It's an estimate that reflects letters found on the Web, in anthologies, biographies, the Library of Congress, the National Archives and Records Administration, presidential libraries, historical societies, company archives, university archives, numerous other archives and manuscript collections, friends' attics, and, in one case, our dentist's mother's house.

Our rules for what we would and would not include evolved. Early on, we decided that memos and telegrams would count as correspondence, but that we should resist the temptation to consider press releases, presidential statements, court opinions, advertisements, or affidavits. A few times, we allowed ourselves to print a letter that was never intended as a private communication but used the form as a conceit. The most famous example of this is Martin Luther King, Jr.'s "Letter from Birmingham Jail," which we felt was too important to exclude. Similarly, James Baldwin's letter to his nephew in *The Fire Next Time* is probably one of the most beautifully written letters in this volume. Though it is more an essay than a letter, you will find it here nonetheless.

We rejected some letters when they turned out to be entirely fictional, parts of epistolary novels that were not labeled as such. We lost other letters when we found out that they were apocryphal. Cary Grant, for example, was once supposed to have received a cable from a magazine fact-checker asking "HOW OLD CARY GRANT?" and to have answered it "OLD CARY GRANT FINE." To our lasting regret we discovered that Grant claimed the story had been made up. According to another, apparently fanciful, tale, some friends of Mark Twain, not knowing where he was, sent out a birthday card addressed "Mark Twain, God knows where." Some weeks later, they supposedly received a note from Twain that said only "He did."

Other letters failed to make the cut because they were written in one period to describe another—for instance, a friend's aunt in 1985 describing Armistice Day: the letter was wonderful, but we had to respect the chronology. Still other letters aren't here because, while fascinating, they were too idiosyncratic. History turns out to be incredibly contradictory when told by one person at a time, and one of our guidelines quickly became not to be *overly* unconventional in the choices we made. We found women with modern morals at the turn of the century; we found immigrants defeated, rather than liberated, by America; we found Edith Wharton—so brilliant in dissecting the relationships of her fictional characters—almost incapacitated when it came to assessing her own. In some cases, we printed the letter that contradicted the assumptions we'd brought to the project. In most, however, we stuck with more comfortable choices. It seemed more important, for example, to have a letter acknowledging Henry Adams for his contribution to American literature than for his undeniable and uniquely pompous anti-Semitism.

If a letter was beautifully written and historically important, it was in. If it was one or the other, it was considered. If it was neither, it was out. With that rule, and with space for only hundreds of letters, this book will no doubt lead readers to note some regrettable omissions. Where, for example, are letters reflecting the 1939 World's Fair, the first moon landing, the 1968 Olympics? We tried in vain to find the right ones. Where were letters about listening to Sinatra? Watching Ali fight? Taking the Pill? And were the people at Woodstock just too stoned to write letters? Perhaps readers will help us fill the gaps in future editions. There are people missing, too. Walter Cronkite, the beacon of the television age, wrote us with characteristic courtesy: "With a regret so deep as to be unfathomable, I am a product of the telecommunications age and my cupboard of correspondence is bare." Apple cofounder Steve Wozniak, by e-mail, promised to look for something, then disappeared into cyberspace—after first admitting he wasn't sure his e-mail was working, which seemed rather like Edison saying he didn't know how to change a lightbulb.

One thing you won't find missing from this book is a single word of any of the letters as we found them. If you come upon an ellipsis in this volume, it's there either because the author put it there or because we were unable to locate the original and complete text, but not because we decided to edit anything out. Digressions of all sorts remain because, as an anonymous author commented in a 1905 book review of Queen Victoria's letters: "It cannot be doubted that a letter is a living thing with an individuality of its own, and if the head and tail are cut off, and two or three pieces taken out of the body, that individuality is lost."

We didn't add anything, either. Sometimes letters end abruptly, without signature or sign-off. Sometimes they start without salutation. With rare exceptions, we didn't correct errors of spelling, punctuation, or grammar, even when a letter writer misspelled a name three different ways in the space of one paragraph. Most letters include mistakes. When you find an error-free letter in this volume, you can assume another editor has been there first. To us, correcting letters for readability seemed too much a slippery slope. It was too short a distance from cleaning up someone's punctuation to cleaning up his or her idioms. We decided to let history speak for itself, even when it mumbled.

Finally, it should be said that we came to this project as writers and editors, with liberal arts educations and no expectation that our selection would be anything but idiosyncratic. We would certainly agree with the famous anonymous statement that "a historian is a person who gets to read other people's mail." But the converse is not equally true. People who get to read other people's mail are not necessarily historians. In our case, they are—as we hope you'll become—people luckily and delightedly browsing through time.

—Lisa Grunwald and Stephen J. Adler
New York City
June 1999

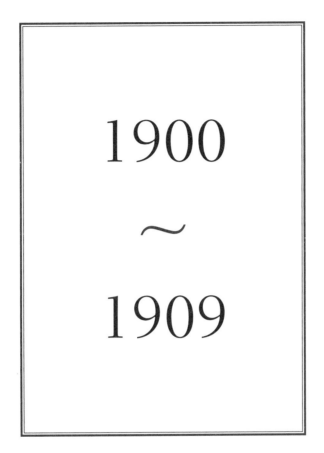

1900
~
1909

People no longer write letters. Lacking the leisure, and,
for the most part, the ability, they dictate dispatches, and
scribble messages. When you are in the humor, you
should take a peep at some of the letters written by
people who lived long ago.

—*Joel Chandler Harris to his son*
April 5, 1900

BETWEEN 1900 AND 1909 . . .

1900: An American boy born this year can expect to live to be 46; a girl to be 48. ★ The U.S population is 75,994,575. ★ Kodak introduces the Brownie, the first camera for amateurs. ★ The International Ladies' Garment Workers' Union is founded in New York City. ★ At Wheaton College in Norton, Massachusetts, only two baths are allowed a week, and students must have written permission from their parents in order to bathe in cold water. ★ Theodore Roosevelt writes his old friend Henry Sprague: "I have always been fond of the West African proverb: 'Speak softly and carry a big stick; you will go far.' " ★ Number of doctors nationwide: 119,749. ★ Average number of people in a household: 4.77. ★ One hundred immigrants an hour are being processed at Ellis Island. ★ Largest city: New York, population 3.4 million. ★ Thirty-sixth largest city: Los Angeles, population 102,000. ★ Number of automobiles in the country: 8,000; number of bicycles: 10 million; number of working horses and mules: 18 million. **1901:** William McKinley is assassinated by the anarchist Leon Czolgosz. Vice-President Roosevelt, 42 years old, becomes the youngest American president in history. ★ Thousands of visitors to the Pan-American Exposition in Buffalo, New York, are duped into thinking the

---

From left to right, top row: the first flight at Kitty Hawk, the Palace Theatre nickelodeon, Little Orphan Annie in a Pittsburgh institution; *second row:* Carry Nation, Evelyn Nesbit, Theodore Roosevelt; *third row:* Mark Twain, a frontier wife; *bottom row:* immigrants at Ellis Island, a patent-medicine advertisement.

"Cardiff Giant," a ten-foot-tall stone statue, is really a primitive petrified man. ★ Number of civilians working for the federal government: 239,476. ★ Walter Reed proves that yellow fever is spread by mosquitoes. ★ J. P. Morgan buys out Andrew Carnegie and creates U.S. Steel. ★ Texas drillers have their first major oil strike, at a drilling ground known as Spindletop, which gushes 80,000 to 100,000 barrels a day. ★ President Roosevelt hosts black leader Booker T. Washington at the White House. **1902:** Featuring luxury dining, smoking, and library cars, the *Twentieth Century Limited* begins 65 years of service between New York and Chicago. ★ Automats, Animal Crackers, and Crayola crayons appear. ★ Scott Joplin writes "The Entertainer." ★ People are singing "In the Good Old Summertime," "Bill Bailey, Won't You Please Come Home," and "Under the Bamboo Tree." ★ In *The Story of My Life*, Helen Keller tells how she was taught to read, write, and speak. **1903:** The Boston Pilgrims beat the Pittsburgh Pirates to win the first World Series. ★ The Wright brothers fly at Kitty Hawk. ★ Singer sells 1.35 million sewing machines. ★ Massachusetts becomes the first state to issue license plates. ★ For the first time, a car is driven all the way across the United States; the trip takes 52 days. ★ King C. Gillette sells 51 razors and 168 blades. **1904:** King C. Gillette sells 90,000 razors and 12.4 million blades. ★ More than a thousand cases of typhoid fever are linked to "Typhoid Mary" Mallon, who carries the disease but refuses to stop taking jobs that require her to handle food. ★ Geronimo appears as part of an exhibit at the St. Louis World's Fair. **1905:** William "Big Bill" Haywood, Mary "Mother" Jones, and Eugene V. Debs help found the Industrial Workers of the World. ★ The first jukebox offers 24 choices, and the newly popular nickelodeons show moving pictures, or "flickers." ★ Coney Island's Dreamland installs a million electric lights, including 100,000 on the 375-foot central tower. **1906:** San Francisco is virtually destroyed by earthquake and fire. ★ Millionaire Harry K. Thaw shoots architect Stanford White to death while singers perform "I Could Love a Million Girls" at the outdoor restaurant atop Madison Square Garden, designed by White. The architect had had an affair with Thaw's wife, Gibson Girl Evelyn Nesbit. ★ The first Times Square New Year's Eve celebration takes place. ★ Upton Sinclair's *The Jungle* is published. **1907:** Oklahoma becomes the 46th state in the Union. ★ J. Murray Spangler, a janitor in an Ohio department store, invents the upright vacuum cleaner and sells the patent rights to W. H. Hoover. **1908:** Henry Ford starts production on the Model T, which sells for $850. ★ The great magician Harry Houdini tours America and Europe, the posters for his underwater escapes proclaiming "Failure Means a Drowning Death." ★ The Dixie Cup and the electric toaster appear. ★ Dinosaur bones are discovered in Utah. **1909:** William Howard Taft becomes president. ★ Sigmund Freud and Carl Jung embark on a U.S. speaking tour. ★ More than 1.3 million telephones are in service. ★ It costs two cents to send a one-ounce letter.

1900: APRIL 5
JOEL CHANDLER HARRIS TO HIS SON

Through his Uncle Remus books, featuring popular characters like Brer Rabbit and Brer Fox, Joel Chandler Harris (1848–1908) introduced Americans to the folk stories, proverbs, and slave lore he had heard as a child in Georgia. Harris was prolific as an author and loyal as a correspondent. But as this letter to his twenty-two-year-old son Evelyn attests, he was one of many in the century who would be premature in mourning the loss of the letter-writing art.

Lithia Springs was a popular spa in Georgia. Essie was Harris's niece. Lucien and Alleen were another son and daughter-in-law.

Thursday Evening, 5th April

Dear Evelyn: Your letter was waiting for me when I came home, but was not the less interesting because I had seen you in the meantime. We usually say more in a letter than we do in conversation, the reason being that, in a letter, we feel that we are shielded from the indifference or enthusiasm which our remarks may meet with or arouse. We commit our thoughts, as it were, to the winds. Whereas, in conversation, we are constantly watching or noting the effect of what we are saying, and, when the relations are intimate, we shrink from being taken too seriously on one hand, and, on the other, not seriously enough.—But people no longer write letters. Lacking the leisure, and, for the most part, the ability, they dictate dispatches, and scribble messages. When you are in the humor, you should take a peep at some of the letters written by people who lived long ago, especially the letters of women. There is a charm about them impossible to describe, the charm of unconsciousness and the sweetness of real sincerity. But, in these days, we have not the artlessness nor the freedom of our forbears. We know too much about ourselves. Constraint covers us like a curtain. Not being very sure of our own feelings, we are in a fog about the feelings of others. And it is really too bad that it should be so. I fear I am pretty nearly the only one now living who is willing to put his thoughts freely on paper even when writing to his own children. This is the result, as you may say, of pure accident. I am really as remote from the activities of the world, and from the commotions that take place on the stage of events as any of the ancients were. It is the accident of temperament, for I am very sure that the temperament has been moulded by circumstances and surroundings. All that goes on has a profound significance for me, but I seem to be out of the way, a sort of dreamy spectator, who must sometimes close his eyes on the perpetual struggle that is going on.— But what is all this? <u>Bang!</u> Let us fire the sunset gun at such prosing, and forcibly bring on the twilight that belongs to modern and contemporary affairs. And the firing was timely, for the report had hardly died away before the door-bell rang and in walked Youth, Beauty, Love and Fashion, all combined in the person of sweet Lula Z., who has arrived to stay with Essie "for the looks of the thing," whatever that may mean. The phrase is a quotation from Mama's guide-book of Etiquette and Propriety. I hope the "thing," whatever it is, will look better now that this charming little filly has appeared in the pasture. It was a great thought to have her here, but it seems to me that I should have preferred, humanly speaking, the girl who has been taking you out among the ruins. But perhaps Age has no right even to hint at the propensities of Youth—especially after it has arrived at that period when it may go about with its trousers unbuttoned without bringing so much as a blush to the pink and sensitive cheeks of Propriety.—But perhaps you have your ears cocked for news. It is useless. We never get out an extra in West End until "Aunt Lol" pays us a visit and it has been a year and a day since she was here. We had Lucien and Alleen to dinner to-day, "for the looks of the thing." Lucien said he liked to go to Lithia on account of the good eating. No doubt this is so, for, of a big hen, only the neck was left when he gave his mouth a final wipe. Mama and Grandma left on time, though she sat up all night for fear the man wouldn't come for the trunk. I haven't heard from her. When she writes I'll send you the letter unless there's some pestiferous piece of confidence in its vitals. You said nothing about money the other day—the fact is we didn't have time to say much of anything—but don't forget that I am to pay your expenses.

Your loving
Daddy.

*   *   *

1900: DECEMBER 9
WALTER REED TO HIS WIFE

Yellow fever had been one of the greatest health problems of the previous century, killing thousands of victims in annual epidemics that beset tropical and coastal cities, especially in the Caribbean. Walter Reed (1851–1902) was an American army surgeon who in 1900 went to Cuba to investigate an outbreak among United States soldiers. By intentionally subjecting volunteers there to bites, he proved Carlos Juan Finlay's theory that like malaria, yellow fever was carried by mosquitoes, not people. In this letter to his wife, Reed revealed the private thrill of his discovery. George M. Sternberg was the United States Surgeon General.

COLUMBIA BARRACKS, Quemados, Cuba
Dec. 9, 1900

It is with a great deal of pleasure that I hasten to tell you that we have succeeded in producing a case of unmistakable yellow fever by the bite of the mosquito. Our first case in the experimental camp developed at 11:30 last night, commencing with a sudden chill followed by fever. He had been bitten at 11:30 December 5th, and hence his attack followed just three and a half days after the bite. As he had been in our camp 15 days before being inoculated and had had no other possible exposure, the case is as clear as the sun at noon-day, and sustains brilliantly and conclusively our conclusions. Thus, just 18 days from the time we began our experimental work we have succeeded in demonstrating this mode of propagation of the disease, so that the most doubtful and sceptical must yield. Rejoice with me, sweetheart, as, aside from the antitoxin of diphtheria and Koch's discovery of the tubercle bacillus, it will be regarded as the most important piece of work, scientifically, during the 19th century. I do not exaggerate, and I could shout for very joy that heaven has permitted me to establish this wonderful way of propagating yellow fever. It was Finlay's theory, and he deserves great credit for having suggested it, but as he did nothing to prove it, it was rejected by all, including General Sternberg. Now we have put it beyond cavil, and its importance to Cuba and the United States cannot be estimated. Major Kean says that the discovery is worth more than the cost of the Spanish War, including lives lost and money expended. He is almost beside himself with joy and will tell General Wood when he goes to town in the morning. Tomorrow afternoon we will have the Havana Board of Experts, Drs. Guiteras, Albertini, and Finlay, come out and diagnose the case. I shan't tell them how the infection was acquired until after they have satisfied themselves concerning the character of the case, then I will let them know. I suppose that old Dr. Finlay will be delighted beyond bounds, as he will see his theory at last fully vindicated. 9:30 p.m. Since writing the above our patient has been doing well. His temperature, which was 102.5° at noon, has fallen to 101° and his severe headache and backache have subsided considerably. Everything points, as far as it can at this stage, to a favourable termination, for which I feel so happy.

1901: MARCH 10
ANDREW CARNEGIE TO HENRY PHIPPS, JR.

After working for more than thirty years to build Carnegie Steel into a lavishly profitable enterprise, Andrew Carnegie (1835–1919) sold his company to J. P. Morgan in March of 1901. Following the completion of the deal, which provided Carnegie personally with $225 million in bonds, he told his former competitor: "Now, Pierpont, I am the happiest man in the world. I have unloaded this burden on your back and I am off to Europe to play." Carnegie turned his attention to giving money away, ultimately donating some $350 million to philanthropic causes.

Henry Phipps, Jr., was one of Carnegie's original business partners.

5 West 51st Street,

Sunday eve.

My dear H. P.

Mr. Stetson has just called to tell me <u>it is closed</u>, all fixed—big times on Stock Exchange tomorrow.

Well, this is a step in my life—a great change, but <u>after a time</u>, when I get down to new conditions, I shall become I believe a wiser and more useful man, and besides live a dignified old age as long as life is granted, something few reach.

Yours,

A. C.

*   *   *

1901: MARCH 12

ANDREW CARNEGIE TO J. S. BILLINGS

Just days after the sale to Morgan, the director of the New York Public Library received this letter from Carnegie, who would go on to endow more than twenty-eight hundred libraries nationwide.

New York 12th March 1901.

Dr. J.S. Billings,
Director New York Public Library.

Dear Mr. Billings,

Our conferences upon the needs of Greater New York for Branch Libraries to reach the masses of the people in every district have convinced me of the wisdom of your plans.

Sixty-five branches strike one at first as a large order, but as other cities have found one necessary for every sixty or seventy thousand of population the number is not excessive.

You estimate the average cost of these libraries at, say, $80,000 each, being $5,200,000 for all. If New York will furnish sites for those Branches for the special benefit of the masses of the people, as it has done for the Central Library, and also agree in satisfactory form to provide for their maintenance as built, I should esteem it a rare privilege to be permitted to furnish the money as needed for the buildings, say $5,200,000. Sixty-five libraries at one stroke probably breaks the record, but this is the day of big operations, and New York is soon to be the biggest of Cities.

Very truly yours,
Andrew Carnegie

1901: JULY 19

MARK TWAIN TO EDWARD DIMMITT

Mark Twain (1835–1910) had long since earned his literary reputation when, on a summer vacation, he received an invitation to return to his native Missouri for its eightieth birthday celebration. He declined, but not without offering one of the organizers of the event a few vintage observations.

Among the Adirondack Lakes, July 19, 1901.

Dear Mr. Dimmitt,—By an error in the plans, things go wrong end first in this world, and much precious time is lost and matters of urgent importance are fatally retarded. Invitations which a brisk young fellow should get, and which would transport him with joy, are delayed and impeded and obstructed until they are fifty years overdue when they reach him.

It has happened again in this case.

When I was a boy in Missouri I was always on the lookout for invitations but they always miscarried and went wandering through the aisles of time; and now they are arriving when I am old and rheumatic and can't travel and must lose my chance.

I have lost a world of delight through this matter of delaying invitations. Fifty years ago I would have gone eagerly across the world to help celebrate anything that might turn up. It would have made no difference to me what it was, so that I was there and allowed a chance to make a noise.

The whole scheme of things is turned wrong end to. Life should begin with age and its privileges and accumulations, and end with youth and its capacity to splendidly enjoy such advantages. As things are now, when in youth a dollar would bring a hundred pleasures, you can't have it. When you are old, you get it and there is nothing worth buying with it then.

It's an epitome of life. The first half of it consists of the capacity to enjoy without the chance; the last half consists of the chance without the capacity.

I am admonished in many ways that time is pushing me inexorably along. I am approaching the threshold of age; in 1977 I shall be 142. This is no time to be flitting about the earth. I must cease from the activities proper to youth and begin to take on the dignities and gravities and inertia proper to that season of honorable senility which is on its way and imminent as indicated above.

Yours is a great and memorable occasion, and as a son of Missouri I should hold it a high privilege to be there and share your just pride in the state's achievements; but I must deny myself the indulgence, while thanking you earnestly for the prized honor you have done me in asking me to be present.

Very truly yours,
S. L. Clemens.

*   *   *

1901: SEPTEMBER 23
THEODORE ROOSEVELT TO HENRY CABOT LODGE

While visiting the Pan-American Exposition in Buffalo, New York, William McKinley (1843–1901) was shot by an anarchist named Leon Czolgosz. Eight days later, the president died, and Vice-President Theodore Roosevelt (1858–1919) assumed office. In his seven and a half years as president, Roosevelt would break up trusts, embrace conservationism, regulate big business, and push through the construction of the Panama Canal. But just a week after McKinley's death, he penned this understandably sober note to Henry Cabot Lodge (1850–1924), the long-term Massachusetts senator.

Washington, September 23, 1901

Dear Cabot: I must just send you a line, hoping it will catch you before you leave, for naturally you have been in my thoughts almost every hour of the last fortnight. It is a dreadful thing to come into the Presidency this way; but it would be a far worse thing to be morbid about it. Here is the task, and I have got to do it to the best of my ability; and that is all there is about it. I believe you will approve of what I have done and of the way I have handled myself so far. It is only a beginning, but it is better to make a beginning good than bad.

I shall not try to give you even in barest outline the history of the last two weeks, and still less to talk of the policies that press for immediate consideration. I hope you can make it convenient to come and see me soon after your return.

I had a very nice talk with Murray Crane. Give my love to Nannie and all.

Ever yours

[Theodore Roosevelt]

1901: OCTOBER 16
ELIZABETH CABOT TO HER HUSBAND

Thomas Edison had invented the incandescent lightbulb in 1879, but electric light was still something worth noticing when, just months before her death, Elizabeth Dwight Cabot (1830–1901) paid a visit to the Plaza Hotel in New York City. Cabot, the wife of James Elliott Cabot and the mother of seven sons, had been a fixture in Boston social life and social work.

The building she described would be torn down in 1905 and replaced with the current hotel in 1907. Minnie Fiske was a well-known actress of the day. The end of this letter has been lost.

Plaza Hotel, New York, Oct. 16, 1901

Dearest,— Here we are in the vortex, but this evening snatching a few moments repose in the "Ladies' Parlor" for domestic life. No one passes the evening in a New York hotel apparently, and we have found it very difficult to find "a place to sit down" in the midst of all this gorgeousness. You will say "What is the matter with your bedroom?" I'll just tell you, you really can't do anything there but wash yourself and go to bed, and those things pall somewhat for evening entertainments. We each have an electric chandelier at least eight feet from the ground, and no ladder convenient to reach it or to sit on to read. No candles or other alleviations. Two gorgeous ladies' parlors downstairs are furnished with tapestry covered furniture and velvet carpets and white grand pianos, but the only lights are chandeliers, closely attached to the ceilings, and again no ladders to reach them, so we have taken refuge in a humble reception room by the entrance, where the door is guarded by a black waiter, who paces the entry like a sentinel, and all kinds of ghastly pictures of sheep and row-boats and various kinds of shipping glare at you from the walls, and a large lamp heavily draped with green and white muslin presides over a vast polished surface of mahogany, which Ella and I are defiling with writing upon it. If I raise my eyes I see a full length figure of myself gazing stupidly at me from a mirror, and feel that I am truly becoming acquainted with American home life.

In spite of these home attractions, however, we managed to arrive at the Horace Mann School at 10.30 a.m., where Mr. Dutton received us most cordially, and showed us the whole institution himself. Ella went back at one o'clock to meet Richard, who went home at three, and I stayed till four, and then came back and we took a hansom and drove in the park and then on the Riverside Drive. The weather is perfect, milder than with us, so that the open cars are still in use and perfectly comfortable. We dined last evening at Mrs. Creighton's little apartment.

After dinner we went down by cars to the Manhattan Theatre to see Mrs. Fiske and were well repaid. She has a charming little theatre, managed by her husband and herself, and her acting is the best I have seen for a long time. She has a delightful voice, which she uses to perfection, and though her part was extremely high wrought, there was never a moment's ranting, but such restraint that it intensified your sympathy for her in a really human way. The play was extraordinarily varied in scenery. It began in a London drawing-room, then removed to our dear Ronda in Spain, then fled to South Africa, and ended in Tangiers.

1901: OCTOBER 17

WILLIAM ROSCOE THAYER TO THEODORE ROOSEVELT

A historian and literary critic who spent most of his career in Cambridge, Massachusetts, William Roscoe Thayer (1859–1923) edited the Harvard Graduates' Magazine. *When he wrote to the new president (a Harvard alumnus), he was expressing an optimism about world peace that the new century would all too quickly contradict.*

Major Henry Lee Higginson, a banker often called Boston's first citizen, had been a member of the class of 1855. He founded the Boston Symphony Orchestra, donated the Harvard Union building, and secured the sites for Harvard's future medical and business schools.

Cambridge, Mass., Oct. 17, 1901

To President Roosevelt
White House, Washington

Dear Mr. President:

Just because everybody has been talking about the culminating episode at the dedication of the Harvard Union Tuesday night, possibly nobody may think to report it to you. Yet, as it concerns you chiefly, you ought to hear of it, and so I write.

Major Henry Higginson, in giving the building to the students and graduates, made one of his matchless addresses—simple, right to the point, and from man's heart to man's heart. After saying how he hoped that the Union would foster friendship in college and loyalty to Harvard, he went on to urge the young fellows never to forget that the final test of education and of character lies in devotion to country. Then he spoke of President McKinley's assassination—"a cowardly treacherous crime," to which "we reply by a renewal of our confession of faith, and by a stern resolve to square our daily thoughts and acts with our national faith and polity."

Presently, Mr. Higginson paused, and we thought that he had done; but in a moment, stepping forward a little, he raised his right hand high, as in benediction, and added, "God bless and guide aright our fellow-graduate, Theodore Roosevelt, President of the United States."

I have never seen anything more solemnly impressive; and for a little while there was a hush over the great audience. For myself, I had rather have such a benediction from Henry Higginson than from a whole chapter of bishops, and you should at least know about it.

I cannot send this without adding my own best wishes. I have often in the past differed from your views on public matters, but I have had the firmest faith in your motives, and now that you are President, I rejoice to think that none of your predecessors ever came to the White House having, as you have, the best wishes of literally the whole nation. That fact alone gives you a greater power for good than any other president has ever had; may you use it to the full and bless our country so that it shall forever bless your memory.

The great needs, the lasting achievements henceforth are in peace not war, in overcoming the moral and intellectual,—not the physical—enemies of civilization. With your courage and your strength, and the knowledge that the nation is behind you, what may you not do! God prosper you! As an old-time friend and as a lover of my country, I cannot say less, and nothing that I could say would mean more.

Ever truly yours
Wm. R. Thayer

1902: SUMMER

MARK TWAIN TO THE PRESIDENT OF

THE NEW YORK WESTERN UNION

Another summer found Twain (see letter page 17) in fine curmudgeonly form, railing against the inefficiencies of modern life.

"The Pines"
York Harbor, Maine.

Dear Sir,— I desire to make a complaint, and I bring it to you, the head of the company, because by experience I know better than to carry it to a subordinate.

I have been here a month and a half, and by testimony of friends, reinforced by personal experience I now feel qualified to claim as an established fact that the telegraphic service here is the worst in the world except that Boston.

These services are actually slower than was the New York and Hartford service in the days when I last complained to you—which was fifteen or eighteen years ago, when telegraphic time and train time between the mentioned points was exactly the same, to-wit, three hours and a half.

Six days ago—it was that raw day which provoked so much comment—my daughter was on her way up from New York, and at noon she telegraphed me from New Haven asking that I meet her with a cloak at Portsmouth. Her telegram reached me four hours and a quarter later—just 15 minutes too late for me to catch my train and meet her.

I judge that the telegram traveled about 200 miles. It is the best telegraphic work I have seen since I have been here, and I am mentioning it in this place not as a complaint but as a compliment. I think a compliment ought always to precede a complaint, where one is possible, because it softens resentment and insures for the complaint a courteous and gentle reception.

Still, there is a detail or two connected with this matter which ought perhaps to be mentioned. And now, having smoothed the way with the compliment, I will venture them. The head corpse in the York Harbor office sent me that telegram altho (1) he knew it would reach me too late to be of any value; (2) also, that he was going to send it to me by his boy; (3) that the boy would not take the trolley and come the 2 miles in 12 minutes, but would walk; (4) that he would be two hours and a quarter on the road; (5) and that he would collect 25 cents for transportation, for a telegram which the h. c. knew to be worthless before he started it. From these data I infer that the Western Union owes me 75 cents; that is to say, the amount paid for combined wire and land transportation—a recoup provided for in the printed paragraph which heads the telegraph-blank.

By these humane and Christian stages we now arrive at the complaint proper. We have had a grave case of illness in the family, and a relative was coming some six hundred miles to help in the sick-room during the convalescing period. It was an anxious time, of course, and I wrote and asked to be notified as to the hour of the expected arrival of this relative in Boston or in York Harbor. Being afraid of the telegraph—which I think ought not to be used in times of hurry and emergency—I asked that the desired message be brought to me by some swift method of transportation. By the milkman, if he was coming this way. But there are always people who think they know more than you do, especially young people; so of course the young fellow in charge of this lady used the telegraph. And at Boston, of all places! Except York Harbor.

The result was as usual; let me employ a statelier and exacter term, and say, historical.

The dispatch was handed to the h. c. of the Boston office at 9 this morning. It said, "Shall bring A. S. to you eleven forty-five this morning." The distance traveled by the dispatch is forty or fifty miles, I suppose, as the train-time is five minutes short of two hours, and the trains are so slow that they can't give a W. U. telegram two hours and twenty minutes start and overtake it.

As I have said, the dispatch was handed in at Boston at 9. The expected visitors left Boston at 9.40, and reached my house at 12 noon, beating the telegram 2 solid hours, and 5 minutes over.

The boy brought the telegram. It was bald-headed with age, but still legible. The boy was prostrate with travel and exposure, but still alive, and I went out to condole with him and get his last wishes and send for the ambulance. He was waiting to collect transportation before turning his passing spirit to less serious affairs. I found him strangely intelligent, considering his condition and where he is getting his training. I asked him at what hour the telegram was handed to the h. c. in Boston. He answered brightly, that he didn't know.

I examined the blank, and sure enough the wary Boston h. c. had thoughtfully concealed that statistic. I asked him at what hour it had started from Boston. He answered up as brightly as ever, and said he didn't know.

I examined the blank, and sure enough the Boston h. c. had left that statistic out in the cold, too. In fact it turned out to be an official concealment—no blank was provided for its exposure. And none required by the law, I suppose. "It is a good one-sided idea," I remarked; "They can take your money and ship your telegram next year if they want to—you've no redress. The law ought to extend the privilege to all of us."

The boy looked upon me coldly.

I asked him when the telegram reached York Harbor. He pointed to some figures following the signature at the bottom of the blank—"12.14." I said it was now 1.45 and asked—

"Do you mean that it reached your morgue an hour and a half ago?"

He nodded assent.

"It was at that time half an hour too late to be of any use to me, if I wanted to go and meet my people—which was the case—for by the wording of the message you can see that they were to arrive at the station at 11.45. Why did your h. c. send me this useless message? Can't he read? Is he dead?"

"It's the rules."

"No, that does not account for it. Would he have sent it if it had been three years old, I in the meantime deceased, and he aware of it?"

The boy didn't know.

"Because, you know, a rule which required him to forward to the cemetery to-day a dispatch due three years ago, would be as good a rule as one which should require him to forward a telegram to me to-day which he knew had lost all its value an hour or two before he started it. The construction of such a rule would discredit an idiot; in fact an idiot—I mean a common ordinary Christian idiot, you understand—would be ashamed of it, and for the sake of his reputation wouldn't make it. What do you think?"

He replied with much natural brilliancy that he wasn't paid for thinking.

This gave me a better opinion of the commercial intelligence pervading his morgue than I had had before; it also softened my feelings toward him, and also my tone, which had hitherto been tinged with bitterness.

"Let bygones be bygones," I said, gently, "we are all erring creatures, and mainly idiots, but God made us so and it is dangerous to criticise."

Sincerely
S. L. Clemens.

1902: SEPTEMBER 15
A TEXAN TO PATTILLO HIGGINS

Spindletop was a drilling ground in Beaumont, Texas, where, for nine days starting on January 10, 1901, an oil well gushed more than a hundred feet into the air and went on to produce an unprecedented eighty thousand to one hundred thousand barrels a day. The discovery made millionaires of drillers Pattillo Higgins and Anthony F. Lucas, and essentially began the petroleum age. By 1902, 285 wells were operating on Spindletop Hill, and nearby landowners like Mr. Johnson (his first name is no longer decipherable) were trying to persuade the drillers to help them become a part of the action.

We have no evidence that Higgins ever visited Johnson.

Port Lavaca, Tex.
Sept 15, '02

Mr. Pattillo Higgins.
Beaumont, Tex.

Dear Sir,—

Seeing your story of Spindletop—and noting the interest you are taking in the developement of oil along the Gulf coast: will write and inform you of the signs of oil here, I have a well about 8 ft. deep. It is drawn out 3 or 4 times day—and each time there is a thin scum of oil on it. About 350 yds from this well another well was dug in '96, that contained so much oil that cattle would not drink it, so it was filled up. Mr. Ragan, from Bmt, was here last winter with his machine, and tested land around here, and said, "that there was more oil on my land than on Spindletop" but I don't put much confidence in his instrument.

but I feel confident that there is oil on my place. Any time you come to this part of the country I will gladly show you around.

Your father and I were quite friends when I lived in that part of the state.

Respecfully yours.

—— Johnson

1902: OCTOBER
SUSAN B. ANTHONY TO ELIZABETH CADY STANTON

Although by the turn of the century a few states were already allowing them to vote, the vast majority of American women could neither cast a ballot nor get information about birth control. Women had extremely limited opportunities for jobs and education, and their pay was dismally low. Two of the people who fought most passionately to change these conditions had been friends since meeting in 1851 and had successfully campaigned for the first laws in New York giving woman control over their property, wages, and children. Elizabeth Cady Stanton (1815–1902) died just days after receiving this letter from Susan B. Anthony (1820–1906). It would be another eighteen years before passage of the Nineteenth Amendment granted women in all states the right to vote.

My dear Mrs. Stanton

I shall indeed be happy to spend with you November 12, the day on which you round out your four-score and seven, over four years ahead of me, but in age as in all else I follow you closely. It is fifty-one years since first we met and we have been busy through every one of them, stirring up the world to recognize the rights of women. The older we grow, the more keenly we feel the humiliation of disfranchisement and the more vividly we realize its disadvantages in every department of life and most of all in the labor market.

We little dreamed when we began this contest, optimistic with the hope and buoyancy of youth, that half a century later we would be compelled to leave the finish of the battle to another generation of women. But our hearts are filled with joy to know that they enter upon this task equipped with a college education, with business experience, with the fully admitted right to speak in public— all of which were denied to women fifty years ago. They have practically but one point to gain—the suffrage; we had all. These strong, courageous, capable young women will take our place and complete our work. There is an army of them where we were but a handful. Ancient prejudice has become so softened, public sentiment so liberalized and women have so thoroughly demonstrated their ability as to leave not a shadow of doubt that they will carry our cause to victory.

And we, dear old friend, shall move on to the next sphere of existence— higher and larger, we cannot fail to believe, and one where women will not be placed in an inferior position but will be welcomed on a plane of perfect intellectual and spiritual equality.

Ever lovingly yours,
Susan B. Anthony

1902: OCTOBER
A YALE STUDENT TO CARRY NATION

Using any tools at her disposal, from religious persuasion to a notorious hatchet, onetime teacher Carry Nation (1846–1911) was well into her crusade against liquor when she received this letter from an anonymous—and almost certainly sincere— Yale student. The menus he enclosed featured such items as claret wine punch, apple dumplings in brandy sauce, roast ham with champagne sauce, and wine jelly.

Dear Mrs. Nation:— Although it pains me deeply, I feel it my duty to inform you that after your soul-stirring address of warning and reproof, the Devil still grins at Yale Dining Hall. The enclosed menus tell the story. The hateful practice of serving intoxicating liquors has not ceased. Capt. Smoke holds open wide the gates of hell. Oh, this is terrible! Satan loves to shoot at brightest marks. Here are eight hundred shining young souls, the cream of the nation's manhood, on the broad road which leadeth to destruction. God Help us. Assist us, Mrs. Nation; aid us; pray for us. Let the world know of this awful condition and rouse the public indignation until it has ceased. Publicity will do it. Let the world know that Yale is being made a training school for drunkards, and Capt. Smoke will never dare to serve liquors again.

Alone, But a Friend of the
Temperance Cause

1903: APRIL 6
WILLIAM DEAN HOWELLS TO CHARLES ELIOT NORTON

William Dean Howells (1837–1920) wrote plays, novels, poetry, criticism, and journalism. His best-known work was The Rise of Silas Lapham. *Friends with Henry James, Mark Twain, and Stephen Crane, he was already considered the dean of American letters when he wrote this letter depicting turn-of-the-century New York social life. Charles Eliot Norton (1827–1908), a fine-arts history professor at Harvard in the late nineteenth century, had been cofounder of* The Nation *and like Howells was a contributor to* The Atlantic Monthly.

John Burroughs was a naturalist and writer. Carl Schurz was a former senator.

48 West 59th st., April 6, 1903.

My Dear Norton:

I am sorry to know that you have been often, but I hope not very much, out of health since I saw you last. Somehow that little visit remains peculiarly precious in my mind, and in spite of the facts, I still have the sense of your continuing to be very well. Once I invented a formula for my brother, or rather tried to console him for some ailment of his later years by saying that when we were young we got well, but now we got better; and I trust this greater triumph is yours. I myself keep on as well as the age, if not my own, will let me; I am not particularly proud of it yet, but I daresay it will look not unhandsome in history. The other night I met at dinner that fine old John Burroughs whom I congratulated on going out to Yellowstone to hold bears for the President to kill; but he seemed to think it not an altogether enviable office, but to have his latent misgivings. I had not then seen a picture of King Edward standing, gun in hand and looking down at the long double line of pheasants he had shot; otherwise I could have told Burroughs that bears were nobler game, and our prince was by so much in advance of the English boy. The dinner was at Carnegie's, where he and his amiable wife entertained a company of New York literati in honor of an Englishman. I sat on Carnegie's left, and had moments of confidence with him in which I could tell him of my pleasure in his offer to buy off a war by paying the debts of a nation. He is a dreamer and in his way a poet, and he seemed to like my notion that this was a stroke of poetry. I found both him and his wife simple-hearted and quite unspoiled. He is quite subject to her, as a husband should be, and suffered being bid do this and that, as her superior social instinct required. The house is subjectively rather than objectively rich, and outside is a triumph of ugliness, though within it is very home-like. The young Scotch painter who has been living there while he painted Mrs. Carnegie and her daughter whispered me that he did not know what to do with his late habits, for every one else in that house was abed by half-past ten. You know that the house is embowered in a ready-made grove of forest trees transplanted full grown to the corner of Fifth Avenue and 90th street, and there is a curious air of establishment in it all. After dinner we had speaking—from Mark Twain, Carl Schurz, Burroughs, and others, and upon the whole it was the pleasantest affair I have been at in New York. I wonder if you have Giusti's Proverbi Toscani? I am writing a grimmish story, which I want to call by a proverb which I seem to remember out of that pleasant book. It is, Iddio non paga sabato, which I propose Englishing into God does not pay Saturdays. Does it afflict you to find your books wearing out? I mean literally. Just now I went to my old Barretti to see whether sabato was spelt with one *b* or two, and it almost came apart in my hand. It was as if I had found an old friend dying. The mortality of all inanimate things is terrible to me, but that of books most of all, and my library is turning into a cemetery.

I am amused when I meet Carl Schurz. We agree entirely, and he comes forward with both hands up and a glad "Ah!" Then we have nothing to say. The man I have most to say with is Mark Twain, but we seldom meet, for he lives up the river where he can see the steamboats passing, and he is kept closely at home by what now seems the hopeless case of his wife. It has changed the poor old fellow, but when he can break away, almost the best talk in the world is left in him.

I wonder if you are looking at James's Ambassadors? It is very good work. But it must appear to you very improbable to find fiction in the North American. Though where will not you find fiction nowadays?

Yours affectionately,

W. D. Howells

1903: DECEMBER 17
ORVILLE WRIGHT TO HIS FATHER

Orville Wright (1871–1948) and his brother Wilbur (1867–1912) spent three years constructing ever more likely gliding and flying machines in their Dayton, Ohio, bicycle shop. Orville sent this telegram home to his father Milton after making the world's first successful powered air flight at Kitty Hawk, North Carolina. The time was in fact fifty-nine seconds, and the telegraph operator misspelled Orville's name.

176 C KA CS 33 Paid.   Via Norfolk Va
Kitty Hawk N C Dec 17
Bishop M Wright
7 Hawthorne St
Success four flights thursday morning all against twenty one mile wind started from Level with engine power alone average speed through air thirty one miles longest 57 seconds inform Press home Christmas. Orevelle Wright 525P

1904: JANUARY 2

IRVING FISHER TO HIS WIFE

---

*The Yale professor and economist Irving Fisher (1867–1947) was still in his thir-
ties when he sent this memorable love letter to his wife. In the next seven years he
would publish four of his most influential books, holding true to the resolve he
shared with her here. They would stay happily married until her death in 1940,
when he wrote: "After the first paroxysm of grief, a miracle happened . . . I felt a
sudden new impulse to live for her . . . it was almost as amazing an experience to
me as was the falling in love with her at the sight of her smile through the crack of
a door in 1891."*

New Haven, January 2, 1904

The spirit moves me to write you a New Year's letter. It means to express first
of all my love for you, as a growing thing and to apply the experience of our past
love-life together to a dream of the years to come.

Five years ago with the Saranac snow like that here today we dreamed, in
sickness, of health and strength. Four years ago in Colorado we still dreamed of
health for me but also of health for you. Three months ago I found I had blun-
dered (about diet), and gave up my lectures to make you an Xmas present of a
well husband. What I still dream of is even closer to my heart. It is that next
Christmas you may give me a similar present.

I am not complaining, sweetheart, but you must let me suggest. That is the
way we can help each other. I want you to help me that way and I'll promise to
curl my moustache and learn all sorts of "young dog's tricks" for you, if you'll follow my suggestions, when you think they are good.

You, then are to take up the hygienic life more earnestly than ever before. I
suppose you are right that you can never equal the alpine-climbing English
woman. But let's see what a year of 366 days without a single day skipped will
do. Then, if we are both here and this letter exists let us read it again and measure the progress. . . .

It is in our power to keep well continuously for many years. The effect on the
children will be like that of sweet music. The effect on my work will be greater
than you imagine. For this I dream of a book a year for three years and several
articles, then a place among those who have helped along my science. It is hard
to put it all in words, but whatever good there is in me you have helped to bring
out. I believe there is more good in me still! And that you are the one who can
bring it out. Is it wrong to tell you that I dream to outgrow my present self like

the chambered nautilus? I want to be a <u>great</u> man. Is it wrong to say to you that I believe I can with your help?

If one little extemporaneous speech can do as much good as the United Church address seems to be doing, don't you think that with growing health, vigor and serenity I can find other and more powerful ways to make myself felt? I don't like to put it more definitely in words. It sounds conceited already. And your mission isn't simply to make a man better but also a son and two daughters. . . .

To do these things means to <u>be</u> what you wish the children to be. I don't know anyone who can fulfill their mission more easily than you. Most persons have to overcome boorishness, selfishness and pride. You don't. You scarcely know what these are as they exist in ordinary persons. All you need is the will to change slightly your health habits and to be less easily disturbed by servants' squabbles and children's naughtiness and a husband's loving interference.

But my own personal ambition for you is not the good you may do others but the good you may get yourself. Your joy is my joy and your discomfiture is mine. Hand in hand let us climb to the delectable mountains of serenity. Let us take ill fortune as it comes. But let us not invite any which need not be. Let us see how far we can go on our journey during 1904.

1904: FEBRUARY 22
BOOKER T. WASHINGTON TO THE <u>BIRMINGHAM AGE-HERALD</u>

Born a slave, Booker T. Washington (1856–1915) was nine years old when the Civil War ended. After graduating from the Hampton Institute, a Virginia school set up for the training of former slaves, he became the first principal of Alabama's Tuskegee Institute at the age of twenty-five. One of the undisputed leaders of the early movement for civil rights, Washington was nonetheless considered by many blacks to be too conciliatory. His usual approach was to urge quiet progress in education and work—even in the face of the type of barbarism he decried in this letter.

Within the last fortnight three members of my race have been burned at the stake; of these one was a woman. Not one of the three was charged with any crime even remotely connected with the abuse of a white woman. In every case murder was the sole accusation. All of these burnings took place in broad daylight and two of them occurred on Sunday afternoon in sight of a Christian church.

In the midst of the nation's busy and prosperous life few, I fear take time to consider where these brutal and inhuman crimes are leading us. The custom of burning human beings has become so common as scarcely to excite interest or attract unusual attention.

I have always been among those who condemned in the strongest terms crimes of whatever character committed by members of my race, and I condemn them now with equal severity; but I maintain that the only protection of our civilization is a fair and calm trial of all people charged with crime and in their legal punishment if proved guilty.

There is no shadow of excuse for departure from legal methods in the cases of individuals accused of murder. The laws are as a rule made by the white people and their execution is in the hands of the white people; so that there is little probability of any guilty colored man escaping.

These burnings without a trial are in the deepest sense unjust to my race; but it is not this injustice alone which stirs my heart. These barbarous scenes followed, as they are, by publication of the shocking details are more disgraceful and degrading to the people who inflict the punishment than those who receive it.

If the law is disregarded when a Negro is concerned, it will soon be disregarded when a white man is concerned; and, besides, the rule of the mob destroys the friendly relations which should exist between the races and injures and interferes with the material prosperity of the communities concerned.

Worst of all these outrages take place in communities where there are Christian churches; in the midst of people who have their Sunday schools, their Christian Endeavor Societies and Young Men's Christian Associations, where collections are taken up for sending missionaries to Africa and China and the rest of the so-called heathen world.

Is it not possible for pulpit and press to speak out against these burnings in a manner that shall arouse a public sentiment that will compel the mob to cease insulting our courts, our Governors and legal authority; cease bringing shame and ridicule upon our Christian civilization.

Booker T. Washington
Tuskegee, Ala.,
February 22, 1904

*   *   *

1904: MARCH 26

MARY HARRIS "MOTHER" JONES TO JAMES PEABODY

The labor movement in America was still in its infancy and Mary Harris "Mother" Jones (1830–1930) was already in her fifties when she began her devoted fight for the rights of coal miners and children. She had been a dressmaker but had lost her shop in the 1871 Chicago fire and turned to the Knights of Labor for help. Impressed by their crusade on behalf of workers, she was soon traveling the country herself, offering feisty speeches and a signature motto ("Pray for the dead, and fight like hell for the living"). In 1898, she helped to found the Social Democratic Party, and in 1905, the Industrial Workers of the World (IWW). She was in her seventies when she wrote this letter to the governor of Colorado, who had ordered her deported from the state for helping strikers. The governor did nothing in response.

Denver, Colorado, March 26, 1904

Governor James H. Peabody:

   Mr. Governor, you notified your dogs of war to put me out of the state. They complied with your instructions. I hold in my hand a letter that was handed to me by one of them, which says "under no circumstances return to this state." I wish to notify you, governor, that you don't own the state. When it was admitted to the sisterhood of states, my fathers gave me a share of stock in it; and that is all they gave you. The civil courts are open. If I break a law of state or nation it is the duty of the civil courts to deal with me. That is why my forefathers established those courts to keep dictators and tyrants such as you from interfering with civilians. I am right here in the capital, after being out nine or ten hours, four or five blocks from your office. I want to ask you, governor, what in Hell are you going to do about it?

Mother Jones

1904: OCTOBER 12

JACOB SCHERER TO DR. C. D. SPIVAK

In 1904, tuberculosis was still the leading cause of death in the United States, and immigrants living in cramped quarters were particularly hard hit. Jacob Scherer was general secretary of the Independent Order Brith Abraham lodge when he was asked to help a TB victim named Hyman Goren find treatment with a Colorado doctor. Goren, a tailor whose Boston lodge had sent him to Scherer, was thirty-six when he contracted the disease. Most immigrants were far less fortunate in finding help, often ending up in unsanitary tent colonies that were popularly known as "Bugsville" or "Lungers Camp."

Goren's name was misspelled in the letter.

UNITED STATES GRAND LODGE

INDEPENDENT ORDER BRITH ABRAHAM

37 SEVENTH STREET

New York,   Oct. 12th, 1904.

Dr. C. D. Spivak,
    Secy. Jew. C. R. Society,
      Denver, Colo.

Dear Sir & Bro:—

Bearer of this letter, Hyman Goron a member of the Rheingold Lodge, of Boston, Mass. is afflicted with consumption, and is advised to go to Denver, in order to get well.

He is absolutely without any means and substance, and his condition is so destitute that it would be impossible for me to describe to you.

The lodge has therefore appealed to us, requesting us to do our utmost and see that he be admitted in your kind home. You will no doubt think me impudent for sending so many letters to you, but no one knows my position, what can I do, when such pitiful pleas for help, come, and when I give a letter they are still hopful, and

I am sure that the above case is worthy of your kind consideration, and trust that you will give it such.

I enclose you herewith a letter which I have received from the above lodge, and which will show you what our lodges think of the Jewish Consumptives Relief Society. In answer to same I said, that they try and give some function, as did our lodges in Hartford, and send the amount realized to your worthy home.

Very respectfully,
Jacob Scherer
Grand Sec'y.

*   *   *

1904: NOVEMBER 10

ULBE ERINGA TO HIS SISTER AND BROTHER-IN-LAW

One of innumerable immigrants who came to farm the rural Midwest in the late nineteenth and early twentieth centuries, Ulbe Eringa (1866–1950) had left the northern part of Holland in 1892 to settle in South Dakota. His letter home, like so many written by immigrants from all nations, expressed both the hopes and hardships of starting a new life.

Tryntje was Eringa's sister in Holland, married to Willem Feitsma. Eringa's wife was Maaike Rypstra. The letter was translated by Eringa's youngest daughter.

Running Water, South Dakota

November 10, 1904

Dear sister Tryntje and brother Willem,

By this letter we are informing you that on Sunday, October 16, our little Trijntje (Thyrza) was born. We are naming her after you so that we keep you in our memory as long as possible. Maaike's sisters each have four girls so their names will stay alive in their own families. Please inform sister Jikke about this too, and tell her I'll write to her sometime this winter. I received a letter from them last week.

I'll write to you some more and hope we'll receive a letter from you too, sometime. Maaike is up and around again and is very busy. To have five children means quite a bit of work when the oldest is only 10 years old. We have a very busy life, and help is scarce and costly. It is a case of "help yourself." But there is one blessing: everything is going well with us. We had a very good crop again this year. I have 20 head of cattle to fatten with corn, and 54 nice pigs. If we are lucky with these, we can pay off another $800 on our land. A person can get ahead better here than in Holland, but he also has to do his best. We now have 320 acres of land. The farm is "20 minutes long and 10 minutes wide" and is square. It is already worth two times as much as when we bought it and will probably go higher in time. We'll get the farm paid for in the near future and then we really are well off.

We are busy picking corn at present. The best pickers earn $2.50 a day each day. A hired hand earns more here in one year in dollars than in Holland in guilders, and for one dollar you can get twice as much as for one guilder. Since a hired man always works with machinery, he can earn more money too.

This year we built a new church towards which we paid $150. We do not have a minister at present. Our congregation is getting bigger all the time since more Hollanders are coming here to live. You should come to visit us sometime, then you could see something of the world. Then you could see us and our children. It's too bad that you don't want to spend the money on it because travelling is very easy nowadays.

The widow of Jan de Roos—Kee Wynia—lives near hear. She still farms with her two youngest sons, Oepke and Pier and one daughter Akke. The three oldest sons and one daughter are married and all live here in Dakota. She often talks about you, that Bauke, Sijtske and she would visit you. That is 33 years ago. Trijntje Baukes Leffinga is married for the second time now. Ulbe Wynia's wife died last year. Old Jan de Roos died over two years ago. His wife died a little before him.

Our children, Grace, Dora and Jessie go to school every day and are able to read quite well already. Dora is a head taller than Grace. Pier is a white-haired boy just like I was in my early years. He is starting to talk a lot. He is fortunately a very bright boy.

Yes, yes, we are getting quite a family. An oversupply of work and responsibilities but "hitherto has the Lord helped us." And we trust that he will continue to supply our needs. My wife and I often say that we are not in this world for pleasure. But neither were our parents and we are no better than they. This life isn't everything and we both hope to live for eternity through our faith in the Lord Jesus Christ as our Savior.

My page is full so I'll end it here.

With hearty greetings from your brother and sister,

U. Eringa

M. Eringa-Rypstra

1905: JANUARY 7

W.E.B. DU BOIS TO VERNEALIA FAREIRA

In 1903, W.E.B. Du Bois (1868–1963) maintained in The Souls of Black Folk *that "the problem of the Twentieth Century is the problem of the color-line." An ardent foe of discrimination, he became a founder of the National Association for the Advancement of Colored People (NAACP) but would ultimately resign as editor of its journal,* Crisis: *his belief that blacks should have separate farms and businesses was considered too radical. Fareira was a black high-school student in Berwyn, Pennsylvania, whose teacher had written to Du Bois that Fareira refused to study because she said her color would deny her "a chance to use her knowledge."*

I wonder if you will let a stranger say a word to you about yourself? I have heard that you are a young woman of some ability but that you are neglecting your school work because you have become hopeless of trying to do anything in the world. I am very sorry for this. How any human being whose wonderful fortune it is to live in the 20th century should under ordinarily fair advantages despair of life is almost unbelievable. And if in addition to this that person is, as I am, of Negro lineage with all the hopes and yearnings of hundreds of millions of human souls dependent in some degree on her striving, then her bitterness amounts to crime.

There are in the U.S. today tens of thousands of colored girls who would be happy beyond measure to have the chance of educating themselves that you are neglecting. If you train yourself as you easily can, there are wonderful chances of usefulness before you: you can join the ranks of 15,000 Negro women teachers, of hundreds of nurses and physicians, of the growing number of clerks and stenographers, and above all of the host of homemakers. Ignorance is a cure for nothing. Get the very best training possible & the doors of opportunity will fly open before you as they are flying before thousands of your fellows. On the other hand every time a colored person neglects an opportunity, it makes it more difficult for others of the race to get such an opportunity. Do you want to cut off the chances of the boys and girls of tomorrow?

1905: NOVEMBER 19
THEODORE ROOSEVELT TO HIS SON

The devoted father of six children, Theodore Roosevelt was famous for entertaining their friends at Sagamore Hill on Long Island and for reading bedtime stories at the White House. Kermit was sixteen years old when his father wrote him this letter, characteristic in its emphasis on courage, physicality, and lack of pretension. Kermit (1889–1943) would grow up to be an author and explorer.

THE WHITE HOUSE
Washington

November 19, 1905

Dear Kermit:

I sympathize with every word you say in your letter, about Nicholas Nickleby, and about novels generally. Normally I only care for a novel if the ending is good, and I quite agree with you that if the hero has to die he ought to die worthily and nobly, so that our sorrow at the tragedy shall be tempered with the joy and pride one always feels when a man does his duty well and bravely. There is quite enough sorrow and shame and suffering and baseness in real life, and there is no need for meeting it unnecessarily in fiction. As Police Commissioner it was my duty to deal with all kinds of squalid misery and hideous and unspeakable infamy, and I should have been worse than a coward if I had shrunk from doing what was necessary; but there would have been no use whatever in my reading novels detailing all this misery and squalor and crime, or at least in reading them as a steady thing. Now and then there is a powerful but sad story which really is interesting and which really does good; but normally the books which do good and the books which healthy people find interesting are those which are not in the least of the sugar candy variety, but which while portraying foulness and suffering when they must be portrayed, yet have a joyous as well as a noble side.

We have had a very mild and open fall. I have played tennis a good deal, the French Ambassador being now quite a steady playmate as he and I play about alike; and I have ridden with Mother a great deal. Last Monday when Mother had gone to New York I had Selous, the great African hunter, to spend the day and night. He is a perfect old dear; just as simple and natural as can be and very interesting. I took him, with Bob Bacon, Gifford Pinchot, Ambassador Meyer and Jim Garfield, for a good scramble and climb in the afternoon, and they all came to dinner afterwards. Before we came down to dinner I got him to spend three quarters of an hour telling delightfully exciting lion and hyena stories to Ethel, Archie and Quentin. He told them most vividly and so enthralled the little boys that the next evening I had to tell them a large number myself.

To-day is Quentin's birthday and he loved his gifts, perhaps most of all the weest, cunningest live pig you ever saw, presented him by Straus. Phil Stewart and his wife and his boy, Wolcott (who is Archie's age) spent a couple of nights here. One afternoon we had hide-and-go-seek bringing down Mr. Garfield and the Garfield boys, and Archie turning up with the entire football team, who took a day off for the special purpose. We had obstacle races, hide-and-go-seek, blind man's buff, and everything else; and there were times when I felt that there was a perfect shoal of small boys bursting in every direction up and down stairs and through and over every conceivable object.

Mother and I still walk around the grounds every day after breakfast. The gardens of course are very, very disheveled now, the snap-dragons holding out better than any other flowers.

Your loving father,
T. R.

1906

A READER TO THE EDITOR OF THE "BINTEL BRIEF"

Between 1881 and 1925, more than two and a half million Jews emigrated from eastern Europe to America, roughly a third of the Jewish population in eastern Europe at the time. With immigrant readers in mind, the Yiddish Jewish Daily Forward *had been started in New York in 1897. Its popular advice column, the "Bintel Brief" (literally, "Bundle of Letters"), offered readers a blend of sympathy, gossip, morality from the Old World, and advice for navigating the New.*

Dear Editor,

I, too, want to take advantage of this opportunity to tell about my troubles, and I ask you to answer me.

Eight months ago I brought my girlfriend from Russia to the States. We had been in love for seven years and were married shortly after her arrival. We were very happy together until my wife became ill. She was pregnant and the doctors said her condition was poor. She was taken to the hospital, but after a few days was sent home. At home, she became worse, and there was no one to tend her.

You can hardly imagine our bitter lot. I had to work all day in the shop and my sick wife lay alone at home. Once as I opened the door when I came home at dinnertime, I heard my wife singing with a changed, hoarse voice. I was terror-stricken, and when I ran to her I saw she was out of her head with fever.

Imagine how I felt. My wife was so ill and I was supposed to run back to the shop because the last whistle was about to blow. Everybody was rushing back to work, but I couldn't leave. I knew that my boss would fire me. He had warned me the day before that if I came late again he wouldn't let me in. But how could I think of work now, when my wife was so ill? Yet without the job what would happen? There would not be a penny coming into the house. I stayed at my wife's bedside and didn't move till four o'clock.

Suddenly I jumped up and began to run around the room, in despair. My wife's singing and talking drove me insane. Like a madman I ran to the door and locked it. I leaped to the gas jet, opened the valve, then lay down in the bed near my wife and embraced her. In a few minutes I was nearer death than she.

Suddenly my wife cried out, "Water! water!" I dragged myself from the bed. With my last ounce of strength I crept to the door and opened it, closed the gas valve, and when I came to, gave her milk instead of water. She finished a glassful and wanted more, but there wasn't any more so I brought her some seltzer. I revived myself with water, and both of us slowly recovered.

The next morning they took my wife to the hospital, and after a stay of fourteen days she got well. Now I am happy that we are alive, but I keep thinking of what almost happened to us. Until now I never told anyone about it, but it bothers me. I have no secrets from my wife, and I want to know whether I should now tell her all, or not mention it. I beg you to answer me.

The Newborn

1906
THE "BINTEL BRIEF" EDITOR TO "THE NEWBORN"

This letter depicting the sad life of the worker is more powerful than any protest against the inequality between rich and poor. The advice to the writer is that he should not tell his wife that he almost ended both their lives. This secret may be withheld from his beloved wife, since it is clear he keeps it from her out of love.

1906: APRIL 24
FREDERICK COLLINS TO HIS FAMILY

An enormous earthquake on April 18, followed by four days of fires set off by over-turned stoves, fallen lanterns, and broken gas pipes, destroyed much of San Fran-cisco. Hundreds of people were killed and thousands injured; four square miles, or 514 city blocks, were devastated; and more than half of the city's 450,000 residents were left homeless. With an estimated Richter scale reading of 8.3, the earthquake would remain one of the century's worst urban disasters. The author of this letter, Frederick H. Collins (1869–1922), was co-owner of a women's clothing shop that was burned in the fire.
Nellie Alice Collins, Fred's sister, was in Oregon at the time. Robert Knox Collins owned a cigar store. Max Koenig was Collins's partner. Floyd McKenny was a reporter for the *San Francisco Bulletin*. Woody was a family friend.

April 24th '06

My Dears—

I don't know when I will get to write again so send this for me to Nell and then you (Nell) send it to mamma—The pouring rain compels us to stay in at Sadies, and our two trips to what was S.F. made us Thank God! to get back.

From the ferry to Van Ness it looks like a gray and black graveyard, as far as you can see, there isn't a house visible until you get within a few blocks of Van Ness. The fire passed way beyond Van Ness on both sides of the City. Rob was wiped out same as Max and I. We haven't heard from nor seen him yet but Floyd McKenny saw him with some of his household goods being driven toward the Park.

Max and I stayed out on Buchanan and Sutter with a friend of ours. But what a night. We felt that if we got home here alive again we would stay here, for no lights of any kind are the houses and they take a shot at you if you are out after 8.30 p.m. So you sit in pitch darkness with a gloomy pall of smoke over your heads and a graveyard silence and an occasional earthquake tremor.

We never closed our eyes that night and it began to rain and a cold mournful wind began to howl around open chimney holes and busted roofs. At 5 o'clock a rifle shot was heard on the block and some young fellow fell dead who was mis-prudent enough to venture out to borrow some whiskey for his sick mother. A soldier ordered him to throw it away and shot him for refusing. This is only one of many cases. When daylight came we helped cook our breakfast in the street where rich and poor alike squat side by side cooking on brick stoves, and then all go stand in line to get their share of provisions. No one is allowed to sell a thing there but every thing left in stores has been distributed, and loads are coming in every day.

We tried to find some of our friends but it's almost impossible. We found Mrs. Young. She has joined the red cross forces and is begging clothes to put on the new born babies in the parks. She had 18 to clothe in one day. Soon as they are born they just have to roll them in some old coat or rags until they find clothes. One woman had triplets.

Then on top of all yesterday, the rain just poured in torrents soaking bedding, grass and ground and peoples' clothes. With it a cold wind. People are draggled with mud, and there is hardly a house left that isn't twisted or unsafe. Some are toppled into the streets. Some are leaning over on their next door neighbors, and stone stairs fallen away from front doors. Church towers of stone have crashed and crushed into homes besides them. Many places crushing the occupants. No one will ever know the hundreds that were killed under fallen buildings and then buried.

Valencia St. has slid 40 feet out of its course and a hotel on that street and Market collapsed, killing 103 out of 106 that were in it. The earth split open there wide enough for a man to fall in and you can hear a running river or creek under it. Another street a little mound raised up and burst open and a little fountain of regular clear mountain spring water is shooting up out of it.

We walked down the north side of Van Ness when we were helping Max's sister in law and baby out of the city and found the earth split and uneven in places and raised in one place enough to tip a big stone mansion over backwards down the hill. Two big houses have fallen together near it and are ready to crash in the street. In places the earthquake has humped iron (or steel) up like arches in places so most of the third of the City left (out in the part beyond Van Ness) is pretty well battered up.

So in a deluge of water Max and I walked to the ferry soaked to the skin making our escape from ruin and (water this time) and dodging quickly along under towering scraps of high stone walls swaying over head in places. Our shoes were full of water and we were happy to get back to Sadies again.

They are dynamiting dangerous walls today over there and an earthquake last night at 11:30 shook down a few more besides scaring the balance of courage out of the people there. We felt it here also. Ann got up and got dressed ready to run last night.

Today it rains in showers at intervals. You know what we have lost of course. Our beautiful store, a fifty thousand dollar stock. Everything at our apartments, my library, your paintings and mine—Bronzes, silver vase. Expensive pictures, our embroidered robes, linens, steins. All good clothes such as black suits, overcoats, hats, shoes, underclothes, shirts. All souvenirs and pictures from Germany, cut glass, all photographs, piano, hand painted china—and so on down to just what useful thing we could rush into a valise and to bundles (enough to cover us in case we had to sleep on the hills) Everything else went. Still we are like all other big losers. We meet it cheerfully and will have to make a new start when all confusion is over and we see if S.F. is doomed to be left or the rest of it demolished.

They have dug "Privy" holes in the middle of streets out in the part that's saved for women to use.

In all the misery there are the usual tearfully funny things—people cross ferry boats that dreadful morning in nightgowns and barefoot and many ran with the crazies and things they had saved. One woman saved a bird and one shoe. Another a few flat irons. One poor Chinaman crossed the bay with a stick of firewood wrapped up, and some ran with an "enlarged picture" of someone of the family as a child. Old women and men were seen dragging chairs loaded with things in the way of clothing and blankets, pulled by a little rope over their backs.

Just had a little shock while writing this—Just got a letter from mamma wanting to know why she can't hear from us. We sent telegram to her the day after the City started to burn. Then Sadie wrote to some of you. We think

Woody must have been killed as he was in the part that collapsed so terribly when the Earthquake came and was soon a raging furnace.

The morning we first went back and wended our way around the flaming City, our store was then the center of the red hot furnace of flames, and our home "The Iroquois" was a pile of hot ashes and stone. One corner of the wall stuck up in the air with one of our window openings left to look through. The rest was in the hot pit below. Sidewalk was even gone and big deep hole with the contents of ten furnished floors. Ashes was all that remained. No chance of even finding a small piece of a glass bottle.

Everything was a complete "wipe out," wholesale and retail both. Never missed one thing on the way, and what ever saved the small part that's left, I can't see—for it was sweeping out all over the Mission and back down through the residence portion on our side of Market, the entire wholesale district, North Beach, Telegraph Hill, Nob Hill mansions, down around Hyde and Lombard, where Rob lived, on out toward the Presidio and at the same time the whole middle of the City in one flaming furnace rushing out at the same time.

They dynamited the side of Van Ness nearest to the oncoming fire Saturday. Whole rows of gun powder along the rows of cannons and shot them all at the buildings then set fire to the ones further down so as to make fire meet fire leaving the space on one side clear that had been blown down. That is the only thing that saved the little they did—Talk about Mt. Vesuvius and Pompeii, this surely beats it all.

The losses go into the Billions—but what hundreds and thousands would have been killed if it had come at about 9 in the evening when theaters were packed and streets were crowded, for nearly every theatre collapsed from the earthquake and the tops of most of the stone and brick buildings fell into the streets and onto sidewalks on both sides. Some buildings fell to the sidewalk right where they stood and some seemed to fall right down into the middle.

Max and I were almost thrown from our beds when the shock came at about 5.15. I rushed to the door casing between bedroom and Turkish room, Max at my heels. We hung onto the sides of the wall while the building seemed to split, groan and crack and rock, expecting each second for the whole big structure of stone and its main floor to crush us at each roll. Stones from the top were falling at our window sills outside and the screams of hundreds of women rushing into the streets half naked.

When the stillness came, I climbed into bed to stop the chatter of my teeth, which seemed to be loose in stiffened jaws. Then we dressed hurriedly and ran to the store over the debris of fallen chimneys and top stories of buildings in the street. Found our store stood it fine. Our wax figures never tipped over but stood unscratched even though the big plate glass windows lay on the sidewalk and glass surrounded them. They stood in a half inch of water with their expensive opera gowns, as the big high jar had tipped over and it was full of water and Easter Lilies.

Inside the store our dressing room was full of fallen plaster but that was all. We even began to clean up and arrange things for business when another shock came and we saw that the City was on fire, so we locked the doors and left the swell store to its fate and went to our home. A little later, when the fire had reached within three blocks. So, expecting the building on our heads any minute, we hurriedly packed some useful clothing, took a farewell look at all our belongings and "hiked" out over the high steep hills and made a circuit to the waters edge and followed that around to the Ferry.

Everything was smoking ruins then right up to the Ferry Building. It seemed the only thing left and they saved that by pumping water on it from the bay.

We can't tell what we are going to do yet as we don't know yet what is going to happen here so will let you know later on. But have hardly recovered from it all yet. All are well here but no fires are allowed here either in stoves as everybody's chimney is in the yards, so it will be a long time before everything is entirely safe. This is to all of you so please forward it as I can't write it all to each of you.

Love from Fred

Haven't found yet where Dr. Fraser is but heard he was safe someplace near French Hospital.

1906: JULY 5
GRACE BROWN TO CHESTER GILLETTE

The nearly month-long trial of Chester Gillette for the murder of Grace Brown was front-page news all over the country, presenting a sordid but riveting tale that would be retold in Theodore Dreiser's An American Tragedy *and the movie* A Place in the Sun. *Gillette, twenty-two, was the privileged nephew of a factory owner in Cortland, New York. Twenty-year-old Brown worked there and became pregnant with Gillette's child in 1906. She may still have been hoping to marry him when she joined him on a trip to the Adirondacks. After two nights together they stopped at Big Moose Lake, where they rented a boat. Sometime that evening she drowned. This desperate letter was the last of several she sent to him, and both jury and spectators wept when they heard it read at Gillette's trial. His defense lawyers insisted it proved his claim that she had committed suicide. But the jury found him guilty of murder, and he would die in the electric chair in March of 1908.*

Thursday night

My dear Chester— I am curled up by the kitchen fire and you would shout if you could see me. Everyone else is in bed. The girls came up and we shot the last firecrackers. Our lawn looks as green as the Cortland House corner. I will tell you all about my Fourth when I see you. I hope you had a nice time.

This is the last letter I can write dear. I feel as though you are not coming. Perhaps this is not right, but I cannot help feeling that I am never going to see you again. How I wish this was Monday.

I am going down to stay with Maude next Sunday night, dear, and then go to DeRuyter the next morning and will get there about 10 o'clock. If you take the 9:45 train from the Lehigh there you will get there about eleven.

I am sorry I could not go to Hamilton, dear, but Mama and Papa did not want me to go and there are so many things I have had to work hard for in the last two weeks. They think I am just going out there to DeRuyter for a visit.

Now, dear, when I get there I will go at once to the hotel and I don't think I will see any of the people. If I do and they ask me to come to the house I will say something so they won't mistrust anything. Tell them I have a friend coming from Cortland; that we are to meet there to go to a funeral or a wedding in some town farther on. Awfully sorry, but we were invited to come and I had to cut my vacation a little short and go. Will that be all O.K. dear? Maybe that won't be just what I will say, but don't worry about anything for I shall manage somehow.

Only I want you to come in the morning. I don't want to wait there in the hotel all day, for if they should see me there, and all day, they would think it funny I did not go to the house. You must come in the morning for I have had to make—you don't know how many plans to fit your last letter—in order to meet you Monday. I dislike waiting until Monday but now that I have I don't think anything only fair that you should come Monday morning. But, dear, you must see the necessity yourself of getting there and not making me wait. If you dislike the idea of coming Monday morning and can get a train up there Sunday, you can come up Sunday night and be there to meet me. Perhaps that would be the best way. All I care is that I don't want to wait there all day or half a day. I think there is a train that leaves the Lehigh at six something Sunday night. I don't know what I would do if you were not there or did not come. I am about crazy now.

I have been bidding goodbye to some places today. There are so many nooks, dear, and all of them so dear to me. I have lived here nearly all of my life. First, I said goodbye to the spring house with its great masses of green moss; then the beehive, a cute little house in the orchard, and, of course, all of the neighbors that have mended my dresses from a little tot up to save me a thrashing I really deserved.

Oh dear, you don't realize what all of this is to me. I know I shall never see any of them again. And Mama! Great heavens, how I do love Mama! I don't know what I shall do without her. She is never cross and she always helps me so much. Sometimes, I think if I could tell Mama, but I can't. She has trouble enough as it is, and I couldn't break her heart like that. If I come back dead, perhaps, if she does not know, she won't be angry with me. I will never be happy again, dear. I wish I could die.

I am going to bed now dear. Please come and don't let me wait there. It is for both of us to be there. If you have made some plans for something Sunday night you must come Monday morning.

Please think, dear, that I had to give up a whole summer's pleasure and you will surely be brave enough to give up one evening for me. I shall expect and look for you Monday forenoon.

Heaven bless you until then.

Lovingly and with kisses, The Kid

I will go to the Tabor House and you come for me there. I wish you would come up Sunday night, so as to be there, and, sweetheart, I think it would be easier for you. Please come up Sunday night, dear.

1906: SEPTEMBER
MARIANNE TO LORNA

Until 1942, when the Supreme Court ruled that a lenient six-week residency requirement would be valid in all states, the "quickie divorce" was a lucrative draw to western states with permissive laws. In 1900, 55,751 Americans—or .7 in 1,000—divorced, many by going west. By 1990, the divorce rate would rise to nearly 5 per 1,000, and the ritual of establishing residency elsewhere would disappear. Yet many of the sentiments of the divorce-bound—including the giddy sense of freedom expressed in this letter—would remain the same.

This letter was published in 1909 in a book called _Letters of a Dakota Divorcee_. Its author was listed as Jane Burr, clearly a pseudonym, as the letters were signed "Marianne." Whether they were fictional or not is unclear.

Duckie Lorna:

Sip a mint julip—slowly, gently, through a long dry straw, then before it dies in you, read my P.O. mark—Sioux Falls, South Dakota,—Yes, I've bolted!

Don't dare to tell anyone where I am for if my husband should find out, he might make me go where I could get a divorce more quickly—You know I'm here for his health. I would splash round in orange blossoms, and this is the result.

My boarding house is a love, furnished with prizes got with soap— "Buy ten bars of our Fluffy Ruffles soap, and we will mail you, prepaid, one of our large size solid mahogany library tables."

Would you believe dear, that these Sioux Fallians have already complained because I bathe my dear, shaggy Othello in the bath tub. And there isn't a human being here with a pedigree as long as his.

If you hear any talk about my being seen in a Staten Island beer garden with Bern Cameron, don't believe one word of it—we didn't go in at all, the place was too smelly. And that fib about his giving me a diamond ring,—deny it please, as I have never shown it to a soul—So you can see how people manufacture gossip.

I walk to the Penitentiary for recreation, as I may have to visit there some day and I never like to be surprised at anything. It isn't refined.

My Attorney is thoroughly picturesque. He wears a coat in his office that his wife must have made. His collar came from Noah's grab bag, and, if you remember, there was no washing machine on the ark. A heavy gold chain meanders down his shirt front to protect his watch from improbable theft. On Sunday he passes the contribution box and is considered a philanthropic pest. I asked how much the fee would be and he said, "One hundred if you furnish witnesses, two hundred if we do." You can hire a man for five dollars out here to swear that he killed you.

When my attorney talks, he sits on his haunches, showing his teeth that would do credit to a shark, and fancies he's smiling when he permits his cracked purple lips to slide back. I wouldn't trust my case to him, only he could not lose if he tried.

Every time I look at him I wonder if there could be a face behind that nose and those whiskers, which give his head the appearance of a fern dish. He wears an old silk hat whose nap is attacked with a skin disease. They say he belongs to one of the first families of this town—first on the way coming up from the station I suppose. He was married years ago, but isn't working at it now. I am so unstrung after our seances that I feel like crawling right out under a bush and eating sage. If I weren't afraid of him I'd raise my umbrella while he talks—his conversation is so showery. In my ingrown heart I hate him so there is no danger for me, tho' I've heard that he's a perfect fusser with the women.

I telephoned the livery stable yesterday and asked if any of the hearse horses were idle, as I'd like to take a ride. The fellow said he'd send me a winner, so I togged up in my bloomers, boots and spurs and stood on the veranda waiting. A young boy galloped up with something dragging behind him. I said: "Do you call that insect a horse?" he answered; "No, but it used to be, m'am." The poor creature was all bones and only waiting for a nudge to push him into the grave. I mounted the broncho, which kept "bronking," but after an encouraging tclk-tclk, I made a detour of the block, then sent the nag to the stable.

There were two children and a dog drowned here yesterday—it almost makes one afraid to go near the tub.

The man who sits on my right at the table, says he's here for nervousness. First time I ever heard a divorce called that, but anyway we all know that he gets out of jail on December, and I will be glad, for the way he plays the anvil chorus with his soup makes me get out of my skin backwards. Hope some day that the Devil will play dominoes with his bones.

The lady on the other end, chews with her lips and of course I'm always excited for fear her dinner will fall overboard. The way she juggles food would get her a job in the vaudeville game any day. She sits up as tho' she'd been impaled, and the shaft broken off in her body.

Long ago—a being, desirous of unhitchment could come here, rent a room, hang her pajamas in the closet and fade away back to Broadway, but times are changed, and you must serve six months or the Judge's wife will not let you have a divorce. The Judge's house is next to mine and the way I look demure when I pass, is a heathenism hypocrisy. But he is under petticoat tyranny and I dread ruffling the petticoat.

Formerly the law was three months, but the Cataract Hotel had the Legislature change it as they could not make enough money.

We had chicken last night and asparagus tips—did you ever notice what a lot of skin a boarding house chicken has? And the tips just missed by one, being tip. The meals are an unsatisfactory substitute for something to eat, and I find myself filling up on bread to keep my stomach and backbone apart.

I am up against old timers that are always to be met at boarding houses—the dear old soldier and the lady "too heavy for light amusements, and not old enough to sit in the corner and knit," as George Ade puts it. She is simply ubiquitous; she is everywhere; she does not gossip! Oh no! Still she wonders if they really are married, you know, and if that strange man is her brother or not? Oh you know the whole tribe! Dear old parasites on the body politic! I have also had sudden paralysis of the jaw from looking into a country mirror and was not again convinced, until consulting my own hand glass during the night that one of my eyes had not slipped down below my nose. I can get along very well if my hair is not parted at all, but I insist upon my features remaining in the same locations.

I am copying down some of the stories that I hear as they are well worth it, and may come in handy some day. I have the advantage of coming upon them suddenly for the first time, with an absolute unbiased mind, which like the Bellman's chart in "The Hunting of the Snark" is "a perfect and absolute blank."

I know I shall go mad before the six months are up, for after ten days, I am down down deep in a bog of melancholy, and so bored that I feel like the president of the gimlet club.

My stomach like nature abhors a vacuum, so me to the strangled eggs and baked spuds which are our unfailing morning diet.

In the name of Charity, send me messages from the world I love.

Devotedly,
Marianne

1907: MARCH 21
WALLACE STEVENS TO ELSIE MOLL

One of the century's most famous poets, Wallace Stevens (1879–1955) was already pursuing two careers—as a writer and a lawyer—when he sent this letter to his future wife. Its callow tone notwithstanding, Stevens would go on to mainstream success in both professional spheres, winning the Pulitzer prize and two National Book Awards, and becoming vice-president of the Hartford Accident and Indemnity Company, where he remained until his death.

Thursday Evening

Dear Elsie:—

I am so full of misery to-night that I am ridiculous. Every Spring I have a month or two of semi-blackness and perhaps the mood is just returning. Perhaps, it is simply a revulsion against old things—habits, people, places—everything: the feeling the sun must have, nowadays, when it shines on nothing but mud and bare trees and the general world, rusty with winter. People do not look well in Spring. They seem grimy and puffy and it makes me misanthropic.—Spring fills me so full of dreams that try one's patience in coming time. One has a desire for the air full of spice and odors, and for days like junk of changing colors, and for warmth and ease, and all the other things that you know so well. But they come so slowly.—Earth and the body and the spirit seem to change together, and so I feel muddy and bare and rusty.—I'd like to wear a carnation every morning and I'd like to see other people decorating themselves like good children.—The winter-nights leave a mark in their faces: the beer and the smoke and the late reading and talking! It makes me want to plunge them all in a crystal pool and bring them out rosy and sparkling. Some of them are young and have gray hair and round shoulders—I'm thinking of one. How lost he would be in our Eden! Elsie (now I could add so many, many more names)—you will never grow old, will you? You will always be just my little girl, won't you? You must always have pink cheeks and golden hair. To be young is all there is in the world. The rest is nonsense—and cant. They talk so beautifully about work and having a family and a home (and I do, too, sometimes)—but it's all worry and head-aches and respectable poverty and forced gushing. Still you must not remember this against me. By gushing I mean: telling people how nice it is, when, in reality, you would give all of your last thirty years for one of your first thirty. Old people are tremendous frauds. The point is to be young—and to be a little in love, or very much—and to desire carnations and "creations"—and to be glad when Spring comes. . . .—Some of us used to lie in the sun at Kissinger's Locks a whole summer long, going home only for meals and to sleep. I can feel the warmth now and remember the laziness of it. Was that in this world—so cloudy and cold and full of winds?—I lost a world when I left Reading. You and I only sip it—I lived it.—Once last summer I went to the level where we ate our lunch—and went swimming in a secluded spot. I left myself float under the water (left should be let, of course) and looked at the blue and brown colors there and I shouted when I came up.—So there is still some of the foolishness and delight in me.—Yet here I am, twenty-seven, practicing law in New-York, and writing letters to my princess. But I am glad to be

Your
Wallace.

1907: NOVEMBER 15
SUSAN LA FLESCHE PICOTTE TO FRANCIS LEUPP

A graduate of Women's Medical College in Philadelphia, Susan La Flesche Picotte (1865–1915) was the first American Indian woman to become an M.D. As her tribe's physician at the Omaha Reservation in Nebraska, she did ceaseless battle with a government bureaucracy that, while small by today's standards, seems to have been every bit as frustrating. Francis Leupp was commissioner of Indian affairs. In his response to this letter, he would inform Picotte that a stenographer had already been authorized, but that due to lack of funds he could not grant the request for another field matron.

Henry Drummond was a British clergyman.

St. Vincent's Hospital
Sioux City Iowa.
Nov. 15th 1907.

Hon. Francis E. Leupp:

Dear Sir:

I am an Omaha Indian and have been working as medical missionary among the Omahas but have broken down from overwork. Altho' I have been here several weeks I have kept in touch with affairs at Macy.

I know what a small figure our affairs cut with all the Department has on its hands, but I also know that if you knew the conditions and circumstances, to be remedied you would do all you could to remedy them.

I understand Mr. Commons, our Agent, has been cut off from a stenographer.

It takes most of his time answering necessary correspondence and the affairs of the Indians have to be neglected.

Mr. Commons is a good man, and does all he can for the Indians, but under the circumstances he can't do clerical work and attend to the Indian's wants too, so we need a stenographer.

Mr. Commons has told me nothing of this.

Second:

We need another Field Matron besides the one we have now, Miss Collett. She is doing fine work and the Indians like her very much, but there is more than enough work for another one. We would like to have Miss Sallie Hagan, who is dayschool teacher, and is known to Maj. Larrabee personally. The Indians are working better and so drinking much less, they are beginning to get interested in the church and now is the time, when they are beginning to climb up, that they need the most help—and this help can be given to them thro' the field matrons. We would want Miss Hagan, for the Indians like her and she is sympathetic, and they would allow her to do things for them, they would not allow anyone else to do.

I asked Mr. Commons and Maj. Hutchings if they tho't the Government would allow us one—they spoke of a man but it's essentially a woman's work, and the man would have to be a second Henry Drummond (and such men are scarce) in order to work successfully among the Indians.

I had intended to do so much work this fall—the Doctor tells me I cannot do any medical work for 6 mos. and I feel that something must be done for the people, such as our field matron is doing now, real missionary work, for you can't rush at the Indians with an open Bible any more than you can the white people.

Will you please give us Miss Hagan besides Miss Collett?

<u>Third</u>:

The spread of Tuberculosis among my people is something terrible—it shows itself in the lungs, kidneys, alimentary track, blood, brain and glands—so many, many of the young children are marked with it in some form. The physical degeneration in 20 years among my people is terrible. I have talked with them and done all I could to prevent infection and contagion, but I want to know if the Gov't can't do for us, what it did for the Sioux, in preventing the spread of this White Plague.

The financial outlay for any of these three requests is but small compared to the amount of good it will bring forth to my people.

Most Respectfully—

Susan La Flesche Picotte, M.D.

1908: APRIL 16
A PATIENT TO DR. JOSEPH COLLINS

The Interpretation of Dreams had been published in 1900, but Sigmund Freud wasn't exactly a household name when, eight years later, a troubled Rhode Island man wrote to a New York neurologist named Joseph Collins (1866–1950) for advice. Today that patient's problem would probably provoke no more than a shrug in the average high-school student, but in 1908, as this letter and the doctor's reply reveal, the province of guilt was still largely uncharted, and even the word "psychotherapy" was new.

Rhode Island, April 16, 1908.

My Dear Doctor:

Your suggestion, when I saw you at your office, that I should write a statement of my complaint, seemed quite reasonable until I began to try to put the facts on paper. Even then it seemed reasonable but also impossible. In the first place, I do not like to write, and in the second place I don't know what to put in and what to leave out. You have seen me and know that I am 21 years old, though I suppose I seem older because I have had to work since I was 14 years old and help to support my mother. This responsibility and the worry that I have had about myself have made me more mature than most young men of 21. I have a good position, and the respect of every one with whom I am associated, but if they knew me as I know myself, very likely I should forfeit them. I attribute all my troubles to masturbation, which I began when about 12 years old. After about three years I learned how injurious it was and stopped it. A few months later I began to have nocturnal emissions which were the result of my foolishness. About this time a great change came over me; I became regretful, remorseful, and self-conscious, and would often break out into a violent perspiration, particularly if I thought any one noticed me. All this was the result of the injury I had done myself. I tried to compensate for this injury by taking every kind of exercise that I was told would be beneficial, by taking cold baths, and paying great attention to what I ate, but none of them did me any good. I continued to have the same feeling and in addition a great deal of indigestion. When I was about 18 years old I was told that if I masticated my food thoroughly I would get rid of the indigestion. I began to do this, taking from an hour to an hour and a half to each meal.

Then it occurred to me that I could accomplish my purpose much better if I were to eat alone. At first I could stand it if persons were in the house, but if anyone were in the room my mouth would become so dry that I could not get the food soft enough to swallow and I would have a queer feeling of contraction in my stomach, and lose my sense of taste. My mother was then having a few lady boarders, mostly school teachers, which I persuaded her to give up because of my inability to take food if they were anywhere about.

Last February my mother went away to make a visit. She was to stay a week, so she cooked some food to do me during her absence. I got my own meals and ate them in my bedroom. During this time that no one was in the house I realized that it was unnecessary to chew my food until it became a liquid, my sense of taste returned, and I gained ten pounds in two weeks. My mother then came home, but I discovered at once that I could no longer eat while she was in the house. No matter if she was in another room I could not eat. I imagined she was listening, my mouth became dry, and this terrible constriction developed in my stomach, and it was impossible to go on eating until she left. I persuaded her to put my meals on the table and then go out away from the house, to visit a neighbor, or to go to a store. Then I ate, but while doing so I was in constant fear that some one would come in. In order to avoid this I ate hurriedly with the result that lately I have had a great deal of indigestion. Now the neighbors are beginning to inquire why she always goes out at meal time, especially when it is raining and storming, and it is often embarrassing to give an explanation. But she must go or I starve, and I must keep up my strength. I always feel the sense of constriction of the stomach when I am in company, when I am talking, riding in the street car, etc., and especially if the person with whom I am in contact has shown more than ordinary interest in a personal or business way. I have it in the most troublesome way when I am with a girl that I know and like very well. It is hard for me to explain it in reference to this particular girl, but I must tell you that I have had lately a feeling that I would never let a woman get the better of me.

This has a queer relationship to what I consider to be the beginning of all my trouble. I have never had any inclination or desire to have certain relations with women; on the contrary, I have had a feeling of profound dislike for even the thought of it or for anything that suggests it. I do not think sexual intercourse is wrong or immoral but I do feel that if it were not for that I should not be in the condition in which I am now. Therefore I never go to a play or to a theater where they have ballet dancing, or where women play in short dresses, or where I would see anything which was likely to suggest these things to produce emission later when I am asleep.

A year ago, when the girl that I spoke about came to ——— to visit, I met her and got to like her very much as a girl; I liked her just because it was she. I never thought of her in any other way than as a boy might think of an automobile. I used to go to see her often, but always after dark. She did not understand at first why I came then, but circumstances favored my calls at such time, and I was more ready to go because in the dark or with very dim light I do not break out into this awful perspiration, and I am not so terribly self-conscious and terrorized as I am at other times.

There are times when I feel perfectly well, even when I am with this girl. For instance I recall that some time ago I was calling upon her and I lay down upon a sofa; she came and sat beside me and caressed me. I felt as if a weight were lifted from me, and I said to myself, "I am perfectly well." If I should plan to repeat this I would get into such a state of excitement and distress, that I think I would go mad. In the first place I have to distinguish this girl from her sex. I am not at all sure that I make clear to you what I mean, but I have the conviction that the sex, meaning women, have had something to do with getting me into this awful condition. If they did not exist, that is, if there had not been something in me which demanded or called for their existence, then I should not be in the condition in which I am. My reasons, then, for not wanting to have anything to do with them is that I want to put this whole question of sex entirely outside my thought, and this is what I mean when I say that I have the feeling that I shall never let a woman get the better of me. But with this particular girl it seems that I don't feel that way and especially when I am with her. When I am not with her she is in the category of her sex, and the thought of her fills me, sometimes, with these extraordinary feelings which are a mixture of fright, anxiety, terror, and despair. I feel sometimes I can't withstand the sensation another minute, and if I don't get relief I'll explode, or go up in the air, or in some other manner cease to be.

I have explained to her a great many of my troubles, but of course she does not know what they come from. Once when she came out to —— I met her at the train and I told her I had to go to ——. She wanted to go with me. I thought I could not stand it, as it would be very light in the train, but finally she persuaded me to take her. The perspiration simply rolled from me all the way and I was most uncomfortable. I kept saying to myself, "If ever I get out of this I'll never get into such a mess again." Had it been dark I should have enjoyed myself. When we returned I went home, changed all my underclothes, which were so wet they dripped when wrung, and then went to her house. The light was low there and I felt all right. To-morrow she is coming up to —— to see a ball game. I am going to play. I shall suffer more than you can imagine because I know she is there. I wish she were not coming. I will have a nervous sensation for fear she will see something in my face that will make her not care for me and I shall avoid her in every possible way. Unless she approaches me it is very probable that I shall go home without speaking to her. She knows I care for her although I have not told her in so many words.

Last summer she wanted to give me a ring. I said, "No, I am not worthy of it." I felt unworthy because I had masturbated and injured myself by so doing. In the winter, however, when she asked me again to take it, and keep it as long as I loved her, I thought "I can do that conscientiously," but I did not say in so many words, "I love you." She is a brilliant girl in company, a wonderful girl, and she is very fond of me.

She has written between forty and fifty letters to me, but I have only written one to her. I cannot bring myself to write because I feel that some time the written letter might be used to my disadvantage. Sometimes, you see, I am so nervous that I can scarcely sign my name.

If I did not have so much worry about eating, that is if I could give time to anything else, I might get well, but I have fallen away terribly, particularly around my chest, although I am pretty good weight, that is I weigh 145 pounds and I am only 5 feet 5 inches high, but I am sure that my body has fallen away a great deal. It is always harder for me to eat dinner than any other meal, and particularly if I have seen a great many people all day or have been excited in any way.

I have had to give up going to church and to entertainments. Occasionally I go alone to the theater, but always I have to have an aisle seat so that if the impulse to get up and go out comes over me I can do so. Once or twice I have been to the theater and had a seat two or three from the aisle but I perspired so all the time and was so painfully self-conscious that I did not have a moment's enjoyment. As a rule when I am in the theater or a similar place, I am able to forget myself only when the lights are turned low. Then of course I can't go anywhere for amusement like other persons. I can't go into a restaurant, I can't go on excursions, I can't go to parties, for the entertainment of all of these is mixed up with eating and with women.

I like crowds; for instance, there are few things I like better than going to a baseball game; then, with a great many people around me, no one observing me, I am without a trace of nervousness. I can talk to anyone at such times, who speaks to me casually and does not take very much interest in me, just as any normal person can.

I am convinced that I brought this all upon myself, and I know I did myself harm. If I don't get out of it I don't know what is going to happen to me. As I have told you, I am falling away around my chest, as anyone can see who will look at it, and I am sure that one can't go on living the way I do.

Another thing that troubles me is that I don't know what to do about this girl. She seems to me to be the finest thing in the world, but I am not able to conduct myself toward her as a man should. Please help me.

Yours faithfully,

[Anonymous]

1908: APRIL 23

DR. JOSEPH COLLINS TO A PATIENT

New York, April 23, 1908.

Dear Sir:

The letter which you wrote to me on April 16 I have received. Despite what you say in the beginning of your letter about your inability to write, it seems to me that you have succeeded in this instance in letting me know something of yourself.

Your case is of the greater interest because it seems, even from the brief recitation that you have made of it, that your obsessions and your delusions are founded upon a sexual basis. A well known Austrian writer, Freud, to whom we are indebted for helping us to interpret such disorders as yours, has suggested that most cases of this kind are founded upon such basis.

I do not believe that the cause which you attribute for your ills, namely onanism, is the fundamental one. In fact, I am not at all convinced that it has had anything to do with your present complaint. In the first place, you must know that the majority of boys at some time in their lives do what you did, and which you are now making such a fuss about. And you must likewise know that no injury flows from it, otherwise the world would be filled with human wrecks. Why should you, a vigorous, robust, young boy, who was addicted to it a very brief time, be wrecked and the countless others go entirely free?

I have no doubt that your disorder is upon a sexual basis but it will require a careful investigation by the so-called psychoanalytic method to determine just what feature of sex disturbance is responsible for it.

It will not cure you to be told that the unnatural sexual indulgence of your boyhood is inadequate to have caused your present condition. It will not suffice you to be assured that if you will exert your will power you will overcome your most distressing symptoms. It will not avail even to convince you by logical argumentation that you must be well nourished to weigh 145 pounds when you are but 65 inches tall, and that therefore the belief that you are falling away is a delusion. In fact argument, persuasion, exhortation, assurance, contempt even (that weapon which pierces the shell of the tortoise) are of little utility in such cases until after the patient has been assisted to a psychic state similar to that which existed when the symptoms first manifested themselves. You ask how this is to be accomplished? And I say to you, I profess to do such things, and I shall be glad to try to do it with you.

Such treatment is called psychotherapy. It is a big word, and now that the public, and here and there an enthusiastic cleric have got hold of it, it is likely to have the vogue that appendicitis had a decade or so ago. It is not at all new in the art of medicine. In fact it antedates Esculapius, and a very fair brand of it was in use at the time of the Pharaohs. However, there came a time when it fell into desuetude in Boston, and so it had to be revived. The renaissance was attended with slight raising of the voice on the part of its sponsors. This is the equivalent of a lyric outburst or of a dramatic apostrophe, or even of an impassioned arraignment, in less cultured centers. Naturally advance has been made in the understanding and application of it during these past few years that have revolutionized every art save that of the poet and artist.

You may do a great deal to assist the physician who essays to cure you. You may assume, for instance, that you are in error about the cause of your symptoms. You need not furnish a cause just at present. Assume that you do not know and leave it to others whose lives are devoted to ferreting out the cause of disease to find out. You may read books whose purpose is the instruction of persons such as you in the nature of their symptoms and diseases. For this purpose I recommend a small book recently published by Lippincott, of Philadelphia, entitled "Why Worry?" from the pen of a physician in a neighboring city long known as the Athens of America, sometimes reviled as the cradle and nursery of "Antis" of every description, but universally recognized as the abiding place of the Ancient and Honorable Artillery. Its author, Dr. George L. Walton, has succeeded in putting the facts about psychoneurotics, of which you are one—if you will forgive me for calling you names—so clearly and so intelligibly that any one can grasp and understand them. More than this, he writes with such insight and sympathy, such candor and simplicity, that the reader cannot fail to appreciate that what is said is founded upon experience, knowledge, and wisdom. You will find in it, I have no doubt, much that will aid me in getting you well.

Finally, don't neglect the poets. They are a great adjuvant to medicine. You will not accuse me of disrespect for the cloth or irreverence for that which it represents symbolically when I say that if I had to choose between Emerson and the Emmanuel Church as an aid to the practice of medicine, I shouldn't hesitate a moment. I don't decry prayer while exalting poetry, for I believe with the Epistler James that the effectual fervent prayer of a righteous man availeth much. While I am speaking of poetry I suggest that you commit to memory the following stanza from Cowper and whenever you get wrestling with the idea that your troubles have flown out of youthful folly counteract it with "Truth," which says:

"Past indiscretion is a venial crime,
And if the youth, unmellowed yet by time,
Bore on his branch luxuriant then and rude,
Fruits of a blighted size, austere and crude,
Maturer years shall happier stores produce,
And 'meliorate the well-concocted juice."

Finally I want to say to you that I am sure that you will recover, and that you and she, "the brilliant girl, the wonderful girl," will live happy together forever afterward.

Yours, very sincerely,
[Joseph Collins, M.D.]

1908: OCTOBER 14

CLARKE SALES COMPANY MANAGER TO JAMES M. JOYCE

As inevitable as it may seem today, the zipper was anything but an overnight success. It evolved over the course of several decades, starting out in 1893 as a gliding, detachable fastener for hooks and eyes and only gradually acquiring its spring clips, its name, and its popularity. Somewhere along the way, a New York company came up with a model called the Plako; like many revolutionary breakthroughs—as this letter to a prospective retailer suggests—the idea had to be sold.

October 14th, 1908.

Mr. James M. Joyce,
  48 Birch St.,
    Lewiston, Me.

Dear Sir:

Our article is a necessity nothing else can take the place of. Go out in the street and look at the back of every skirt worn and then count and see if nine out of every ten doesn't need an invisible and secure fastener to close the skirt opening. Ask every woman you know and see if she won't agree with you that all her neighbors' skirts are not fastened neatly.

Some placket openings will gap; some eyes will be pulled off. The majority of placket and waist backs will lack the neat appearance every self-respecting woman requires in the rest of her attire.

Big field for an absolutely secure and invisible method of closing the skirt and in which our PLAKO Fastener has no competitor.

How easy to sell a fastener for the waist which eliminates gaping or opening when on, and wonder of wonders, THE WEARER CAN FASTEN THE BACK OF HER OWN WAIST!

Sell it also to the men: they know what a great need there is for the PLAKO Waist Fastener.

Don't forget that PLAKO is an ideal trousers fastener. This is where the men are interested for their own clothes.

Given this great want of humanity, and an article to satisfy this want, will this not result in a rush of customers and a large profit with so easy a seller?

Every month that your orders equal one gross we will credit you with four dollars on every gross and will send it in check or in goods the following month, as you choose.

Take the PLAKO we are sending you under separate cover, show it to your friends, and get their opinion of it. You will find that you will have a number of orders to fill even before you have purchased your set of samples as described in the circular enclosed, "What We Have For You."

Customers?	Everybody.
Selling?	Easy.

None in Stores.

Send your order in quickly and hustle.

> Yours very truly,
> CLARKE SALES COMPANY.
> SALES MGR.

1909: JANUARY 14
O. J. ELDER TO COLUMBUS PITTMAN

Despite persistent attempts by journalists to expose them, patent-medicine makers in the early twentieth century were still flourishing. Hawking dubious potions for everything from consumption and deafness to alcoholism and "female weakness," they also relied heavily on shameless endorsement letters like the one below to boost their sales.

Physical Culture was a monthly magazine that, according to its slogan, was "Devoted to health, strength, vitality, muscular development and the care of the body."

PHYSICAL CULTURE

ADVERTISING DEPARTMENT

O.J. ELDER, MANAGER

2078 METROPOLITAN BLDG., NEW YORK

New York, N.Y., Jan. 14, 1909.

Columbus W. E. Pittman,
    Chapel Hill, N.C.

Dear Sir:

We have your letter of January 7th making inquiry in regard to the Cartilage Co. of Rochester, N.Y. Will say that this Company has been successful with their apparatus in increasing the height of thousands of people. The writer knows of several persons who have used the Cartilage System with excellent results. Of course, we cannot guarantee absolutely that the use of the Cartilage System will enable you to increase your height three or four inches, but we can guarantee that you will receive beneficial results. The exercises which go with this System are excellent and well worth the price asked.

Very truly yours,

Physical Culture,

O. J. Elder.

1909: FEBRUARY
ARCHIBALD BUTT TO HIS SISTER

Born in Georgia and known throughout his life for his southern grace, Archibald Butt (1865–1912) served as the devoted personal aide to President Theodore Roosevelt and, starting in 1909, to his successor, William Howard Taft (1857–1930). Yet despite Butt's acclaimed social skills and his profound understanding—so clear in this letter—of Washington diplomacy, he would be unable to make peace between the two men when Roosevelt split the Republican party by running against Taft in the 1912 election. Butt's loyalty torn, he would take a leave of absence in Europe. He would become one of the most notable people to die on the Titanic. *Said one survivor: "When the order to take to the boats came . . . you would have thought he was at a White House reception, so cool and calm was he."*
Taft had been Roosevelt's secretary of war.

Washington, D.C.,

February

Dear Clara:

I am often amused at people saying that Mr. Taft has such a wonderful memory for names. In manner he is the politician carried to the nth power. I have presented the army and public to him both in Washington and the Philippines, and he never receives a delegation without someone to announce their names. His instructions to Cloman and myself have always been never to let a person get by without getting his or her name, but when they do get by, as they often will, especially when they think they are old friends and, therefore, want to demonstrate the fact that they are remembered as such, it would be impossible for any one not knowing him well to realize that he has no idea whatever who they might be.

I shall never forget once, several years ago now, trying to get a visitor to give me his name, and he simply refused to do so, saying:

"Oh, the Secretary and I are old friends and were schoolmates."

"That may be so," I said, "but it is my duty to announce you by name."

"Oh, that does not make any difference; he will remember me."

As he got up to the Secretary I saw him stretch out his hands in a peculiar way old friends have of doing, which gave the Secretary some idea as to what his expectations might be. The Secretary turned hopelessly to me, but I was unable to help him out, so he drew back his arm as if he were going to strike the man and made a sweep through the air and grasped his hand and gave a greeting that no one else had had during the day.

The guest began to pin him rather closely, so to extricate himself he said:

"Helen" (or "Nellie," as he calls her, I think), "you remember our dear old friend here."

Before "Nellie" could say she did not, which she would have said had she been given the chance, the Secretary was busy recognizing some other old friend.

At the first lull in the line, Mrs. Taft turned to the Secretary and said:

"Will, I never knew that man's name even. I wish you would give the names of your intimate friends when I am expected to be especially cordial."

"My darling, I have not the faintest idea who he is but I saw he was an intimate friend by the way he stood poised on one foot waiting to be recognized."

I could but laugh later when this same man passed me in the hall with his coat and said: "I told you there was no need to present me."

When the President does not remember a name or face he gives a cordial greeting, but he never makes any effort to deceive the man or woman into the belief that he does remember them when he doesn't. . . .

Good-night,
Archibald.

1909: APRIL 1

CARL VAN DOREN TO HIS MOTHER

Carl Van Doren (1885–1950) was a critic and biographer who taught English at Columbia University. He would become literary editor of The Nation *and* The Century *and would go on to win the Pulitzer prize for his biography of Benjamin Franklin. In 1909, however, he was still a young man studying for his Ph.D. at Columbia and indulging in some deep, and thoroughly timeless, wallowing.*

1 April 1909

My lovely Mother,

I have caught a miserable cold in some way and have been sitting about my room all morning and a part of the afternoon studying and half seduced from attention by the warm day outside. My indisposition is nothing, just enough to put me in a melancholic mood—of the kind that will come now and then, no matter how little there is really to bring it on, or how hard I fight against its coming. It seems to me that I have wasted and still waste so much time and get so little done. They tell me here my learning is perhaps the largest among the graduate students in English (altho that is by no means sure) and yet I am the youngest of them all. Next year too I am to have the fellowship. I have the best parents in the world and everything that their kindness can get me. Is it not strange then that I should have sat all these past few hours kicking my heels in sullenness? I can see the folly, well enough, but I cannot forget how much of a dissipation of energy is obligatory upon me. My roommate is wholly bent upon the study of the law. He has a good head and great industry, and what he is doing is a preparation for the thing he most wants. He can grudge every minute stolen from his work, while I am divided. My whole ambitions are for original work, but here I must plod dully on in scholarly pursuits, filling my head with a vast deal of dusty lumber that seems very far from a prospect of ever being useful, and letting my imagination rust in its sheath. I wonder whether it is fair that professors of literature should be obliged in the corrupted currents of this world to do something outside of literature to earn their bread and butter and give only the fagged out hours of their leisure to the only thing they live for. Some days I grow a despicable coward, and am nearly tempted to turn my back upon all the bright ideal to which I have been true now for nearly a third of my life, and drop my energies to a slighter task where there is a chance of wealth and ease after a time. I know I could be rich—but I don't care to be—and I suppose I could attain some kind of worldly preferment. What is the good of all this feverish distracted effort, and all this silent sacrifice? I ask myself, and then I grow ashamed and vow that I will use the wretched talents that have been given me, and tho I may curse with all my hate the cruelty that gave me a giant's ambition and a child's powers, I will not be downed, but hold my head erect, tho it reach no further than the waist of most of my companions.

On such a day I wish I could be in Urbana again to greet all my beloved ones, and to walk about the kind, quiet old streets until a little calm could find its way into my angry peevish heart. But for your sake it is just as well I am here.

I send you all as much love as you can hold and all I have. There is no one in this world so dear to me.

Your loving son, Carl

*　　*　　*

1909: SEPTEMBER 6
ROBERT PEARY TO THE WORLD

It took Admiral Robert E. Peary (1856–1920) eighteen years and eight expeditions to reach the North Pole—and five months to return to civilization after he had done so. Once at Indian Harbour, Labrador, he sent off this exuberant cable, the truth of which would later be disputed, reaffirmed, and debated anew.

Stars and Stripes nailed to the North Pole.

—Peary.

1909: DECEMBER 8
ELIZABETH COREY TO HER MOTHER

Since the passage of the Homestead Act in 1862, the United States government had granted parcels of western land to more than half a million settlers in exchange for a nominal fee and a promise to live on the land for at least five years. Elizabeth "Bachelor Bess" Corey was twenty-one years old and carrying a suitcase and a parasol when she left her family in Iowa to become a homesteader in South Dakota in 1909. Her claim was the usual 160 acres, but it was infested with rattlesnakes and located two miles from the one-room schoolhouse where she taught.

Rusks were a kind of sweet bread. Howard, sixteen years old, was one of Bess's students and neighbors.

Dear Ma,— It is a quarter of nine but I must write you a few lines any way.

Last week was a caution—it started to rain Tuesday evening and Wednesday morning I went to school in the rain then it turned cold and stormed to beat the band so I went home with the Speer Children. Thursday it was a little better and I came home then Friday it stormed so that Mr Speer came after the children and insisted that I go home with them again—I didn't want to but he said it was no use for me to start out as I'd never make it in such a storm he said he would <u>try</u> it in a case of absolute nescessity but not other wise so I thought I better not try what a man wouldnt risk so I staid with Speers again and went home about noon Saturday.

Saturday afternoon I sorted the apples and washed them all—canned up the ones with spots in them—had about six qts and then as it seemed to be getting colder every minute I dyed some flour sacks and got them ready to cover a comfort it was about eleven that night when I went to bed. Sun I baked bread, pumpkin pies and rusks—the bread and pies are fine but the rusks are what I suppose Mr Speer would call "Cranky like de devil" They are surely fierce.

You folks <u>think</u> you know something about cold weather but you dont. I had got used to having my hair, eyebrows and eyewinkers covered with frost and ice till I looked like Santa Clause when I got to school but Sun. night beat that all hollow. I went to bed with the covers over my head and just a little air hole over my right eye and when I woke up in the night I found when I put up my hand to turn down the covers that my hair and the blanket were covered with hoar frost

Monday morning it was blazing cold—I put that heavy gray wool skirt on for an under neath skirt—and wrapped as warm as I could. I got to school at five minutes till eight but the stove is in such a bad condition it took me fifteen minutes to clean out the ashes and start the fire. About that time my feet began to feel queer and by the time I was through sweeping I was ready to dance the "Highland Fling." I saw Mr Stone coming with Myrtle and when he got there I had a note written to Mrs Stone asking if she had any thing in the house of which I could make bloomers as I got so cold about the branches and if she would send to town for some woolen stockings for me first time she got a chance. Plague take Mr Stone he read the note and it tickled him so he had to tell Speers about it. Mrs Speer said the wording of the note most killed him off. Mrs Stone sent me a pair of her woolen stockings and Miss Hunts bloomers that night when Mr. Stone came after Myrtle.

Howard wanted me to go home with them Monday evening—he said it was far colder than in the morning and I'd frieze to death—he talked till he was red in the face and then gave it up. When he got to the door he turned back and said "Well if you do start home you'll find how cold it is by the time you get to the dam and you better turn of there and cut a crossed to our place" When Mr Stone came for Myrtle he said I was to go home with him or down to Speers but he thought I better go down to Speers and I got there just as Mrs Speer finished: "Well if Miss Corey tries to go home such a night as this she needs a right good thumping"

I guess my heels were pretty well nipped and should have been thawed with snow Mr Stone said. I walked the floor most of the forenoon and sometimes I could hardly keep my voice steady but when it began to shake all the other voices began to shake too—even Howards so I <u>had</u> to keep a stiff upper lip.

My but Howard is good to me! He brings my dinner to school and takes the pail home, gets in coal, sharpens my pencils and all sorts of such things

Tuesday Mr Speer went to town and I sent for some heavy union suits, some woolen stockings and heavy dark brown outing flannel for bloomers. I staid all night there again last night and got into some warmer duds.

The chill Monday morning caused a postponement and the warm clothes acted the other way. I was "took" before noon today.

I came home tonight to find every thing froze up tight as a brick both up stairs and down cellar—apples potatoes and all—they rattle around like stones.

By the time I got my fire started I felt rather tipsy and jarred up against the oven and the stove pipe came unjointed. I would have sat down and cried for my maw but I knew it wouldn't do any good so I just worked till I got it fixed and whistled "Good Old Summer Time" while I was at it. Yes honestly I've whistled most all the evening.

A pack of wolves passed the school house yesterday afternoon. Howard says its school ma'am they're after. He says they like school ma'ams better than any-thing else and can scent them a long ways off. He said if they ever attact me to pursuade them to let me off for a week or two till I faten up a little better then perhaps I can get a gun befor I meet them again.

I realy must beg, borrow or steal money enough to get me a gun and a licence for there isn't a tree or telaphone pole to climb here

Did I tell you about my dinner pail? Just as big around as a pint cup and twice as high. One day it didn't seem to hold enough and I remarked that I guessed I'd have to put sideboards on it. That tickled the children and they took it home. Now <u>that</u> is going the rounds and is applied to all sorts of things. Its always "We'll have to put sideboards on it like Miss Corey said about her dinner pail."

Say Mr. Stone woke up Monday night and found one of his ears friezing. He says this is colder than he ever saw since he came out here.

When I got home last Saturday I saw about the first thing that my ink bottle had been having a swell time so will have to use a pencil in real Soddie style here after.

I have twelve flour sacks the color of the piece enclosed

Mr Stone went to town today so will not seal this till I see what mail I get. When some of you are feeling rich I wish you would get that jewelry of mine at Nielsons and pay the bill I'd make it square with you.

Did you ever settle up our accounts to see how much I owe you? And did you give Toad that ten spot I owe him?

If you have any means of finding out anything of L. Wilkins of Guthrie Cen-ter and his daughter Leana who married a fellow named Share I wish you would—find out if she is at home at present—it might save a heap of trouble if it could be learned quietly Do you suppose Uncle John would know any thing of them

Your card rec'd Monday eve. Must close and retire it is almost eleven so

Good Night—Bess

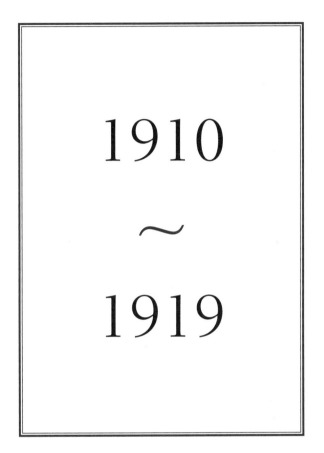

1910
~
1919

We have disasters for breakfast; mined ships for luncheon;
burned cities for dinner; trenches in our dreams, and
bombarded towns for small talk.

—Walter Hines Page to his son
December 20, 1914

BETWEEN 1910 AND 1919 . . .

1910: Almost 50 million Americans live in rural areas, about 42 million in cities. ★ The U.S. population is 91,972,266. ★ The country is home to 2,433 daily newspapers. ★ Roughly 4 percent of Americans have a college diploma. ★ Norfolk, Virginia, buys the state's first motor-powered fire truck. ★ Residents of Chicago board up their windows, coal miners refuse to go below ground, suicide rates climb, and people take "comet pills" to protect against supposedly deadly gas—all because the tail of Halley's comet passes within 400,000 kilometers of the Earth. ★ The Boy Scouts and electric washing machines appear. **1911:** A hundred people die this year in aviation accidents. ★ Edith Wharton publishes *Ethan Frome*. ★ *Photoplay* is the first fan magazine. ★ Declaring both organizations guilty of restraint of trade, the Supreme Court breaks up Standard Oil and American Tobacco. ★ At the Triangle Shirtwaist Factory in New York City, 146 workers, mostly immigrant women and children, die when trapped by fire. **1912:** The *Titanic* sinks. ★ Woodrow Wilson is elected president. ★ Slang thrives: "Sure!" "It's a cinch!" "You look flossy!" ★ Mack Sennett starts the Keystone studios, soon to be home of Buster Keaton, Charlie Chaplin, and the Keystone Kops. ★ Seeking decent wages as well as humane treatment, mill workers in Lawrence,

---

From left to right, top row: The Birth of a Nation film poster, Woodrow Wilson, W.E.B. Du Bois; *second row:* John Reed, night attack in France, war poster; *third row:* suffragists marching, Harry Houdini; *bottom row:* Laura Ingalls Wilder, the *Titanic*.

Massachusetts, stage the "Bread and Roses" strike; James Oppenheimer writes: "Our lives shall not be sweated from birth until life closes / Hearts starve as well as bodies, give us bread but give us roses." ★ Life Savers are invented by a Cleveland chocolate maker who wants to sell something sweet that won't melt in the summer heat. ★ In Wytheville, Virginia, a powerful, clannish patriarch named Floyd Allen is found guilty of assault and sentenced to one year in prison. In the courtroom, he declares: "Gentlemen, I ain't goin'," and his son and other members of the family promptly shoot five people to death, including the judge, the prosecutor, and a member of the jury. **1913**: Floyd Allen and his son Claude are electrocuted in Richmond, Virginia, 11 minutes apart. ★ Federal income tax is permitted by the Sixteenth Amendment. ★ The Ford Motor Company is now producing a complete Model T every 93 minutes. ★ At the International Exhibition of Modern Art, better known as the Armory Show, more than 300,000 visitors pay to be inspired, shocked, and/or mystified by the 1,300 paintings and sculptures created by European artists, including Picasso, Duchamp, and Matisse. ★ According to the Chicago Court of Domestic Relations, 46 percent of unhappy homes are caused by drinking, 14 percent by "immorality," 12 percent by disease, 11 percent by "ill temper and abuse," and 7 percent by "intemperance of parents." ★ On the day before President Wilson's inauguration, 5,000 suffragettes march down Pennsylvania Avenue, demanding the right to vote. **1914**: In a Flag Day speech, Secretary of the Interior Franklin K. Lane begins: "This morning, as I passed into the Land Office, the Flag dropped me a most cordial salutation, and from its rippling folds I heard it say: 'Good morning, Mr. Flag Maker!' " **1915**: On the eve of his execution for the murders of a grocer and his son, IWW organizer and itinerant songwriter Joe Hill writes: ". . . let the merry breezes blow / My dust to where some flowers grow. / Perhaps some fading flower then / Would come to life and bloom again." The next morning, despite the lack of witnesses or motive, he is shot by a firing squad. ★ D. W. Griffith's *The Birth of a Nation* premieres in New

York City, offering both blatantly racist views and utterly revolutionary cinematic techniques. ★ Nearly 1,200 people—including more than 100 U.S. citizens—are killed when the *Lusitania*, a British ship, is sunk off the Irish coast by a German submarine; yet despite repeated calls to enter the war in Europe, America stays neutral. ★ Popular songs include "M-O-T-H-E-R, a Word That Means the World to Me." **1916**: In Fort Worth, Texas, a doctor advertises efficient cures for "blood poisoning, gonorrhea, gleet piles, fistula, cancer, night emissions and lost vitality." ★ Woodrow Wilson is reelected on the slogan "He kept us out of war." ★ Architect Frank Lloyd Wright's son, John, invents the children's building toy Lincoln Logs. ★ Enamel bathtubs with flat bottoms begin to replace cast-iron ones with feet. ★ Six thousand people die, and thousands more are left crippled, by a polio epidemic that strikes nearly 30,000 victims in the summer and fall. **1917**: The first jazz recording is "The Darktown Strutters' Ball" by the Original Dixieland Jazz Band. ★ The fashion craze is for short, or "bobbed," hair. ★ Congress passes a law requiring immigrants to be literate in some language. ★ The United States declares war on Germany. ★ George M. Cohan writes: "We'll be over, we're coming over / And we won't come back till it's over over there." Within three months, 400,000 copies of the sheet music have sold. **1918**: The first regular airmail service connects Washington, D.C., and New York City. ★ A worldwide flu epidemic kills more than 21 million people this year alone. ★ The Raggedy Ann doll is new. ★ Warner Bros. Pictures and Louis B. Mayer Pictures are both organized. ★ President Wilson introduces the Fourteen Points plan for peace, including formation of a League of Nations. **1919**: The Treaty of Versailles formally ends World War I. ★ The Chicago White Sox, heavily favored to win the World Series, lose five games to three to the Cincinnati Reds, setting off rumors of a fix. ★ Telephone users can now dial numbers themselves instead of going through operators.

1910: MARCH 21

PRESCOTT HALL TO WHOM IT MAY CONCERN

In the late nineteenth century, a group of Harvard alumni, mainly lawyers and scholars, had founded the Immigration Restriction League. It was the first official anti-immigrant organization, and one of its central tenets was the superiority of the white race. Its practical goal was to push the federal government to create legislation that would limit the number of new immigrants to the United States. But the first decade of the new century saw the influx of unprecedented numbers of newcomers, with nearly nine million admitted between 1901 and 1910. In an effort to drum up fresh enthusiasm for its cause, the IRL's executive committee secretary sent this form letter to many notables of the day, finding support from, among others, the presidents of Stanford and Harvard; the publisher Henry Holt; Alexander Graham Bell; and the original vice-squad enforcer, Anthony Comstock.

Boston, March 21, 1910

Dear Sir:—

The Immigration Restriction League is a non-political and non-sectarian organization, with members from all parts of the United States. Since 1894, it has led the agitation for the better enforcement of existing immigration laws, and the enactment of needed legislation. It is opposed only to such immigration as lowers the mental, moral and physical average of our people.

Immigration the coming year will again near the 1,000,000 mark. Of recent immigration, 1–4 over 14 years of age could not read or write in any language; 3–5 were of the Slavic and Iberic races of Southern and Eastern Europe; nearly 1–3, including women and children, had no occupation; 3–5 were destined for only 4 States.

In 1908, the foreign-born population of 13.6 per cent furnished 15.6 per cent of the criminals, 20.8 per cent of the paupers, and 29.5 per cent of the insane. Between 1904 and 1908, the aliens in these institutions increased 34%.

The League feels that facts like these show that the present laws governing the admission of aliens are inadequate to protect our social and political standards and institutions from deterioration. Those pecuniarily interested in lax immigration laws are strongly organized to influence legislation, while those who believe in a proper selection of the aliens coming to us are scattered. This letter is written with the purpose of getting in touch with those who agree with the attitude of the League.

We should much appreciate a letter from you, stating whether you favor

1. Further selective tests for immigrants.

2. Obliging aliens to be able to read in some language.

3. Increasing the present head-tax of $4, and if so to what amount.

4. Requiring immigrants to be in possession of an amount of money sufficient to support them while seeking work.

We should also be glad to have your views on this subject, outside of the questions noted above.

Very truly yours,

Prescott F. Hall

Secretary of the Exec. Com.

1910: MAY 1
AART PLAISIER TO HIS COUSIN

Aart Plaisier was living in Grand Rapids, Michigan, when he wrote home to his cousin, Cornelius Van der Waal, in Holland. Plaisier had emigrated in 1910 and was joined by his parents and six siblings a year later. His cousin never came to America.

May 1, 1910

Dear cousin,

Having received your letter just this Wednesday, I will sit down to write back to you. Usually I go to church on Sunday mornings, but because it is raining, I will go this evening instead. . . . It is a great pleasure to hear everything about the fatherland from you. I will try to answer all your questions in full.

During our first four weeks here we had beautiful growing weather, but in the last two weeks it was different—and at times rather cold. But we are getting closer to summer.

At work things are going well too. We work from 7:00 a.m. to 5:00 p.m., with an hour's rest. That is, then, ten hours per day, just as in Holland. But the work here in the factory is very different. You have to learn a great deal at first. There are many Hollanders here in the factory, which makes it very easy for me, but it does not help in learning English. But I will not stay with this job for very long. As soon as I have acquired enough English usage, I will go to another factory where everyone is English, and I will learn much more.

You asked about autos. They ride along by the hundreds, and they frequently have serious accidents. The other day one had to go up a high hill, and when it was near the top, a chain broke, and it came rolling crazily down again. Then it ran against a lamppost. There was hardly anything left of the auto worth saving. Often you can see children, that is boys or girls of sixteen or seventeen years, fly through the city in large autos. It is shocking sometimes, but people here are not surprised by this. Also, women are often seen driving horses and wagons. And women also ride with the horse between their legs—and galloping too. It is a treat to the eyes. But it is very ordinary here.

There are also many lovely girls here, but you must be careful. If you try to stop and say hello to such a girl, she calls a police agent, and then you go to jail or pay $18.00. Yes, the stinkers do, in fact, have such a law here. Sometimes the girls walk along the streets and show off like peacocks. But then, when I am inclined to get involved, I remind myself, there are plenty of Holland girls equally attractive. And they know it too. Furthermore, there are those among them who will not run off to call the police agent. For example, when you sit in church on Sunday, some are pleased to come and sit next to you. The seats are all free. Now, enough of that. . . .

You were certainly fortunate with your colts and mares. And to hear that Adrian is doing well is no surprise to me. If any person, and especially the lovely girls of Ridderkerk, are curious about me, just tell them to send a letter or postcard, and I will answer them quickly.

The food here is very good—you could get fat here quickly. Meat in abundance all the time, and eggs and fruit. More than you can eat at every meal. But people here say that you need more food than in Holland—that it has something to do with the climate. But we eat three times daily—six in the morning, at noon, and 6:30 in the evening. The style of clothing here is about the same as in Holland. For example, no one here notices that I wear a Dutch coat.

I don't know much about flowers and birds because it's not yet summer, but I have heard that the summer brings a delightful display of flowers. Everyone plants flowers around their houses, and the parks are beautiful at that time. You have seen the postcard of John Ball Park; well, I have been there once, and, although it was cloudy and cold out, I could still see the nice arrangement of things. The place is all hills and valleys, and some are high above the city. When you stand at the top you can see the whole city.

Bonjour

[Aart Plaisier]

1910: WINTER
EDITH WHARTON TO W. MORTON FULLERTON

When she wrote this letter to her lover, Edith Wharton (1862–1937) was already an acclaimed American novelist. She would publish Ethan Frome *the following year and would become the first woman to win the Pulitzer prize (for* The Age of Innocence*) in 1920. Yet in this letter, her protestations of pride notwithstanding, she revealed her deep insecurities about—and her vulnerability to—Fullerton, a correspondent for the London* Times *who would be best remembered for his association with her. The affair with Fullerton would end in 1912, and her marriage a year after that.*

A *petit bleu* was a letter card sent through Paris's pneumatic post.

Sunday night—

Mon ami, I sent you just now—in haste, with people waiting for me—a word which may have seemed impatient and irritated.—That is the last note I wish to sound.

Three or four times I have given you the opportunity to make, gaily & good-humouredly, the transition which seems to me inevitable; & you have not chosen to do it. Therefore I will give you my "motives," though they could hardly, I think, be "unrevealed," even to perceptions much less fine than yours.— What you wish, apparently, is to take of my life the inmost & uttermost that a woman—a woman like me—can give, for an hour, now & then, when it suits you; & when the hour is over, to leave me out of your mind & out of your life as a man leaves the companion who has accorded him a transient distraction. I think I am worth more than that, or worth, perhaps I had better say, something quite different. . . . Don't imagine that I expect to see you often, or even to hear from you regularly. I know that a relation like ours has its inevitable stages, & that <u>that</u> stage is past. I know you haven't time to come, often haven't time to write; but I know also that sometimes you have a moment, & that when one loves one never fails to use such a moment. Poor human nature has only a limited number of signs by which to express itself—& these signs, in cases like ours, are always much the same!—You hoped to find me last Thursday, in order to ask if I were free for Saturday. But I was out—& no other possibility of reaching me occurred to you!—Non, mon ami, ne me dites pas de ces choses-là. . . . Don't you see that, if you accepted the solution I offer, you would not have to rack your brains to find such explanations? My friends are free to see me or not see me, think of me or not think of me, as they please! They find me when they choose to, & when they are otherwise preoccupied they don't have to assure me that they still feel an affection for me.

But I do ask something more of the man who asks to be more than my friend; & so must any woman who is proud enough to be worth loving . . . No, Dear, I know you haven't time to write; but one word would suffice me—You haven't time to seal & stamp an envelope; but a post-card addressed by you would be a message in itself!

And if a woman asks these signs, it is not necessarily because she is "sentimental," or jealous, or wishes to dominate a man, or restrict his freedom; but because these are the ways in which the heart speaks, & because, when two people are separated, there are no other ways available.

There are my "motives," Dear, once for all; & the request prompted by them springs from the fear—I really believe—that even the letters in question should constitute a kind of silent importunity!

I wanted to spare you this explanation, & for that reason, left every door open; & a week ago last Saturday, when you came to luncheon, I quite sincerely thought we were in accord on the subject, & that "the reign of the spirit" was to begin!—You wished otherwise, apparently—yet, after we said goodbye, you could let nine days pass—living at my very door—without concerning yourself to know if I were well or ill, happy or unhappy, here or away.—

Don't see the least hint of a reproach in what I have written. It is a frank explanation of the <u>reason why</u>—that's all!—

8 p.m.—Your telephone message has just come & I see that, as I feared, my hurried petit bleu must have seemed impatient.

I am therefore sending you just what I had written, to show how earnestly I wish that you should feel no unkindness in what I ask.—It is unreasonable for me to expect you to arrange the matter for me tomorrow, however; & if I don't leave till Tuesday night, Tuesday will do as well. Or we can wait till I come back, if it is more convenient.

I will let you know if I can lunch tomorrow, but probably not.

In case it's <u>not</u>, please remember that, for me, there is much, much left be-tween us. It is less so for you, I know; but there are women of whom I have heard you speak affectionately, & with regard. Let me be one of them, won't you?

1910: DECEMBER 22
L. VERNON BRIGGS TO OWEN COPP

At the beginning of the century, some states required sterilization of the mentally ill, and mental hospitals employed all sorts of would-be cures, from insulin doses and hydrotherapy to lumbar punctures and physical restraints. A Boston-based psychia-trist, Dr. L. Vernon Briggs (1863–1941) tirelessly lobbied the Massachusetts legisla-ture to enact groundbreaking bills that decreased the use of physical restraints and introduced the idea of occupational therapy. Briggs would also be largely responsi-ble for the creation of the Boston Psychopathic Hospital in 1912 and later for the enactment of the Briggs Law, requiring psychiatric evaluation for certain criminals.

64 Beacon Street, Boston, December 22, 1910.

Dr. Owen Copp, Executive Officer, State Board of Insanity,
State House, Boston, Mass.

My Dear Dr. Copp:—After I got back to my house last night, I did not feel at all satisfied that the State Board of Insanity had seriously taken up all the points which I was to bring before them, Mr. Whittemore excepted.

It seemed to me that the State Board had chosen an hour when they were not prepared to listen to what I had to say. Four members were present; one mem-ber immediately got up and retired without saying anything. Dr. Howard, who I appreciate is an extremely busy man, was on the <u>qui vive</u> all the time, and you personally, owing to your enthusiasm about what was being done and planned, did not always give me a chance to state clearly what I wanted to say. In a gen-eral way I feel you know what I am working for, but facts and figures are the only things which count with me. General statements I have no use for.

What I wish to put before the Board, among other things, is the following: That some plan and action be taken for the regular employment of patients in each of the State hospitals. I came away with no assurance that this was going to be done. What I further wanted the Board to do, was to take some action for improving the class of attendants, who now are only custodians of our insane people, many of whom are herded like so many cattle in the enclosures and grounds of the hospitals, where attendants are loafing as well as the patients, and where attendants are used to prevent the patients from committing overt acts, and otherwise have little occupation. These attendants should be instructed in manual training. They never should be idle. They should always be helping the patients to do something in the way of occupation or entertainment. This is more true on stormy days when the patients are indoors, where the demoralizing effect of the sight of patients sitting about on benches in corridors, doing nothing, makes one feel that the State of Massachusetts is rather making people more insane instead of less. Patients have said to me: "For God's sake, take me out of this place where I can only think of my condition, and where I am not allowed to do any work." I think it is true that quite a number of insane criminals at Bridgewater would gladly return to the State Prison for occupation alone.

Some of the other questions which I wished to bring up before the Board, but was unable to, were the separation of the almshouse cases from the insane, the separation of the criminal insane from those innocent of any crime, the separation of epileptics and idiots from the other insane, the manner of bathing patients, and the punishment used to make them work. One more question which I did bring up, but on which I came away without any more satisfaction than I had previously had, was the closer and more intimate relations which should be established between the physicians and the hospitals. It may be true that certain physicians are invited to conferences, or that certain hospitals employ this method. I will say that, with the exception of McLean Hospital, I have never been invited to any conference after sending a patient to a hospital. Committing patients is an act that I avoid, if possible, for many reasons, so that the number of my committals is not large; but I have asked men who have committed many more cases than I have, and I have failed to find one who has been invited to a conference after committing a patient.

I went to the Board meeting hoping that some definite action would soon be taken in regard to this plan. I came away feeling that nothing definite would be done at present.

The matter of restraint, about which I have been interested, seems to be progressing in the right direction. I feel that when a more intelligent handling of the attendants as to instruction and employment is used, then a different class of men who want to work and help these people will be attracted and take the place of the present loafer. I believe that when more medical work is done with the patients on systematic lines, such as is planned in some of the hospitals today, the service will attract a higher class of physicians than it does at present, and that the two cries now—that you cannot get good attendants, and that you cannot get enough desirable physicians to fill the places—will not be heard.

I have written thus fully because I do not feel like asking for any more time of such a busy Board, and because I can put more concisely what I have to say in writing.

Very truly yours,
L. Vernon Briggs.

1911: MARCH 26
MORRIS BUTLER TO THE NEW YORK TIMES

On March 25, 1911, a fire broke out at the Triangle Shirtwaist Factory in lower Manhattan, killing 146 workers, many of whom were forced to leap to their deaths. The fire dramatized the dangerous conditions of the sweatshops that had begun to appear at the turn of the century, and it served as a rallying point for women trade workers and suffragists. Though the International Ladies' Garment Workers' Union (ILGWU) had been founded in 1900, it had not been able to attract much attention, and it would only begin to effect real changes in the aftermath of the tragic fire.

Dear Mr. Editer

i Went down town with my daddy yesterday to see that terrible fire where all the littel girls jumped out of high windows My littel cousin Beatrice and i are sending you five dollars a piece from our savings bank to help them out of trubble please give it to the right one to use it for sombody whose littel girl jumped out of a window i wouldent like to jump out of a high window myself.

Yours Truly
Morris Butler

1912: FEBRUARY 10
ROBERT FROST TO SUSAN HAYES WARD

Robert Frost (1874–1963) was still more than a decade away from receiving the first of his four Pulitzer prizes when he wrote this letter—archetypal Frost, with its description of the solitary figure confronting himself in the New England landscape—to the literary editor of the New York Independent.

Ward's "Sweet Singer" was a book by Julia Moore, a sentimental poet known as the Sweet

Singer of Michigan who was generally criticized for having created, as one critic put it, "a mile-post in the history of bad poetry." The *Youth's Companion* was a weekly magazine for children.

10 February 1912   Plymouth

Dear Miss Ward:—

You should receive almost simultaneously with this your long-lost Sweet Singer. I ought to say that I don't think I laughed at her as much as I should have if I had been a hearty normal person, and not something of a sweet singer myself. She is only a little more self-deceived than I am. That she was not altogether self-deceived I conclude from the lines in which she declares it her delight to compose on a sentimental subject when it comes into her mind just right. There speaks something authentic anyway.

Two lonely cross-roads that themselves cross each other I have walked several times this winter without meeting or overtaking so much as a single person on foot or on runners. The practically unbroken condition of both for several days after a snow or a blow proves that neither is much travelled. Judge then how surprised I was the other evening as I came down one to see a man, who to my own unfamiliar eyes and in the dusk looked for all the world like myself, coming down the other, his approach to the point where our paths must intersect being so timed that unless one of us pulled up we must inevitably collide. I felt as if I was going to meet my own image in a slanting mirror. Or say I felt as we slowly converged on the same point with the same noiseless yet laborious strides as if we were two images about to float together with the uncrossing of someone's eyes. I verily expected to take up or absorb this other self and feel the stronger by the addition for the three-mile journey home. But I didn't go forward to the touch. I stood still in wonderment and let him pass by; and that, too, with the fatal omission of not trying to find out by a comparison of lives and immediate and remote interests what could have brought us by crossing paths to the same point in the wilderness at the same moment of nightfall. Some purpose I doubt not, if we could but have made it out. I like a coincidence almost as well as an incongruity. Enclosed is another in print. The Marion C. Smith you were talking of when I was with you I was very certain I had heard of somewhere, but I didn't know where. It must have here. Heard of her? Yes it is almost as if I had met her in the pages of the Companion.

Nonsensically yours
Robert Frost

*   *   *

1912: MARCH 1
MARY DREIER TO VICTOR BERGER

In 1912, the average pay for textile workers in Lawrence, Massachusetts, was sixteen cents an hour. When the legislature reduced the fifty-six-hour workweek by a paltry two hours and mill owners cut pay accordingly, thousands of outraged workers— mainly women and children—stopped their looms and marched in the "Bread and Roses" strike. The Massachusetts militia attempted to drive the laborers back to work, causing at least two deaths—and profound outrage among countless unions in the country. After a month, the number of strikers in New England had reached fifty-thousand. Led by Mother Jones and Bill Haywood, the IWW kept the strikers organized and gained new momentum in the Northeast.

Mary Dreier was president of the Women's Trade Union League of New York. Victor Berger was a Socialist congressman from Milwaukee.

New York, March 1, 1912

Hon. Victor Berger,
House of Representatives, Washington, D.C.:

Not since the days of negro slavery has there occurred so flagrant an outrage on personal liberty as that exhibited in the treatment of the Lawrence strikers by the local and State authorities in forbidding parents from sending their children to friends and sympathizers. The attack of the police upon the mothers of the children was an act of brutality which aroused the indignation of every public-spirited citizen. The situation is aggravating by the fact that these women were from a foreign country and had come to America expecting to find the high standard of living and regard for personal liberty of which we boast, on which our Republic is founded. They have found neither. In the name of the 55,000 working people of New York, the Women's Trade Union League of that city urges upon Congress the passage of the bill calling for immediate action of Congress and the Federal authorities.

Mary E. Dreier, President.

*   *   *

1912: APRIL 18

GUS COHEN TO HIS GIRLFRIEND

At nineteen, Gershun "Gus" Cohen was an out-of-work printer from Whitechapel, England, who was heading for America to seek his fortune. He borrowed the money to buy a third-class ticket on the Adriatic *but discovered at the pier that he would be able to sail on the maiden voyage of the* Titanic *instead. This letter was written after the great ship sank and Cohen was picked up by the rescue ship* Carpathia.

18/4/12

Dear Hettie:

I've arrived, rescued and my-self safe at New York. I suppose you heard about the "Titanic" and I suppose you thought I was drowned, but, thank God, I just managed to escape.

I will explain how the accident happened. At 10-30 we were all sent to bed, lively shouting and singing and doing everything. About 11:45 we were awakened as about a dozen crewmen came by our decks. We did not take the slightest notice and went to bed again, but we were awakened by the sailors to put on lifebelts. I did not have any because I could not find one, and still I was making a lark of it and people were singing and playing the piano' the band was also playing.

I went on the Third Class Deck and saw great lumps of ice and realised we had struck an iceberg. But we still did not realise there was any danger.

Later things looked serious and I knew that it was time to fend for myself. I realised that I had to find a lifebelt which I did. I went back to my birth to find some of my belongings and as I walked through the gangway, I was told by some merchant seamen that things were serious, so I decided to go back on deck.

While walking on the deck, I saw quite a few people praying and holding rosaries to be saved. I thought to myself, I will pray when I am rescued.

It was then about 200 feet high from the water where I was standing. As I was not afraid of the danger, I knew I must do something. I was standing near the davits with ropes hanging down climbed on the davits, crawled across and jumped for one of the ropes. I was wearing gloves and that saved my hands partially. I had to jump 5 feet horizontally to reach them.

I clutched the ropes and when I got to the end of these, I still found I had to jump into the sea and was kept up by my lifebelt. After being in the water for several minutes, I was picked up. The boat that rescued me had children and women but was not filled to capacity. Our boat picked up several men from the water. I believe one or two died of exposure.

Then the bung of my lifeboat began to leak, so my job was to bale the water. We sailed through the night in a calm see. We were lucky and every star we saw in the sky we thought theses were lights from boats, but we were only seeing mirages.

At about 7:00 a.m. when it became light, we saw a boat in the distance, which we found out was the CARPATHIA. When we reached the CAR-PATHIA, we had to climb on board this boat by rope ladder.

I had lost all my money, barring a few coppers, but my valuables was with the purser, which included a farewell watch from my boys club which I belonged.

Gus

1912: APRIL 19

ARTHUR FIFIELD TO GERTRUDE STEIN

American author Gertrude Stein (1874–1946) had recently published the short-story collection Three Lives *and was already ensconced in her famous Parisian salon when she received this letter from a prospective publisher. The woman who would be famous for writing the line "Rose is a rose is a rose is a rose" (in her poem "Sacred Emily") would survive this and countless other parodies of her self-consciously repetitive literary style.*

13, Clifford's Inn,
London, E.C.,
Apr 19, 1912

Dear Madam,

I am only one, only one, only one. Only one being, one at the same time. Not two, not three, only one. Only one life to live, only sixty minutes in one hour. Only one pair of eyes. Only one brain. Only one being. Being only one, having only one pair of eyes, having only one time, having only one life, I cannot read your M.S. three or four times. Not even one time. Only one look, only one look is enough. Hardly one copy would sell here. Hardly one. Hardly one.

Many thanks. I am returning the M.S. by registered post. Only one M.S. by one post.

Sincerely yours,
A. C. Fifield

*   *   *

1912: DECEMBER 12

WALT KUHN TO WALTER PACH

Walt Kuhn (1877–1949) began his contribution to American art with a series of cartoons and illustrations for magazines and newspapers. For most of the rest of his career, he painted—vibrantly and prolifically—with special emphasis on circus people. Along the way, as this letter to artist and critic Walter Pach (1883–1958) attests, he brought unmatched enthusiasm to planning the revolutionary Armory Show of 1913. Exhibiting some thirteen hundred paintings and sculptures, the show introduced Americans to the works of such artists as Manet, Monet, Cézanne, Gauguin, Van Gogh, Duchamp, and Matisse.

The painter Arthur B. Davies (1862–1928) was Kuhn's partner in organizing the show. *Der Bien muss* is an ungrammatical way of saying "the bee must" in German.

> Fort Lee
>
> Dec 12

Dear Pach—

I should have written you before this but Davies and myself have been on the jump every minute since we landed. Today I gave the papers the list of European stuff which we know of definitely. It will be like a bomb shell, the first news since our arrival.

You have no idea how eager everybody is about this thing and what a tremendous success it's going to be. Everybody is electrified when we quote the names etc. The outlook is great, and after having figured up the likely income we stand to come out ahead of the game as far as money goes. The articles appearing from now on will increase the desire to help by the moneyd "classes." We owe you a tremendous lot for your indispensable help and advice, but you know that we are all in the same boat for this great chance to make the American think. I feel as though I had crowded an entire art education into those few weeks. Chicago has officially asked for the show, and of course we accepted.

I am very anxious to get a "thumb nail" biography of <u>all</u> the important men. Will you see what you can get for me every little bit helps, anything of interest. The papers are also interested in portrait-photos of the men themselves. Everything you can send me in this line will be of enormous help in securing good press notices. I have planned a press campaign to run from now right through the show, and then some—a snapshot of the Duchamp Villon brothers in their garden, for instance will help me get a special article on them. I await your story on them, also Redon. We are going to feature Redon big (BIG!). You see the fact that he is so little known will mean a still bigger success in publicity.

John Quinn, our lawyer and biggest booster, is strong for plenty of publicity, he says the New Yorkers are worse than rubes, and must be told. All this is not to my personal taste, I'd rather stay home and work hard at my pictures shoving in some of the things I have learned, but we are all in deep water now and have got to paddle—Don't disappoint me on this—Our show must be talked about all over the U.S. before the doors open.

I hope that the letter I mailed you at Queenstown was clear to you, and that I covered everything. Got a letter from "Moderne Gallerie" Munenchen stating all O.K. also one from Flechsheim Düsseldorf (Rousseau) also O.K. of course that's all settled by this time. If you should be thrown down on any of the important things at the last minute, do not hesitate to apply to Cassirer Berlin, or Dr. G. F. Reber Barmen, Germany. Reber is in someway connected with Rosenberg (dealer) Paris and has some of the best Cezannes and Van G's in Germany, he's a sort of semi dealer. He said that he would gladly loan some of his things.

If Munch the Norwegian is willing to send and there is still time get a couple of his, insist on his most advanced ones, they could be added to Chenue's shipment from London. The Norwegian show here is very very tame, and it would be fine for us to show even better Scandinavian stuff than they have—Munch (Edward, HVISTLEN Norway. I shall send you press clippings as they appear. The ball is on now and there will be lots doing.

We have a great opportunity in this show, and must try to make it truly wonderful and get all the people there, which owning to the extremely short duration of the show is very hard, and can only be done through the press. So don't ignore my plea for minor information, it may me undignified but it brings the desired result. We want this old show of ours to make the starting point of the new spirit in art, at least as far as America is concerned.

I feel that it will show it's effect even further and make the big wheel turn over both hemispheres. I suppose you are thinking there he goes again, but I guess its better to say "there he goes" than "doesn't he look natural!" as Tod says.

Guy du Bois in on "arts & crafts" (off the Journal) and will devote a whole issue to the show, he's in strong I hear. Expect to see him tomorrow.

Remember me to the Duchamp Villons and all the others you may see. I shall not wait another ten years before I drop in on old Paree. We will have an office in town a sort of information bureau. The business end of this thing is enormous. I expect to give practically all my time to it, but do it gladly if we can really do what we hope to do. Did you ever hear the story of the Russian Bee keeper? A friend looking at the bee hive of a Russian says: "but that ball is much too small, no bee can enter that hive"—the Russian answered in his funny German

Der Bien muss!

I have a lot of other stories, which I will save until you show up in New York.

Remember me to Mrs. Smythe, too bad we missed connections in London.

Talking about London, it has about as much modern art as Paducah Ky. but I tell you I'd like to board in the British Museum for about a year. I sure went batty on that antique glass, and the Assyrian lion hunt. (sculpture)—

Had supper in Child's tonight

Oh you Laperouse!

1913: FEBRUARY 1
HARRY HOUDINI TO C. HOWARD WATSON

Harry Houdini (1874–1926) was probably the most famous American magician of the century, and with his breathtaking ability to escape from jails, handcuffs, strait-jackets, and milk cans, one of its greatest showmen. His water-torture cell, which he introduced while on a British tour, was, despite the concerns he expressed in this letter, an unlikely source of imitation. It required that Houdini be suspended by manacled ankles and lowered, head first, into a full tank of water.

REGISTERED.

Hull,
England,
Feb. 1st 1913.

C. Howard Watson, Esq.
2 Buckingham St.
Strand.

Dear Sir:

Pardon the liberty I am taking in addressing this letter to you, but I wish to warn Managers and the Profession in General that I have invented another sensation viz:—

THE WATER TORTURE CELL.

which is the greatest feat I have ever attempted in strenuous career and hereby wish to give notice that I have

SPECIAL LICENCE FROM THE LORD CHAMBERLAIN (Granted May 2nd 1913)

as a Stage Play and I will certainly stop anyone infringing on my rights.

I am notifying the Managers in the United Kingdom by Registered Post explaining the trick, also enclosing colored illustration of the New Mystery and will hold them responsible for any infringement.

Sincerely Yours,

Harry Houdini

Enroute Moss Tour,

IMPORTANT NOTICE.

The above effect consists of the performer being locked into a narrow Water Torture Cell filled with water, whilst standing on head ankles clamped and locked above in centre of massive cover, and escaping therefrom in this Up-side-Down position.

Harry Day, Business Manager, 1, Arundle Street, Strand London.

1913: AUGUST
CHARLIE CHAPLIN TO HIS BROTHER

Charlie Chaplin (1889–1977) wrote this letter to his brother Sydney while touring the United States and Canada with the Fred Karno Repertoire Company. Chaplin would make his first film for the Keystone Film Company the next year, and his overnight success would lead steadily toward a series of increasingly profitable—and productive—screen contracts. In 1919, he would join forces with Mary Pickford, Douglas Fairbanks, and D. W. Griffith to create United Artists, gaining control over every aspect of his films. The first truly international movie star, he would ultimately write, act in, and direct more than eighty films and would contribute to American culture the indelible character of the lovable, silent Little Tramp.

Sonny Kelly was the brother of Chaplin's first love, Hetty, and would one day become an executive at United Artists. Fred Mace had become famous as the "Chief of the Keystone Kops." The "S.C." was the Sullivan and Considine vaudeville circuit. Alfred "Alf" Reeves managed Chaplin's 1910 Karno tour and would later manage the Chaplin Film Corporation. Adam Kessel, Jr., was an executive with Keystone's parent corporation.

My Dear Sid,

I hope you received my letter all right. I know there wasn't much news in it—"they say no news is good news" but not in this case. I have quite a lot of news to tell you this time. Did I tell you I met Sonny Kelly in New York? Yes, I met him and had a grand time—he took me all over the place. He has a lovely apartment on Madison Avenue which you know is the swell part of New York. Hetty was away at the time—so I never saw her but still I am keeping correspondence with Sonny and he tells me I am always welcome to his place when in New York. I do nothing else but meet people and old friends—right here in Winnipeg I met one of the old boys who use to be in the Eight Lancashire Lads. I dont know wether you would know him or not—Tommy Bristol—he use to be my bigest pal—now he's working the Orpheum turns with a partner getting about 300 dollars per—I tell you they are all doing well, even me. I have just to sign a contract for <u>150 Dollars a week</u>. "Now comes the glad news." Oh' Sid I can see you!! beaming now as you read this, those sparkling eyes of yours scanning this scrible and wondering what coming next. I'll tell you how the land lyes. I have had an offer from a moving picture company for quite a long time but I did not want to tell you untill the whole thing was confirmed and it practically is settled now—all I have to do is to mail them my address and they will forward contract. It is for the New York Motion Picture Co., a most reliable firm in the States—they have about four companies, the "Kay Bee" and "Broncho" "Keystone" which I am to joyne, the Keystone is the Comedy Co. I am to take Fred Mace place. He is a big man in the movies. So you bet they think a lot of me—it appears they saw me in <u>Los Angeles, Cal</u>. playing the Wow-Wows then they wrote to me in Philadelphia which was a long time after. I could have told you before but I wanted the thing settled. We had a week's lay-of in Phili so I went over to New York and saw them personaly. I had no idea they would pay any money but a pal of mine told me that Fred Mace was getting four hundred a week well I ask them for two hundred. They said they would have to put it before the board of Directors ("dam this pen!") Well we hagled for quite a long time and then I had to do all my business by writing them and you bet I put a good business letter together with the help of the dictionary. Finaly we came to this arrangement i.e. A year's contract. Salary for the first three months 150 per week and if I make good after three months 175 per week with no expences at all and in Los Angeles the whole time. I don't know whether you have seen any Keystone pictures but they are very funny, they also have some nice girls ect. Well that's the whole strength, so now you know. Of course I told them I would not leave this company until we finished the S.C. circuit, so I will join them by about the beginning of Dec that will be about the time we get through. I have told Alf and of course he doesn't want me to leave but he says I am certainly bettering myself and he can't say otherwise. Mr Kessel tells me there is no end of advancement for me if I make good. Just think Sid £35 per week is not to be laugh at and I only want to work about five years at that and then we are independent for life. I shall save like a son of a gun. Well I am getting tired now so will draw to a close. Don't tell anybody about what Alf said because it may get to the Guvnor's ears and he will think Alf had been advising me. And if you know of any little Ideas in the way of synaros ect. don't forget to let me have them. Hoping you are in good health and Mother improving also I would love her and you to be over hear. Well we may some day when I get in right.

Love to Minnie
and yourself
Your loving Brother,
Charlie.

1913: DECEMBER 3
W. FRANKLIN TO THE KEELEY INSTITUTE

The Anti-Saloon League had been founded in 1893, and two decades later had become a leading and very vocal proponent of the Eighteenth Amendment, establishing Prohibition. This letter, which was written to the head of an alcoholics' sanatorium, was reprinted by the league in leaflet form and distributed as an example of the evils made possible by alcohol.

Kansas City, Mo.
Dec. 3, 1913.

Keeley Institute
Dwight, Illinois.

Gentlemen: Our customers are your prospective patients. We can put on your desk a mailing of over 50,000 individual consumers of liquor. The list is the result of thousands of dollars of advertising.

Each individual on the list is a regular user of liquor. The list of names is new, live and active. We know this because we have circularized it regularly. We furnish this list in quantities at the prices listed below. Remittances to accompany each order.

40,000 to 50,000 . . . .$400
20,000 . . . .$300
10,000 . . . .$200

We will not furnish this list in lots less than 10,000. Discontinuance of business January 1, is the occasion for selling our mailing list.

Yours truly,
Kentucky Distillers' Co.
W. Franklin, President

1914

OTISVILLE SANATORIUM TO PATIENTS

Located in the Catskills and designed for charity patients only, Otisville was New York City's municipal tuberculosis sanatorium. The notice below, despite the severity of its tone, would have been received with enormous relief. It was not until 1944, with the discovery of streptomycin, that a true treatment for the "White Plague" would be developed.

NOTICE TO ACCEPTED CANDIDATES
FOR OTISVILLE SANATORIUM
READ THIS NOTICE CAREFULLY

You have been accepted as a suitable case for treatment at Otisville Sanatorium. Your name has been placed on a waiting list. When a vacancy occurs you will be notified to present yourself at the Admission Bureau, 426 First Avenue, Borough of Manhattan, for Admission.

If under the influence of liquor or smelling of the same you will be rejected. You must not take liquor with you.

All patients who have been accepted must supply themselves with a complete outfit of articles described in this circular.

These outfits should be packed in a suit case or bundle. They will be inspected at the Admission Bureau on the day you start for Otisville Sanatorium. <u>Do not bring a trunk.</u>

1914: MARCH 21

HENRY JAMES TO HENRY ADAMS

Two of the most celebrated American writers of the late nineteenth and early twentieth centuries, Henry James (1843–1916) and Henry Adams (1838–1918) were nearing the ends of their lives when James, in London, sent this letter to Adams. It was apparently a response to a letter that has not survived but that contained Adams's reaction to James's memoir, Notes of a Son and Brother. *Adams's letter to another friend at the time offers a glimpse of what he might have written to James. With characteristic gloominess, Adams had asked, "Why did we live? Was that all? . . . Poor Henry James thinks it all real, I believe . . ."*

21 Carlyle Mansions
Cheyne Walk S.W.

My dear Henry

I have your melancholy outpouring of the 7th, & I know not how to acknowledge it than by the full recognition of its unmitigated blackness. Of course we are lone survivors, of course the past that was our lives is at the bottom of an abyss—if the abyss has any bottom; of course too there's no use talking unless one particularly wants to. But the purpose, almost, of my printed divagations was to show you that one can, strange to say, still want to—or at least can behave as if one did. Behold me therefore so behaving—& apparently capable of continuing to do so. I still find my consciousness interesting—under cultivation of the interest. Cultivate it with me, dear Henry—that's what I hoped to make you do; to cultivate yours for all that it has in common with mine. Why mine yields an interest I don't know that I can tell you, but I don't challenge or quarrel with it—I encourage it with a ghastly grin. You see I still, in presence of life (or of what you deny to be such,) have reactions—as many as possible—& the book I sent you is a proof of them. It's, I suppose, because I am that queer monster the artist, an obstinate finality, an inexhaustible sensibility. Hence the reactions—appearances, memories, many things go on playing upon it with consequences that I note & "enjoy" (grim word!) noting. It all takes doing—& I do. I believe I shall do yet again—it is still an act of life. But you perform them still yourself—& I don't know what keeps me from calling your letter a charming one! There we are, & it's a blessing that you understand—I admit indeed alone—your all-faithful

Henry James

1914: NOVEMBER 20
LEO FRANK TO ADOLPH OCHS

Leo Frank was a twenty-eight-year-old New York Jew living in Atlanta when he was arrested for the murder of a fourteen-year-old National Pencil Company employee named Mary Phagan. In a highly publicized trial, Frank, who had been the factory's superintendent, was convicted and sentenced to death. After receiving an estimated hundred thousand appeals, many from citizens and from newspapers that saw the case as one of rampant anti-Semitism, Governor John M. Slaton commuted Frank's sentence from death by hanging to life imprisonment. Yet less than a year after writing this letter to the owner and publisher of the New York Times, *Frank would be dragged from his jail cell and lynched.*

National Pencil Company
Office and Factory
37-41 S. Forsyth St.
Atlanta, GA.

November 20, 1914.

Hon. Adolf Ochs,
    New York City.

Dear Sir:

I have read with deep interest and appreciation the editorials, bearing on my case, appearing in your issues of the "Times," November 16th and 17th. I feel that your editorials, with rare insight, have accurately diagnosed the issues of the proposition, and have accentuated the crux of the situation.

Far and away more important than the shell of legal intricacies and technicalities, is the reality beneath the shell—the question of human right and justice. The question to be decided is whether or not an unruly mob, operating in an atmosphere of smoldering violence and prejudice, may, with impunity and the apparent seal of judicial approval, invade our courts, and compel verdicts. Are the safeguards thrown about defendants, and which have been developed and insisted upon during the many years past as fundamental at common law, to be cast ruthlessly aside, just because a howling, violent mob threatens?

Our motion "to set aside" becomes not the invoking of a technicality which may be lightly sidetracked because procedure is, or is not, thus and so; but it invokes a basic human right, a right grounded in the fibre of Anglo-Saxon intelligence and civilization. Orderly trial by jury is one thing, and the rank disorder of a lynch-crazy mob is another. They are diametrically opposed; one cannot be justified or substituted for the other. One is right, the other dastardly.

It surely cannot obtain that truth and innocence be forever throttled. It never, surely, is too late to do right, and to hear the truth. This outrageous charge against me was hastily conceived, in error, and brought forth in prejudicial hate. I cannot believe that, in this day, with still time to right the wrong, a judicial murder will be promulgated. They may take human life, and attempt to annihilate human honor, but I am confident that the truth cannot be strangled to death.

I am grateful that you have seen the truth in this horrible affair. That you have seen fit to air the facts in the "Times" bespeaks your courage.

Be assured, dear sir, of my high regard and best wishes,

respectfully yours,
Leo M. Frank

1914: DECEMBER 20

WALTER HINES PAGE TO HIS SON

Walter Hines Page (1855–1918) had been editor of Forum *and* The Atlantic Monthly *and a founder of the Doubleday publishing company before being appointed ambassador to Britain by President Woodrow Wilson (1856–1924). Six months after the war in Europe began, Page wrote this letter from London to his twenty-seven-year-old son Frank, who would grow up to be a newspaper editor, and later, head of an electrical company. The letter's celebration of America is at odds with its offensive racial slur. But the restlessness the letter revealed was in keeping with Page's conviction—often expressed to Wilson—that America must show its strength by entering the "war to end all wars."*

Kitty was Frank's younger sister, Katharine Alice Page. Their mother had gone home for a visit.

Sunday, December 20, 1914

Dear Old Man:

I envy both you and your mother your chance to make plans for the farm and the house and all the rest of it and to have one another to talk to. And, most of all, you are where you can now and then change the subject. You can guess somewhat at our plight when Kitty and I confessed to one another last night that we were dead tired and needed to go to bed early and stay long. She's sleeping yet, the dear Kid, and I hope she'll sleep till lunch time. There isn't anything the matter with us but the war; but that's enough, Heaven knows. It's the worst ailment that has ever struck me. Then if you add to that this dark, wet, foggy, sooty, cold, penetrating climate—you ought to thank your stars that you are not in it. I'm glad your mother's out of it, as much as we miss her. And miss her? Good gracious! There's no telling the hole her absence makes in all our life. But Kitty is a trump, true blue and dead game, and the very best company you can find in a day's journey. And, much as we miss your mother, you mustn't weep for us; we are having some fun and are planning more. I could have no end of fun with her if I had any time. But to work all day and till bed time doesn't leave much time for sport.

The farm—the farm—the farm—it's yours and Mother's to plan and make and do as you wish. I shall be happy whatever you do, even if you put the roof in the cellar and the cellar on top of the house.

If you have room enough (16 by 12 plus a fire and a bath are enough for me), I'll go down there and write a book. If you haven't, I'll go somewhere else and write a book. I don't propose to be made unhappy by any house or by the lack of any house nor by anything whatsoever.

All the details of life go on here just the same. The war goes as slowly as death because it <u>is</u> death, death to millions of men. We've all said all we know about it to one another a thousand times; nobody knows anything else; nobody can guess when it will end; nobody has any doubt about how it will end, unless some totally improbable and unexpected thing happens, such as the falling out of the Allies, which can't happen for none of them can afford it; and we go round the same bloody circle all the time. The papers never have any news; nobody ever talks about anything else; everybody is tired to death; nobody is cheerful; when it isn't sick Belgians, it's aeroplanes; and when it isn't aeroplanes, it's bombarding the coast of England. When it isn't an American ship held up, it's a fool German-American arrested as a spy; and when it isn't a spy it's a liar who <u>knows</u> the Zeppelins are coming tonight. We don't know anything; we don't believe anybody; we should be surprised at nothing; and at 3 o'clock I'm going to the Abbey to a service in honour of the 100 years of peace! The world has all got itself so jumbled up that the bays are all promontories, the mountains are all valleys, and earthquakes are necessary for our happiness. We have disasters for breakfast; mined ships for luncheon; burned cities for dinner; trenches in our dreams, and bombarded towns for small talk.

Peaceful seems the sandy landscape where you are, glad the very blackjacks, happy the curs, blessed the sheep, interesting the chin-whiskered clodhopper, innocent the fool darkey, blessed the mule, for it knows no war. And you have your mother—be happy, boy; you don't know how much you have to be thankful for.

Europe is ceasing to be interesting except as an example of how-not-to-do-it. It has no lessons for us except as a warning. When the whole continent has to go fighting—every blessed one of them—once a century, and half of them half of the time between, and all prepared even when they are not fighting, and when they shoot away all their money as soon as they begin to get rich a little, and everybody else's money too, and make the world poor, and when they kill every third or fourth generation of the best men and leave the worst to rear families, and have to start over fresh every time with a worse stock—give me Uncle Sam and the big farm! We don't need to catch any of this European life. We can do without it all as well as we can do without the judge's wigs and the court costumes. Besides, I like a land where the potatoes have some flavor, where you can buy a cigar, and get your hair cut and have warm baths.

Build the farm, therefore, and let me hear at every stage of that happy game. May the New Year be the best that has ever come to you.

Affectionately,
W.H.P.

1915: MAY 11
WILLIAM ROSCOE THAYER TO MARGARET FOSTER

William Roscoe Thayer (see letter page 21) sent this message to a British friend four days after the sinking of the British ship Lusitania *by a German submarine. Nearly 1,200 people, including more than 120 Americans, were killed in the incident, which led many Americans to assume—wrongly—that President Wilson would immediately enter the war.*

Horatio Kitchener was a British field marshal and statesman who had led successful campaigns in the Sudan and South Africa; in World War I he became secretary of state for war.

8 Berkeley St.
Cambridge, Mass.,
May 11, 1915

Dear Margaret:

There is too much to say about the destruction of the <u>Lusitania</u>, & so I will say nothing. But I send you some cartoons which will show you that American public opinion is mightily aroused. Except when Sumter was fired on—if even then—there has been no such deep, solemn, leashed-in indignation.

The only question here is, What to do? We can't hurt Germany's Army and Navy—even if we had Army & Navy of our own capable of doing much hurt to any large power. We more than half suspect that Germany wants us to declare war, because she hopes that we can't then ship food & arms to the Allies.

Don't let the English think for a moment that our hesitation proceeds from timidity. I saw a good many representative men at the Harvard Overseers' Meeting yesterday, and the single regret of all of them was that no way can yet be seen for throwing all our weight against the Common Outlaw of Civilization. Before this reaches you—if it ever does—Wilson will probably have given his decision. I can't believe that it will show the faintest sign of wavering.

This monstrous crime has had the beneficial effect already of causing many German-Americans to declare that they are loyal. I predict that before the end hyphens will be very unfashionable over here for a long time.

Really, Margaret, I stand still—mentally—every day and pinch myself, to see whether I am not dreaming—so incredible—so horribly grotesque, do the acts of these German barbarians seem: deliberately making wolves, fiends, demons of themselves, and glorying in it. I may not live to see the day when the exorcism of these devils shall be accomplished—but that day will surely come, in five years or in fifty: because they can no more carry on the world in their way, permanently, than they could build a town in the crater of a live volcano.

But let me tell you that we are all anxious about the slowness of England. Hasn't John Bull waked up? Does he cling to his old comfortable belief that somehow or other he is sure to muddle through? Woe unto him, and Europe, and the world, if he does. For he is facing such a danger now as he never faced before. Even had Napoleon won, England would have survived; but if these German demons win, there will be no more England.

I don't want to alarm you needlessly; but I wish you could prod & urge every Englishman till he thoroughly understands the danger—& acts accordingly. The reports we get here of your ammunition factories running on short hours; of multitudes of workmen going off two or three days a week for gin; and the steadily increasing range & activity of the German submarines makes us anxious. I enclose a clipping from today's Herald which might do good if it could be circulated in England.

Goodnight. All are well here. Ben saw your grandson a few days ago, & found him as fascinating—almost—as his grandma. In these times, there is nothing more invigorating than the familial ties and friendships.

> Love from all.
> Affectionately yours,
> W. R. Thayer

Of course I don't mean this letter to be too pessimistic—but to let you know how many of us feel here.

So far as the campaign on the Continent has gone in the past fortnight, there's nothing to discourage us. But it is almost time for "Kitchener's two millions" to be heard from, encouragingly.

1915: AUGUST 18

ALEXANDER SAMUELSON TO THE UNITED STATES PATENT OFFICE

The formula for Coca-Cola had been invented in 1886 by a druggist named John "Doc" Pemberton, then purchased and closely guarded by marketing whiz Asa Candler. Countless imitators soon followed. Candler decided the company needed to make the soft drink's packaging inimitable—a bottle that, according to a direc-tive of the time, "a person could recognize in the dark, so shaped that, even if bro-ken, a person could tell at a glance what it was." In 1915, that challenge was met by Alexander Samuelson of the Root Glass company of Terre Haute, Indiana. By 1921, more than a thousand Coca-Cola bottling plants would be in operation.

To all whom it may concern:

Be it known that I, ALEXANDER SAMUELSON, a citizen of the United States, residing at Terre Haute, in the county of Vigo and State of Indiana, have invented a new, original, and ornamental Design for Bottles or Similar Articles, of which the following is a specification, reference being had to the accompany-ing drawings, forming a part thereof.

Figure 1 is a perspective view of a bottle showing my design. Fig. 2 is a bot-tom plan view of the same.

I claim:

The ornamental design for a bottle or similar article, as shown.

Alexander Samuelson.

1915: AUGUST 26
WOODROW WILSON TO EDITH GALT

Widowed in office after twenty-nine years of marriage, Woodrow Wilson (1856–1924) was still in his first term as president when he met Edith Galt, a forty-two-year-old Washington widow. Though beset by the war in Europe, Wilson quickly fell in love, and Galt wrote to him: "I . . . love the way you put one dear hand on mine, while with the other you turn the pages of history." Then as now, such attachments were difficult to keep secret in the nation's capital. Though his advisers warned him about damaging his 1916 reelection prospects, Wilson re-mained devoted and, in the letter below, was strikingly frank in describing the link he saw between "intimate love" and presidential effectiveness. He married Galt in December of 1915.

26 August 1915
Thursday evening

My own Darling,

. . . I must beg you, my sweet Darling, not to attach too much importance to Washington gossip, or to what anyone is saying. If we keep within bounds, as we shall, and give them no proofs that they can make use of, we can and should ignore them. And there are some very big reasons why we should ignore them, within the limits we, of course, mean to observe. Our happiness is not an ordinary matter of young lovers; it is, for me a matter of <u>efficiency</u>.

I hate to argue the matter in my own interest, but I know you are thinking of that side of it, too, and will, in your generosity, forgive my speaking of it. I can of course practice self-denial to any extent—spend any proportion of my energy upon it that is required—so far as it is a mere question of strength and resolute self-control; but it costs me more than anyone but you and I can know, and I doubt if it is my duty to use myself up in that way any more than is unavoidable. I am absolutely dependent on intimate love for the right and free and most effective use of my powers and I know by experience—by the experience of the past four weeks—what it costs my <u>work</u> to do without it to the extent involved in entire separation from you. And so we are justified in taking risks.

If during this dreadful week that has just gone by—the most anxious week of my whole term as President, when loneliness sat upon me like a pall—I could have had you actually at my side, if only once or twice a week, I would have <u>laughed</u> at the strain and carried it with a light heart . . .

Friday, 6:40 a.m.

Good morning, my precious One! I love you with all my heart, and it is sweet to be closeted here again alone with my thoughts of you, the sweetest, most delightful thoughts a man's heart could desire . . .

I am worried about the small amount of rest and sleep you take. I wish with all my heart it were much more. I wonder if I can teach you better habits? Ah, if I could only steal in and sit by your bedside and watch you as you sleep and throw loving thoughts about you to make sleep sweeter, as I used to do in the half light by the davenport in the morning room! I would not touch you: that would startle you, for you would not be expecting me. I would only sit and watch that lovely face . . .

Woodrow

1915: SEPTEMBER

HARRY BUTTERS TO HIS PARENTS

Harry Butters was twenty-three when he wrote this letter home to his parents in California. He would die the next year fighting for the Allies.

Delenda est Germania means "Germany must be destroyed."

France, September, 1915.

. . . And now, just a word to reassure you, my dearest folks, and to lessen, if possible, your anxiety on my account. I am now no longer untried. Two weeks' action in a great battle is to my credit, and if my faith in the wisdom of my course or my enthusiasm for the cause had been due to fail, it would have done so during that time.

I find myself a soldier among millions of others in the great Allied Armies, fighting for all I believe to be right and civilized and humane against a power which is evil and which threatens the existence of all the rights we prize and the freedom we enjoy, although some of you in California as yet fail to realize it. It may seem to you that for me this is all quite uncalled for, that it can only mean the supreme sacrifice for nothing or some of the best years of my life wasted, but I tell you that not only am I willing to give my life to this enterprise (for that is comparatively easy, except when I think of you), but that I firmly believe if I live through it to spend a useful lifetime with you, that never will I have an opportunity to gain so much honorable advancement for my own soul, or to do so much for the cause of the world's progress, as I have here daily, defending the liberty that mankind has so far gained for himself against the attack of an enemy who would deprive us of it and set the world back some centuries if he could have his way.

I think less of myself than I did, less of the heights of personal success that I aspired to climb, and more of the service that each of us must render in payment for the right to live and by virtue of which only can we progress.

Yes, my dearest folks, we are indeed doing the world's work over here, and I am in it to the finish. "Delenda est Germania!" is our faith. "For God, for Liberty, For Honor," the call that so many have answered, if not all from as far as I.

Back me up, all of you, my nearest and dearest, and write to me often to show that you do.

Always and forever,
Most devotedly
H.A.B.

1915: SEPTEMBER 21
LAURA INGALLS WILDER TO HER HUSBAND

A working farmwife for most of her life, Laura Ingalls Wilder (1867–1957) would not publish the first of her popular Little House *books until she was in her sixties. She wrote this letter to her husband when she went west to visit her daughter Rose, then twenty-nine and a writer. The exhibits Wilder described so delightedly were at the World's Fair, called the Panama-Pacific International Exposition.*

"Manly" was short for Almanzo.

San Francisco
September 21, 1915

Manly Dear,

Yesterday I saw the "Dogs of all Nations" and was rather disappointed in them. There were some interesting ones, among them some of Perry's team who went to the North Pole. Then there was an Irish Wolf Hound, which breed the man in charge said was very rare. The one we saw was as large as a yearling steer and was only thirteen months old and thin. They said he was worth $3,000, perhaps like Mr. Quigley's thousand-dollar one, but this one was certainly a monster. It seemed impossible that it could be a dog and be so large.

We saw some fine Percheron horses and some Belgian horses and the dearest little Hungarian ponies. They are the size of Shetlands. One was a dapple gray with silver mane and tail. He was beautiful. The man said he was worth $500. While he was having the pony play around on the end of the halter a man came by with a very large Belgian horse and they looked so funny as they passed by each other.

There were some lovely Kentucky race and riding horses, and believe me, they can all have their automobiles that want them. I would have me a Kentucky riding horse if I could afford it.

And OH I saw the Carnation milk cows being milked with a milking machine. And it milked them clean and the cows did not object in the least. The man in charge took your address and if you get any literature be sure and save it, for this machine is certainly a success and I can tell you about it when I come.

I have had a trip on the bay out into the sunset. It was wonderful and the more the boat rolled on the waves the better I liked it. I did not get dizzy at all. We went out to the highest fort in the world and around the quarantine station on Angel Island and then back to the anchorage. The fog rolled up and came down on us and we could not see the land in any direction. The ocean swell came in through the Golden Gate and rocked the boat and we could imagine we were away out on the ocean. It was just a little steam yacht we were on and Rose and I stood up in the very front and let the spray and the mist beat into our faces and the wind blow our hair and clothes and the boat roll under our feet and it was simply glorious.

Since then we have taken the ferry boat and gone down the bay to Sausalito. We took a loaf of bread with us and threw it to the sea gulls and they followed us clear across the bay. We would throw a piece of bread out and they would try to catch it but it usually fell into the water and then they would drop down after it and squall and try to get it away from each other. I enjoyed the boat ride very much but it was not so good as the other because the boat was larger and would not pitch. We got off at Sausalito and stayed over two boats. We walked around the town, which is built all up and down the sides of the hills and the streets are crooked and no two houses built on the same level. It is a beautiful little place.

It was getting twilight when we took the boat back and we went out and up the path of the moon on the waves. We counted thirty-one ships and small motor boats anchored in the harbor as we came away. It was a beautiful sight, and we stood out on the deck as close as we could get to the water all the way home.

The lights at the Exposition made it look like fairyland and the lights of the city rising on the hills, row after row behind, linked it all with the stars until one could not tell where the lights stopped and the stars began. San Francisco is a beautiful, wonderful city and the people in it all seem so friendly—I mean the people one meets on the streets who are perfect strangers.

There seems to be a spirit of comradeship and informality among men and women alike. I thought it was because of the Fair but Rose says it is always that way. Perhaps it is because of the fire when they all got so well acquainted.

Sunday we went for a twelve-mile streetcar ride in all directions over the city and it only cost a nickel apiece because of transfers.

We saw the old mission that was the first of San Francisco, founded by the priest who put the stone cross on the hill for the ships at sea. This old mission church is decorated by the Indians of those early days. The rafters and beams of the ceiling are stained in Indian designs and the pictures and wall decorations are the work of the Indians also. Before the mission runs the "King's Road" which reached all up and down the coast. It was traveled in those days by the priests as they went from one mission to another and of course by Indians and others. There were bells on all the highest points and there was a system of ringing the bells in such a way as to carry news from point to point so that it could travel all up and down the coast.

After we left the mission we went on out five miles to where they are starting a new suburb of the city. There is a beautiful view of the bay. Then we came back through Butcher Town and passed the China Basin and up town again where we stopped at a moving picture show and saw Charlie Chaplin, who is horrid. I mean we saw him act in the pictures.

I am tired and must go to bed early so I can go to San Jose tomorrow. Besides I must leave something to tell you when I come home or you will not be glad to have me.

Lovingly,
Bessie

The foghorn on Alcatraz is crying out at regular intervals so it must be that the fog is getting thick. Every few minutes I hear the bellow of a steamer's whistle as it comes in or meets or passes another boat. The foghorn on Alcatraz is the most lonesome sound I ever heard and I don't see how the prisoners on the island stand it.

1915: DECEMBER 22
RUTH GORDON TO HER PARENTS

As exuberant as she would remain through a long career as screenwriter (Adam's Rib) *and actress* (Harold and Maude), *Ruth Gordon (1896–1985) was nineteen when she sent this letter home. She enclosed Alexander Woollcott's positive mention of her debut performance as one of the Lost Boys in a production of* Peter Pan. *"Ruth Gordon," he wrote in the* New York Times, *"is ever so gay as Nibs."*
Maude Adams gave more than fifteen hundred performances as Peter Pan.

December 22, 1915

Dear Mama and Papa,

Well, it's all over and you can be proud of me. I wish you could have been there. That was truly the only thing missing. It was the worst day of my life and the greatest night. No matter how old I live I will never experience such emotions. I'll begin from the worst, it was my period and, Mama, you know what pains I have, but nothing could equal yesterday. Thank fortune I had a good sleep although how I had the courage to, the night before my first opening night, I don't know! I really think I am wonderful. But this horrible pain woke me up. I could just groan and our good colored maid looked in. She asked me if I ever had gin. Mama, I <u>didn't</u> drink any. Ida fixed me up some of the Penny Royal tea from Wollaston. I thought I would throw up, but I didn't and it worked.

That was my terrible day. My night made up for all that and for all the rest of my life. In a big envelope I am sending you something will prove why. I don't care how hard it is or how terrible, I would rather be an actress than live. In other words, if I could not be an actress, I would gladly take my life. I can say that without fear because I <u>can</u> be an actress and <u>will</u> be, as proven by what it says in the other envelope. Papa, I know you like the Boston Globe, but wait till you see this envelope!

At the Empire Theatre I dress one flight up with Angela Ogden, who kind of slips me little hints of what to do, without exactly letting on she's doing it. Also in the dressing room is Miss Keppel, who is sweet and subdued. They are all too old, except me, to play the Lost Boys, but most of them are friends of friends of Miss Adams or been with her since the year one. Angela Ogden is a very wonderful actress, who, they say, stole the show from Miss Adams when they played <u>Quality Street</u>, so Miss Adams won't put that one on any more, but will revive <u>The Little Minister</u> where Angela has a nice part that's no competition.

Well, I better get back to opening night. Did I write you I wear a suit of sort of like teddy bear fur? It goes all over me except my face and is quite hot and cumbersome, but the Lost Boys have to wear them. Well, the curtain went up and I thought I would die of fright, but the scenes in the Darlings' nursery are before I come on, so I recovered. Our scene started in the Never Never Land and I was in my place inside the tree trunk when I heard my cue and came out and said my line and got a huge laugh. I was so pleased. They tell me no one ever got that laugh before, so it made quite an impression.

All went swimmingly. It was a very fashionable audience, all the Fifth Avenue set. Miss Adams is a big society draw. They said all the men wore silk hats and white ties and tails and the ladies were quite decolleté and heavily jewelled. After my dance Miss Adams beckoned me to take three bows and our orchestra leader Henri Deering stood up and applauded. Gratifying after all I've been through. And Miss Adams has no jealousy like Alice Claire Elliot says many stars have. My cup runneth over and I guess when you read this yours will, too.

Then came the final curtain with Miss Adams alone in the treetop house after having waved goodbye to Wendy who flew home and everybody including the cast in the wings were crying when down came the curtain to thunderous applause and we all took our rehearsed bows, then rushed back and stood in the wings. That means just out of sight in the scenery. Miss Adams took one of her calls alone then came over and said 'Nibs' and led me on and while the audience applauded she broke off a rose from the immense bouquet that had been passed over the footlights and handed me a long-stemmed American Beauty rose that must have cost I don't know how much and I will treasure and preserve forever.

Well, that's about all. All the people in the dressing room including those I mentioned and Mrs. Buchanan, quite a swell, and Miss Clarens, extremely elegant, told me I had made a most auspicious start. And when you see the other envelope you will note they are right.

Your loving actress daughter,

Ruth Gordon

(a name you will one day see in lights)

December 22, 1915, my favorite day of my life.

R.

1916:

THE SURGEON GENERAL TO WHOM IT MAY CONCERN

Over the course of five months in 1916, twenty-seven thousand cases of polio and six thousand related deaths were reported in twenty-six states. The mortality rate of victims in New York City was roughly one child in four. In the summer, public panic about the spread of polio reached a new high, and officials, partially reinforcing and partially responding to a fear of dirt, germs, and immigrants, began to use quarantine to try to control the spread of the disease. In Paterson, New Jersey, no "nonresidents" were allowed into the town. And cities all along the eastern seaboard issued letters like the following.

This card is furnished for the aid of interstate travelers. It should be retained and shown upon demand to proper authorities.

U.S. PUBLIC HEALTH SERVICE,

Baltimore, Md., ... , 1916.

To whom it may concern:

This certifies that . . . .

traveling { from . . . .

to . . . .

with . . . . children under 16 years of age has presented a satisfactory health certificate from the health authorities at point of departure that his premises are free from poliomyelitis (infantile paralysis). The children accompanying traveler have been inspected and show no evidence of that disease.

RUPERT BLUE,

Surgeon General, U.S. Public Health Service.

By . . . .

1916: FEBRUARY 14
A SUFFRAGETTE TO EDWARD WILLIAM POU

Still four years away from passage of the Nineteenth Amendment, women continued to champion the cause of suffrage, relying on many different methods of persuasion, including this anonymous valentine.

TO CONGRESSMAN EDWARD WILLIAM POU, HOUSE RULES COMMITTEE
>The rose is red,
>The violet's blue,
>But VOTES are better
>Mr. Pou.

1916: MAY 15
LELLA SECOR TO HER MOTHER

Though she had been raised in Battle Creek, Michigan, and had spent part of her early twenties homesteading in the state of Washington, Lella Secor (1887–1966) seemed by 1916 largely unfazed by New York City. A journalist and a passionate peace activist dedicated to the "war against war," she was fighting an uphill battle as talk of preparedness increased. She was also, according to one historian, "blessed with a mop of golden red curls and total self-confidence." The following year, she would marry a teacher named Philip Florence. With their two sons, they would move to England in 1921, where she would found the Cambridge Birth Control Clinic and continue to speak about women's rights.

Benjamin W. Huebsch was a publisher and one of Secor's closest advisers in New York. A hug-me-tight was a short crocheted jacket.

Monday

May 15, 1916

Dear Mother and All:

I feel as though I must stop and write a few lines before I go out this morning. . . . Unless I keep at my correspondence every day, it piles up until I don't know where I'm at. . . .

I am devoting every spare moment these days to the fight against prepared-ness, and if I neglect you, you will know it is because I am giving my minutes to a good cause. Last Saturday the Navy League—backed of course by the muni-tions makers and the political preparedness crowd—had a tremendous parade in New York. There were over 400,000 people in line, and it lasted from nine in the morning until ten o'clock at night. They have, of course, all the money they need, and there were bands and banners galore. Anne Herendeen, Mrs. Lane of the Woman's Peace Party, and a few other young women decided that the day ought not to pass without some protest on the part of those who see the thing as it is and are not deceived or scared by the munitions crowd. So we planned a lit-tle stunt which worked beautifully, and we were able to reach thousands of peo-ple with our ideas.

Needless to say, the experience was a brand new one for me, and one which I shall never forget. The plan was to have a crowd of girls all dress in white and with identical hats, so as to stand out from the mob, and circulate among the crowds distributing literature which would set forth the other side of the ques-tion. We wanted to carry sandwich boards—a sign which covers the person both front and back, the like of which I don't remember having seen out West—but we found that almost anything we might wish to do would infringe upon the law, and we had every reason to believe that the strictest censorship would be exer-cised over all those not with the preparedness crowd. It was I, fortunately, who finally struck upon a happy idea. I suggested that we paint the legend on the back of our middy blouses. Thus it would become part of our clothes, and policemen would be unable to do anything about it. Out of this suggestion evolved the final plan of using large black letters which were pasted on, and looked really quite startling. When we walked in front of anyone, he had to read this sign: "Real Patriots Keep Cool." We all wore white skirts and middies—I borrowed mine from Louise—and little ten-cent open-work sea-shore hats. Sort of hyphenated hats it would appear from this description.

I had to finish some work at home before going down Saturday morning, so that by the time I reached Fifth Avenue, the parade was well started. I have never had anything affect me more deeply. In spite of my best efforts, I could not keep back the tears, and for blocks down Fifth Avenue I wept over the piti-ful spectacle. I could not look at those long lines of fine looking men, marching so gaily along, and with so little realization of what it all means, without a fresh outburst of tears. How little they realized that they were endorsing a system which means that great armies of splendid manhood shall go forth and slay other great armies. And why? Because stupid diplomats were too avaricious, too selfish, too ambitious to sanely handle the affairs entrusted to their care. All the lunatics turned loose from all the hospitals in the world could not have made so sorry a mess of things as have the diplomats of Europe. And yet we, blind and stupid as we are, are rushing into the same horrible cataclysm.

In a flash I was back in Europe, on the streets of Holland, watching the steady tramp, tramp, tramp of young men and boys being trained in the gentle art of murder. But their faces bore none of the lightness and frivolity which could be seen on the faces of those marchers Saturday. By the time I reached the peace headquarters, I was so wrought up that I could hardly control myself long enough to speak to anyone. Only those who have been to Europe during this brutal war, and have seen the horrible results of militarism, can realize or understand completely what it means. Anne Herendeen and I decided to go out together, but first we went for lunch, though I was scarcely able to eat anything.

Then, with white bags slung over our shoulders and filled with pamphlets, we started out. New York women, who have fought for suffrage and free speech and social betterment and every other thing, are accustomed to such stunts. But I confess that my heart was beating like a trip hammer. We started down Fifth Avenue, and almost the first person we met was Mr. Huebsch, with whom I have been carrying on a polite little quarrel over certain differences of opinion. He disapproved of our plan, and did not want me to go in on it. At first I pretended not to see him and was going to pass by, for I was in such a state anyway that I hardly felt fit to undertake anything more. Then I thought that very cowardly, and turned to overtake him and show him how I looked and what I was doing. As I turned, he turned also to come back to me. We exchanged just a few words, and then I went on. This morning I have a note from him telling me how charming I looked, etc., just by way of amelioration. But I am not so easily satisfied.

We began to hand out our pamphlets, and were astonished at the eagerness with which people took them and read them. We had 50,000 copies, and within a few hours they were all handed out. We met with courtesy on every hand, and only those violently pro-English or pro-German had anything to say against our program. On the other hand, when people read the signs on our back, they would often come up by the dozens, asking for our pamphlets, so that many times it was difficult to hand them out fast enough. There were many comments such as, "That's the dope!" "I sympathize with this idea!" "I'm interested in this; give me all the different kinds you have!" etc. By evening my spirits had risen. I began to feel that after all the preparedness parade did not represent such prodigious strength as it appeared to represent. As someone suggested, most of the preparedness people were marching, and the crowds on the street were either against preparedness or mildly indifferent.

Hundreds of those who marched did so not because they sympathize with the effort to line the munitions makers' pockets with more money, but because they were practically compelled to do so by their employers. A number of them came to our headquarters after their part was over, and signed a petition to Congress asking that no great preparedness program be entered into.

The "war against war"—as we peace people like to call ourselves—contingent has opened an exhibit on Fifth Avenue which is attracting much attention. At six o'clock, the woman who had it in charge, and who had already worked eight hours, announced that the place was to be closed. I felt that this was a big mistake, since the parade was still to be in progress for several hours. So Anne and Mr. and Mrs. Seltzer and a few others, with myself, offered to remain and keep the place open. Anne and her husband took me to a fine restaurant near by for dinner, and then we began our work of the evening.

Little groups gathered here and there for discussion, and the first thing I knew, I was the center of a large crowd which had gathered to listen to my debate with a man who favored preparedness. We thrashed the thing out, and the crowd agreed that I had won. It's thrilling work, and I love it, especially since I feel confident that whenever folks are started thinking on the right lines, they will see the thing for themselves as it really is. This idea that vast armaments is going to preserve peace is the biggest fallacy that was ever perpetrated on a reasonable people. But I must stop preaching on this subject. I am sending copies of our literature which we handed out. Oh how I wish that I might be financed so that I could simply devote my whole time to this work. I CAN grip the attention and interest of an audience. Everyone who has heard me speaks of it, and I feel it myself. So I think it seems like sort of a waste of talent which might be used to good advantage in this needed field. Over 11,000 people visited the exhibits on that one day. . . .

I have been having little spells of homesickness lately, which of course I must put out of the way. I cannot afford to waste any time mooning. But New York is such a deadly place to live in that I can't help sometimes longing for the green fields of home. There seems to be something about this place which saps my vitality. I am perfectly well—I'm sure I weigh more than I have for some time—but I seem to have no energy. I think it is because I do not get enough fresh air, so I am going to try to go into the country somewhere every Sunday as soon as the weather is better. This morning it is raining and cold, so cold that I am uncomfortable, even in my hug-me-tight. . . .

Don't stay home from prayer meeting to write me, Mother. Of course I do miss your letters when they are long in coming, but I don't want you to deny yourself any pleasure in order to write.

. . . I don't believe I'll bother about piecing down that blue dress, for I only wear it around the house, and skirts are so short now anyway. . . .

Now I must stop, for the morning is slipping away, and I still have loads to do. . . .

Lovingly,
Lella

1916: AUGUST 1

JESSE DAY TO THE OREGON SECRETARY OF STATE

In 1916, three years before ratification of the Eighteenth Amendment forbade the consumption, sale, or manufacture of liquor nationwide, Oregon passed its own state prohibition law. But as temperance rhetoric flourished there, so did marketing innovation. The Astoria Soda Works came up with "Wine-o," a nonalcoholic drink made with fruit and berry juices. A company called Starbird advertised the "Ice Cream High-Ball." And Jesse Day, a trademark applicant, offered his own blunt commentary with the name he submitted for his temperance drink.

APPLICATION

TO

REGISTER A TRADE-MARK IN THE STATE OF OREGON

Bend, Oregon, August 1st, 1916

To the Secretary of State:

Jesse W. Day, whose place of business is No. 846 Wall Street, City of Bend, County of Crook, State of Oregon, desiring to secure within the State of Oregon the sole and exclusive use of a TRADE-MARK in accordance with the provisions of "An Act to provide for the registration by any person, partnership, firm or private corporation, desiring to secure within the State of Oregon, the exclusive use of any Trade-Mark, etc.," filed in the office of the Secretary of State, February 18, 1911, hereby presents this application for the registration of each TRADE-MARK, described as follows:

the word, NOTHING,

a facsimile of which is marked "Exhibit A," hereto attached. This TRADE-MARK, as shown in the Exhibit, is to be placed upon the following articles of merchandise:

a temperance beverage, receipt for the compounding of which will be furnished upon application if required.

And by reason of priority of adoption of the TRADE-MARK herein described and shown in the Exhibit hereto attached, the said Jesse W. Day hereby claims the right to the sole and exclusive use of the same within the State of Oregon for the use and purposes herein stated. A fee of Five Dollars ($5.00) provided by law for issuing Certificate of Registration for such Trade-Mark is tendered herewith.

Jesse W. Day

NOTE—Enclosed with the application should be two (2) extra facsimiles of Trade-Mark printed, impressed or made upon thin, durable paper for attaching to the book of Records of Trade-Marks. A fee of $5.00 must be sent with the application.

1916: OCTOBER 10
W.E.B. DU BOIS TO WOODROW WILSON

Anticipating the 1916 election, Du Bois (see letter page 36) and his fellow NAACP board members sent this letter to President Wilson and a similar one to Charles Evans Hughes, the Republican nominee.

New York, October 10, 1916.

To the President of the United States
Sir:

As an organization representing the Negro race and thousands of their friends we are deeply interested in the presidential election.

During the last campaign, believing firmly that the Republican Party and its leaders had systematically betrayed the interests of colored people, many of our members did what they could to turn the colored vote toward you. We received from you a promise of justice and sincere endeavor to forward their interests. We need scarcely to say that you have grievously disappointed us.

We find ourselves again facing a presidential campaign with but indifferent choice. We have waited for some time to gather from your writings and speeches something of your present attitude toward the colored people. We have thought that perhaps you had some statement or explanation which would account for the dismissal of colored public officials, segregation in the civil service, and other things which have taken place during your administration. You must surely realize that if Negroes were Americans—if they had a reasonable degree of rights and privileges, they need ask for no especial statement from a candidate for the high office of President; but being as they are, members of a segregated class and struggling against tremendous prejudices, disabilities and odds, we must for their own salvation and the salvation of our country ask for more than such treatment as is today fair for other races. We must continually demand such positive action as will do away with their disabilities. Lynching is a national evil of which Negroes are the chief victims. It is perhaps the greatest disgrace from which this country suffers, and yet we find you and other men of influence silent in the matter. A republic must be based upon universal suffrage or it is not a republic; and yet, while you seem anxious to do justice toward women, we hear scarcely a word concerning those disfranchised masses of the South whose stolen votes are used to make Rotten Boroughs of a third of the nation and thus distort and ruin the just distribution of political power. Caste restrictions, fatal to Christian civilization and modern conceptions of decency, are slowly but forcibly entering this land and making black folk the chief victims. There should be outspoken protest against segregation by race in the civil service, caste in public travel and in other public accommodations.

As Negroes and as their friends; as Americans; as persons whose fathers have striven for the good of this land and who ourselves have tried unselfishly to make America the land of just ideals, we write to ask if you do not think it possible to make to the colored and white people of America some further statement of your attitude toward this grievous problem such as will allow us at least to vote with intelligence.

We trust, Sir, that you will not regard this statement and request as beyond the courtesy due you or as adding too much to the burdens of a public man.

We beg to remain, Sir,

> Very respectfully yours,
> National Association for the
> Advancement of Colored People
> W. E. Burghardt Du Bois
> Director of Publications and
> Research

1916: OCTOBER 17
JOSEPH TUMULTY TO W.E.B. DU BOIS

*Charles Evans Hughes offered no reply to Du Bois beyond an official acknowledg-
ment. Joseph Tumulty, secretary to the president, sent the following as Wilson's response. Fellow NAACP board member Oswald Garrison Villard would tell Du Bois:
"It is an amazing statement that the President makes through Tumulty and a false
one." Du Bois ultimately endorsed Hughes over Wilson.*

Asbury Park, N.J., October 17, 1916

Personal

My dear Dr. DuBois:

The President asks me to acknowledge the receipt of your letter of October
10th, and to say that he stands by his original assurances. He can say with a
clear conscience that he has tried to live up to them, though in some cases his
endeavors have been defeated.

Sincerely yours,

J. Tumulty

Secretary to the President

1917: JANUARY 19
ARTHUR ZIMMERMANN TO JOHANN VON BERNSTORFF

*Arthur Zimmermann (1864–1940) was the German foreign secretary, and Count
Johann von Bernstorff (1862–1939) the German ambassador to the United States.
The "Zimmermann telegram," as this document came to be called, was intercepted
by the British Naval Intelligence Service and sent on to the U.S. Department of
State. With its unconcealed belligerence and its shocking promise of three American states in exchange for Mexico's alliance with Germany, it galvanized public
opinion and caused Wilson to break off diplomatic relations with Germany. Three
months later, the United States entered the war.*

Berlin, January 19, 1917

On the first of February we intend to begin submarine warfare unre-
stricted. In spite of this it is our intention to keep neutral the United States of
America.

If this attempt is not successful we propose an alliance on the following basis with Mexico: That we shall make war together and together make peace. We shall give general financial support, and it is understood that Mexico is to reconquer the lost territory in New Mexico, Texas, and Arizona. The details are left for your settlement.

You are instructed to inform the President of Mexico of the above in the greatest confidence as soon as it is certain there will be an outbreak of war with the United States, and we suggest that the President of Mexico on his own initiative should communicate with Japan suggesting adherence at once to this plan; at the same time offer to mediate between Germany and Japan.

Please call to the attention of the President of Mexico that the employment of ruthless submarine warfare now promises to compel England to make peace in a few months.

Zimmermann.

1917: APRIL
THE DETROIT CLUB TO ITS MEMBERS

Detroit was the first major city in the United States to prohibit the sale and consumption of alcohol. Days before the new law was to be enforced, a local club demonstrated the gallows humor that would soon become popular all over the country. This invitation was sent out under the title "In Memoriam."

GREETINGS.

Hereby, ye are commanded to be present in body and person (members only) at the Detroit Club House, on the night of Saturday, April 20th, at Seven O'clock, to attend the obituary of one long in our midst—

Mr. John Barleycorn

And, ere thou eschew the frivolities of the crimson beak, to bathe thy spirit in the laughing waters of Lethe. And, in the manner of the true gourmet, to encompass

One Beefsteak Dinner

garnished with rare condiments and spices, steeped in Nectar, and fragrant as the Attar of the festive onion.

These obsequies being the Vale ere thou steppeth on that aqueous chariot, known by the mundane as the "water-wagon," which will away from the "Milky Way" at 12:01 a.m., May the first.

And ye are commanded to desist cutting coupons long enough to trim the below card from this summons, under pain of relentless remorse, and return it in an envelope addressed to the Entertainment Committee.

AT THE   DETROIT CLUB
CASS AND FORT STREETS
SATURDAY, APRIL 20TH
SEVEN O'CLOCK

(NO LADIES)

1917: APRIL 20

A SOUTHERN MIGRANT TO THE <u>CHICAGO DEFENDER</u>

Throughout the second part of the decade, the offices of the Chicago Defender *were deluged with letters from southern blacks hoping for help in coming north. Many factors inspired the migration. For some, poor treatment by former slave owners, slim economic opportunities, and Mississippi River floods were making the South increasingly unpleasant. At the same time, educational opportunities, economic improvement, and the wartime decrease in European immigrant labor were making the North seem more attractive. Some hopefuls had even heard about offers of free railroad passes—occasionally distributed by northern recruiters—like the ones referred to below.*

Lapne, Alabama April 20, 1917

Sir:

I am writing you to let you know that there is 15 or 20 familys wants to come up there at once but cant come on account of money to come with and we cant phone you here we will be killed they dont want us to leave here & say if we dont go to war and fight for our country they are going to kill us & wants to get away if we can if you send 20 passes there is no doubt that every one of us will com at once. We are not doing any thing here we cant get a living out of what we do now some of these people are farmers and som are cooks barbers and black smiths but the greater part are farmers & good workers & honest people & up to date the trash pile dont want to go no where These are nice people and respectable find a place like that & send passes & we all will come at once we all wants to leave here out of this hard luck place if you cant use us find some place that does need this kind of people we are called Negroes here. I am a reader of the defender and am delighted to know how times are there & was glad to know if we could get some one to pass us away from here to a better land. We work but cant get scarely any thing for it & they dont want us to go away & there is not much of anything here to do nothing for it Please find some one that need this kind of people & send at once for us. We dont want anything but our wareing and bed clothes & have not got no money to get away from here with & beging to get away before we are killed and hope to here from you at once. We cant talk to you over the phone here we are afraid to they dont want to hear one say that he or she wants to leave here if we do we are apt to be killed. They say if we dont go to war they are not going to let us stay here with their folks and it is not anything that we have done to them. We are law abiding people want to treat ever bordy right. these people want to leave here but we cant we are here and have nothing to go with if you will send us some way to get away from here we will work till we pay it all if it takes that for us to go or get away. Now get busy for the south race. The conditions are horrible here with us. its going to be a famine just like they are treating us. they wont give us anything to do & say that we dont need anything but something to eat & wont give us anything for what we do & wants us to stay here. Write me at once what you will do for us we want & opertunity thats all we wants in to show you what we can do and will do if we can find some place. we wants to leave here for a north drive somewhere. We see starvation ahead of us here. We want to immigrate to the farmers who need our labor. We have not had no chance to have anything here thats why we plead to you for help to leave here to the North. We are humans but we are not treated such we are treated like bruts by our whites here we dont have no privlige no where in the south. We must take anything they put on us Its hard if it fair. We have not got no cotegeus diseases here. We are looking to here from you soon.

Yours truly.

[Anonymous]

1917: JULY 19
DAISY WESTBROOK TO LOUISE MADELLA

The war years were not good ones for race relations. In the South, tensions rose over the prospect of black Americans becoming soldiers. In the North, competition for jobs was becoming fierce. On July 2, in East St. Louis, Illinois, thirty-nine blacks and nine whites died, hundreds more were injured, and hundreds of buildings were destroyed in a savage race riot that would remain the most deadly of the century. The author of this letter, Daisy Westbrook, had worked as director of music and drawing at Lincoln High School. Along with her sister, mother, grandmother, and an adopted baby, she had lived in the so-called Black Valley section of that city—in a house that was at first spared by rioters, perhaps because of its stately appearance. Several weeks after the riot, Westbrook recalled the terrible events in a letter to a friend.

3946 W. Belle
St. Louis, Mo.

Dearest Louise:

Was <u>very</u> glad to hear from you. Your letter was forwarded from what used to be my house.

Louise, it was <u>awful</u>. I hardly know where to begin telling you about it. First I will say we lost everything but what we had on and that was very little—bungalow aprons, no hats, and sister did not have on any shoes.

It started early in the afternoon. We kept receiving calls over the 'phone to pack our trunks & leave, because it was going to be <u>awful</u> at night. We did not heed the calls, but sent grandma & the baby on to St. Louis, & said we would "stick" no matter what happened. At first, when the fire started, we stood on Broadway & watched it. As they neared our house we went in & went to the basement. It was too late to run then. They shot & yelled some thing awful, finally they reached our house. At first, they did not bother us (we watched from the basement window), they remarked that "white people live in that house, that is not a nigger house." Later, someone must have tipped them that it was a "nigger" house, because, after leaving us for about 20 min. they returned & started shooting in the house throwing bricks & yelling like mad "kill the 'niggers,'" burn that house.

It seemed the whole house was falling in on us. Then some one said, they must not be there, if they are they are certainly dead. Then some one shouted "They are in the basement. Surround them and burn it down." Then they ran down our steps. Only prayer saved us, we were under tubs & any thing we could find praying & keeping as quiet as possible, because if they had seen one face, we would have been shot or burned to death. When they were about to surround the house & burn it, we heard an awful noise & thought probably they were dynamiting the house. (The Broadway Theatre fell in, we learned later). Sister tipped to the door to see if the house was on fire. She saw the reflection of a soldier on the front door—pulled it open quickly & called for help. All of us ran out then, & was taken to the city hall for the night—(just as we were). The next morning, we learned our house was not burned, so we tried to get protection to go out & get clothes, & have the rest of the things put in storage. We could not, but were sent on to St. Louis. Had to walk across the bridge with a line of soldiers on each side—in the hot sun, no hats, & scarcely no clothing. When we reached St. Louis; we tried to get someone to go to our house & get the things out, but were not successful.

On Tuesday evening at 6 o'clock our house was burned with two soldiers on guard. So the papers stated. We were told that they looted the house before burning it. We are in St. Louis now trying to start all over again. Louise it is so hard to think we had just gotten to the place where we could take care of our mother & grandmother well, & to think, all was destroyed in one night. We had just bought some new furniture & I was preparing to go away, & had bought some beautiful dresses. Most of my jewelry was lost also. I had on three rings, my watch bracelet and LaValliere—Everything else was lost. 9 rings, a watch, bracelet, brooch, locket, and some more things. I miss my piano more than anything else.

The people here are very nice to us. Several of our friends have brought us clothing, bed clothes etc.

Tell me how you got in the Gov. Printing Office. Do you take an examination, if so what does it consist of. I might take it. I have had a good position in E. St. L., but don't know whether there will be enough children to teach there this fall or not. People are moving out so fast. The papers did not describe all the horrors. It was awful. People we being shot down & thrown back into fire if they tried to escape. Some were shot & then burned; others were dragged around with ropes about their necks, one man was hung to a telegraph post. We saw two men shot down. One was almost in front of our house. One man & his wife, a storekeeper, were burned alive, a cross in front of our house.

I must close now it makes me blue to talk about it Write again.

Tell Miss Black I received her card. Will you tell Florence & Mrs. Bowie, I haven't their address. Will expect to hear from you real soon. All send love.

> Lovingly,
> Daisy

1917: DECEMBER 4
KENNETH MACLEISH TO HIS FIANCÉE

In March of 1917, a month before the United States entered the war, Kenneth MacLeish (1894–1918) had enlisted in the Naval Reserve as a member of the elite flying "First Yale Unit." He was originally from Glencoe, Illinois, and his older brother was Archibald MacLeish, who would become a celebrated poet. Kenneth had met Priscilla Murdock when he was a freshman at Yale. He proposed to her—

and she accepted—just before he left for the war. He wrote this letter to her while awaiting orders in Paris. He would die flying a scouting mission a few weeks before the armistice.

Paris, 4 December 1917

Beloved,

I'm beginning to understand why so many American soldiers and sailors go wrong in Paris. Of course the temptations now in Paris are perfectly frightful. I have never been out walking in the evening that at least two girls didn't come up to me and grab my arm. They're so darn persistent that they're repulsive to me, but just lately some ideas have entered my head that scared me. Of course, what has always kept me straight was the thought that I owed it to my family, and the girl I would marry, and to my own pride and education. But what if I never see my family again? Danger demands its rewards in excitement. The greater the danger, the stronger the desire. Why should I refrain? These are some of the thoughts that have arisen lately. They aren't very powerful with me because I've decided to live, while I live, in a way which would make you happy and, if I must die, in a way which would make you proud. But I guess there are many men in our service who aren't as lucky as I am. Perhaps the girl they love has turned them down; perhaps their families have turned them out. I don't blame them nearly so much now. I'm inclined to pity them. They don't need to have what remnants of their religion remain to them collected and strengthened. Their crying need is something practical and tangible which will drive the old saying, "Eat, drink, and be merry for tomorrow you may die," out of their heads. That's why I think people and churches back in America are on the wrong track.

England has suffered terribly because of a frightful mistake the War Department made. They didn't give the men leaves of absence at regular intervals. The result was that wives went two years without seeing their husbands. They went wrong. When the husbands finally came back, well. . . . Conigsby Dawson told me that there were two hundred applications for divorce in the British headquarters every week. And that's why I'm afraid. Our government won't give us leave because it's too far to go. Do you think conditions will ever be that awful in the States? Lord, I hope not. . . .

My next letter from you should contain news of the arrival of my first letter to you. I wish I knew when we left. I want to get out of this city.

*   *   *

1917: WINTER

ROSE WINSLOW TO HER HUSBAND AND FRIENDS

For nearly a year, dozens of suffragettes picketed the White House, demanding the vote. Their almost daily presence, not to mention their placards ("Mr. President What Will You Do For Woman Suffrage") were a constant affront to Woodrow Wilson— and an embarrassment with visiting dignitaries. Beginning in June of 1917, different groups of women were arrested on charges of obstructing traffic. The early protesters were pardoned, but Rose Winslow was among those sentenced to seven months in prison. Once jailed, she and others staged a hunger strike, demanding that they be treated as political, not criminal, prisoners. As a result, they were brutally force-fed. The letter below was actually a series of notes smuggled out from the prison hospital to Winslow's husband and her friends.

If this thing is necessary we will naturally go through with it. Force is so stupid a weapon. I feel so happy doing my bit for decency—for <u>our</u> war, which is after all, real and fundamental. . . .

The women are all so magnificent, so beautiful. Alice Paul is as thin as ever, pale and large-eyed. We have been in solitary for five weeks. There is nothing to tell but that the days go by somehow. I have felt quite feeble the last few days— faint, so that I could hardly get my hair brushed, my arms ached so. But to-day I am well again. Alice Paul and I talk back and forth though we are at opposite ends of the building and a hall door also shuts us apart. But occasionally— thrills—we escape from behind our iron-barred doors and visit. Great laughter and rejoicing! . . .

My fainting probably means nothing except that I am not strong after these weeks. I know you won't be alarmed.

I told about a syphilitic colored woman with one leg. The other one was cut off, having rotted so that it was alive with maggots when she came in. The remaining one is now getting as bad. They are so short of nurses that a little colored girl of twelve, who is here waiting to have her tonsils removed, waits on her. This child and two others share a ward with a syphilitic child of three or four years, whose mother refused to have it at home. It makes you absolutely ill to see it. I am going to break all three windows as a protest against their confining Alice Paul with these!

Dr. Gannon is chief of a hospital. Yet Alice Paul and I found we had been taking baths in one of the tubs here, in which this syphilitic child, an incurable, who has his eyes bandaged all the time, is also bathed. He has been here a year. Into the room where he lives came yesterday two children to be operated on for tonsillitis. They also bathed in the same tub. The syphilitic woman has been in that room seven months. Cheerful mixing, isn't it? The place is alive with roaches, crawling all over the walls, everywhere. I found one in my bed the other day. . . .

There is great excitement about my two syphilitics. Each nurse is being asked whether she told me. So, as in all institutions where an unsanitary fact is made public, no effort is made to make the wrong itself right. All hands fall to, to find the culprit, who made it known, and he is punished. . . .

Alice Paul is in the psychopathic ward. She dreaded forcible feeding frightfully, and I hate to think how she must be feeling. I had a nervous time of it, gasping a long time afterward, and my stomach rejecting during the process. I spent a bad, restless night, but otherwise I am all right. The poor soul who fed me got liberally besprinkled during the process. I heard myself making the most hideous sounds, like an animal in pain, and thought how dreadful it was of me to make such horrible sounds. . . . One feels so forsaken when one lies prone and people shove a pipe down one's stomach. . . .

This morning but for an astounding tiredness, I am all right. I am waiting to see what happens when the President realizes that brutal bullying isn't quite a statesmanlike method for settling a demand for justice at home. At least, if men are supine enough to endure, women—to their eternal glory—are not.

They took down the boarding from Alice Paul's window yesterday, I heard. It is so delicious about Alice and me. Over in the jail a rumor began that I was considered insane and would be examined. Then came Doctor White, and said he had come to see "the thyroid case." When they left we argued about the matter, neither of us knowing which was considered "suspicious." She insisted it was she, and, as it happened, she was right. Imagine any one thinking Alice Paul needed to be "under observation!" The thick-headed idiots! . . .

Yesterday was a bad day for me in feeding. I was vomiting continually during the process. The tube has developed an irritation somewhere that is painful.

Never was there a sentence like ours for such an offense as ours, even in England. No woman ever got it over there even for tearing down buildings. And during all that agitation <u>we</u> were busy saying that never would such things happen in the United States. The men told us they would not endure such frightfulness. . . .

Mary Beard and Helen Todd were allowed to stay only a minute, and I cried like a fool. I am getting over that habit, I think.

I fainted again last night. I just fell flop over in the bathroom where I was washing my hands and was led to bed when I recovered, by a nurse. I lost consciousness just as I got there again. I felt horribly faint until 12 o'clock, then fell asleep for awhile. . . .

I was getting frantic because you seemed to think Alice was with me in the hospital. She was in the psychopathic ward. The same doctor feeds us both, and told me. Don't let them tell you we take this well. Miss Paul vomits much. I do, too, except when I'm not nervous, as I have been every time against my will. I try to be less feeble-minded. It's the nervous reaction, and I can't control it much. I don't imagine bathing one's food in tears very good for one.

We think of the coming feeding all day. It is horrible. The doctor thinks I take it well. I hate the thought of Alice Paul and the others if I take it well. . . .

We still get no mail; we are "insubordinate." It's strange, isn't it; if you ask for food fit to eat, as we did, you are "insubordinate"; and if you refuse food you are "insubordinate." Amusing. I am really all right. If this continues very long I perhaps won't be. I am interested to see how our so-called "splendid American men" will stand for this form of discipline.

All news cheers one marvelously because it is hard to feel anything but a bit desolate and forgotten here in this place.

All the officers here know we are making this hunger strike that women fighting for liberty may be considered political prisoners; we have told them. God knows we don't want other women ever to have to do this over again.

1918: MAY 11
HOWARD HERRICK TO J. J. MCAULIFF

By the end of the century, it would be startling for the U.S. government to make as direct a request of a news organization as the one made in the telegram below. But with no signs of the war ending, it was considered patriotic to use every medium available for stirring public sentiment.

Howard Herrick worked for the Committee on Public Information, a government agency created in 1917 to produce propaganda films. J. J. McAuliff, managing editor of the *St. Louis Globe Democrat*, was one of many editors to receive this request.

TELEGRAM
COMMITTEE ON PUBLIC INFORMATION
10 JACKSON PLACE
WASHINGTON

May 11th, 1918

No. 76 10.00 A.M.

J.J. McAuliff,
Managing Editor
Globe Democrat
St. Louis, Mo.

UNDER THE AUSPICES OF THE UNITED STATES GOVERNMENT THERE WILL BE SHOWN AT THE AMERICAN THEATRE WEEK BEGINNING MAY NINETEENTH THE FIRST OFFICIAL AMERICAN WAR FILM ENTITLED "PERSHINGS CRUSADERS" AS IT IS MOST DESIRABLE THAT THESE PICTURES OF THE ACTIVITIES OF OUR BOYS IN KHAKI OVER THERE AND OVER HERE BE SEEN BY AS MANY PEOPLE AS POSSIBLE THIS COMMITTEE WILL GREATLY APPRECIATE WHATEVER UNUSUAL PUBLICITY YOU MAY GIVE TO THE PRESENTATION TO HIT THE HUN PROPAGANDA IN THE SOLAR PLEXUS IS THE AIM OF THIS PICTURE WE HOPE THAT YOU WILL DO YOUR BEST TO HELP US LAND THIS PUNCH.

COMMITTEE ON PUBLIC INFORMATION
DIVISION OF FILMS
HOWARD HERRICK
PUBLICITY MANAGER

1918: JUNE
KARL SPENCER TO HIS MOTHER

Of the eight thousand marines who fought the advancing German army in early June near the River Marne in France, only two thousand escaped injury or death. Sergeant Karl Spencer was one of the survivors.

My dear mother: I am taking this opportunity to write. The Lord only knows when I will be able to get the letter off. Yesterday and today I received beaucoup first-class mail and a package of eats from Paris, plum pudding and chocolate bars. Believe me, Mother, one appreciates such luxuries after existing for six days on Argentine bully beef, French bread, salmon and water. Twice the Red

Cross and Y.M.C.A. (God bless them!) have sent us jam and cakes and chocolates and cigarettes. I smoke cigarettes (when I have them) like a trooper, and especially when I am lying in my hole in the ground and the shells are breaking all around; they quiet one's nerves, I believe.

In my last letter I spoke of our moving to the rear; instead, that very day word came for us to go into the front line that night. Were we disgusted? Gee, but you should have heard us rave and swear! We have been in the trenches since March 14th, and in this sector nearly four weeks; no leaves; no liberty; no rest; they must think the Marines are supermen or maybe mechanical devices for fighting. But then we have it straight from General Pershing that what's left of the Marine Corps will parade in Paris July 4th. Glory be, if this is only true. According to the fighting we've done we rate something out of the ordinary, and, of course, you know the Marines are credited with saving Paris. You have read exaggerated accounts of our exploits, perhaps you would be pleased to hear the truth. It is a long, long story so don't weaken.

Get you a map, locate Château-Thierry, back up ten kilometres toward Paris by way of Meaux (Meaux was being evacuated when we arrived), and there you find the location of our battle-ground. The Germans were advancing ten kilometres a day when in swept the Marines, relieving the retreating boys and with the Eighty-second and Eighty-third Companies in skirmish formation, attacking, the Huns were stopped and in three hours lines were pushed back four kilometres. Our losses were slight, for the Germans were not prepared to meet a stone wall resistance such as they bumped up against and certainly they had no idea of an offensive movement being launched.

The German infantry had been moving at so rapid a pace that their artillery could not keep up with them. As a result it was easy sailing for us. You should have seen those Huns running; they dropped everything and started toward Berlin. Twenty German planes were counted overhead that evening; they wanted to find out what the devil had interfered with their well-laid plans; what they saw was a wheat-field full of Marines and for miles behind the lines hundreds of trucks going forward at full speed, loaded with men, provisions and munitions. The Kaiser certainly had a set-back.

To continue with the battle, our objective was a railway station, but between us and our objective was a machine-gun Hill 142, and here the Germans made a last stand. The hill is a sort of plateau rising out of Belleau Woods, but between it and the woods are patches of wheat and beyond the hill the ground slopes gently down to the railway station. The hilltop is covered with immense rock and behind these the Germans placed their machine guns and made their stand, and held out for three weeks. The Eighty-second and Eighty-third made one attack against this position. We formed in the wheat-field in wave formation, and with our captain and major leading we rushed up that hill in the face of twenty machine guns. The woods were also full of German snipers.

The attack failed; we lost all our officers and half our company. We were just starting when out from behind a rock comes an unarmed German with arms up in the air shouting "Kamerad!" A dozen Marines rushed forward with fixed bayonets and stuck that man full of holes—orders were to take no prisoners. Many a brave Marine fell that day. That was our last attack. Since then six separate attacks were made on that hill and not until the other night did the Marines take it. Between the time of our attack and the successful one, the German artillery was moved up and we suffered much from shell fire.

The attack of the 25th was wonderfully successful. We, the Eighty-second Company, were in support, but were not called upon. At 3 p.m. the American artillery opened up on the hill. The Germans suspected something and immediately began gassing our rear and shelling the support—us. After two hours of fearful bombarding, at 5.05 p.m. two companies of Marines marched up that hill in wave formation and never halted until they had taken the position. Their losses were heavy, for the whizz-bangs, 77's, and other German guns were playing a tune all over that hill and about one hundred Maxims were spitting fire into the ranks of our brave men, but at heart those Germans are cowards, and when they saw the jig was up they surrendered. Six hundred prisoners, old men, and boys of eighteen and nineteen years old, and fifty machine guns were taken. One Marine private took sixty prisoners, and by himself marched them away.

The inevitable followed. A counter-attack. Four hundred Huns attempted to retake the hill; a great many were taken prisoners, and several hundred gassed by our battery. To-day we hold the hill and the prospect of an early relief is bright. Not a great deal is to be feared from these defeated divisions, for the Marines have their "Nanny."

Finish to-morrow, Mother, for it's getting too dark to write.

June 28, 1918. I saw a wonderfully thrilling sight several days ago—an air battle. For several hours a Hun plane had been flying low, up and down our lines, observing our activities and probably signaling his artillery our range. He was loafing over our position, when out from the clouds above darts a frog plane straight for the Hun, when within range the frog opened up with his machine gun and the next minute the German plane was nothing but a ball of fire. The aviator tried his best to get back to the German lines, but the wind was blowing our way, so Heinie darn near burned himself to death: but he turned and vol-planed toward our line, and when within a few feet of the ground he sprang out of his machine, killing himself. Three Boche planes were down that day in this one sector. Some of the men went out this morning to salvage the dead Germans. They returned with watches, razors, iron crosses, pictures, knives, German money, <u>gats,</u> and all sorts of souvenirs. I don't like salvaging, for the odor of a dead German is stifling. Nix on that stuff. The only souvenir I care to bring back to U.S.A. is yours truly.

This has been a banner day for us. Our ration detail returned this A.M. with Y.M.C.A. donations—chocolate, cookies, raisins, sugar and syrup, and cigarettes. This p.m. more mail arrived, K.C. papers and two pair of white lisle sox from Jones Store, Paris. I put one pair on immediately, although my feet were dirty and darn near black, due to the absence of water and abundance of sand. Two weeks ago I had a bath. That was a memorable day. The major decided that his boys needed washing, so he marched the whole battalion about twelve kilometres to the rear to a small village on the Marne River. The town had been evacuated, so we made ourselves at home. New potatoes, green peas, onions, and honey. I had honey that day, but I certainly paid for it. Several of us put on respirators, wrapped up well and invaded the beehives. I finished with eleven bee stings and a great quantity of excellent honey. After that escapade I filled my tummy and then went for a plunge in the river Marne. We were a happy crew that evening.

Water up here is scarce. We send after drinking-water at night. One dares not wander very far from his hole during the day, except on duty, of course, for those deadly whizz-bangs are very muchly in evidence. A whizz-band (so-called because of the sound it makes when hitting near by—you hear the whizz and immediately the bang) is a trench-mortar affair, calibre 88 cm., shot from a small gun about one and one half to two feet long, and smooth-bore. The shell has very little trajectory (in fact, the Germans use them for sniping), is filled with shrapnel, and its concussion is terrific. Damn it, I certainly hate these things! You can hear other shells coming and quite often can dodge them, but these whizz-bangs come fast and low.

The only writing I shall ever do when I return home will be a theme or so for some English Prof. There will be so much war bunk after this affair is over that the people will become sick of the word "war." I used to be ambitious. I desired a war cross and honor, but my ideas have changed. I have seen too many men with those ambitions go down riddled with bullets. (One of our lieutenants was shot twenty times while trying to rush a machine-gun position.) So I've come to the conclusion that I am of more value and credit to my country, to you and myself, as a live soldier, obedient and ready for duty, than as a dead hero. No grand-standing—just good honest team work and common sense. Don't be disillusioned—if I live long enough I may rate a sir. . . .

Sunday afternoon, June 30, 1918. Oh, what a relief! Last night we were relieved on the front line. . . . We were many miles behind the lines. We struck camp in a large woods. At 3 a.m. we had a hot meal; turned in later and slept until 11 a.m. when we ate again. Since then I have been swimming and feel like a different man. Received your June 10th letter a short while ago. More Y.M.C.A. supplies blew in, so with a full stomach and a feeling of security from those "Dutch" shells I am fairly happy. From a reliable source we are told that our battalion will parade in Paris July 4th and will be decorated for the fighting we have done this month. Will write you later whether or not this comes to pass.

1918: JUNE 17
LINCOLN STEFFENS TO JOHN REED

Journalist, intellectual, and avowed Communist, John Reed (1887–1920) had witnessed the Bolshevik revolution in 1917. But the notes he would eventually use to write his classic, Ten Days That Shook the World, *were confiscated by the U.S. government when he returned to New York from Russia. In early June he wrote to his old friend, the influential and left-leaning journalist Lincoln Steffens (1866–1936), to see if Steffens could help get the papers back. Steffens's response, written five months before World War I ended, warned of the nation's general lack of sympathy for the Bolsheviks, who had taken Russia out of the war.*

Walter Lippmann was one of the country's most prominent journalists. The writer Louise Bryant was Reed's wife.

850 FRANCISCO STREET

SAN FRANCISCO, CALIFORNIA

June 17, 1918.

Dear Jack:—

I'll do what I can about your papers. That's what is uppermost in your mind, apparently. I can't promise anything. I haven't much hope of accomplishing any result, but I'll try. And you should see meanwhile Walter Lippmann. Maybe you have, & if he failed, it may mean nothing at all. For the government is disjointed.

Both the old parties are in power, and, as in Europe, the crooks & the tories know what they want. <u>They</u> are the real traitors these days. They are using the emergency to get even with their enemies & fight for their Cause. It's fierce.

But it's exactly that which is sure to cause a reaction & bring on their troubles. I hoped the war would end in reasonable progress; but the Reactionaries won't permit it. They are showing what they care about law & order, constitution & precedents. Talk about scraps of paper!

But Jack, you do wrong to buck this thing. In the first place, the war was inevitable; in the second place, the consequences of the war, its by-products, are normal & typical; & in the third place, the public mind is sick. This last is what I learned in my experiences with it. I gave pain. I tried to speak always with the consciousness that an audience was in trouble: psychologically, & I was just as tender as I could be. And I often did my job without hurting them very much. But sometimes I saw that what I said had cut like a surgeon's knife into a sore place, & I was sorry. Really. I think it is wrong to try to tell the truth now. It must wait. You must wait. I know it's hard, but you can't carry conviction. You can't plant ideas. Only feelings exist & the feelings are bewildered. I think it is undemocratic to try to do much now. Write, but don't publish.

When the war is over, & it will not be long now,—then the world will divide normally again, & it will need light, & take facts. I have stopped myself; cut all engagements & have sat down here to write,—stories. I am pulling close financially, however, not yet recovered even from my Russian trip & unable to earn anything lecturing. I hope to make some money writing. But my stories are all so irrelevant; the effect, I suppose, of the suppression, that I don't believe I shall be able to place them. I think I'll just sit tight & write some stuff for publication after the war. And I don't know whether to stay here & do it, or go East.

Write again, & I will, Jack. The last letter from Louise was more like a cry than a letter. She said among other things that she didn't believe people wanted what they said they wanted! I'm afraid Louise is seeing the world.

Yours affectionately,
L. Steffens

1918: JUNE 29
JOHN REED TO LINCOLN STEFFENS

Still worried about the return of his notes, Reed rejected Steffens's arguments about delaying his book.

Croton-on-Hudson, N.Y.   June 29

My dear Steff—

I wouldn't ask Walter L. for anything for the whole world. I have other friends in the State Department, however—but they don't appear to be able to do anything. Meanwhile of course I am getting cold on the whole business, and I fear that it will be too late to write my book into the bargain. It is really tragic, I think. I have the story, and I am deliberately kept from writing it, without the shadow of a given reason. The Government is of course disjointed; much worse than the Russian government which everybody criticizes so much. I believe with you that the war will end in utter violence.

However, Steff, I am not of your opinion that it is undemocratic to buck this thing. If there were not the ghost of a chance, if everybody were utterly for it, even then I don't see why it shouldn't be bucked. All movements have had somebody to start them, and if necessary go under for them. Not that I want particularly to go under—but—

And you are wrong to think that this business is unanimous. There are many—oh so many—who crowd to my meetings—thousands; and <u>they</u> are with us. And it's growing, growing fast. I don't seem to give pain. My people weep with joy to know that there is something like dreams-come-true in Russia. And moreover I have seen what is happening abroad, and I'm not troubled any more at all myself.

Come east, and come here to Croton, where you can do what you please and live alone if you wish—or with us—in this beautiful and ineffably quiet growing spot.

Yours
Reed

You can live in a little out-house—very comfortable all to yourself or in the big house. Most of the time you'd be alone.

1918: AUGUST 1
JOHN D. ROCKEFELLER, JR., TO JOHN D. ROCKEFELLER

The senior Rockefeller (1839–1937) spent several decades building the Standard Oil Company from a single refinery into a monopoly—and nearly as many years methodically transferring the fortune he'd made to his son and namesake. After graduating from Brown in 1897, John D. Rockefeller, Jr. (1874–1960), had joined the family business, where he would ultimately help his father contribute more than three billion dollars to philanthropic causes, including Rockefeller University and the Rockefeller Foundation. The letters below are two of dozens that were nearly identical both in the coolness with which millions of dollars were given and the formality with which they were received.

Pocantico Hills was the site of Kykuit, the Rockefeller family home.

Seal Harbor, Me.

August 1st, 1918

Dear Father:

Your letter of July 30th, telling me of the securities which you have given me, came last night, and quite overpowered me.

I was only just beginning to fully realize the significance of the previous gift, which you made me just before I left Pocantico, and now this further gift of equal magnitude has come.

Dear Father, I thank you from the bottom of my heart for your great generosity, and this further evidence of your confidence and affection.

The opportunities for doing good which you have made possible to me are unlimited and wonderful.

I can only hope and pray that I shall be as conscientious in my stewardship as you have always been in yours, and I shall strive to be as wise and generous.

In the hope that you may never have cause to regret having placed this great responsibility upon me, and again with profoundest thanks and truest love, I am,

Affectionately,

John

1918: SEPTEMBER 1
BILL HAYWOOD TO JOHN REED

William Dudley "Big Bill" Haywood (1869–1928) grew up in the West and started work as a miner; by 1905, he was helping found the IWW. An active and militant Socialist, he was an organizer of the "Bread and Roses" strike in Lawrence and a charismatic speaker who called for American workers to organize into "one big union." In 1907, he was acquitted of murdering former Idaho governor Frank Steunenberg, but eleven years later, he and dozens of other Wobblies (as IWW members were called) were found guilty on a total of ten thousand counts of sedition for opposing the war. Three years later Haywood, facing twenty years in prison, would jump bail and flee to Russia, where like John Reed (see letter page 128), he would remain until his death.

The Liberator, which had just started publication in March of 1918, was a Socialist periodical edited by Max Eastman.

Cook County Jail
Sept. 1/18

Jack Reed,

Dear Jack,

The big game is over we never won a hand. The other fellow had the cut, shuffle and deal all the time, personally we didn't lose much just a part of our lives that is all, some of us as high as twenty years.

All in the world they had against was morsels of fragmentary evidence, not enough to convict a ward heeling politician, but we were off our field, we will do better when we get organized and can tie into them on the Industrial ground.

Everybody feeling fine. Write would like other friends to do the same, Yours Haywood

over

Haven't got a copy of the Liberator as yet, there is just one in the jail it is going the round, tell Art Young we got the loose photos of his drawing.

Address Temporarily
Wm D Haywood
1001 N. Madison St.
Chicago, Ill.

1918: SEPTEMBER 12
JOHN D. ROCKEFELLER TO JOHN D. ROCKEFELLER, JR.

Golf House
Lakewood, N.J.
September 12, 1918

Dear Son:

Answering yours of the 9th, you could not have enjoyed the visits of the past two weeks which we have had together more than I did.

You are very busy, but you never seem too busy to put yourself out to come and visit me. These visits I appreciate more and more, and I don't tell you so nearly as much as I ought to.

What a Providence that your life should have been spared to take up the responsibilities as I lay them down! I could not have anticipated in the earlier years that they would have been so great, nor could I have dreamed that you would have come so promptly and satisfactorily to meet them, and to go beyond, in the contemplation of our right attitude to the world in the discharge of these obligations.

I appreciate, I am grateful, beyond all I can tell you. There is much for you to accomplish in the future. Do not allow yourself to be overburdened with details. Others must look to these. We will plan and work together. I want to stay a long time to help do my part. I hope you will take good care of your health. This is a religious duty, and you can accomplish so much more for the world if you keep well and strong.

Affectionately,
Father

1918: SEPTEMBER 29
AN ARMY DOCTOR TO A COLLEAGUE

Worldwide, the Great War killed approximately nine million people during the course of its four years. But an outbreak of influenza killed more than twenty million in one year alone. The month after a doctor stationed at an army camp near Boston wrote this letter to a friend, nearly two hundred thousand deaths would be reported in the United States.

Cyanosis is discoloration of the skin due to lack of oxygen in the blood. Rales are abnormal chest sounds.

Camp Devens, Mass.
Surgical Ward No. 16
29 September 1918

My dear Burt,

It is more than likely that you would be interested in the news of this place, for there is a possibility that you will be assigned here for duty, so having a minute between rounds I will try to tell you a little about the situation here as I have seen it in the last week.

As you know, I have not seen much pneumonia in the last few years in Detroit, so when I came here I was somewhat behind in the niceties of the Army way of intricate diagnosis. Also to make it good, I have had for the last week an exacerbation of my old "Ear Rot" as Artie Ogle calls it, and could not use a stethoscope at all, but had to get by on my ability to "spot" 'em thru my general knowledge of pneumonias. . . .

Camp Devens is near Boston, and has about 50,000 men, or did have before this epidemic broke loose. It also has the base hospital for the Division of the

Northeast. This epidemic started about four weeks ago, and has developed so rapidly that the camp is demoralized and all ordinary work is held up till it has passed. All assemblages of soldiers taboo. These men start with what appears to be an attack of la grippe or influenza, and when brought to the hospital they very rapidly develop the most viscous type of pneumonia that has ever been seen. Two hours after admission they have the mahogany spots over the cheek bones, and a few hours later you can begin to see the cyanosis extending from their ears and spreading all over the face, until it is hard to distinguish the coloured men from the white. It is only a matter of a few hours then until death comes, and it is simply a struggle for air until they suffocate. It is horrible. One can stand it to see one, two or twenty men die, but to see these poor devils dropping like flies sort of gets on your nerves. We have been averaging about 100 deaths per day, and still keeping it up. There is no doubt in my mind that there is a new mixed infection here, but what I don't know. My total time is taken up hunting rales, rales dry or moist, sibilant or crepitant or any other of the hundred things that one may find in the chest, they all mean but one thing here—pneumonia—and that means in about all cases death.

The normal number of doctors here is about 25 and that has been increased to over 250, all of whom (of course excepting me) have temporary orders— "Return to your proper station on completion of work"—Mine says, "Permanent Duty," but I have been in the Army just long enough to learn that it doesn't always mean what it says. So I don't know what will happen to me at the end of this. We have lost an outrageous number of nurses and doctors, and the little town of Ayer is a sight. It takes special trains to carry away the dead. For several days there were no coffins and the bodies piled up something fierce, we used to go down to the morgue (which is just back of my ward) and look at the boys laid out in long rows. It beats any sight they ever had in France after a battle. An extra long barracks has been vacated for the use of the morgue, and it would make any man sit up and take notice to walk down the long lines of dead soldiers all dressed up and laid out in double rows. We have no relief here; you get up in the morning at 5:30 and work steady till about 9:30 p.m., sleep, then go at it again. Some of the men of course have been here all the time, and they are tired.

If this letter seems somewhat disconnected overlook it, for I have been called away from it a dozen times, the last time just now by the Officer of the Day, who came in to tell me that they have not as yet found at any of the autopsies any case beyond the red hepatitis stage. It kills them before it gets that far.

I don't wish you any hard luck Old Man, but do wish you were here for a while at least. Its more comfortable when one has a friend about. The men here are all good fellows, but I get so damned sick o' pneumonia that when I eat I want to find some fellow who will not "talk shop" but there ain't none, no how. We eat it, sleep it, and dream it, to say nothing of breathing it 16 hours a day. I would be very grateful indeed if you would drop me a line or two once in a while, and I will promise you that if you ever get into a fix like this, I will do the same for you.

Each man here gets a ward with about 150 beds (mine has 168), and has an Asst. Chief to boss him, and you can imagine what the paper work alone is— <u>fierce</u>—and the Government demands all paper work be kept up in good shape. I have only four day nurses and five night nurses (female) a ward-master and four orderlies. So you can see that we are busy. I write this in piecemeal fashion. It may be a long time before I can get another letter to you, but will try.

Good-by old Pal,

"God be with you till we meet again"

Keep the Bouells open.

Roy

1918: OCTOBER 5
SMEDLEY BUTLER TO HIS PARENTS

A Pennsylvania Quaker and the son of a congressman, Smedley Butler (1881–1940) served in the Marine Corps for most of his adult life, becoming a major general during World War I. Stationed in France immediately after his arrival, he wrote home to describe the effects of the flu epidemic there. By December, half a million American soldiers and sailors, including fully a quarter of the navy, had contracted the virus, and thirty thousand of those would die.

The first paragraph is a reference to wartime censorship. Though the epidemic was known as the Spanish flu, it seems to have originated in America.

Brest, France
October 5th 1918

Dear Father and Mother:

This letter is going to you via an officer so I can speak a little more freely than under ordinary circumstances.

We had a "hell" of a trip over, an epidemic of Spanish influenza breaking out among us the second day out and to make things worse shifting swiftly into pneumonia towards the last of the trip. Our officers, medical and line, worked like the devil to save the men but were almost powerless to overcome such terrific odds—we had at one time fully 500 cases of influenza and over 90 of pneumonia. I myself went down the second day with influenza and could not get up until the day we landed. Was not seriously or dangerously sick but felt terribly and the Doctors feared I was getting pneumonia but I did not.

However, by almost superhuman efforts they pulled two thirds of the cases through and I am grateful for that.

Poor little Francis Logue died as did Majors Torrey and MacLachlin, both splendid fellows and fine officers. They caught it from the men they fought so hard to save. We had a very rough passage and were greatly crowded. I suppose it is one of the awful results of this devilish war but nevertheless it is terribly hard to bear, this loss of your men when you can't help them.

As soon as we landed we put our sick in the hospitals and they are nearly all back to duty now so we are all right again. Our experience was not exceptional, many of the ships coming in had identical experiences, another ship in our convoy had a greater percentage of loss than we had so I feel not quite so badly. We have a splendid lot of Doctors and they did wonders, am on their side forever.

. . . We have been inspected by every and all sorts of Army Officers all of whom state that we are the finest troops who have come through this enormous camp. I myself have never seen such men. We get together in the mud and rain in the evenings, after a rain soaked supper, and sing more beautifully than ever we did at Quantico, keep it up too until after dark. All our working details always sing on the roads and are neat and far cleaner than any Army soldiers who go by our camp. It brings a big lump into my throat whenever I see them, which is all the time in fact as my little tent is right in the middle of theirs. We all eat the same food and are determined to fight it out together.

Now for the awful rub.

Orders have come breaking up our Regt. and distributing all along the coast of France for guard duty in the ports. I am not even allowed to go with them but am ordered to command this concentration camp, the least desirable and lowest job in France. It has not been commanded except by an officer who has been sent back in disgrace from the front. However I am in France and will do all in my power to make these poor miserable, wretched sick soldiers who pass by the thousands through here, as comfortable and happy as my poor strength will let me. The strength of this post varies from 15,000 to 50,000 men, depending on arrivals so were it not for its past history of canned officers in command it would be a good job if one were not allowed to go to the front, which is my case.

. . . Just think we have not had one single man misbehave in or around this City, and we are the only troops who ever came here for a stay of this length without getting a <u>single</u> mans name on the Military Police Records, and they have done it I know because I asked them to behave as that was the best way to make a good reputation and get to the front. We are all going to fight it out together, each man and officer doing his best to be ready when the chance comes to get together.

The Commander of this Base is old Brig. General Harries from Washington, says he knows thee well and has had me to a very good lunch. . . .

Admiral Wilson was very pleasant when I called to pay my respects but has paid no other attention to us, naturally not as we are now in the Army. . . .

Should thee have an opportunity thee might tell the Secretary of the Navy about our smash up, <u>but don't complain</u> for all we asked was to get to France and we will make our own way. I have asked to keep Joe Daniels with me here to see that nothing happens to him. He is a fine boy and looks better physically every day, queer how things go in the health line. . . .

Your loving son

Smedley D. Butler

1918: NOVEMBER 4
PERCIVAL GATES TO HIS FATHER

Percival Gates was born January 3, 1897, the seventh child of Frederick Gates, who was adviser to John D. Rockefeller. Percival enlisted in the air service in September of 1917. After training in the States, he sailed for Europe in late May of 1918 and served in France until the end of the war, which was a week away when he wrote this letter. Its tone reveals what, at the time, was an all too common familiarity with death. Russell Gates was one of Percival's older brothers.

Dear Father:

In case of accident you should write to . . . and either have him take the remainder of the payment out of my "six months pay," which the government gives after the death of an officer, or else have him send back the money I have already paid with interest. All that of course is in case of accident. I am bringing up all these things because we have so much trouble with other fellows' stuff if they go missing as they sometimes do.

As to my personal belongings, according to AEF regulations backed up by the 1st Pursuit Group, all belongings of a man who is missing in action for over 10 days are packed up and sent to the "effects depot." There, everything except the most personal things, such as watches, picture albums, diaries, letters, jewelry etc, are sold or thrown away and the proceeds are sent home. Since this is the case, we have a custom here of selling everything except the personal things to fellows here in the group, such as blankets, bedding rolls, cots, leather goods, and toilet articles. However if the goods is claimed from the "effects depot" by a member of the family, it is given over intact.

I tell you this and I am writing the same to Russell so that you will understand the red tape that has to be gone through. This is purely a business letter; I will try to write a more interesting one to Mother a little later. Don't think I am in any special danger. I am merely getting things straightened out that I should have attended to long ago.

> Your loving son,
> Percival

1918: NOVEMBER 7
ELIZABETH STEARNS TYLER TO MISS R.

Elizabeth Stearns Tyler worked for the Red Cross in France during World War I. In 1919, after her death from bronchitis, her letters were privately printed.

In French, *recueillement* means "meditation." No information was available about "Miss R."

Paris, November 7

Just think, tonight everybody says that the Armistice has been signed with Germany and that there will be peace. I think the first feeling is of absolute incredulity. It doesn't seem possible that the war can really be over. I keep thinking of the infinite joy of the people whose men are at the front. After the strain of the four years I should think the joy would almost kill one, the relief from the strain. If only <u>all</u> our soldiers could go home at once, so that all these hospitals, filled more by grippe than by the fighting, might be emptied. It has all been so horrible. Do you suppose people <u>ever</u> could start up another? Did the world have the same feeling of nightmare, the same exhaustion in 1815 and have we merely lost the experience through the generations in between? I pin my faith to the idealistic, youthful—naïve, if you like—determination of the American people that this shall be the last war. I don't think any of these European people, for all their suffering is so much greater than ours, feel the crusade against war as we do. It seems a part of our God-given richness of opportunity that our people feel <u>able</u> to change the old order which these people, however much more they suffer, more passively accept. I have a better idea of what war means than before, for I have just been with Miss May to take some things to a hospital near the front and we went, en route, through villages that were fought over last July. There is no use trying to describe it. Along the highways we saw only soldiers, their blue uniforms lightening a little the gray forlornity of the country. But off in the hills the little villages would be <u>absolutely</u> deserted. Somehow it is the <u>silence</u> that comes back to me most strongly now. Do you remember our discussing once why ears gave so much more intimate impressions than eyes? Somehow all I saw does not stay with me or bring the impression as much as the <u>absolute</u> stillness. It was an autumn day, most beautiful, like the Indian summer Emily Dickinson describes, and the haunting sense of past life and growth in her poem just went with the spell of that place. I shall always see the mute, broken arches of an old church, raising themselves silently out of the ruins against a hillside colored by lovely autumn soft colors or scarred by dead trees and trenches. It was dreadful. I am very glad to have gone once, but I never want to go again until the reconstruction work begins. When you are there, intellectual curiosity runs away with you. I walked miles through deep trenches, looked down the steps of dug-outs that went down thirty feet under the floor of the trench, collected empty shells, helmets, etc., looked at the unexploded shells, <u>hated</u> myself for wanting to see it all and wondered how I could. But once away, when the little village relapses into the silence and tragic <u>receuillement</u> which you have interrupted, then the spell gets you again and you are defenceless against it. Its very <u>inarticulateness</u> is expressive of what it has seen. . . .

1918: NOVEMBER 10
EDWARD HOUSE TO WOODROW WILSON

Colonel Edward M. House (1858–1938), for many years Wilson's closest adviser, was sent by the president to Europe in the waning days of World War I to help negotiate the armistice between German and Allied forces. His cablegrams to the president reported the progress of the talks, which culminated in the signing of the peace agreement on November 11, 1918.

Colonel T. Bentley Mott was American military attaché in France. Marshal Ferdinand Foch had been commanding the unified British, French, and U.S. armies since April of 1918.

Paris, November 10, 1918

The following has just been received by me from Colonel Mott: "The German Government has announced by wireless that they accept the terms of the Armistice. The signing of the Armistice as far as we know has not taken place. No information has yet come from Marshal Foch that any paper has been signed."

House

1918: NOVEMBER 10
EDWARD HOUSE TO WOODROW WILSON

Paris, November 10, 1918

Would suggest when the Armistice is signed that you read the terms to Congress and use the occasion to give another message to the world. You have a right to assume that the two great features of the Armistice are the defeat of German military imperialism and the acceptance by the Allied Powers of the kind of peace the world has longed for. A steadying note seems to me necessary at this time. A word of warning and a word of hope should be said. The world is in a ferment and Civilization itself is wavering in the balance.

Edward House

1918: NOVEMBER 11
EDWARD HOUSE TO WOODROW WILSON

Paris, November 11, 1918

Autocracy is dead. Long live democracy and its immortal leader. In this great hour my heart goes out to you in pride, admiration and love.

Edward House

1919: MARCH 7
AGNES VON KUROWSKY TO ERNEST HEMINGWAY

As an ambulance driver in Italy in 1918, Ernest Hemingway (see letter page 172) was wounded in the leg by an explosion and taken to a hospital in Milan. There he fell in love with Agnes von Kurowsky, an American Red Cross nurse. He had just turned nineteen; she was twenty-six. For him, the affair was far more serious than it proved to be for her. It inspired him to create the character of Catherine in A Farewell to Arms. *It inspired her to pen one of the great Dear John letters.*

March 7, 1919

Ernie, dear boy,

I am writing this late at night after a long think by myself, & I am afraid it is going to hurt you, but, I'm sure it won't harm you permanently.

For quite awhile before you left, I was trying to convince myself it was a real love-affair, because, we always seemed to disagree, & then arguments always wore me out so that I finally gave in to keep you from doing something desperate.

Now, after a couple of months away from you, I know that I am still very fond of you, but, it is more as a mother than as a sweetheart. It's alright to say I'm a Kid, but, I'm not, & I'm getting less & less so every day.

So, Kid (still Kid to me, & always will be) can you forgive me some day for unwittingly deceiving you? You know I'm not really bad, & don't mean to do wrong, & now I realize it was my fault in the beginning that you cared for me, & regret it from the bottom of my heart. But, I am now & always will be too old, & that's the truth, & I can't get away from the fact that you're just a boy— a kid.

I somehow feel that some day I'll have reason to be proud of you, but, dear boy, I can't wait for that day, & it is wrong to hurry a career.

I tried hard to make you understand a bit of what I was thinking on that trip from Padua to Milan, but, you acted like a spoiled child, & I couldn't keep on hurting you. Now, I only have the courage because I'm far away.

Then—& believe me when I say this is sudden for me, too—I expect to be married soon. And I hope & pray that after you have thought things out, you'll be able to forgive me & start a wonderful career & show what a man you really are.

> Ever admiringly & fondly
> Your friend,
> Aggie

1919: SEPTEMBER 16
THOMAS EDISON TO WILLIAM FEATHER

Thomas Edison (1847–1931) had already invented the phonograph, the kineto-graph (a forerunner of the movie camera), and the first practical incandescent light-bulb before the turn of the century. His patents would ultimately number more than a thousand, but he would be most famous for the electric light and the way it changed the world. When William Feather, a business writer, asked Edison if it was true that, because of electric lights, he and his assistants could work longer hours and get by with a minimum of sleep, Edison offered this reply.

FROM THE LABORATORY OF THOMAS A. EDISON
ORANGE, N.J.

September 16, 1919

Dear Mr. Feather:

I received your letter of September 10 in regard to sleep. Until the last six years, and over a period of 40 years, I and my experimental assistants worked on an average 18 hours daily. New men found it very difficult to get used to 4 or 5 hours sleep, but in a short time they became accustomed to it and I have never heard of any one of them being injured.

I find that men who once worked with me for a number of years and then left, kept up the habit of working long hours. I think any person can get used to it. One remarkable thing that they all agree on is that it stops dreaming. This is perhaps due to a deeper sleep.

If the world had been differently arranged and the sun had shone continuously, I do not think that anybody would require or take sleep. There seems to be no actual reason why we should sleep, from a scientific standpoint.

I noticed in automobiling through Switzerland that the towns which had electric lights had many new buildings and the people were active and on the streets at 12:00 o'clock, midnight, whereas in towns without electric lights, everybody was in bed about 8:30 and the town was a dead one.

Thomas A. Edison

1919: DECEMBER 3
BERTRAND BROWN TO CHARLES DILLINGHAM

Vaudeville was still in its heyday and Charles Bancroft Dillingham (1868–1934) was one of its leading producers when an ambitious innovator sent off this proposal. We were unable to learn whether the spectacle, which prefigured the 1988 film *Big*, was ever constructed. The Hippodrome, managed by Dillingham and located on Forty-third Street in Manhattan, was billed as the "Largest Theater in the World."

Room 362, 1 Madison Ave.
New York, N.Y.
December Third
1919

Mr. Charles B. Dillingham
Broadway & 46th Street,
New York, N.Y.

My dear Mr. Dillingham:—

An idea has occurred to me which I believe would make a good spectacle for production at the Hippodrome.

It embodies the erection on the stage of a huge set of manuals of a pipe organ. These would be attached to one or more large organs. They would provide a unique setting for both a beautiful ballet number and a comedy number, the idea, of course, being that the dancers should aid in playing their own accompaniment by stepping on the proper keys at the proper intervals. A solo toe dancer doing a number with chromatic runs on such an instrument would, it seems to me, be an innovation.

Should the suggestion be new, and should you like to use it, I would like to submit one or more song manuscripts for use in connection with it.

Cordially yours,
BERTRAND BROWN.

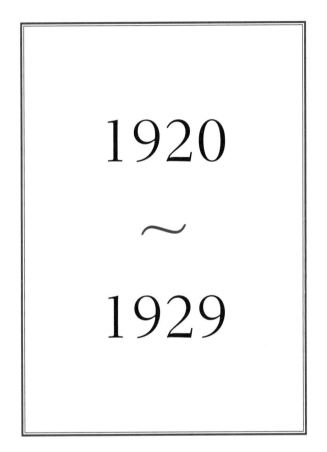

1920

~

1929

We are over-sexed these days. From the shrouded and veiled mystery that Grandma knew, we have reacted too strongly and are now at the outer extreme of vulgar display and a harsh frankness that appalls most of us even while we pretend to take it all as a matter of course.

—*A former flapper to Nancy Brown*
September 6, 1923

BETWEEN 1920 AND 1929 . . .

1920: For the first time, more Americans live in cities than in rural areas. ★ The U.S. population is 105,710,620. ★ Average number of Americans per square mile: 35.6. ★ Prohibition begins at 12:01 on the morning of January 16, after a night of subdued drinking and mock funerals for "John Barleycorn." ★ In Springfield, Ohio, a judge hangs an "ankle curtain" in the courtroom so that women jurors will not have to show their bare ankles. ★ Warren G. Harding is elected president. ★ Cleveland Indians shortstop Ray Chapman is hit by a pitch and killed. ★ Women get the vote. ★ More than 6,000 suspected Communists are rounded up in raids authorized by Attorney General A. Mitchell Palmer. **1921:** New word: "robot." ★ New fragrance: Chanel No. 5. ★ New tradition: the Miss America pageant in Atlantic City, New Jersey, with contestants showing bare knees. The first winner: Margaret Gorman, five feet, one inch tall; 108 pounds; 16 years old. ★ Charlie Chaplin's first full-length movie, *The Kid,* becomes a smash hit. **1922:** *The Reader's Digest* begins publication. ★ Harrison Jones, Coca-Cola's vice-president in charge of sales, sees a man struggling to carry a 24-bottle case of Coke, and comes up with the idea of the 6-pack. ★ In Schenectady, New York, radio station WGY

From left to right, top row: Prohibition tombstone, George Washington Carver, Charlie Chaplin and Jackie Coogan; *second row:* Sacco and Vanzetti, F. Scott and Zelda Fitzgerald, Amelia Earhart; *third row:* bathing beauties; *bottom row:* Margaret Sanger, the stock market crash, an early radio.

broadcasts the first sound effect: a slamming door suggested by two pieces of wood banged together. **1923:** A female teacher's contract in Utah declares, in part, "Teacher is not to marry. Teacher is not to keep the company of men. Teacher may not loiter downtown in ice cream parlors. Teacher may not dye her hair." ★ The first issue of *Time* magazine is published. ★ More than 13 million cars are in circulation. ★ Warren Harding dies in office, and Calvin Coolidge becomes president. **1924:** With the accompaniment of the Paul Whiteman Orchestra, George Gershwin premieres *Rhapsody in Blue*. ★ Membership in the Ku Klux Klan is now estimated to be in the millions. ★ Defended by Clarence Darrow, teenagers Nathan Leopold, Jr., and Richard Loeb receive life sentences instead of the electric chair for their part in the "thrill kill" of Loeb's 14-year-old cousin, Bobby Franks. ★ Notebooks are made with spiral bindings. ★ The Citizenship Act declares all American Indians to be U.S. citizens. ★ Seen for the first time: frozen food, Little Orphan Annie, and Kleenex. **1925:** Howard Johnson borrows $500 to turn a Quincy, Massachusetts, patent-medicine shop into an ice cream stand. ★ F. Scott Fitzgerald publishes *The Great Gatsby*. ★ John T. Scopes is arrested for teaching evolution in the town of Dayton, Tennessee; the trial begins with a ten-foot-long banner proclaiming Read Your Bible hanging behind the judge's bench. ★ In *The New Republic*, Bruce Bliven describes the current skimpy women's fashions this way: "Ladies who used to go away for the summer with six trunks can now pack twenty dainty costumes in a bag." **1926:** Biggest box-office star of the year: Rin Tin Tin. ★ Among flappers, especially, good things are called "the berries," "the cat's meow," "the cat's pajamas," "swell," "hotsy-totsy," or "the bee's knees." ★ Bootlegging is estimated to be a $3.6 billion business. **1927:** Clara Bow is the "It" Girl. ★ Piloting the *Spirit of St. Louis*, Charles Lindbergh becomes the first man to fly solo across the Atlantic Ocean. ★ Babe Ruth hits 60 home runs. ★ Al Jolson stars in *The Jazz Singer*, the first feature-length "talkie." **1928:** Herbert Hoover is elected president. ★ Popular songs include "Makin' Whoopee" and "I Wanna Be Loved by You." ★ Bubble gum, broccoli, and Mickey Mouse make their first appearances. ★ Bootleg liquor kills 1,565 Americans. 1929: The first Academy Awards ceremony, lasting five minutes, is held in the Blossom Room of Los Angeles's Roosevelt Hotel. ★ On February 14 in Chicago, in what will become known as the St. Valentine's Day Massacre, a bystander and six members of the Bugs Moran gang are lined up against a garage wall and shot, presumably on orders from Al Capone. ★ In Kansas City, Gypsy Rose Lee performs as a stripper for the first time. ★ Ernest Hemingway publishes *A Farewell to Arms*, Thomas Wolfe publishes *Look Homeward, Angel*, and William Faulkner publishes *The Sound and the Fury*. ★ U.S. radio sales surpass $900 million. ★ Weekly movie attendance is 100 million. ★ California astronomer Edwin Hubble declares that the universe is expanding. ★ The stock market crashes.

The greatest sports scandal of the century began with the rumor that eight members of the favored Chicago White Sox had agreed to throw the 1919 World Series. Charles Comiskey (1859–1931) was owner of the White Sox and, though famously tightfisted, offered $200,000 in reward money for information that would prove the fix. More than a year later, the eight players—among them the very popular Shoeless Joe Jackson—received this telegram. Though several of the players confessed, they were ultimately found not guilty at trial. Still, all eight would be banned from the game for life.

CHICAGO, ILL. TO CHARLES RISBERG, FRED MCMULLIN, ETC.

YOU AND EACH OF YOU ARE HEREBY NOTIFIED OF YOUR INDEFINITE SUSPENSION AS A MEMBER OF THE CHICAGO AMERICAN LEAGUE BASEBALL CLUB. YOUR SUSPENSION IS BROUGHT ABOUT BY INFORMATION WHICH HAS JUST COME TO ME, DIRECTLY INVOLVING YOU AND EACH OF YOU IN THE BASEBALL SCANDAL NOW BEING INVESTIGATED BY THE GRAND JURY OF COOK COUNTY, RESULTING FROM THE WORLD SERIES OF 1919.

IF YOU ARE INNOCENT OF ANY WRONGDOING, YOU AND EACH OF YOU WILL BE REINSTATED; IF YOU ARE GUILTY, YOU WILL BE RETIRED FROM ORGANIZED BASEBALL FOR THE REST OF YOUR LIVES IF I CAN ACCOMPLISH IT.

UNTIL THERE IS A FINALITY TO THIS INVESTIGATION, IT IS DUE TO THE PUBLIC THAT I TAKE THIS ACTION EVEN THOUGH IT COSTS CHICAGO THE PENNANT.

CHICAGO AMERICAN LEAGUE BB CLUB
BY CHARLES A. COMISKEY

1921: JANUARY 20
GERTRUDE LAITINEN TO EUGENE V. DEBS

Gertrude Laitinen was a Fitchburg, Massachusetts, schoolgirl when she wrote this letter to Eugene V. Debs (1855–1926). At the time, the famous union leader and Socialist was in prison on sedition charges for his vocal opposition to the war. The year before, he had gathered nearly a million votes in the last of five campaigns for the presidency. In December he would be released from jail.

Lord Baltimore and Roger Williams were early founders of the American colonies. General John Joseph Pershing commanded the American Expeditionary Force in Europe during World War I.

January 20, 1921
Fitchburg, Massachusetts

Dear Comrade

I just happened to think how you are shut behind the bars, and thought it would make you feel happy for awhile, if I send these few words.

I am eleven years old and I am in seventh grade, my teacher questioned me at history period in front of my class, she asked me if I like Lord Baltimore or Roger Williams and I answered I dont know whom I like best, then she asked if I like Washington I said no, if I like Lincoln. I said yes. she asked why? I answered "Yes because he freed the slaves and rose from a poor boy to a president; then she asked if I like Pershing I said NO! she asked why? then I said because he is a capitalist in mind. then also she aked if I like Foch I said No! then she said I suppose for same reason

Then she asked what capitalists are I said they are the ones who rob the workers she said, "Well they never have robbed me of any money, I said they dont always rob of money but something more precious than money then I said its our lives also as I considered it, then I was allowed to take my seat, She continued to talk about socialism and said people who are not Christians or loyal Americans ought to go to the land they like and then she said some children in my room are not loyal and I suppose she meant me. I dont think she is a proper kind of a teacher.

I play the violin a little and I love this instrument, the weather was beautiful the first of January but today it has been very cold. Jack Frost almost pinches your nose off when I am out. As the clock is quite late Ill tell you its half past ten and you will forgive me if my writing is so bad

Yours for the Bolshevik
Revolution
Gertrude Laitinen

1922: JANUARY 9

GEORGE WASHINGTON CARVER TO A STUDENT

George Washington Carver (1861–1943) had become head of the agriculture department at Booker T. Washington's Tuskegee Institute in 1896. He would remain there until his death, researching the development of products made from peanuts and sweet potatoes, among other natural resources. His advice to his departing students was both universal in subject and timeless in spirit.

January 9, 1922

Mr. L. Robinson

I wish to express through you to each member of the Senior class my deep appreciation for the fountain pen you so kindly and thoughtfully gave me Christmas.

This gift, like all the others, is characterized by simplicity and thoughtfulness, which I hope each member will make the slogan of their lives.

As your father, it is needless for me to keep saying, I hope, except for emphasis, that each one of my children will rise to the full height of your possibilities, which means the possession of these eight cardinal virtues which constitutes a lady or a gentleman.

1st. Be clean both inside and outside.

2nd. Who neither looks up to the rich or down on the poor.

3rd. Who loses, if needs be, without squealing.

4th. Who wins without bragging.

5th. Who is always considerate of women, children and old people.

6th. Who is too brave to lie.

7th. Who is too generous to cheat.

8th. Who takes his share of the world and lets other people have theirs.

May God help you to carry out these eight cardinal virtues and peace and prosperity be yours through life.

Lovingly yours,
G. W. Carver

1922: JANUARY 31

DAVID SARNOFF TO OWEN YOUNG

Radio was still in its infancy, with only five thousand home receivers in operation, when David Sarnoff (1891–1971) proposed that the recently formed Radio Corporation of America transform radio into a mass entertainment medium. A for-

mer Marconi operator, Sarnoff had achieved fame in 1912 for supposedly picking up the first wireless message about the sinking of the Titanic. *Whether he actually did this is doubtful, but Sarnoff's initiative, as well as his penchant for self-promotion, are undisputed. Recognizing his talents, RCA chairman Owen D. Young (1874–1962) asked Sarnoff in 1920 to assess the commercial prospects for radio. Having failed to spur the company to move as aggressively as he had hoped, Sarnoff reiterated and updated his key points two years later in the following letter. By 1929, U.S. radio sales would total $950 million. Sarnoff would lead RCA for some forty years.*

E. J. Nally was general manager of Marconi Wireless.

January 31, 1922

O. D. Young, Esquire
Chairman, Board of Directors,
Radio Corporation of America,
120 Broadway, N.Y.C.

Dear Mr. Young,   <u>BROADCASTING</u>

Now that the idea of radio broadcasting and the sale of devices for use at home in connection therewith, have met with such great enthusiasm and interest, you may wish to review that part of my report to you dated January 31, 1920, or <u>two years ago</u>, on Prospective Radio Business, which dealt with the broadcasting field and from which you will note that the plan was conceived and worked out in commercial detail in 1915, or <u>seven years ago</u>.

I quote from my report to you as follows:

<u>"Sales of 'Radio Music Box'</u>
<u>for Entertainment Purposes"</u>

"For some years past I have had in mind a plan of development which would make radio a 'household utility' in the same sense as a piano or phonograph. In 1915 I presented the plan in detail to Mr. Nally, but the circumstances attending our business at that time and since then have not been such as to make practicable serious consideration of this subject. However, I feel that the time is now ripe to give renewed consideration to this proposition which is described below:

<u>"The idea is to Bring Music into the House by Wireless"</u>

"While this has been tried in the past by wires, it has been a failure because wires do not lend themselves to this scheme. With radio, however, it would seem to be entirely feasible. For example—a radio telephone transmitter having a range of say 20 to 50 miles can be installed at a fixed point where instrumental or vocal music or both are produced. The problem of transmitting music has already been solved in principle and therefore all the receivers attuned to the transmitting wave length should be capable of receiving such music. The receiver can be designed in the form of a simple 'Radio Music Box' and arranged for several different wave lengths, which should be changeable with the throwing of a single switch or pressing of a single button.

"The 'Radio Music Box' can be supplied with amplifying tubes and a loud speaking telephone, all of which can be neatly mounted in one box. The box can be placed on a table in the parlor or living room, the switch set accordingly and the transmitted music received. There should be no difficulty in receiving music perfectly when transmitted within a radius of 25 to 50 miles. Within such a radius there reside hundreds of thousands of families; and as all can simultaneously receive from a single transmitter, there would be no question of obtaining sufficiently loud signals to make the performance enjoyable. The power of the transmitter can be made 5 kw if necessary, to cover even a short radius of 25 to 50 miles; thereby giving extra loud signals in the home if desired. The use of head telephones would be obviated by this method. The development of a small loop antenna to go with each 'Radio Music Box' would likewise solve the antennae problem.

"The same principle can be extended to numerous other fields—as for example—receiving lectures at home which can be made perfectly audible; also events of national importance can be simultaneously announced and received. Baseball scores can be transmitted in the air by the use of one set installed at the Polo Grounds. The same would be true of other cities. This proposition would be especially interesting to farmers and others living in outlying districts removed from cities. By the purchase of a 'Radio Music Box' they could enjoy concerts, lectures, music, recitals, etc. which may be going on in the nearest city within their radius. While I have indicated a few of the most probable fields of usefulness for such a device, yet, there are numerous other fields to which the principle can be extended.

*   *   *   *   *   *   *   *   *   *   *   *

"In connection with this idea I have had in mind for some time the possibility of connecting up the 'Wireless Age' with the plan, thereby making the Wireless Press a profitable venture. What I have in mind is this:

"Every purchaser of a 'Radio Music Box' would be encouraged to become a subscriber of the 'Wireless Age' which would announce in its columns an advance monthly schedule of all lectures, music recitals, etc. to be given in the various cities of the country. With this arrangement the owner of the 'Radio Music Box' can learn from the columns of the 'Wireless Age' what is going on in the air at any given time and throw the 'Radio Music Box' switch to the point (wave length) corresponding with the music or lectures desired to be heard.

"If this plan is carried out the volume of paid advertising that can be obtained for the 'Wireless Age' on the basis of such proposed increased circulation would in itself be a profitable venture. In other words, the 'Wireless Age' would perform the same mission as is now being performed by the various motion picture magazines which enjoy so wide a circulation.

"The manufacture of the 'Radio Music Box' including antenna, in large quantities, would make possible their sale at a moderate figure of perhaps $75.00 per outfit. The main revenue to be derived will be from the sale of 'Radio Music Boxes' which if manufactured in quantities of one hundred thousand or so could yield a handsome profit when sold at the price mentioned above. Secondary sources of revenue would be from the sale of transmitters and from increased advertising and circulation of the 'Wireless Age'. The Radio Corporation would have to undertake the arrangements, I am sure, for music recitals, lectures, etc. which arrangements can be satisfactorily worked out. It is not possible to estimate the total amount of business obtainable with this plan until it has been developed and actually tried out but there are about 15,000,000 families in the United States alone and if only one million or 7% of the total families thought well of the idea it would, at the figure mentioned, mean a gross business of about $75,000,000, which should yield considerable revenue.

"Aside from the profit to be derived from this proposition the possibilities for advertising for the Radio Corporation are tremendous; for its name would ultimately be brought into the household and wireless would receive national and universal attention."

——— ——— ——— ——— ——— ——— ———

On March 3rd, 1920, in response to a request from Mr. E. W. Rice, Jr. for an estimate of prospective radio business, I wrote:

"The 'Radio Music Box' proposition requires considerable experimentation and development; but, having given the matter much thought, I feel confident in expressing the opinion that the problems involved can be met. With reasonable speed in design and development, a commercial product can be placed on the market within a year or so.

"Should this plan materialize it would seem reasonable to expect sales of one million (1,000,000) 'Radio Music Boxes' within a period of three years. Roughly estimating, the selling price at $75,000,000 can be expected. This may be divided approximately as follows:

			Actual business done by RCA
1st Year— 100,000 Radio Music Boxes	$ 7,500,000	'22	$11,000,000
2nd Year—300,000 Radio Music Boxes	$22,500,000	'23	$22,500,000
3rd Year— 600,000 Radio Music Boxes	$45,000,000	'24	$50,000,000
Total $75,000,000			$83,500,000

— — — — — — — — —

At the time the foregoing reports were made there was in existence neither a practical radio telephone transmitter for sending out such information as is at present being broadcasted, nor suitable device in compact form for reception. The technical developments of the past two years and the exchange of patent rights which resulted in the present "set-up" have made both possible.

The next step is to so organize radio broadcasting on the transmitting end as to render real service without confusion or overlapping, thus making possible the dream of bringing entertainment into the home by radio. Efforts are now being directed towards accomplishing this result.

> Very truly yours,
> David Sarnoff
> General Manager

1922: FEBRUARY 7
BRITON HADDEN TO HIS MOTHER

Briton Hadden (1898–1929) and Henry Luce (1898–1967) had only recently graduated from Yale when they came up with the idea of a magazine that would amass and condense the world's increasingly dizzying supply of news. In this letter to his mother, a somewhat defensive Hadden explained why he would be leaving his job. But the magazine he envisioned—originally called Facts, *not* Time—*would soon be embraced and emulated around the globe. It would also, despite Hadden's death from a strep infection at age thirty-one, eventually yield a publishing empire.* Herbert Bayard Swope *was a Pulitzer prize–winning reporter and an editor for the* New York World. *Bill was Hadden's stepfather, Dr. William Pool.*

2/7/22
Monday Night

Dearest Mother:—

I tendered my resignation to Editor-in-Chief Harwood this afternoon, interviewed City Editor Steuart at his home tonight, and (aided and abetted by his own good Rye) succeeded in getting him to agree to the following plan:—

1) Luce and I are to leave Baltimore Wednesday night.

2) Any time up to April 1 we are privileged to return to Baltimore and continue at our present jobs on The News at $40 per.

3) We can also return to these jobs any time after April 1—provided The News is not over-manned.

4) Nothing but the very best of feelings exists between us and The Baltimore News, etc. etc.

I am confident that in the 7 weeks prior to April 1 we shall be able to determine whether or not the paper FACTS is going to be brought into existence. We propose to devote our time in New York to working out our ideas and having them criticised by able journalists of the Swope type. This process of criticism is bound to result in either one of two ways. Either our plans will meet with such approval that we shall feel justified in going out and "getting the money". Or our plans will receive such universal condemnation as will warrant our immediate and prodigal return to Baltimore. At any rate, we intend to prove this paper FACTS either a potential success or a potential failure sometime before April 1.—

Provided FACTS proves a failure during the 7 weeks, I figure that I shall have lost this much:

1) Seven weeks salary at $40 per ($280).

2) Seven weeks experience of small city reporting.

3) Several bucketfuls of respect of my friends and acquaintances, who will know well that I have been without visible means for support for 7 weeks and that I have been backing a potential failure.

4) Ten dollars per week from my present capital ($100). (I intend to pay myself that salary while I am living at home; and I swear I can live within its limits.)

To offset these losses, I shall have gained this much provided FACTS proves a potential failure:

1) Several cornucopias full of information relative to all the details of the

publishing business relative to the organizing of a new paper. (Since there is no doubt but that I shall organize a real paper or magazine some day, the time thus spent on FACTS can hardly be termed time wasted.)

In the events that FACTS proves a potential success during the 7 weeks, great is my reward and obvious.

You will note that all through the above I have spoken of the paper FACTS as a "potential" success or a "potential" failure. It won't be, of course, a real success or a real failure until I ask somebody to put money into it. I don't intend to invite anybody to invest one copper penny until I have thoroughly explored every fraction-of-an-inch of the way. I'm not in any hurry. If necessary, I'll spend a year in planning this thing—provided I am financially able to pay myself $10 per week and provided I continue to receive encouragement from able journalists of the Swope type.

)))--

In order to defray expenses and eliminate the necessity of paying myself $10 per week, it is quite possible that I shall write a bit of "Sunday stuff" for The World at $8 per column. I think Swope will let me do this. I shan't allow it to interfere with my vital work on FACTS, however.

Sudler (in Chicago) has been ordered to drop his job ($10,000?) and report for duty in New York at once. He shall spend his time in <u>Business Department</u> research; Luce and I in <u>Editorial Department</u> research.

I feel sure that you and Bill will read this letter calmly and will make a sincere endeavor to see things through my point of view.

Also I am gratefully cognizant of the fact that (even though you may not agree with a single statement that I have here made) you will give me your moral and material support in the venture and will not bawl out: "We told you so!" if the scheme (during the 7 weeks) crashes.

The following men to date have stated have stated: "Your plan will succeed and pay large dividends provided you raise capital enough." ($10,000 to $200,000, they have estimated as "enough".)

Neal, Adv. Mgr. of Doubleday Page and Co.

Eaton, Circulation Mgr. of ditto.

Everitt, Treas. of ditto.

Strother, Managing Editor of World's Work.

Farrar, Editor of Bookman. (Circulation doubled during year he's been in office.)

Canby, Editor of N.Y. Post Literary Review. (Circulation more than doubled during yr in office.)

Williams, head of biggest advertising firm in Chi.

However, Ridgeway, Business Mgr. New York Herald, has given the plan his unqualified disapproval. Ridgeway, who dropped close to a quarter of a million dollars of his own money on a magazine somewhat similar to the embryo FACTS, is reputed to be one who "knows".

Several bushel baskets full of love and regards and hopes and apologies from

Brit

1922: JULY 16
G. W. PRICE TO FELLOW KLANSMEN

Begun after the Civil War by a group of Confederate veterans, the Ku Klux Klan had lynched, burned, whipped, and persistently intimidated the South's newly freed slaves. After three violent years, during which America had its first glimpse of the white robes and hoods that were meant to frighten as well as to mask, the Klan had been disbanded nationally in 1869 by order of the chief, or Grand Wizard. But local groups remained active, and in 1915, the Klan was reorganized. By the early 1920s it had attracted an estimated four million members nationwide and had added Jews, Catholics, Communists, union members, and immigrants to its list of targets. It had also developed the matter-of-fact voice—and the banal bookkeeping concerns—of any large organization.

IMPERIAL PALACE

KNIGHTS OF THE KU KLUX KLAN

DATED AT   LOS ANGELES CALIF. JULY 16TH 1922.

Cyclops or Kligrapp.
Fresno.
Calif.

My Esteemed Klansman:—

This will introduce to you Mr. T. A. McCarty, who is out of the Atlanta office making audit of the various Klans in the State of California.

It is requested that you assist him in obtaining what information he desires. He will require a copy of your Roster to date; All donations received; Robes ordered and received; Robes ordered and not received; Resignations, if any, and applications on file who have not been obligated.

> Yours in Sacred and Unfailing Bond,
> G. W. Price
> King Kleagle Realm of California

1922: AUGUST

A MOTHER OF TWO TO MARGARET SANGER

A former nurse who had seen too many impoverished women struggling with unwanted pregnancies, Margaret Sanger (1879–1966) set up the first birth-control clinic in 1916 and the American Birth Control League (later renamed Planned Parenthood) in 1921. Telling women about methods of birth control was still a crime when the letter below was printed in the organization's magazine. But almost every issue of The Birth Control Review *featured letters, often anonymous, from mothers looking to Sanger for information or advice, despite the risks. Sanger herself was jailed and faced numerous legal battles in her pioneering attempts to educate women about their choices.*

Dear Mrs. Sanger:

I am writing these few lines, trusting you won't think me too forward. I am a sufferer from kidney trouble, and when my first baby was born in the hospital, I spent three months there before the baby was born at all, and then they gave me up and said they did not think I would get over it. When the baby was born and I was sent home, they told me never to have another baby. When I asked the doctor how was I to stop that he said, "Learn." But when my first baby was six months old, I was two months with another baby, so you see I had no rest at all when I had to go back to the same hospital with the same trouble. They said, "I thought I told you not to have any more babies." I said, "Yes, I know you did, but why don't you do something for me?" He said, "If I was to do that for you, I would be put out of this hospital." So I had to suffer this time more than the last, and I asked God to please let me die. When the second was born and I was home again with two small babies and a man out of work and myself so weak that I could die and be glad, I was soon ready for another. So you see Mrs. Sanger six months after every time I am ready for another, and I am only 25 now and my two babies are one year and two years old, and I would have had two more if a good kind doctor had not helped me. But I can't go on forever doing away with them because no one will help me. I am just slowly killing myself. So I am writing to you, Mrs. Sanger, if you will only do something to help me. I can get proof and show that I am not fit to have babies. I should be glad to have them if I was in good health, but I am not. Trusting you will do something for me.

1922: DECEMBER 23
A TRAIN CONDUCTOR TO THE LADIES' HOME JOURNAL

Prohibition had been in place for three years when the Ladies' Home Journal *printed this reassuring letter in praise of it.*
The A.E.F. was the American Expeditionary Force.

The Ladies' Home Journal, Philadelphia:

I read today in your December number an article by Charles A. Selden on the Enemies of Prohibition. In my opinion prohibition is getting more and better results daily. I hear the rabble say it is worse by far than it was before the adoption of the Eighteenth Amendment. I am a passenger-train conductor and have been on busy runs for a good many years, the years before September, 1917. On a certain run when it came just before a Saturday and Sunday or a holiday or circus day or something of that sort, I would lay off and lose the time rather than make the return trip. I left every third day at six o'clock p.m., and on Saturdays and Sundays there were always more drunken persons to encounter than at other times.

I went over to France with the A.E.F. in 1917, and came back in October, 1919, when I went to work on my old run. I have been on it ever since, and in somewhat over three years I do not recall having had more than two drunken men on my train. So if there are so many getting drunk—as some of our people would try to make us believe—they must be staying quietly put in some place until they get over it and not showing up on the trains I run at any rate.

I have heard the argument that the Eighteenth Amendment was put over while two millions of soldiers were out of the country. That is the veriest rot. Had the amendment been put to the vote of the soldiers it would have been a divided vote, I think, with much the larger per cent of them in favor of the amendment.

From my experience, I think it likely that there are comparatively few who get drunk now, while four years ago there were many.

I was at the American Legion meeting in New Orleans in October last. My son—who is also an overseas soldier—was with me. It was, I think, a big boost for the young men of America that there was evidently such an absence of the desire for anything to drink; I am confident that the bootlegger's business with the exsoldiers in New Orleans did not make the rum runners rich.

I am giving you this bit of testimony, as I come in contact with from three hundred to five hundred people every day.

1923: JANUARY 19
CARL VAN VECHTEN TO THEODORE DREISER

One of countless Americans who had found a way to circumvent the liquor ban, Carl Van Vechten (1880–1964) was willing to give fellow author Theodore Dreiser a few tips. Van Vechten, a music critic and novelist, was the author of the acclaimed Nigger Heaven. *Dreiser (see letter page 201) wrote, most famously,* Sister Carrie *and* An American Tragedy.

The ellipsis is Van Vechten's.

19 January 1923   151 East 19th Street
                                                                New York City

Dear Mr. Dreiser, I saw the man I spoke to you about today, and gave him your name. So, when you want something, telephone him, mentioning my name:

   His is   William Linehan
              Kingsbridge 1228.

Over the telephone one is discreet and calls gin: <u>white</u> . . . mention the number of bottles you want. Scotch is <u>gold</u>. If he isn't in, leave your name and number and he will call you. I hope we may get together again soon.

                           very sincerely,
                           Carl Van Vechten

1923: JULY 4
CLARENCE DARROW TO THE <u>CHICAGO TRIBUNE</u>

John Thomas Scopes (1900–1970) had yet to be arrested for teaching evolution in his Dayton, Tennessee, biology class, and it would be another two years before Clarence Darrow (1857–1938) would defend Scopes against William Jennings Bryan (1860–1925) in the celebrated "Monkey Trial." But in the questions he posed in this letter to the editor of the Chicago Tribune, *Darrow struck many of the themes that would dominate that case. With a line of inquiry intended to show that the Bible could not, as fundamentalists claimed, be literally true, he foreshadowed one of the most famous cross-examinations in history: that of Bryan himself by Darrow.*

Editor of the Tribune: I was very much interested in Mr. Bryan's letter to <u>The Tribune</u> and in your editorial reply. I have likewise followed Mr. Bryan's efforts to shut out the teaching of science from the public schools and his question-naires to various college professors who believe in evolution and still profess Christianity. No doubt his questions to the professors, if answered, would tend to help clear the issue, and likewise a few questions to Mr. Bryan and the fundamentalists, if fairly answered, might serve the interests of reaching the truth—all of this assumes that truth is desirable.

For this reason I think it would be helpful if Mr. Bryan would answer the following questions:

Do you believe in the literal interpretation of the whole Bible?

Is the account of the creation of the earth and all life in Genesis literally true, or is it an allegory?

Was the earth made in six literal days, measured by the revolution of the earth on its axis?

Was the sun made on the fourth day to give light to the earth by day and the moon made on the same day to give light by night, and were the stars made for the benefit of the earth?

Did God create man on the sixth day?

Did God rest on the seventh day?

Did God place man in the Garden of Eden and tell him he could eat of every tree except the tree of knowledge?

Was Eve literally made from the rib of Adam?

Did the serpent induce Eve to eat of the tree of knowledge?

Did the eating of this fruit cause Adam and Eve to know that they were naked?

Did God curse the serpent for tempting Eve and decree that thereafter he should go on his belly?

How did he travel before that time?

Did God tell Eve that thereafter he would multiply the sorrows of all women and that their husbands should rule over them?

Did God send a flood covering the whole earth, even the tops of the highest mountains and destroy "all flesh that has the breath of life," excepting the in-mates of the ark?

Did God command Noah to build an ark for him and his family and to take on board a male and female of every living species on earth?

Did he build the ark and gather the pairs of all animals on the earth and the food and water necessary to preserve them?

As there were no ships in those days, except the ark, how did Noah gather them from all the continents and lands of the earth?

Did he then cause it to rain forty days and forty nights and destroy every living thing on the earth?

Did all these living things enter the ark on the second month and 17th day of the month?

Were all the high mountains on all the earth covered?

Did the waters prevail on the earth for 150 days?

Did the ark rest on Mount Ararat in the seventh month and the tenth day of the month?

Did God set a rainbow in the heavens for a token that the world would not again be destroyed by flood?

Was this the first rainbow that ever appeared?

According to the old testament, was this not about 1,750 years B.C.?

Is not history full of proof that all colors and kinds of people lived over large and remote parts of the earth within fifty years after this time?

Were the pairs of animals sent to every quarter of the earth after the flood?

How could many species that are found nowhere but in Australia or other far off places get there and why did they not stop on the way?

Was there any more water on the earth in Noah's day than any other time before or since?

Is not all the water that falls drawn from the reservoirs of water on the earth?

Is it possible to increase the amount of water in any part of the earth without drawing it from another part?

Does not water seek its level?

Shortly after the flood was the whole earth of one language?

Did the inhabitants begin to build the Tower of Babel so they might reach the heavens?

Did God confound their language so they could not complete the tower?

How high would the tower have had to be built to reach the heavens?

Was the confounding of tongues at the Tower of Babel the cause of the many languages spoken by the people of the earth?

Did the Lord prepare a big fish to swallow Jonah and did he lie for three days and three nights in the whale's belly when he was spewed out on dry land?

Was Lot's wife turned into a literal pillar of salt for turning back and looking at Sodom and Gomorrah when she was fleeing from their destruction?

Did Balaam's ass speak to him in human language?

Did the walls of Jericho fall down flat from the soldiers and priests marching around it and blowing on the ram's horn?

Did the sun stand still to give Joshua time to fight a battle?

If the sun had stood still, would that have lengthened the day?

If instead of the sun standing still, the earth had stopped revolving on its axis, what would have happened to the earth and all life thereon?

Under the biblical chronology, Was not the earth created less than 6,000 years ago?

Were there not many flourishing civilizations on the earth 10,000 years ago?

According to the same chronology, Was not Adam created less than 6,000 years ago?

Are there not evidences in writing and hieroglyphics and the evidence of man's handiwork which show that man has been on the earth more than 50,000 years?

Are there no human remains that carry their age on the earth back to at least 100,000 years?

Has not man probably been on earth for 500,000 years?

Does not geology show by fossil remains, by the cutting away of rock for river beds, by deposit of all sorts, that the earth is much more than a million years and probably many million years old?

Did Christ drive devils out of two sick men and did the devils request that they should be driven into a large herd of swine and were the devils driven into the swine and did the swine run off a high bank, and were they drowned in the sea?

Was this literally true, or does it simply show the attitude of the age toward the cause of sickness and affliction.

Can one not be a Christian without believing in the literal truth of the narrations of the Bible here mentioned?

Would you forbid the public schools from teaching anything in conflict with the literal statement referred to?

Questions might be extended indefinitely, but a specific answer to these might make it clear what one must believe to be a "fundamentalist."

Very truly yours,
Clarence Darrow

1923: SEPTEMBER 6

A FORMER FLAPPER TO NANCY BROWN

Nancy Brown (1870–1942), the Ann Landers of her day, wrote a long-running advice column called "Experience" in the Detroit News *that attempted to sort through the sometimes contradictory impulses of the young century. The Roaring Twenties had just begun when Brown replied to this reader's letter: "As you say, there are thousands of girls like 'Reformed,' who play the wild parties solely because they think the men they love admire that. Yet all the time these men are being disgusted with the girls' laxness of morals."*

Dear Nancy Brown:

Please let me thank you for the pleasure your daily Column has given me. I enjoy the published letters of your correspondents and find in them a poignant sincerity that goes straight to my heart.

I am a stranger in your city—a bride of recent date, with a dear little apartment and a wonderful boy-husband. Sometimes after a perusal of other people's problems, I feel as though I have a monopoly of the world's happiness. My only sore spot is loneliness for my mother. We were very close friends, she and I, and the thought that half a continent separates us now is not a very cheerful one. I miss our twilight conversations and in lieu of them, I have turned to your Experience Column in The News, with something more than pleasure—a real need.

I want to comment on a letter that appeared signed "Reformed"—the girl who attended wild parties through fear of losing her "only one." My sympathy goes out to that girl. I know of hundreds such. Pretending recklessness, drinking, smoking, countenancing roadside petting parties just to be in with the rush. Afraid of being called "slow"—it is an old story these days. In a set like that, every girl is guessing as to how far the other girl goes—and no one is sure.

My knowledge of these things is first hand because my marriage meant to me deliverance from that crowd. I just happened to be lucky where "Reformed" was unfortunate, and now my hubby and I are ideally happy in each other's happiness. We've both sowed our wild oats—and we got tired of it, so we quit. My mother trusted me, and in the real sense of the word I proved true to her trust—though no one would have suspected it.

I was in Rome and did as the Romans did. Three a.m. was no unusual hour, and cigarettes never made me sick. Even after my engagement was announced, Hubby and I went around a lot together and separately. I never slacked up till the day of the wedding, but it is well over and done with now. Personally, I am none the worse for my experiences and I honestly believe that at least 80 per cent of the modern young people react as I have done. There are many who fall by the wayside, either from ignorance or from curiosity. Very few, I assure you, are knocked down by force! The survival of the fittest has been the slogan of the world since man was man—and applies here.

Of course, I grant this—we are over-sexed these days. From the shrouded and veiled mystery that Grandma knew, we have reacted too strongly and are now at the other extreme of vulgar display and a harsh frankness that appalls most of us even while we pretend to take it all as a matter of course. Sometimes it seems as though we have lost all sense of delicacy and are wallowing in a slough of realism whose quicksands threaten to drag us under.

There is no rule of conduct, but God gave every one a tiny inner voice called intuition, instinct, or conscience, as you will, and that was my only guide. Mother counselled, advised and admonished, of course, but in the long run I was thrown back upon my own resources in my dealings with the men who made up our crowd. Not one of us was really bad, at least I don't think so, and I know that the sacred ambition of one of our wildest "neckers" was to have a home and a baby. And that's that!

I didn't mean to write at such great length, but now I'm glad I did. I had the urge to explain—and oh, I hope, Nancy Brown, that you understand I am not discussing something I know nothing about, but something that until three months ago was my own life. I insist that I had a marvellous time, but that I'm too glad for words to be definitely out of it. And every blessed one of us felt the same way, though I would never have admitted it then any more than they.

Thank you for the precious time I've taken up, and believe me a sincere well-wisher. May I come again?

Ex-Flapper

1923: DECEMBER
THE THEATRE GUILD TO GEORGE BERNARD SHAW

When it was first written, Saint Joan *by George Bernard Shaw (1856–1950) was six acts long, with an epilogue. For its staging at New York's Garrick Theatre, the Theatre Guild cut it down to four acts and an epilogue. Then came this request—and Shaw's response.*

NEW YORK NY

GEORGE BERNARD SHAW
AYOT SAINT LAWRENCE
HERTFORDSHIRE ENGLAND

PLEASE ALTER FOURTH ACT OF "ST. JOAN" SO COMMUTERS CAN CATCH
LAST TRAIN TO SUBURBS.

THEATRE GUILD

1923: DECEMBER
GEORGE BERNARD SHAW TO THE THEATRE GUILD

HERTFORDSHIRE ENGLAND

THE THEATRE GUILD, PRODUCER
"ST. JOAN"
GARRICK THEATRE
NEW YORK NY

ALTER THE TRAINS.

SHAW

1924: FEBRUARY 20
GEORGE WHARTON PEPPER TO HARRY DAUGHERTY

Scandals involving members of the Warren Harding cabinet lingered after the president's sudden death in office. Most famous was the lucrative secret leasing of drilling rights to naval oil reserves at Teapot Dome, Wyoming, by Secretary of the Interior Albert B. Fall. Harry M. Daugherty (1860–1941), who continued as attorney general under Calvin Coolidge, was himself accused of conspiring to defraud the government. In this letter, Pennsylvania Senator George Wharton Pepper (1867–1961) urged Daugherty to resign. Despite the quaintly civil language, the thrust and parry of political accusation appear not to have changed much in seventy-five years.

Truman Handy Newberry, a Michigan senator, had been convicted of election fraud in 1921; though his conviction was reversed by the Supreme Court, he nonetheless resigned.

UNITED STATES SENATE
Washington

February 20, 1924.

Dear Mr. Attorney-General:

I have just done as hard a thing as I have ever been called upon to do, and I want to play fair with you by telling you of it. As one of two Senators delegated for the purpose I went to the White House and told the President that, in the opinion of practically all the Republicans in this body, he ought to intimate to you that your resignation would be for the good of the party.

In speaking to him I expressed the opinion that it is not a question of justice or injustice—but a case in which you are on the wrong side of an issue in the mind of the public—and that when a man gets into that position, as was the case with Newberry, the rightness of his position is immaterial; nobody can save him—and he must go.

You have been considerate to me and to Mrs. Pepper. You have gained and will retain our friendship—if you care to have it. You have helped me and my state politically; and my contacts with your Department have proved its efficiency.

But I have felt that in this thing I must act impersonally; and something in me makes me want to tell you so. If you resign and face your accusers as a free man—free, I mean, from the complication of placing the President and the Party upon trial—you will, it seems to me, put yourself in the best position to refute whatever is charged against you. To resign and to insist on a hearing seems to me the part that a man of your spirit ought to play in the terrible drama which is now being enacted.

Yours sincerely,
George Wharton Pepper.

To The Hon. H. M. Daugherty,
Attorney-General.

1924: FEBRUARY 21

HARRY DAUGHERTY TO GEORGE WHARTON PEPPER

His reply notwithstanding, Daugherty would indeed resign. Though not convicted of any crime, he subsequently devoted himself to clearing his name.

February 21, 1924.

Hon. George Wharton Pepper
United States Senate
Washington, D.C.

My dear Senator:

Please accept my thanks for your very kind note of yesterday. Your complimentary reference to my administration of the Department of Justice is, at this time, most highly appreciated. I note with amazement your suggestion that my interests are not to be decided on the basis of "justice or injustice," even though my honor, reputation and all that I hold dear in this world are at stake. Your expressions of personal regard are most gratifying and keenly appreciated, and I am sure that nothing will ever happen to change our friendly relations.

Coming now to the subject matter of your letter, I am interested in your statement that I am on the wrong side of an issue in the mind of the public. I assume you have in mind the resolution of Senator Wheeler and his speech on the floor of the Senate. You have then concluded that I am on the wrong side of an issue, without hearing, without evidence, and accepted as final the baseless, scandalous and defamatory charges of my political adversaries.

You further imply that the public has also concluded that I am on the wrong side of an issue without evidence, on ex-parte statements, and baseless charges of those same adversaries. You must realize, as I do, that these charges against me, made on the eve of a Presidential election, are made with other motives than that of injuring me. My destruction is but the accomplishment of one phase of the program which will be immediately followed by other and more drastic demands by these same adversaries.

My elimination, voluntarily or otherwise, will be a confession of the truth of all the baseless charges of our adversaries, and will justify them in claiming that we have thereby admitted their truth, and such admission will accomplish the ultimate end and purpose most gratifying to such adversaries.

I will never be a party to such a program.

You say that my fate does not involve a question of "justice or injustice." My dear Senator, my personal interests sink into insignificance when compared with the magnitude of the issues now involved. Is the preservation of the orderly processes of the law, and the preservation of constitutional rights of no importance? Shall reputations be destroyed and public officials driven from office by clamor, insinuation and falsehood?

The basest criminal standing before the bar of justice has a right to a trial by his peers. Am I to be denied a right granted to even the basest criminal?

If I am on the wrong side of the issue to which you refer, and it has already been concluded against me by the Senate, to which forum I have no access, without evidence of the truth or falsity of the charges against me; and if the public has likewise, as you claim, without evidence, concluded that I am on the wrong side of such issue, then nothing remains for me to do except to plead my cause before the bar of public opinion. And in order to do so accept some of the numerous invitations to make addresses throughout the country and present before that great tribunal all of the facts bearing upon these matters. That tribunal, my dear Senator, by which we will all ultimately be tried—the one before whose verdict we must all bow with respectful humility.

Very sincerely yours,
H. M. Daugherty,
Attorney-General

1924: AUGUST 28
HUEY LONG TO CHARLES STAIR

Huey P. Long (1893–1935) was one of the most flamboyant and demagogic politicians of the century. He had been born poor but managed despite little formal education to pass the bar in 1915, and he came to power and popularity by challenging the authority of the local utility companies. He was still four years away from his first term as Louisiana governor when he wrote this letter, characteristic in both its populist agenda and its threatening tone.

August 28, 1924

Mr. Chas. A. Stair, La. Mgr.,
Cumberland Telephone & Telegraph Co.,
New Orleans, La.

Dear Sir:

It doesn't make a bit of difference with me how many telephones you promised. What I am interested in is one thing only:

I want every damned man who wants a telephone to have a telephone, and I want you to get your affairs in such shape that you can give every human being a phone who wants one. No other kind of program is worth anything to me or this state. I am covered up, knee deep, with people in this town and the surrounding territory trying to get telephones and can't get them. We are in just as bad shape as ever, so far as I am concerned. I have been pretty patient with this thing, but my patience has reached the absolute extreme limit. I am damned disgusted with the way it has been running and don't intend to continue to condone it.

Now, this means exactly the words and terms stated here.

Sincerely yours,

Huey P. Long

1925: JANUARY
WILLIAM FAULKNER TO HIS MOTHER

It may be hard to believe that this "Billy" would eventually win a Nobel prize and two Pulitzers. One of the greatest American novelists, William Faulkner (1897–1962) was in New Orleans when he sent this letter home. His first book, a collection of poetry called The Marble Faun, *had been published with the help of a friend in December of 1924. Faulkner left for Europe in July of 1925. He would publish* The Sound and the Fury *four years later. But it would be decades before he achieved true critical recognition, and he was beset by financial hardship throughout his career.* Colonel James Edmonds was managing editor of the New Orleans *Times-Picayune*. Faulkner had purchased an edition of Samuel Pepys for his mother.

Dear Mother—

I have turned in 5 of my ~~sketches~~ stories and collected $20.00 for them. I write one in about 3 hours. At that rate I can make $25.00 a week in my spare time. Grand, isn't it? They want some short things—about 200 words with a kick at the end. I can knock off one of them while I'm waiting for my teakettle to boil. They pay $1.00 for each of them. The others run so much a column. I believe, if I'd work eight hours a day at it, I could earn $50.00 a week. That is, as long as they take them. The first will appear in the Sunday magazine a week from next Sunday. I am trying to get a contract at, say $10.00 per week, while I am touring Europe, with him. I have told you Col. Edmonds is going to give me a contract when I get back, haven't? He thinks the trip abroad will be the making of me, that I can write something no other paper can duplicate exactly. $20.00. Hot dog. When I get established with him, I'm going to dump all that stuff I have scribbled and left at home, on him. All's well, and the twilight is like spring—vague azure and green and silver.

Billy

OVER.

I have had two more letters from strange females who saw my photo in the paper. One about 40, gushing, you know; and the other about 14—on pink paper and terrible spelling.

Pepys cost $6.00. No, I have got no check from you for it. I gave my own money for it.

1925: JULY 1
ERNEST HEMINGWAY TO F. SCOTT FITZGERALD

Although its clipped syntax and its references to bullfights and fishing may make this letter sound like a parody, it was in fact written by Ernest Hemingway (1899–1961) to his friend and fellow novelist F. Scott Fitzgerald (see letter page 203). Hemingway was in Spain at the time, on his way to see the running of the bulls at the fiesta of San Fermin.

<u>Burguete</u>, Navera.

July 1—

Dear Scott—

We are going in to Pamplona tomorrow. Been trout fishing here. How are you? And how is Zelda?

I am feeling better than I've ever felt—havent drunk any thing but wine since I left Paris. God it has been wonderful country. But you hate country. All right omit description of country. I wonder what your idea of heaven would be—A beautiful vacuum filled with wealthy monogamists. All powerful and members of the best families all drinking themselves to death. And hell would probably an ugly vacuum full of poor polygamists unable to obtain booze or with chronic stomach disorders that they called secret sorrows.

To me a heaven would be a big bull ring with me holding two barrera seats and a trout stream outside that no one else was allowed to fish in and two lovely houses in the town; one where I would have my wife and children and be monogamous and love them truly and well and the other where I would have my nine beautiful mistresses on 9 different floors and one house would be fitted up with special copies of the Dial printed on soft tissue and kept in the toilets on every floor and in the other house we would use the American Mercury and the New Republic. Then there would be a fine church like in Pamplona where I could go and be confessed on the way from one house to the other and I would get on my horse and ride out with my son to my bull ranch named Hacienda Hadley and toss coins to all my illegitimate children that lined the road. I would write out at the Hacienda and send my son in to lock the chastity belts onto my mistresses because someone had just galloped up with the news that a notorious monogamist named Fitzgerald had been seen riding toward the town at the head of a company of strolling drinkers.

Well anyway were going into town tomorrow early in the morning. Write me at the / Hotel Quintana

    Pamplona

    Spain

Or don't you like to write letters. I do because it's such a swell way to keep from working and yet feel you've done something.

    So long and love to Zelda from us both—

                        Yours,

                        Ernest

1925: JULY 14?

H. L. MENCKEN TO RAYMOND PEARL

With his renowned ear for hypocrisy, H. L. Mencken (1880–1956) understood immediately the importance of the trial of John Scopes in the summer of 1925. It was Mencken who had helped persuade Clarence Darrow to defend the biology teacher arrested for teaching evolution, and Mencken who then described the trial for the Baltimore Evening Sun *in a celebrated series that pulled no punches.*

Raymond Pearl was a prominent biologist and statistician at Johns Hopkins University. *Sus scofa* is the Latin term for "pig." Mencken had cofounded *The American Mercury* magazine in 1924. Dudley Malone was part of the Scopes defense team.

Dear Pearl:—

This is far worse than anything you could imagine, even under the bowl. Every last scoundrel in sight is a Christian, including the town Jew. I begin to realize what life must have been in Judea 1925 years ago. No wonder the Romans finally bumped off the son of Joseph. After an hour on the main street, listening to the bawling, I feel like loading a cannon with the rejecta of the adjacent hogs (Sus scrofa) and letting fly. The thing is genuinely fabulous. I have stored up enough material to last me 20 years.

I expected to be poisoned by corn liquor, but have had to drink only one drink of it. That I got down out of politeness to the local Russell Sage. He is a frantic Prohibitionist, but usually half stewed. They tell a charming story of him. He arrived home one night in his cups, and told his wife that he was sick and that she would have to do the evening praying alone. She got on her knees and began: "Oh, Lord, throw the mantle of Thy mercy around my drunken husband". He cut in with: "Great God, woman, don't tell the old scoundrel I'm drunk; say I'm sick!"

Chattanooga is full of excellent Scotch. There is also one beer saloon. I had hardly got in before Founder Subscribers to the Mercury began to show up with jugs under their coats. I actually got four quarts the first night. Ever since then it has been pouring in—very good stuff. Even the Scotch of the bootleggers is drinkable, and they charge but $7.50 a bottle, by the bottle. Dudley Malone has rented a house here in Dayton, laid in a couple of cases, and sent for dancing women.

The trial is superb—an obscenity of the very first calibre. I'll be back in time for the club dinner Sunday, barring acts of God.

Mencken

1925: JULY 27
EDGAR LEE MASTERS TO EDWIN REESE

William Jennings Bryan died several days after the end of the Scopes trial. He had first become famous as a Nebraska congressman supporting the free coinage of silver, a position popular among debtors in the agrarian South and West, who believed that more circulating money would help them pay their debts. With his famous declaration, "you shall not crucify mankind upon a cross of gold," he had won the 1896 nomination of the Democratic party. That led to the first of three presidential losses. Yet Bryan remained ever visible—and audible—as a champion of populism and fundamentalist Christianity. He had been secretary of state under Wilson until resigning in protest as America prepared to enter the war. The poet Edgar Lee Masters (1868–1950) had published his famous Spoon River Anthology *in 1915.*

"Lewd Puckett" was a pseudonym Masters used when writing to old friends, of whom Edwin Reese was one. Masters's typing was almost aggressively inaccurate.

July 27 1925

Dear Fool: Do you remember 29 years ago this summer that you and I in Lewistown were editing the News fro Brayn, and that you with a Civil War heritage and a republican father were fighting for free silver. Now the man who flashed upon that stormy convention at the Coliseum has goen the way o all flesh, as simply as did the late Charles Metcalf. To me Brayn is a great study. He at the first had a sort of argumenative mind of lievly energy, but of no depth; he had a great forensic fluencey; a gerat will, a strong body, a fine presence. But when 96 ended he ceased to grow. He had little education and he added nothing to it. By much talking and little thinking his mentality ran dry. But a more profound thing is the matter of the man's vision, his moral nature. If he had wil ed to be a brother of the light, instead of willing to master those who had defeated him, and to vindicate his own persoanlity by victory, he might have been something considerable I believe; because I see man's choices and will free within ceratain boundaries. I am not a hard and fast determinist. The truth is that his moral nature was asshallow as his mind. It was made of texts and quotations, and operated through negatives. It made no great sacrifieces. It took no great chances. And I feel that his gravytaing to religion was an expedient by which he made and held on to a constituency for the puropse of escaping death in life—an intolerable thing to a amn who has tasted of the necatr of applause. Bu he didn't have the depth to toil for place and remembrance by digging deeply inot life and laying deep foundations, and abiding his time. Like an American life had to give him something at once, and all the time. He started as an octavo of C. Porter Johnson (how well you and I knoe the type), and after a great hold on to the people peterde out almost as much as C.Porter did. As Leonardo said memory leads to quotation; but thought explores. Bryan never could think; his first debates won him a low place on thought as they used to say; and so going on he got to the pass where he couldn't tell a fact from a fancy, nor a good syllogism from a metaphor. It is a monumenatl catstrophe, and some biographe applying the new psycho;ogy will make a master study of this type, which once was plentiful, but I hope has disapperade from American life. There is a picture of him in the World to day as he sat in the court room at Dayton; and to me it is one of the most tragic faces iin the wolrd. Defeat had made its marks on his soul in spite of masking smiles (they wore off too); his pride fought against the constant disappo nntment of his ambitions, and righ thorugh to the Wilson administartion and in it and after he was booed over the land. He was hooted out. Unlike Doglas who took to drink when Lincoln defeated him, Bryan took to smiles and religion; and they were make believes, Christian scinece anadynes; all the while the fooling with his own nature worked deteriorations. He was unwise as a liver too. Afflicted with diabetes for years, he was gormandizing, and eating too much starchy food. He lacked wisdom there, if he wante to live; and he did no doubt. If he woke in another life, he surely found no Methodist heaven, no pit ching of golden crwons around the glassy sea, and no lamb; but he found great powers and forces and strange wonderful proceses moving to orlds not realized; and perahsps smiled thta he had be n such a fool and made so much trouble for his countrymen.

Well, with his passing it makes me feel that life is a strageg weird thing, a joke and a tragedy combined. In ten years no one will speak his name. No oration of his will live. He got off nothing so good as Wilson's speech at the dedication of the Lincoln memorial at Hodgensville; and nothing comparable to Ingersoll's best, not to say Webster's. And he has given the world not one thought—nor one love; but something of hate. Here endeth many lessons.

As Ever

Lewd.

P.S. AS diabetes affects the mind, I am satisfied that Bryan was mentally pathologica and had be n so for several years.

1926: MARCH
A READER TO THE <u>WOMEN'S HOME COMPANION</u>

In the 1920s, the General Federation of Women's Clubs surveyed homeowners and found that they owned more cars, phones, and radios than vacuum cleaners, sewing machines, or washtubs. On the basis of this discovery, a Women's Home Companion *writer named Mary Sherman came to the remarkable conclusion that, because housewives were not buying new household equipment, they had no desire to escape the drudgery of their lives. Mrs. C. S. was one of many readers who begged to differ—and in doing so, offered a glimpse of women's daily life in the twenties.*

I have read and pondered over your article in the November <u>Companion</u>, "What Women Want in Their Homes," and I feel that you missed the spirit of the average woman—that the statistics veiled the ideal we hold. I am one of the hardworking mothers, with primitive equipment and seven little ones ranging from the baby-in-arms to a twelve-year-old. We have practically nothing of value except a good sewing machine.

You mention the automobile as a luxury. Yet had you visited a farm home twenty years ago and, noting poor kitchen equipment, condemned the big team standing in the barn it would have been as unreasonable. The automobile is one of the tools of life now. My sisters live in small towns near large cities, their husbands go to and from work in their automobiles. The fact that their cars can also mean pleasant hours no more detracts from their usefulness than the fact that Old Kate and Fanny were often hitched up to take the family to the fair.

Then the radio, the piano, and so on, elbowing the washboard and tubs, are viewed with amazement. Here is where you lost the meaning of it all.

The mother doesn't have time, in her inefficient kitchen routine, to enjoy these things, as you suggested. Her life is a perpetual round of recurring tasks. Why, then, did she consent to the purchase of these things?

Her job is to make a happy home. She must establish good conditions for the family, to secure normal lives for the children, and hold them in a charmed circle until they are strong enough for the world's temptations, despite the poverty of the little group. She robs Peter to pay Paul. The radio is her answer to the call of the pool-hall. Her daughters must have the advantage of piano instruction, that their lives be brighter and better than her own. She stands deep in mire herself, but holds her family up in the sunlight.

If to-morrow some great fortune would grant me three hundred dollars would I cast away my tubs and washboard, with which I weekly grind out the family washings? Or equip my ancient kitchen with the loveliness of linoleum, gas range, kitchen cabinet? Or indulge in refrigerator, washer and electric iron?

Alas, no, though my heart yearns for them. I would buy a piano, that these children might learn right now, as they should, the love of music. I would buy good books and some better furniture to make the home brighter for them. For now is the time they need such things so badly, not a few years later, say after Mother has had her kitchen modernized. If I wait till after that, their home years are gone. If I wait for my plans for a handy home, but make a home after all, it may be that I shall never have those wonderful things, but I will have succeeded in my big job, after all.

That is what the statistics you gathered say to me, a humble but ambitious mother.

Mrs. C. S.,
Washington

1927: FEBRUARY 26
WILLIAM ALLEN WHITE TO GABRIEL WELLS

The legendary Emporia Gazette *editor William Allen White (1868–1944) had made a name for himself upholding liberal Republicanism. He became a firm believer in Prohibition, which he defended in this letter to Gabriel Wells (1862–1946), an author and bookseller. Prohibition would not be repealed until 1933.*

February 26, 1927.

Dear Mr. Wells:

It all comes down to the definition of liberty, doesn't it? I have tried to indicate my feeling that liberties are inexorably restricted as civilization becomes more complex. This liberty to drink what one wants to drink, and to buy it where one wants to buy it, is a perfectly defensible liberty in a simple civilization. But in a complex civilization, that liberty is not defensible because, although we will both admit that not more than ten persons drink to excess, the presence of ten persons in a hundred, a hundred persons in ten thousand, ten thousand persons in a million who are drinking to excess, this number endangers the lives, property, and security of too many people. Machinery requires a calm, steady nerve. Poisoned nerves at throttles, levers, and key places, make a tremendous waste in a complicated civilization hence it is the duty of the nine people who do not overdrink, as it seems to me, to give up their liberties so far as drink goes for the good not of the one man who abuses the privilege but for the ten thousands who are his potential victims. That is the whole philosophy of prohibition. If it cannot stand on that, it goes. That is my answer to your question about the relation of the soul of democracy to personal liberty.

As I said in my last letter, I am beginning to raise a question whether or not, with the many substitutes for boredom which civilization is presenting, that is the radio, the moving picture, the cheap automobile, and a diverting environment— man may not lose his vicious appetite for alcohol and use it as wisely as they do around the Mediterranean where they have become immunized to alcohol. If new conditions have changed the relation of man to booze, then of course our legal attitude toward it must change also.

There is no such thing as an essential liberty. Liberty, as I see it, is the largest use of one's personal desires consistent with the common good. The liberty to sell the milk of one's cow, which looks like a primitive liberty, is now being restricted, and very properly. The liberty to sell the flesh of one's pig when one will and where one will and how one will is properly restricted, because it conflicts with the right of the majority to clean milk and undiseased pork. Once a man had a right to dispose of his daughter as a chattel, a right which he doubtless cherished as sacredly as the bootlegger cherishes his right to sell his liquor, but another element entered in. New conditions make new morals. No liberty, as I see it, is stable. Morals after all are customs.

Thank you for your patience with me, and also I thank you for your kind words about my article in Harper's. I have enjoyed tremendously having your letters.

Sincerely yours,
[William Allen White]

*   *   *

1 9 2 7 : MAY 18

WILLIAM BREEN TO HIS WIFE

Prohibition created a huge traffic in illegal importation of alcohol, and many fisher-
men along the eastern seaboard turned to rum-running. As one fisherman's wife
said: "You knew right away when a man stopped fishing and started running rum. In
the first place, his family began to eat proper." William J. Breen was master and
owner of a schooner called the Carrie L. Hirtle. *She was lying off the Maine coast,*
holding more than five hundred cases of alcohol, when she was boarded by the U.S.
Coast Guard. Breen confessed to having altered the ship's manifest to conceal his
haul, but he claimed to be farther offshore than the Coast Guardsmen believed—
and thus outside U.S. jurisdiction. While he was making his case, this letter
dropped from the folds of a chart. He tore it up and threw it in the ocean. Coast
Guardsmen fished it out and pieced it together.

Portland Maine

May 18, 8 p.m.

My Dear Pal

Just a line, old sweetheart thought you might be getting a little uneasy. But I
have had a little hard luck the cutter pulled me in from of Machias Seal Island.
I was 15 miles off at the time but he said I was 9. I laid their becalmed and
couldn't get off. How I did wish I had the Engine in while I was praying for wind
But none came Instead, when the fog glened up along comes a Bran New Patrol
Boat What you say their picture in the Motor Boat magazine Just out on his first
trip. Luck for him I suppose But Hell for me. He wouldn't lister to no reasons,
as their Skipper was a Square Head, and he thought he owned the world with
his 5 or 6 armed men with him. However he says your only 9 miles off and Im
going to tow you in. I told him we was 15 But he wouldn't listen, so here he
brought me They don't Just Know yet if they will proceed to Boston tomorrow or
leave me here. Ile know tomorrow But I suppose youl see this in the paper before you get this letter. Well at any rate don't worry Old Pal. If that dam Nelson
had of been on his Job, this thing wouldn't have happened. Cause if he had of
made preparations I would have now been in Metegan. However dont worry I
guess all they can do is to take the Vessel But thats bad enough at that I cant
write much at present as I dont know who I can trust to mail this letter. Only
Just dont worry no matter what turns up. Ile be in a better position tomorrow to
Know what they are going to do. But for a sure Bet I know Vessel Cargo will be
held and perhaps forfeited. Now then Ile close and don't you worry one Bit and

Keep well and perhaps Ile go home and stay with you and pick berries all summer. Im getting so now I hate to stay away from you over night. Well good bye for now Dear Pal Ile write more particulars as soon as I get the information. So good Bye a little while worlds of love & Kisses from your poor Old Pal Bill I may be down Kid But I'm not out, not By a jug ful Worlds of Love to you my Dear Old P

1927: AUGUST 21
BARTOLOMEO VANZETTI TO DANTE SACCO

In April of 1920, Bartolomeo Vanzetti (1888–1927) and Nicola Sacco (1891–1927), a fish peddler and a shoemaker, were arrested for the murders of two shoe-factory workers. Liberals at the time—and panels of impartial judges later—agreed that the evidence against them was too scant to justify their convictions. But the charges stuck, largely because the pair were political anarchists at a time when revolutions abroad and fears at home were making a "Red menace" of all radicals. After seven years of trials and controversy, and despite the confession of a convicted killer, Sacco and Vanzetti died in the electric chair. This letter was written to Sacco's son the day before the executions.

Ines was Sacco's daughter. Susie was a family friend with whom Sacco's wife and children had been living.

August 21, 1927. From the Death House of Massachusetts State Prison

My dear Dante:

I still hope, and we will fight until the last moment, to revindicate our right to live and to be free, but all the forces of the State and of the money and reaction are deadly against us because we are libertarians or anarchists.

I write little of this because you are now and yet too young to understand these things and other things of which I would like to reason with you.

But, if you do well, you will grow and understand your father's and my case and your father's and my principles, for which we will soon be put to death.

I tell you now that all that I know of your father, he is not a criminal, but one of the bravest men I ever knew. Some day you will understand what I am about to tell you. That your father has sacrificed everything dear and sacred to the human heart and soul for his fate in liberty and justice for all. That day you will be proud of your father, and if you come brave enough, you will take his place in the struggle between tyranny and liberty and you will vindicate his (our) names and our blood.

If we have to die now, you shall know, when you will be able to understand this tragedy in its fullest, how good and brave your father has been with you, your father and I, during these eight years of struggle, sorrow, passion, anguish and agony.

Even from now you shall be good, brave with your mother, with Ines, and with Susie—brave, good Susie—and do all you can to console and help them.

I would like you to also remember me as a comrade and friend to your father, your mother and Ines, Susie and you, and I assure you that neither have I been a criminal, that I have committed no robbery and no murder, but only fought modestily to abolish crimes from among mankind and for the liberty of all.

Remember Dante, each one who will say otherwise of your father and I, is a liar, insulting innocent dead men who have been brave in their life. Remember and know also, Dante, that if your father and I would have been cowards and hypocrits and rinnegetors of our faith, we would not have been put to death. They would not even have convicted a lebbrous dog; not even executed a deadly poisoned scorpion on such evidence as that they framed against us. They would have given a new trial to a matricide and abitual felon on the evidence we presented for a new trial.

Remember, Dante, remember always these things; we are not criminals; they convicted us on a frame-up; they denied us a new trial; and if we will be executed after seven years, four months and seventeen days of unspeakable tortures and wrong, it is for what I have already told you; because we were for the poor and against the exploitation and oppression of the man by the man.

The documents of our case, which you and other ones will collect and preserve, will prove to you that your father, your mother, Ines, my family and I have sacrificed by and to a State Reason of the American Plutocratic reaction.

The day will come when you will understand the atrocious cause of the above written words, in all its fullness. Then you will honor us.

Now Dante, be brave and good always. I embrace you.

P.S. I left the copy of <u>An American Bible</u> to your mother now, for she will like to read it, and she will give it to you when you will be bigger and able to understand it. Keep it for remembrance. It will also testify to you how good and generous Mrs. Gertrude Winslow has been with us all. Good-bye Dante.

Bartolomeo

1927: DECEMBER 23
PAUL WINTER TO ALFRED SMITH

In 1925, forty thousand Klansmen marched in Washington, D.C., and two years later, membership in the Ku Klux Klan remained in the millions. To one member of a Long Island chapter, it seemed reasonable to appeal to the governor of New York on behalf of the Klan's constitutional rights.

IMPERIAL PALACE

INVISIBLE EMPIRE

KNIGHTS OF THE KU KLUX KLAN

December 23rd, 1927

P.O. Lock Box 57

Jamaica, L.I., N.Y.

OPEN LETTER.

Hon. Alfred E. Smith,
Governor's Mansion,
Albany, N.Y.

Honorable sir:

Again I am desirous of drawing your attention to the maladministration of justice in Queens County, New York City, relative to the attack precipitated by the police of New York City on a peaceful parade of native-born Americans last Memorial Day, May 30, 1927, in Jamaica, Long Island.

Despite the fact that the Grand Jury of Queens County has placed the blame for the attack on the shoulders of the police and in their decision called upon the Mayor to punish the guilty parties, Mayor James J. Walker has consistently "whitewashed" the affair on the basis that the Klan is illegally operating in the State of New York.

This attitude has not the semblance of an excuse, but merely justifies the clubbing and beating of innocent men and women because they differ religiously with him and have endeavored to exercise their Constitutional rights. The parade of the Klan on Memorial Day was covered by a legal permit and was conducted in compliance with the Walker Law.

You are perfectly acquainted, and I believe Mayor Walker is also, with the fact that the Klan incorporated as a Greek letter society and exercising its perogative changed its name later to the Knights and Women of the Ku Klux Klan.

This act made it a legally constituted organization with the same rights enjoyed by any other organization, even the Fascisti.

As the field representative of the Klan in Queens County I am appealing to you in an effort to see that justice is administered and I am making this request for the purpose of determining whether you can separate your religious feelings from things political.

Trusting that the injured feelings of thousands of citizens in Queens County might healed in the interest of true Americanism, I am

Respectfully yours,

Paul M. Winter

1928: JANUARY 13

A KANSAS MOTHER TO THE CHILDREN'S BUREAU

---

*For several decades in the early part of the century, the U.S. Department of Labor's Children's Bureau tried to educate women about how to care for themselves and their children. The bureau was well known for distributing two pamphlets—*Infant Care *(1913) and* Prenatal Care *(1914)—to millions of women who, like Mrs. E. S., frequently had no other access to basic health information, let alone to advice about birth control.*

Dear Sirs:—

I have followed your book on Infant Care and found it Wanderful. But I'm comming with my largest problem. I am Mother of 2 little boys 1 yr apart & expect to be mother again this summer. Im only in my twenties. We Rent a farm & find it a hard row to hoe to provide food & clothe for us all. We can not meet expenses. My health is going down hill from hard Work & Bearing babies. My husband works hard & worries, also has the Asthama so bad in Winter I find My self doing a Man's Work. This is hard to be Mother, Wife, & especially the out side Work.

Now what I Want to know is Why can't We poor people be given Birth Control as well as Dr's. & the Rich people that could provide & Dr. their families. We need help to prevent any more babies. After this next one comes Im going to seek advice if Possible so We can live more happy. Don't you think it better to be Parents of 3 which we are willing to work & do all we can for them, to raise & provide food for us all, then to hafto have 6 or more that would take us down into the grave & leave 6 or more for poverty to take & be Motherless? I think it unfair Dr's. & Rich seek Birth Control & the poor can't seek nothing, only

Poverty & more babies. Any safe Advice of where to go or do. Im willing to undergo anything after our next baby comes to make me steral. Birth Control, I blieve in it strong to keep down divorce cases & Poverty, also so many a Criminal Case. Please advice us. Thanking you in advance. Please don't publish this letter with my name signed to it thou I'm sure it would be enjoyed by the Poor class of people.

I am Resp.

[Mrs. E. S.]

1928: AUGUST 28
MAXWELL PERKINS TO A READER

Maxwell Perkins (1884–1947), the legendary Scribner's editor who published Ernest Hemingway, Thomas Wolfe, and F. Scott Fitzgerald, wrote this letter to a reader outraged by Fitzgerald's The Great Gatsby, *which had been published in 1925.*

Aug. 28, 1928

Dear ——:

We have read with interest your letter in criticism of "The Great Gatsby" by F. Scott Fitzgerald, and we thank you for it. Probably if you had read the book through, you would not have felt any the less repugnance to it, but you would no doubt have grasped its underlying motive, which is by no means opposed to your own point of view.

The author was prompted to write this book by surveying the tragic situation of many people because of the utter confusion of ideals into which they have fallen, with the result that they cannot distinguish the good from the bad. The author did not look upon these people with anger or contempt so much as with pity. He saw that good was in them, but that it was altogether distorted. He therefore pictured, in the Great Gatsby, a man who showed extraordinary nobility and many fine qualities, and yet who was following an evil course without being aware of it, and indeed was altogether a worshipper of wholly false gods. He showed him in the midst of a society such as certainly exists, of a people who were all worshipping false gods. He wished to present such a society to the American public so that they would realize what a grotesque situation existed, that a man could be a deliberate law-breaker, who thought that the accumulation of vast wealth by any means at all was an admirable thing, and yet could have many fine qualities of character. The author intended the story to be repugnant and he intended to present it so forcefully and realistically that it would impress itself upon people. He wanted to show that this was a horrible, grotesque, and tragic fact of life today. He could not possibly present these people effectively if he refused to face their abhorrent characteristics. One of these was profanity—the total disregard for, or ignorance of, any sense of reverence for a Power outside the physical world. If the author had not presented these abhorrent characteristics, he would not have drawn a true picture of these people, and by drawing a true picture of them he has done something to make them different, for he has made the public aware of them, and its opinion generally prevails in the end.

There are, of course, many people who would say that such people as those in the book should not be written about, because of their repulsive characteristics. Such people maintain that it would be better not to inform the public about evil or unpleasantness. Certainly this position has a strong case. There is, however, the other opinion: vice is attractive when gilded by the imagination, as it is when it is concealed and only vaguely known of; but in reality it is horrible and repulsive, and therefore it is well it should be presented as it is so that it may be so recognized. Then people would hate it, and avoid it, but otherwise they may well be drawn to it on account of its false charm.

Very truly yours,
Maxwell Perkins

1929: MAY 8
MARY GOLD TO HER SISTER

Ellwood was the name of an L-shaped brick house in Clarke County, Virginia, that had been built in the 1840s by the sons of a Scotch-Irish immigrant named John Gold. By the next century, his great-granddaughter Mary, an independent-minded farmer and devoted Baptist, had inherited the house. Despite her ardent struggle to hold on to it, she would be forced to sell in 1933.

Governor Harry Flood Byrd was a neighboring landowner. Uncle Ben and Uncle Joe were servants. Felix McManus was a cousin. Hugh Baker was the last tenant on the property before it was sold. Lewis Glover was a banker. Frank Walter was a nephew.

Ellwood, Virginia
May 8, 1929

Darling Child,

I thought I would hear from you yesterday, but I know how busy you are and how disturbed in mind about useless me as well. This letter came from the

Governor day before yesterday. You see what his position is and how it affects mine. The Governor is my only chance—shall I take it? Let me tell you of last week.

Uncle Ben was taken ill on Monday with a sharp heart attack, was in bed till Friday with the Dr. coming every day. I myself was so sick with a heavy cold and sore throat that I could hardly muster, but muster I had to. Uncle Joe was here. He and Uncle Ben had to be fed. Uncle Joe can do very little now, and is so horribly dirty that it takes Christian grit to endure him.

I make the fires and do all the cleaning, beside the cooking—including the two dogs, and they are a big count though mighty dear.

Uncle Joe is slowly, slowly cutting the grass in the front yard. A prospect for a garden is as remote, even more so, than Paradise. I am wondering if the Lord is taking this way to show me, convince me, that I cannot stay here any longer. I pray and pray for unmistakable guidance, and it looks like all doors are being shut but one.

I was lying out on the porch in Felix's chair yesterday. The sun was so good, the view of the lawn and the trees so lovely, so soft, so dear, and the two pretty, contented horses moving around so happily. I thought nowhere could I find such a porch, such a scene, such sweetness, and that I could not leave it.

I happened to raise my eyes—my chair was back against the storeroom at the end of the porch, out of the wind and in the sunshine. There I could see how the sleeping porch above was in dreadful need of paint, and more than that needing a new cornice under the piping—all rotted and ready to fall.

I was in the cellar after the heavy rain the other day—it was flooded. I thought I had it all fixed against that, but investigation showed the foundation under the outside cellar entrance was rotted and sprung entirely out of place, letting the water flow in. Uncle Ben cannot fix it. Mr. Baker would never get around to it.

I see daily what entirely nice people the Bakers are—I simply do not know people of better instincts of honor and right feeling; yet they never get things done! They have no eye to the main chance, no ability to make all edges cut, no capacity to make both ends meet. They are just like me, in fact!

Lewis Glover from the bank is coming this afternoon to go over the situation with me. What can he tell me what I do not already know? What phase of it all have I not debated with myself?

If I sold off the eastern end of the farm—$15,000 or thereabouts—it would leave me a very slight margin for living and running a little farm. And of course there would be no great income from such a little farm. The right man could do it, but where is he?

Mr. Byrd would let me stay here "for a term of years", but that would have many drawbacks. Yet to have no suitable place for you all to come to ever again! It will mean the utter loss of the children out of my life. My hold is slight now—will be nothing then. This breaks my heart. Then my two pretty, dear old horses and the dogs! Do you remember little Frank exclaiming one day, "O isn't Jack happy on this old place?"

There are so many birds this Spring. I saw a yellow hammer sitting bolt upright in the big bed of purple violets the other day.

Love, my own Dear.

Do you remember Felix gave me this typewriter with the stipulation: "On demand pay to Felix R. McManus in Washington D.C. one crock of Ellwood clabber, one pitcher of cream, one pound of brown sugar". So funny. Poor Felix.

1929: OCTOBER 29

EARNEST ELMO CALKINS TO THE <u>NEW YORK TIMES</u>

On Black Tuesday—the day before this letter was written—16 million shares of stock were sold at declining prices. The damage, estimated at $9 billion, would grow into a $30 billion rout by mid-November, leading thousands to lose fortunes and millions to lose jobs, and ushering in the Great Depression. In his letter to the Times, *advertising man Earnest Elmo Calkins (1868–1964) argued vehemently, if futilely, that the country was overreacting.*

To the Editor of the <u>New York Times</u>:

I have a feeling that fewer persons are affected by the stock market drop than one would infer from the figures, just as fewer persons were affected by the previous rises. I am judging by my own situation. Among the stocks I happen to own are some that suffered the greatest losses last week, such as Tel. and Tel., American Tobacco, Union Pacific and Western Union, but my income from them remains the same as before.

As far as I am concerned a group of men, technically known as the Stock Exchange, gets together and decides that my Tel. and Tel. stock is worth $310 a share, and I experience a momentary glow of elation. A few days or weeks later they get together and decide that it is worth only $232, and I have a feeling of disappointment, also momentary. It is unlikely that the slump will affect the continued use of the telephone or that the company will be unable to continue to pay the $9 a share. I bought my stock at an average price of $98 a share, so even at the present low—or high, according to the point of view—it is worth more than double what I paid for it.

Doesn't it seem probable that mine is the situation of a great majority of holders of this and other good stocks? That they have merely lost some of their spectacular gains, but their stocks are still quoted at and worth more than they paid for them?

It seems to be the practice to compute the total loss in such a recession, and multiply it by the total number of shares outstanding, and imply that somebody or the country has lost that vast amount. Headlines last week said that the loss was about $4,000,000,000. In Monday's market only 87,100 shares of Tel. and Tel. were traded in. That is a very small percentage of the 13,203,093 shares outstanding. How many of the holders of these shares have actually lost anything? I am just where I was a few weeks ago. When Tel. and Tel. first crossed 232 I thought that was pretty good, and I still think so now that it has receded to 232, and I felt the same about American Tobacco when it first touched 196, Union Pacific when it first touched 240, and Western Union when it first touched 191. My profits the last few weeks have been paper profits, and my losses last week are paper losses, and one cancels the other.

It reminds me of the farmer who told a neighbor that Josh Stebbins had offered two hundred dollars for his horse.

"Josh Stebbins ain't got two hundred dollars."

"Yes, I know, but ain't it a good offer?"

Earnest Elmo Calkins.
New York, October 29, 1929

1929: NOVEMBER 14

WILLIAM RANDOLPH HEARST TO HERBERT HOOVER

Publisher of some twenty newspapers and half a dozen magazines, creator and resident of the palatial San Simeon, William Randolph Hearst (1863–1951) was owner of the world's largest publishing empire. A month after the Crash, he sent some optimistic advice to the president. But by 1937 even Hearst would be nearly bankrupt, and it would take the industrial needs of World War II to rebuild his empire.

Honored Sir:

The present unwarranted depression in the value of sterling securities is due partly to the vicious manipulation of bear interests and partly to the alarm of the public at the sudden and unjustifiable collapse of values.

Such panics, as President Wilson said, are largely a matter of psychology.

Lack of confidence is contagious; but, on the other hand, so is confidence contagious.

And, in the opinion of many of your earnest friends, some reassuring utterance by the President of the United States, accompanied by vigorous action in stimulating the legitimate activities of the Federal Reserve, would do much to restore the confidence of the public and make them realize that the present situation is not a disaster, but an opportunity for legitimate investment under the most favorable circumstances.

Your very able and greatly respected Secretary of the Treasury recently took occasion to say, and to say truthfully, that stocks were too high.

He could undoubtedly say with equal truth today that stocks are too low, and that sound dividend-paying stocks must eventually return to twice their present value.

A statement from this authoritative source would have a great psychological effect and would do much to make the investing public realize the unusual opportunity that is now offered them.

The people expect as much from you, Mr. President, an able, an active and experienced business man, as they would have expected from your strenuous predecessor, Mr. Roosevelt, under similar circumstances.

Surely your administration could assemble the banking and financial leaders of the nation and insist that they cooperate with the government in reviving confidence and restoring normal prices.

Undoubtedly President Roosevelt would have taken some such vigorous action, and the Wall Street leaders would have known that he was in earnest and would not have hesitated to cooperate with his administration to the utmost.

Secretary Mellon, whose department would doubtless initiate any such action, has the full confidence of the financial interests, and all that the President of the United States under the circumstances need do is to compel respect for the sincerity and the determination of the administration.

William Randolph Hearst.

*   *   *

1929: NOVEMBER 14

IRVING NORTON FISHER TO HIS FATHER

Son of the famous economist (see letter page 30), Irving Norton Fisher (1901–1979) dispatched this overly optimistic letter to his father the month after the Crash. The stock market would indeed go lower, and "talkies" would provide escapist entertainment to millions during the bleak depression years to come.
The stock to which Fisher refers was Remington Rand. Irving Norton Fisher would become a drama critic and author.

IRVING NORTON FISHER
68 TAMALPAIS ROAD
BERKELEY, CALIFORNIA

Nov. 14, 1929.

Dear Father:—

Yours of the 10th just here. For which many thanks, as I know how pressed for time you must be. It's incredible that the stock market can go any lower, and yet each new day seems to be worse than the day before. I haven't yet seen your talkie comment on the situation but shall today or tomorrow. I naturally shall not hold you to your promise to turn over 600 more shares of Rem Rand to me, if releasing such a number of shares can ease the situation even a little.

I'm free to confess I don't entirely agree with all you say about "talkies" replacing the theatre. Any more than I believe that artificial flowers can ever replace those produced by nature. There is no mechanical way of thrilling the human mind as the actual presence of an actor or singer thrills it. And from what Sidney Howard said after directing three "talkies" in Hollywood himself, the whole thing is still in the balance. No talkie has yet paid for itself.—They are so much more expensive than other films, and the whole foreign market (formerly so lucrative) is automatically cut out, except for English-speaking countries. Formerly, movies didn't <u>begin</u> to make money until the returns began accumulating from the small towns in U.S. (which are still unequipped for "talkies") and from foreign countries. Of course Hollywood is optimistic, who wouldn't be if his livelyhood depended on it, but it is by no means an assured thing!

Naturally I'm eager to see "Disraeli" when it is released here, but unless I'm mistaken you won't be seeing very many more like it. It is one in a thousand.—But if I say more, you'll be thinking "He doth protest too much, methinks!"

Your very loving son,

Irving N. Fisher

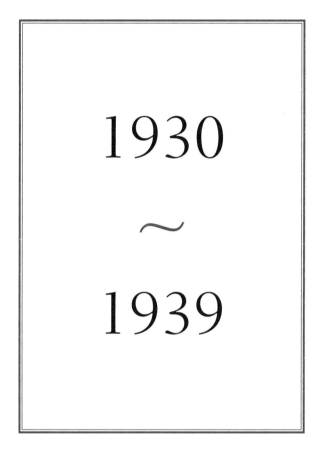

1930

~

1939

We work, ten hours a day for six days. In the grime and
dirt of a nation. We go home tired and sick—dirty—disgusted—
with the world in general, work—work all day, low pay . . .
slaves—slaves of the depression! I'm even tired as
I write this letter—, a letter of hope—

—a Brooklyn worker to Frances Perkins
March 29, 1935

BETWEEN 1930 AND 1939 . . .

1930: One of every five Americans now owns a car. ★ The U.S. population is 122.7 million. ★ Life expectancy of the average American is 61 years. ★ Median age for all living Americans: 26.4. ★ More than 1,300 banks close. ★ Fred MacMurray sings a song by George Olsen and His Music: "I'll have to see my broker / Find out what he can do. / 'Cause I'm in the market for you." ★ More than 14 million Americans are foreign-born, the highest number there will be in the United States for another six decades. ★ The planet Pluto is discovered by 24-year-old astronomer Clyde Tombaugh. ★ An article on bridal showers suggests that guests hunt for souvenirs: "such things as a ten-cent wedding ring, toy wash-boards and other articles suggestive of marriage and housewifery." ★ The first installment of the comic strip *Blondie* appears. ★ Grant Wood paints *American Gothic*. **1931:** Between four and five million Americans are unemployed. ★ "The Star-Spangled Banner" is made the national anthem by an act of Congress. ★ Two white women claim they have been raped onboard a freight train in Alabama; despite scant evidence, nine black youths who will become known as the Scottsboro boys—because the trial takes place in Scottsboro, Alabama—are convicted. ★ Al Capone is ordered to pay a $50,000 fine and more than twice that in back taxes and is

---

From left to right, top row: an apple seller's sign, Social Security poster, Margaret Mitchell; *second row:* Albert Einstein, the Dust Bowl; *third row:* the *Hindenburg,* Al Capone; *bottom row:* George Balanchine, the 1939 World's Fair.

sentenced to 11 years in prison for tax evasion. ★ James Cagney crushes a grapefruit into his girlfriend's face in the film *The Public Enemy*. ★ President Hoover takes a 20 percent pay cut. **1932:** Franklin Delano Roosevelt is elected president after promising a "new deal" for the American people. ★ On NBC and CBS, prices can now be mentioned in radio commercials. ★ Popular songs include Jay Gorney and E. Y. Harburg's "Brother, Can You Spare a Dime?" Irving Berlin's "Let's Have Another Cup of Coffee," and Cole Porter's "Night and Day." ★ The dead body of kidnapped baby Charles Lindbergh, Jr., is found in the woods near the Lindberghs' home. ★ Radio City Music Hall, Skippy peanut butter, and Zippo lighters are new. ★ Moving to radio, *New York Daily Mirror* columnist Walter Winchell begins his entertainment news and gossip show with the words "Good evening, Mr. and Mrs. America, and all the ships at sea." **1933:** At New York's Cotton Club, a 16-year-old Lena Horne makes her debut. ★ FDR broadcasts his first "fireside chat." ★ Gasoline costs 18 cents a gallon. ★ With its billboard inviting customers to SIT IN YOUR CAR, SEE AND HEAR MOVIES, the first drive-in movie theater opens, in Camden, New Jersey. ★ Prohibition is repealed. ★ Formerly found in packs of cigarettes, baseball cards are now packaged with gum as well. **1934:** In separate incidents, Bonnie Parker and Clyde Barrow, John Dillinger, Baby Face Nelson, and Pretty Boy Floyd are all gunned down. **1935:** Louisiana's governor, the demagogic, 42-year-old Huey Long, is shot to death by Dr. Carl Austin Weiss. ★ The Works Progress Administration is created by an executive order. ★ The Social Security Act becomes law. ★ Massive dust storms ravage the prairie states. ★ Alcoholics Anonymous is founded by Bill Wilson and Dr. Robert H. Smith. ★ Pan American Airways becomes the first airline to serve hot meals in the air. **1936:** Margaret Mitchell's first and only novel, *Gone With the Wind,* sells a million copies in six months. ★ The Waring blender and *The Joy of Cooking* are introduced. **1937:** Amelia Earhart disappears over the Pacific Ocean. ★ The German airship *Hindenburg* explodes over Lakehurst,

New Jersey. ★ San Francisco's Golden Gate Bridge is opened. ★ In gratitude for their increased sales, American spinach growers erect a six-foot-tall painted statue of the comic-strip character Popeye in Crystal City, Texas. **1938:** Tanks are set up outside Gimbel's department store so swimmers can show that the newly invented ballpoint pen will write underwater. ★ In spite of four explanatory announcements during the show, panic sweeps the nation when Orson Welles, 23, and his Mercury Theatre broadcast a radio version of *War of the Worlds*, complete with reports of "poisonous black smoke . . . death rays [and] monstrous Martians." **1939:** Acclaimed black contralto Marian Anderson, denied the right to perform in Constitution Hall, sings before 75,000 people at the Lincoln Memorial. ★ *Gone With the Wind*, *The Wizard of Oz*, *Mr. Smith Goes to Washington*, *Dark Victory*, and *Wuthering Heights* are among the movies released in what is arguably Hollywood's best year ever. ★ Baseball can be seen on television for the first time. ★ Frank Sinatra is hired by band-leader Harry James as lead vocalist. ★ It takes 22 hours (and $675 per passenger, round trip) to cross the Atlantic Ocean on Pan Am's new commercial Clipper service. ★ The Perisphere and the Trylon grace the New York World's Fair and become symbols of its optimistic theme "Building the World of Tomorrow."

MICHAEL CULLEN TO THE PRESIDENT OF KROGER

The year this letter was written, Kroger was one of the largest chain grocery-store operators in the country, and Michael J. Cullen was an ambitious forty-six-year-old food merchandiser with a vision—and messianic zeal. Eventually famous as "King Kullen," the name he put on his supermarkets, Cullen led a revolution in retailing, introducing innovations—many of which are detailed in this letter—that changed both the landscape and the buying habits of America.

When products are shipped FOB, or "free on board," transportation costs are paid by the buyer. William K. Henderson owned a radio network in the South and Midwest. On air, he solicited $12 fees payable to his "Merchants' Minute Men," who would supposedly defend local commerce by battling the chain stores.

My grocery equipment would cost two thousand five hundred dollars. My meat equipment would cost about $4,500.00 complete. A total outlay of $7,000.00 for equipment and a $23,000.00 stock of merchandise in each store. In other words, I would have an investment in each store of $30,000.00. My operating expenses would be as follows:

1 Grocery Manager		$50.00 per week
1 Fruit Man		$25.00 per week
1 Assistant Fruit Man		$18.00 per week
1 Assistant Grocery Manager		$25.00 per week
2 Male Clerks	$18.00	$36.00 per week
1 Cashier		$15.00 per week
3 Lady Clerks	$12.00	$36.00 per week
1 Male Clerk		$15.00 per week
12 Extra Saturday Clerks	$ 2.50	$30.00 per week
Total Salaries		$250.00 per week

I expect to do a grocery business of $8,500.00 per week per store, a fruit and vegetable business of $1,500.00 per week, per store. In other words, the kind of stores I have in mind should do a grocery business of $10,000.00 a week and a meat business of $2,500.00 per week. On the grocery business, including fruit and vegetables, I can operate on a gross profit of 9%. My complete operating expenses on a $10,000.00 a week grocery business would be as follows:

Help	$250.00	2.50%
Rent	58.00	.58
Investment on Money	30.00	.30
Insurance	10.00	.10
Light-heat-water	7.00	.07
Taxes	10.00	.10
Depreciation	10.00	.10
Supervision	20.00 ⅕ 5 stores	.20
Paper, bags, etc.	75.00	.75
Income tax	30.00	.30
Hauling	20.00	.20
Advertising	50.00	.50
Buying	40.00 ⅕ 5 stores	.40
M. J. Cullen	40.00 ⅕ 5 stores	.40
Total		6.50%

Our meat department sales per store would be at least $2,500.00 per week, and we would make a net profit of at least 3% on this meat business. This is the kind of cut-rate Chain of Wholesale selling direct to the public that I want to operate.

I want to sell 300 items at cost.
I want to sell 200 items at 5% above cost.
I want to sell 300 items at 15% above cost.
I want to sell 300 items at 20% above cost.

I want to gross 9% and do a grocery, fruit and vegetable business of $10,000.00 per week, and make a net profit of 2½% on the grocery department, and 3% on the meat department.

You need have no fear regarding the present overhead of the Chain Stores.

My buying, advertising and hauling expense of $110.00 per week per store is more than enough to take care of the buying under my supervision; and this could be reduced twenty-five points after I had my fifth store opened.

I would bill all merchandise to the stores at cost, and adopt a cash register check system, that stealing or dishonesty would be impossible. I would inventory these stores every month at cost and their stock gain less all current expenses would be our net profit per month per store.

It would be a little difficult to begin with to buy for my first store, but after my fifth store was opened, I could buy the minimum shipments and ship 80% of same FOB to the store direct, thereby eliminating entirely a warehouse, which is not necessary when these monstrous stores could show a turnover such as I would get.

Can you imagine how the public would respond to a store of this kind? To think of it—a man selling 300 items at cost and another 200 items at 5% above cost—nobody in the world ever did this before. Nobody ever flew the Atlantic either, until Lindbergh did it.

When I come out with a two-page ad and advertise 300 items at cost and 200 items at practically cost, which would probably be all the advertising that I would ever have to do, the public, regardless of their present feeling towards Chain Stores, because in reality I would not be a Chain Store, would break my front doors down to get in. It would be a riot. I would have to call out the police and let the public in so many at a time. I would lead the public out of the high-priced houses of bondage into the low prices of the house of the promised land.

I would convince the public that I would be able to save them from one to three dollars on their food bills. I would be the "miracle man" of the grocery business. The public would not, and could not believe their eyes. Week days would be Saturdays—rainy days would be sunny days, and then when the great crowd of American people came to buy all those low-priced and 5% items, I would have them surrounded with 15%, 20% and in some cases, 25% items. In other words, I could afford to sell a can of Milk at cost if I could sell a can of Peas and make 2¢, and so on all through the grocery line.

The fruit and vegetable department of a store of this kind would be a gold mine. This department alone may make a net profit of 7% due to the tremendous turnover we would have after selling out daily and not throwing half the profit away, which is done at the present time in 25% of the Chain Stores throughout the land.

Then the big meat department. This would be a beehive. We would have the confidence of the public. They . . . that every other grocery item they picked up they saved money on same, and our meat department would show us a very handsome profit. It wouldn't surprise me if we could not net 5% in this meat department.

How long are you and your Company going to sit by and kid yourself that in a few weeks this Henderson Radio Stuff and Home Owned Retailed Store propaganda will pass by?

The reason that I know that this proposition can be put over is that I have already put over a similar proposition right here in Southern Illinois. I operated Bracy's Warehouse store in West Frankfort before Bracy bought out Limerick, and did as high as $19,000.00 per week, $9,000.00 on groceries, $3,000.00 on meats and made a net profit of $15,000.00 on this one single store year before last, 1928, and I did this in a mining town of 14,000 people, mines only working half time, with A&P in the same city and Limerick doing a big business in this same city.

I was never so confident in my life as I am at the present time; and in order to prove to you my sincerity and my good faith, I am willing to invest $15,000.00 of my own money to prove that this will be the biggest money maker you have ever invested yourself in.

A salary expense of 2½%, I know seems ridiculous to you. You perhaps think this is almost impossible. I have had a great many stores under me in the past, and their weekly salary was only 3% with less than $3,000.00 sales. So this 2½% salary basis on a $10,000.00 weekly business is not only reasonable but is practical.

Again you may object to my locating two or three blocks from the business center of a big city. One great asset in being away from the business section is parking space. Another is, you can get generally the kind of store you want and on your own terms. The public will walk an extra block or two if they can save money, and one of our talking points would be, the reason we sell at wholesale prices are that we are out of the high rent district.

My other percent of store expenses I believe you will agree, are not excessive. If anything, I am a few points too high.

Don't let the buying worry you in any way whatever. I can handle the buying in fine shape. I could buy goods, ship them direct to my stores, 3% cheaper than you could buy them, store them in a warehouse, and put them all through the red tape that all Kroger items go through before they are sold. If this proposition appeals to you, there is not a question but that Reock and I could work together. It would be an asset, but what I am trying to bring out is, I would put this over without any assistance from Reock.

Before you throw this letter in the wastebasket, read it again and then wire me to come to Cincinnati, so I can tell you more about this plan, and what it will do for you and your company.

The one thought always uppermost in mind—How can I undersell the other fellow? How can I beat the other fellow? How can I make my company more money? The answer is very simple: by keeping my overhead down, and only by keeping this overhead down can I beat the other fellow.

What is your verdict?

1930
LAWRENCE MATTINGLY TO C. W. HERRICK

Notorious Chicago mobster Al Capone (1899–1947) was a master at evading capture and was never convicted of bootlegging, gambling, or murder. In 1930, however, he made a big mistake: he hired an honest lawyer, Lawrence Mattingly, to handle his tax problems. In this letter to an agent of the Internal Revenue Service, Mattingly provided the evidence that would lead to Capone's 1931 conviction and imprisonment—for federal income tax evasion.

The address given for Capone was that of the Lexington Hotel.

Dear Sir:

Mr. Alphonse Capone, residing at 2135 South Michigan Avenue, Chicago, Ill., has authorized me to make an exact computation of income tax liability for the year 1929 and prior years, the amount of which he will pay as soon as determined. Mr. Capone has never filed income tax returns.

1930: APRIL 3
THEODORE DREISER TO YVETTE SZEKELY

Author Theodore Dreiser (1871–1945) began an affair with Yvette Szekely when she was seventeen and he was fifty-eight. In this letter, written to her a year and a half later, Dreiser expressed a profound optimism about the future that was quite at odds with his novels' candid and often grim descriptions of the country. Despite his ongoing marriage and a number of other affairs, Dreiser's relationship with Szekely continued on and off for sixteen years, until his death in 1945 at seventy-five. Szekely later married the author and editor Max Eastman.

Margaret Monahan, Szekely's mother, had originally introduced her to Dreiser and his circle.

SANTA RITA HOTEL

M. EDWARD OLSON, MANAGER

TUCSON, ARIZ.

April 3rd 1930

Dearest:

Just now I received such a doleful and yet really vital and interesting letter from you. Your so unhappy. You see no future or—you are falling all unprepared into one from the great height—youth. And no parachute. Excellent. Excellent. At seventeen and a half you are thinking more than most men and women at sixty. You have weltschmerz—that most upbuilding disease that can attack youth. You really feel so bad that your going to do something about it, by George! Excellent, baby. I can think of nothing more healthful and encouraging. It even inspires me at three and a half times your age. . . . But what is going to please you most is that you are going to get somewhere. You have youth, brains, health, and looks. Kids at your age are—where they have real brains—always dispairing as to their future. But you are going to live in a period of enormous social changes here in the U.S.A. People are going to read. A heavy percentage are going to weary of numbskullery and fol-de-rol and sigh for worlds to conquer. There are going to be vital changes in government. If you want to be in on things—read first chemistry, physics, bio-chemistry and all phases of science. And then sociology. It would pay you to read law—and pay well. A law course would be invaluable in your case. Also a course in philosophy. But read now— and at once. Will Durants Story of Philosophy. And if youve never read it H. G. Wells—Outline of History (which reminds me that I owe him a letter). Get Schopenhauers The World as Will and Idea and read that. If you want to go to college perhaps that can be arranged. If you were to study science enough you could become a technical assistant at good wages & learn besides. Dont forget too, that the movies are going to provide an enormous field for educational ideas. People are going into Hollywood pretty soon who are going to construct social and scientific documents in film form—things that are going to teach & change the world enormously. Bother the communists over here. Turn your face to gay, thrilling instruction—the conquest of more & more amazing natural facts. Just now I have a bid to go to Hollywood (Warner Brothers) for some such work. If so I may give you a lift. But I am not going to leave New York. Not permanently. And should I go for awhile I'll send for you because I feel you can be of help to me—and to yourself. And even should I go—I'll be back before I go— and arrange some things with you. Will you come? Will Margaret have sense enough to let you. You see how interested I get on the mental side. But there'll be <u>moments</u>—too, when you'll want me to "<u>Hold me.</u>" Well, I will.

Its still marvellous here. No rain. No clouds yet. All sunshine. They say it rains but I havent seen any. And I'm feeling better. No coughing at night at all. And none in the day to speak of. I still wish you were here. It would be fun strolling around with you here. And how.

Write me. Cheer up. Eat an apple every day. Get to bed by noon. And blow me a few kisses and a few hot thoughts. No hot thoughts—no great ideas. I gotta have moments.

T

1930: SUMMER?
F. SCOTT FITZGERALD TO ZELDA FITZGERALD

Author of The Great Gatsby *and* The Last Tycoon, *F. Scott Fitzgerald (1896–1940) coined the phrase "the Jazz Age" to describe the dissolute 1920s, and he spent a good part of the decade demonstrating what the phrase meant. A writer of astonishing talent, he was also known for his drinking, and when he married Zelda Sayre in 1920 he embarked upon one of the most famously turbulent marriages on record. He wrote her this letter several months after she had had the first of many nervous breakdowns.*
Author and publisher Robert McAlmon ran Contact Editions and published Gertrude Stein, among other members of the modern movement. Zelda had been treated at the Valmont clinic in Switzerland. John S. Sumner was secretary of the New York Society for the Suppression of Vice.

When I saw the sadness of your face in that passport picture I felt as you can imagine. But after going through what you can imagine I did then and looking at it and looking at it, I saw that it was the face I knew and loved and not the metalic superimposition of our last two years in France. . . .

The photograph is all I have: it is with me from the morning when I wake up with a frantic half dream about you to the last moment when I think of you and of death at night. The rotten letters you write me I simply put away under Z in my file. My instinct is to write a public letter to the Paris Herald to see if any human being except yourself and Robert McAlmon has ever thought I was a homosexual. The three weeks after the horror of Valmont when I could not lift my eyes to meet the eyes of other men in the street after your stinking allegations and insinuations will not be repeated. If you choose to keep up your wrestling match with a pillar of air I would prefer to be not even in the audience.

I am hardened to write you so brutally by thinking of the ceaseless wave of love that surrounds you and envelopes you always, that you have the power to evoke at a whim—when I know that for the mere counterfeit of it I would perjure the best of my heart and mind. Do you think the solitude in which I live has a more amusing decor than any other solitude? Do you think it is any nicer for remembering that there were times very late at night when you and I shared our aloneness?

I will take my full share of responsibility for all this tragedy but I cannot spread beyond the limits of my reach and grasp. I can only bring you the little bit of hope I have and I don't know any other hope except my own. I have the terrible misfortune to be a gentleman in the sort of struggle with incalculable elements to which people should bring centuries of inexperience; if I have failed you is it just barely possible that you have failed me (I can't even write you any more because I see you poring over every line like Mr. Sumner trying to wring some slant or suggestion of homosexuality out of it)

I love you with all my heart because you are my own girl and that is all I know.

1931: FEBRUARY 7
AMELIA EARHART TO GEORGE PALMER PUTNAM

Five times, the publisher George Putnam asked the renowned aviatrix Amelia Earhart (1897–1937) to marry him. He was twelve years older than she and had been married before. She was a maverick and a free spirit. On the morning of their wedding, she handed him this letter, which he later called "brutal in its frankness but beautiful in its honesty." They were still married six years later, when her plane disappeared over the Pacific Ocean.

Dear GP,

There are some things which should be writ before we are married. Things we have talked over before,—most of them.

You must know again my reluctance to marry, my feeling that I shatter thereby chances in work which means so much to me. I feel the move just now as foolish as anything I could do. I know there may be compensations, but have no heart to look ahead.

In our life together I shall not hold you to any medieval code of faithfulness to me, nor shall I consider myself bound to you similarly. If we can be honest I think the differences which arise may best be avoided.

Please let us not interfere with each other's work or play, nor let the world see private joys or disagreements. In this connection I may have to keep some place where I can go to be myself now and then, for I cannot guarantee to endure at all times the confinements of even an attractive cage.

I must exact a cruel promise, and this is that you will let me go in a year if we find no happiness together.

I will try to do my best in every way.

A.E.

1931: JUNE 4

STARR FAITHFULL TO A FORMER BOYFRIEND

It was front-page news when twenty-five-year-old Starr Faithfull was found dead, bruised, and partly clothed on the sand at Long Beach, New York, on Monday, June 8, 1931. Faithfull, memorable for her name as well as for the rumor that she had been seduced at eleven by a former mayor of Boston, had apparently been addicted to ether—and to reckless behavior. "Death by drowning," the local district attorney declared, "brought about by someone interested in closing her lips." But the following letter, written the day before Faithfull died, suggested suicide. The case, never solved, became one of the most notorious of the early part of the century, and would be the foundation for the John O'Hara novel Butterfield 8.

Hello Bill Old Thing:

It's all up with me now. This is something I am GOING to put through. The only thing that bothers me about it, the only thing I dread, is being outwitted and prevented from doing this—which is the only possible thing for me to do. If one wants to get away with murder one has to jolly well keep one's wits about one. It's the same with suicide. If I don't watch out I will wake up in a psychopathic ward, but I intend to watch out and accomplish my end this time. No ether, allonal or window jumping. I don't want to be maimed. I want oblivion. If there is an after life it would be a dirty trick—but I'm sure fifty million priests ARE wrong. That is one of the things one <u>knows</u>. Nothing makes any difference now. I love to eat and can have one delicious meal with no worry over gaining. I adore music and I am going to hear some good music. I believe I love music more than anything. I am going to drink <u>slowly</u> keeping <u>AWARE</u> every second. Also I am going to enjoy my last cigarettes,—I won't worry because men flirt with me in the streets—I shall encourage them—I don't care who they are. I wish I got more pleasure with men. It's a great life when one has 24 hours to live. I can be rude to people—I can tell them they are too fat or that I don't like their clothes, and I don't have to dread being a lonely old woman, or poverty, obscurity, or boredom. I don't have to dread living on without ever seeing you, or hearing rumours such as "The women all fall for him"—and "he entertains charmingly". Why in hell shouldn't you!—But it's more than I can cope with—this feeling I have for you. I have tried to pose as clever and intellectual thereby to attract you, but it was not successful and I couldn't go on writing those long, studied letters. I don't have to worry because there are no words in which to describe this feeling I have for you. The words Love, adore, worship have become meaningless.—There is nothing I can do but what I am going to do. I shall never see you again. That is extraordinary. Although I can't comprehend it any more than I can comprehend the words—"always" or "time". They produce a very merciful numbness.

Starr

1931: JULY 31
GEORGIA O'KEEFFE TO HENRY MCBRIDE

Georgia O'Keeffe (1887–1986) had been given her first one-woman show in New York City in 1917 and was well established as a leading American modernist painter when she wrote this letter from Alcalde, New Mexico. She was on one of her earliest trips to the part of the country that would yield some of her most memorable subjects—desert bones, rocks, and clouds. The paintings she refers to had been done in 1929. Henry McBride was an art critic and friend.

Mabel Dodge Luhan had written a not entirely positive profile of O'Keeffe. "That man" was the photographer Alfred Stieglitz, O'Keeffe's husband and the first exhibitor of her work.

2:45—a.m.

A night when I can not sleep—I think the first one since I am out here——bright moonlight on my door—everything so still but for a very persistent mocking bird—somewhere out there in the night.—I thought to myself—What can I read?—There isn't a printed word in the place as far as I know except that Creative Art with Mabels article on me—I hadn't at all been able to face the idea of reading it before—but now I got up and read it—

Well—I doubt if it reads to anyone else as it reads to me tonight—rather

beautiful—a bit disjointed—something of a lie—because she doesnt say something poisonous she wants to say—and that wouldn't be true either—And one
picture losing all the point there is to it by standing on its left ear—the
Lawrence tree. The bottom of it as it is printed should be the left hand side.
That tree should stand on its head——And the Ranchos Church seems to be
cut up all round—that I really think quite inexcusable——specially when there
is no note about the reproduction being only a part of the picture—

—I dont know what it is all about. I look through the rest of the book and decide that frankly—I dont know what Art is all about—

It all puzzles me very much. Ten weeks away from New York—most of it
spent by the roadside—in that famous Ford that I now drive very well—
attempting to paint landscape—I must think it important or I wouldnt work so
hard at it—Then I see that the end of my studio is a large pile of bones—a
horses head—a cows head—a calfs head—long bones—short bones—all sorts
of funny little bones and big ones too—A beautiful rams head has the center of
the table—with a stone with a cross on it and an extra curly horn

And then I wonder what painting is all about What will I do with those bones
and sticks and stones—and the big pink sea shell that I got from an Indian—it
looks like a rose—and the small katchina—indian doll—with the funny flat
feather on its head and its eyes popping out—it has a curious kind of live
stillness

—There is also a beautiful eagle feather

When I leave the landscape it seems I am going to work with these funny
things that I now think feel so much like it

—but maybe I will not.

—The days here are very good. They are mostly days alone—out of doors all
day—I hate being under a roof—it galls me that I haven't the courage to sleep
out there in the hills alone—but I haven't—

I will be going East soon. I dont seem to remember what its like there but I'll
be finding out. Cant leave that man alone too long—The things I like here seem
so far away from what I vaguely remember of New York.

I wonder if you would like it here—We are thirty five miles from town—
Santa Fe—without even a telephone—

I hope your summer is going well——I heard you went to Europe—

I hope you are home digging postholes by now—I some way seem to feel it
would be a healthier thing for an Art Critic to be doing

The daylight is coming Henry McBride—I am going up on the roof and watch it come——we do such things here without being thought crazy—it is nice—isn't it.

fondly
Georgia

1932: MARCH 4
BRUNO HAUPTMANN TO CHARLES LINDBERGH

A hundred thousand people were waiting at Paris's Le Bourget airfield on May 21, 1927, to watch Charles Lindbergh (1902–1974) land the Spirit of St. Louis. *Having made the first solo transatlantic airplane trip, "Lucky Lindy" inspired vast hero worship—not to mention a host of daredevil pilots, a dance craze, and numerous songs. Five years later, the kidnapping and murder of his twenty-month-old son horrified the nation. The letter below was received three days after the baby disappeared and was one of some dozen ransom notes. Hauptmann, a German immigrant, was ultimately arrested for the crime and electrocuted, but he proclaimed his innocence until the end.*

Dear Sir. We have warned you note to make anyding public also notify the police now you have to take consequences—means we will have to holt the baby until everyding is quite. We can note make any appointment just now. We know very well what it means to us. It is (is it) realy necessary to make a world affair out of this, or to get your baby back as soon as possible to settle those affair in a quick way will be better for both—don't by afraid about the baby—keeping care of us day and night. We also will feed him according to the diet.

We are interested to send him back in gut health. And ransom was made aus for 50000 $ but now we have to take another person to it and probably have to keep the baby for a longer time as we expected. So the amount will be 70000 20000 in 50 $ bills 25000 $ in 20$ bill 15000 $ in 10$ bills and 10000 in 5$ bills Don't mark any bills or take them from one serial nomer. We will form you latter were to deliver the money. But we will note do so until the Police is out of the cace and the pappers are qute. The kidnaping we prepared in years so we are prepared for everyding.

*   *   *

1933

WILLIAM RANDOLPH HEARST TO HIS EDITORS

His most famous, though possibly apocryphal, decree was uttered on the eve of—and in pursuit of—the Spanish-American War: "You provide the pictures, I'll provide the war." But as this memo to his editors illustrates, William Randolph Hearst (see letter page 188) had no shortage of advice, or confidence, about how to create his empire-building brand of journalism.

Have a good exclusive news feature as often as possible.

PAY LIBERALLY for big exclusive stuff and encourage tipsters. Get reporters with acquaintance.

When a big story must get in all the papers, try to have notably the best account in your paper.

Try to get scoops in pictures. They are frequently almost as important as news. I don't mean pictures of chorus girls, but pictures of important events.

Make the paper thorough. Print all the news. Get all the news into your office and see that it gets into the paper. Condense it if necessary. Frequently it is better when intelligently condensed BUT GET IT IN.

Get your best news on your first page and get as much as possible on that page. Don't use up your whole first page with a few long stories, but try to get a large number of interesting items in addition to your picture page and your two or three top head stories.

Of course, if your feature is big enough it must get display regardless of everything, but mere display does not make a feature. When you have two features it is frequently better to put one on the first page and one on the third, so as not to overcrowd the first page.

Get important items and personal news about well-known people on the first page, and sometimes condense a big news story to go on the first page rather than make it run longer inside. Make your departments complete and reliable so that the reader will know that he can find a thing in your paper and that he can find it right.

Make a paper for the NICEST KIND OF PEOPLE—for the great middle class. Don't print a lot of dull stuff that they are supposed to like and don't.

Omit things that will offend nice people. Avoid coarseness and slang and a low tone. The most sensational news can be told if it is written properly.

Make the paper helpful and kindly. Don't scold and forever complain and attack in your news columns. Leave that to the editorial page.

Be fair and impartial. Don't make a paper for Democrats or Republicans, or Independent Leaguers. Make a paper for all the people and give unbiased news of ALL CREEDS AND PARTIES. Try to do this in such a conspicuous manner that it will be noticed and commented upon.

PLEASE BE ACCURATE. Compare statements in our paper with those in other papers, and find out which are correct. Discharge reporters and copy readers who are persistently inaccurate.

Don't allow exaggeration. It is a cheap and ineffective substitute for real interest. Reward reporters who can make THE TRUTH interesting, and weed out those who cannot.

Make your headlines clear and concise statements of interesting facts. The headlines of a newspaper should answer the question, "WHAT IS THE NEWS?" Don't allow copy readers to write headlines that are too smart to be intelligible.

Don't allow long introduction to stories, or involved sentences. Don't repeat unnecessarily. Don't serve up the story in the headlines and then in the introduction and then in the box. Plunge immediately into the interesting part of the story.

Run pretty pictures and interesting layouts, but don't run pictures just to "illuminate the text." If a picture occupies a column of space it should be as interesting as a column of type. Pictures of pretty women and babies are interesting. Photographs of interesting events with explanatory diagrams are valuable. They tell more than the text can, and when carefully and accurately drawn people will study them. . . . Make every picture worth its space.

Please sum up your paper every day and find wherein it is distinctly better than the other papers. If it isn't distinctly better you have missed that day. Lay out plans to make it distinctly better the next day.

If you cannot show conclusively your own paper's superiority, you may be sure the public will never discover it.

A succession of superior papers will surely tell.

When you beat your rivals one day try harder to beat them the next, for success depends upon a complete victory.

1933: MARCH 13

J. F. BANDO TO FRANKLIN ROOSEVELT'S SECRETARY

The Depression was at its depth, with more than fifteen million Americans unemployed, when the newly elected president, Franklin Delano Roosevelt (1882–1945), began broadcasting his series of "fireside chats." It was a revolutionary use of radio—and of political charisma. Roosevelt's fatherly reassurances and matter-of-fact tone provided, as this letter from a listener noted, a soothing influence in a bleak time.

2232 78th Street
Brooklyn, N.Y.
March 13th 1933

Secretary to the President
The White House
Washington, D.C.

Dear Sir:

Being a citizen of little or no consequence I feel the utter futility of writing to the President at a time such as this, but I trust you will accept this letter in the spirit in which it was written.

For me to sit down to write to any public official, whoever he may be, it must be prompted by a very special and appealing occasion or personality. That happened last evening, as I listened to the Presidents broadcast. I felt that he walked into my home, sat down and in plain and forceful language explained to me how he was tackling the job I and my fellow citizens gave him. I thought what a splendid thing it would be if he could find time to do that occasionally.

Needless to say, such forceful, direct and honest action commands the respect of all Americans, it is certainly deserving of it.

My humble and sincere gratitude to a great leader. May God protect him.

Respectfully,
J. F. Bando

1933: JULY 16
LINCOLN KIRSTEIN TO A. EVERETT AUSTIN, JR.

The writer and impresario Lincoln Kirstein (1907–1996) met the Russian choreographer George Balanchine (1904–1983) in London in 1933 and promised him that before Kirstein turned forty, Balanchine would have an American ballet company and theater. Only a year behind that schedule, in 1948, the New York City Ballet was founded, with Balanchine as its director and, eventually, the choreographer of most of its extensive repertoire. This letter, written from London, launched American ballet.

A. Everett Austin, Jr., was, apart from being Kirstein's good friend, director of the Wadsworth Atheneum museum in Hartford, Connecticut.

Batt's Hotel
Dover Street, W.1
July 16: 1933.

Dear Chick:

This will be the most important letter I will ever write you as you will see. My pen burns my hand as I write: words will not flow into the ink fast enough. We have a real chance to have an American ballet within 3 years time. When I say ballet, I mean a trained company of young dancers—not Russians—but Americans with Russian stars to start with—a company superior to the dregs of the old Diaghilev company which will come to N.Y. this winter and create an enormous success purely because though they aren't much they are better than anything New York will have seen since Nijinsky.

Do you know Georges Balanchine? If not he is a Georgian called Georgei Balanchivadze. He is, personally, enchanting—dark, very slight, a superb dancer and the most ingenious technician in ballet I have ever seen. For Diaghilev he composed <u>The Cat</u>, <u>The Prodigal Son</u>, <u>Apollon Musagète</u>, <u>Le Bal</u> of Chirico, <u>Barabau</u> of Utrillo, <u>Neptune</u> of the Sitwells, and many others. This year he did Tchelitchew's <u>Errante</u>, Bérard's <u>Mozartiana</u>, Derain's <u>Competition</u> and Bérard's <u>Cotillon</u>. He is 28 yrs. old, a product of the Imperial schools. He has split from the Prince de Monaco as he wants to proceed, with new ideas and young dancers instead of going on with the decadence of the Diaghilev troupe, which I assure you, although it possesses many good, if frightfully overworked dancers, is completely worn-out, inartistic, commercial. Now Balanchine has with him Tamara Toumanova, the daughter of a general Toumanov, and a Circassian princess. She is 14 yrs. old. I enclose what the best ballet critic in England says about her. Her technique is phenomenal. Preobrajenska, her teacher and Pavlova's great rival says she is unbelievable, in 3 yrs. a real phenomenon. Balanchine adores her, has really created her: made her blossom out. Toumanova is so <u>photogenique</u> she has refused 2 movie contracts: She wants to dance above all. <u>"Il faut danser."</u> The Monte Carlo Ballet wanted her on a <u>10</u> yrs. contract. Balanchine refused to tie her up for so long: they dismissed her. Enclosed are her photos. Balanchine also has her partner Roman Jasinsky. He is a Pole from the Warsaw School. He is extremely beautiful, a superb body and by way of becoming a most remarkable dancer. He promises far more than Lifar who is absolutely spoiled and is artistically through, a terrible snob and cabotin. Jasinsky works all the time, is a fine mime, modest, a bit dumb, but marvelous in an expert's hand like Balanchine. I wish you could have seen him in the marvelous pas de deux in

Mozartiana. Toumanova is a sombre little girl, a tragic face and a rather firm heavy build, a dancer in whom the masculine strength and feminine art is superbly intertwined. Jasinsky is older, about twenty: but less mature. But his pirouettes, his entrechats are fine and he will be a superb artist. These 3 have <u>nothing</u> to do now. I prepared the following and they are willing and eager to do it.

To have a school of dancing, preferably in Hartford: it is distant from New York—plenty of chance to work in an easy atmosphere. Balanchine is socially adorable, but he hates the atmosphere both of society, as such (Lifar loves it) and the professional Broadway Theatre. For the first he would take 4 white girls and 4 white boys, about sixteen yrs. old and 8 of the same, <u>negros</u>. They would be firmly taught in the classical idiom, not only from <u>exercises</u> but he would start company ballets at once so they could actually <u>learn</u> by doing. As time went on he would get younger children from 8 yrs. on. He thinks the negro part of it would be amazingly supple, the combination of suppleness and sense of time superb. Imagine them, masked, for example. They have so much abandon—and disciplined they would be <u>nonpareil</u>. He could start producing within 3 months. Now, if you could work it he could use your small theatre: . . . a department of the museum a school of dancing could be started—entirely from the professional point of view. But since <u>no</u> tuition fee will be charged, the dancers will be picked for their <u>perfect</u> possibilities and they will have to sign contracts to prevent them from appearing anywhere else, except in the troupe for 5 years. This will obviate the danger of movies or Broadway snatching them up after they have been trained—better than anybody else in the country. In the meantime Balanchine and Jasinsky and Toumanova will serve as demonstrators and models. Thus, you can already see in a girl not yet 15 and a boy of 20, finished dancers, artists of <u>conviction</u>. Now, Madame Nijinsky, her name is very important, has given me the rights to <u>Sacre du Printemps</u>, <u>Jeux</u>, <u>Faun</u>, <u>Tyl Eulenspiegel</u> and <u>4</u> unproduced ballets, the benefit of his <u>untried</u> system of training of dancers. She also volunteers to lecture with me, at these demonstrations where one could also see the dancing of Toumanova and Jasinsky. I intend to get engagements charging $100 a lecture from Harvard, Boston, <u>Worcester,</u> Springfield, Northampton, Bennington, New Haven, New London, Poughkeepsie, Bryn Mawr, Wesleyan, Philadelphia and 3 or 4 times in N.Y. This will prepare the way for the company, which will give performances <u>not</u> at the theatre, but always kept on an educational level, with museums. This takes us out of the competition class, obviates us from theatres—managers etc. In the meantime Balanchine, Jasinsky, Toumanova and her mother must live. Toumanova can't go anywhere without her <u>ma</u>. She is a nice woman, has starved for years and could keep house and cook for them which she has always done. It would be necessary to have $6000 to <u>start</u> it. That guarantees them for one year with passage back and forth. I count this sum as dead loss. Though it won't be at all because by February you can have four performances of wholly new ballets in Hartford. Balanchine is willing to devote all his time to this for 5 yrs. He believes the future of ballet lies in America as do I. I see a great chance for you to do a hell of a lot here. The expense can be under<u>written</u>, say I glibly, but you must realize how much this means. So I have to be arrogant, by Phil <u>Johnson</u> who is willing, myself, <u>Jim Sobey,</u> Jere, the Lewisohns, the <u>Cotters</u> etc. in N.Y. who are willing and I feel sure there are others. This school can be the basis of a national culture as intense as the great Russian Renaissance of Diaghilev. We must start small. But imagine it. We are exactly as if we were in 1910, offered a dancer only less good than an unformed Nijinsky, an incipient Karsavina, a maître de ballet as good as Fokine, who would also be delighted to cooperate. It will be not easy. It will be hard to get good young dancers willing to stand or fall by the <u>company</u>. <u>No</u> first dancers. NO STARS. A perfect ESPRIT DE CORPS. The ballets I have discussed with Balanchine out of American life are these—

<u>Pocahontas:</u> classical ballet with décor from American primitives: music from 17th century English suite de danses.

<u>Doomsday: décor</u> by John Benson after New England gravestones. Libretto on Salem themes by Katherine Anne Porter, the superb biographer of Cotton Mather. She is working on it now.

<u>Uncle Tom's Cabin:</u> ballet au grand serieux avec apotheose: by E. E. Cummings. He is doing it now on my suggestion. Music by Stephen Foster. Décor by WHOEVER.

<u>Defeure of Richmond:</u> Dèbacle dansé on a libretto of John Peale Bishop. I've spoken a lot about this to him. Virgil Thomson is excited about the music. All about Southern <u>swords</u> and roses.

<u>Flying Cloud:</u> a ballet of the days of clipper ships: a dock in New Bedford or <u>Moby Dick</u> by Jere Abbot.

<u>Custer's Last Stand:</u> After Currier and Ives, the circling Indians: corps de ballet shooting at the chief dancers in the center. Ponies: Ritual of scouts going out, Indian dances <u>stylisé</u>.

Then there are Balanchine's own ideas: a great erotic ballet which is to die. Nijinsky undone ballet to an organ and Bach's preludes and fugues—abstract in the baroque manner, and so much else.

I know Stokowski will cooperate musically. It is absolutely necessary to keep

Balanchine to ourselves. Not let either Stokowski, the <u>League</u> of Composers, the <u>Juilliard</u> or the Curtis Institute get ahold of him. He is an honest man, a serious artist and I'd stake my life on his talent. In two years, unhindered by petty intrigue, by rows between Tchelitchew and Bérard, between the Monte Carlo ballet, Lifar and the Paris Opéra, unworried about how he could both live and call his soul his own which he has not done since Diaghilev died, he could achieve a miracle, and right under our eyes: I feel this chance is too serious to be denied. It will mean a life work to all of us, incredible power in a few years. We can command whom we want. We will be developing new talent. It will not be a losing proposition. Conceived as an educational institution under the title of The American Ballet, or the School of Classical Dancing of America or something, it could travel, on small tours, at first, simply <u>as</u> a school and get a considerable return. We would have to do a little theatrical camouflage at first. A few leaps by Jasinsky or a few <u>fouettés</u> by the adorable Toumanova will lift a roomful off their feet, cheering. I wish to God you were here: that you could know what I am writing is true, that I am not either over-enthusiastic or visionary. Please, please, Chick, if you have any love for anything we do both adore, rack your brains and try to make this all come true. If not as I outline, then some other way must be feasible. WE have both done harder things than to raise $6000. Hartford is a perfect place for it, I think. You will adore Balanchine. He is no trouble, i.e. not personally difficult in any way. He could come over in October or even sooner. When you have thought of this, considered it, talked it over with Russell, Jere, Joe Marvell, even Winslow Ames and Francis Taylor—talk to Muriel Draper too. She knows a lot about such things. But please wire me, give me some inkling as to how you will receive this letter. If not I can't sleep. I won't be able to hear from you for a week, but I won't sleep till I do. Just say <u>Proceed</u> or <u>Impossible</u>. If <u>Impossible</u>, I will try to think of something else, but as I see it, Hartford is perfect. It will involve no personal loss. The $6000 is just a guarantee, for poor Balanchine, who is responsible for Toumanova and Jasinsky: he has been tricked so often.

We have the future in our hands. For Christ's sweet sake let us honor it.

Yours devotedly,
Lincoln

<u>Wire</u> me here

*   *   *

1933: SEPTEMBER 19
GEORGE "MACHINE GUN" KELLY TO CHARLES URSCHEL

From Al Capone to Baby Face Nelson, gangsters flourished during the Depression. Among the most notorious was George "Machine Gun" Kelly (1895–1954), a bootlegger, bank robber, and kidnapper. In July of 1933, Kelly kidnapped millionaire oilman Charles Urschel in Oklahoma City and took him to a Texas ranch owned by "Boss" Shannon and his son "Potatoes." Kelly demanded—and received—$200,000 in ransom. But when the FBI and police raided the Shannon ranch in August, Kelly fled—and sent this chilling message to his former hostage. Captured in Tennessee a week later, he would be sentenced to life in prison the following month.

Just a few lines to let you know that I am getting my plans made to destroy your so-called mansion, and you and your family immediately after this trial. And young fellow, I guess you've begun to realize your serious mistake. Are you ignorant enough to think the Government can guard you forever. I gave you credit for more sense than that, and figured you thought too much of your family to jeopardize them as you have, but if you don't look out for them, why should we. I dislike hurting the innocent, but I told you exactly what would happen and you can bet $200,000 more everything I said will be true. You are living on borrowed time now. You know that the Shannon family are victims of circumstances the same as you was. You don't seem to mind prosecuting the innocent, neither will I have conscious qualms over brutally murdering your family. The Shanons have put the heat on but I don't desire to see them prosecuted as they are innocent and I have a much better method of settling with them. As far as the guilty being punished you would probably have lived the rest of your life in peace had you tried only the guilty, but if the Shannons are convicted look out, and God help you for he is the only one that will be able to do you any good. In the event of my arrest I've already formed an outfit to take care of and destroy you and yours the same as if I was there. I am spending your money to have you and your family killed—nice—eh? You are bucking people who have cash—planes, bombs and unlimited connection both here and abroad. I have friends in Oklahoma City that know every move and every plan you make, and you are still too dumb to figure out the finger man there.

If my brain was no larger than yours, the Government would have had me long ago, as it is I am drinking good beer and will yet see you and your family like I should have left you at first—stone dead.

I don't worry about Bates and Bailey. They will be out for the ceremonies—your slaughter.

Now say—it is up to you: if the Shannons are convicted, you can get another rich wife in hell, because that will be the only place you can use one. Adios, smart one. Your worst enemy,

GEO. R. KELLY

I will put my fingerprints below so you can't say some crank wrote this.

1934: APRIL 10
CLYDE BARROW TO HENRY FORD

Along with Bonnie Parker (1911–1934), Clyde Barrow (1909–1934) was accused of committing twelve murders during a two-year crime spree chiefly in the American Southwest. Notorious even in their lifetimes, they were gunned down together six weeks after Clyde wrote this letter.

Tulsa Okla
10th April

Mr. Henry Ford
Detroit Mich.

Dear Sir:—
  While I still have got breath in my lungs I will tell you what a dandy car you make. I have drove Fords exclusively when I could get away with one. For sustained speed and freedom from trouble the Ford has got ever other car skinned, and even if my business hasn't been strickly legal it don't hurt enything to tell you what a fine car you got in the V8.

Yours truly
Clyde Champion Barrow

1934: JULY 24
SAMUEL COWLEY TO J. EDGAR HOOVER

John Dillinger (1902–1934) was the Federal Bureau of Investigation's original Public Enemy Number One, a distinction that apparently did little to deter him from his infamous crime spree. Beginning on May 10, 1933, when he was paroled after eight years in Indiana State Prison, Dillinger terrorized the Midwest, killing at least ten people, wounding almost as many others, robbing banks, and staging jail breaks. When he crossed the state line into Illinois in a stolen sheriff's car, he came under the jurisdiction of young FBI director J. Edgar Hoover (1895–1972). Hoover would make his name with the Dillinger case, despite the fact that it was fraught with embarrassing misses. Finally, on Saturday, July 21, the bureau received the crucial tip from a Gary, Indiana, madam who wanted to avoid deportation. The rest was reported to the director in this telegram.

SAC stands for Special Agent in Charge. Melvin Purvis was Cowley's Chicago partner.

DIV INVEST   CGO   7-24-34   1–10 AM
DIRECTOR

JODIL

About 5-30 PM Sunday Confidential informant telephoned that she would accompany Dillinger and girl friend to either Marbro or Biograph Theatre in Chicago about 8 PM Sunday. At 7-30 PM SAC Purvis and Agent Brown proceeded to a point near Biograph Theatre, 2433 Lincoln Avenue, while Sergeant Zarkovich, East Chicago Police Department, and Agent Winstead proceeded to Marbro Theatre. All agents remained in Chicago office awaiting telephone advice concerning which theatre Dillinger actually attended. At 8-50 PM Dillinger and two women companions were observed entering the Biograph Theatre and this information was telephoned to the Chicago office. Special agents C O Hurt and H E Hollis together with Officers Sopsic and Stretch were assigned to seize Dillinger as he was leaving the theatre. Agents J P McCarthy and R G Gillespie were to close in towards Dillinger from the north side. Agents J R Welles and A E Lockerman were to close in towards Dillinger from south side. Special agents E L Richmond,—C G Campbell, J J Metcalfe and Val C Zimmer were on opposite side of street. Agents T J Connor, M F Glynn and R C Suran covered the exits in the alley at the southeast corner of the Biograph Theatre, while agents J T Mclaughlin, W C Ryan, Woltz and D P Sullivan covered the emergency exits in the alley on the north side of the theatre. Agent Brown remained in a car parked on the same side of the street as the theatre, while SAC Purvis was stationed near the Biograph Theatre. Agent Winstead and Sergeant Martin Zarkovich were advised by telephone that Dillinger was at Biograph Theatre and they immediately proceeded to that place, Winstead taking a position with Agents Hurt and Hollis. Immediately upon receiving word that Dillinger was at the Biograph Theatre, I proceeded to the vicinity of the theatre accompanied by Timothy O'Neil and Sergeant Conroy, I was in a roving position and kept in touch with all agents in order to see that all points were being covered properly. About 10-30 PM, Dillinger accompanied by two women companions emerged from the theatre—walking south on Lincoln Avenue. SAC Purvis gave a signal and the agents began to close in. Dillinger became apprehensive and started to run—grabbing for his gun. Agent Winstead fired one shot which was immediately followed by one shot each by agents Winstead and Hurt—followed by another shot by Winstead. Dillinger was removed to the Alexian Brothers Hospital, arriving there at 10-55 PM where he was pronounced dead. He was later taken to the county morgue. Examination of Dillingers body disclosed two fresh wounds on his chest, one of which was just below his heart. A third fresh bullet wound appeared to have been caused by a bullet entering the rear of the skull and emerging from lower portion of the right eye above the cheek bone. In addition to clothes worn by him there were found 1 gold 17 jewel Hamilton watch works number 3444347 case number 0558384 money in bills and change amounting to $7.70, three keys, a loaded automatic .380 calibre pistol and one loaded automatic clip, and one red stoned ring.

Inquest held at Cook County Morgue by Coroner Frank J Walsh at 11-30 AM July 23 and pronounced justifiable homocide jury took occasion to commend the work of the division. The coroner criticized the precinct no. 37 of the Chicago Police Department in which Dillenger was killed for not having a representative present. Agent Richmond testified as to fingerprint identification and I testified as to general facts. Theresa Paulus, 2920 Commonwealth Avenue received a slight flesh wound in hip and was taken to the Grant Hospital where she remained seven hours hospital bill is $3.00. Mrs Eta Natalsky, 2429 Lincoln Avenue was shot in leg between knee and thigh and is now in the Columbus Hospital injury not serious.

END   COWLEY

1934: JULY 31

AN UNEMPLOYED WORKER TO FRANKLIN ROOSEVELT

As the Depression deepened, desperate Americans wrote to the president for help.

7/31/34

West Point Ga

East 7th St

Dear Mr President I dont no Just How to rite to you But I want to ask Your Help   I am a old Citizen of West Point and I am about 75 or 6 years old and

Have Labored Hard all My days until depression Came on and I Had No Job in three years and I Have a Little Home I Bought when times was good and I managed to Pay my state and County tax But they Claim I owe about 15 fifteen dol City tax and going to sell my Little Home for that and will you Please sir Help me out the government Can Have a Lean on the Little House until I Get some way to Pay Back Please Sir do what you Can for me I am to old to be turned out of doors   I tried to get a Job on the CWA But they wanted younger men   Ive Never gave the City any troube Have always stood in fear of god and ben Law abiding and Ben a Hard Worker all my days and Is able and Can work   Now if I get any thing to do   its Just about a quarter of an ace and a 2 room House and it Need Fixing Bad aint No account Much But I toil so Hard to get it I dont want to Loose it so Please Sir Help me I am and old Colored Man and seems like they Just want to take my Place I aint got Nothing and Cant get Nothing if ever a Poor Person Need Help I do   Please Sir Let Me Hear from you at once I Havent got but a few days to get the Money up   they Supose to sell it some time in Aug I dont No the excat day

Yours and oblige your
Humble Servent
D. A.
West Point Ga

1934: AUGUST 29
GEORGE DRAPER TO FRANKLIN ROOSEVELT

George Draper (1880–1959) had been FDR's doctor during his crippling bout with polio and had been a friend since their years together at Harvard. Still, he was typical of the country's wealthy conservatives in believing that Roosevelt had gone too far in putting forth his New Deal programs.

33 East 68th St.
N.Y. City
Aug. 29.'34.

Dear Franklin:—

There is a giant lying supine across the Continent. He is paralysed in arms & legs—a victim of infantile paralysis. He is in the hands of a most earnest & conscientious doctor. But the doctor is over-treating him.

My experience with the disease has convinced me that more cases with potential recovery possibilities are ruined by too vigorous treatment of the weakened muscles than are helped by it.

I recall one case, known also to you, who was protected by pain from too early & too vigorous treatment.

Would not the giant, stretched supine across the country, react more quickly & completely if the current prescription of massage & specialized exercises were interrupted for a period.

Nature works in mysterious ways to heal wounds. The ideas of man often interfere with natural processes.

Good luck
Sincerely
George W. Draper

1934: SEPTEMBER 6
FRANKLIN ROOSEVELT TO GEORGE DRAPER

President Roosevelt was still in only the second of his twelve years in office when he offered Draper this response, characteristic in its humor as well as its firmness.

Hyde Park, N.Y.
September 6, 1934.

Dear George:—

I like your supine giant and I should like to stop the treatment were it not for the fact that sixteen million little cells out of the one hundred and twenty million cells in his body would lose their circulation, starve and die, if we were to stop the very gentle massage which keeps some blood running into these sixteen million little cells. That is the only treatment being given at the present time. Also, in cases like this medical history proves that if treatment is suddenly stopped the giant is very apt to leap from his bed and either commit suicide or die of an epileptic fit.

Enough said!

Hope to see you soon.

As ever yours,
[FDR]

Dr. George W. Draper,
33 East 68th Street,
New York, N.Y.

1934: OCTOBER 26
WALTER WHITE TO DAVID SHOLTZ

Claude Neal, a young black worker, was arrested in Marianna, Florida, on October 19 and charged with murdering a white woman named Lola Cannidy. During the next week, as local reaction intensified, Neal was moved from prison to prison, but a week later a mob found him in Brewton, Alabama, and took him back to Florida, where newspapers and radio had actually advertised his lynching. Walter White, head of the NAACP, sent this telegram to the governor of Florida in an attempt to prevent the violence. But on Saturday, October 26, more than two thousand people gathered for the gruesome event. In a bacchanalian atmosphere, Neal was stabbed, tortured, castrated, shot, and finally hanged, another of the thousands of people, mostly black, who had died by lynching in America since the 1880s. His case became a rallying point against a practice that was already on the wane.

Received at
JNB418 125 5 EXTRA=NEWYORK NY 26 522P
HON DAVID SHOLTZ, GOVERNOR=
TALLAHASSEE FLO=

ASSOCIATED PRESS JUST INFORMED US THAT JOHN P HARRELL SHERIFF OF WASHINGTON COUNTY HAS ANNOUNCED THAT TONIGHT BETWEEN EIGHT AND NINE OCLOCK A MOB WILL TAKE CLAUDE NEALE CHARGED WITH MURDER TIE HIM TO STAKE NEAR GREENWOOD AND PERMIT FATHER OF DEAD GIRL TO LIGHT FIRE TO BURN NEALE TO DEATH STOP EVERY DECENT PERSON NORTH AND SOUTH LOOKS TO YOU TO TAKE EVERY POSSIBLE STEP TO AVOID THIS DISGRACE UPON THE STATE OF FLORIDA STOP DOTHAN ALABAMA EAGLE ALSO ANNOUNCES THAT NEGRO IS BEING HELD BY MOB FOUR MILES FROM SCENE WHERE HE IS TO BE BURNED AT STAKE STOP WE URGE UPON YOU TO TAKE IMMEDIATE STEPS TO RESCUE NEGRO FROM MOB AND PLACE HIM IN SAFE CUSTODY=
WALTER WHITE   SECRETARY NATIONAL ASSOCIATION FOR THE ADVANCEMENT OF COLORED PEOPLE   SIXTY NINE FIFTH AVENUE.

*   *   *

1934: OCTOBER 27
E. J. HUMPHRIES TO JEANNIE CORNELL

Not everyone was disgusted by the Neal lynching. Some were appalled by those who were appalled. E. J. Humphries, a White Supremacist, lived in Florida.
Jeannie Cornell was chairman of the Florida chapter of the Association of Southern Women for the Prevention of Lynching.

In this morning's paper I read of your sending a telegram to call out the troops in defense of Neal, the negro brute that assaulted and mutilated the body of a white girl. How could you a white woman ask such a request? Suppose it was a female of your family met with such a fate, would you wait for troops? Oh, no, you would cry out for vengeance. I pray the Southern men will always stand shoulder to shoulder for White Supremacy, and clear the earth of such reptiles as Neal and his kind, by rope, fire or anything at hand. You let the negroes think that they are somebody, and you will have a job on your hands hard to get rid of. I cannot comprehend a Southern woman (if you are one) coming out in defense of a low down nigger. Wake up. . . . Stand firmly for White Supremacy, right or wrong, White Supremacy. I wish I was eloquent enough to express myself more forcibly.

1935: JANUARY 2
AN EXPECTANT MOTHER TO ELEANOR ROOSEVELT

Despite the abundance of legislation passed at the beginning of the New Deal, it would be another five years before war production put an end to the Depression. In the meantime, a struggling housewife in Troy, New York, needed clothes for her new baby and turned to the president's wife. Eleanor Roosevelt (see letter page 251) was renowned for her compassionate support of the underprivileged and would remain a powerful influence on the president's policies.
The outcome of Mrs. H.E.C.'s request is unknown.

Troy, N.Y.
Jan. 2, 1935

Dear Mrs. Roosevelt,

About a month ago I wrote you asking if you would buy some baby clothes for me with the understanding that I was to repay you as soon as my husband got enough work. Several weeks later I received a reply to apply to a Welfare Association so I might receive the aid I needed. Do you remember?

<u>Please</u> Mrs. Roosevelt, I do not want charity, only a chance from someone who will trust me until we can get enough money to repay the amount spent for the things I need. As a proof that I really am sincere, I am sending you two of my dearest possessions to keep as security, a ring my husband gave me before we were married, and a ring my mother used to wear. Perhaps the actual value of them is not high, but they are worth a lot to me. If you will consider buying the baby clothes, please keep them (rings) until I send you the money you spent. It is very hard to face bearing a baby we cannot afford to have, and the fact that it is due to arrive soon, and still there is no money for the hospital or clothing, does not make it any easier. I Have decided to stay home, keeping my 7 year old daughter from school to help with the smaller children when my husband has work. The oldest little girl is sick now, and has never been strong, so I would not depend on her. The 7 year old one is a good willing little worker and somehow we must manage—but without charity.

If you still feel you cannot trust me, it is allright and I can only say I donot blame you, but if you decide my word is worth anything with so small a security, here is a list of what I will need—but I will need it very soon.

2 shirts, silk and wool. size 2

3 pr. stockings, silk and wool, 4½ or 4

3 straight flannel bands

2 slips—outing flannel

2 muslim dresses

1 sweater

1 wool bonnet

2 pr. wool booties

2 doz. diapers 30 × 30—or 27 × 27

1 large blanket (baby) about 45" or 50"

3 outing flannel nightgaowns

If you will get these for me I would rather no one knew about it. I promise to repay the cost of the layette as soon as possible. We will all be very grateful to you, and I will be more than happy.

Sincerely yours,

Mrs. H.E.C.

*　　*　　*

1935: MARCH 13

WILLIAM CARLOS WILLIAMS TO HIS SON

The poet William Carlos Williams (1883–1963) had not yet written his most famous work, the epic poem Paterson, *when he sent this letter to his elder son, then a college senior. "No ideas but in things" would be the poet's famous declaration in that work: a judicious credo befitting the hands-on doctor Williams remained, the ordinary language he espoused—and the down-to-earth advice he dispensed.*

March 13, 1935

Dearest Bill:

This I can say for certain, you seem not far different from what I was myself at your age. I don't mind saying I went through hell, what with worrying about my immortal soul and my hellish itch to screw almost any female I could get my hands on—which I never did. I can tell you it is almost as vivid today as it was then when I hear you speak of it. Everything seems upside down and one's self the very muck under one's foot.

It comes from many things, my dear boy, but mostly from the inevitable maladjustment consequent upon growing up in a more or less civilized environment. Any bum on the street, any crook who is his own master at the expense of the law is happier than the man who is trying to mould himself to a society which revolts his entire manhood. We do not want to fit into anything, we want to be free, potent, self-reliant—and that society cannot and will not permit. Nor would we be really satisfied if we found ourselves antisocial in our success. That is the situation of the great fortunes, the Morgans, the Vanderbilts, as well as the Al Capones of the world. They are "free" but at a terrific cost.

But more immediately, your difficulties arise from a lack of balance in your daily life, a lack of balance which has to be understood and withstood—for it cannot be avoided for the present. I refer to the fact that your intellectual life, for the moment, has eclipsed the physical life, the animal life, the normal he-man life, which every man needs and craves. If you were an athlete, a powerful body, one who could be a hero on the field or the diamond, a <u>Big</u> Hero, many of your mental tortures would be lulled to sleep. But you cannot be that—so what? You'll have to wait and take it by a different course.

And after all, the athletes haven't it as easy as it seems. They may be soothed during the difficult years but they've got to face the music some day, and that some day may be too late. They can't always be physical figures, and when the real test comes later, they often fold up and disappear completely.

You, dear Bill, have a magnificent opportunity to enjoy life ahead of you. You have sensibility (even if it drives you nuts at times), which will be the source of keen pleasures later and the source of useful accomplishments too. You've got a brain, as you have been told <u>ad nauseam</u>. But these are the very things which are tormenting you, the very things which are your most valued possessions and which will be your joy tomorrow. Sure you are sentimental, sure you admire a man like Wordsworth and his "Tintern Abbey." It is natural, it is the correct re-action of your age in life. It is also a criticism of Wordsworth as you will see later. All I can say about that is, wait! Not wait cynically, idly, but wait while looking, believing, getting fooled, changing from day to day. Wait with the only kind of faith I have ever recognized, the faith that says I wanna know! I wanna see! I think I will understand when I do know and see. Meanwhile I'm not making any final judgments. Wait it out. Don't worry too much. You've got time. You're all right. You're reacting to life in the only way an intelligent, sensitive young man in a college can. In another year you'll enter another sphere of existence, the practical one. The knowledge, abstract now, which seems unrelated to sense to you (at times) will get a different color.

Sooner or later we all of us knock our heads against the ceiling of the world. It's like breaking a record: the last fifth of a second, which marks the difference between a good runner and a world beater is the hardest part of the whole pro-ceeding. I mean that you, Bill, will be one of the minds of the world tomorrow. You will be the one, you and your generation, who will have to push knowledge of all sorts that inch ahead, which will make life tolerable in your day. Knowl-edge is limited, very limited, and it is only because you are in the preliminary stages of knowing that you think men, certain men, know so much more than you do. They may know a little more, but not the great amount that you imag-ine. For this reason, wait! Believe in yourself and your generation. Take it with a smile. That's what they mean when they speak of humor. It doesn't mean a guf-faw or a grin. It means steadiness of nerves that is willing to bide its time, cer-tain that with time a human adjustment can and will be made. It is the most that any man has ever been able to do.

Jumping to practical things: Have the Ford put in condition up there if you think the local mechanics can be trusted. Send me the bill. . . .

Mother and I both send love. Don't let <u>anything</u> get your goat and don't think you have to duck anything in life. There is a way out for every man who has the intellectual fortitude to go on in the face of difficulties.

Yours,
Dad

1935: MARCH 29

A BROOKLYN WORKER TO FRANCES PERKINS

At its worst, the Depression is estimated to have put nearly a quarter of all Americans out of work; in 1932, thirty-four million Americans had no income. But those who did work suffered as well, slogging for longer hours and for lower pay than usual, often in dreadful conditions, with the threat of unemployment ever present.

Frances Perkins (1882–1965) was Roosevelt's secretary of labor and the first female Cabinet member.

Brooklyn, New York,
March 29, 1935

Dear Miss Perkins:

Reading about you as I do I have come to the understanding, that you are a fair and impartial observer of labor conditions in the United States. Well, I'll have to get a load off my chest, and tell you of the labor conditions in a place which is laughingly called a factory. We work in a Woolstock Concern. We handle discarded rags. We work, ten hours a day for six days. In the grime and dirt of a nation. We go home tired and sick—dirty—disgusted—with the world in general, work—work all day, low pay—average wage sixteen dollars. Tired in the train going home, sitting at the dinner table, too tired to even wash ourselves, what for—to keep body and souls together not to depend on charity. What of N.R.A.? What of everything—? We handle diseased rags all day. Tuberculosis roaming loose, unsanitary conditions—, slaves—slaves of the depression! I'm even tired as I write this letter—, a letter of hope—. What am I? I am young— I am twenty, a high school education—no recreation—no fun—. Pardon ma'am—but I want to live—! Do you deny me that right—? As an American citizen I ask you—, what—what must we do? Please investigate this matter. I sleep now, yes ma'am with a prayer on my lips, hoping against hope—, that you will better our conditions. I'll sign my name, but if my boss finds out—, well—Give us a new deal, Miss Perkins. The address of the concern is Simons Wool Stock, 20 Broadway, Brooklyn, N.Y.

Yours hoping,
J. G.

*   *   *

1935: JUNE 30
CAROLINE HENDERSON TO A FRIEND

In 1931, the first dust storms swept through the southern plains states, coating the landscape with millions of tons of dirt. For four years, there was no significant rainfall. Farmers like Caroline Henderson, who with her husband had worked the land for twenty-seven years, were forced to make the impossible choice between staying and leaving. She described her plight in a letter to a friend in Maryland.

Eva, Oklahoma
June 30, 1935

My dear Evelyn:—

Your continued interest in our effort to "tie a knot in the end of the rope and hang on" is most stimulating. Our recent transition from rain-soaked eastern Kansas with its green pastures, luxuriant foliage, abundance of flowers, and promise of a generous harvest, to the dust-covered desolation of No Man's Land was a difficult change to crowd into one short day's travel. Eleanor has laid aside the medical books for a time. Wearing our shade hats, with handkerchiefs tied over our faces and vaseline in our nostrils, we have been trying to rescue our home from the accumulations of wind-blown dust which penetrates wherever air can go. It is an almost hopeless task, for there is rarely a day when at some time the dust clouds do not roll over. "Visibility" approaches zero and everything is covered again with a silt-like deposit which may vary in depth from a film to actual ripples on the kitchen floor. I keep oiled cloths on the window sills and between the upper and lower sashes. They help just a little to retard or collect the dust. Some seal the windows with the gummed-paper strips used in wrapping parcels, but no method is fully effective. We buy what appears to be red cedar sawdust with oil added to use in sweeping our floors, and do our best to avoid inhaling the irritating dust.

In telling you of these conditions I realize that I expose myself to charges of disloyalty to this western region. A good Kansas friend suggests that we should imitate the Californian attitude toward earthquakes and keep to ourselves what we know about dust storms. Since the very limited rains of May in this section gave some slight ground for renewed hope, optimism has been the approved policy. Printed articles or statements by journalists, railroad officials, and secretaries of small-town Chambers of Commerce have heralded too enthusiastically the return of prosperity to the drouth region. And in our part of the country that is the one durable basis for any prosperity whatever. There is nothing else to build upon. But you wished to know the truth, so I am telling you the actual situation, though I freely admit that the facts are themselves often contradictory and confusing.

Early in May, with no more grass or even weeds on our 640 acres than on your kitchen floor, and even the scanty remnants of dried grasses from last year cut off and blown away, we decided, like most of our neighbors, to ship our cattle to grass in the central part of the state. We sent 27 head, retaining here the heifers coming fresh this spring. The shipping charge on our part of the carload was $46. Pasture costs us $7.00 for a cow and calf for the season and $5.00 for a yearling. Whether this venture brings profit or loss depends on whether the cattle make satisfactory gains during the summer and whether prices remain reasonable or fall back to the level that most people would desire. We farmers here in the United States might as well recognize that we are a minority group, and that the prevailing interest of the nation as a whole is no longer agricultural. Hay for the horses and the heifers remaining here cost us $23 per ton, brought by truck from eastern Oklahoma.

The day after we shipped the cattle the long drouth was temporarily broken by the first effective moisture in many months—about one and one-quarter inches in two or three gentle rains. All hope of a wheat crop had been abandoned by March or April.

Contrary to many published reports, a good many people had left this country either temporarily or permanently before any rains came. And they were not merely "drifters," as is frequently alleged. In May a friend in the southwestern county of Kansas voluntarily sent me a list of the people who had already left their immediate neighborhood or were packed up and ready to go. The list included 109 persons in 26 families, substantial people, most of whom had been in that locality over ten years, and some as long as forty years. In these families there had been two deaths from dust pneumonia. Others in the neighborhood were ill at that time. Fewer actual residents have left our neighborhood, but on a sixty-mile trip yesterday to procure tractor repairs we saw many pitiful reminders of broken hopes and apparently wasted effort. Little abandoned homes where people had drilled deep wells for the precious water, had set trees and vines, built reservoirs, and fenced in gardens,—with everything now walled in or half buried by banks of drifted soil,—told a painful story of loss and disappointment. I grieved especially over one lonely plum thicket buried to the tips of the twigs, and a garden with a fence closely built of boards for wind protection, now enclosing only a hillock of dust covered with the blue-flowered bull nettles which no winds or sands discourage.

It might give you some notion of our great "open spaces" if I tell you that on the sixty-mile trip, going by a state road over which our mail comes from the railroad, and coming back by a Federal highway, we encountered only one car, and no other vehicles of any sort. And this was on Saturday, the farmers' marketing day!

The coming of the long-desired rain gave impetus to the Federal projects for erosion control. Plans were quickly made, submitted to groups of farmers in district gatherings, and put into operation without delay.

The proposition was that, in order to encourage the immediate listing of abandoned wheat ground and other acreage so as to cut down wind erosion, the Federal Government would contribute ten cents per acre toward the expense of fuel and oil for tractors or feed for horses, if the farmers would agree to list not less than one fourth of the acreage on contour lines. Surveys were made promptly for all farmers signing contracts for either contour listing or terracing. The latest report states that within the few weeks since the programme was begun in our county 299,986 acres have been ploughed or listed on these contour lines—that is, according to the lay of the land instead of on straight lines with right-angled turns as has been the usual custom.

The plan has been proposed and carried through here as a matter of public policy for the welfare of all without reproach or humiliation to anyone. It should be remembered that 1935 is the fourth successive year of drouth and crop failure through a great part of the high plains region, and the hopelessly low prices for the crop of 1931 gave no chance to build up reserves for future needs. If the severe critics of all who in any way join in government plans for the saving of homes and the restoration of farms to a productive basis could only understand how vital a human problem is here considered, possibly their censures might be less bitter and scornful.

At any rate the contour listing has been done over extensive areas. If rains come to carry forward the feed crops now just struggling up in the furrows, the value of the work can be appraised. The primary intention of the plan for contour listing is to distribute rainfall evenly over the fields and prevent its running off to one end of the field or down the road to some creek or drainage basin. It is hoped that the plan will indirectly tend to lessen wind erosion by promoting the growth of feed crops, restoration of humus to denuded surfaces, and some protection through standing stubbles and the natural coverage of weeds and unavoidable wastes. One great contributing cause of the terrible dust storms of the last two years has been the pitiful bareness of the fields resulting from the long drouth.

I am not wise enough to forecast the result. We have had two most welcome rains in June—three quarters of an inch and one-half inch. Normally these should have been of the utmost benefit, though they by no means guarantee an abundant feed crop from our now sprouting seeds as many editorial writers have decreed, and they do nothing toward restoring subsoil moisture. Actually the helpful effects of the rains have been for us and for other people largely destroyed by the drifting soil from abandoned, unworked lands around us. It fills the air and our eyes and noses and throats, and, worst of all, our furrows, where tender shoots are coming to the surface only to be buried by the smothering silt from the fields of rugged individualists who persist in their right to do nothing.

A fairly promising piece of barley has been destroyed for us by the merciless drift from the same field whose sands have practically buried the little mulberry hedge which has long sheltered our buildings from the northwest winds. Large spaces in our pastures are entirely bare in spite of the rains. Most of the green color, where there is any grazing, is due to the pestilent Russian thistles rather than to grass. Our little locust grove which we cherished for so many years has become a small pile of fence posts. With trees and vines and flowers all around you, you can't imagine how I miss that little green shaded spot in the midst of the desert glare.

Naturally you will wonder why we stay where conditions are so extremely disheartening. Why not pick up and leave as so many others have done? It is a fair question, but a hard one to answer.

Recently I talked with a young university graduate of very superior attainments. He took the ground that in such a case sentiment could and should be disregarded. He may be right. Yet I cannot act or feel or think as if the experiences of our twenty-seven years of life together had never been. And they are all bound up with the little corner to which we have given our continued and united efforts. To leave voluntarily—to break all these closely knit ties for the sake of a possibly greater comfort elsewhere—seems like defaulting on our task. We may <u>have</u> to leave. We can't hold out indefinitely without some return from the land, some source of income, however small. But I think I can never go willingly or without pain that as yet seems unendurable.

There are also practical considerations that serve to hold us here, for the present. Our soil is excellent. We need only a little rain—less than in most places—to make it productive. No one who remembers the wheat crops of 1926, 1929, 1931, can possibly regard this as permanently submarginal land. The newer methods of farming suggest possibilities of better control of moisture in the future. Our entire equipment is adapted to the type of farming suitable for this country and would have to be replaced at great expense with the tools needed in some other locality. We have spent so much in trying to keep our land from blowing away that it looks foolish to walk off and leave it, when somewhat more favorable conditions seem now to "cast their shadows before." I scarcely need to tell you that there is no use in thinking of either renting or selling farm property here at present. It is just a place to stand on—if we can keep the taxes paid—and work and hope for a better day. We could realize nothing whatever from all our years of struggle with which to make a fresh start.

We long for the garden and little chickens, the trees and birds and wild flowers of the years gone by. Perhaps if we do our part these good things may return some day, for others if not for ourselves.

Will joins me in earnest hopes for your recovery. The dust has been particularly aggravating to his bronchial trouble, but he keeps working on. A great reddish-brown dust cloud is rising now from the southeast, so we must get out and do our night work before it arrives. Our thoughts go with you.

1935: SEPTEMBER 30
FRANKLIN ROOSEVELT TO MARGARET SUCKLEY

Shortly after Margaret Lynch "Daisy" Suckley died in 1991 at the age of ninety-nine, friends found a worn black suitcase under her bed. In the suitcase were letters to and from FDR, written during the last twelve years of his life and recording the development of their intimate friendship.

Dutchess refers to Dutchess County, New York, where FDR and Daisy, who were distant cousins, had both grown up.

Monday Eve, Sept. 30th

I wish so much my dear that you could have been at Boulder Dam today—Nothing I could say would give you a picture of the <u>immensity</u> of the whole canvas—A huge peak—bigger than a hundred other peaks near by—was clear at seventy-five miles. The colors marvelous—yet not a tree or grass in sight—Do you know the pictures of Gustave Doré illustrating Milton's <u>Paradise Lost</u>?—I love the desert and the rocks—but not to live among—still true to Dutchess!

Some day though you must see this country—It has been a successful trip—really happy crowds of people—even bigger than last year—and there is no doubt of the great great gains in prosperity. My difficulty is in having to keep on my "braces" from early morn till nearly midnight—because at every stop—even a water tower—a crowd surrounds the rear platform & I cannot disappoint them by refusing to go out and say "Howdy"—

This p.m. we took a glorious drive up a canyon on a new narrow road, which greatly alarmed the newspaper men but was really not dangerous.

Tomorrow a day in Los Angeles—a huge gathering in the Coliseum—110,000 people—and I am to appear, drive slowly around & say a few kind words—I can't make out if I am the lion in the Roman Arena or the Early Christian Martyr—I have a new sympathy for both.

I will add to this tomorrow in San Diego—but in the meantime there is no reason why I should not tell you that I miss you <u>very</u> much—It was a week ago yesterday—

Allowing for three hours' difference in time you are now very soundly asleep at 3 a.m. in Rhinebeck and I hope you are having very happy dreams. I look forward so to my letter on the ship—

<u>Tuesday midnight!</u> Safely here at Coronado Beach (San Diego) and <u>both</u> your letters are here & constitute the real news—It is a long long road to Panama.

1935: OCTOBER 1
MARGARET SUCKLEY TO FRANKLIN ROOSEVELT

In their letters, FDR and Daisy referred to each other as "a Certain Person," or C.P. for short.

Alexis Carrel, a French scientist, had written *Man, the Unknown*, which became a bestseller.
Anna Eleanor Roosevelt was FDR's oldest child.

. . . <u>Tuesday</u> Oct. 1st The papers have just come, telling about your trip up that mountain road—<u>please</u> don't do such things again! There's no point in being frightened after it's over—but I really feel that way—the idea of whoever was responsible getting you into a thing like that! It's awful—But perhaps the papers made the most of it—I hope so—Boulder Dam must be most inspiring—Someday I'm going to tour <u>all</u> the big dams & mountain tops: I loved your speech there—the whole tone of it—

<u>Oct. 1st Evening</u>—I'm still frightened about that mountain road! You'll really have to get some more responsible person to manage your trips! They shouldn't <u>allow</u> a Pres. of the U.S. to get into such a dangerous position! And at least they should have made you get out of the car when they turned! Now—if <u>I'd</u> been driving you—oh my—I fear I might have wanted to go up that road too!

—Let me see—(denotes deep thought!)—San Diego tomorrow—Speech at about 5 p.m. E.S.T.—Sails right afterward—A letter <u>may</u> have been mailed there during the day—<u>Should</u> get to the East <u>within</u> a week?!?

We go to 399 Park on Oct. 10th—

Shall I confess something? These trips of yours—in crowds—on trains—near precipices—<u>really</u> worry me—I'll be relieved when I know you are safely at sea—

Aren't we humans something like the pieces of a jig-saw puzzle? Each one touches others at small points, & they in turn touch each other at entirely different points. When we touch at several points we are friends. The tragedies are where no points seem to fit! Dr. Carrel claims <u>everyone</u> has a certain amount of telepathic power—our sixth sense—perhaps—It would account for Friendships that can live & flourish even when people see little of each other.

The picture in the paper of you & Anna at the Pawling games is perfect—"looking out" at one, as I like a photograph to do—It's you, at least as I see you—it's you—

Early this morning I had a <u>very</u> serious talk with a Certain Person.

I told her she must come to earth, attend to her job, and stop looking at the moon (there is a particularly silvery new one)— She took it <u>very</u> nicely—agreed with me <u>perfectly</u>—said I was <u>entirely</u> right—She will reform for at least for about two weeks <u>after</u> Oct 10th, and then for an indefinite period <u>after</u> Nov. 5th! I really <u>had</u> to speak to her rather severely, for she spends entirely too much time writing letters.

<u>Wednesday</u>—Oct. 2nd 5.45 p.m. Eastern Standard Time: You have <u>just</u> left the San Diego Stadium; <u>do</u> you realize how wonderful and inspiring your speech was—I wish I could tell you how I loved the spirit behind it. I sat in a western window watching a brilliant red sunset, & realizing that that same sun was high up over San Diego. I think you are the best example of "the good neighbor"—and of countless <u>other good</u> things— This must <u>really</u> end! This letter—

Au revoir & good luck,
D.

1935: NOVEMBER 1
HELEN KELLER TO ALEXANDER WOOLLCOTT

Illness had left Helen Keller (1880–1968) both blind and deaf before she was two years old. With the help of her remarkable teacher, Anne Sullivan, Keller nonetheless learned to read and write, graduating cum laude from Radcliffe College in

1904 and dedicating most of her life to helping the deaf and blind. The method she described to Alexander Woollcott (see letters pages 237 and 273)—of "hearing" a singer by feeling the vibrations of his voice—was one she first used with Sullivan in order to learn to speak.

John McCormack (1884–1945) and Enrico Caruso (1873–1921) were renowned operatic tenors.

7111 Seminole Avenue
Forest Hills, New York
November 1, 1935

Dear Alexander Woollcott,

Since we listened to you over the radio Sunday night, I have had it in mind to suggest to you the name of a song I am fond of which it would please me to have sung at one of your broadcasts. It is "My Wild Irish Rose"——the one John Mc-Cormack sings so beautifully.

Once we happened to be at the hotel where McCormack was staying. His publicity man arranged to have him sing "My Wild Irish Rose" for me. A number of the singer's friends and ours were gathered in the sitting-room for the performance. I was all expectation and excitement. My fingers were on his lips, but no sound came from them for several seconds. Then he cried, "I can't, I can't!" his tears wet my hand, and turning away he ran into his bedroom. I loved him for that tenderness which seemed to me the flower of the Irish heart.

How different Caruso was when we met under similar circumstances! To get to him I walked down the corridor through a double line of kneeling guests of the hotel listening while the great tenor practiced. When I entered his room, Caruso was being shaved. A pretty girl was manicuring his nails. A masseur with sleeves rolled up had just finished with him. "Ah! you have come," Caruso said, and seized my two hands and clapped them on his great chest, which was bare, and with almost terrifying intensity burst into Samson's lament over his blindness. I never dreamed that a human chest could expand as his did, nor that a throat could emit such a volume of sound. An hour or so later he appeared on the verandah as radiant as a day in June and, raising my hand to his lips, cried "Behold your Caruso!"

To come back to "My Wild Irish Rose," I love it because I remember my teacher as a wild Irish rose when she came to me. It is no hyperbole to say that when I touched that rose, happiness skipped to my side. The wild-rose tells a wondrous story in my life of growth and beauty. Its perfume is the fragrance of God's Goodness and of a Love that passeth knowledge.

I am glad you are coming out Monday. If my tongue was more nimble, I should say what I have just written to your attentive ear, but experience has taught me that when I particularly want to say anything, I'd better write it.

I'm sorry you didn't manage to come up to see us at Arkville this summer. It would have been pleasant to sit and chat among the hills and firs.

Until Monday good-bye.

Cordially yours,
Helen Keller

1935: NOVEMBER 5
BILLY GOBITAS TO THE MINERSVILLE
SCHOOL DISTRICT BOARD

Billy Gobitas (1925–1989) was ten years old when, along with his twelve-year-old sister Lillian, he refused to salute the flag at his Minersville, Pennsylvania, school. Raised as Jehovah's Witnesses, the children had been instructed that saluting and pledging allegiance to the flag—as required by their public school—were acts of idolatry. The day after this letter was written, the board voted to expel the two for insubordination. After years of legal cases, the Supreme Court would rule in 1943 that the government could not compel anyone to salute or pledge allegiance to the flag.

Minersville, Pa.
Nov. 5, 1935

Our School Directors

Dear Sirs

I do not salute the flag because I have promised to do the will of God. That means that I must not worship anything out of harmony with God's law. In the twentieth chapter of Exodus it is stated, "Thou shalt not make unto thee any graven image, nor bow down to them nor serve them for I the Lord thy God am a jealous God visiting the iniquity of the fathers upon the children unto the third and fourth generation of them that hate me. I am a true follower of Christ. I do not salute the flag not because I do not love my crountry, but I love my crountry and I love God more and I must obey His commandments.

Your Pupil,
Billy Gobitas

1935: NOVEMBER 22

ALEXANDER WOOLLCOTT TO PAUL HARPER

A member of the famously literary Algonquin Round Table, Alexander Woollcott (1887–1943) was a drama critic, sometime actor, and, in his later years, the host of a radio program called The Town Crier. *It was in this role that he took on Mussolini and Hitler, and when that proved potentially unpopular, a man who represented the ad agency that handled the show's sponsor.*

Sir John Buchan was a Scottish writer who was governor general of Canada and the author of *The Thirty-nine Steps*. Father Charles Coughlin was an American priest and right-wing activist.

New York City

November 22, 1935

My dear Harper:

This is an answer to your official letter of November 22nd in which you announce that:

"The Cream of Wheat Corporation is unwilling to continue the broadcasts after December 29th unless you will agree to refrain from including in your broadcasts material of a controversial nature which, in our opinion, would be offensive to individuals or groups in the radio audience."

This paragraph would be unintelligible to anyone who had not previously read your letter of November 14th in which you transmitted this message from Mr. Thomson and Mr. Clifford of the Cream of Wheat Corporation:

"They went on to say that they preferred that you didn't make any more caustic references to people like Hitler and Mussolini as there are large racial groups who are apt to be antagonized by these references."

Now, in these broadcasts the Town Crier has for several years been freely reporting his likes and dislikes on the books, plays, pictures, prejudices, manners and customs of the day. In undertaking such an oral column, he could not with self-respect agree in advance never to take pot shots at such targets as Hitler or Mussolini. Or, for that matter, at any other bully, lyncher or jingo whose head happened to come within shooting distance. If he did embark upon a series thus hamstrung in advance, his own interest in the broadcasts would so dwindle that they would deteriorate in short order.

I am entirely in sympathy with the viewpoint of Mr. Bull and his Cream of Wheat associates. If they think an occasional glancing blow antagonizes old customers or drives away new ones it would be folly for them to address their advertising to such an audience as I might assemble. It is my own guess that the allusions complained of have no such effect. It would seem to me as reasonable to expect every crack at Hitler to send all the Jews in America rushing to the grocery stores to stack up with Cream of Wheat. It would be as reasonable to assume that the Buchan broadcast (which Mr. Bull so highly approved) with its hands-across-the-sea, England-and-America shoulder-to-shoulder theme, alienated from Cream of Wheat every Irish listener and all those whom Mr. Hearst and Father Coughlin have industriously filled with a distrust of the English. It would be as reasonable to fear that the November 10th broadcast, which you yourself loudly applauded, may have so infuriated the Scotch that they all reverted to oatmeal in a body. I have said enough to make clear what a blank check I would be signing if I recklessly promised to omit all controversial material. Before each broadcast, you see, there would be so much honest disagreement as to what material was controversial. The irony of this impasse lies in my own suspicion that it is these very elements which most promote interest in the series. The only reason I don't indulge in them oftener is because I believe they are more effective when infrequently used. They lend the series salt, provoke discussion, whip up attendance and enlarge the audience. The sponsor is therefore most worried by the broadcast which serves him best. At least, that is my guess, which may be as good as Mr. Bull's but need not be any better. And after all, it is his business and not mine.

I have overheard enough of the experiences of other broadcasters to suspect that it would be difficult to find anywhere among the big national advertisers a sponsor who would be as considerate, liberal and agreeable as the Cream of Wheat people have been throughout all our dealings. This would seem to indicate that the Town Crier is unlikely to find any other sponsor willing to meet the terms he must insist on so long as he uses the now established formula which inevitably represents him as one citizen leaning over the fence and talking freely to his neighbors. And since all the good time on the great networks has been pre-empted by advertisers, that in turn would mean I must drop out of national broadcasting altogether, which, as you know, would be a solution entirely acceptable to me. I would merely be driven back to the comparative privacy of the printed page where, in my own opinion, I belong and where, at long last, I might get some writing done.

Yours sincerely,

Alexander Woollcott

P.S. By the way, in your final paragraph you say that I have "declined to accept any restrictions made by the sponsor" in my choice of material. When you wrote that sentence you must have been either absent-minded or disingenuous. I told you yesterday that I had no objection whatever to letting your representative cut out of my script any joke, anecdote or phrase which, in his opinion, was either coarse or suggestive. If you still do not recall this promise, Brown may be able to refresh your memory.

One other point. You yourself asked why I should ever need to introduce controversial matter into a broadcast since I could so easily let off steam in the various publications to which I can always contribute. Unfortunately, this suggestion is impractical. I find the weekly preparation of the next broadcast and the consequences of the preceding one so time-consuming that when I am broadcasting I am unable to do any other kind of work. I haven't even time left to write a post card to the folks.

A. W.

1936
DOROTHY PARKER TO GERALD MURPHY

Dorothy Parker (1893–1967) contributed her stories and reviews to Vanity Fair, Esquire, *and most notably,* The New Yorker. *Along with her friend Alexander Woollcott (see preceding letter), she became a regular of the Algonquin Round Table, providing a deeply sardonic presence and frequently quotable quips. She first went to Hollywood in 1933, where she received credits on more than fifteen screenplays, including* A Star Is Born.

The exact date of this letter is unknown. The painter Gerald Murphy and his wife, Sara, were friends to Parker and many other writers of the period.

SELZNICK INTERNATIONAL PICTURES, INC.

9336 WASHINGTON BOULEVARD

CULVER CITY, CAL.

Dear Gerald,

So last week, the board of directors of Selznick Pictures, inc., had a conference. The four members of the board sat round a costly table in an enormously furnished room, and each was supplied with a pad of scratch paper and a pencil. After the conference was over, a healthily curious young employee of the company went in to look at those scratch pads.

He found:

Mr. David Selznick had drawn a seven-pointed star; below that, a six-pointed star; and below that again, a row of short vertical lines, like a little picket fence.

Mr. John Hay Whitney's pad had nothing whatever on it.

Dr. A. H. Giannini, the noted California banker, had written over and over, in a long, neat column, the word "tokas," which is Yiddish for "arse".

And Mr. Meryan Cooper, the American authority on technicolor, had printed, in the middle of his page, "RIN-TIN-TIN".

The result of the conference was the announcement that hereafter the company would produce twelve pictures a year, instead of six.

I don't know. I just thought you might like to be reassured that Hollywood does not change.

With love and nostalgia,
Dorothy

1936: JUNE 1

MARGARET MITCHELL TO JOSEPH HENRY JACKSON

Margaret Mitchell (1900–1949) published Gone With the Wind *in June of 1936. The book was an instant sensation, and by April of 1937 would earn its author the Pulitzer prize and more than half a million dollars in royalties. Mitchell had never written a book before and would never write another. On the first of June, responding to a* San Francisco Chronicle *critic who had seen an early copy, Mitchell went to great lengths to thank him personally, little knowing how many other glowing reviews she would soon receive.*

Atlanta, Georgia
June 1, 1936

Mr. Joseph Henry Jackson
San Francisco Chronicle
San Francisco, California

My dear Mr. Jackson:

I am Margaret Mitchell, author of the book "Gone With the Wind," of which you wrote so kindly in the "Chronicle" on May 13 and 14. It is my first book and I am so new and green at the business of authoring that I do not even know if it is good form for an author to write to a critic. But your columns gave me so much pleasure and happiness that I have to write you and say thank you.

I suppose you would call my reactions "pleasure and happiness" even if I did have to go to bed with a cold pack on my head and an aspirin after I read your words. God knows I'm not like my characters, given to vapors and swooning and "states," but I was certainly in a "state." I have always been able to bear up nobly under bad news but your good news floored me. I suppose it was because it was so unexpected.

I wrote the book nearly ten years ago, beginning it some time between 1925 and 1926 and laying it aside, minus a few chapters, sometime around 1927 or 1928. It seemed, to be quite frank, pretty lousy and I never even submitted it to any agent or publisher. In fact, I had about forgotten it when Mr. Latham of the Macmillan Company came here on a visit and exhumed it and bought it. Since then, I've been in a twitter ducking at every sound and expecting brickbats—and prepared for brickbats. So when I read what you had to say—and you were the first critic who had written anything about it—I was overcome. Like the old lady in the nursery rhyme I feel like, "Lawk and a mercy on me! This is none of I!"

I was very interested in what you wrote in the Chronicle of May 14 (New York date line May 10) about the new novelists turning their attention to "destruction and rebirth" and the "upheavals." I was interested because, as I stated above, I wrote this book when the Great American Boom was at its height and the high tide of the Jazz Age was with us. Everyone I knew had a car, a radio, an electric ice box and a baby that they were buying on time (everybody except me!). Everyone had money, or thought they had, and everyone thought that life was going to continue just as it was. Heaven knows I didn't foresee the Depression and try to write a novel paralleling it, in another day. I was writing about an upheaval I'd heard about when I was a small child. For I spent the Sunday afternoons of my childhood sitting on the bony knees of Confederate Veterans and the fat slick laps of old ladies who survived the war and reconstruction. And I heard them talk about friends who came through it all and friends who went under. They were a pretty outspoken, forthright, tough bunch of old timers and the things they said stuck in my mind much longer than the things the people of my parents' generation told me.

And all during my childhood I'd been told to be prepared for the next time the world turned over. My family live to incredible ages and have incredible memories and I was brought up on stories of the hard times after the Revolution and what happened to kinfolks after the Seminole Wars and who went under in the panic during Andy Jackson's regime and what happened to people after 1865 and how bad things were in the panics of 1873 and 1893 and 1907. So I suppose that explains why I wrote a book about hard times when the country was enjoying its biggest boom.

I do thank you, too, for your kind remarks about my style—if you could call it a "style." I haven't any literary style and I know it but have never been able to do anything about it. I am very conscious of my lack in this particular and I was expecting more brickbats about it than any other thing. I wish I could tell you how very happy you have made me! Just saying thank you seems so inadequate!

1936: JULY 6
MARION DICKENS TO THE FEDERAL WRITERS' PROJECT

One assignment of the New Deal's Works Progress Administration was the compilation of state guidebooks by the Federal Writers' Project. In Arkansas, hundreds of questionnaires were sent to local communities in an attempt to find out what sort of conveniences were available for black travelers. It was with neither apology nor evident dismay that the president of one Arkansas chamber of commerce answered a WPA researcher's questions.

Newport, Arkansas, July 6, 1936

Dear Madam:—

In regard to your letter of June 26th, 1936, please pardon the delay. Will try and give you the information you request. I do not think that there is any section in the state of Arkansas that the negro would be discriminated against as long as he knows his place and most of our southern negroes do. However, the negroes from the north and east are not familiar with the conditions and laws in the south especially, in Arkansas, and would possibly have a right to feel that they are being discriminated against. For reason they are not allowed certain privileges of the white people. Namely, eating at the same table, rooms at the same hotel, riding in the same sections on trains. Divisions are made of the passengers in buses, trolley cars and other conveyances. These are laws our state enforces very rigidly.

However, I assure you that in the negro tourist traffic through Arkansas he must resort to negro tourist camps or colored quarters. I am sure you will find the same conditions in all southern states.

There is no feeling against the colored race as far as his being a tourist is concerned. He has the same road protection that any other person would have.

Hoping this is the information you desire.

Yours very truly,
Marion Dickens,
President, Chamber of
Commerce

*   *   *

1936: AUGUST 30

FRANK LLOYD WRIGHT TO EDGAR KAUFMANN

Frank Lloyd Wright (1867–1959) was already in his sixties when he designed Fallingwater, possibly the most famous private home in the world, for Edgar Kaufmann. A local Pennsylvania builder was hired to construct it, but the first stone walls had to be rebuilt, and a worried Kaufmann tried to have his own engineers check Wright's computations for the reinforced slabs. The letter below was the result of Kaufmann's attempt to second-guess the famously confident architect. But by the end of the twentieth century, Fallingwater—specifically its concrete slabs— would indeed be in need of restoration.

After Dankmar Adler's death in 1900, Louis Sullivan continued with their firm of Adler and Sullivan, remaining among the most influential architects of his time. His famous tenet that "form follows function" was a profound influence on Wright, his most illustrious student.

August 30, 1936
Mr. E. J. Kaufmann
Kaufmann's Department Stores
Pittsburgh, Pennsylvania

If your engineer was consistent in his checkup of our details he would have had to reject not only the reinforcement in the beams he questioned but throughout the building from start to finish—not only steel but concrete as well.

For this reason—

I have learned from experience with the earthquake proof Imperial Hotel and other buildings that the fibre stress in steel is safe at 25 to 30,000 lbs and that the compression on concrete of 1500 is entirely safe.

We have had those stresses in order to save you waste because we are not operating under contract conditions to meet the hazards of which the assumptions of your engineer were made. So why waste money to actually weaken structure by excess weight.

Also it had never been the practice of Adler and Sullivan with whom I served an apprenticeship of seven years (nor my own practice since—the earthquake-proof Imperial Hotel included) to assume a live load on reinforced concrete constructions in dwellings.

By these assumptions we have not only saved you more than two thousand five hundred dollars but given you a stronger building.

Now if you had been above board in your dealing with your architect you might have saved your own engineer from demonstrating his incompetence and saved your money as well. Incompetence because by applying the standards set for him he put his finger upon only two spots in the structure where the sheer waste of standardized ignorance should be applied whereas he should have condemned the whole structure if he was consistent and reliable.

In interfering as you have you have set up a condition where we have no recourse but to accept an accusation that we do not know how to build our building without your help—and deliberately given current gossip a good break against us. Why? I thought I had found a man and a client.

But is this your usual method in dealing with men?

If so I will make a prophecy—in ten years time no one will work for you for either love or money.

I have worked for much of one in your case and a little of the other. So damned little of the other (money) that it hardly matters in the consideration of the whole. And for this you hand me this betrayal to solve your own fear—if you were afraid why didn't you say so?

In short Mr. E. J. Kaufmann (client No. 199) these assumptions of your engineer, to wit: 750 lbs for concrete—plus a 40 live load—20,000 for steel would double the cost of your construction because not only is there double the cost of your structure but the increase to carry the increase in weight would be considerably more.

Now maybe these pearls of wisdom gained by experience have been cast before swine, and not only do the swine refuse to eat the pearls but turn and rend us.

What do you think?

Does any client really know when he is well off?

Frank Lloyd Wright, Architect

1937: MAY 6

P. E. FOXWORTH TO J. EDGAR HOOVER

Radio broadcaster Herbert Morrison was on hand at the U.S. naval base in Lakehurst, New Jersey, to do a field recording for a broadcast about the routine landing of the German zeppelin Hindenburg. As it burst into flames, Morrison lost control, uttered the famous cry "Oh the humanity!," went off the air, vomited, and then returned to declare: "There is not a possible chance for anyone to be saved!" Despite that dire assertion, sixty-one of the ninety-seven passengers survived. Most of the

others died within seconds. The disaster—which was probably the result of atmo-
spheric electricity and a hydrogen leak—was initially thought to have been the
work of anti-Nazi sympathizers. This memo from an FBI agent to the director, apart
from being a reminder of how slowly news still traveled in 1937, was in keeping
with the bureau's ultimate conclusion: no sabotage was involved.

FEDERAL BUREAU OF INVESTIGATION

UNITED STATES DEPARTMENT OF JUSTICE

WASHINGTON, D.C.

May 6, 1937

Time—

MEMORANDUM FOR THE DIRECTOR

SAC Devereaux of the Newark Division telephoned me and said that a flash
had just come over the wires to the effect that the Hindenburg had blown up in
midair just as it was about to land at Lakehurst, New Jersey. Mr. Devereaux said
that inasmuch as this is on a government reservation, he thought he had better
go down there and look the situation over.

I told Mr. Devereaux that he could go down there, but under no circumstances should he start any investigation without notifying the Bureau of the
facts involved so that a determination might be made as to whether the Bureau
is justified in making an investigation. I told Mr. Devereaux that after he gets
down there and looks the situation over, he should call us and advise us of the
situation.

Time—11:55 p.m.

Mr. Devereaux telephoned me from Lakehurst, and said that the Hindenburg started to circle the field for a landing at about 6:19 p.m., standard time.
After dropping the landing ropes at 6:25 p.m., the ship came in for a landing,
and when about 210 feet from the ground, fire broke out, due to an explosion
approximately 100 feet in front of the rear fin. The dirigible was demolished by
the fire. Of the 61 members of the crew and 36 passengers, 44 of the crew and
20 of the passengers are alive. Twenty-six unidentified bodies have been recovered, and seven bodies are still missing. The explosion was due to a hydrogen explosion. The American Zeppelin Transport operated the airship, which was in
command of Captains Lehmann and Pruss.

Secretary of Commerce Roper is en route and is due to arrive in about 15 minutes. Several high officials of the Navy are also coming there. There appears to be nothing the Bureau can do at the present time.

Mr. Devereaux wanted to know whether he and Mr. Connelley, who went down there with him, should get a list of the crew so that the information would be available for future reference. I told him that he should do nothing further on this matter at this time; that if we need the names of the crew, that information will undoubtedly be available from a number of sources later on. I told him that at this time, there is nothing to indicate that the Bureau has any investigative jurisdiction, and consequently, nothing should be done in the premises. Mr. Devereaux and Mr. Connelley are returning at once to Newark.

Respectfully,

P.E. Foxworth.

1937: OCTOBER 3
CAREY MCWILLIAMS TO LOUIS ADAMIC

The labor movement was gaining momentum in the 1930s when Carey McWilliams (1905–1980), a civil-liberties lawyer and journalist, spoke to a group of cannery workers in Los Angeles. He described the night to Louis Adamic (1899–1951), a novelist who had been born in Slovenia and wrote frequently about immigrant life.

October 3, 1937

A few nights ago I spoke to 1,500 women—women who work picking walnuts out of shells. It was one of the most amazing meetings I've ever attended. The remarks of the speakers were translated into five different languages. There were Russians, Armenians, Slavs, Mexicans, etc. All ages of women, from young girls to old women. A whole row of old Russian women who couldn't speak a word of English, dressed in their shawls and scarfs. The meeting was presided over by a young slip of a girl—president of the union—she was about 19. This was the first meeting these people had ever attended—that is, their first union meeting. You should have been there to <u>feel</u> the thing: the excitement, the tension. And you should have watched some of these women as they got up to their feet and tried to tell about their experiences. They had to struggle with themselves to get a word or words. But the profound meaning that they conveyed! I felt, honestly, very weak, meaningless, and ineffectual. They were kind and listened to what I had to say about the National Labor Relations Act. But they wanted to hear their own leaders—Mary and Vera, and the others. The employers recently took their hammers away from them—they were making "too much money." For the last two months, in their work, they have been cracking walnuts with their fists. Hundreds of them held up their fists to prove it—the lower portion of the fist being calloused, bruised, swollen. They told of the hatred they feel for their miserable stooges who spy upon them, speed up their work, nose into their affairs. They were really wonderful people. You had the feeling that here, unmistakably, was a section of the American people. And you felt stirred, profoundly stirred, by their wonderful good sense, the warmth and excitement in their faces, their kindliness, their sense of humor. Someone complained of working conditions, etc., the fact that the floors were not swept and that they were constantly falling on shells. One woman jumped up, tossed back her skirts, and laughingly exhibited a huge bruise well above the knee, and in the general vicinity of her ass. The others howled and poor Mary, the president, had to pound with her hammer to get them back into any kind of order. It was a warm evening, sticky hot. They packed the hall, stood on benches, crowded the doorways. I've never seen so many women at one time in my life! And such extraordinary faces—particularly the old women. Some of the girls had been too frequently to the beauty shop, and were too gotten up—rather amusingly dressy and so forth. But occasionally you would see a young girl, like the president of the union, simple, fresh, eager, smiling—very charming. It was a real meeting and I thought of you throughout the meeting, wishing you could be there.

1938: MARCH 7
JOHN STEINBECK TO ELIZABETH OTIS

As conditions in the Dust Bowl worsened, more farmers began moving west in search of work. John Steinbeck (1902–1968) would immortalize those migrants in his novel The Grapes of Wrath *(1939), for which he would win a Pulitzer prize and a National Book Award.*

Elizabeth Otis was Steinbeck's literary agent.

Los Gatos
March 7, 1938

Dear Elizabeth:

Dear Elizabeth:

I shouldn't have repeated that for the sake of the letter but it was true enough in intention and quite unconscious. I guess unconscious is very correct as an evaluation of my condition. Just got back from another week in the field. The floods have aggravated the starvation and sickness. I went down for Life this time. Fortune wanted me to do an article for them but I won't. I don't like the audience. Then Life sent me down with a photographer from its staff and we took a lot of pictures of the people. They guarantee not to use it if they change it and will send me the proofs. They paid my expenses and will put up money for the help of some of these people.

I'm sorry but I simply can't make money on these people. That applies to your query about an article for a national magazine. The suffering is too great for me to cash in on it. I hope this doesn't sound either quixotic or martyrish to you. A short trip into the fields where the water is a foot deep in the tents and the children are up on the beds and there is no food and no fire, and the county has taken off all the nurses because "the problem is so great that we can't do anything about it." So they do nothing. And we found a boy in jail for a felony because he stole two old radiators because his mother was starving to death and in stealing them he broke a little padlock on a shed. We'll either spring him or the district attorney will do the rest of his life explaining.

But you see what I mean. It is the most heartbreaking thing in the world. If Life does use the stuff there will be lots of pictures and swell ones. It will give you an idea of the kind of people they are and the kind of faces. I break myself every time I go out because the argument that one person's effort can't really do anything doesn't seem to apply when you come on a bunch of starving children and you have a little money. I can't rationalize it for myself anyway. So don't get me a job for a slick. I want to put a tag of shame on the greedy bastards who are responsible for this but I can best do it through newspapers.

I'm going to see the Secretary of Agriculture in a little while and try to find out for my own satisfaction anyway just how much of the government's attitude is political and how much humanitarian. Then I'll know what course to take.

I'm in a mess trying to catch up with things that have piled up in the week I was gone. And of course I was in the mud for three days and nights and I have a nice cold to beat, but I haven't time right now for a cold so I won't get a very bad one.

Sorry for the hectic quality of this letter. I am hectic and angry.

Thank you for everything.

> Bye,
> John

*   *   *

1938: JUNE 23

AN UNWED MOTHER TO DR. VALERIA PARKER

A physician, marriage counselor, and lecturer, Dr. Valeria Parker received this letter after writing an article about unwed mothers for a popular magazine.

Blairs, Va.
June 23, 1938.

Dear Dr. Parker:

Reading your letters in the Romantic Story, I am asking you to please help me. Its like this:

Last December I went to visit my Uncle in Richmond and I met a boy and fell in love with him and he said he loved me and showed it in many ways. Well, in January I was in a wreck with my Uncle and stayed in the hospital three weeks with a broken knee. I came home in April and found I was going to have a baby. I had to go back for trial and told him he promised to marry me. In fact he wanted to marry me before but his foster mother objected (he is an orphan). Well, Dr. Parker, I came home again. He promised to write but two weeks passed and I did not hear from him so I wrote begging him to do something. He never answered and so I forgot my pride and wrote again.

That has been two months ago and still I haven't head a word from him. I sent the letters to a boy I knew I could trust as I couldn't send them to him on account of his foster mother. Now I don't know what to do. It would kill my Daddy and brother to know what I've done, but I love him and it couldn't be so terribly wrong loving him as I did.

My Daddy worries over everything and has the heart trouble and I'd rather die than for him to know. I've even thought of ending it all but then the whole world would know. And I haven't any money to go away and my Daddy is a poor man and he paid all my hospital bills and I can't ask him for money, if he had it. I have thought of just disappearing and never be heard from again but the thought of what it would cause makes me want to die and I love my brother so much. He's the only brother I have. My Mother has been dead since I was small. I have one sister but Dr. Parker I can't bear to have them know.

My life has been lonely. My sister married young to get away from my step-mother. I am desperate; have no one to help me; no money. If I went away I'd have to go and write them that I had a job far away so they couldn't find and see my condition and it's been three months now and Dr. Parker I can't stay here much longer. The wreck was the other man's fault and Daddy is going to sue him and if they don't have the trial soon I'll have to be gone and stop that and I'm in such a terrible state I don't know what to do. I was hoping and praying they would have it before I'd have to go off so Daddy could get back what he paid out on me—all his hard earned money.

I have thought of just going as far as my lame knee would carry me, where I'm not known and just do oh I don't know what. Please understand if you can. I've heard of homes where girls like I am can go. I thought maybe you could tell me some place where I could work for my board until then and after maybe the Good Lord will help me. I want to keep my baby, if possible. Is there some place I could go?

Won't you help me please? I'll have to tell them I have a job and they won't want me to then but I'll have to slip away. Please, Dr. Parker, don't think I'm bad. I loved him and no man ever made me have the feeling I did. I'm 21 and he is just 18. Is that why he has forgotten me? He said he loved me and I believed him.

I am miserable because I am beginning to show some and I'm afraid to go any place. I just want to die but I know I'm not fit to now, so please Dr. Parker, if you can help me, won't you write and tell me which way to turn?

I am enclosing a self-addressed envelope and am anxiously waiting to hear from you and please don't print this letter.

Just a heart-broken girl

1938: AUGUST 12
THOMAS WOLFE TO MAXWELL PERKINS

At Scribner's, Maxwell Perkins (see letter page 184) had been editor, muse, and champion to Thomas Wolfe (1900–1938) during the writing of Look Homeward, Angel *and* Of Time and the River. *They had broken off with each other after these two books, and Harper's had published Wolfe thereafter. Just a month before his early death, after two operations for a brain infection brought on by pneumonia, Wolfe wrote Perkins this memorable letter, which would prove to be his last.*

Providence Hospital
Seattle, Washington
August 12, 1938

Dear Max:

I'm sneaking this against orders—but "I've got a hunch"—and I wanted to write these words to you.

I've made a long voyage and been to a strange country, and I've seen the dark man very close; and I don't think I was too much afraid of him, but so much of mortality still clings to me—I wanted most desperately to live and still do, and I thought about you all a 1000 times, and wanted to see you all again, and there was the impossible anguish and regret of all the work I had not done, of all the work I had to do—and I know now I'm just a grain of dust, and I feel as if a great window has been opened on life I did not know about before—and if I come through this, I hope to God I am a better man, and in some strange way I can't explain I know I am a deeper and a wiser one—If I get on my feet and out of here, it will be months before I head back, but if I get on my feet, I'll come back.

—Whatever happens—I had this "hunch" and wanted to write you and tell you, no matter what happens or has happened, I shall always think of you and feel about you the way it was that 4th of July day 3 yrs. ago when you met me at the boat, and we went out on the cafe on the river and had a drink and later went on top of the tall building and all the strangeness and the glory and the power of life and of the city was below—

Yours always,
Tom

1939: FEBRUARY 28
ELEANOR ROOSEVELT TO MRS. HENRY M. ROBERT, JR.

When the Daughters of the American Revolution barred the great black singer Marian Anderson (1897–1993) from performing at its Washington, D.C., Constitution Hall, First Lady Eleanor Roosevelt (1884–1962) fired off this letter to the DAR's president general. Less than two months later, on Easter Sunday, seventy-five thousand people would gather in front of the Lincoln Memorial to hear Anderson sing at a public recital organized by the federal government.

February 28, 1939

My dear Mrs. Henry M. Robert Jr.:

I am afraid that I have never been a very useful member of the Daughters of the American Revolution, so I know it will make very little difference to you whether I resign, or whether I continue to be a member of your organization.

However, I am in complete disagreement with the attitude taken in refusing Constitution Hall to a great artist. You have set an example which seems to me unfortunate, and I feel obliged to send in to you my resignation. You had an opportunity to lead in an enlightened way and it seems to me that your organization has failed.

I realize that many people will not agree with me, but feeling as I do this seems to me the only proper procedure to follow.

Very sincerely yours,

[Eleanor Roosevelt]

1939: AUGUST 2
ALBERT EINSTEIN TO FRANKLIN ROOSEVELT

Like many scientists in Germany, Albert Einstein (1879–1955) fled the Nazis to come to America. He accepted a teaching post at Princeton University in 1933 and remained there until his death. A realist though an ardent pacifist, the Nobel prize–winning author of the theory of relativity felt the need to write this letter of warning to the president.

Enrico Fermi and Leo Szilard, working at the University of Chicago, developed the first self-sustaining nuclear reactor.

Albert Einstein
Old Grove Rd.
Nassau Point
Peconic, Long Island
August 2nd, 1939

F. D. Roosevelt
President of the United States
White House
Washington, D.C.

Sir:

Some recent work by E. Fermi and L. Szilard, which has been communicated to me in manuscript, leads me to expect that the element uranium may be turned into a new and important source of energy in the immediate future. Certain aspects of the situation seem to call for watchfulness and, if necessary, quick action on the part of the administration. I believe, therefore, that it is my duty to bring to your attention the following facts and recommendations.

In the course of the last four months it has been made probable—through the work of Joliot in France as well as Fermi and Szilard in America—that it may become possible to set up nuclear chain reactions in a large mass of uranium, by which vast amounts of power and large quantities of new radium-like elements would be generated. Now it appears almost certain that this could be achieved in the immediate future.

This new phenomenon would also lead to the construction of bombs, and it is conceivable—though much less certain—that extremely powerful bombs of a new type may thus be constructed. A single bomb of this type, carried by boat or exploded in a port, might very well destroy the whole port together with some of the surrounding territory. However, such bombs might very well prove to be too heavy for transportation by air.

The United States has only very poor ores of uranium in moderate quantities. There is some good ore in Canada and the former Czechoslovakia, while the most important source of uranium is the Belgian Congo.

In view of this situation you may think it desirable to have some permanent contact between the administration and the group of physicists working on chain reaction in America. One possible way of achieving this might be for you to entrust with this task a person who has your confidence and who could perhaps serve in an unofficial capacity. His task might comprise the following:

(a) To approach government departments, keep them informed of further developments, and put forward recommendations for government action, giving particular attention to the problem of securing a supply of uranium ore for the United States.

(b) To speed up the experimental work which is at present being carried on within the limits of the budgets of the university laboratories, by providing funds, if such funds be required, through his contacts with private persons who are willing to make contributions for this cause, and perhaps also by obtaining the cooperation of industrial laboratories which have the necessary equipment.

I understand that Germany has actually stopped the sale of uranium from the Czechoslovakian mines which she has taken over. That she should have taken such early action might perhaps be understood on the ground that the son of the German Undersecretary of State, von Weizsäcker, is attached to the Kaiser Wilhelm Institute of Berlin, where some of the American work on uranium is now being repeated.

Yours very truly,

A. Einstein.

* * *

1939: OCTOBER 20

DAVID SELZNICK TO WILL HAYS

President from 1922 of the industry-created Motion Picture Producers and Dis-
tributors of America, William Harrison Hays (1879–1954) established a produc-
tion code in 1930 to regulate the use of profanity, the depiction of sexual behavior,
and the treatment of material deemed to be unpatriotic. Throughout the thirties
and early forties, producers such as David O. Selznick (1902–1965) lobbied "the
Hays office" repeatedly for the right to include certain material—in this case, ex-
tremely famous material—in their films.

Mr. Will H. Hays   October 20, 1939

Motion Picture Producers and Distributors of America, Inc.

28 West 44th Street

New York, N.Y.

bcc: Mr. Whitney, Mr. Calvert

Dear Mr. Hays:

As you probably know, the punch line of Gone With the Wind, the one bit of dialogue which forever establishes the future relationship between Scarlett and Rhett, is, "Frankly, my dear, I don't give a damn."

Naturally I am most desirous of keeping this line and, to judge from the reactions of two preview audiences, this line is remembered, loved, and looked forward to by the millions who have read this new American classic.

Under the code, Joe Breen is unable to give me permission to use this sentence because it contains the word "damn," a word specifically forbidden by the code.

As you know from my previous work with such pictures as David Copperfield, Little Lord Fauntleroy, A Tale of Two Cities, etc., I have always attempted to live up to the spirit as well as the exact letter of the producers' code. Therefore, my asking you to review the case, to look at the strip of film in which this forbidden word is contained, is not motivated by a whim. A great deal of the force and drama of Gone With the Wind, a project to which we have given three years of hard work and hard thought, is dependent upon that word.

It is my contention that this word as used in the picture is not an oath or a curse. The worst that could be said against it is that it is a vulgarism, and it is so described in the Oxford English Dictionary. Nor do I feel that in asking you to make an exception in this case, I am asking for the use of a word which is considered reprehensible by the great majority of American people and institutions. A canvass of the popular magazines shows that even such moral publications as <u>Woman's Home Companion</u>, <u>Saturday Evening Post</u>, <u>Collier's</u> and the <u>Atlantic Monthly</u>, use this word freely. I understand the difference, as outlined in the code, between the written word and the word spoken from the screen, but at the same time I think the attitude of these magazines toward "damn" gives an indication that the word itself is not considered abhorrent or shocking to audiences.

I do not feel that your giving me permission to use "damn" in this one sentence will open up the floodgates and allow every gangster picture to be peppered with "damns" from end to end. I do believe, however, that if you were to permit our using this dramatic word in its rightfully dramatic place, in a line that is known and remembered by millions of readers, it would establish a helpful precedent, a precedent which would give to Joe Breen discretionary powers to allow the use of certain harmless oaths and ejaculations whenever, in his opinion, they are not prejudicial to public morals.

Since we are trying to put <u>Gone With the Wind</u> into the laboratory this week, I should appreciate your taking this matter under immediate consideration. Mr. Lowell Calvert, our New York representative, has a print of the scene referred to, which will take you literally only a few seconds to view. . . . However, you may feel it possible to give the consent without viewing the film.

The original of the line referred to is on page 1035 of the novel, <u>Gone With the Wind,</u> and you might have your secretary secure it for you.

We have been commended by preview audiences for our extremely faithful job on <u>Gone With the Wind</u>, and practically the only point that has been commented on as being missing is the curious (to audiences) omission of this line. It spoils the punch at the end of the picture, and on our very fade-out gives an impression of unfaithfulness after three hours and forty-five minutes of extreme fidelity to Miss Mitchell's work, which, as you know, has become an American Bible.

Thanking you for your cooperation in this,

Cordially and sincerely yours,
[David O. Selznick]

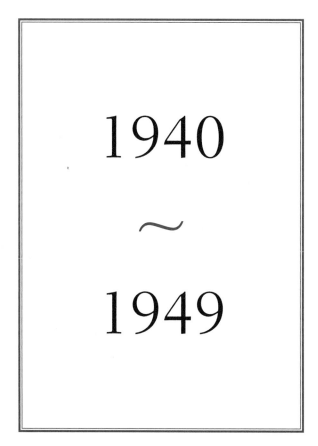

1940

~

1949

Darling, they *can't* take you—the finest, sweetest boy that
ever lived, and send you away—it just tears my heart out
to think of it. Everyone in town is talking war, war war! . . .
There are some sad hearts over this world tonite.
And none sadder than mine.

—Rubye Seago to Richard Long,
December 7, 1941

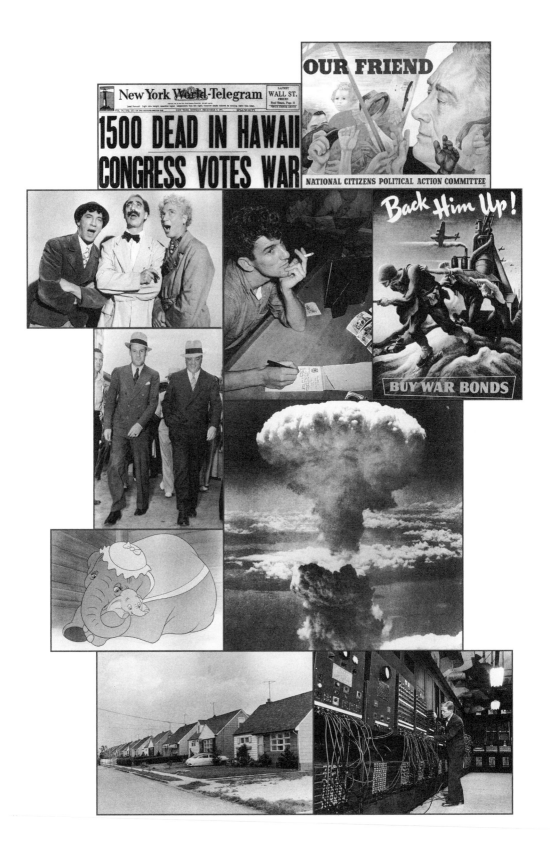

BETWEEN 1940 AND 1949 . . .

1940: A third of American farms have electricity. ★ The U.S. population is 131.6 million. ★ Only 4.2 percent of Americans cannot read. ★ Franklin Delano Roosevelt is elected to a third term. ★ The Selective Service System is created by Congress, requiring all American men between the ages of 21 and 36 to register for military service. ★ Walt Disney releases *Fantasia*. ★ Color television, jeeps, and Bugs Bunny are new. ★ Vermont widow Ida May Fuller receives the first Social Security check—for $22.54. ★ The Bald Eagle Protection Act is passed, mandating that "No person within the United States shall possess, sell, purchase, barter, offer to sell, transport, export, or import, at any time or in any manner, any bald eagle or any golden eagle, alive or dead, or any part, nest or egg." **1941:** Orson Welles's *Citizen Kane* is released. ★ At the University of Georgia, the boys of Sigma Chi elect their annual sweetheart on the sole basis of height and weight. ★ The Japanese attack Pearl Harbor. ★ The United States declares war on Japan. ★ Germany and Italy declare war on the United States. **1942:** 110,000 Japanese-Americans—most of them U.S. citizens—are taken from their homes and moved to internment camps in western states. ★ The Kodacolor process creates the first color

---

From left to right, top row: December 8, 1941 headline, Ben Shahn FDR poster; *second row:* the Marx Brothers, a Coast Guardsman writing home, Thomas Hart Benton war bonds poster; *third row:* Clyde Tolson and J. Edgar Hoover, Nagasaki; *fourth row:* Dumbo; *bottom row:* Levittown, ENIAC.

print. ★ On February 10, the last new American car comes off the assembly line; henceforth, while under the direction of the War Production Board, America's automakers will produce only tanks, jeeps, and planes. ★ With produce scarce, 40 percent of America's vegetables are grown in approximately 20 million backyard "victory gardens." ★ New York City outlaws pinball machines as Mayor Fiorello La Guardia complains that boys are stealing coins from their mothers' purses. ★ Construction begins on the Manhattan Project's Los Alamos, New Mexico, laboratory for the development of an atomic bomb. **1943:** Leading a USO troupe of four, Bob Hope makes his first trip into a combat area. ★ Because of the shortage of rubber, sneakers are scarce: all over America, soles made from recycled rubber leave black marks on school gym floors. ★ Roughly a fifth of all beef produced by the U.S. ends up being sold on the black market. ★ With its revolutionary use of dance as part of the score and story, *Oklahoma!* opens on Broadway at the St. James Theater to run for 2,212 performances. ★ The Triple Crown is won by Count Fleet, who injures his leg at Belmont and is put out to stud. ★ Beginning a beloved tradition, the *New York Times*'s Al Hirschfeld conceals the name of his newborn daughter Nina in one of his caricatures. **1944:** NBC presents the first televised network newscast. ★ In radio commercials, Patti Clayton sings "I'm Chiquita Banana and I've come to say / Bananas have to ripen in a certain way. . . ." The jingle is an attempt by the United Fruit Company to give its bananas a brand name and thus rescue them from generic anonymity. ★ On D day, the Allies land at Normandy with 176,000 soldiers and 20,000 vehicles; within the month, there will be more than a million men, 600,000 tons of supplies, and 200,000 vehicles; by the end of July, the Germans will begin to withdraw. ★ Offering a uniquely American style of ballet, Jerome Robbins's first choreographic work, *Fancy Free*, debuts at the Metropolitan Opera House. **1945:** Churchill, Roosevelt, and Stalin meet at Yalta. ★ FDR dies of a cerebral hemorrhage at the age of 63, and Harry S Truman becomes president. ★ Germany surrenders. ★ Piloted by Paul

Tibbets, Jr., the *Enola Gay* drops the world's first atomic bomb on Hiroshima: 100,000 Japanese die outright; three days later Nagasaki is hit, and 75,000 Japanese immediately perish. ★ Japan surrenders. ★ Number of births in the U.S. this year: 2,858,000. **1946:** Number of births in the U.S. this year: 3,411,000. ★ The Roosevelt dime is issued by the mint. ★ *The New Yorker* devotes an entire issue to John Hersey's *Hiroshima.* ★ ENIAC—the Electronic Numerical Integrator and Computer—performs its first computations. ★ Congress establishes the Indian Claims Commission. ★ Dr. Benjamin Spock publishes *The Common Sense Book of Baby and Child Care.* **1947:** Piloting the X-1 plane, dubbed *Glamorous Glennis* for his wife, Chuck Yeager, 24, breaks the sound barrier over the desert at Muroc, California. **1948:** Former State Department official Alger Hiss is indicted for perjury. ★ Jack Kerouac coins the term "the beat generation." ★ A million American homes now have television sets. **1949:** William Levitt sells the first of his Levittown houses, for less than $8,000 each. ★ A new Cadillac costs $5,000; a pack of cigarettes costs 21 cents; a Coke costs 5 cents; a quart of milk costs 21 cents. ★ A useless synthetic rubber developed by General Electric is divided into one-ounce pieces, placed in plastic cases, named Silly Putty—and sold for a dollar apiece by an advertising man named Peter Hodgson; it becomes a huge success.

1940: OCTOBER 1
GEORGE PATTON, JR., TO DWIGHT EISENHOWER

Dwight D. Eisenhower (1890–1969) served briefly under George S. Patton, Jr. (1885–1945) in 1919, when Patton brought the U.S. Tank Corps home from France. Eisenhower had still not made colonel when he received this letter from Patton, already a brigadier general. Before World War II ended, however, Eisenhower would be the Supreme Commander of the Allied forces, and Patton's otherwise brilliant career would be clouded by a notoriously aggressive incident (see letter page 300).

Patton was referring to tank production.

It seems highly probable that I will get one of the next two armored divisions which we firmly believe will be created in January or February, depending on production. If I do, I shall ask for you either as Chief of Staff, which I should prefer, or as a regimental commander. You can tell me which you want, for no matter how we get together we will go PLACES.

If you get a better offer in the meantime, take it, as I can't be sure, but I hope we can get together. At the moment there is nothing in the brigade good enough for you. However, if you want to take I will ask for you now. . . .

Hoping we are together in a long and BLOODY war.

1941: MAY 4
JESSIE BERNARD TO HER UNBORN CHILD

Jessie Bernard (1903–1996) was at a relatively early stage in what would prove to be a long and spirited career as a teacher, sociologist, and feminist when she wrote this letter. She was six months pregnant at the time, and the war in Europe had been going on since September of 1939.

Bernard's daughter, Dorothy Lee, would be born on July 23.

4 May 1941

My dearest,

Eleven weeks from today you will be ready for this outside world. And what a world it is this year! It has been the most beautiful spring I have ever seen. Miss Morris (a faculty colleague) says it is because I have you to look forward to. She says she has noticed a creative look on my face in my appreciation of this spring. And she is right. But also the world itself has been so particularly sweet, aglow with color. The forsythia were yellower and fuller than any I have ever seen. The lilacs were fragrant and feathery. And now the spirea, heavy with their little round blooms, stand like wonderful igloos, a mass of white. I doff my scientific mantle long enough to pretend that Nature is outdoing herself to prepare this earth for you. But also I want to let all this beauty get into my body. I cannot help but think of that other world. The world of Europe where babies are born to hunger, stunted growth, breasts dried up with anxiety and fatigue. That is part of the picture too. And I sometimes think that while my body in this idyllic spring creates a miracle, forces are at work which within twenty or twenty-five years may be preparing to destroy the creation of my body. My own sweet, the war takes on a terrible new significance when I think of that. I think of all those mothers who carried their precious cargoes so carefully for nine long months— and you have no idea how long nine months can be when you are impatient for the end—lovingly nurtured their babies at their breasts, and watched them grow for twenty years. I think of their anguish when all this comes to naught. Your father thinks parents ought to get down on their knees and beg forgiveness of children for bringing them into such a world. And there is much truth in that. But I hope you will never feel like that. I hope you will never regret the life we have created for you out of our seed. To me the only answer a woman can make to the destructive forces of the world is creation. And the most ecstatic form of creation is the creation of new life. I have so many dreams for you. There are so many virtues I would endow you with if I could. First of all, I would make you tough and strong. And how I have labored at that! I have eaten vitamins and minerals instead of food. Gallons of milk, pounds of lettuce, dozens of eggs . . .Hours of sunshine. To make your body a strong one because everything on that. I would give you resiliency of body so that all the blows and buffets of this world would leave you still unbeaten. I would have you creative. I would have you a creative scientist. But if the shuffling genes have made of you an artist, that will make me happy too. And even if you have no special talent either artistic or scientific, I would still have you creative no matter what you do. To build things, to make things, to create—that is what I covet for you. If you have a strong body and a creative mind you will be happy. I will help in that. Already I can see how parents long to shield their children from disappointments and defeat. But I also know that I cannot re-make life for you. You will suffer. You will have moments of disappointment and defeat. You will have your share of buffeting. I cannot spare you that. But I hope to help you be such a strong, radiant, self-integrated person that you will take all this in your stride, assimilate it, and rise to conquer . . .

Eleven more weeks. It seems a long time. Until another time, then, my precious one, I say good-bye.

Your eager mother

1941: DECEMBER 6
FRANKLIN ROOSEVELT TO HIROHITO

Japan's expansionist policies during the thirties and early forties led to escalating tensions with the United States. These tensions rose further in July, when Japan occupied French Indochina and Roosevelt froze Japanese assets in the U.S. Throughout the autumn, both countries still pursued diplomatic solutions, but on December 1, Tokyo's privy council voted to go to war against the U.S. After writing this telegram to the emperor in a last-ditch effort to stave off Japanese aggression, FDR told Eleanor: "This son of man has just sent his final message to the son of God."

His Imperial Majesty the Emperor of Japan:

Almost a century ago the President of the United States addressed to the Emperor of Japan a message extending an offer of friendship of the people of the United States to the people of Japan. That offer was accepted, and in the long period of unbroken peace and friendship which has followed, our respective nations, through the virtues of their peoples and the wisdom of their rulers, have prospered and have substantially helped humanity.

Only in situations of extraordinary importance to our two countries need I address Your Majesty messages on matters of state. I feel I should now so address you because of the deep and far-reaching emergency which appears to be in formation.

Developments are occurring in the Pacific area which threaten to deprive each of our nations and all humanity of the beneficial influence of the long peace between our two countries. Those developments contain tragic possibilities.

The people of the United States, believing in peace and in the right of nations to live and let live, have eagerly watched the conversations between our two governments during these past months. We have hoped for a termination of the present conflict between Japan and China. We have hoped that a peace of the Pacific could be consummated in such a way that nationalities of many diverse peoples could exist side by side without fear of invasion; that unbearable burdens of armaments could be lifted for them all; and that all peoples would resume commerce without discrimination against or in favor of any nation.

I am certain that it will be clear to Your Majesty, as it is to me, that in seeking these great objectives both Japan and the United States should agree to eliminate any form of military threat. This seems essential to the attainment of the high objectives.

More than a year ago Your Majesty's Government concluded an agreement with the Vichy Government by which five or six thousand Japanese troops were permitted to enter into northern French Indochina for the protection of Japanese troops which were operating against China further north. And this Spring and Summer the Vichy Government permitted further Japanese military forces to enter into southern French Indochina for the common defense of French Indochina. I think I am correct in saying that no attack has been made upon Indochina, nor that any has been contemplated.

During the past few weeks it has become clear to the world that the Japanese military, naval, and air forces have been sent to southern Indochina in such large numbers as to create a reasonable doubt on the part of other nations that this continuing concentration in Indochina is not defensive in its character.

Because these continuing concentrations in Indochina have reached such large proportions and because they extend now to the southeast and the southwest corners of that peninsula, it is only reasonable that the people of the Philippines, of the hundreds of Islands of the East Indies, of Malaya, and of Thailand itself are asking themselves whether these forces of Japan are preparing or intending to make attack in one or more of these many directions.

I am sure that Your Majesty will understand that the fear of all these peoples is a legitimate fear inasmuch as it involves their peace and their national existence. I am sure that Your Majesty will understand why the people of the United States in such large numbers look askance at the establishment of military, naval and air bases manned and equipped so greatly as to constitute armed forces capable of measures of offense.

It is clear that a continuance of such a situation is unthinkable.

None of the people whom I have spoken of above can sit either indefinitely or permanently on a keg of dynamite.

There is absolutely no thought on the part of the United States of invading Indochina if every Japanese soldier or sailor were to be withdrawn therefrom.

I think that we can obtain the same assurance from the Governments of the East Indies, the Government of Malaya, and the Government of Thailand. I would even undertake to ask for the same assurance on the part of the Government of China. Thus a withdrawal of the Japanese forces from Indochina would result in the assurance of peace throughout the whole of the south Pacific area.

I address myself to Your Majesty so that Your Majesty may, as I am doing, give thought in this definite emergency to ways of dispelling the dark clouds. I am confident that both of us, for the sake of the peoples not only of our own great countries but for the sake of humanity in neighboring territories, have a sacred duty to restore traditional amity and prevent further death and destruction to the world.

Franklin D. Roosevelt

1941: DECEMBER 7
DOROTHEA TAYLOR TO HER BROTHER

Dorothea Taylor had come to Hawaii to be nurse and companion to a woman named Jessie Miles Campbell; Taylor was living in Honolulu when the Japanese attacked Pearl Harbor. She wrote this letter to her brother, P. H. Taylor, who was living in Ohio, just a few hours after the bombing. More than twenty-three hundred American servicemen were killed and eleven hundred injured in the space of several hours. More than three hundred planes and numerous ships were destroyed.

A. J. Cronin's *The Keys of the Kingdom* was a popular novel, published in 1941, about a Catholic missionary in China.

Honolulu, Dec. 7, 1941

This morning was as delightful a Sunday morning as ever. There was a cool breeze, for rain had fallen in the night. I wakened about seven. There was the sound of heavy firing in the distance as there so often is when our brave defenders are practicing. I thought it peculiar the paper was not in the box. When I stepped up to the street to look at the ocean I noticed heavy black smoke, as from oil rising from the region of Pearl Harbor. My first thought was that an accident had set fire to one of the oil tanks, or worse still, aircraft, which did not amaze me as they are often shot for practice.

Calmly I sat down to my coffee and doughnuts to listen to the broadcast of the Salt Lake City Choir. The singing was interrupted by the announcer stating that a sporadic attack had been made on Pearl Harbor and one Japanese plane had been shot down. Civilians were forbidden to use the telephone or to go on the streets. We were advised to keep our radios on and bulletins would be given as fast as they came in. We were told to be calm and stay where we were, that everything was under control. The announcer had to repeat a number of times that this was a real attack, not practice maneuvers.

Bulletins and orders continued at intervals. All firemen were called to duty. All army and navy men told to report to their stations. Disaster wardens were sent to their districts and the meeting places named for each ward. Mine is at the Robert Louis Stevenson school, just down the steps from my gate. Explosions and anti-aircraft firing continued. I went to the top of the reservoir across the street where most of my frightened neighbors had congregated. With my binoculars I could see numerous large fires in Pearl Harbor and Hickam Field. It made me sick at heart to see all the oil going up in clouds of black smoke, for of what good will our ships and planes be without oil? The loss is already disastrous. I heard two shells whistle overhead. The fire siren sounded every few minutes. KGU announced a bomb had hit about 50 ft. from their building, and there were some other craters elsewhere. As a precaution I packed up all the valuable things in the apartment in small baggage, so it could be moved easily. I filled everything with water, inside and out, and Miss Davis did the same, and asked everyone to draw water into every container in their apartments. There was smoke raising from two large fires in Makiki district, about a mile away, but I have not yet learned what started them or how much damage was done. Governor Poindexter spoke on the radio at 11 a.m., but unfortunately that is just when my set went bad so I could not get any broadcasts. It has been acting up for some time, and has not been serviced for a year. I had to depend on my neighbor's radio for further bulletins. One bomb fell on a place on Lillian Street, about two miles from me. No one hurt.

Parachute troops were reported to have landed on St. Louis heights—a mostly bare steep hill, far from any military objectives—and guards were directed by radio to deal with them. I never learned whether the suspects were our own men who had to bail out of a plane or whether they were enemies. By mid-afternoon there was no smoke from fires that I could see, which was a relief because the wind was blowing quite strongly all day, and still is.

Most of my time was spent trying to calm and divert these young navy wives. They have husbands on cruisers and destroyers and in the air force, but they cooked meals with each other and insisted I eat supper with them, which I did.

They packed their suitcases and stayed at home. About three o'clock martial law was declared, so we now have to obey all orders and give an account of our every move. Two civilian men are left on the place and they were made Civilian Defense wardens and act as police in the neighborhood. Tonight there is a complete blackout. Millions of stars not otherwise seen make the heavens shine with a soft glow. I believe the moon rises about 10. I am sitting in my dressing-room closet with the door shut, and heavy green paper over the narrow high screened opening in the shower. Very little air gets in through the cracks, so I go out and cool off every few minutes. I am not excited, nor a bit afraid. I have plenty of food on hand. We were instructed to boil all our drinking water in case the open reservoirs had been meddled with.

I resort to my knitting when I get a little nervous. I am in the midst of Cronin's book <u>Keys to the Kingdom</u>, but it was hard to concentrate on any reading or study today. Now night has come, everything is silent and peaceful. It has been a tense day, and with no lights on, everyone seems to have retired. You people on the mainland have probably had a lot more news of this incident than I have while right on the spot. One announcement stated a naval battle was going on west of Oahu. It was said a Japanese ship flying the American flag with planes marked with U.S. insignia came within range and started all the trouble. It has been an Incident. We are all wondering what tomorrow will bring forth.

Most affectionately,
Dorothea

1941: DECEMBER 7
RUBYE SEAGO TO RICHARD LONG

Rubye Seago and Richard Long met in October of 1940 when he went to register for the draft in Lawrenceville, Virginia. They would be married three years later in New York City. In between those two events came the Japanese attack on Pearl Harbor. This letter was written while Richard was still in basic training at Camp Wheeler, Georgia.

Pete was a lodger at the Seagos'.

Lawrenceville, Sunday Nite, Dec. 7, 1941

My Darling:

I know you feel exactly like I do right now. I've just been listening to the radio. I've never been so blue or heartsick as I am right this minute. Oh, my darling—if it were possible I'd charter a plane—do anything—just to see you for a few minutes . . .

Honestly, Dick, if I don't get to see you I'm going to lose my mind. Isn't there <u>any</u> thing you can do? 'Cause if you don't do it now do you realize we may <u>never</u> see each other again? Of course you do—you realize how serious the situation is, even more then I. Darling, they <u>can't</u> take you—the finest, sweetest boy that ever lived and send you away—it just tears my heart out to think of it.

Everyone in town is talking war, war war! Everyone is sure it will be declared tomorrow. There are some sad hearts over this world tonite. And none sadder than mine. And your poor mother.

There isn't any use of me pretending to feel other than the way I do. It's too serious now. And you'd know I was pretending, if I tried to write a cheerful letter.

. . . Pete is in the bathroom crying her eyes out. I think she'd marry Jack tonite. I don't blame her. She'd have that much. It's better than not having anything—to remember. This is awful—I know I'm hurting you. And I can't help it. Every word is coming from my heart.

I love you, Dick, more than anybody in the world. You know it already, but I want to tell you again. And I'll always love you to the end of my life. I love you because you're fine and good and just the kind of man I always wanted to meet and love. You meet all the requirements, Darling.

I'd give everything I own, or ever hope to have, to see you right now. Isn't there anything we can do?

Please don't let anything happen without letting me know. Wire me or call me or something. If it's possible.

Forever yours,
Rubye

1941: DECEMBER 17
FRANKLIN ROOSEVELT TO THE
PRESIDENT OF THE UNITED STATES IN 1956

Captain Colin P. Kelly, Jr., was the first American to die for his country after the United States declared war on Japan on December 8. Somehow finding the time to think past the mounting crisis, Roosevelt wrote this letter. The president in 1956, Dwight Eisenhower, would honor FDR's request and appoint Colin P. Kelly III to West Point.

December 17, 1941

To the President of the United States in 1956:

I am writing this letter as an act of faith in the destiny of our country. I desire to make a request which I make in full confidence that we shall achieve a glorious victory in the war we are now waging to preserve our democratic way of life.

My request is that you consider the merits of a young American youth of goodly heritage—Colin P. Kelly III, for appointment as a candidate in the United States Military Academy at West Point. I make this appeal in behalf of this youth as a token of the nation's appreciation of the heroic services of his father who met his death in the line of duty at the very outset of the struggle which was thrust upon us by the perfidy of a professed friend.

In the conviction that the service and example of Captain Colin P. Kelly, Jr., will be long remembered, I ask for this consideration in behalf of Colin P. Kelly III.

Franklin D. Roosevelt

1941: DECEMBER 18
LESTER MARKEL TO ARTHUR HAYS SULZBERGER

Invented in nineteenth-century England, the crossword puzzle first appeared in America in the New York World *in 1913. But for decades the* New York Times *held out against this novelty, even editorializing against it as "a primitive form of mental exercise." Then America entered the war, and distractions were suddenly valued in a new way.*

Lester Markel edited the *Times*'s Sunday supplements. Arthur Hays Sulzberger was the newspaper's publisher. Margaret Farrar would edit the *Times*'s crosswords for nearly three decades. Charles Merz edited the editorial page.

December 18, 1941

Mr. Sulzberger:

We have had a number of meetings with Mrs. Farrar on the cross word puzzle thing, and she has prepared several samples, one of which was worked out by Mr. Merz. After this exploration, I am convinced of these things:

1. That we ought to proceed with the puzzle, especially in view of the fact that it is possible that there will now be bleak black-out hours—or if not that, then certainly a need for relaxation of some kind or other. (That, in turn, raises the question of whether we ought not to

have a cross word puzzle in the daily also—but that's a different story.)

2. That we ought not to try to do anything essentially different from what is now being done—except to do it better.

I attach a memorandum from Mrs. Farrar which sums up her conclusions.

Shall we proceed?

L. Markel

From Mrs. John Farrar
Scarborough, N.Y.

Memo for Mr. Markel:
Re: CROSS WORD PUZZLES for the Sunday Magazine

In the experimenting I have done for you, I think certain conclusions present themselves.

(1) The great majority of puzzle solvers want a large, challenging, rather hard puzzle, with terse dictionary definitions plus occasional literary, historical and news references. Such a puzzle gives an hour or two of real satisfaction to everyone who tries it.

(2) The smaller puzzle, which could occupy the lower part of the page, could provide variety each Sunday. It could be topical, humorous, have rhymed definitions or story definitions or quiz definitions.

The combination of these two would offer meat and dessert, and catch the fancy of all types of puzzlers.

The Herald Tribune runs the best puzzle page in existence so far, but they have gotten into a bit of a rut. Their big puzzle never ventures even one imaginative definition, and lacks the plus quality that I believe can be achieved and maintained. Their two diagramless puzzles have, in my experience, a limited appeal. We could, I dare to predict, get the edge on them with the above plan.

I don't think I have to sell you on the increased demand for this kind of pastime in an increasingly worried world. You can't think of your troubles while solving a cross word. After seventeen years of editing the blooming things, on The World and in the 52 Simon & Schuster books, I know this to be true.

I am profoundly aware that a New York Times puzzle page must establish and maintain a reputation for excellence that would be in keeping with the standing of the newspaper itself. From our conferences and experiments, I hope I have proved to you that it can be done.

1942: JANUARY 12
ALEXANDER WOOLLCOTT TO WALT DISNEY

Notwithstanding the war, Alexander Woollcott (see letter page 237) was not alone in finding true illumination in Dumbo. *Presenting a guileless hero who begins as a victim of snobbery and prejudice and ends in triumph over his oppressors, Walt Disney, according to one review of the time, "strips off the masks under which hide our foibles, frailties, fears, and . . . gives us a true-view reflection of what we really look like . . . the face behind the mask." Before long, Disney (1901–1966) would be turning his inspirational skills to the war effort; by the middle of the year, government contracts would account for almost all of his studio's production.*

Humorist Frank Sullivan was a sometime member of the Algonquin Round Table.

Bomoseen, Vt.
January 12, 1942

My dear Disney:

This is a letter of thanks from the bottom of my heart. Having been over to England, done a dozen broadcasts there, come back and delivered a dozen lectures here, I blew myself to a spot of rest. In fact, during the Christmas holidays, I did nothing but sleep, dine with Frank Sullivan, listen to Churchill, and go to see Dumbo. That's what I call a good life.

After seeing Dumbo for the third time, I suspect that if we could get far enough away to see it in its place, we would recognize it as the highest achievement yet reached in the Seven Arts since the first white man landed on this continent. This cautious tribute is paid by one who was several degrees short of nuts about Snow White and a little bored by Pinocchio. I was as afflicted by what went agley in Fantasia as anyone in this country, with the possible exception of yourself. But Dumbo is that once far-off divine event toward which your whole creation has moved.

After some thought, I have decided that you are the most valuable person alive, so for God's sake take care of yourself.

Yours to command,
Alexander Woollcott

1942: JANUARY 15
FRANKLIN ROOSEVELT TO KENESAW MOUNTAIN LANDIS

Attendance at professional baseball games fell dramatically in 1942; in addition to prospective fans, a large percentage of major and minor league players were fighting the war. Nevertheless, Roosevelt offered Kenesaw Mountain Landis, baseball's first commissioner, a "green light" to keep the games going.

THE WHITE HOUSE
Washington

January 15, 1942.

My dear Judge:—

Thank you for yours of January fourteenth. As you will, of course, realize, the final decision about the baseball season must rest with you and the Baseball Club owners—so what I am going to say is solely a personal and not an official point of view.

I honestly feel that it would be best for the country to keep baseball going. There will be fewer people unemployed and everybody will work longer hours and harder than ever before.

And that means that they ought to have a chance for recreation and for taking their minds off their work even more than before.

Baseball provides a recreation which does not last over two hours or two hours and a half, and which can be got for very little cost. And incidentally, I hope that night games can be extended because it gives an opportunity to the day shift to see a game occasionally.

As to the players themselves, I know you agree with me that individual players who are of active military or naval age should go, without question, into the services. Even if the actual quality of the teams is lowered by the greater use of older players, this will not dampen the popularity of the sport. Of course, if any individual has some particular aptitude in a trade or profession, he ought to serve the Government. That, however, is a matter which I know you can handle with complete justice.

Here is another way of looking at it—if 300 teams use 5,000 or 6,000 players, these players are a definite recreational asset to at least 20,000,000 of their fellow citizens—and that in my judgment is thoroughly worthwhile.

With every best wish,

Very sincerely yours,
Franklin D. Roosevelt

Hon. Kenesaw M. Landis,
333 North Michigan Avenue,
Chicago,
Illinois.

1942: FEBRUARY 18

WALTER UNDERWOOD TO FRANK KNOX

Several months after Pearl Harbor, Japanese and Japanese-American West Coast residents were increasingly being seen as a national threat. Between February 26 and March 2, 1942, dozens of letters like the one below were read before a congressional committee that had been set up to examine "the problems of evacuation of enemy aliens and others from prohibited military zones." The sentiments expressed in this letter—from the head of an Oregon chamber of commerce—were typical of the rationale that would lead to the establishment of internment camps for more than a hundred thousand Japanese and Japanese-Americans.

James W. Mott was a U.S. congressman from Oregon; Oregon senator Charles L. McNary was minority leader.

Astoria Chamber of Commerce,
Astoria, Oreg., February 18, 1942.

Hon. Frank Knox,
Secretary of Navy, Washington, D.C.

Dear Sir: Business interests of this community are much concerned over the presence of enemy aliens in this area. According to statements just made by the President of the United States, even cities as far inland as Detroit may be justified in expecting bombings. It therefore would appear absolutely essential that we protect ourselves for all possibility of sabotage, especially in such strategic areas such as the lower Columbia.

It is therefore our wish to acquaint you with the wish of this community as expressed in the enclosed telegrams and a petition which has been forwarded to the President of the United States, requesting and urging designation of this area as a defense zone from which enemy aliens shall be removed.

You will find attached copies of wires sent to Congressman Mott, Senator McNary, and wire sent on February 14 to the President of the United States, which telegram was duplicated by the labor council. Also a petition signed by 50 citizens of Hammond, Oreg., has been forwarded to the President.

There can be little doubt that the great majority of public opinion in this area favors removal of these aliens, particularly as at present these aliens cannot find lucrative employment here and many of them individually desire to be removed to areas where they may safely be employed to earn a livelihood.

We also understand that interested parties along the water front in this area have formed a committee for the protection of the water front, and that this committee will communicate with the Government requesting removal of these aliens.

Sincerely,
Walter W. Underwood,
Managing Secretary.

1942: MAY 6
JONATHAN WAINWRIGHT TO FRANKLIN ROOSEVELT

Hoping to capitalize on the disarray of the American forces after Pearl Harbor, the Japanese had quickly attacked a series of Pacific targets: Wake Island, Malaya, and, in January, Manila. General Douglas MacArthur withdrew to the nearby peninsula of Bataan, where a combined force of American and Filipino solders held out until April 9. After their surrender, some seventy-six thousand soldiers were taken to prison camps on the notorious sixty-five-mile "Bataan death march." Along the way, many thousands died from hunger or disease or were bayonetted and tortured to death by their captors. On May 5, the Japanese landed on the tiny island of Corregidor, just south of Bataan, where General Jonathan Wainwright (1883–1953) was forced to surrender the remaining fifteen thousand American and Filipino troops. Wainwright explained the situation, which was one of the low points of the war, to FDR in this letter.

URGENT

From: Fort Mills
To: Chief of Staff

No Number May 6, 1942

For the President of the United States. It is with broken heart and head bowed in sadness but not in shame that I report to your Excellency that I must today go to arrange terms for the surrender of the fortified Islands of Manila Bay–Corregidor (Fort Mills) Caballo (Fort Hughes) El Fraile (Fort Drum) . . .

With many guns and anti-aircraft fire control equipment destroyed, we are no longer able to prevent accurate bombardment from the air. With numerous batteries of heavy caliber emplaced on the shores of Bataan and Cavite the enemy now brings devastating crossfire to bear on us, outranging our remaining guns.

Most of my batteries, seacoast, anti-aircraft and field, have been put out of action by the enemy. I have ordered the others destroyed to prevent them from falling into enemy hands. In addition, we are now overwhelmingly assaulted by Japanese troops on Corregidor.

There is a limit to human endurance, and that limit has long since been past. Without prospect of relief, I feel it is my duty to my country and to my gallant troops to end this useless effusion of blood and human sacrifice.

If you agree, Mr. President, please say to the nation that my troops and I have accomplished all that is humanly possible and that we have upheld the best traditions of the United States and its Army.

May God bless and preserve you and guide you and the nation in the effort to ultimate victory.

With profound regret and with continued pride in my gallant troops I go to meet the Japanese commander. Good-by, Mr. President.

Jonathan Wainwright

1942: MAY 21
JOSEPH BREEN TO JACK WARNER

Back home, the Hays office's Joseph Breen continued the fight for cinematic "decency" via the production code. But in this case—as all Casablanca *fans will gratefully attest—the rules weren't strictly applied.*

Jack Warner (1892–1978) was president of Warner Bros., which he had founded with his three brothers in 1918.

Mr. J. L. Warner
Warner Brothers
Burbank, California

Dear Mr. Warner:

We have received part II, also pages of changes dated May 19th, for your proposed picture CASABLANCA. As we indicated before, we cannot, of course, give you a final opinion until we receive the complete script.

However, the present material contains certain elements which seem to be unacceptable from the standpoint of the Production Code. Specifically, we cannot approve the present suggestion that Capt. Renault makes of practice of seducing the women to whom he grants visas. Any such inference of illicit sex could not be approved in the finished picture.

Going through this new material, we call your attention to the following:

Pages 70 and 71: The dialogue in scenes 125 and 126 is unacceptable by reason of its sex suggestiveness.

Page 76: The following dialogue is unacceptable for the above reasons. "By the way—another visa problem has come up; show her in".

Page 85: The line "You'll find it worth your while" is unacceptably sex suggestive.

Page 86: The suggestion that Ilsa was married all the time she was having her love affair with Rick in Paris seems unacceptable, and could not be approved in the final picture. Hence we request the deletion of Ilsa's line "Even when I knew you in Paris."

We will be happy to read the balance of the script, and to report further, whenever you have it ready.

Cordially yours,
Joseph I. Breen

1942: MAY 24
SHIZUKO HORIUCHI TO HENRIETTE VON BLON

In the spring of 1942, Shizuko Horiuchi became one of the more than one hundred thousand Japanese and Japanese-Americans who were evicted from their homes in the western United States and sent first to crude temporary "assembly centers" and then to inland internment camps, where many would spend the remainder of the war. In a 1976 proclamation, President Gerald Ford would officially condemn the evacuation as a "national mistake," and in 1988, President Ronald Reagan would sign into law a bill providing reparations for surviving former internees.
The Von Blon family had been dear friends of the Horiuchis and would travel two hours by bus and some miles by foot to visit them.

May 24, 1942

Dear Mrs. Von Blon,

It does seem as if it's getting to be a habit of mine to be neglectful in writing, but truly, I'm so busy, I haven't found much time.

It's been a one round of washing, ironing with all the dust, soot from the mess hall kitchen, that it isn't an easy life for us. Especially with three children, it's double work.

This is a very belated thank you, but I sincerely mean it. Thank you ever so much for your kindness and thoughtfulness. Your visits to our home made us very happy. I guess it would be hard to convey our dire feelings in these times. And to be brightened by our dear American friends is really more than words can express.

The life here cannot be expressed. Sometimes, we are resigned to it, but when we see the barbed wire fences and the sentry tower with floodlights, it gives us a feeling of being prisoners in a "concentration camp." We try to be happy and yet, oftentimes, a gloominess does creep in. When I see the "I'm An American" editorial and write-ups, the "equality of race, etc." . . . it seems to be mocking us in our faces. I just wonder if all the sacrifices and hard labor on part of our parents has gone up to leave nothing to show for it? Well, I hope after this is all over, they'll find some compensation waiting for them.

While Hitonie is sleeping, I'd better have my work done, so I'll be closing now. Please extend our best regards to Mr. Von Blon, Marie Adele and Philip. We do think of all of you often.

Very sincerely yours,

Shizuko

1942: SEPTEMBER 2
DOROTHY PARKER TO ALEXANDER WOOLLCOTT

Dorothy Parker (see letter page 239) married Alan Campbell, an aspiring actor and screenwriter, first in 1934 and again (with a divorce in between) in 1950. Their friend Gerald Murphy, apparently impressed with Campbell's decision to enlist in the war as a private, gave him a watch engraved Qui Sensat Acet *("He who feels, acts"). Other friends, who had watched Parker begging Campbell to enlist, were less moved. Writer Robert Benchley claimed the watch should have read "Whose wife feels, acts."*

"Goodbye Dolly Gray" was a traditional Civil War song.

FOX HOUSE

Pipersville, Bucks County

Pennsylvania   September second.

Dear Alec, Private Campbell has just gone, and I'm afraid I'm feeling a little like Dolly Gray. So I thought I would—Oh hell, I wanted to talk to you. So here's this letter.

I am this minute back from Philadelphia, where I went with him to see him off. Seeings-off are usually to be regretted, but I am so glad that I went. Twice before he had had a card with a date and had appeared with his bag, all ready, but each time—that cutting off of that dog's tail by those inches—they had told him to go home and wait. Even today, the sergeant said to him, "Are you <u>sure</u> you want to do this?" Yes. He was sure he wanted to do this.

The enlistment office in Philadelphia is in the customs house—it is a great, bare room, used, I suppose, as a sort of warehouse before. Along one wall are a couple of benches, packed tight with men sitting down, and beyond them is a line of men, moving up, man by man, as a man vacates the bench to go to the enlistment sergeant, and the sitting men move up to give another place, and the standing men move along a place for their turn. They are the men coming that day to enlist in the army. All the while we were there, that line kept lengthening, and men were still coming in when we left. That goes on every day, all day, Jesus, Alec, I guess we're all right.

Most of them look poor—I mean by that, they haven't got coats on, they have soiled shirts and stained pants, their working clothes. The Lord God knows, those men who have made up their minds don't look poor in any other way and aren't poor! The majority of them are very young—"heart-breakingly young", I read in a piece by a lady who watched the troops go by and threw them roses, which were their immediate need. They are not in the least heart-breaking, and I think if you called them that they would turn out to be neck-breaking. They are young, certainly—several even had women standing beside them in line, their mommas, come to give consent to a minor's enlistment—but they're all right. There were many older men, too, carefully dressed, and obviously prosperous in their businesses—which they were willing to leave. There was nothing whatever pathetic about them, either. There were numerous Negroes. And nobody avoided them, as they stood in line with the whites, nobody shied away from them or stood in silence. They all talked with one another, in the lowered voices you decently accord a big office full of busy men, but a man in line talked to the men on both sides of him.

(Look, Alec, I'm not going to make any more pencil corrections. I know you will know what I mean.)

The greater part of the room is for the men who are going to camp that day. They all have their bags, and the only time I busted was at the sight of a tall, thin young Negro—"lanky" I believe is the word almost always employed—carrying a six-inch square of muslin in which were his personal effects. It looked so exactly like a bean-bag . . . And then I realized I was rotten to be tear-sprinkled. He wasn't sad. He felt fine. . . . I was ashamed of myself. And yet, dear Alec, I defy you to have looked at that bean-bag, and kept an arid eye. That, of course, has nothing to do with war. Except, also of course, that a man who had no more than that was going to fight for it. . . .

Well, anyway, there were a few camp-stools—not enough, many were standing—for mothers and wives and friends and various interested parties. Many women had brought their kids, certainly beacuse there were no nurses to leave them with, and the little ones pooped about and fought and whined and demanded drinks of water and in general conducted themselves like swine. But theirs was the only bad behavior. Not one woman but was fine. They were not quite of all classes. There were no stinking rich nor fantastically poor. They were lower-to-middle and middle-to-upper. There wasn't one that didn't look proud and respecting, both of herself and of the man because of whom she was there.

The men who were to go to camp—they didn't know where they were going, they are not told until they go, and that is, of course, quite right—stood in line, filed along to desks, filled out forms, and were finger-printed. They were not yet in the army. It was impressed upon them that they could get the hell out then, if they wanted to. No one went.

Then a segeant called the roll of their names. I was astonished, Alec, at the preponderance of the short, quick English or Scottish or American names—Marsh, Kent, Brown, Downs, Leith. We think—due I am afraid to the news-papers—of factory workers, and most of these men were obviously those, as a mess of consonants. God knows that is nothing against them, but it just hap-pens that this especial day, those men who had volunteered were of plain, famil-iar names. There were only a couple of Cazzonottis and Schecovitxixzes. But, as I say, this is only this day. There was also, God help us, only one to represent my side—a lone Levy. I am delighted to say he was a fine looking young man.

They formed in two blocks of thirty men each—six men across, five men down. Then they took the oath of induction into the army of the United States. I had never heard it before, never seen men take it. It was a fine and solemn and stirring thing. It is flat simple and direct, as to what they pledge themselves to do, and it is in the form of a question—it begins "Do you—"? When the sergeant had finished reading it to them, those sixty men said "I do" as one man. I never heard a thing like that. There were no stragglers, no piping voices, no quavers. Precise and proud and strong it came, from sixty men—"I do". Jesus, Alec. I will not soon forget that sound.

Then the sergeant talked to them, as decent a talk as I have ever heard. Then he said, "men on the right are to go to Fort Cumberland, men on the left to Fort Meade." Then he turned to the Fort Cumberland group and called "Private Campbell!" I had one horror-stricken moment when I thought he was going to say "stop biting your nails." But it turned out, when our private stepped forward looking pretty sheepish, that Private Campbell was to have charge of his detail, that the men were to report to him at the station, and obey his orders on the way to camp. I saw Private Campbell for a moment before they left for the station. Private Campbell said only, "I'm going to see they don't leave the car messy." Dear Alec, he will be a brigadier-general by Tuesday.

Fort Cumberland, by the way, is where you go for a few days, to get your clothes and take your tests and be assigned to what they think is best for you. And I must say, I have the deepest respect for the way they seem to be trying to assign a man to his most useful job. From there, they are sent on some place else. I will let you know as soon as I know.

Then we went to the station. The Mothers and wives and friends all came too, and so did the kids, but the kids felt something and behaved superbly. The men were lined up intwo rows, each man with his bag beside him—the varying kinds of bags, Alec! Ah, it really is a democratic war!—and Private Campbell, giving orders. I couldn't hear much—drat those acoustics in the Penn station at Philadelphia—but I did hear him say something and then add, "That is, if it's all right with you." I love Alan. Don't you, Alec?

In the station, it was a little bad. Oh, I don't mean everybody didn't go on being swell—but you know how it is, when a train's going out. The mothers and wives and girls all had tears in their eyes, and they all looked carefully away from one another, because you can be fine, yourself, but when you see tears, you're gone. Jesus, what fine people, Alec!

So while we were standing there, there came up to me a fat, ill-favored, dark little woman, who said to me, "Parn me, but aren't you Dorothy Parker? Well, I've no doubt you've heard of me, I'm Mrs. Sig Greesbaum, Edith Greesbaum, you'd probably know me better as, I'm the head of our local chapter of the Better Living Club, and we'd like to have you come talk to us, of course I'm still a little angry at you for writing that thing about men not making advances at girls who wear glasses, because I've worn glasses for years, and Sig, that's my husband, but I still call him my sweetheart, he says it doesn't matter a bit, well, he wears glasses himself, and I want you to talk to our club, of course we can't pay you any money, but it will do you a lot of good, we've had all sorts of wonderful people, Ethel Grimsby Loe that writes all the greeting cards, and the editor of the Doylestown Intelligenser, and Mrs. Mercer, that told us all about Italy when she used to live there after the last war, and the photographs she showed us of her cypresses and all, and it would really be a wonderful thing for you to meet us, and now when can I put you down to come talk to us?"

So I said I was terribly sorry, but if she didn't mind, I was busy at the moment. So she looked around at the rows of men—she hadn't seen them before, apparently; all they did was take up half the station—and she giggled heartily and said, "Oh, what are those? More poor suckers caught in the draft?"

And an almighty wrath came upon me, and I said, "Those are American patriots who have volunteered to fight for your liberty, you Sheeny bitch!" And I walked away, already horrified—as I am now—at what I had said. Not, dear, the gist, which I will stick to and should, but the use of the word "sheeny", which I give you my word I have not heard for forty years and have never used before. The horror lies in the ease with which it came to me—And worse horror lies in the knowledge that if she had been black, I would have said "You nigger bitch"—Dear God. The things I have fought against all my life. And that's what I did.

Well, so anyway, then they came down to the train, and then I left before the train pulled out, because flesh and blood is or are flesh and blood.

Alec, the private is a good man. He could have had a commission; he saw in Washington the men commissioned as majors and colonels and lieutenant colonels—cutters and directors and producers and assistants. He said—and that's all he ever said about it—"I don't think this is that kind of war." He enlisted without telling one soul. He had a job at which he was extremely good and at which he got a preposterous, in anybody's terms, salary. Just before he left, he had an offer of a six-months contract at Hollywood at twelve hundred and fifty dollars a week.

Of course it is right that he did what he has done—but no one told him what was right, except himself. He had had a bad time. When he was a kid, he liked his father; he has apparently always hated his mother. When he was fourteen, sensitive and cognizant, his mother divorced his father, took Alan, and never allowed him to see his father again. (His father died some three years after.) His resentment against his mother increased to the point where he cannot remain in the room with her—although she gives him some curious guilt, as only Southern mothers can, about his lack of filial duty. He went to New York after V.M.I—because his father went there; he himself loathed a military college—did what he could and damn near starved. Hollywood was all assurance to him. He was good at what he did, he did it with all his conscience, he said whatever it was, it was honest work—not what came out of it, but what he put into it.

And I behaved like a shit to him, Alec. I screamed about Hollywood. I had much right on my side, but I used all the wrong things. I yipped about lowering of standards and debasing of principles. There was a lot in what I said. But there was nothing in what I thought I understood. Private Campbell's standards are not low.

He's given up a lot. His job, the house here he builded—no, I don't mean built, I mean Builded—which, I think, means more to him than anything. Anything, of course, except what he must do. I know other men have done as much, but sometimes I see the other side. I hear men who say, "Gee, I'd certainly like to do something in the war—but there's my business I've got to look after, and everything." I hear women who say, "Well, let them take everybody but George. Goodness knows they don't need him—they've got enough men." They are not the natives or the workers around here, who are all we've seen, day by day. But when we've been in to New York, we've heard those things.

Now about Alan's mother. She always comes up to expectations, but this time she has outdone them and herself. When she heard Alan had enlisted, she made a scene that shook the oat fields. "Selfish", "heartless", "never thinks of me"—oh, it was great. Then when she found that did not induce him to desert the army, she found a happier—for her—role. She became the gold-star mother. Her heart was broken. She went all about the country side—she has a B card, I guess for being Southern—telling all the neighbors of the sacrifice she was making for her country. In most cases the act flopped; their sons had gone before hers. But she got some of them. There was a little delegation that came up here and talked to Alan and me about that poor sick woman living all alone. Alan spoke to them. We ended friends.

Then she tried heart attacks. We brought our doctor, who pronounced her in perfect shape. She then, of course, hated him and us. I am not a vengeful woman, no matter what you have said—possibly for the perfectly working reason that if you just sit back and wait, the bastards will get theirs, without your doing anything about it, and it will be fancier than anything you could ever have thought up. But I would, for the sake of immediate action, give quite a large bit of my soul if something horrible would happen to that woman for poisoning Alan's last days here.

You see, there is no basis for it, Alec, but her insane selfishness. It isn't that she is not going to see him for a while. When he was in Hollywood for a year or so at a crack, when he was in New York, when he first came, for four years without once seeing her, that never worried her. Nor can it be the dread of immediate or even eventual danger for him. When he was in Spain, being bombed and shelled and machine-gunned and sniped at, she sat under a magnolia tree and waved her fan. (I may say, when we came back from Spain, she said to me, "well, that old war wasn't goin' on while you were there, was it?" So I said, with what I thought was blasting irony, "Oh, no, they stopped the war while your son was there". So she said, smiling elegantly, "Well, I tho't so.") It's just that she must do everything to make everything wretched for everybody but herself and her importance. I know. I know it is pathetic that she can achieve importance in no other way. Only, you know, it isn't.

She lives perhaps five miles from us, in a most horrible little house, horrible because of her decor. ("Awways sayude ah could be inteya decraytuh") It is how-ever, a little house, if you consider four bedrooms, three baths and the usuals lit-tle, which I do not. She refers to it as her "rotten lil ole shayukah". (That is meant to spell the way she says "shack", but I guess it doesn't actually convey it.) The fact that Alan and I bought her the shayukah at great expense, and keep it going at greater, means nothing. She wants to come live here. I don't know what the hell she would do here. Here I am with no servants, no telephone, no gasoline—even if I could drive. The farmer and his wife and children live over in the barn, a good stone's throw if you had a pitching arm. I can't stay on here. In the first place, I've got to root up some work, and in the second nobody could do it. But she is obsessed to move in here, and settle. And if you say "Why not?" I can only say we tried that once, while we were in Hollywood, and she fired our farmer—and oh boy, are they hard to replace—fired our servants, and set fire to our drawing-room.

This isn't lousy. She could go back to Richmond, where she lives with an enormous family of brothers and sisters all of whom she has buffaloed, and a circle of illiterate friends. But she won't do it. She wails about her horrible lone-liness here, and when Alan—who is afraid of her, there's no good saying he isn't and so for that matter am I—suggests that she go back home, she says that Richmond is too dangerous—she's just sure they're goin to bomb it. She says she'd only feel real safe in this house. . . .

Oh, the hell with her. I don't want to talk about her any more. Anyway she'll be here any minute—because she'll always be here any minute, no matter what time—and I'll have to face it.

And who am I to talk about people's families? On the way back from Phila-delphia, I telephoned my brother and sister—whom I had neglected to inform that I was back in the East. I got my sister, and said Alan had enlisted and had gone. She said, "Oh, isn't that terrible? Well, it's been terrible here, too, all Sum-mer. I never saw such a Summer. Why, they didn't even have dances Saturday nights at the club."

So then I tried my brother, who is not bad, but I got my sister-in-law. I told her about Alan. She said, "Oh, really? Well, of course, he's had a college education. That's what's holding Bertram back—he never had a college education". (She has a son named Bertram, approximately thirty-five) "He'd just love to be an aviator, but of course he hasn't got a college education". I skipped over Bertram's advanced age for the aviation corps, and explained that the college-educated Alan had enlisted as a private. "Oh, really?" she said. "Oh, listen, Dot, we're going to take a new apartment, the first of October. It's got two rooms that the sun simply POURS in—and you know how I love sun!" I don't, Alec.

Honestly, if you were suddenly to point a finger at me and say, "Dorothy Parker, what is your sister-in-law's opinion of sun?" I should be dum-founded.

Jesus Christ. People whose country is at war. People who live in a world on fire, in a time when there have never before been such dangers, such threats, such murders. . . .

Well. On the other hand, and so far outbalancing them, thank God, there are those boys in their sweat-stained shirts streaming in to enlist, there are those sixty men saying "I do" in one strong voice, there is Private Campbell, U.S.A.

I think I'd like to write a story about that enlistment place. That isn't being phoney, is it?

I've got to write a lot of stories—if, of course, I can. I've got the farm to keep going, I've got myself, I've got Alan's mother. I've been feeling pretty guilty about not doing any war work. But if I can keep all this swinging, I'll be releasing a man for the front just as much as if I were welding in a factory. I am proud to think that and to know it.

Dear Alec, I'll be here for a few days, and then I'm going in to the Ritz Tower. Alan knew the manager and got me a room, much less expensive than you think, though still too expensive. I will, though, as often as the hired man can spare gas to meet me at the station, come out here, because there are alterations going on, and I should say a few words. This address is always the one for me. Please, dear Alec, please. I'll be embarrassed when this letter is sent. It's so long. I can only say, if I had had more time, it would have been longer. I think you know that my friendship could not be deeper and higher than writing you this, and knowing you understand why and to whom I write it.

Dear Alec——

Dorothy—

*   *   *

1942: SEPTEMBER 6
GUS FALEN TO EDDIE HOFFMAN

Eddie Hoffman first met Gus Falen at a restaurant called the Peek-in-Grill in Buf-
falo, New York, where Hoffman was bartender. Falen, twenty-five, had been a truck
driver and a member of the New York State National Guard before the war, and
Hoffman, thirty-five and the father of three, befriended him. Lieutenant Falen
would end up marrying his army nurse, and after twenty-seven years in the military
would retire as a field commander with the rank of major.

Ft. Benning, Ga.
Sept. 6, 1942

Dear Eddie,

You should have seen me last week on Payday. I got 205 bucks. We have a great & beautiful Officers' Club here at Benning. There are many snobbish officers who look at you. But I don't give a damn.

I round up a couple extra crazy Parachute Officers and we call up the Army Nurses. Boy, they're always crazy to go out . . . cause they can only go out with officers ('cause they're 2nd Lts.) and most officers here are married.

And these Army Nurses in their pretty blue uniforms are crazy about Paratrooper Officers. They know we make $271 a month and they—poor kids—only make $90 a month. Eddie, we have some <u>real wild</u> times! . . . .

Eddie, I didn't write lately—not because I was busy (I'm never too busy to write to you) but because I was scratched up a little bit.

From one of my jumps from high tower on a bad windy day—I landed hard on my neck & shoulder. Perfect landing!

Dislocated my right shoulder & pulled several ligaments out, fractured my right knee cap, and busted 2 ribs on my left side. Not counting the bloody nose, etc.—being scraped along ground. I was more dead than alive. Now, 2 weeks later, I'm almost healed up. They wanted to disqualify me. Had orders to send me back to Infantry. So, I, Gus Falen, went to see General Howell—Commander of all Paratroopers & Airborne Command.

It took a lot nerve for me—just a 2nd Lt. to see the <u>General</u> but I did it!

He smiled & liked me—listened to me as I stood snappy at attention & explained my story.

So, tomorrow I start jumping from towers again. Then 5 jumps from plane next week. It's fun jumping from towers with a 'chute but oh those plane jumps—we all "sweat" them out.

It takes lot of nerve to haul yourself out into the clouds and dangle thru space before your 'chute opens up.

In last 2 jumps (of 5 jumps) we act as Jump masters.

Well, each one of us officers takes 12 enlisted men up in a plane with him. I lay on my belly on the floor of the plane with my head sticking out door (plane doing 150 m.p.h.) When I see I'm getting near my "X" on ground, I give 4 commands. "Stand up!" "Hook up!" "Check your equipment." "Stand at door"—"Go!" and I jump first. They all follow me out.

It's bad enough that I'm shaking like a leaf, then I have to check over all those 12 boys who are privates & corporals & 1 sergeant. My Sergeant (who is my 2nd in Command) jumps last.

I'll be so damn scared but I'll try my damndest to hide it so my men won't see their officer is scared.

I'll just swallow hard, say a short prayer, & go. . . .

In a week, if I'm alive, (and I hope to be) I'll tell you all about it.

Guess I'll say g'nite now.

Have damn good time with gang.

> Your nervous sky-jumpin' pal,
> Gus Falen

PS: You've got a little souvenir comin'. And I'll send you those bars first chance I get.

1942: OCTOBER 30?
DWIGHT EISENHOWER TO MAMIE EISENHOWER

Eisenhower was serving as U.S. commander of the European theater of operations when he wrote this birthday letter to his wife. He was in London, on the brink of leading the Allied invasion of North Africa. Eisenhower would go on to command all Allied forces in Europe, direct the D day invasion, head the NATO forces in Europe after the war, and serve two terms as president.

Milton and Helen were Eisenhower's brother and sister-in-law. His naval aide's wife, Ruth Butcher, shared an apartment with Mamie during the war. The "do not open" instruction was written on the envelope.

Not to be opened until November 14

HEADQUARTERS

United States Army Forces

in

The British Isles

My sweet heart—

By the time you read this your newspapers will probably have told you where I am and you will understand why your birthday letter had to be written some time in advance. You will also realize that I have been busy—very busy—and any lapses in the arrival of letters will be explained to you. Knowing that all this will be plain to you by the time you read this I am not compelled to violate rules of secrecy and censorship in order to tell you what I am planning to do.

I hope you won't be disturbed or worried. War inevitably carries its risks to life and limb—but the chances, in my case, are all in my favor—a fact which you must always remember. Moreover—even if the worst should ever happen to me, please don't be too upset. In 31 years as a soldier I've been exposed to few of the risks that most have encountered. If I had been in the Theatre of Operations during the World War I, I might easily have long since been gone. And, while I don't mean to be fatalistic or too philosophical—I truly feel that what the U.S. and the world are facing today is so much bigger than anyone of us can even comprehend, that personal sacrifice and loss must not be allowed to overwhelm any of us.

Anyway—on the day you open this letter you'll be 46. I'd like to be there to help you celebrate, and to kiss you 46 times (multiplied by any number you care to pick). I imagine Ruth will have some little party for you, or maybe Helen & Milton will try to get hold of you. In any event I will be with you in thought, and entirely aside from the usual congratulations and felicitations I will be thinking with the deepest gratitude of the many happy hours and years you've given me. I am quite aware of the fact that I'm not always easy to live with—that frequently I'm irascible and even mean—and my gratitude is all the greater when I realize how often you've put up with me in spite of such traits.

The crowning thing you've given me is our son—he has been so wonderful, unquestionably because he's so much you—that I find I live in him so very often. Your love and our son have been my greatest gifts from life, and on your birthday I wish that my powers of expression were such as to make you understand that thoroughly—clearly and for always. I've never wanted any other wife—you're mine, and for that reason I've been luckier than any other man.

I feel this war is so big—so vast—that my mind completely refuses to visualize anything beyond its possible end. But I do hope that all through it I do my duty so well, so efficiently, that regardless of what may happen to me you and John can always be proud that we three are one family. I do <u>not</u> seek rank—I don't even seek acclaim, because it is easily possible that a commander can receive credit (and <u>blame</u>) for which he is no wise responsible. But if my own conscience tells me I've done my duty—I will always come back to you in the certainty that you'd understand any fall from the high places, and that my place in your heart would be as big as ever.

Again—love and kisses on your birthday!

1943: FEBRUARY
ALLEN SPACH TO HIS FATHER

Guadalcanal, the largest of the Solomon Islands in the southwest Pacific, constituted a strategic prize for which the United States and Japan battled fiercely. On August 7, 1942, the first wave of marines landed there; Curtis Allen Spach was among them. He stayed on the front lines for 110 days, until December 9, when his division was relieved and sent to Australia. The island was eventually captured by the Allies in February of 1943.

Dear Dad,

I think you will find this letter quite different than the others which you've received from me. My health is well as could be expected as most of us boys in the original outfit that left the States together about CENSORED of us are still here. The other are replacements. The missing have either been killed, wounded or from other various sources mainly malaria fever.

On May 16 '42 we left New River N.C., and went to the docks at Norfolk. On the 20th at midnight we hit the high seas with 7,000 marines aboard the U.S.S. Wakefield. We went down through the Panama Canal and past Cuba. On the 29th we crossed the international date line, latitude 0°, 0′, 0″ longitude 85°, 45′, 30″. Was continually harassed by submarines as we had no convoy whatsoever.

We landed in New Zealand 28 days later and they were wonderful to us as we were the first Americans to arrive there. We lived aboard ship at the dock for about a month loading equipment on incoming ships getting ready for "<u>The Day</u>." After working day and night we left and went to one of the Fiji Islands for four days. I was aboard the U.S.S. Fuller picked up in New Zealand. In our convoy were about 100 ships including 3 aircraft carriers and the battleship, North Carolina. We also had air protection from Flying Fortresses coming from Australia. On August 6 we had our last dinner aboard ship and they gave us all we wanted with ice cream and a pack of cigarettes. Just like a man doomed for the electric chair he got any kind of food for this last meal. That was our last for a while. Each one of us received a letter from our commanding officer, the last sentence reading Good Luck, God Bless You and to hell with the Japs. On the morning of the 7th I went over the side with the first wave of troops as Rifle Grenadier, just another chicken in the infantry. With naval bombardment and supreme control of the air we hit the beach at 9.47. All hell broke loose. Two days later our ships left taking our aircraft with them, never to have any sea and air protection for the next two CENSORED. In the meantime the Japanese navy and air force took the advantage and gave us hell from sea and air. I won't say what the ground troops had to offer us yet. I can say we never once retreated but kept rushing forward taking the airport first thing.

Left to do or die we fought hard with one purpose in mind to do, kill every slant eyed bastard within range of rifle fire or the bayonet which was the only thing left to stop their charge. We were on the front lines 110 days before we could drop back for a shave, wash up. Don't many people know it but we were the first allied troops to be on the lines that long, either in this war or the last. We have had to face artillery both naval and field, mortar bombings sometimes three or four times a day, also at night, flame throwers, hand grenades, tanks, booby traps, land mines, everything I guess except gas. The most common headache caused by machine gun fire, snipers, rifle fire, and facing sabers, bayonet fighting, the last most feared by all. A war in five offensive drives and also in defense of our own lines. I've had buddies shot down on both sides of me, my closest calls being a shot put through the top of my helmet by a sniper. Once I had to swim a river when we were trapped by the enemy.

With no supplies coming in we had to eat coconuts, captured rice, crab meat, fish heads. We also smoked their dopey cigarettes. We also captured a warehouse full of good Saba Beer, made in Tokyo. Didn't shave or have hair cut for nearly four months, looked rather funny too. Wore Jap clothing such as underwear, socks, shoes. Had plenty of thrills watching our boys in the air planes dog fighting after they sent us some planes to go on the newly finished field that they had built. We found field pieces and pictures of American girls and mothers on Japs that we killed. They were taken off the Marines at Wake Island. They used explosive and dum dum bullets in their long rifles so we cut the ends of ours off with bayonets so that when they were hit the bullet would spread making a hell of a hole in them. You had to beat them at their own tricks. What few of the old fellows here are scarred by various wounds and 90% have malaria. I've been down with it several times but I dose heavy with quinine till I feel drunk. It gets you so that you feel as if your eyes are popping out and very weak and lousy. We want to come home for a while before seeing action again which is in the very near future, but they won't do it even though the doctors want us to. We were continually bombed and strafed but took it pretty good. The average age of the boys was 21 and were around 18 to 20. When we were finally relieved by the army who were all larger and older they were surprised to find us kids who had done such a good job. My best buddie at the time was caught in the face by a full blast of machine gun fire and when the hole we were laying in became swamped by flies gathering about him and being already dead, I had to roll him out of the small hole on top of the open ground and the dirty SOBs kept shooting him full of holes. Well anyway God spared my life and I am thankful for it. I know that your and dear Mama's prayers helped bring me safely through the long months of it. I hope that you will forgive me of my misdoings as it had to take this war to bring me to my senses. Only then did I realize how much you both had done for me and Dear God, maybe I can come through the next to see you and my friends again. . . .

God bless the whole world and I'm looking forward to the days when Italy and Germany are licked so that the whole might of the allied nations can be thrown in to crush Japan and the swines that are her sons, fighting to rule the white race. I heard an English speaking Nip say that if he didn't die fighting, that is if he didn't win or if he was captured and later came to Japan, he would be put in prison for 17 years and that all his property would be taken over by the government. That's his point of view. Where ever we go us boys will do our best always till the end when we don't have the strength to press a trigger.

Please understand that I didn't write this so as to worry you anymore than I already have but I wanted you to know I am doing my best for your Uncle Sam. Maybe some day I will be able to sleep in that thing called a bed and eat from a table. Just simple everyday things, but they mean a lot when you have to live in jungles and lay in filthy stinking surroundings day after day. If you let the folks over there see this, cut out the names of the ships and certain countries which I mentioned, for they shouldn't be discussed. Wishing you all health and happiness, will say goodby for now. Give Mother and the kids my love.

Love always,
Your son,
Allen

1943: APRIL 26

JOHN BRAINERD TO HAROLD PENDER

The first general-purpose electronic digital computer, called ENIAC, was originally designed for the U.S. War Department (under the code name "Project PX") to calculate ballistics trajectories. Harold Pender was dean of the Moore School at the University of Pennsylvania, where ENIAC was developed, and John G. Brainerd supervised the ENIAC team, led by John W. Mauchly and J. Presper Eckert, Jr. Once operational, the machine used eighteen thousand vacuum tubes, consumed 174 kilowatts of electrical power, weighed more than thirty tons, and had a footprint of eighty feet by three feet. Fifty years later, to celebrate ENIAC's birthday, students at the University of Pennsylvania would use transistors, electronic switches, and a PC to create an "ENIAC" on an eight-by-eight-millimeter chip. But however cumbersome the original was, it did constitute the beginning of the computer age.

Dean Harold Pender
Dr. J. G. Brainerd
April 26, 1943
Proposed Army Project

As you know, we have had numerous conferences recently with representatives of the Ordnance Department of the Army concerning the possibility of developing and constructing an electronic difference analyzer and computer. These conversations have progressed unexpectedly rapidly, and I therefore want to place before you in writing the situation as it now stands. If the proposed project continues to move as swiftly as it has in the past month, there is a possibility that we might have a letter of intent within another month. We would, consequently, like to have at this time approval for continuing the discussions, the goal of which would be a definite proposal which might be submitted to the Executive Committee.

1. The electronic difference analyzer and computer is a proposed device never previously built, which would perform all the operations of the present differential analyzers and would in addition carry out numerous other processes for which no provision is made on present analyzers. It is called a "difference" analyzer rather than a "differential" analyzer for technical reasons.

2. The proposed project would be sponsored by the Ordnance Department and the difference analyzer, when and if built, would be for the specific use of the Ballistic Research Laboratory of the Army, at the Aberdeen Proving Ground Maryland.

3. The reasons for the Ordnance Department's interest in this device is that its speed of operation would be very considerably greater than that of any present analyzer, and in addition it would carry out many processes not now performed on differential analyzers, but which are required in ballistic computations.

The simplest way of illustrating the desirability of developing the proposed new difference analyzer is probably to point out that the calculations now being performed on the Moore School differential analyzer have fallen far behind the need for them. In the specific case of sidewise firing from airplanes, construction of directors for guns has been held up several months because it has been a physical impossibility to supply to the manufacturers the necessary ballistic data. The proposed electronic difference analyzer would, if successfully developed, not only eliminate such delays but would permit far more extensive ballistic calculations than are now possible with available equipment.

4. The cost of the development of the proposed electronic analyzer is estimated at $150,000. The tenor of the recent conversations with Ordnance Department officers has been that most of this money would be made available to the Moore School if the project were undertaken. It is desirable, however, and we have recommended to the Ordnance department, that one of the numerous units in the proposed new device be developed in the RCA Research Laboratories. This would leave about nine-tenths of the work at the Moore School.

It is not anticipated that a contract for $150,000 would be received immediately. Instead it is probable that money would be supplied for development, and as soon as the various needed units were developed the balance necessary for completion of the difference analyzer would be made available.

5. To provide personnel for the project under discussion we might plan to use the men now working on PL #2 (contract expires June 30) and on PZ #3 and #4 on which work will be completed in the near future. Most of these men are research engineers employed specifically for war research. The two staff members concerned could carry their normal teaching loads.

6. A brief chronological outline of the steps in the development of this project will serve to illustrate how the Moore School has come to be a central factor in it. In August 1942 a group on the staff discussed the possibilities of an electronic difference analyzer and a brief typewritten discussion was circulated. Nothing was done at that time. However, late in March 1943 the Ordnance officer in charge of the Ballistic Research Laboratory's unit now stationed in the Moore School chanced upon the memorandum. He mentioned it at Aberdeen, and we were asked to prepare a report, which was done on April 2. A more com-

plete report was prepared on April 9, when Moore School representatives made a trip to Aberdeen at the Army's request. Shortly thereafter Colonel Simon, in charge of the Ballistic Research Laboratory, indicated that he was inclined to include $150,000 in his budget for the project. Following this, numerous conferences have been held and it is my understanding that after the conclusion of a conference on April 20, Colonel Gillon of the Office of the Chief of Ordnance stated that the possibilities were so important that the Army should invest the money in the development. It has been pointed out both to Colonel Simon and Colonel Gillon that this is a development project and that there is no certainty that the desired result can be achieved. It is, however, a reasonable chance.

At the present time the situation is that Colonel Gillon is calling a meeting in Washington some time next week to review details and to discuss procurement and other problems.

J. G. Brainerd

1943: JUNE 29
FRANKLIN ROOSEVELT TO J. ROBERT OPPENHEIMER

With physicist J. Robert Oppenheimer (1904–1967) heading its Los Alamos, New Mexico, laboratory, the Manhattan Project had been started the summer before this letter was written. It would culminate two summers later, on July 16, 1945, with the first experimental detonation of the atomic bomb.

Dr. Vannevar Bush, an electrical engineer who had invented the differential analyzer in 1928, headed the U.S. Office of Scientific Research and Development during World War II. General Leslie Groves was the military director of the Manhattan Project.

THE WHITE HOUSE
Washington

June 29, 1943

<u>Secret</u>

My dear Dr. Oppenheimer:

I have recently reviewed with Dr. Bush the highly important and secret program of research, development and manufacture with which you are familiar. I was very glad to hear of the excellent work which is being done in a number of places in this country under the immediate supervision of General L. H. Groves and the general direction of the Committee of which Dr. Bush is Chairman. The successful solution of the problem is of the utmost importance to the national safety, and I am confident that the work will be completed in as short a time as possible as the result of the wholehearted cooperation of all concerned.

I am writing to you as the leader of one group which is to play a vital role in the months ahead. I know that you and your colleagues are working on a hazardous matter under unusual circumstances. The fact that the outcome of your labors is of such great significance to the nation requires that this program be even more drastically guarded than other highly secret war developments. I have therefore given directions that every precaution be taken to insure the security of your project and feel sure that those in charge will see that these orders are carried out. You are fully aware of the reasons why your own endeavors and those of your associates must be circumscribed by very special restrictions. Nevertheless, I wish you would express to the scientists assembled with you my deep appreciation of their willingness to undertake the tasks which lie before them in spite of the dangers and the personal sacrifices. I am sure we can rely on their continued wholehearted and unselfish labors. Whatever the enemy may be planning, American science will be equal to the challenge. With that thought in mind, I send this note of confidence and appreciation.

Though there are other important groups at work, I am writing only to you as the leader of the one which is operating under very special conditions, and to General Groves. While this letter is secret, the contents of it may be disclosed to your associates under a pledge of secrecy.

Very sincerely yours,
Franklin D. Roosevelt

Dr. J. R. Oppenheimer,
Post Office Box 1663,
Santa Fe,
New Mexico.

1943: JUNE 30
ROBERT HENDON TO CLYDE TOLSON

J. Edgar Hoover (see letter page 353) ruled the FBI for forty-eight years, serving under eight presidents, until his death in 1972. Robert Hendon and Clyde Tolson were both FBI assistant directors. Tolson was also Hoover's closest colleague, best friend, and frequent companion on weekends and vacations. Despite their evident homophobia, they were rumored to have been a gay couple themselves, a charge to which, as this memo suggests, Hoover was particularly sensitive. The fact that a

women's bridge game could attract the notice of the federal government gives some
indication not only of the reach, but also of the paranoia, of the FBI director.

Tolson would become associate director in 1947. He would resign from the bureau within a
day of J. Edgar's Hoover's death.

FEDERAL BUREAU OF INVESTIGATION

ROH:DW   June 30, 1943

PERSONAL AND CONFIDENTIAL

   As a matter of record, SAC Guerin telephoned from New Orleans on
June 26. He advised that NAME WITHHELD, Cleveland, Ohio, is an aunt of
Special Agent NAME WITHHELD assigned to the New Orleans Office whom
she is visiting at the present time. NAME WITHHELD advised Agent NAME
WITHHELD for the benefit of the Bureau and Agent NAME WITHHELD im-
mediately advised SAC Guerin that on June 11, 1943, a bridge party was held at
her home in Cleveland. In attendance at this party were the following:
   NAME WITHHELD Cleveland
   NAME WITHHELD Cleveland
   NAME WITHHELD Lakewood, Ohio
   NAME WITHHELD Lakewood, Ohio
   NAME WITHHELD Titusville, Pennsylvania
   NAME WITHHELD New Brighton, Pennsylvania
   NAME WITHHELD stated that NAME WITHHELD had formerly been
connected with the Emerson High School in Cleveland. NAME WITHHELD
stated that during the course of the bridge party the Director's name was men-
tioned at which time NAME WITHHELD made the statement that the Direc-
tor was a homosexual and kept a large group of young boys around him. NAME
WITHHELD said that one person in the party immediately took NAME
WITHHELD to task for this statement pointing out that it just did not line up
with the responsibilities and reputation of the Director.
   After advising the Director of this matter telephonically, I contacted
SAC Boardman at Cleveland and instructed him to vigorously take NAME
WITHHELD to task for her gossip. SAC Boardman advised me telephonically
yesterday that NAME WITHHELD, whose maiden name was NAME WITH-
HELD, had been an old maid school teacher at Emerson High School until
her marriage five years ago to NAME WITHHELD. Her husband is a motion
picture operator NAME WITHHELD. Their reputation and background are
satisfactory.

Boardman called NAME WITHHELD into his office and severely chastised her, pointing out that he personally resented such a malicious and unfounded statement as she had made and that he could not understand what would lead her to make any such libelous statement concerning a man in such a responsible position as the Director who had in his hands the internal security of the country in wartime

NAME WITHHELD was deeply sorry and indicated she did not blame Mr. Boardman for being indignant. She explained that while on a trip with her husband in the fall of 1941 they were eating in Millers Restaurant in Baltimore. At an adjoining table were several young men who were having a riotous time and who were discussing various personalities. They mentioned that Herbert Hoover was at the time on a fishing trip and then one of them said that on that day he had seen J. Edgar Hoover of the FBI go through Baltimore with his chauffeur. To this one of the men stated that the chauffeur was Mr. Hoover's sweetheart and that Hoover was queer.

NAME WITHHELD claimed that she never said anything about this nor had she thought anything about it until the day of this bridge party. She said during the course of the bridge party there was the ordinary small talk and some mention was made of the Director. One of the girls pointed out that the Director was a bachelor and she wondered why. To this NAME WITHHELD said that she replied she understood Mr. Hoover was queer. She said there was no discussion of this and immediately after she made the statement she thought it should not have been made and she could not understand why she had made it. She stated that those in attendance at the bridge party had been gathering like this for a period of eleven years and she was going to point out to each of those present that her statement was not founded on fact and that she was deeply sorry that she had made it and it should not have been made at all. She is going to advise Boardman when this has been done.

Boardman emphasized that he had chastised her most vigorously and that she thoroughly understood the untruth of her statements and the serious nature of her action in having made them.

Respectfully,
Robert C. Hendon

director fully advised
RH

*   *   *

1943: JULY 4

WILLIAM FAULKNER TO MALCOLM FRANKLIN

Malcolm Franklin (1923–1977) was the stepson of William Faulkner (see letter page 171) and would serve as a combat medic in Europe during World War II.
Jim was Faulkner's nephew. Pantelleria, an Italian island strategically located between Sicily and Tunisia, was used as a base by Mussolini until the Allies destroyed its installations by air in 1943. A ukase is an edict.

Sunday

Dear Buddy:

Mr Robert Haas is vice president of Random House. They publish my books. During the times when I would be broke, year after year sometimes, I had only to write him and he would send me money—no hope to get it back, unless I wrote another book. He's a Jew.

He had an only son, and a daughter. In '40, the son withdrew from Yale and became a Navy pilot. In '41, the girl about 20, joined that Womens' Ferry Squadron, is now flying, ferrying aeroplanes from factories to bases. The boy was flying torpedo planes off carriers (what Jim is training for) in the Pacific. He was killed last week. The girl is still flying. All Jews. I just hope I dont run into some hundred percent American Legionnaire until I feel better.

There is a squadron of negro pilots. They finally got congress to allow them to learn how to risk their lives in the air. They are in Africa now, under their own negro lt. colonel, did well at Pantelleria, on the same day a mob of white men and white policemen killed 20 negroes in Detroit. Suppose you and me and a few others of us lived in the Congo, freed seventy-seven years ago by ukase; of course we cant live in the same apartment hut with the black folks, nor always ride in the same car nor eat in the same restaurant, but we are free because the Great Black Father says so. Then the Congo is engaged in War with the Cameroon. At last we persuade the Great Black Father to let us fight too. You and Jim say are flyers. You have just spent the day trying to live long enough to learn how to do your part in saving the Congo. Then you come back down and are told that 20 of your people have just been killed by a mixed mob of civilians and cops at Little Poo Poo. What would you think?

A change will come out of this war. If it doesn't, if the politicians and the people who run this country are not forced to make good the shibboleth they glibly talk about freedom, liberty, human rights, then you young men who live through it will have wasted your precious time, and those who dont live through it will have died in vain.

Pappy

1943: AUGUST 3
JOHN KENNEDY TO THE TOWN OF RENDOVA

Future president John F. Kennedy (1917–1963) used a jackknife to scratch this message into a coconut husk after his navy patrol torpedo boat, PT109, was destroyed by a Japanese ship in the Pacific. After his rescue, the coconut was returned to him. Years later, encased in plastic, it would be a fixture on his presidential desk.

NAURO ISL
COMMANDER　　　NATIVE KNOWS
POS'IT　　HE CAN PILOT　　11 ALIVE
NEED SMALL BOAT　　　KENNEDY

1943: AUGUST 16
PERRIN LONG TO THE SURGEON, NATOUSA

Eisenhower, by now Supreme Commander of the Allied Expeditionary Force, forwarded this letter to his old friend Patton, writing, "I hope you can assure me that none of [these allegations] is true." No such assurance was possible. But the incidents and the news of them closely followed Patton's victorious invasion of Sicily and capture of Palermo—and no official reprimand resulted. Patton, however, was called upon to make a public apology. The story soon spread, and the "slapping incident" became notorious. Writing in his journal after receiving these reports, Patton admitted that his "method was wrong," but insisted, "My motive was correct because one cannot permit skulking to exist."

An E.M.T. was an emergency medical tag.

Letter, Lt. Col. Perrin H. Long, Medical Corps, to The Surgeon, NATOUSA, August 16, 1943, subject: Mistreatment of Patients in Receiving Tents of the 15th and 93d Evacuation Hospitals

Exhibit No. 1—Pvt. Charles H. Kuhl, L Company, 26th Infantry, 1st Division, was seen in the . . . aid station on August 2, 1943 . . . where a diagnosis of "Exhaustion" was made . . . He was evacuated to C Company, 1st Medical Battalion. There a note was made on the patient's E.M.T. that he had been admitted to Company C three times for "Exhaustion" during the Sicilian Campaign. From C Company he was evacuated to the clearing company . . . There he was put in "quarters" and was given sodium mytal . . . On 3 August '43, the following note appears on the E.M.T. "Psychoneurosis anxiety state—moderate severe (soldier has been twice before in hospital within ten days. He can't take it at the front, evidently. He is repeatedly returned.)" . . . He was evacuated to the 15th Evacuation Hospital. While he was waiting in the receiving tent . . . Lt.. Gen. George S. Patton, Jr., came into the tent with the commanding officer and other medical officers . . . The General spoke to the various patients in the receiving tent and especially commended the wounded men. Then he came to Pvt. Kuhl and asked him what was the matter. The soldier replied, "I guess I can't take it." The General immediately flared up, cursed the soldier, called him all types of a coward, then slapped him across the face with his gloves and finally grabbed the soldier by the scruff of his neck and kicked him out of the tent. The soldier was immediately picked up by corpsmen and taken to a ward tent. There he was found to have a temperature of 102.2 degrees F and he gave a history of chronic diarrhea for about one month, having at times as high as ten or twelve stools a day. The next day his fever continued and a blood smear was found to be positive for malarial parasites. The final disposition diagnosis was chronic dysentery and malaria. This man had been in the Army eight months and with the 1st Division since about June 2d.

Exhibit No. 2—Pvt. Paul G. Bennett, C Battery, 17th Field Artillery, was admitted to the 93d Evacuation Hospital . . . 10 August '43. This patient was a 21 year old boy who had served four years in the regular Army. His unit had been with II Corps since March and he had never had any difficulties until August 6th, when his buddy was wounded. He could not sleep that night and felt nervous. The shells going over him bothered him. The next day he was worried about his buddy and became more nervous. He was sent down to the rear echelon by a battery aid man and there the medical officer gave him some medicine which made him sleep, but still he was nervous and disturbed. On the next day the medical officer ordered him to be evacuated, although the boy begged not to be evacuated because he did not want to leave his unit.

Lt. General George S. Patton, Jr., entered the receiving tent and spoke to all the injured men. The next patient was sitting huddled up and shivering. When asked what his trouble was, the man replied, "It's my nerves," and began to sob. The General then screamed at him, "What did you say?" The man replied, "It's my nerves, I can't stand the shelling any more." He was still sobbing. The General then yelled at him, "Your nerves, hell; you are just a Goddamned coward, you yellow son of a bitch." He then slapped the man and said, "Shut up that Goddamned crying. I won't have these brave men here who have been shot at seeing a yellow bastard sitting here crying." He then struck the man again, knocking his helmet liner off and into the next tent. He then turned to the admitting officer and yelled, "Don't admit this yellow bastard; there's nothing the matter with him. I don't have the hospitals cluttered up with these sons of bitches who haven't got the guts to fight." He then turned to the man again, who was managing to sit at attention though shaking all over and said, "You're going back to the front lines and you may get shot and killed, but you're going to fight. If you don't, I'll stand you up against a wall and have a firing squad kill you on purpose. In fact," he said, reaching for his pistol, "I ought to shoot you myself, you Goddamned whimpering coward." As he left the tent, the General was still yelling back to the receiving officer to send that yellow son of a bitch back to the front line. Nurses and patients attracted by the shouting and cursing came from adjoining tents and witnessed this disturbance.

The deleterious effects of such incidents upon the wellbeing of patients, upon the professional morale of hospital staffs, and upon the relationship of patient to physician are incalculable.

It is imperative that immediate steps be taken to prevent a recurrence of such incidents.

1944: FEBRUARY 2
GEORGE MARSHALL TO HERBY FUNSTON

General George C. Marshall (1880–1959) was U.S. Army Chief of Staff when he took the time to respond to a letter from young Herby Funston of Keota, Iowa.

February 2, 1944

My dear Herby,   I like your letter, the fact that you want to do your full part in licking these Japs, and that you are training every day to prepare to serve the country as a soldier.

It is true "that selling and buying bonds and stamps and salvaging is fighting a war". These things must be done, so somebody must do them and that seems to be your duty at the present time. But I sympathize with you in your desire to avenge the "nice kid" from your town who became a prisoner in the Philippines.

Be patient and don't give up the effort you are now making, but I must confess to you that it makes me sad as well as very angry to think that these Japs and

Nazis have brought us to such a pass that fine, clean young boys like you must be thinking of killing men, of machine guns, bombs and other deadly tools of war. We are in the terrible business of staightening out this demoralized world so that you and your friends and millions of boys and girls like you may think more of kindness than of death and hatreds and may live useful lives in a peaceful world. But today your older brothers and your fathers and cousins need your backing at home every day of the week.

Faithfully yours,

George C. Marshall

1944: MAY 14
AYN RAND TO FRANK LLOYD WRIGHT

Ayn Rand (1905–1982) was best known for her novel The Fountainhead, *which was published in 1943 after having been rejected by twelve publishers. A cult classic, especially after it was made into a movie starring Gary Cooper, it celebrated the spirit of individualism as personified by the character of the self-interested, headstrong architect Howard Roark.*

Wright (see letter page 243) made drawings for a Rand house, but it was never built.

May 14, 1944

Dear Mr. Wright,

Thank you. Your letter was like the closing of a circle for me, the end of ten years of my life that began and had to end with you. I felt that The Fountainhead had not quite completed its destiny until I had heard from you about it. Now it is completed.

Thank you for your very gracious sentence: "So far as I have unconsciously contributed anything to your material you are welcome." You know, of course, that you have contributed a great deal, and I think that you know in what way. I have taken the principle which you represent, but not the form, and I have translated it into the form of another person. I was careful not to touch upon anything personal to you as a man. I took only the essence of what constitutes a great individualist and a great artist.

I have thought that you might resent Howard Roark, not for the things in which he resembles you, but precisely for the things in which he doesn't. So I would like to tell you now that Howard Roark represents my conception of man as god, of the absolute human ideal. You may not approve of it and it may not be the form in which you see the ideal—but I would like you to accept, as my tribute to you, the fact that what I took from you was taken for the figure of my own god.

Am I really "sensationalizing" my material? If I am, I think it is in the same way in which your buildings are "sensationalized." Your buildings are not designed for sloppy, "homey" living, not for flopping around in bedroom slippers, but for standing straight and making each minute count. I felt, whenever I entered a building of yours, that one could never relax here—relax in the sense most people do all their lives, that is, feel small, mean, slothful and comfortably insignificant. I felt that here one had to be a hero and lead a heroic life. Most people live in a kind of disgusting everyday stupor, and they experience a higher sense of existence only on very rare occasions, if at all. In your buildings one would have to experience it all the time. I think that is the way you build. Well, that is the way I write. No, my characters and events are not of the "century of the common man." They are not little people nor average people nor "just like the folks next door." You don't build for the way people live, but for the way they should live. I don't write about people as they are, but as they could be and should be. There are no such people in real life? Why, yes, there are. I am one of them.

You said, when I met you here, that I was too young and couldn't have suffered enough to write about integrity. Do you still think so?

I <u>have</u> been "set up in the market place" (the review of my book which you read in the <u>Architectural Forum</u> is just a little sample of that), but I can't be "burned for a witch," because I think I am made of asbestos.

I am not afraid of what Hollywood might do to my book. So far, it looks as if I will win the battle, and the book will be preserved on the screen. I am willing to take the chance, because my producer's enthusiastic. But should others interfere and succeed in ruining the story, even a ruined screen version will attract the attention of some proper readers to my book. And that is all I want. I have stated my complete case in the book. I want those who can hear me to hear me.

Now, would you be willing to design a house for me? You said you had to be interested in a person before you accepted him or her as a client. I don't know yet when and whether I will be able to go East to buy the land—but if I can go, would you care to design the house? I should like to know that before I buy the land.

Will you forgive me now for Roark's long legs and orange hair?

Gratefully—and always reverently,

[Ayn Rand]

1944: JULY 9

H. W. CRAYTON TO THE PARENTS OF RAYMOND HOBACK

Despite the hope expressed in this letter, both Raymond Hoback and his brother Bedford had been killed in action on June 6 at Omaha Beach.

Cpl. H. W. Crayton
6657549 A.S.N.
453 A. & C.
A.P.O. 230
c/o P.M. N.Y.C. NY

July 9, 1944
Somewhere in France

Dear Mr and Mrs Hoback:

I really don't know how to start this letter to you folks, but will attempt to do something in words of writing. I will try to explain in the letter what this is all about. While walking along the beach D-Day plus 1 I came upon this Bible and as most any person would do I picked it up from the sand to keep it from being destroyed. I knew that most all bibles have names and addresses within the cover so I made it my business to thumb through the pages until I came upon the name above. Knowing that you no doubt would want the book returned I am sending it knowing that most Bibles are a book to be cherished. I would have sent it sooner but have been quite busy and thought it best if a short period of time elapsed before returning it.

You have by now received a letter from your son saying he is well. I sincerely hope so. I imagine what has happened is that your son dropped the book without any notice. Most everybody who landed on the beach D-Day lost something. I for one as others did lost most of my personal belongings, so you see how easy it was to have dropped the book and not known about it. Everything was in such a turmoil that we didn't have a chance until a day or so later to try and locate our belongings.

Since I have arrived here in France I have had occasions to see a little of the country and find it quite like parts of the U.S.A. It is a very beautiful country, more so in peace time. War does change everything as it has the country. One would hardly think there was a war going on today. Everything is peaceful and quiet. The birds have begun their daily practice, all the flowers and trees are in bloom, especially the poppies and tulips which are very beautiful at this time of year.

Time goes by so quickly as it has today. I must close hoping to hear that you received the Bible in good shape.

Yours very truly,
Cpl. H. W. Crayton

1945: FEBRUARY
E. B. WHITE TO WILLIAM SHAWN

Author of Stuart Little *(1945) and* Charlotte's Web *(1952), E. B. White (1899–1985) was also an essayist of unique charm and elegance. In 1959, he would revise William Strunk, Jr.'s* The Elements of Style, *a classic handbook for writers. Both his humor and his attention to stylistic detail were evident in this memo to the editor of* The New Yorker, *where he remained a contributor for nearly sixty years.* The "comment" to which White refers was a short article about Life *magazine.*

Shawn:

In the comment on <u>Life</u>'s storage wall, I wrote: ". . . a pretty good case can be made out for setting fire to it and starting fresh." Some studious person, alone with his God in the deep of night, came upon the word "fresh" and saw how easily it could be changed to the word "afresh," a simple matter of affixing an "a." So the phrase became "starting afresh" and acquired refinement, and a sort of grammatical excellence.

I still think people say "start fresh." I shall continue to write "start fresh," to say "start fresh," and, in circumstances which require a restart, I shall actually <u>start</u> fresh. I don't ever intend to start <u>a</u>fresh. Anybody who prefers to start <u>a</u>fresh is at liberty to do so, but I don't recommend it.

An afresh starter is likely to be a person who wants to get agoing. He doesn't just want to get going, he wants to get <u>a</u>going. An afresh starter is also likely to be a person who feels acold when he steps out of the tub.

Some of my best friends lie abed and run amuck, but they do <u>not</u> start afresh. Never do. However, if there is to be a growing tendency in the <u>New Yorker</u> office to improve words by affixing an "a," I shall try to adjust myself to this amusing situation. Characters in my stories will henceforth go afishing, and they will read Afield & Astream. They will not be typical people, they will all be atypical. Some of them, perhaps all of them, will be asexual, even amoral.

Amen.
E. B. White

1945: FEBRUARY 12
HENRY GILES TO JANICE HOLT

Henry Giles (1916–1986) and Janice Holt (1909–1979) met on a bus in the sum-
mer of 1943. She was thirty-four. He was twenty-seven. She was on vacation from
her job as a secretary and was on her way to Texas to visit an aunt. He was wearing
an army uniform and heading back to camp from a furlough. There were only two
empty seats when Giles boarded the bus, one of them next to Holt. They were to-
gether for forty-eight hours of the ride and wrote each other throughout the war.
Married the day he came home, they would stay married until her death thirty-four
years later.

Henry would return to run a forty-acre farm in Kentucky, and Janice would become a writer,
eventually producing several dozen works of fiction and nonfiction.

Monday, February 12, 1945

My only love:—

It's our "anniversary" again and after nineteen months of knowing you darling, I love you so much that words don't begin to express what you mean to me.
In some ways (a day at a time) it seems an awful long time, but on the whole, it
seems to have passed quick enough. It doesn't matter how long we may have to
wait, we will still be loving each other more with every day that passes. One day,
we <u>will</u> be together again.

I've heard the song, "Don't Let Your Sweet Love Die," but I don't know it. In
fact, I've almost forgotten all songs I ever knew. Robert sent me a song but I've
never heard it. "Mother's Prayers Guide Me." Beautiful words, but I can't match
them with the music.

Did I ever tell you of reading Bob Hope's book, <u>I Never Left Home</u>? You
should read it, if you like his programs. There's a lot of laughs all the way
through it. That reminds me that my comics still haven't come through. Probably still following me through the Replacement Depots. The letters I've had so
far are direct from the states.

Yes, I remember the letter I wrote Christmas day and I did express my feelings a little too freely. I try not to sound too gloomy when I write, but sometimes
I guess it will show up. But Christmas <u>was</u> an exceptionally blue day.

Oh yes, I thought you remembered the bet I made when we left Nashville. I
bet you I would kiss you before we were in Memphis. When you called it so
quick like, I figured I had made a bad bet, so I immediately called it off. Remember it now?

I had to laugh at your learning to sleep with the covers tucked in just for me. That <u>is</u> real love. But you shouldn't bother yourself on such a small a thing as that. Guess we'll both be kicking them off some. I'll stop here sweetheart, by telling you again I love you and I'm living for the day I can come home to you.

   <u>All my love always,</u>

Henry

1945: MARCH 19

HARRY TOWNE TO HIS MOTHER

The American flag had been raised on Iwo Jima's Mount Suribachi on February 23, but there was almost another month of hard fighting before the Allies won the island from the Japanese—and with it, the strategic location for a U.S. air base. Corporal Harry Towne was wounded four days after the flag was raised. One of twenty-eight thousand U.S. casualties of the battle, he would receive the Purple Heart and the Navy Cross.

March 19, 1945

Central Pacific

Dear Mom:

I don't know if you have heard that I was wounded or not Mom. I asked a Chaplain to write to you, so you probably know about it.

   I am coming along fine now and expect to be in the States before long. I was wounded quite badly, Mother, but the Navy Medical Corps will fix me up like new again. In a year or less I shall be able to walk just as before.

   Don't let this be a shock to you, Mother, I will be in almost as good shape as before now that they have these new artificial limbs. Yes, Mother, I have lost my right leg, but it isn't worrying me a bit. I shall receive a pension for the rest of my life and with the new artificial limb, you can hardly tell anything is wrong . . .

   I lost my leg on the front lines of Iwo Jima on February 27, but have been moved around so much I couldn't write. I would like to write to Alma, but somehow I can't force myself to do it. You write and tell her, Mother. I'll try to write to her later on.

   Don't worry, Mom, the war for me is ended and I should be seeing you by fall.

Love,

[Harry]

*   *   *

1945: APRIL 7

THE CAPTAIN OF THE <u>HOWORTH</u> TO MRS. ORVILL RAINES

Like Iwo Jima, the island of Okinawa was seen as a crucial step toward Allied victory in the Pacific. On April 1, about sixty thousand U.S. troops landed there. On April 6, the Japanese launched 355 kamikaze air raids, and the Howorth *was one of many ships hit. Among those on board was Yeoman James Orvill Raines, twenty-six, who had been a reporter for the* Dallas Morning News *before enlisting in the naval reserve. Gasoline fires forced him overboard, badly burned. Later, it would be learned that Seaman First Class Russell A. Bramble held on to him in the icy water until he died. By the time the campaign ended in July, it would leave more than twelve thousand Americans dead and thirty-six thousand wounded.*

April 7, 1945

Dear Mrs. Raines:

It is with deep regret that I inform you of the details regarding your husband Orvill who is missing in action following an enemy air attack upon this ship during the afternoon of April sixth. I presume the Secretary of the Navy has informed you so I will try to clarify the picture for you insofar as security allows me.

The ship was at Battle Stations most of the afternoon. Friendly fighter planes were engaged in dog fights with Japanese planes, and were more than keeping the situation under control until the enemy's excess in numbers allowed some to get through. After the ship shot down five dive bombers which fell flaming into the sea nearby, the sixth crashed out of control onto the ship in the vicinity of Orvill's battle station. Several men, including Orvill, were observed to jump or were blown overboard and were seen in the water. It is possible that one of the several ships close by picked him up. We have no information as to whether he was injured or has been recovered as yet.

All of his personal effects are being shipped to you. Please do not expect them too soon as they have a long way to travel. They are being shipped in two packages—one with papers and valuables, the other with clothes. . . .

Your husband was very popular among the officers and men on board this ship. There was certainly no finer bluejacket to be found anywhere. I only wish I could give you more information but you will receive it as fast as humanly possible from the Navy Department if he is recovered.

If I can be of any further assistance or clarify anything for you, please do not hesitate to write me. . . .

As the war in Europe came slowly to an end, Corporal Fred Diamond (1926–) was among the American soldiers assigned to liberate the Nazi camps, where more than six million Jews, as well as millions of other people who had been racial, religious, or political targets, are estimated to have died. This letter was written from Ohrdruf in Germany, the first camp to be liberated. Eisenhower himself would tour the camp with Patton, who chose not to enter a room filled with corpses because he said the sight would make him sick. Less than a month later, on May 7, the Germans would surrender, and the full extent of the atrocities they committed would begin to be known.

13 April 45

Today I was in a town called Ohrdruff. It's a nice little town—one of those spared in the engulfment of the area by the roaring tide of allied armor. On a hillside just outside the town one can see what seems to be barracks, but behind the high barbed-wire fences lies a tale of horror beyond the fertile imagination of a Poe.

If you haven't the stomach for this sort of thing, read no further. This camp was another Lublin, where hundreds of innocent Russians and Poles were brutally tortured, killed, and disposed of.

There is the perceptible odor of rotten flesh upon entering this death camp. The "barracks"—stables would be a more appropriate word—are now empty of the survivors and the less fortunate. But the empty shacks still bear the evidence of the heinous deeds committed against people whose only crime was to encounter these barbarous SS troops. Their beds were the filth and straw-covered floor which is still covered with small pools of blood. Around remain a few crumbs of black bread and some weak soup, which was all the food they received.

The bodies had been earlier removed from the shed where they had been stacked before their disposal. Now they were laid out atop a small hill in preparation for burial. Their bodies showed the lustful brutality of Hitler's elite.

The corpses were little more than skeletons. Mere skin and bones, their arms and legs were not thicker than broomstick handles. Their ribs protruded greatly and their abdomens were now hollow pits. Their skin, now turned grey, was stretched like drums over the emaciated bodies.

Starvation was the least of the privation these poor people suffered. Their bodies were covered with bruises, and were enormously swollen, particularly in the region of the groin. The heads of many bore lacerations; others had had their eyes gauged out. Others had been stabbed in the chest approximately half a dozen times. Many had their misery ended with a bullet through their heads.

The bodies were being disposed of by the Germans about a half a mile away. The ashes tell the story. Mingled with a pile of railroad ties burned are charred skulls and bones. All one can see in stench-filled nearby pits is a protruding charred arm.

This is eugenics as practiced by the Master Race.

. . . .

There is an epilogue to this story. This evening, some German civilian was guiding some U.S. soldiers around the area. Two Russians recognized him as one of the SS men and immediately began beating him, watched by the Yanks. He now lies with the others, his head bashed in, his body swollen. His chest bears about a dozen bayonet wounds. No one is interested in how these un-armed men got the weapon.

1945: APRIL 24
HENRY STIMSON TO HARRY TRUMAN

Nominated for vice-president by the Democratic convention in 1944, Harry S Truman (1884–1972) joined FDR in his fourth and last term, succeeding previous Roosevelt vice-presidents John N. Garner and Henry A. Wallace. Truman was sworn in as the thirty-third president of the United States following FDR's death on April 12. As vice-president, he had met with FDR only twice, and he knew nothing about the Manhattan Project. Twelve days into Truman's presidency, Secretary of War Henry L. Stimson (1867–1950) sent him this letter. Across the bottom the new president scrawled: "Put on list tomorrow, Wed. 25, HST."

April 24, 1945.

Dear Mr. President:

I think it is very important that I should have a talk with you as soon as possible on a highly secret matter.

I mentioned it to you shortly after you took office but have not urged it since on account of the pressure you have been under. It, however, has such a bearing on our present foreign relations and has such an important effect upon all my thinking in this field that I think you ought to know about it without much further delay.

Faithfully yours,
Henry L. Stimson
Secretary of War

The President,
The White House.

1945: MAY 8

HARRY TRUMAN TO HIS MOTHER AND SISTER

In this letter to his mother, Martha Ellen, and his sister, Mary Jane, Truman showed a typical inclination to discuss momentous events in plain language. "Mama & Mary" would indeed come to visit the new president in May. Martha Ellen was ninety-two and making not only her first voyage to the nation's capital but her first plane trip. Disembarking, she took one look at the encroaching Washington press and with typical Truman directness declared, "Oh, fiddlesticks!"

May 8, 1945

THE WHITE HOUSE
Washington

Dear Mama & Mary:—

I am sixty-one this morning, and I slept in the President's room in the White House last night. They have finished the painting and have some of the furniture in place. I'm hoping it will all be ready for you by Friday. My expensive gold pen doesn't work as well as it should.

This will be a historical day. At 9:00 o'clock this morning I must make a broadcast to the country: announcing the German surrender. The papers were signed yesterday morning and hostilities will cease on all fronts at midnight tonight. Isn't that some birthday present?

Have had one heck of a time with the Prime Minister of Great Britain. He, Stalin and the U.S. President made an agreement to release the news all at once from the three capitals at an hour that would fit us all. We agreed on 9 a.m. Washington time which is 3 p.m. London and 4 p.m. Moscow time.

Mr. Churchill began calling me at daylight to know if we shouldn't make an immediate release without considering the Russians. He was refused and then he kept pushing me to talk to Stalin. He finally had to stick to the agreed plan—but he was mad as a wet hen.

Things have moved at a terrific rate here since April 12. Never a day has gone by that some momentous decision didn't have to be made. So far luck has been with me. I hope it keeps up. It can't stay with me forever however and I hope when the mistake comes it won't be too great to remedy.

We are looking forward to a grand visit with you. I may not be able to come for you as planned but I'm sending the safest finest plane and all kinds of help so please don't disappoint me.

Lots & lots of love to you both.

Harry

1945: MAY 14
META MAASS TO ALFRED AND MILA GRÜNWALD

Born in Vienna in 1911, Meta Maass was the daughter of Alfred Grünwald, a well-known librettist, and his wife, Mila. After spending the war years in occupied Holland, Meta and her husband, Walter, would emigrate to America in 1946, where they would live together until her death in 1987. Technically, of course, her letter is not an American letter, because she was not yet an American. But it is one of the most vivid and extraordinary letters we've read, and this book's coauthor had the privilege of being Meta's niece.

The letter was written in English.

Waardenburgh, Holland
May 14th. 1945.

Dearest parents,

You surely can imagine how wonderful it was to have direct news from you again, to hear that you are both well and in good health. Through all these years that thought sustained us: you, at least, are safe, safe in America, in the free world, far from Europe's war theatre.

In the meantime you got our first and reassuring news from us, you know now that we are alive and well. The thought that you had no ways of finding out anything about our whereabouts and that you would fear for our lives, may-be give up hope completely, was tormenting, but there was nothing we could do to communicate with you after America entered the war and even the Red Cross letters had to stop.

Now, all this lies behind us and we are free again. I do not know when we shall see you again, most likely not for a long time. Surely you want to know how we managed to survive the war and the German occupation in the Netherlands. Later I hope to be able to give you more details, about the many kind people who helped us once the German occupation began, about how we were forced to move several times and to take on new identities, to disappear underground, "onder water" as the Dutch called it.

For now I will start with April the 26th, 1944. By then we were renting rooms in the house of Mevrouw and Mijnheer van der Bergh. Walter, who had managed to find work as a chemist, left in the morning as usual. I was supposed to go to the Hague to get more rationcards. I left my room around 12 o'clock, went to the library to pick up some books, then on to the railroad station. I deposited my bags with the books in the storage room, got a ticket with a number for it, and boarded my train. The outskirts of The Hague were already in sight, when, suddenly, I noticed great unrest amongst the passengers. Before I had time to think or to get scared, a young, arrogant-looking man in his beige/brown S.S. uniform stopped in front of me.

"Your papers."

The officer looked at the papers, then at me, then held the papers against the glass of the window and finally put them into his pocket.

"These papers are forged. The watermark is uneven. You are under arrest. Come with me!"

When the train stopped we got out.

"Are you Jewish?"

"No!" My only chance to survive, if at all, is never, never to admit my real identity.

"Why the forged papers, then?"

We went to a small police station in the Hague. I had one hour to prepare myself for my interrogation. In this one hour only this became clear to me. At all cost, whatever happened, never, never confess who I am. If I confess not only is my life lost, but with me this of Walter, of the family van der Bergh, of all our friends in the underground. With a start I remembered the ticket from the storage room, the only thing I had on me that could give a clue. I looked around, seemed unnoticed, bent my head and swallowed it.

After a while a tall man in civil clothes approached.

"Name? Nationality? Age? Adres?"

Stubbornly I refused to answer.

This went on for some time. At first he was polite, then shouted, threatened, tried to intimidate me. I still did not answer.

He lost his temper finally.

"Zum Donnerwetter, name, age, adres, nationality! What are you? German? French? Dutch? Hongarian? Russian? English?"

"Yes."

I did not know why I said this. It simply was an inspiration of the moment.

"Na endlich! Why did you not say this right away. Name?"

"Mary Nicholson."

Now my mind worked feverishly. I have an english girlfriend by this name and of course my own middelname is Mary. To my greatest amazement he put this down on the paper in front of him. All right then, this was it. From now on I was english, unmarried, remember this good.

The trolley took us to Scheveningen, the beautiful and famous vacation place, now the infamous prison the dutch called the "Hotel Orange", taken over by the enemy and overflowing with their victims.

A momentary panic seized me when we got off. I tried to run away. As a result the officer binds my hands.

We walked for an hour before we reached the prison. At that moment I was devoid of feelings. A tiny door in the huge, somber building opened and we stepped into a big room crowded with German officers. I was unable to distinguish faces, merely seeing brown caps, boots, uniforms and more boots. In the middle of the room, sitting at a desk, a young blond officer, the haughtiness and lust for power, the hatred and contempt against everything that was not German clearly written on his pale face. Another short interrogation, more papers filled. Then on to the court of the prison, waiting, my face against the wall. After a while another officer.

"Who are you? Papers!"

Someone gave them to him.

"Hm, you are english? Jewish?"

"No." I said with strong conviction.

"Don't lie so infamously, we will get the truth out of you yet! And what about your attempt to escape and why the forged papers?"

To this I had no answer ready, so I thought it better to be silent.

This seemed to infuriate him even more.

"If you were a man I would know how to get you talk—with this here—" he swept his whip across my face, without striking me though—"but as you are a mere woman, I am not interested just now. Abtransportieren!"

A sadistic looking creature with black hair, small piercing eyes behind glasses in an ugly, livid face, pushed cold fingers into my back.

"Come along."

A small room. Three women in blue uniforms.

"Jewish?"

"No."

They grinned incredulously.

"Well, we will find out soon enough. We have our means, they never fail, you know! Get undressed. Completely!"

Standing there, naked, in front of these merciless, cold creatures, I had to close my eyes in shame and humiliation. They searched me carefully, with German thoroughness. My coat, dress, slip, bag, hair. When they could not find anything to rouse suspicion, I got my things back and got escorted to my cell. 381. That was my number. The door closed behind me. I was alone. My cell had radiator pipes on one side of the wall. A small table with a tin mug, wooden plate and spoon on it. On the other side 2 buckets, one empty, one filled with water. A coatstand in the corner.

Exhausted I sat down. My eyes fell on the various inscriptions on the wall, evidently drawn with some sharp instrument. There were poems, names, calenders, varied etchings, in different languages, all with a deeper meaning. Keep smiling. Always answer with "I do not know." May the Lord be your sheppard. In God we trust. Quand on n'a pas ce qu'on aime, il faut aimer ce qu'on a. And many, many more. With a nail that I soon found, my unstable fingers tried to draw the word: "STERKTE." Strength. There it was, and in moments of despair—and there were many to come—that word would sustain me.

This first night in solitary confinement was hard to take. I had difficulty from refraining to scream, to shout, to run my head against these enclosing walls, cold and hot shivers went through my body, until, in helpless defeat I finally realized there was nothing I could do. So, when the room darkened, I took off my dress and went to bed. Dead tired with suspense and worry my thoughts now drifted to Walter. Soon he will come home and not find me. In a few hours he will know something terrible must have happened. The thought of his anguish and despair was unbearable. It will not only mean worry and pain about my own fate but also another hiding place, new contacts, new handicaps for himself. How will he be able to live through this new ordeal? And what, what will I tell them when the interrogation starts, this very night yet may-be, how mislead the Gestapo, how erase any possible link or clue so that our friends in the underground could unharmed continue their vital work? At that moment I had no answer ready, my brain refused to work.

Through the high window the stars looked in, first one, then many, many more. Later hundreds and hundreds of allied bombers crossed the sky, oh welcome, welcome sound!

My right hand tried to trace Walter's face on the wall, his eyes, nose, mouth and chin—yes, that's it—and finally, now not so alone any more—I fell asleep.

The next morning: heavy knocks against the door. I had to get up, bring my bed in order, clean my cell. Then my morning coffee. I sat and waited, walked up and down. At noon potatoes and vegetables, twice a week soup, evenings more coffee and bread.

The second night approached. The door opened to let a bent, thin woman in, clad in deep black from head to toe, two shiny red apples clutched in her hands. Tiredly she sank down on the chair. Slowly, haltingly, she told her story. Her name was Claire. For a year she and her husband had lived in hiding in the house of their more fortunate gentile daughter-in-law, confined to their room and yet betrayed in the end, by some suspicious neighbours.

"And you?" she finally asked.

"Mary," I answered. "English," while my face grew red and hot. To lie to her, to one of my own race was hard, felt like a cowardly act of desertion. Shameful, I turned my head away from her look. But I would not help her by admitting the truth. Claire stayed with me for a week. I admired her for her unfailing courage. When they finally came for her, all she said was: "I will be reunited with my husband and son, we will die together."

She left a strange emptiness behind.

Another day: "Come on out. Take your towel."

The bath was wonderful. I relished in it.

Back at my cell I found a new guest.

"Eva," she introduced herself and we shook hands. After 3 weeks in prison in Brussels, she had been transferred back to her native country.

"It was much nicer there, livelier, not so sad! We have to change things a bit around here! Come, I have something good for you." And she gave me delicious bits of chocolate, sugar, fruit, cookies. "Red Cross parcel. I hid it in my handkerchief."

Then she opened her hair, let it fall down to her shoulders, looking younger now, more vulnerable. From under her curls out came a lipstick, rouge, powder—oh, that smelled nice—and a small pencil.

With Eva around life indeed changed for the better. Full of stamina and cheer, she tried to brighten up our cell, draping a colourful handkerchief around the shelves, rolling the sac of straw into a fancy pillow, picking a flower when we went out to the court for our "airing." She was a law student, her fiancé, Pim, a member of the underground movement in Leiden.

"I only hope he takes good care of my dog Flickie. I miss him badly."

"And why are you here, Eva?"

"Well, bad luck. I smuggled english and american pilots that had come down here over the border, hundreds of them. One night they caught me."

This was very serious, she had but a slim chance. Still she was always cheerful, entertaining us with songs, trying to make us laugh.

Next evening, our next guest.

"Mevrouw Potter," she introduced herself. A strikingly dressed woman in a fashionable suit, hat with veil and flowers, high heeled shoes, a large foxcape. We could only gasp, this here, in our "Hotel Orange."

"My son was supposed to go to a labor camp in Germany, he tried to hide, his hairdresser—durty traitor—gave him up," she told us, furious. "Now I am supposed to confess where I got the forged papers for him. Well, a nice story I told them, not one word of truth in it, they'll get nothing out of me, no! What are you doing here, how do you kill the time? We could play some cards, some Rommy may-be?"

Play? Rommy? We looked at each other. It was a thought! Sure, we had toiletpaper and a pencil. Eagerly we drew figures and faces on the paper and within an hour our set of cards was ready.

When it got too dark and the light had to go out, Mevrouw Potter, being the oldest, got our bed, we others on the floor. Her silken slip smelled sweet and clean—how faded and gray our things looked.

"I cannot sleep with these filthy blankets next to my skin! Huh, it is cold in here! Give me my foxcape, please, it will keep me warm."

And there she lay then in our cell in Scheveningen, a tragic-comic figure. We burst out laughing, and laughed and laughed until the tears were streaming down.

My first week was over and no interrogation yet. I lived between hope and fear. Then, one morning, footsteps outside, keys in the door.

"Nicholson. Come. Interrogation!"

In the corridor a tall man in civil clothes, waiting for me.

"Who are you? Name? Nationalit? What language do you speak?"

A rain of questions, I answered slowly, hesitatingly. We came to a better part of the prison with soft rugs and lighter colors. In front of a small door he stopped, let me enter the room first, very politely.

"Sit down. Do you smoke? No? You are english? Do you speak any german?"

"Yes. Some."

"That is good, makes things easier for me. We shall understand each other better."

And then the questioning started. I did my best to speak a broken german, trying not to give myself away, concentrating hard. He asked, I answered. He put everything I said down on paper, carefully, thoroughly. What I told him was the most phantastic, the most incredible fairy-tale. Instinctively I felt he did not know what to make of me.

When he rested for a while, I tried to divert him. How did he like it in Holland? Was he married? Did he have a family in Germany? For a few short moments we talked like human beings. Then, again and again:

"Are you Jewish? No? Why then the forged papers?"

"I was afraid to get interned."

"We do not harm our foreign internes. Nothing would have happened to you in our internment camp. But now we shall have to establish proof of your identity. We have our means. The Red Cross in Geneva. I shall send a cable. Within three days I'll have the answer. And now tell me about your family. Married? No? Parents alive?"

"Yes. My father is a famous playwright." This at least is true and I do not have to invent.

Somehow this seemed to interest him.

"Oh, a playwright, you say? And famous? You must like the theatre then. And how about you? Any hidden talents? No? Have you ever tried? May-be you would like to try now and tell us the story of your life—in english, please, with all possible details. I'll see to it that you get paper and pen and ink. You have a week's time. Perhaps I'll get a nice romance to read."

With this the ordeal was over. Only now I noticed that the door had been locked. He escorted me back to my cell.

"Good afternoon, Miss Mary. I shall see you again."

Eva wanted to know what had happened. But first my story had to be written down, exactly as I had told it. Of course he would compare word for word with his notations. And what if, next time, he confronts me with a genuine Englishman? And the cable to the Red Cross? For the moment, though, I was relieved.

"Lena," said our new guest in a soft, timid voice that belonged and went well with her fragile, modest appearance. We liked her immediately. It took a while though, before she warmed up to us and started talking. After becoming close friends, we discovered a fierce and violent defiance in this quiet, sincere girl and also that she played a big part in the underground movement. Luckily, the Gestapo did not know this yet. Lena, always brave, sympathetic, understanding, careful to look neat and tidy in her dark red woolen dress, did not easily give way to her emotions, to fear or despair. And if she allowed herself that luxury she did it quietly, retreating to a corner to get a good cry. We tried to look away, making believe not to notice.

And then, when Truusje came, we were four in a cell built for one. But we did not mind to have even less space now. Truusje, a small girl with intelligent eyes, was a vivacious, witty person with a sharp tongue and quick tempered. Days and nights we sat and talked, discussing music and books and philosophy and religion and art. Sometimes we were daydreaming: happy, wonderful phantasies about "afterwards." "We'll all celebrate at the Beukenhof, Pim and Walter in white dinnerjackets, and we all in fancy eveningdresses, dancing, and sipping champagne, of course!"

For two long weeks I was able to hold on to my pretense, though I felt that the girls did not really believe me. One evening, finally, I did not want to be silent any longer. Here, in this enforced confinement, thrown together, sharing every hour of the day and night, fighting a common enemy, each in our own way, this became too great a burden for me. Afterwards, when all was told, I felt so wonderful and so relieved. I slept light and deep this night, and the sketch on the wall, Walter's face, suceeded well.

The next day: Noise and movement outside, across the corridor.

"What do you want? What happened to my fiance?" This from an excited voice in anguish, obviously belonging to a young girl.

"Your fiance is condemned to be executed within the hour, he will die together with 18 others, all members of the underground."

"Oh, let me die with him, let me die, I can not live without him!"

"You should be ashamed of yourself," was the stern answer in a deep man's voice. "18 years old and wants to die! Think of your parents! Come now, we'll take you to Germany—"

"I don't want to go, let me die, let me die!"

"Stop this! Get ready and pack your things. I'll come for you within an hour. Understand?"

Within an hour we heard the shots of the fussilade-cordon. Later, that same night, from somewhere, the voice of a man: "Allons enfants de la patrie, le jour de gloire est arrive!" La Marseillaise. We all took over. Thousands and thousands of voices, throughout the prison, we sang. God safe the King. The American National Anthem. Stronger and stronger our voices. Free world, America, France, England, did you hear?

The 6th of June. Lena had her first interrogation. It went pretty well, nothing they could pin on her, a promise to release her soon. We rejoiced with her and saw a chance to get some news to our families. After she had carefully learned all names and adresses by heart, she came up with a plan: the casement that enclosed the bones of her corset would make a fine hiding place for a letter to Walter. Carefully we ripped out the bones to make room for my message, written on a piece of paper folded into the smallest possible roll:

"Dearest! Lena will bring you news about me. Please tell Mother and Father I was killed in an air-raid, that would be less painful to them. Thank you for all your love and happiness you gave me during our 10 years of togetherness. Please do not stay alone and get married soon again. Mary."

At noon we got our bath, washed our hair and set it in curlers we had made from the strong brown paper that held our Red Cross parcels.

2 o'clock. Coffee. Waiting. Waiting.

All of a sudden commotion outside, running, excited shouting, unusual at this hour of the day and against the routine. Someone pushed the window in our door open: "Get ready! Immediately! The prison is going to be evacuated."

In silent bewilderment we faced each other. Something serious must have happened. Feverishly we got our things ready. It did not take us long. An hour later we assembled in the corridor. With a loaf of bread pushed into our hands we marched through the part of the building where the men used to live. The cells were empty, doors wide open. Officers, wardens, officials, all of them looking alarmed, confused, visibly frightened. The huge building with its zoo-like fences looked forlorn and deserted now. Green busses waiting for us outside. We rode to a small station in the Hague, where a train would take us to our next destination. German soldiers behind each tree, their guns ready, guarded us well. No chance to escape. A soft rain started to come down. After many hours a train rolled in.

"Get in. Transportation to Vught, Germany, Poland."

Truusje, Eva, Lena and I sat down in a small compartment with 12 other prisoners. The train seemed to be only sparsely guarded. Only now and then one of the soldiers looked in, shouting: "Get away from the window, otherwise I shoot. Silence!"

In the meantime I had made up my mind. Vught, Germany, Poland, that meant torture for me and death. No. If I had to die let it be here then, in this country with its good and gentle people. As we rolled on it grew dark outside and night came. It must have been about 2 o'clock in the morning, I guessed. We passed a long bridge, the Waal, may-be. I motioned to Lena. Softly she opened the door, which, unlocked, fell open. The other women in the compartment covered their eyes and mouths, suppressing a cry that could give me away and alarm the guards. I stepped on the running-board and let myself fall.

A sharp pain shot through me as I hit the rails, my head and back felt torn to pieces. A thousand stars—Walter—this is the end. But no. I am not dead. I was alive, blood running down my face. I tried to move my arms, my legs, they functioned, I was able to get up, though my back hurt badly.

Filled with enormous, grateful relief, feeling reborn, free, I looked around, noticing a faint light somewhere at a distance. In the dark night, heavy rain pouring down, this light, somehow, seemed symbolic, meaning life, hope, some human beings there, and I marched towards it. A small house, and five railroad-workers sat inside. Noticing that I was wounded, they listened to my story, some incredulous. Again my faint but still traceable austrian accent rousing suspicion.

"Who knows if she is not a German spy?"

But one of them, an older man, pitying me, took me on his byke. In his house I found shelter, warm food and a clean shining white bed. Unbelievable chance of fate, his wife, being a nurse, knew where to find a doctor, who came quick to stitch my head-wounds. Now I finally learned that indeed it was the day of the invasion in Normandy. With a feeling of immense, overwhelming gratitude, I fell asleep.

In the morning, upon awakening, I found a stranger sitting next to my bed.

"Luke," he introduced himself. "Who are you?"

My story, my true story this time, sounded incredible to him.

"Can you name someone I could contact to verify what you have told me? You see, I take an enormous risk if I help you, I am a leader in the underground. You understand that, don't you?"

I nodded. "Of course."

"Without proof, I would be forced to keep you here until the end of the war. Nothing would happen to you, but you would not be free."

This was a difficult decision. To let Walter know that I am alive, to give him new hope, to learn about his fate, was a great temptation. On the other hand, what if Luke gave me up to the Gestapo and with me Walter and our friends? For a long night I thought this over. Next morning Luke came again, his face honest, open.

"Here I brought you something to give you strength." He laid a bible in my hands. "Come, trust me. I trust you too." Finally I gave him Walter's name and the adres of Frans, and Luke was on his way to find them.

After two days he was back, having good news from Walter and our friends, they were all alive and well. Luke decided I should not go back to the Hague, where Walter now lived. He told me I was in the southern part of Holland, a good many hours from where I had come. He already had pulled his strings. In case my escape to this house had been discovered it was better not to stay on. I was to go to Waardenburgh, a small village where a doctor would give me shelter. After safely crossing the bridge, a hazardous undertaking, as all bridges and roads were carefully guarded, we reached the doctor's house. Within three weeks I was fully recovered and a new chapter of my life began.

Waardenburgh was a small village, Henk, the most beloved doctor in the community, "Huize Zomerland" a beautiful, stately house where I lived with the doctor's wife and their three children. I had my own room in the attic and, though restricted to the house and garden, I felt at home, grateful and safe.

From time to time Luke brought news from Walter. The situation in the city was growing worse; the invasion, though successful, had not brought the quick liberation we had so fervently hoped for. Walter's life became untenable. There was no gas, no light, no food, no fuel, all men between the age of 18 and 40, regardless of race or religion, were summoned to forced labor in Germany. Once Walter had to hide for 10 hours in an icy cold shaft under the floor while S.S. troops raided the house. In December food mainly consisted of beets and tulip bulbs. Henk, doubling the hazard of risking his own neck and the life of his family, offered to give Walter shelter. Luke cleverly smuggled Walter out of the city, defying raids, man-hunts and controls along the roads, and one morning Walter stood outside in our garden. After 10 months of separation we were together again.

He looked haggard and near starvation, but soon regained strength.

Until mid-april all was quiet, then german parachute troops got billetted on us. It was somewhat uncomfortable to have them around, but they paid little attention to us and left us unharmed. Now the number of allied airbombers crossing our country on their way to Germany increased steadily. English and German artillery fired at each other across the river, often our house shook and trembled, but withstood all attacks.

On April 1st the German radio announced the death of the Fuhrer. At the same time allied bombers dropped their first food parcels over Holland. After five years the German guns on the ground were silent, while allied flying fortresses circled the sky. The people in the streets were crying, some knelt down in grateful prayer. Embittered, pale, the German soldiers watched.

April 2nd. Berlin fell. The parachute troops in our house assembled in the garden to be sworn in. Their new Fuhrer is Admiral Donitz. Once more we have to witness the enormous swastika spread across the green of our grounds, once more the sound of the Horst Wessel Lied.

April 4. At 9 o'clock p.m. the B.B.C. announced the capitulation of the German forces in the Netherlands. Not really believing it yet, we assembled in our hall, while the parachute troops still live in our house. Tears streaming down our faces, we sang the dutch National Anthem. Paul brought down the flag, now leaving its long hiding place. But the soldiers in our house had no official order to leave.

May 6th. 1945. A German soldier had been attacked by an overzealous dutch civilian outside our house. The parachute troops, in a last attempt to prove their superiority, assembled us in the living-room.

"You will all be executed in the morning."

They searched the house for hidden weapons, found a dead grenade that one of the children had wanted to keep as a souvenir. Confused, alarmed, disappointed, embittered, partly drunk, their mood was dangerous and spelled disaster. Finally, at 4 o'clock in the morning, the official announcement over the German radio:

"Capitulate."

A few hours later our parachute troops marched home.

March 10, 1945. At last. The first allied soldiers in our village. A small group of musicians assembled in our garden to play "God Save the King." When a car with 2 canadian soldiers rolled along, we stopped them and triumphantly raised them on our shoulders.

Now only are we really free.

We tried to put down our story for you. Much of it will seem phantastic and incredible. Yet you know, of course, that everything happened just as I tell it to you. Walter and I are both well and anxious to hear from you soon. Greet America for us, we hope to see it some day.

Much love,
Meta

*   *   *

1945: MAY 24

O. C. BREWSTER TO HARRY TRUMAN

Not all of the work of the Manhattan Project was confined to Los Alamos. O. C. Brewster was an engineer who, while employed by a laboratory at the Kellex Corporation, worked on the separation of the uranium isotope. Despite extremely limited information, Brewster managed to perceive the essence of what would be the atomic age. Copies of his letter were sent to Truman and Stimson. Whether or not Truman ever saw it is unknown. Stimson was impressed with it, and in passing it on to Marshall called it a "remarkable document."

Herrenvolk is the German word for "master race." The OSRD was the Office of Scientific Research and Development.

O. C. Brewster
23 East 11th Street
New York

May 24, 1945

The President of the United States
The White House
Washington, D.C.

My dear Mr. President:

Presented herewith is a matter which I believe to be one of the <u>gravest</u>, if not the gravest, questions now confronting the United States and the entire world. It has to do with the policy to be adopted as to the future handling of the Clinton Engineer Works (near Knoxville, Tennessee) and associated projects. This communication is being directed to you through the special channels provided by the Army for material on this subject, but this fact should in no way be construed as Army endorsement of any of the ideas presented but is merely in recognition of my right as a citizen to bring those ideas before you, and on my part it is so done in recognition by me of the continued urgent necessity for the security of this undertaking and my compulsion to avoid any act that would jeopardize that security. Copies of this communication have also been directed to the Secretaries of State and of War through the same channels in the belief that it is proper to bring the matter before them at the same time that it is presented to the President.

This matter is presented with the full knowledge on my part that it is undoubtedly being given very serious attention already by far better minds than mine and yet I know myself to hold the unpopular and minority view on the question and therefore feel it my duty as a loyal citizen to attempt to place before you these ideas on the chance that they have not been presented to you before and on the further chance that, while I can lay no claim to any knowledge of statesmanship or world politics, some of these ideas may turn out to be correct and of importance to world peace. The question is of such appalling urgency that I would be derelict in my duty in not bringing it to your attention in the absence of definite information that it was being fully considered from all points of view.

I have been associated with this project since February 1942 as an engineer with The Kellex Corporation, and while not in possession of all the facts under the wise ruling that for the sake of security no one should have such knowledge, I do know enough about it to realize its possible effect upon our modern civilization and I have given a great deal of thought to it over the past three years. My knowledge of the so called "K-25" plant (that engineered by The Kellex Corporation and now going into operation under Carbide and Carbon Chemicals Corporation) is quite detailed and specific, but as to the other projects— Tennessee-Eastman (Y-12 and X-10), DuPont (in Washington State), Perclave (S-50), and Chicago University on end use (in Texas, I believe)—my information is second hand and general and may be inaccurate although obtained from informed sources. Moreover I am not qualified as a physicist to judge as to the correctness of the estimates of the possible effectiveness of the material involved and there again I can only pass on what I have been told and believe to be substantially true.

*   *   *   *   *   *   *   *   *   *   *   *

In order to present my views adequately I feel forced to go into rather extensive detail, with much of which you are already undoubtedly familiar, in order that the facts on which I base my conclusions may be verified so that if my information is faulty my conclusions may be accordingly discounted.

The project as a whole is a mammoth undertaking on which many hundreds of millions of dollars are being spent and hundreds of thousands of people are directly or indirectly involved. It is rapidly approaching completion—wherein lies great danger, as I hope to show—and represents a modern miracle of science and engineering and even today, unfinished, shows enough promise of success to stand as a monument to the genius of the men whose tireless devotion has, in the face of almost insuperable difficulties, delays, and discouragement, brought it to its present state.

The purpose of the project is to produce in useable quantities the one known material from which can be liberated, by scission of the atom, energy locked up in the atom in such huge quantities relative to the weight of material handled that it is impossible to grasp its full significance. On my introduction to the project I was told that one fifty pound bomb utilizing this material would be equivalent to twelve thousand tons of TNT—in other words, about five hundred thousand times as effective, pound for pound. Furthermore such a bomb would completely destroy an area the equivalent of Manhattan and, due to induced radio activity, all life in this area would be impossible for a period of years. I have been told that this estimate is a gross exaggeration, but I have also been told that experimental work is demonstrating the material to be useable with something approaching its theoretical potentiality and that all signs pointed to its living up to expectations as an explosive. My work is not involved with the end use of the material and I have made no effort to verify these facts. The exact figure is of little importance—if its effectiveness were only five hundred times that of TNT instead of five hundred thousand, my conclusions would only be in error to a degree.

This material, under controlled conditions, also has tremendous potentiality as a concentrated fuel for power generation, one pound being equivalent to many tons of coal or oil, making possible a revolution in ship propulsion as one example.

While much of this was known for several years before the war and much was written on the subject, no serious effort to produce this material in anything but microscopic quantities was made until, under the compulsion of war, the effort became necessary. This is due to the enormous difficulty in its production, as it involves the separation of a relatively small portion of a fairly rare metal by separating means which are very difficult. The result is that a plant to do this job on any worthwhile scale is so costly that no individual and few nations could undertake it and then only under the great stress of war when cost becomes a secondary consideration. The Clinton Engineer Works represents the effort of this country to produce this material, and since the whole undertaking was an enormous experiment for which at the start there was no assurance of success of any one of a number of proposed methods, all of these methods which showed any promise on a minute laboratory scale were undertaken in parallel in the hope that one at least might succeed. The "Y-12" plant, which had the chance of securing production most quickly, was intended to supply only small quantities for research and experimentation but due to the shorter time element in its construction could yield invaluable data. The "K-25" plant was designed for relatively large production of the ultimate product but was later altered to produce material of only moderate concentration. The DuPont plant in Washington was also for large production, but I understand it has been a disappointment. "S-50" came along as a later idea and is a plant capable of producing in relatively large quantities but of unusably low concentration and is thus used to produce feed for "Y-12."

At present "Y-12" is in moderately successful production of sufficient material, I believe, for experimental purposes. K-25 is in partial operation, producing a large quantity of material of low concentration which is being used as feed to "Y-12," thereby augmenting its production of highly concentrated product. K-25 is rapidly being pushed to completion and, as now set up, will upon completion and upon completion of K-27, a newly authorized addition to K-25, be able to furnish such a supply of moderately highly concentrated material that, when this is fed to Y-12, the ultimate production of highly concentrated material will be equal to or greater than that originally planned for K-25.

The K-25 plant, with which I am quite familiar, shows every prospect of success. Many units of this plant have been in operation for months and their performance exceeds expectations. Except for final proof by actual complete operation, the plant now stands as a vindication of the genius and skill of those who have given their untiring devotion to it through periods of greatest trial and discouragement. Nothing which I advocate as the policy to be pursued as to these plants is intended to detract in any way from the success of the patriotic effort which has been put into them.

*   *   *   *   *   *   *   *   *   *   *   *

The destructive possibilities of the material as I have described it are obvious. With aviation what it is today, it should be possible, with planes based in any country on the globe, to destroy at one fell swoop almost any great city in the world and wipe out the manufacturing, the fleets, and the supply bases of any other country without warning, thereby rendering it helpless almost before it realized it had an enemy.

The country producing such a weapon during the course of a war would gain such an enormous advantage over its enemy that victory would be almost assured regardless of its condition just prior to putting it to use. I do not know whether this weapon could be applied in sufficiently homeopathic doses to make it efficient against combat troops, but certainly against massed supplies, manufacturing centers, nations' capitals, and great cities the effectiveness is apparent.

Before we were forced into the war it was known that Germany was working to produce this material. It was known that a great horde of her ablest physicists, chemists, and engineers had been drawn into the project. It was known and recognized that if Germany succeeded in this effort the victory was irrevocably Germany's and that the rest of the world could look to nothing other than slavery under the Nazi yoke.

Thus before our entry into the war the OSRD had already started a research program looking toward the production of this material. After Pearl Harbor this program was enormously enlarged and with the cooperation of Britain, who was already at work, a fantastic race with Germany was begun, with the full knowledge that Germany had a head start of possibly as much as two years. Before the research was even well started enough encouraging results by several methods had been obtained that, without waiting for further development, full sized facilities for the large scale production of this material were started. The fact that any success at all was achieved constitutes the modern miracle I mentioned earlier because these plants were built on scanty research,—they were built on hunch, on prayers, and on what at times appeared to be wishful thinking, but by dogged determination coupled with some of the most brilliant scientific and engineering work they have succeeded or given every promise of success and Germany for some reason, which I think all of us are entitled to know some day, has failed.

*   *   *   *   *   *   *   *   *   *   *   *

From my first association with this project I have been convinced, and have been appalled by the conviction, that the successful production of this material by any nation meant the inevitable destruction of our present day civilization. This is not an original thought with me but is shared by many of my associates. One of the most earnest hopes of many of us was that it might be conclusively proved that the thing was impossible. Obviously, however, so long as there was any chance that Germany might succeed at this task there was only one course to follow and that was to do everything in our power to get this thing first and destroy Germany before she had a chance to destroy us. We must forget about the destruction of civilization or at least we must agree that, if civilization is to be destroyed, we should do it our way and prevent Germany from doing it the Nazi way. Thus this project became the most important thing of its kind before the country and still it remained, by what seems another miracle, one of the best kept secrets of our time.

The idea of the destruction of civilization is not melodramatic hysteria or crack-pot raving. It is a very real and, I submit, almost inevitable result. It cannot, of course, be proven until it occurs—and then it would be too late.

The possession of this weapon by any one nation, no matter how benign its intentions, could not be tolerated by other great powers. Those who could not produce the weapon themselves would watch our every move. Our elections, our foreign policy, everything we did would be viewed with suspicion and distrust. If we urged our views on the world on any subject we would be charged with threatening to use this weapon as a club. We would be toadied to and discriminated against, all the world would do lip service as our friends and conspire and intrigue against us behind our backs. We would be the most hated and feared nation on earth.

Meantime others would not sit by idly but would also build plants for production of this material. Our best friend could not permit us to be the only possessor of this thing. How could they know where our friendship might be five, ten, or twenty years hence? Others, not our best friends, would be still more anxious for their own legitimate self protection to prepare themselves. I submit that we, the United States, could not rest complacently if, say, Mexico, or France, or Russia, or even Britain were the sole possessor of this means of sudden destruction.

As I say, our intentions toward the world may be most benign, but competition would start—other countries would get it—every country would eye every other country askance, and sooner or later the spark would be struck that would send the whole world up in one flaming inferno of a third world war which would dwarf the horror of the present one.

There are further dangers. Repeating that our intentions now may be most benign, the human mind and soul are far from perfect and the possession of great power is a corrupting influence which many men cannot resist. Even this country, knowing that it could, if it chose, rule the world, could in the course of time acquire the same Herrenvolk complex that led to the destruction of Germany—but which might lead to the destruction of the world the next time. Going along a slightly different line, the possession of this power by our country would offer a prize more tempting to the corrupt and venal demagogue than had ever been dangled before the eyes of man. Such a man, given the great ability which many of them have, could lay his plans with greatest care, could set aside twenty, thirty, or forty years to gain his end, could build his organization, attract his following and, with never a word of his real intention, finally get himself into power in this country and then, and only then, he could turn on us and the world and conquer it for his own insane satisfaction.

I would be supremely vain if I set myself up to say just what would happen, but I know that things such as I have mentioned could happen. I know the course of events might follow some other unpredictable track but with the same general cataclysmic result, and I know that if this thing exists on earth while men still have greed and hate and lust of power, I know as well as I know that God is in his Heaven that something of this kind will happen without the slightest shadow of a doubt.

*   *   *   *   *   *   *   *   *   *   *   *

This thing must not be permitted to exist on this earth. We must not be the most hated and feared people on earth however good our intent may be. So long as the threat of Germany existed we had to proceed with all speed to accomplish this end. With the threat of Germany removed we must stop this project. Peace is possible, and we and we alone today have it in our power to bring peace to this earth for the first time and this very weapon which we have today almost in our grasp is the means whereby we can help to bring this about.

If this world has learned nothing from this war then we had best give up and revert to the dark ages. The world has learned at least that war must not happen again. But it will happen if this weapon, permitting a war to be fought and won possibly in a matter of days, if not even hours, is found upon this earth.

I know nothing of statesmanship or diplomacy or power politics, but I believe we today can go before the world and say something like this:

"We now possess this weapon. We will show it to you and demonstrate what it can do. We will soon have it in quantity and can before any one can stop us be in a position to control and enslave the world.

"We do not want to do this. We do not care to rule the world. We want peace on earth, and we realize there can be no peace if this weapon exists.

"We therefore say to you that we will give up this weapon if you, the rest of the world, will so organize with us that no country on earth shall ever produce this material in a form which can be used for destructive purposes.

"We propose that every power on earth, great and small, shall agree that it shall not produce this material.

"We know that agreements are only made to be broken, so we further propose that this agreement be implemented somewhat as follows:—

1. A group of international observers shall watch the industry of every

country. The production of this weapon is such a gigantic undertaking that no country under these conditions could attempt to build the necessary plant in secret.

2. If any country starts this work the rest of the world shall as one take it over by force and prevent this thing from happening. The time necessary to build the plant would give time to do this.

3. All known sources of supply of the raw material shall be supervised by an international commission and every pound of the raw material be accounted for. (The sources of raw material in quantity are few—Canada, Czechoslovakia, the Belgian Congo, and probably the Urals. The material is widely distributed in low grade deposits but the difficulty of recovery would be great and could be observed).

4. Research (perhaps under international sponsorship) should continue as to the properties of the material and as to methods of production. Particular emphasis should be placed on a search for any easy and simple method since such a method, if it exists, as it well may, would greatly increase the hazard and make necessary more rigid control.

5. The use of this material for power may be permitted if it can be conclusively proven that when in form useable for power it cannot be used for destruction and cannot be used as the first and perhaps most difficult stage of manufacture for destructive purposes.

"We are showing you our good faith in this by having stopped our plant almost on the point of success. We are prepared to proceed with this plant and will proceed and finish it if world agreement is not reached. We will in self defense proceed against any nation which we believe is building a similar plant."

I believe something like that, in substance, would get the desired result. I am sure Britain and France would gladly fall in line, and I have enough faith in human nature to believe that Russia would see the light and agree to the restraints and supervision which at present appear repugnant to her. Germany and later Japan can, of course, be forced to abide by the program.

Many of us are so afraid of Russia we fairly jump when the name is mentioned. I pretend to know nothing of Russia, but surely she has learned that war is a sorry business and surely it must be possible to convince her that this must be done.

*   *   *   *   *   *   *   *   *   *   *   *

The war with Japan goes on and I have almost been accused of treason by some for proposing the stoppage of this work before Japan is brought to terms. This is not my idea. The present facilities are, I believe, capable of producing in the near future an amount of the material sufficient to serve as a demonstration, and I see no reason why Japan should not serve as the target for such demonstration. I question whether added production would be necessary to bring about the surrender of Japan. This is of course a matter of opinion wherein my opinion is admittedly not well informed.

On the other hand, the full plant—utilizing K-27 only recently undertaken—cannot be in production until 1946 and when its production would be ready for use is something I do not know, but I think it likely that it will certainly be post-war.

I do not of course want to propose anything to jeopardize the war with Japan, but, horrible as it may seem, I know that it would be better to take greater casualties now in conquering Japan than to bring upon the world the tragedy of unrestrained competitive production of this material.

It is obvious that many other better minds than mine are earnestly considering this problem, but I am sincerely disturbed by the following considerations. From its very nature this project has been and must be wrapped in the greatest secrecy. Only a small proportion of those working on the project really know what we are making. For that reason the only people who know about it are those who are most deeply interested in it. The men of the Corps of Engineers, the OSRD, the scientists, engineers, and manufacturers who have given their all to make this thing a success,—none of us are capable of viewing the problem objectively and disinterestedly and therefore are not the proper ones to advise or decide what should be done.

Without discrediting the humanitarianism or honesty of the Army at all, surely it is not the one to decide the future course of this project. Such a weapon is the answer to all the prayers of the professional soldier. He cannot be expected to forego willingly such a potent means of bringing victory to or preparing the defense of his country.

The rest of us—the civilians in the project—are so intent on making it succeed that the suggestion that it should be stopped is rank heresy, if not treason, to most.

But these are practically the only people who know about it and therefore the only ones who can think about it. Also there is the old saw of the scientist that "you cannot stop progress." In this case I disagree, if indeed it be "progress," since the task of manufacture is so great that it can be controlled and stopped if the world as a whole can be made to agree that this must be done.

It therefore seems to me most urgent, Mr. President, that you should consult with others before it is concluded that this project should proceed full force according to the view of the great majority of those who know about it. In the name of the future of our country and of the peace of the world, I beg you, sir, not to pass this off because I happen to be an unknown, without influence or name in the public eye. I am definitely in the small minority of those now in a position to form an opinion on this matter. I respect and maintain the right of those who oppose me to their opinion just as some of them respect my opinion, but I do not believe that any of us can offer sound disinterested counsel on this question.

There surely are men in this country, however, to whom you could turn, asking them to study this problem, secure the facts, and come to a conclusion unbiased by their own deep and sincere interest in the project. Only on the judgment of such men could there be faith that full consideration had been given to all sides of this desperately grave question. I hope I do not appear presumptuous in this. I assure you I have full faith and confidence, and that the whole country has full faith and confidence, in you in fulfilling the enormous task that has befallen you and that you are going to lead us and with us the world into an era of lasting and just peace and security and that you are the best judge as to where and to whom you should turn in solving the multitude of problems which no man can be expected to solve unaided.

Most respectfully submitted,

O C Brewster

1945: JUNE 14

WILLIAM LEAHY TO THE JOINT CHIEFS OF STAFF

While he had now been informed about the Manhattan Project, Truman was still weighing more conventional approaches to the war in the Pacific as the summer of 1945 began. Among these were a traditional invasion of Japan and a massive naval blockade. In the following memo, Chief of Staff Admiral William D. Leahy (1875–1959) laid out Truman's desire to seek all available information on the likely consequences of a conventional attack. On August 6, 1945, the first atomic bomb would be dropped on Hiroshima.

Washington

14 June 1945

URGENT—IMMEDIATE ACTION
MEMORANDUM FOR

THE JOINT CHIEFS OF STAFF:

The President today directed me to inform the Joint Chiefs of Staff that he wishes to meet with the Chiefs of Staff in the afternoon of the 18th, in his office, to discuss details of our campaign against Japan.

He expects at this meeting to be thoroughly informed of our intentions and prospects in preparation for his discussions with Churchill and Stalin.

He will want information as to the number of men of the Army and ships of the Navy that will be necessary to defeat Japan.

He wants an estimate of the time required and an estimate of the losses in killed and wounded that will result from an invasion of Japan proper.

He wants an estimate of the time and the losses that will result from an effort to defeat Japan by isolation blockade, and bombardment by sea and air forces.

He desires to be informed as to exactly what we want the Russians to do.

He desires information as to what useful contribution, if any, can be made by other Allied nations.

It is his intention to make his decisions on the campaign with the purpose of economizing to the maximum extent possible in the loss of American lives.

Economy in the use of time and in money cost is comparatively unimportant.

I suggest that a memorandum discussion of the above noted points be prepared in advance for delivery to the President at the time of the meeting in order that he may find time later to study the problem.

WILLIAM D. LEAHY

1945: JULY 31

HARRY TRUMAN TO HENRY STIMSON

Truman's final order—which referred, according to prior arrangement, both to a press release and to the bomb itself—was handwritten in pencil.

Sec War
    Reply to your 41011
    suggestions approved
    Release when ready
    but not sooner than
    August 2

                                            HST

1945: AUGUST 6
HENRY STIMSON TO HARRY TRUMAN

Truman was given this message on board the Augusta, *heading home from Potsdam, where he had met with Churchill and Stalin to discuss plans for a postwar Europe. The president turned to the sailors standing around him and said: "This is the greatest thing in history. It's time for us to get home."*
When the bomb was dropped, it was August 5 in Washington, but already August 6 in Japan.

TO THE PRESIDENT
FROM THE SECRETARY OF WAR

    Big bomb dropped on Hiroshima August 5 at 7:15 p.m. Washington time. First reports indicate complete success which was even more conspicuous than earlier test.

1945: AUGUST 11
JANE POULTON TO HER HUSBAND

Jack Poulton had reported for navy duty on August 31, 1942, and had gone home to Richmond, Virginia, for a leave in April of 1945. Jane's letter to him suggests just how poorly the events of August 6 were initially understood.

                                    August 11, 1945
                                        Saturday

    I was hoping that this would be V-J Day. Maybe tomorrow.
    I was so keyed up yesterday and have felt all let down by this suspense as you are too no doubt. I heard over the radio that your boys on Island X had to get in foxholes to avoid the celebration bullets. Now I have to worry about you and the

horrors of peace! Of course the big question now is when do you get home. Your being a hero as long as the war was on was all right with me but now I wish you would bend every effort to come home. The victrola won't work, the baby is coming, the kitchen light switch is on the blink and besides all that, I can get you a teaching job next year at school. And you can walk the floor when the baby has a tummy ache.

When you get this letter it will all be decided. Radio says Japanese are considering peace terms. Suspense is awful.

I am surprised at your continued interest in my figure. It's not lush as it is all going to the tummy as of now. Mother brought me home some maternity clothes from Front Royal today. I want to look good next winter but everything costs so much. I have a few things for the baby to wear and he will be better dressed than his mother.

Had a gorgeous dream about you night before last. Not printable, however.

1945: AUGUST 13
JACK POULTON TO HIS WIFE

This was sent from Okinawa.

August 13, 1945
Monday

I can't seem to get much excited over the Peace news. I ought to be, I know, but it just doesn't register. I said to Mom in a letter night before last that we have succeeded better than we had thought and it has come to seem the normal thing and peace is nearly as incomprehensible as the war was when it came. But there are stirrings of happiness in me, and I think I will be feeling more and more excited as time goes by.

I haven't any idea, of course, though you will be wondering, what will happen to us. The best guess I can make is that we will come home on a point system pretty much like the Army's and ought surely to be home within a year. That will make the baby somewhere between one and seven months old and I think I'll be right lucky to be able to see so much of his/her babyhood. Nobody seems to have been much excited around here—there was a little feeble yelling the night the news was announced but it sounded forced and soon stopped. There was considerable shooting on another part of the island. People firing flares and tracers in lieu of fireworks and it looked pretty from here but I didn't see much sense in it. But I can tell you this, when they DO sign the terms I am going to take a whole day off and get VERY drunk. You would be ashamed of me or maybe drunker.

I would be glad to teach a night course in Calculus. I don't remember a thing about it but I can brush up and I suspect it would be fun.

1946

GROUCHO MARX TO THE WARNER BROTHERS

The Marx Brothers had already produced major movie hits, including Animal Crackers *(1930),* Duck Soup *(1933), and* A Night at the Opera *(1935) by the time they were wrapping up a movie called* A Night in Casablanca. *Inquiries and legal threats came from the Warner brothers, who were apparently worried about potential similarities to* Casablanca, *which they had made four years earlier. In this letter and the two that follow, Groucho (1890–1977) tried to set them straight.*

Dear Warner Brothers:

Apparently there is more than one way of conquering a city and holding it as your own. For example, up to the time that we contemplated making this picture, I had no idea that the city of Casablanca belonged exclusively to Warner Brothers. However, it was only a few days after our announcement appeared that we received your long, ominous legal document warning us not to use the name Casablanca.

It seems that in 1471, Ferdinand Balboa Warner, your great-great-grandfather, while looking for a shortcut to the city of Burbank, had stumbled on the shores of Africa and, raising his alpenstock (which he later turned in for a hundred shares of the common), named it Casablanca.

I just don't understand your attitude. Even if you plan on re-releasing your picture, I am sure that the average movie fan could learn in time to distinguish between Ingrid Bergman and Harpo. I don't know whether I could, but I certainly would like to try.

You claim you own Casablanca and that no one else can use that name without your permission. What about "Warner Brothers"? Do you own that, too? You probably have the right to use the name Warner, but what about Brothers? Professionally, we were brothers long before you were. We were touring the sticks as The Marx Brothers when Vitaphone was still a gleam in the inventor's eye, and even before us there had been other brothers—the Smith Brothers; the

Brothers Karamazov; Dan Brothers, an outfielder with Detroit; and "Brother, Can You Spare a Dime?" (This was originally "Brothers, Can You Spare a Dime?" but this was spreading a dime pretty thin, so they threw out one brother, gave all the money to the other one and whittled it down to, "Brother, Can You Spare a Dime?")

Now Jack, how about you? Do you maintain that yours is an original name? Well, it's not. It was used long before you were born. Offhand, I can think of two Jacks—there was Jack of "Jack and the Beanstalk," and Jack the Ripper, who cut quite a figure in his day.

As for you, Harry, you probably sign your checks, sure in the belief that you are the first Harry of all time and that all other Harrys are imposters. I can think of two Harrys that preceded you. There was Lighthouse Harry of Revolutionary fame and a Harry Appelbaum who lived on the corner of 93rd Street and Lexington Avenue. Unfortunately, Appelbaum wasn't too well known. The last I heard of him, he was selling neckties at Weber and Heilbroner.

Now about the Burbank studio. I believe this is what you brothers call your place. Old man Burbank is gone. Perhaps you remember him. He was a great man in a garden. His wife often said Luther had ten green thumbs. What a witty woman she must have been! Burbank was the wizard who crossed all those fruits and vegetables until he had the poor plants in such a confused and jittery condition that they could never decide whether to enter the dining room on the meat platter or the dessert dish.

This is pure conjecture, of course, but who knows—perhaps Burbank's survivors aren't too happy with the fact that a plant that grinds out pictures on a quota settled in their town, appropriated Burbank's name and uses it as a front for their films. It is even possible that the Burbank family is prouder of the potato produced by the old man than they are of the fact that from your studio emerged "Casablanca" or even "Gold Diggers of 1931."

This all seems to add up to a pretty bitter tirade, but I assure you it's not meant to. I love Warners. Some of my best friends are Warner Brothers. It is even possible that I am doing you an injustice and that you, yourselves, know nothing at all about this dog-in-the-Wanger attitude. It wouldn't surprise me at all to discover that the heads of your legal department are unaware of this absurd dispute, for I am acquainted with many of them and they are fine fellows with curly black hair, double-breasted suits and a love of their fellow man that out-Saroyans Saroyan.

I have a hunch that this attempt to prevent us from using the title is the brainchild of some ferret-faced shyster, serving a brief apprenticeship in your legal department. I know the type well—hot out of law school, hungry for success and too ambitious to follow the natural laws of promotion. This bar sinister probably needled your attorneys, most of whom are fine fellows with curly black hair, double-breasted suits, etc., into attempting to enjoin us. Well, he won't get away with it! We'll fight him to the highest court! No pasty-faced legal adventurer is going to cause bad blood between the Warners and the Marxes. We are all brothers under the skin and we'll remain friends till the last reel of "A Night in Casablanca" goes tumbling over the spool.

> Sincerely,
> Groucho Marx

1946

GROUCHO MARX TO THE WARNER BROTHERS

Warner Bros.' legal department replied that the Marx Brothers should explain what the story was about. This was Groucho's answer.

Dear Warners:

There isn't much I can tell you about the story. In it I play a Doctor of Divinity who ministers to the natives and, as a sideline, hawks can openers and pea jackets to the savages along the Gold Coast of Africa.

When I first meet Chico, he is working in a saloon, selling sponges to barflies who are unable to carry their liquor. Harpo is an Arabian caddie who lives in a small Grecian urn on the outskirts of the city.

As the picture opens, Porridge, a mealy-mouthed native girl, is sharpening some arrows for the hunt. Paul Hangover, our hero, is constantly lighting two cigarettes simultaneously. He apparently is unaware of the cigarette shortage.

There are many scenes of splendor and fierce antagonisms, and Color, an Abyssinian messenger boy, runs Riot. Riot, in case you have never been there, is a small night club on the edge of town.

There's a lot more I could tell you, but I don't want to spoil it for you. All this has been okayed by the Hays Office, Good Housekeeping and the survivors of the Haymarket Riots; and if the times are ripe, this picture can be the opening gun in a new worldwide disaster.

> Cordially,
> Groucho Marx

1946

GROUCHO MARX TO THE WARNER BROTHERS

---

*Apparently still confused, the lawyers asked for further explanations. Despite every-
thing, the film was released, as planned, in 1946.*

Dear Brothers:

Since I last wrote you, I regret to say there have been some changes in the
plot of our new picture, "A Night in Casablanca." In the new version I play Bordello, the sweetheart of Humphrey Bogart. Harpo and Chico are itinerant rug
peddlers who are weary of laying rugs and enter a monastery just for a lark. This
is a good joke on them, as there hasn't been a lark in the place for fifteen years.

Across from this monastery, hard by a jetty, is a waterfront hotel, chockfull of
apple-cheeked damsels, most of whom have been barred by the Hays Office for
soliciting. In the fifth reel, Gladstone makes a speech that sets the House of
Commons in an uproar and the King promptly asks for his resignation. Harpo
marries a hotel detective; Chico operates an ostrich farm. Humphrey Bogart's
girl, Bordello, spends her last years in a Bacall house.

This, as you can see, is a very skimpy outline. The only thing that can save us
from extinction is a continuation of the film shortage.

Fondly,

Groucho Marx

1947?

FRED ALLEN TO EARL WILSON

---

*Fred Allen (1894–1956) had begun his career in vaudeville, but large audiences
were first introduced to his wit and exquisite timing in 1932, when he debuted
on radio. He performed on numerous programs before starring on* Town Hall
Tonight *from 1934 to 1939, when it was renamed the* Fred Allen Show. *Along with
other denizens of "Allen's Alley," Allen stayed on the air for another decade. Earl
Wilson (1909–1987), also a New York institution, was a syndicated Broadway
columnist.*

Jane Russell, Hedy Lamarr, Lana Turner, and Paulette Goddard were actresses. Jack Egan and
Jack Haley were actors. Oscar Levant was an actor and composer. Cole Porter was the height
of sophistication as a playwright, composer, and raconteur. Sherman Billingsly owned the
swank Stork Club. Toots Shor's and the Copacabana were also popular nightspots. Lindy's,

the Automat, and Hamburger Heaven were less tony restaurants. Yellow jack is a kind of fish. The film *Life With Father* opened in 1947.

dear earl . . .

sorry i can't write a guest column for you. column writing isn't my metier. (metier is french for racket) i could never be a bistro balzac, a saloon sandburg or a diva de maupassant.

an m.c. on a quiz program once told me that einstein knows more about space than any columnist. i told him that a columnist fills more space in a week than einstein can hope to fill in a lifetime. einstein keeps going for years with one lousy theory. to weather a day, you need two columns of facts.

and what facts! i could never take your place.

with gay abandon you write of falsies and girdles and elaborate on their contents. i blush when i see breast of chicken on a menu. the first time i saw jane russell i wondered how she got her kneecaps up in her sweater.

press agents date hedy lamarr, lana turner and paulette goddard for you to interview.

the last blind date i had i opened one eye and it was broadway rose.

you are welcomed at all of the fine eating places. mr. billingsly, they say, carries you over the threshold of his stork club nightly.

the last time i ate in lindy's the tongue in my sandwich gave me the raspberry through a small hole in the top slice of bread. when i complained to lindy he put his head in the sandwich and gave me another raspberry through a small hole in the bottom slice of bread.

when you walk down broadway, you meet scores of interesting people.

when i walk down broadway i meet jack benny or some other actor who is out of work.

the nights you go into toots shor's, oscar levant, between sips of coffee, is bellowing epigrams. to wit: "i ran myself through an adding machine today and found that i didn't amount to much."

the nights i go into shor's toots is generally talking to himself in a low voice. i can't even hear what he is saying. the only time i could hear him, toots was mumbling "why you big crum bum, you're so stupid you think yellow jack is chinese money."

when you go to an opening, noel coward stops you at intermission and regales you with the story that is currently sweeping london. to wit: the one about the young innocent girl whose father told her about the flowers but neglected to tell her about the b's. the girl went to hollywood and made three bad pictures.

the last opening i attended (life with father) a guy named dwight gristle, who was selling black market tassels, told me a broken-down gag about a new cheese store—it was called "limberger heaven."

how could i ever get enough good jokes together to be "earl for a day?"

last night, i walked around town. here's what happened to me.

at the health food store, on 50th street, i saw a sign "hubert frend has switched to yogurt."

at the copa, jack eigan told me about the latest in hollywood styles: an undertaker is featuring a suede coffin.

at the automat, jack haley told me about the picture star who thought he was a banana. his psychiatrist found the picture star had a split personality. his is the first banana split personality on record.

you can see, earl, the whole thing is futile. i can never be a columnist. i know the wrong people. i hear the wrong things. i go to the wrong places.

i will end up like the old man who lived in the cannon for twenty years—he was always hoping to be a big shot, but he never quite made it.

sorry to have to let you down with the guest column.

regards . . .

fred allen

1947: JUNE 30
E. G. HALL TO THE NEW YORK TIMES

Hemlines rose and fell with national fortunes. The scarcity of fabric during the war had dictated shorter skirts, but after the war ended, Christian Dior introduced American women to "the New Look," with cinched waists and long, full skirts. Not everyone was pleased.

To the Editor of the New York Times:

I am writing to your influential paper in the hope that you will publish this letter, to help bring to an end a frumpish fashion. I mean these horrible longer skirts and dresses that the dictatorial fashion experts have brought out. They are a definite offense to the gaze and an insult to a Maker who gave women legs to show, not conceal behind a screen of cloth.

I wouldn't walk two yards with a woman in a long skirt. Why can't women have character and individuality enough to wear what they desire, and not what fashion says? Prudery and narrow-mindedness are the sinister forces working behind the fashion designers.

American Women, I call on all of you to resist to the utmost a hideous fashion. Wear your skirts as short as you desire in the name of beauty and freedom of movement. How can you move with a horrible old sack of skirt flopping around? This is 1947 not 1847.

> E. G. Hall
> Northampton, Mass., June 30, 1947

1947: JULY 8
FBI DALLAS TO J. EDGAR HOOVER

Something crashed in Roswell, New Mexico, in the summer of 1947. After that came official explanations (weather balloon, spy balloon) and unofficial theories (extraterrestrial visitors, alien autopsies, massive government cover-ups, and the planting of alien technologies at IBM and Bell Laboratories). The memo below, unlike many other Roswell documents, is authentic. What it proves, if anything, continues to be the object of endless debate.

FBI DALLAS   7-8-47   6-17 PM
DIRECTOR AND SAC, CINCINNATI   URGENT
FLYING DISC, INFORMATION CONCERNING. MAJOR CURTAN, HEADQUARTERS EIGHTH AIR FORCE, TELEPHONICALLY ADVISED THIS OFFICE THAT AN OBJECT PURPORTING TO BE A FLYING DISC WAS RE COVERED NEAR ROSWELL, NEW MEXICO, THIS DATE. THE DISC IS HEXAGONAL IN SHAPE AND WAS SUSPENDED FROM A BALLON BY A CABLE, WHICH BALLON WAS APPROXIMATELY TWENTY FEET IN DIAMETER. MAJOR CURTAN FURTHER ADVISED THAT THE OBJECT FOUND RESEMBLES A HIGH ALTITUDE WEATHER BALLOON WITH A RADAR REFLECTOR, BUT THAT TELEPHONIC CONVERSATION BETWEEN THEIR OFFICE AND WRIGHT FIELD HAD NOT . . . BORNE OUT THIS BELIEF. DISC AND BALLOON BEING TRANSPORTED TO WRIGHT FIELD BY SPECIAL PLANE FOR EXAMINATION. INFORMATION PROVIDED THIS OFFICE BECAUSE OF NATIONAL INTEREST IN CASE AND FACT THAT NATIONAL BROADCASTING COMPANY, ASSOCIATED PRESS, AND OTHERS ATTEMPTING TO BREAK STORY OF LOCATION OF DISC TODAY. MAJOR CURTAN ADVISED WOULD REQUEST WRIGHT FIELD TO ADVISE CINCINNATI OFFICE RESULTS OF EXAMINATION. NO FURTHER INVESTIGATION BEING CONDUCTED.

> WYLY

END

1947: DECEMBER 30

DALTON TRUMBO TO A MOTION PICTURE ASSOCIATE

The U.S. House Committee on Un-American Activities (HUAC) was created in 1938 to investigate extreme political groups. By 1945, when it became a standing committee, it was focused on Nazi and other pro-Axis sympathizers. In the years after the war, it turned its attention to suspected American Communists. Screenwriter Dalton Trumbo (1905–1976) was one of the original Hollywood Ten, a group of writers, producers, and directors called before HUAC in October of 1947. Refusing to answer questions about their political affiliations, they were jailed for contempt and blacklisted by the film industry. The recipient of this letter had written to Trumbo earlier in the fall, enclosing a check to help fight the blacklist and telling Trumbo of his great affection in spite of political differences. Trumbo returned the check.

After writing for years under assumed names, Trumbo—as "Robert Rich"—would win an Academy Award in 1957 for his screenplay of *The Brave One.* "The Guild" was the Screen Writers Guild. Neither the recipient of the letter nor the contents of Trumbo's "original letter" is known.

Lazy T Ranch

Frazier Park, California

December 30, 1947

Dear ——:

I am told you take it badly that I have not yet answered your note, and that you consider my original letter to you insulting.

I am astonished to find you still so sensitive: for I have grown quite accustomed to abuse lately—not only the quietly slanderous kind which impels you to raise political bars against me in my trade union, but also that which comes from your less genteel colleagues and obliges me to hide my mail lest the children see letters addressed quite openly to "Traitor Trumbo," "Bolshevik Dalt T.," "Jew-lover Trumbo," "Red Rat Trumbo" and other epithets of like nature. No criminal, no murderer nor rapist can safely be called the names which with impunity are now applied to me: there lives no man so foul or so low that he may not elevate himself a little in the esteem of society by spitting upon my name and proscribing my work.

I say this to you because for long years you have been a political hermaphrodite, lifting your voice in the defense of no man, espousing no principle which smells of danger. But now you are a politico. You have found a faith to fight for. You have embarked upon a crusade—not <u>for</u> something, to be sure, but at least against something. Hence you must prepare yourself for a certain amount of re-crimination. You must callous yourself and harden your heart a little, for there is much work to be done before your objective is fully achieved.

Your crusade isn't a very new one. Its first disciples felt the call in Germany immediately after the Reichstag fire, when hundreds of thousands rushed forth to sanctify political discrimination a good four years before it blossomed at Nuremberg into racial and religious discrimination. You belong to the legion of men who traditionally sacrifice their brothers to gain a little more time for themselves—the shuddering, exquisite, sensitive men who quietly deplore injustice while dining upon its victim. This is your right, ——, and your choice and your destiny.

But you should not, in your letter to me, assume a whore's virtue at confession by using the word "affection." My affection caused me to assert your ability to producers when you were out of favor; yours impelled you to cry out against me in the most fatal hour of my career. Mine persuaded me to spend long hours in discussion of your story problems when you sought to re-establish yourself; yours led to organizational meetings calculated to deprive me of my rights within the Guild, to destroy my good name and to make it impossible for me to work in my profession. Give me no more such affection, ——: I stagger beneath that already conferred. Give me rather your hatred and let me console myself by the exchange of a weak friend for a strong enemy.

And do not attribute, as you did in your letter, the destruction of our friendship to political differences. Political opposition I have freely given and taken both in victory and in defeat. But I have never advocated the savagery of second-class citizenship for anybody, nor sought to impose it, nor tolerated its suggestion. There can be no real political differences between you and me because you have no politics but expediency, no standard of conduct but deceit, no principle but self-love.

I did not wish to write this letter, and would not have done so but for your characteristically widespread complaints. With it—and with your last kiss still hot upon my cheek—I bid you farewell.

Dalton Trumbo

1948: MAY 6

ALFRED KINSEY TO ALBERT ELLIS

Sexual Behavior in the Human Male, *the first volume of what came to be known as the Kinsey Report, was published in 1948. It became an immediate bestseller and an instant source of controversy. It also made a target of its author, Dr. Alfred Kinsey (1894–1956). Later biographies of Kinsey would reveal a sometimes bizarre, certainly experimental, side to his own sexual life. Those revelations, along with the number and profile of the original participants in the study, have long since called his results into question. But Kinsey's first reports—about the prevalence of masturbation, infidelity, and homosexuality among American men—were groundbreaking in their frankness and were, as this letter attests, passionately defended by their author.*

Albert Ellis (1913–), a psychologist and author, developed rational-emotive psychotherapy, which placed an emphasis on conscious as well as unconscious emotions; he would write *Sex Without Guilt* in 1966. Albert Deutsch wrote about science and medicine. Dorothy Thompson wrote a column for the *Ladies' Home Journal*. Rosalind Ives had written a short favorable article in *Good Housekeeping*. Fulton Oursler, Jr., was an editor for *The Reader's Digest*. The "100% samples" that Kinsey defends here were groups in which all the participants had agreed to give him their sexual histories. This kind of universal participation sometimes resulted from Kinsey giving free lectures in exchange for the chance to solicit a group's membership list. In Germany between the wars, Magnus Hirschfeld was considered an authority on homosexuality.

May 6, 1948

Dr. Albert Ellis
New Jersey State Hospital
Greystone Park, New Jersey

Dear Dr. Ellis:

I have been out-of-state and this has been my first opportunity to look over the review which you were good enough to send me. I regret that I still have not had time to go over it in detail.

I appreciate your general interest in the furtherance of our research, and your general overall approval. I think it fair to tell you, however, that I think there is no more damnable way to prevent the continuation of this research than to write the sort of review that you have. Albert Deutsch has recently written to one of the psychoanalysts that this continual emphasis on the inadequacies is something that will invite John Sumner and his vice society, and the Watch and Ward society to crawl in bed with them. It is exactly the sort of half baked stuff which you are writing which allows people like Dorothy Thompson in the LADIES HOME JOURNAL and Ives in the GOOD HOUSEKEEPING, and Oursler in the June and July issues of the READERS DIGEST to suggest that there be public action against the continuation of the research. I am serious about this, and I hope that the revisions which you suggest you have already had in mind, since hearing me speak in New York, will bear this in mind.

I have considerable respect for your analytic mind, and I congratulate you on the quality of several of the things which you have done. I have no question of your honesty, and I know that the error that you fall into is due to your inexperience. I would not tell you this if I did not think that you have considerable ability and promise, and if I did not like you and hope to see you become a psychologist of considerable significance.

Your total lack of experience in actual interviewing and surveying of the sort that we have done is the source of your error. For instance, the way in which you discount the quality of our 100% samples could be completely changed if you could spend a few hours in the midst of one of these groups where we have gotten such samples. You suggest that people tell us what is supposed to be accepted in their community. This is another question that would never be raised if you were to spend a few days with us in a community and see how we work. In many a community we have the entre to homes where we can meet the people involved, know who is sleeping with whom on a particular night, and the 100 and one other details that completely substantiate the more statistical record that we have abstracted from our histories.

If humans were pictures on a pack of playing cards, you could deal them and sample them in accordance with all the rules which you would emphasize for playing cards. It is beyond possibility with human material, and our problem has been to determine how much likelihood of error there is after we have done our best at sampling. To compare the way we have gone after our sample with the way Hirschfield went after his sample is far from correct. You make innumerable remarks on what we have and have not done which are not in accord with the fact. There is about 30% of our population that came from 100% groups, and there is a very high proportion of the remainder that come from groups where we got anywhere from 70%–95% of the group. I question very much whether complete 100% sampling would have modified the figures any more than 2% or 3%, or the 5%–10% which we allow on certain items, as discussed in Chapter 4.

I would not have written this way if I had not known you so well, and if I did not believe in your ability, nor would I have written this way if I thought your review were just one more item in the archives of scientific journals. On the other hand, I can see that possibly it might be the sort of thing that adds one more straw to the burden of opposition which can mean long years of court action and, possibly, stoppage of the research for a long time to come. This is a much more serious and immediate issue than apparently you begin to comprehend. For the people who are writing supercilious reviews and emotionally charged objections, I have no particular concern. A review that attempts to be technically correct, however, can do more damage when it fails to keep the overall objectives of the project in mind.

I suggest that you read the chapter by Leo Crespi, psychologist at Princeton University and statistical advisor to the Gallup Poll, which is in the book edited by Albert Deutsch, and just published by Prentice-Hall of New York.

Alfred C. Kinsey
Professor of Zoolozy

1948: AUGUST 3
ALGER HISS TO J. PARNELL THOMAS

Alger Hiss (1904–1996) had been law clerk to Supreme Court Justice Oliver Wendell Holmes. He had served in the agriculture, state, and justice departments and had been an adviser to Roosevelt at Yalta: In 1946, he had been elected president of the Carnegie Endowment for International Peace. The day he learned that Time *editor and confessed spy Whittaker Chambers had called him a Communist, he sent this telegram to the chairman of the House Committee on Un-American Activities. With Hiss's denial, the battle lines were drawn for a series of congressional hearings and two trials that would present one of the most debated cases in the nation's history.* New Jersey congressman J. Parnell Thomas was chairman of HUAC.

My attention has been called by representatives of the press to statements made about me before your committee this morning by one Whittaker Chambers. I do not know Mr. Chambers and insofar as I am aware have never laid eyes on him. There is no basis for the statements made about me to your committee. I would appreciate it if you would make this telegram a part of your committee's record, and I would further appreciate the opportunity to appear before your committee to make these statements formally and under oath. I shall be in Washington on Thursday and hope that that will be a convenient time from the committee's point of view for me to appear.

✳   ✳   ✳

1948: SEPTEMBER 7
AGNES MAXWELL PETERS TO FREDRIC WERTHAM

The Cold War was setting in, but not all the perceived threats were red. This letter, written by a California mother, was typical of the correspondence that Dr. Frederic Wertham (1895–1981) received during the forties and fifties. In the complaints of despairing parents, Wertham found support for his argument that mass culture was having a harmful effect on "delinquent youth." Wertham would publish Seduction of the Innocent *in 1954, a book that became famous for its indictment of the violence in comic books. A "Comics Code" would be created in response, and comic books would take on a much purer tone. But neither the debate nor the complaints about children's exposure to violence would cease.*

Dear Dr. Wertham:

We have two boys, 7 and 13, with unusually high intelligence and excellent ability in school and in sports. . . . They have a library of fine books of their own, and read library books almost daily, yet in the presence of comic books they behave as if drugged, and will not lift their eyes or speak when spoken to. . . . What we would like to know is, what can be done about it before it is too late? My boys fight with each other in a manner that is unbelievable in a home where both parents are university graduates and perfectly mated. We attribute the so-called "hatred" that they profess for each other to the harmful influence of these books, plus movies and radio. . . .

We consider the situation to be as serious as an invasion of the enemy in war time, with as far reaching consequences as the atom bomb. If we cannot stop the wicked men who are poisoning our children's minds, what chance is there for mankind to survive longer than one generation, or half of one?

1948: NOVEMBER 3
BOB HOPE TO HARRY TRUMAN

Winning the election despite predictions to the contrary, President Truman flashed a buoyant grin as he showed off the famously erroneous Chicago Daily Tribune *headline "DEWEY DEFEATS TRUMAN." Then the comedian Bob Hope (1903–) sent him this telegram.*

November 3, 1948

PRESIDENT HARRY S TRUMAN
THE WHITE HOUSE
WASHINGTON, D.C.

UNPACK.

BOB HOPE

1948: NOVEMBER 29
ZIPPORAH BOROWSKY TO HER FAMILY

A year before this letter was written, the United Nations voted to split Palestine into two states, and the first of many Arab-Israeli wars began with the declaration of the State of Israel in May. Zipporah "Zippy" Borowsky left America for Palestine in 1947 for what was intended to be a year of study at the Hebrew University in Jerusalem. But she soon became caught up in Israel's War of Independence, joined the underground defense forces, served as a nurse, and stayed on. Eventually, she became a freelance journalist.

This letter was sent from Haifa Bay, Israel.

Dearest Mother, Dad and Naomi,

From the roof of the hospital, I watched this morning's parade, a parade of soldiers of the Jewish State. Not partisans or underground fighters. Soldiers, standing erect and proud, in rain puddles six inches deep, wearing shabby outfits—winter uniforms still haven't reached us—listening to lofty words of accomplishment and tribute.

I, too, listened but my thoughts wandered—drifted back to last November 29th, 1947, Jerusalem, the courtyard of the Sochnut building, the spontaneous joy that filled the streets when the United Nations resolution calling for a Jewish State was approved.

And now we march, we form ranks, we listen to speeches, we salute officers; Natan, as they taught him in the Russian army; Lev, as he learned in the RAF; Aryeh, as they do in the Polish army; Uzi (the Sabra), reluctantly; Moshe, in Turkish style. All of them, saluting the Jewish Officer in Command, representing <u>Tzva Haganah LeYisrael</u> (Israel Defense Forces). The same people who were partisans last year are soldiers today, and civilian citizens of the State of Israel tomorrow. I wondered whether "tomorrow" would be another year or an eternity?

The command rang out, "<u>Chofshi</u>" (dismissed). The ranks broke to the count of three and everyone dashed to the canteen where they mimicked each other marching, saluting and even drinking tea. Nobody mentioned the words we had heard, nobody referred to the historic importance of the day or the momentous events that had transpired, transforming us into a State with an Army. Nobody marveled at the wonder of it all. Were these miracles already being taken for granted?

For me, this pathetic parade was a fulfillment, a consummation. I kept thinking that it had been mustered from all the lands of the world, had taken not one year but <u>two thousand years</u> to materialize. Next year, the parade will probably be more impressive. We'll have smart uniforms, everyone will salute in the same way, stand in straight lines and know all the marching commands. We will have learned so much and, possibly, forgotten so much.

The talk in the canteen was about leave time, the latest movie, tonight's party, who has an extra blanket or what's the biggest gripe of the day. I looked at the faces of those around me and thought of the patriots who had fought the American Revolution. Faced with a Fourth of July celebration 1948-style, would they have the same sober thoughts I was having?

Like everything else here, it has happened very fast, too fast—the twenty-ninth of November is just a red-letter day on the calendar. A fighting people hasn't time to be sentimental.

But I couldn't help thinking of Moshe, Oded, Zvi, Amnon, Yaakov, Aryeh, Matty, Nachum and a hundred others in Jerusalem, who a year ago danced and sang through the night with me, but didn't live long enough; they fell before the dream came true. The lump in my throat was too big in my mouth.

Was it only a year ago? No, it was worlds ago, each a separate world: the University, the Haganah, Deir Yassin, the Burma Road, Sheikh Jarrah, Katamon, Talpiot, Tel Aviv, Haifa—worlds of people, places and events.

I can't believe this year. So much has happened, but the most important thing by far is the birth of the State. I've been part of it and it will forever be part of me. I guess that means I am telling you I intend to see this war through and then remain on, whatever happens. This is now my HOME.

Love,

Zippy

* * *

1949: JANUARY 14
J. EDGAR HOOVER TO FBI COMMUNICATIONS SECTION

Like "pumpkin papers" and "prothonotary warbler," the phrase "Woodstock type-writer" became inseparable from the Alger Hiss case. It was on this brand of machine, Whittaker Chambers claimed, that Hiss had copied a series of incriminating documents. The search for the famous typewriter was lengthy and far-reaching—and undertaken by J. Edgar Hoover in deadly earnest. Ultimately it was Hiss's defense team that tracked down the typewriter. Though Hiss claimed that the FBI had planted and doctored the machine, he was convicted of perjury and jailed for nearly four years. He would spend the rest of his life insisting on his innocence.
WAS stands for wide-area surveillance. Priscilla was Hiss's wife.

FEDERAL BUREAU OF INVESTIGATION
UNITED STATES DEPARTMENT OF JUSTICE

To: COMMUNICATIONS SECTION.
JANUARY 14, 1949
Transmit the following message to:

SAC'S NEW YORK   URGENT
BALTIMORE
CHICAGO
PHILADELPHIA

JAY DAVID WHITTAKER CHAMBERS, WAS; ALGER HISS, ET AL; PERJURY; ESPIONAGE—R. RE PHILA TEL JANUARY THREE INST REQUESTING BUREAU TO ESTABLISH SERIAL NUMBER LIMITS IN THE SEARCH FOR HISS WOODSTOCK TYPEWRITER. SEARCH FOR WOODSTOCK SHOULD BE LIMITED TO MACHINES MANUFACTURED BETWEEN JANUARY ONE, NINETEEN TWENTY-SIX AND JANUARY ONE, TWENTY-NINE, THAT IS, MACHINES HAVING SERIAL NUMBERS FROM ONE HUNDRED FORTY FIVE THOUSAND TO TWO HUNDRED FOUR THOUSAND, FIVE HUNDRED. IN VIEW OF THE FACT ALGER HISS ALLEGES PRISCILLA HISS SOLD WOODSTOCK TO A SECONDHAND TYPEWRITER CONCERN OR TO A SECONDHAND DEALER IN WASHINGTON, D.C. SOME TIME AFTER NINETEEN THIRTY-EIGHT, CHICAGO SHOULD ASCERTAIN FROM FACTORY IF ANY MACHINES WITHIN ABOVE RANGE HAVE BEEN RETURNED TO THE FACTORY FROM WASHINGTON

AFTER NINETEEN THIRTY-SIX OR FROM NYC AFTER NINETEEN FORTY-SIX. OBTAIN SERIAL NUMBERS OF ANY MACHINES RETURNED WITHIN THE ABOVE RANGE AND ASCERTAIN WHO RETURNED THE MACHINES TO THE FACTORY. INVESTIGATION REFLECTS POSSIBILITY HISS MIGHT HAVE TAKEN WOODSTOCK TO NYC IN NINETEEN FORTY-SEVEN AND THERE-FORE, MACHINE MAY HAVE BEEN DISPOSED OF THERE.

HOOVER

1949: MAY 14
MARY CHURCH TERRELL TO THE <u>WASHINGTON POST</u>

The first president of the National Association of Colored Women, Mary Church Terrell (1863–1954) was raised in relative comfort by middle-class parents who had been born into slavery. A graduate of Oberlin, Terrell was a writer, a teacher, a suffragist, and a lecturer. She was also both outspoken and extremely modern in her concerns about the power of language to perpetuate—or to combat—racial stereotypes.

Theodore Bilbo was a notoriously racist Mississippi senator.

Dear Sir:

Please stop using the word "Negro". Several days ago "BAN ON WORD ASKED" was the Post's title of an appeal made by a leper who stood before a congressional committee urging that the Federal Government ban the use of the word "leper." He said the word "leper" should be removed from the dictionary because of its unjust and shameful stigma which hurts its victims and efforts to control and wipe the disease out. He wants the affliction to be called "Hanson's Disease," because lepers are treated unfairly owing to "public misunderstanding."

For a reason similar to the one given by the leper I am urging the Post and others willing to advance our interests and deal justly with our group to stop using the word "Negro". The word is a misnomer from every point of view. It does not represent a country or anything else except one single, solitary color. And no one color can describe the various and varied complexions in our group. In complexion we range from deep black to the fairest white with all the colors of the rainbow thrown in for good measure. When twenty or thirty of us are meeting together it would be as hard to find three or four of us with the same complexion as it would be to catch greased lightning in a bottle. We are the only human beings in the world with fifty seven variety of complexions who are classed together as a single racial unit. Therefore, we are really, truly colored

people, and that is the only name in the English language which accurately describes us.

To be sure the complexion of the Chinese and Japanese is yellow. But nobody
refers to an individual in either group as a colored man . . . They say he is Chinese. . . . When I studied abroad and was introduced as an "American," (generally speaking, everybody from the United States used to be called an "American"
in Europe) occasionally somebody would say "you are rather dark to be an
American, aren't you?" "Yes" I would reply, "I am dark, because some of my
ancestors were Africans." I was proud of having the continent of Africa part of
my ancestral background. "I am an African-American," I would explain. I am
not ashamed of my African descent. Africa had great universities before there
were any in England and the African was the first man industrious and skillful
enough to work in iron. If our group must have a special name setting it apart,
the sensible way to settle it would be to refer to our ancestors, the Africans,
from whom our swarthy complexions come.

There are at least two strong reasons why I object to designating our group as
Negroes. If a man is a Negro, it follows as the night the day that a woman is a
Negress. "Negress" is an ugly, repulsive word—virtually a term of degradation
and reproach which colored women of this country can not live down in a thousand years. I have questioned scores of men who call themselves "Negroes", and
each and every one of them strenuously objected to having his wife, or daughter
or mother or any woman in his family called a "Negress".

In the second place, I object to . . . Negro because our meanest detractors
and most cruel persecutors insist that we shall be called by that name, so that
they can humiliate us by referring contemptuously to us as "niggers", or "Negras" as Bilbo used to do. Some of our group say they will continue to classify us
as Negroes, until an individual referred to as such will be proud of that name.
But that is a case of wishful thinking and nothing else. For the moment one
hears the word Negro in this country, instantly, automatically, in his mind's eye
he sees a human being who is ignorant, segregated, discriminated against, considered inferior and objectionable on general principles from every point of
view. God alone knows how long it will take our minority group under prevailing
conditions in this country to reach such heights that a representative of it will
be proud to be called a Negro. That would be a double, back action, super-
duper miracle indeed! . . .

It is a great pity the word "Negro" was not outlawed in the Emancipation
Proclamation as it certainly should have been. After people have been freed, it
is a cruel injustice to call them by the same name they bore as slaves. It is

painful and shocking indeed that those in our group who have enjoyed educational opportunities; that officials in the National Association for the Advancement of Colored People, founded forty years ago which repudiated the word "Negro" should continue to use the slave term and thereby increase the difficulties of their group in their effort to reach the worthy goal toward which they strive.

The founders of the N.A.A.C.P. which has been and still is waging such a holy warfare against disfranchisement, segregation and discrimination of all kinds certainly deserves our gratitude for not naming that wonderful, powerful instrument for good "The National Association for the Advancement of Negroes".

1949: AUGUST 8
HELEN SELLERS TO JACKSON POLLOCK

Jackson Pollock (1912–1956) was still being dismissed by many art critics as "Jack the Dripper" when a South Carolina mother sent along this fan letter on behalf of her son. Pollock, who had begun his career as a conventional painter, had taken up what was then called action painting just two years before this letter was written. He would soon be revered as one of the founders of the abstract expressionist movement.

August 8

Dear Mr. Pollock,

Just a few lines to tell you that my seven year old son Manning couldn't get over your picture Number Nine. Frankly, it looked like some of his finger-painting at school to me. However, he insisted that I write you to tell you that he cut it out of the "Life" and put it in his scrape-book—the first painting that he has ever cut out—

He really has quite good taste as you can tell by the Cocker—Snafu—he is holding. He wanted you to have his picture in exchange for his copy of No. 9—which he loves—

Sincerely,
Mrs. Helen K. Sellers

*   *   *

1949: AUGUST 8

LEVITT AND SONS TO A PROSPECTIVE BUYER

Between 1947 and 1951, William J. Levitt (1907–1994) built the first Levittown—17,500 simple houses, as well as schools, shops, community centers, and play-grounds—on four thousand acres of Long Island potato fields. Designed with the young postwar GI's family in mind, Levittown was affordable, popular—and fre-quently criticized for being too crowded and too uniform. But its design was not the company's only attempt to homogenize the American dream: A standard early lease, later justified by Levitt as being both common practice and good for business, required tenants to promise "not to permit the premises to be used or occupied by any person other than members of the Caucasian race."

August 8, 1949

Dear Sir:

The next allocation of houses in Levittown will be held on Monday evening, August 15. Since we expect a large number of people that evening, we ask you to please follow the instructions below carefully so as to make it most conve-nient for everybody.

1. These houses are for occupancy in late November and December.

2. The allocation will be held at the VILLAGE BATH CLUB IN MAN-HASSET on August 15. Please be there at 10:00 p.m. Since a different time is assigned to various groups, PLEASE DO NOT ARRIVE BEFORE THE TIME SHOWN. It will merely crowd us and you and will slow up things.

3. Enclosed are pictures of all five types of houses. Make your decision in ad-vance so that you will know when you get there just what house you want. To play safe, bring the pictures with you.

4. At the time shown above, or shortly thereafter, you will be called by name.

5. No further payment is necessary. You have already made your deposit, and after you move in it will be refunded. Please remember that all we are doing on August 15 is allocating houses. NO OTHER BUSINESS OF ANY KIND CAN BE TRANSACTED THAT EVENING.

6. It is not necessary for both husband and wife to be there.

7. The Village Bath Club is directly in back of the Altman Department Store on Northern Boulevard (Route 25A) in Manhasset. By car, take Grand Central Parkway to Exit 27, Shelter Rock Road. Drive north on Shelter Rock Road to Northern Boulevard. Turn right on Northern Boulevard about a mile and a half

to B. Altman and Co. (on the right hand side). Turn right about 300 feet to the Village Bath Club. By train, take the Long Island Railroad to Manhasset and a taxi from the station to the Village Bath Club.

Very truly yours,

LEVITT AND SONS, INC.

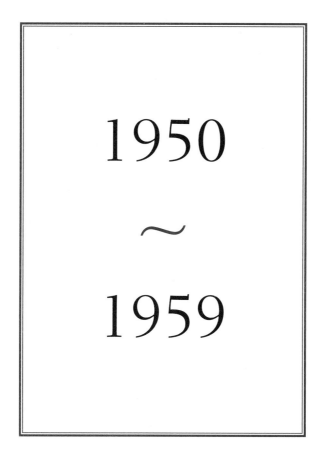

1950

~

1959

I do not like subversion or disloyalty in any form . . . But to hurt innocent people whom I knew many years ago in order to save myself is, to me, inhuman and indecent and dishonorable. I cannot and will not cut my conscience to fit this year's fashions . . .

—*Lillian Hellman to John Wood*
May 19, 1952

BETWEEN 1950 AND 1959 . . .

1950: Sixty-four percent of Americans live in cities. ★ The U.S. population is 150.6 million. ★ For the first time, television viewers' watching habits are tracked by A. C. Nielsen. ★ The first credit card—made of cardboard and usable at 28 places—is offered to 200 members of the New York Diners' Club. ★ *The Betty Crocker Cookbook* is published. ★ At a meeting of the Wheeling, West Virginia, Republican Women's Club, Senator Joseph McCarthy declares: "I have here in my hand a list of 205 . . . names that were known to the Secretary of State as being members of the Communist Party." Despite the fact that he offers no evidence, his speech creates a huge shock and sets off a Cold War witch hunt. ★ The Korean War begins. ★ Nat King Cole's "Mona Lisa" sells more than three million copies. **1951:** There are 1.5 million television sets in the United States, ten times the number in the previous year. ★ *I Love Lucy* debuts. ★ Ronald Reagan stars in *Bedtime for Bonzo*. ★ J. D. Salinger publishes *The Catcher in the Rye*. **1952:** On CBS, the computer Univac correctly projects Dwight D. Eisenhower's presidential victory. ★ Faced with accusations about an $18,235 slush fund created by his millionaire supporters, Senator Richard M. Nixon goes on television to declare that he has used none of the money for personal expenses. Conceding that he was given a

---

From left to right, top row: campaign buttons, map of Korea, Elvis Presley; *second row:* Joseph McCarthy, Marilyn Monroe; *third row:* polio poster, model of DNA, Jack Kerouac; *bottom row:* the Edsel, Howdy Doody.

dog, named Checkers, by his daughter Tricia, the vice-presidential candidate vows: "We're gonna keep it!" ★ Television audiences are introduced to *The Adventures of Ozzie and Harriet*, while movie audiences don red-and-green 3-D glasses to watch *Bwana Devil*, in a short-lived Hollywood craze. ★ Norman Vincent Peale's *The Power of Positive Thinking* becomes a bestseller. ★ There are 15,000 pizzerias in the United States. **1953:** While a report from the Sloan-Kettering Institute of Cancer Research links tobacco to cancer in mice, L&M cigarettes are advertised as being "just what the doctor ordered." ★ Convicted of passing atomic secrets to the Soviets, Ethel and Julius Rosenberg die in the electric chair. ★ *Go Tell It on the Mountain*, by James Baldwin, is published. ★ James Watson and Francis Crick discover the structure of DNA. ★ Parts of 13 midwestern states are declared disaster areas because of a vast drought. ★ Marilyn Monroe appears nude in a calendar photo in the first issue of Hugh Hefner's *Playboy*. **1954:** Sports events are aired live and in color. ★ The Salk polio vaccine is administered to children for the first time. ★ The case of *Brown* v. *Board of Education of Topeka* reaches the Supreme Court, which outlaws segregation of public schools by race. ★ Responding to parents' fears about the unwholesome content of comic books, a group of publishers forms the Comics Code Authority to monitor comics' contents. **1955:** William F. Buckley, Jr.'s *National Review* begins publication. ★ Rosa Parks, 43 years old and black, sits in the front of a Montgomery, Alabama, bus; when she refuses to give up her seat to a white man, she is arrested. ★ Allen Ginsberg reads the epic beat poem "Howl" at the Six Gallery in San Francisco. ★ Kay Thompson's *Eloise* is published. ★ Disneyland opens on 244 acres in Anaheim, California. **1956:** The minimum wage is one dollar. ★ Grace Kelly marries Prince Rainier, and Marilyn Monroe marries Arthur Miller. ★ Elvis Presley hits the pop charts with "Heartbreak Hotel," "Don't Be Cruel," and "Blue Suede Shoes"; 54 million viewers watch him perform on *The Ed Sullivan Show*. ★ Eisenhower is reelected, beating Adlai Stevenson in a landslide.

★ The Dow Jones Industrial Average hits a high of 521.05. ★ Advertisements for Miss Clairol hair dye ask: "Does she or doesn't she?" **1957:** The Frisbee, originally called the Pluto Platter Flying Saucer, is introduced by the Wham-O Manufacturing Company, whose PR man had seen Yale students throwing metal Frisbee Pie Company tins back and forth. ★ With the help of 1,000 paratroopers and 10,000 members of the Arkansas National Guard, Little Rock Central High School is integrated. ★ *West Side Story* opens on Broadway. ★ Dr. Seuss's *The Cat in the Hat* is published. **1958:** It costs four cents to send a one-ounce letter. ★ The first United States earth satellite is launched. ★ The American Express card makes its first appearance. ★ Median U.S. family income is $5,087. **1959:** The microchip, Barbie, *Some Like It Hot,* and panty hose are seen for the first time. ★ Singer Buddy Holly dies in a plane crash. ★ Alaska and Hawaii become the 49th and 50th states in the Union. ★ In only its third year, the Ford Edsel is discontinued.

1950: JUNE 25
BILLY GRAHAM TO HARRY TRUMAN

Billy Graham (1918–) started preaching his version of Protestant fundamentalism when he was still a student. In the late forties he gained widespread attention with the first of a series of national evangelical campaigns. After troops from North Korea invaded South Korea, Graham sent this telegram to the president, whom he would meet three weeks later. Its message typified both Graham's politics (he would later support U.S. intervention in Vietnam) and his boldness.

MILLIONS OF CHRISTIANS PRAYING GOD GIVE YOU WISDOM IN THIS CRISIS. STRONGLY URGE SHOWDOWN WITH COMMUNISM NOW. MORE CHRISTIANS IN SOUTHERN KOREA PER CAPITA THAN ANY PART OF WORLD. WE CANNOT LET THEM DOWN.

1950: OCTOBER 29
JOHNNY GRZEGORCKY TO BARBARA CLEGG

The Korean War lasted until July 27, 1953. Estimates are that 1.3 million South Koreans were killed, one million Chinese, five hundred thousand North Koreans, and fifty-four thousand Americans. Among them was Sergeant Edward L. Clegg, twenty-four years old. He left behind Barbara, his twenty-one-year-old wife, and three children, ages three, two, and one.

Johnny Grzegorcky had come from Chicago and had been a buddy of Clegg's at Camp Carson, Colorado.

Oct 29, 1950

Dear Barbara,

Here I am writing you a letter which I have to admit I hate to write. You see Barbara it is pretty hard to write and takes much courage. I was going to write you some time ago, but I couldn't find the words or the courage.

You see Ed and I were good friends and soldiered at the same time for a while before disaster had taken effect. As in any war it does. There were 16 of us around this one position we were to defend and were under constant fire all day.

That night when we got hit out of the sixteen only two of us were unhurt, I being one of them one of my comrades being another. The other which name I will not mention for reasons was in the same hole with Ed. When we got back to battalion I spoke with him and he mentioned Ed. He also mentioned that Ed never knew what hit him, he died fast and didn't suffer any. We didn't get to see Ed after that you see five days after that we were able to retake that position and we couldn't get too close to the bodies because of the odor. But we did get Ed's watch ring and pen, which our platoon leader probably sent you or will.

We buried Ed there and I guess Graves Registration hasn't caught up to their graves yet. You see Barbara there were four of us which used to pal around together and today there is only one left which is me. And I have a job to do over here which needs to be done. I have yet to notify the other two families of their sons that were killed fighting this cause so that our families may be safe at home and free.

Well Barbara I hope this letter finds you in the best of health and may God bless you. Before I finish this letter which I so much hate to write I would like you know that Ed thought of you people before he died he took you pictures and put them close to his heart for he really thought very much of his family. If there is anything I can do to help let me know. I must sign off for now my duty calls me. So til later.

Always a friend
Johnny

1950: DECEMBER 1
ROBERT WARD TO HIS MOTHER

Technical Sergeant Robert J. Ward (1925–) was twenty-five years old and fighting in Korea when his mother, who had lost two other sons in World War II, wrote to the Marine Corps commandant, asking to have Robert transferred to a noncombat zone. From his new desk job in Tokyo, Ward sent this letter to his mother in Inglewood, California. Just before Christmas, she wrote the commandant again, honoring her son's request. He was ultimately allowed back into combat.

Little Squaw was Ward's baby daughter, and Bettye his wife.

Dec. 1, 1950

Dear Mother:

I'm no hero, but I also have responsibilities to Little Squaw and Bettye and you.

If these people aren't stopped here on their own ground, we will have to share the thing so many have died to prevent their loved ones from sharing, the sight of death in our own backyard; of women and children being victims of these people.

I went on the warpath for the right to do my bit to keep our people free and proud and now I'm shackled to a useless job.

I ask you, my mother, to free me so I can once again be free to help my boys.

They placed their faith in me and I brought them all back and now someone else leads them and I know they need me.

Maybe in a sense I need them, my dirty, stinking and loyal platoon.

Once I cried before you when I thought I'd lost someone whom I loved very dearly, and once again did I cry when I was told I must leave my men.

So I ask you the one thing which your heart does not want to do, release me to fight.

I pace my room feeling useless, being no good to anyone. I'm no barracks, parade-ground marine. I'm a Cherokee Indian and I'm happiest being miserable with my own people up on those mountains.

I know you'll understand that your blessings will go with me into whatever the future holds in store for us.

Write to the commandant and release me, explain to them as only you can that I have a job to do and that you understand.

> Your loving son,
> Robert

1950: DECEMBER 6
HARRY TRUMAN TO PAUL HUME

On December 5, President Truman's daughter, Margaret, an aspiring opera singer, gave a concert at Constitution Hall before a glittering Washington audience of thirty-five hundred. In the Washington Post *the next morning, music critic Paul Hume offered a straightforward opinion. "Miss Truman," Hume wrote, "cannot sing very well." Responding to the review in this note, Truman made no pretense of presidential neutrality, exercising what he later told Margaret was the right to be both a president and a human being.*

Hardly an old man, Hume was thirty-four. Westbrook Pegler was a Pulitzer prize–winning, often controversial, journalist.

THE WHITE HOUSE
Washington

Mr. Hume:

I've just read your lousy review of Margaret's concert. I've come to the conclusion that you are an "eight ulcer man on four ulcer pay."

It seems to me that you are a frustrated old man who wishes he could have been successful. When you write such poppy-cock as was in the back section of the paper you work for it shows conclusively that you're off the beam and at least four of your ulcers are at work.

Some day I hope to meet you. When that happens you'll need a new nose, a lot of beefsteak for black eyes, and perhaps a supporter below!

Pegler, a gutter snipe, is a gentleman alongside you. I hope you'll accept that statement as a worse insult than a reflection on your ancestry.

H.S.T.

1951

MYRNA CHASE TO A MEDICAL SECRETARY

The author of this letter spent sixteen years as a medical secretary in a successful surgeon's office. When she married, she promised to train her replacement. After a few initial conversations, she began sending letters of instruction, demonstrating standards of efficiency, sincerity, and professionalism that virtually define the phrase "the good old days."

My dear Mary:

In my last letter I listed all the things you'll be expected to do as Dr. Barrie's secretary. If you have recovered from the shock, I'll continue with an outline of a typical day. Your time will always be well filled and sometimes crowded, so care must be given to planning in advance. Otherwise you'll come to the end of the day with a feeling of being rushed and muddled instead of poised and satisfied. It's a good idea to have a definite schedule and stick to it.

Your day really begins the night before, when you take a warm bath, brush your hair, cream your face, and relax in bed for at least eight hours' sound sleep.

When your alarm goes off, you rise, eat a nourishing breakfast without hurrying, and get to the office five minutes <u>before</u> 9.

Promptness in opening the office is one of the things Dr. Barrie insists upon. There is no surer way to annoy him than to have patients try to reach him at home because they called the office at 9 o'clock and could get no reply.

In your office you are required to wear a white uniform. This is an excellent idea even though you are not a trained nurse; for it gives you a fresh, hygienic look and has a comforting psychological effect on patients. I'm sure I don't need to caution you against the horror of a dark slip under a white uniform. A light slip (one that doesn't sag) is as essential to your professional attire as are light stockings and white shoes.

To insure the correctness of the picture, avoid ornamentation. One ring and a plain wrist watch are all the jewelry compatible with good taste if you are in uniform. No beads, no earrings, and please—no brightly-bordered handkerchief flaring out of your breast pocket and no flower, however beautiful, pinned on your shoulder. Light nail polish and carefully adequate make-up are requisites. You may choose to wear a white cap if it is becoming to you, but wear it only in the office. To neglect these little warnings will stamp you as unacquainted with professional training and make you appear a little foolish to those "in the know."

Just imagine, as you dress, that you're about to appear on the stage as a doctor's assistant. Then look as immaculate and smart as if this were really the case. Remember, too, that white in a doctor's office must always be just a little whiter than white.

It is now 9:10. By 9:30, allowing time out for answering several telephone calls, you should have opened the windows, aired out the office, arranged the flowers in the reception room, and be seated at your desk ready to start your work.

You begin by opening the mail and disposing of it through the proper channels. You also make up the bank deposit for the day. This takes you to 10 o'clock.

As you know, Dr. Barrie and his assistant, Dr. Carl, spend their mornings at the hospital and making calls. Dr. Carl arrives at the office at noon and Dr. Barrie at 1:30. This means that you have the reception room to yourself for three precious hours. During that time you should complete all your noisy work, all your private work, and all work requiring deep concentration.

Never, during the later hours when patients are sitting about watching you, be guilty of pounding the typewriter in their ears (except, of course, for an emergency letter). And shun as you would the plague any dunning telephone calls in their presence. Instead, squeeze these things into the morning hours when doctors and patients are not present.

At 10:00 you start to type. You continue until you have finished all the dictation of the day before. Letters are placed on Dr. Barrie's desk to be signed; carbon copies and histories are filed. The remainder of the time before lunch may then be divided between bookkeeping and collections.

When the noon hour arrives, stop your work promptly. Dr. Carl will come in at that time and answer the telephone while you go to lunch. It's a good idea to take a brisk walk in the fresh air, dropping in at the bank with the day's deposit.

Try to return in time to go into one of the private rooms and lie down for fifteen minutes, relaxing completely. Believe me, this will make a world of difference in your afternoon's efficiency.

Just before the office hours begin, see that all furniture, magazines, and office appointments are in as perfect order as if you were about to give a high tea in your own home. Check the doctor's desk equipment as you would the setting of your table; and be sure that no speck of dust is visible anywhere. I know you will not feel it beneath you to supplement the efforts of the overworked janitress with a good dustcloth of your own. Place on the doctor's desk blotter a typewritten list of the appointments for the afternoon, with the time allotted to each. Remove from the files and place on the left side of his desk the case histories of all patients who have appointments. Then smooth your hair, renew your make-up, and return to your own desk.

It is now 1:25. Office hours will begin in five minutes.

Look over the appointments for the day. Speak the names to yourself so you can say them readily when their owners arrive. Try to call to mind the appearance of patients you've seen, so you won't have to check the appointment book before you address them by name.

When office hours begin, your job will be that of receiving patients, making appointments, answering the telephone, ushering patients into the doctor's presence, answering the buzzer, assisting the doctor in the examining room, accepting payment on bills, issuing receipts, and a dozen other things. Though this precludes any desk work requiring concentration, make a point of having some desk work to do during lulls, so that you need not sit idle. If patients see you idle, they get the impression that the doctor isn't very busy either. To read a book or magazine in their presence is a thoughtless form of rudeness, both to them and to your employer.

The afternoon is an excellent time to post accounts. They must without fail be kept up to date. If you work on them a little while each day, it will be easy. Afternoon is also a good time to do the part of the bookkeeping that requires only copying and not figuring.

About 5 o'clock, when the last patient has gone, the doctor will summon you to his office. Take with you your stenographic notebook and pencil, the appointment book, and the little black book containing the most frequently used telephone numbers. (You will know most of these later by heart.)

Dr. Barrie will probably ask you to get several persons on the telephone for him. He'll dictate histories and notes about the patients he has seen that day. Then he'll indicate the charges for the day in the appointment book. At this juncture, he may want to let the mail go until tomorrow; if so, it is your duty to urge him tactfully to clean it all up before he leaves.

If he is not in too great a hurry to get away, you may at this time ask him anything you wish about the work. You will always find him ready to explain. Ask him to make any suggestions he can that will improve your work.

When the doctor is ready to leave, usher him out and tell him good-night as if he were the guest of honor. Your respect and admiration can never be too great for a man who is following the finest profession in the world. Your usefulness to humanity depends largely upon your usefulness to him.

Now you are alone. You pick up the scattered magazines and arrange them neatly on the table. You place in the lower righthand drawer of your desk all dictation, letters, and histories that you will type in the morning. You change quickly into your street clothes and skip off into your other life, where you must forget all about this one so it will be fresh and new tomorrow. I'll write you again soon. Meanwhile—good luck!

1951: MAY 22

THE TRAVELERS TO JACKIE ROBINSON

The first black baseball player to join the major leagues in the twentieth century (there had been two in the nineteenth century), Jackie Robinson (1919–1972) was signed by the Brooklyn Dodgers' president, Branch Rickey (see letter page 392), in 1945 and brought up to Brooklyn two years later. This note arrived before a double-header in Cincinnati. Robinson hit a home run in the first game.

NOTE
WE HAVE ALREADY
GOT RID
OF SEVERAL
LIKE YOU
ONE WAS FOUND IN RIVER

JUST RECENTLY
ROBINSON
WE ARE GOING
TO KILL YOU
IF YOU ATTEMPT
TO ENTER A
BALL GAME AT
CROSLEY FIELD

THE TRAVELERS

1951: SEPTEMBER 14
IRVING MEYERS TO IRA MARION

A goofy-looking puppet whose wooden face was painted with forty-eight freckles (one for each state in the pre-Hawaii, pre-Alaska union), Howdy Doody was responsible for the first children's television craze. By 1953, six years into its thirteen-year run, The Howdy Doody Show *would be seen by fifteen million viewers daily— more than* Barney *was seen weekly in 1997. Then as now, parents of young fans were shameless in their attempts to achieve the impossible.*

Meyers did manage to get the tickets. His son, who would also grow up to be an attorney, writes to us: "I still remember meeting Clarabelle, and receiving a free miniature bottle of Welch's Grape Juice."

LAW OFFICES

MEYERS AND ROTHSTEIN

188 WEST RANDOLPH STREET, SUITE 1116

CHICAGO 1

September 14, 1951

Mr. Ira Marion
Radio Writers' Guild
6 East 39th Street
New York, NY

Dear Ira:

My wife, Thelma and son, Peter (4 years old) will be in New York City a week, Monday, September 17th. My son's greatest desire at the moment is to be in the peanut gallery of the "Howdy-Doodie" show.

I have told my wife to call you at your office to see if you could get tickets for it. Can you bring influence to bear to get tickets? From what I understand, not even box tops or box bottoms help. However, Radio Writers, 4As, joined with the A.F. of L. and your position may be able to get tickets.

Thanks very much.

Yours sincerely,
Irving Meyers

1952

ELAINE DE KOONING TO WILLIAM THEO BROWN

A painter, teacher, and art critic, Elaine de Kooning (1920–1989) met her husband, the renowned abstract expressionist Willem de Kooning (1904–1997), in 1938. She became his model, student, lover, and muse, and she married him in 1943. Together they dominated the downtown New York art world of the 1950s, as Willem's studies of women, many of which Elaine had inspired, became increasingly graphic and increasingly controversial. The show she describes, at the Janis Gallery, provided a milestone in de Kooning's career.

Collectors Leo and Ileana Castelli would open their first American gallery in 1957. William Theo Brown, Conrad Marca-Relli, Herbert Ferber, Robert Motherwell, Grace Hartigan, Jane Freilicher, Bradley Walker Tomlin, and Nicolas de Staël were all artists. Giovanni Tiepolo was an eighteenth-century Venetian painter. Jane Kootz was the wife of gallery owner Samuel Kootz. Edwin Denby was a dance critic. Thomas B. Hess (T.B.H., or Tom) was editor of *Art News* and at various times a lover of Elaine's. Harold Rosenberg was a leading art critic.

Dear Bill: Don't think I haven't been missing you because of these long stretches betwixt letters but life is crowded, packed teeming and how does the human constitution take it is what I want to know. Right now my human constitution is very much under the weather which is very lovely might I add, what with the tree across the street sprouting its new green leaves which are moving gently in the breeze which is also moving gently through my studio and hair so things could be worse even though I am exceedingly hung over from this party last night which ended at four this morning after I agreed to spend the summer in Mexico with the De Marcareeli's who are driving there in a huge station wagon because they can't afford to live in Easthampton and have proved conclusively to me that I could live more luxuriously and cheaply with them there and paint more and see more bullfights than I could in Easthampton with the

Castellis, which information I imparted to Bill (de K) at 4:30 AM and to which he replied with great (and characteristic) logic that if he could could get a re-entry permit from or to Mexico then he could get one from or to Holland in which case he would go to Holland where he could see his mother who is pining away to come here which would be exceedingly complicated for the De Koonings with their unconventional hours and habits so this may all turn out or it may all come to naught but whichever way it will be decided upon within a fortnight.

I had an excellent argument all prepared for you to come to Easthampton because despite the fact that it is crowded and expensive, it is possible to get a good, cheap place without any trouble with our contacts. There is for instance a rooming house which offers a room and kitchen facilities for 15 dollars a week but also, there are groups of attractive artists who are taking houses and who could find room to take in another attractive artist without crowding themselves.

But, if I decide to go to Mexico, then I would naturally try to persuade you to go to Mexico so wait a week until I know what in hell I'm doing of which fact I will apprise you and you can take it from there unless you've already made your plans.

I would also just as soon stay in New York which I love in the summer and not move being a victim of a pleasant and fruitful inertia and also my studio seems so cool and New York has its profound attractions—but how exhausting.

Now, as to Bill's show and remarks thereabout:

The elevator man (Boswell) of the Janis gallery to Bill: "You alive? Why I thought you was dead. Last artist we had he hung himself and he didn't have as many people at his opening as you."

Herbert Ferber (to Bill with an appropriate doleful expression at the opening) "Hm. I feel sorry for Elaine."

Jackson Pollock (to an outsider who reported it back). "He can't do that."

Unknown art students to Donald Droll. The show is conclusive proof that de Kooning is a homosexual. Why? The bullet holes of course. What bullet holes? Why, the ones in that gal's chest. (The bullet holes, be it known, are very chic rubies which stick to the skin unaided or abetted by pins or chains—a device de Kooning saw in Harpers Bazaar and never forgot.)

Time Magazine in print—. . . as ripe as Tiepolo's baroque matrons . . . fully clothed and mighty ugly with ox eyes, balloon bosoms, pointy teeth, vaguely voracious little smiles . . . terribly tough, big-city, mid-20th century dames . . . . one of the most original artists of the day.

Motherwell (on seeing me in a bathing suit, at Easthampton) Oh now I get it. Bill is painting Elaine.

Grace Hartigan (to me) That one's you. That one's me. That one's Jane Freilicher.

Mercedes (to me). That one's you. That one's me. That one's Jane Kootz.

Me (to Edwin Denby) That one's you. All the rest are Me.

Art Digest: De kooning is painting the woman in himself.

     "   "   " wreaking his vengeance on the muse of painting.

     "   "   " a misogynist.

Her image exists in the vast area between something scratched on the wall of a cave and something scratched on the wall of a urinal.

Does de Kooning love her? Not with any romantic passion. IN a gesture that paralells a sexual act, he has vented himself with violence on the canvas which is the body of this woman. . . . . If he got lost. . . . it is. . . . . for a worthwhile reason—woman. He has gone too far, but that is the only place to go.

I liked the Art Digest articles—there were two, April 1 and 15 I guess—and, of course, thought Tom's was brilliant but that, you must have read. And except for T.B.H. the fascinating thing about all the comments was that no one talked about the painting. They all talked about THE WOMAN. Big surprise for Bill who was quite pleased to discover he had shocked the avant garde.

Two big paintings were sold, one to Mrs. John D. Rockefeller, and about eight pastels were sold, so it wasn't a financial flop although by no means a great success that way, considering that De Stael sold out his large pistachio colored confections at the opening.

Last Monday we all went to a funeral that looked like an opening, what with the familiar faces of museum directors dealers and all of us at St Bartholomew's, an elegant church on Park opposite the Waldorf. Bradley Tomlin was the man in the box, who had, two days previous bought himself a house next to Jackson Pollock, and who no doubt realized that he was not going to be able to contend with Jackson roaring drunk and his wife peering disapprovingly through the window at her next door neighbor who would dare to paint in competition with the great JP. The future, one can imagine, looked bleak so Bradley did the sensible thing the quiet way.

And tomorrow night we all go to hear Nebuchadnezzur Rosenberg's last lecture on death, which has been a gay and gorgeous subject on 15 (count em)

Monday nights. Will write again next week when I know more about Easthampton vs Mexico.

Love
E.

1952: MAY 19
LILLIAN HELLMAN TO JOHN WOOD

Lillian Hellman (1905–1984) was a playwright, essayist, and screenwriter. She was most celebrated for her works of social commentary, including her plays The Children's Hour, The Little Foxes, _and_ Watch on the Rhine. _Surprisingly few letters contain truly famous lines. This one, featuring Hellman's refusal to "cut her conscience," is an exception._

John S. Wood was chairman of the House Committee on Un-American Activities from 1951 to 1954.

May 19, 1952

Honorable John S. Wood
Chairman
House Committee on Un-American Activities
Room 226 Old House Office Building
Washington 25, D.C.

Dear Mr. Wood:

As you know, I am under subpoena to appear before your Committee on May 21, 1952.

I am most willing to answer all questions about myself. I have nothing to hide from your Committee and there is nothing in my life of which I am ashamed. I have been advised by counsel that under the Fifth Amendment I have a constitutional privilege to decline to answer any questions about my political opinions, activities and associations, on the grounds of self-incrimination. I do not wish to claim this privilege. I am ready and willing to testify before the representatives of our Government as to my own opinions and my own actions, regardless of any risks or consequences to myself.

But I am advised by counsel that if I answer the Committee's questions about myself, I must also answer questions about other people and that if I refuse to do so, I can be cited for contempt. My counsel tells me that if I answer questions about myself, I will have waived my rights under the Fifth Amendment and could be forced legally to answer questions about others. This is very difficult for a layman to understand. But there is one principle that I do understand: I am not willing, now or in the future, to bring bad trouble to people who, in my past association with them, were completely innocent of any talk or any action that was disloyal or subversive. I do not like subversion or disloyalty in any form and if I had ever seen any I would have considered it my duty to have reported it to the proper authorities. But to hurt innocent people whom I knew many years ago in order to save myself is, to me, inhuman and indecent and dishonorable. I cannot and will not cut my conscience to fit this year's fashions, even though I long ago came to the conclusion that I was not a political person and could have no comfortable place in any political group.

I was raised in an old-fashioned American tradition and there were certain homely things that were taught to me: to try to tell the truth, not to bear false witness, not to harm my neighbor, to be loyal to my country, and so on. In general, I respected these ideals of Christian honor and did as well with them as I knew how. It is my belief that you will agree with these simple rules of human decency and will not expect me to violate the good American tradition from which they spring. I would, therefore, like to come before you and speak of myself.

I am prepared to waive the privilege against self-incrimination and to tell you anything you wish to know about my views or actions if your Committee will agree to refrain from asking me to name other people. If the Committee is unwilling to give me this assurance, I will be forced to plead the privilege of the Fifth Amendment at the hearing.

A reply to this letter would be appreciated.

> Sincerely yours,
> Lillian Hellman

1952: OCTOBER 12
JACK KEROUAC TO JOHN CLELLON HOLMES

Jack Kerouac (1922–1969) coined the term "the beat generation" in 1948, the same year he started writing his best-known work, On the Road. *When the book was finally published in 1957, it became the touchstone for a generation of anti-establishment seekers, many of whom would emulate Kerouac's cross-country wanderings, others of whom would merely long to. This letter was written while Kerouac was working as a student brakeman for the Southern Pacific railroad and trying to save enough money to go to Mexico. John Clellon Holmes had met Kerouac at a party and was the author of the 1952 book* Go, *which, like* On the Road, *included portraits of many beat generation figures.*

The Town and the City, Kerouac's first novel, had been published in 1950. Beverly Burford and Ed White were Denver friends. Neal Cassady, himself a beat legend, would appear as Dean Moriarty in *On the Road* as well as in *Go.* Carolyn was Cassady's wife. Allen was the poet Allen Ginsberg. Mary Carney had been Kerouac's high-school idol.

Sunday Oct. 12

As ever, whereabouts is <u>dead secret</u>

c/o Cassady

1047 East Santa Clara St.

San Jose, Calif.

Dear John—

Here I sit in my little room in Frisco Skid Row, the first time in weeks I've had to sit & write in response to your letter and check. I just come in from work, will be going out again in 8 hours, work sometimes 24 hours a day, have no time whatever for anything but sleep, I get in my double bed with bop on the radio, a poorboy half-bottle of Tokay wine, the shades drawn, & I try to rest and think: "Some lost song is beating in my soul, that I have not sung, and cannot sing"— the star of my sister, I remember her pale little face in holy snows of Lowell, now, like all America, she's grown cold-hearted, blank, money-anxious—ah, she used to make little holy cards—my mother angrily retorted, in a letter, "So you want to roam & leave—well, <u>don't you dare do anything that will dishonor your father's name</u>—(!)"— . . . The days of <u>The Town and The City</u> are all forgotten—I start West in the rain—John, you think I'm a self-made martyr? I go 3,000 motherfucking miles, sleep on railroad porches, in Salvation flops, eat out of cans—in Hickey, N.C. I stand in the drizzle exhausted, one saves me—I stay at Ed White's in Beverly's backyard—we cook weenies, drink Tokay—I make love to big Swedish student-girl Edeltrude—Mrs. White motherly packs me lunch, I hitch to Salt Lake (after a day spent sketching Neal's entire Denver area) and sleep in motel garage, hitch straight to Neal's door via wild trips, including Australian history professor anxiously from top of oil pole, in Nevada desert, scanning horizon for swimming hole—"nothing I like better than swimming, ya know?"—we end up on little slimy rocks of Tuckee River . . . I was bored with the job in Rocky Mount, with $5 in my pocket I lifted my seabag up and walked out my sister's backdoor ("Never mind presents from China, just mail me $50 room & board for the month of August.")

. . . In San Jose, Neal's big house, Neal's frantic working with me out on railroad—I learn—can't stand position in his house, leave to live in my Skid Row retreat (near the Wildest Corner in America, 3rd & Howard, around the corner from the Little Harlem where they blew so much in 1949)—Neal I don't like any more; he's somewhat insultingly abrupt & even beginning to put on that familiar American pseudo-virility of workingman & basket ball players, "tough guy"—when I try to talk about literature he makes it a point to change the subject to money or work or "bills," him & his bloody bills— . . . I'm not American, nor West European, somehow I feel like an Indian, a North American Exile in North America—in New York I'm a Peasant among the Solomons, that's why I never make a cent off the huge productivity of my crazy pen—there's something else in me—maybe because I have an Indian great-great-grandmother—or have strong Quebec Plain Peasant feeling and general weird Catholic mysticism—& a streak of truly Celtic superstitiousness— . . . I accept your $50 in the spirit of gratitude, and I need it too, it will be added to my winter writing stake—I'm ready to write a super <u>Town & City</u>, a book of 1,000 pages. <u>On the Road</u> it will have to be called, The Neal Road I'll change to "Visions of N.P."—Already started my super book, not only about the hip generation but another fictional arrangement of my family life— . . . If it wasn't for the railroad now, people would instantly recognize me as a true hobo—the bo's on Third St. all do—A HOBO LIVES LIKE AN INDIAN.—Nevertheless, the glory of it all is, I am a gifted writer and my soul is pure—& big to live— . . . Write to me care of Neal's, I get my mail there—we hardly talk to each other but Carolyn is close to me and I go there to drink wine with her—Neal apparently wrote another letter to Allen explaining why he can't talk to me—I ought to throw my 2c in & explain why I can't talk to him—but I would say this, it was him stuck his head in my door in Ozone Park and outlined the reasons why we should be friends—now that he has the soul of a baboon clearly showing, I wonder I forgot seeing it then right in the door—Gad, the mistakes I've made, the time wasted—the forgetting of lonely nights in cheap hotel rooms with my father & mother making little cold suppers cheerfully—every time we'd touch the lace curtains a shower of dust fell, & Pop would say, "Perk up, Jackie pauvre Jackie, we won't always be poor & abandoned," and my mother'd say, "Oui, and look, here's the bread, the ham, the butter, the coffee, the little cups, we've got everything we need."—and how I loved Mary Carney's dark sad face, & wanted to marry her at 16 and be a brakeman on the Boston & Maine railroad—only an ounce of my hundredweight life—to have a real asshole like Cassady come along & con me like a yokel into listening to his crap & believing in his kind of franticness & silly sexfiend ideas—it will all come back, John—Please stay my friend thru life, it'll be long & dark.

As ever,

Jack

1953: MARCH 12
JAMES WATSON TO MAX DELBRÜCK

James Watson (1928–) was only in his early twenties when, along with the British biophysicist Francis Crick (1916–), he began the work that would change the field of biology forever. Using X-ray diffraction techniques that had been developed by Maurice Wilkins (1916–), Watson and Crick set about discovering the chemical nature of heredity, and thus of life. It was in the spring of 1953 that Watson first surmised that the four basic components of the molecule must be linked in definite pairs. This insight led the two scientists to develop the now familiar double-helix model for DNA. In 1962, Watson would share the Nobel prize with Crick and Wilkins.

Max Delbrück (1906–1981), another gifted biologist and eventual Nobel winner, was a pioneer in the field of molecular genetics. American chemist and Nobel winner Linus Pauling was also working on a model of DNA; Jerry Donohue was one of his former graduate students. William Cochran was a crystallographer at Cavendish. William Thomas Astbury had, in the 1930s, been among the first to investigate biological molecules. William Hayes was researching the reproductive patterns of bacteria. Alfred Tissières was a Swiss biochemist. Manny was Delbrück's wife.

UNIVERSITY OF CAMBRIDGE   DEPARTMENT OF PHYSICS

Telephone

Cambridge 55478

Cavendish Laboratory

Free School Lane

Cambridge

March 12, 1953

Dear Max,

Thank you very much for your recent letters. We were quite interested in your account of the Pauling Seminar. The day following the arrival of your letter, I received a note from Pauling, mentioning that their model had been revised, and indicating interest in our model. We shall thus have to write him in the near future as to what we are doing. Until now we preferred not to write him since we did not want to commit ourselves until we were completely sure that all of the van der Walls contacts were correct and that all aspects of our structure were stereochemically feasible. I believe now that we have made sure that our structure can be built and today we are laboriously calculating out exact atomic coordinates.

Our model (a joint project of Francis Crick and myself) bears no relationship to either the original or to the revised Pauling-Corey-Shoemaker models. It is a strange model and embodies several unusual features. However since DNA is an unusual substance we are not hesitant in being bold. The main features of the model are (1) the basic structure is helical—it consists of two intertwining helices—the core of the helix is occupied by the purine and pyrimidine bases—the phosphates groups are on the outside (2) the helices are not identical but complementary so that if one helix contains a purine base, the other helix contains a pyrimidine—this feature is a result of our attempt to make the residues equivalent and at the same time put the purines and pyrimidine bases in the center. The pairing of the purine with pyrimidines is very exact and dictated by their desire to form hydrogen bonds—adenine will pair with thymine while guanine will always pair with cytosine. For example

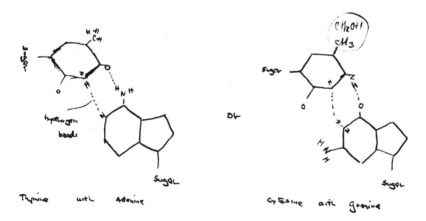

Thymine   with   Adenine   Cytosine   with   guanine

While my diagram is crude, in fact these pairs form two very nice hydrogen bonds in which all of the angles are exactly right. This pairing is based on the effective existence of only one out of the two possible tautomeric forms—in all cases we prefer the keto form over the enol, and the amino over the imino. This is definitely an <u>assumption</u> but Jerry Donohue and Bill Cochran tell us that for all organic molecules so far examined, the keto and amino forms are present in preference to the enol and imino possibilities.

The model has been derived almost entirely from stereochemical considerations with the only X-ray consideration being the spacing between the pairs of bases 3.4 A which was originally found by Astbury. It tends to build itself with approximately 10 residues per turn in 34 Å. The screw is right-handed.

The X-ray pattern approximately agreed with the model, but since the photographs available to us are poor and meager (we have no photographs of our own and like Pauling must use Astbury's photographs), this agreement in no way constitutes a proof of our model. We are certainly a long way from proving its correctness. To do this we must obtain collaboration from the group at King's College London who possess very excellent photographs of a crystalline phase in addition to rather good photographs of a paracrystalline phase. Our model has been made in reference to the paracrystalline form and as yet we have no clear idea as to how these helices can pack together to form the crystalline phase.

In the next day or so Crick and I shall send a note to Nature proposing our structure as a possible model, at the same time emphasizing its provisional nature and the lack of proof in its favor. Even if wrong I believe it to be interesting since it provides a concrete example of a structure composed of complementary chains. If by chance it is right then I suspect we may be making a slight dent in the manner in which DNA can reproduce itself. For these reasons (in addition to many others) I prefer this type of model over Pauling's which if true would tell us next to nothing about the manner of DNA reproduction.

I shall write you in a day or so about the recombination paper. Yesterday I received a very interesting note from Bill Hayes. I believe he is sending you a copy.

I have meet Alfred Tissières recently. He seems very nice. He speaks fondly of Pasadena and I suspect has not yet become accustomed to being a fellow of Kings.

My regards to Manny

Jim

P.S. We would prefer your not mentioning this letter to Pauling. When our letters to Nature is completed we shall send him a copy. We should like to send him coordinates.

1953: JUNE 10
DWIGHT EISENHOWER TO CLYDE MILLER

Julius and Ethel Rosenberg (see letter page 385) had been arrested for espionage in 1950. The chief witness against them, Ethel's brother David Greenglass, testified that the couple led a spy ring during World War II and persuaded him to pass secrets about the atomic bomb to the Soviets. The Rosenbergs insisted on their innocence, but were convicted in 1951 and sentenced to death. National and international protests followed, but the Supreme Court voted six to three in favor of their execution, and for the reasons he offered in this letter, President Eisenhower refused to grant the Rosenbergs clemency.

Clyde Miller was a professor at Columbia University; Eisenhower had been the university's president from 1948 to 1950.

THE WHITE HOUSE
Washington

June 10, 1953.

<u>Personal and Confidential</u>

Dear Clyde:

Thank you very much for your thoughts on the Rosenberg conviction. It is extremely difficult to reach a sound decision in such instances. Not all the arguments are on either side.

I started studying the record of the case immediately after Inauguration, and have had innumerable conferences on it with my associates.

Several of the obvious facts which must not be forgotten are these. The record has been reviewed and re-reviewed by every appropriate court in the land, extending over a period of more than two years. In no single instance has there been any suggestion that it was improperly tried, that the rights of the accused were violated, that the evidence was insufficient, or that there was any factor in the case which justified intervention on the part of the Executive with the function of juridical agencies.

As to any intervention based on considerations of America's reputation or standing in the world, you have given the case for one side. What you did not suggest was the need for considering this kind of argument over and against the known convictions of Communist leaders that free governments—and especially the American government—are notoriously weak and fearful and that consequently subversive and other kind of activity can be conducted against them with no real fear of dire punishment on the part of the perpetrator. It is, of course, important to the Communists to have this contention sustained and justified. In the present case they have even stooped to dragging in young and innocent children in order to serve their own purpose.

The action of these people has exposed to greater danger of death literally millions of our citizens. The very real question becomes how far can this be permitted by a government that, regardless of every consideration of mercy and compassion, is also required to be a <u>just</u> government in serving the interests of all its citizens. That their crime is a very real one and that its potential results are as definite as I have just stated, are facts that seem to me to be above contention.

Another factor that appeals, quite naturally, to Americans is that one of these criminals—indeed the more strong-minded and the apparent leader of the two—is a woman. But the question presents itself—if the Executive should interfere because of this fact, would we be justified in encouraging the Communists to use only women in their spying process?

I assure you that I appreciate receiving your thoughts on the matter. You not only have the right of any citizen to submit your suggestion, but, of course, our old friendship at Columbia assures that I would give special attention to your convictions. But when it comes to the decision to commute such a sentence—which would mean that these arch criminals would be subject to parole at the end of fifteen years—I must say I have not yet been able to justify such an action.

I have answered your letter at some length, because I know that you wrote it out of a deep sense of duty and friendship. I realize that your desire to protect America is as great as mine, but I doubt that you have had to consider some of the results that could spring from the action you recommend.

We shall, of course, have another clemency petition presented this week, from which we will see whether there are additional considerations to take into account.

With personal regard,

Sincerely,
[Dwight D. Eisenhower]

Professor Clyde Miller
Butler Hall
Columbia University
New York 27, New York

1953: JUNE 13

HUGH HEFNER TO NEWSSTAND SELLERS

With this letter, Hugh Hefner (1926–) launched the Playboy empire, a publishing enterprise but also a symbol of sexual liberation and frank hedonism. Before founding the magazine Playboy, Hefner had worked for the Publishers' Development Corporation, as well as for Esquire. He bought the rights to the Marilyn Monroe

*nude photograph for $500 from a calendar publisher. The same afternoon, he sat
down to write this letter to the newsstand sellers.*

The "group of people from *Esquire*" was a group of one: Hefner himself.

Dear Friend:

We haven't even printed our letterhead yet, but I wanted you to be one of the
very first to hear the news. STAG PARTY—a brand new magazine for men—
will be out this Fall and it will be one of the best sellers you've ever handled.

It's being put together by a group of people from ESQUIRE who stayed here
in Chicago when that magazine moved east—so you can imagine how good it's
going to be. And it will include male-pleasing figure studies, making it a sure hit
from the very start.

But here's the really BIG news! The first issue of STAG PARTY will include
the famous calendar picture of Marilyn Monroe—in <u>full colour</u>! In fact—every
issue of STAG PARTY will have a beautiful, full-page, male-pleasing nude
study—in full natural colour!

Now you know what I mean when I say this is going to be one of the best sellers you've ever handled.

STAG PARTY will sell for 50c and you'll receive your copies at a profitable
38c. It will be supplied to you on a <u>fully returnable</u> basis and, of course, we will
pay all shipping costs.

Fill out the postage-paid AIR MAIL reply card enclosed and get it back to me
as quickly as possible. With 4 colour printing on the inside pages, we've got to
confirm our distribution quantities right away.

It will be nice doing business with you again—especially with a title as good
as this one.

Cordially,
Hugh M. Hefner
General Manager.

---

*Julius and Ethel Rosenberg (1918–1953 and 1915–1953, respectively) were to-
gether when Ethel wrote this letter from Sing Sing prison. They were electrocuted
later the same day, the first U.S. civilians to be put to death for espionage.*

The Rosenbergs' children, Michael and Robert, were ten and six. "Julie" was signed in Julius's
handwriting.

June 19, 1953

Dearest Sweethearts, my most precious children,

Only this morning it looked like we might be together again after all. Now that this cannot be I want so much for you to know all that I have come to know. Unfortunately I may write only a few simple words; the rest your own lives must teach you, even as mine taught me.

At first, of course, you will grieve bitterly for us, but you will not grieve alone. That is our consolation and it must eventually be yours.

Eventually, too, you must come to believe that life is worth the living. Be comforted that even now, with the end of ours slowly approaching that we know this with a conviction that defeats the executioner!

Your lives must teach you, too, that good cannot really flourish in the midst of evil; that freedom and all the things that go to make up a truly satisfying and worthwhile life, must sometimes be purchased very dearly. Be comforted, then, that we were serene and understood with the deepest kind of understanding, that civilization had not as yet progressed to the point where life did not have to be lost for the sake of life; and that we were comforted in the sure knowledge that others would carry on after us.

We wish we might have had the tremendous joy and gratification of living our lives out with you. Your Daddy who is with me in these last momentous hours sends his heart and all the love that is in it for his dearest boys. Always remember that we were innocent and could not wrong our conscience.

We press you close and kiss you with all our strength.

Lovingly,

Daddy and Mommy—

Julie   Ethel

1953: JULY 21

KEN BIERLY TO RAYMOND BELL

With Senator Joseph McCarthy (1908–1957) now leading the anti-Communist crusade, each Hollywood studio was supposed to do its own checking for questionable affiliations among its employees. Ken Bierly, a former FBI agent, ran the Research and Security Corporation: for a fee, he would rate someone "See" (could find nothing), "Bee" (questionable background), or "Very Que" (very questionable). Peter Viertel had been one of the screenwriters credited with the adaptation of The African Queen; *despite Bierly's report, Viertel went on to write novels and more screenplays, including the 1990 Clint Eastwood film* White Hunter, Black Heart, *which was loosely based on Viertel's experience filming in Africa.*

Raymond Bell was an executive at Columbia Pictures. Hanns Eisler was a German composer. Budd Schulberg wrote the screenplays for *A Face in the Crowd* and *On the Waterfront.* Martin Berkeley and Elizabeth Wilson were screenwriters who testified before HUAC. Along with Dalton Trumbo (see letter page 345), Lester Cole, John Howard Lawson, and Ring Lardner, Jr., were among the Hollywood Ten.

Dear Ray:

For identification purposes, Peter Viertel is reported to have been born in Dresden, Germany, Nov. 15, 1920. His name appeared on the Amicus Curiae brief in support of the Hollywood Ten in September 1949. The coast reports he was a friend of Hanns Eisler and it appears he joined with Eisler in issuing an invitation to a social function at Malibu, Calif., in Feb., 1948. The return address appearing on the invitation at that time was Box 10, Route 1, Bonsall Drive, Calif.

Viertel's wife, Virginia, was formerly married to Budd Schulberg. She was identified as a Communist Party member by Martin Berkeley and Elizabeth Wilson, who testified in Sept. of 1951. From their testimony it appears Virginia Schulberg was a Communist in 1937 and later, and there is nothing in the record which would indicate she subsequently disaffiliated from the Communist Party.

There is some confusion about Peter Viertel's mother. The records indicate his mother's name is Salomea, and that his father's name is Berthold. A Salka Viertel has been active in several Communist enterprises on the coast. It is possible that Salka is a contraction of Salomea, that Salka is Peter's sister and not his mother, or, that Salka is no relation to him. In any event, Peter Viertel's mother is reported to have been friendly with Hanns Eisler and to have served on a Committee in his support in Dec. of 1947. <u>Salka</u> Viertel's name appeared on the Amicus Curiae brief for Lawson and Trumbo, in support of the Hollywood Ten, and she has also been listed as a member of the Progressive Caucus (Communist) within the Screen Writers Guild, who supported Lester Cole and Ring Lardner Jr. for office in Nov. of 1948.

In view of the foregoing, I would suggest Peter Viertel be listed as <u>very que</u>. It is true that information linking him to the Communist apparatus is scant. Nevertheless, the fact that there is a record of a slight degree of affiliation, plus the fact that his wife has been identified as a Party member, plus the fact that his mother has been identified with Communist organizations and causes, makes Viertel's present status highly questionable and suspect. Unless he is able to clear up these points in a statement, I feel his employment might be highly embarrassing to the Studio.

With best regards,

[Ken Bierly]

1954: JANUARY 26
NUNNALLY JOHNSON TO THORNTON DELEHANTY

As a screenwriter, Nunnally Johnson (1897–1977) added dozens of films to Hollywood's golden age, including The Grapes of Wrath, The Three Faces of Eve, *and* The Desert Fox. *His* How to Marry a Millionaire *starred Marilyn Monroe, Lauren Bacall, and Betty Grable. The clipping to which he refers in this letter showed him at the film's premiere, escorting Monroe and Bacall while his wife, Dorris, was being pushed aside by photographers.*

Delehanty was *Redbook's* Hollywood representative and a film reviewer for the *New York Evening Post*. Darryl Zanuck was already legendary as a producer and screenwriter. George Sanders was a popular character actor most celebrated for his portrayal of Addison De Witt in 1950's *All About Eve*. He would marry two Gabor sisters, Zsa Zsa and Magda. Porfirio Rubirosa was a notorious ladies' man. Mae Marsh, Marjorie Main, and Martha Raye were all actresses. Knute Rockne was the famously determined Notre Dame football coach. Clare Boothe Luce, a playwright, was the wife of *Time* founder Henry Luce.

January 26, 1954

Dear Thorny:

Will you be good enough not to answer my letters promptly? You answer quickly, I answer quickly, you answer quickly, I answer quickly. Pretty soon I've got time for nothing else, just answering your letter quickly. Then one day I'd get mad and drop the whole correspondence. Otherwise, if I tried to keep at it, my work would fall off, Zanuck would speak sharply to me two or three times, and next year they wouldn't pick up my option. This wouldn't bother me at first, but presently I'd learn that the word had got about that all I did was correspond with you. I suppose we could sell the house but we'd have to take a pretty big loss on it. I'm sure the studio would give Dorris some kind of stock job, like Mae Marsh's, and at least the children wouldn't starve, but I can't pretend that they would be able to have much of a childhood. So for God's sake, cut it out, will you?

The clipping I enclose shows me on a typical evening out. Sometimes I'll have Marjorie Main too, or maybe Martha Raye, but all in all, this is about as fair a picture of the way I step out in the evening as any other. Dorris? God only knows.

You may want to hear what happened to my friend Zsa Zsa the other evening. Christmas Eve, in fact. George Sanders, who tells the story, said that his lawyers and Zsa Zsa's had come to a property settlement agreeable to both parties until it came to the point of Zsa Zsa's signing the paper. Then she refused and began to ask for more and more and more. This irked George. But he figured it wouldn't be difficult to get something on her.

So on Christmas Eve, that holy day, he prepared to raid her home to catch Rubirosa in the hay with her. He planned to lean a ladder against a second-floor balcony and enter her bedroom through the French doors there, but he couldn't remember whether the doors opened in or out, so, being a careful fellow, he sent a gift over to Zsa Zsa that afternoon by his butler, who was also instructed to nip upstairs and get information on the door situation. They opened out.

Around two-thirty that night, while every son-of-a-bitch and his brother in town was singing "Silent Night," George got in a car with four Sam Spades and set out for the house in Bel-Air. His operatives were such horrible looking fellows that he thought it best to take along something in the shape of a gift for Mrs. Sanders by way of alibi if the Bel-Air cops stopped him. So he wrapped up a brick in some holly paper. They found Rubirosa's car parked outside and the Sam Spades all went through a "Dragnet" routine of jotting numbers and photographing fingerprints and then George and his friends sneaked around the house and set up the ladder.

The rules, it seems, call for the husband to enter first. Otherwise, charges of breaking and entering can be lodged against outsiders. The ladder turned out to be a little shaky and George got quite nervous. As he explained, "I felt it would be most embarrassing if I fell and broke my leg and Rubirosa had to take me to the hospital." But he made it to the balcony all right and found the windows open. Zsa Zsa likes fresh air. So he dashed in bravely and found himself in a scramble with a Venetian blind. Through them he saw two naked forms break the record for the dash to the bathroom, where the light was on. As soon as he could untangle himself from the blinds, George rallied at the head of his operatives and all made a dash for the privileged sanctuary. Rubi and Zsa Zsa had slammed the door shut but in their excitement they forgot that it could also be locked. The door opened inward and it then became a head-on push between George and Rubi, Rubi trying to hold the door shut, George trying to bull it open. Now according to George, he was hitting low, just like Knute Rockne always said, and with a powerful lunge he managed to get the door open about a foot, which to his astonishment brought him face to face with Rubirosa's organ, whereupon, in a moment of whimsy, he shook it heartily and called Merry Christmas to them both. This mortified Rubirosa. It was then that Zsa Zsa called out, "Now, George, really! Please be seated and I'll be out in just a moment." She emerged in a diaphanous negligee, leaving the shy Mr. Rubirosa skulking in the can.

George says her conduct then was above and beyond reproach. In the most elegant fashion, like a veritable Clare Luce, she greeted her husband and his four thugs and invited them to sit down and talk it over. While the thugs stared, George mentioned the lateness of the hour and that he felt that they should be pushing on. But when they started to exit by way of the balcony and the ladder, Zsa Zsa was shocked that they should believe she would not show them to the front door as she would any guest in her home. So she led them downstairs and was reminded on the way of the Christmas tree. "You haven't seen it, George! You must! It's perfectly beautiful!" So she led them all into the living room and they all admired it. "Did you get your gift?" she asked. George said he hadn't, but the evening could be taken as an entirely adequate gift so far as he was concerned. "Never mind, it'll be there bright and early in the morning," she assured him. Then she opened the front door for them, shook hands all around, and they all exchanged God bless you's.

1954: MAY 21

JO ANN ROBINSON TO W. A. GAYLE

Jo Ann Robinson (1912–) was a professor at Alabama State College and the initial organizer of the Montgomery bus boycott, during which the city's black residents refused to ride its segregated buses. The protest, which would begin in 1955 after Rosa Parks's arrest for failing to move to the back of a Montgomery bus, lasted for almost a year. This letter was inspired by the Supreme Court's decision in Brown v. Board of Education *and foreshadowed the historic effort.*

Harriet St.
Montgomery, Ala.
May 21, 1954

Honorable Mayor W.A. Gayle
City Hall
Montgomery, Alabama

Dear Sir:

The Women's Political Council is very grateful to you and the City Commissioners for the hearing you allowed our representatives during the month of March, 1954, when the "city-bus-fare-increase case" was being reviewed. There were several things the Council asked for:

1. A city law that would make it possible for Negroes to sit from back toward front, and whites from front toward back until all the seats are taken;
2. That Negroes not be asked or forced to pay fare at front and go to the rear of the bus to enter;
3. That busses stop at every corner in residential sections occupied by Negroes as they do in communities where whites reside.

We are happy to report that busses have been stopping at more corners now in some sections where Negroes live than previously. However, the same practices in seating and boarding the bus continue.

Mayor Gayle, three-fourths of the riders of these public conveyances are Negroes. If Negroes did not patronize them, they could not possibly operate.

More and more of our people are already arranging with neighbors and friends to ride to keep from being insulted and humiliated by bus drivers.

There has been talk from twenty-five or more local organizations of planning a city-wide boycott of busses. We, sir, do not feel that forceful measures are necessary in bargaining for a convenience which is right for all bus passengers. We, the Council, believe that when this matter has been put before you and the Commissioners, that agreeable terms can be met in a quiet and unostensible manner to the satisfaction of all concerned.

Many of our Southern cities in neighboring states have practiced the policies we seek without incident whatsoever. Atlanta, Macon and Savannah in Georgia have done this for years. Even Mobile, in our own state, does this and all the passengers are satisfied.

Please consider this plea, and if possible, act favorably upon it, for even now plans are being made to ride less, or not at all, on our busses. We do not want this.

Respectfully yours,

The Women's Political Council

Jo Ann Robinson, President

1954: JUNE 15
BRANCH RICKEY TO THE PITTSBURGH PIRATES

Branch Rickey (1881–1965) was late in his life—and in his Hall of Fame career as an executive—when he signed on as general manager with the Pittsburgh Pirates. But his scouting report on pitcher Don Drysdale (1936–1993) showed Rickey's knack for spotting talent. Ultimately signed not by the Pirates but by the Brooklyn Dodgers, Drysdale would go on to win the Cy Young Award in 1962 and to lead the National League in strikeouts for three years.

Hollywood, Cal.

June 15, 1954

<u>DON DRYSDALE</u>

6'4", 185 pounds, 18 years of age. A lot of artistry about this boy. Way above average fast ball. It is really good. Direction of the spin and the speed of rotation the same on all fast ball pitches,—angle of delivery the same, stride is wide, and his body is in all pitches. Fine pitching hand, and placement on fast and curve ball needs no coaching. Let him alone on all his fingering. He is good. I don't know about his agility or whether or not he has body control or can field his position, but his work on the hill itself has an unusual amount of perfection. Intelligent face and manner, shows good breeding.

This boy's curve is fairly good, and he shows control of it also. He has a change-up on his curve that is usable. Change-up on the fast ball is too fast and he lets up on his delivery. This will take considerable work but I am very sure that this particular chap will acquire an effective change on his fast ball.

It is my judgment that his aptitude would be far above average. He is a definite prospect. With proper handling, I could see this boy on the Pittsburgh club in two years. He impresses me very much,—the same as Dangleis did two years ago,—with one thing in his favor, namely, more speed, but Dangleis was more finished with four pitches.

It is probable that this chap is worth whatever it takes except that Pittsburgh is in no position to make him a bonus player.

And here is a secret for you, Bob. Rather than lose him, I would sign him to a Pittsburgh contract, for I think he would come within the three years, but his first contract must not be above $4,000, for he should go out of course. If he were to stay with our club, however, his salary would be the minimum in the major leagues, viz, $6,000.

This boy had a high scholastic record,—almost a straight A.

BRANCH RICKEY

1954: OCTOBER 23

DWIGHT EISENHOWER TO NGO DINH DIEM

In July of 1954, the Geneva Accords marked the end of French control in Viet-nam and made it illegal for any foreign power to intervene there militarily. Ngo Dinh Diem was the newly named premier of the anti-Communist South Vietnam, and with this letter, Eisenhower made a cautious offer of economic aid. However guarded the overture was, it constituted one of the first U.S. steps toward eventual involvement in the Vietnam War.

Donald R. Heath was U.S. ambassador to South Vietnam.

Dear Mr. President:

I have been following with great interest the course of developments in Viet-Nam, particularly since the conclusion of the conference at Geneva. The implications of the agreement concerning Viet-Nam have caused grave concern regarding the future of a country temporarily divided by an artificial military grouping, weakened by a long and exhausting war, and faced with enemies without and by their subversive collaborators within.

Your recent requests for aid to assist in the formidable project of the movement of several hundred thousand loyal Vietnamese citizens away from areas which are passing under a <u>de facto</u> rule and political ideology which they abhor, are being fulfilled. I am glad that the United States is able to assist in this humanitarian effort.

We have been exploring ways and means to permit our aid to Viet-Nam to be more effective and to make a greater contribution to the welfare and stability of the Government of Viet-Nam. I am, accordingly, instructing the American Ambassador to Viet-Nam to examine with you in your capacity as Chief of Government, how an intelligent program of American aid given directly to your

Government can serve to assist Viet-Nam in its present hour of trial, provided that your Government is prepared to give assurances as to the standards of performance it would be able to maintain in the event such aid were supplied.

The purpose of this offer is to assist the Government of Viet-Nam in developing and maintaining a strong, viable state, capable of resisting attempted subversion or aggression through military means. The Government of the United States expects that this aid will be met by performance on the part of the Government of Viet-Nam in undertaking needed reforms. It hopes that such aid, combined with your own continuing efforts, will contribute effectively toward an independent Viet-Nam endowed with a strong government. Such a government would, I hope, be so responsive to the nationalist aspirations of its people, so enlightened in purpose and effective in performance, that it will be respected both at home and abroad and discourage any who might wish to impose a foreign ideology on your free people.

Sincerely,

Dwight D. Eisenhower

1955: MARCH 26

JONAS SALK TO ELEANOR ROOSEVELT

Dr. Jonas Salk (1914–1995) began to study polio in 1947, while he was head of viral research at the University of Pittsburgh. By 1952, the year a record fifty-eight thousand cases were reported in the United States, Salk began field-testing his vaccine. Two years later, after he had tested the vaccine on himself, his family, and on former polio patients, nearly two million American children took part in clinical trials. Knowing that the successful results would soon be announced, Salk wrote this letter to the widow of the most famous polio victim in the country.

26 March 1955

Mrs. Eleanor Roosevelt

Hyde Park

New York

Dear Mrs. Roosevelt:

A desire I have had for a long time has overtaken me. I suppose this has occurred because the time is drawing quite near when a report will be made which, I expect, will indicate that a means for preventing paralytic poliomyelitis is available. Since you were the person closest to the man to whom society owes so great a debt, I wanted you to know that my thoughts, in the past few years, have been with you and your late husband more often than I can count.

The scientific report, that may mark the beginning of the end of the scourge of polio, is to be made on the Tenth Anniversary of Mr. Roosevelt's untimely death. Wherever you may be, or whatever your thoughts, I would like you to know that a part of his great spirit will be within me, living as it was during his great life, while we all share the knowledge that may bring the fulfillment of the dream he had many years ago.

Sincerely,

Jonas E. Salk, M.D.

1955: APRIL 13
JOANNA SHURBET TO JONAS SALK

The Salk vaccine was announced the day before this letter was written. In an instant, Salk became a national hero, and although his vaccine would soon be supplanted by Albert Sabin's live-virus oral version, it was Salk who would remain most famous for discovering a way to prevent polio.

Old Mountain Rd.

Nyack, N.Y.

April 13, 1955

Dear Doctor Salk—

Not the least among the many honors a grateful world bestows upon you are the blessings of a million mothers to whom your discovery means freedom from a most tragic fear. When I realize that my young daughter and another child as yet unborn will never suffer from polio, I am more grateful than words can express to you and to all the others who have made this possible.

Most sincerely,

Joanna H. Shurbet

1955: AUGUST 31
WILLIAM HENRY HUFF TO HUGH WHITE

In the summer of 1955, the mutilated body of a black fourteen-year-old named Emmett Till was pulled from Mississippi's Tallahatchie River. His apparent offense, the result of a dare, had been embracing a white store owner and yelling at her, "Bye, baby." The images of his body, displayed in an open casket and photographed by Jet *magazine, became a major catalyst in the modern civil rights movement.*

William Henry Huff was chairman of the NAACP's legal redress committee. Hugh White was governor of Mississippi.

THOSE WHO COMMIT SUCH DASTARDLY ACTS ARE THEMSELVES ENEMIES TO OUR COUNTRY, AND THOSE WHO DO NOTHING TOWARD BRINGING SUCH CRIMINALS TO JUSTICE ARE THEM-SELVES PARTIES TO THE CRIME.

1955: AUGUST 31
HUGH WHITE TO THE NAACP

In September, the husband and brother-in-law of the store owner would go on trial for Till's murder. Despite eyewitness testimony from Till's uncle, who had seen the teenager dragged away, an all-white jury would take only an hour and seven minutes to acquit the pair. Clearly contradicting the sentiments expressed in this telegram, one of the jurors said that if they hadn't "stopped to drink pop . . . it wouldn't have taken that long."

PARTIES CHARGED WITH THE MURDER ARE IN JAIL. I HAVE EVERY REASON TO BELIEVE THAT THE COURT WILL DO THEIR DUTY IN PROSECUTION. MISSISSIPPI DOES NOT CONDONE SUCH CONDUCT.

1955: OCTOBER 19
THE FORD MOTOR COMPANY TO MARIANNE MOORE

Marianne Moore (1887–1972) was a leading American poet who had won the Pulitzer prize for her Collected Poems *in 1952. Science, history, and exotic animals were frequently featured in her poetry, as was a certain irony. This may help explain why she was approached, in the letter below, by the Ford Motor Company's manager of marketing research, David Wallace. Wallace's associate, Robert B. Young, was married to a woman who had met Moore at a Mount Holyoke College luncheon. On that slim footing, and initially using Young's signature instead of his own, Wallace began a remarkable correspondence.*

October 19, 1955

Dear Miss Moore:

This is a morning we find ourselves with a problem which, strangely enough, is more in the field of words and the fragile meaning of words than in car-making. And we just wonder whether you might be intrigued with it sufficiently to lend us a hand.

Our dilemma is a name for a rather important new series of cars.

We should like this name to be more than a label. Specifically, we should like it to have a compelling quality in itself and by itself. To convey, through association or other conjuration, some visceral feeling of elegance, fleetness, advanced features and design. A name, in short, that flashes a dramatically desirable picture in people's minds.

Over the past few weeks this office has confected a list of three hundred-odd candidates which, it pains me to relate, are characterized by an embarrassing pedestrianism. We are miles short of our ambition. And so we are seeking the help of one who knows more about this sort of magic than we.

As to how we might go about this matter, I have no idea. One possibility is that you might care to visit with us and muse with the new Wonder which now is in clay in our Advance Styling Studios. But, in any event, all would depend on whether you find this overture of some challenge and interest.

Should we be so fortunate as to have piqued your fancy, we will be pleased to write more fully. In summary, all we want is a colossal name (another "Thunderbird" would be fine). And, of course, it is expected that our relations will be on a fee basis of an impeccably dignified kind.

Respectfully,
Robert B. Young
Marketing Research Department

Miss Marianne Moore
260 Cumberland Street
Brooklyn 5, New York

1955: NOVEMBER 19
MARIANNE MOORE TO THE FORD MOTOR COMPANY

Moore accepted the challenge. The following three letters contain many, but by no means all, of her suggestions for what to name the car.

November 19, 1955

Some other suggestions, Mr. Young, for the phenomenon:

THE RESILIENT BULLET

or intelligent bullet

or bullet cloisoné   or bullet lavolta

(I have always had a fancy for the THE INTELLIGENT WHALE—the little first Navy submarine, shaped like a sweet-potato; on view in our Brooklyn Yard).

THE FORD FABERGÉ (That there is also a perfume Fabergé seems to me to do no harm for here, allusion is to the original silversmith).

THE ARC-en-CIEL (the rainbow)

ARCENCIEL?

Please do not feel that memoranda from me need acknowledgment. I am not working day and night for you; I feel that etymological hits are partially accidental.

Sincerely yours,

Marianne Moore

The bullet idea has possibilities, it seems to me, in connection with mercury (with Hermes and Hermes trismegistus) and magic (white magic).

I seem to admire variety in the sections of your address!

1955: NOVEMBER 28

MARIANNE MOORE TO THE FORD MOTOR COMPANY

November 28, 1955

To: Mr. Robert B. Young

From: Marianne Moore

MONGOOSE CIVIQUE

ANTICIPATOR

REGNA RACER (couronne à couronne) sovereign to sovereign

AEROTERRE

fée rapide (aerofée, aero faire, fée aiglette, magi-faire) comme il faire

tonnère alifère (wingèd thunder)

aliforme alifère (wing-slender a-wing)

TURBOTORC (used as an adjective by Plymouth)

THUNDERBIRD allié (Cousin Thunderbird)

THUNDER CRESTER

DEARBORN diamanté
MAGIGRAVURE
PASTELOGRAM
    I shall be returning the sketches very soon—

M.M.

1955: DECEMBER 8
MARIANNE MOORE TO THE FORD MOTOR COMPANY

December 8, 1955

Mr. Young:
    May I submit UTOPIAN TURTLETOP?
Do not trouble to answer unless you like it.

Marianne Moore

1956: NOVEMBER 8
THE FORD MOTOR COMPANY TO MARIANNE MOORE

November 8, 1956

Dear Miss Moore:

    Because you were so kind to us in our early and hopeful days of looking for a suitable name, I feel a deep obligation to report on events that have ensued.

    And I feel I must do so before the public announcement of same come Monday, November 19.

    We have chosen a name out of the more than six-thousand-odd candidates that we gathered. It has a certain ring to it. An air of gaiety and zest. At least, that's what we keep saying. Our name, dear Miss Moore, is—Edsel.

    I know you will share your sympathies with us.

Cordially,
David Wallace, Manager
Marketing Research

P.S. Our Mr. Robert Young, who corresponded with you earlier, is now and temporarily, we hope, in the services of our glorious U.S. Coast Guard. I know he would send his best.

DW

*   *   *

1957: MAY 11

JAMES SNODGRASS TO WHOM IT MAY CONCERN

In its first ten weeks on television, The $64,000 Question *was watched by forty-seven million viewers. Imitators soon followed, and at the height of the quiz shows' popularity, crime in America dropped during the broadcasts. Eventually, rumors started to spread that the shows were rigged, and in 1959 a congressional investigation would reveal that some popular players—most notably the literary scion and Columbia University teacher Charles Van Doren—had been coached. The letter below, written by a contestant on* Twenty-One *named James Snodgrass, provided hard proof. Snodgrass sent the letter to himself by registered mail and kept it sealed; dated and posted before the show it described had taken place, it detailed the questions he would be asked.*

To whom it may concern:

The following are some of the questions, specifically the ones I will be asked for the television quiz show "Twenty-One" on the night of May 13 (Monday).

First category: "Movies"—I take 11 points. The question is worth 11 points.

In the story of "Snow White and the Seven Dwarfs," after she is banished from the palace of her stepmother, the Queen, Snow White goes to live in the forest with seven dwarfs. In the Walt Disney version, what were the names of the seven dwarfs?

(I shall answer in this sequence—Sleepy, Sneezy, Dopey, Happy (pause) the grouchy one, Grumpy (pause) Doc (pause) Bashful.

Second category: "England"—I take 10 points.

What was the name of the ruling houses to which the following monarchs belonged—Richard II, Henry VII, Edward V, George VI?

(I shall answer something like this. Richard II was the last of the Plantagenets; Henry VII was a Tudor. I shall then ask to come back to Edward V. George the Sixth of course was the House of Windsor. Then I think about Edward V and mention that he was the kid murdered in the Tower of London by Richard III; he was not a Tudor, he was of the House of York.)

That ends the first game with a score of 21. Presumably Bloomgarden and I shall be tied.

First round game 2: "Presidents."

The first President of our country was a General as was President Eisenhower. Identify the following Presidents who also were generals. This man won fame by defeating the British at New Orleans during the War of 1812? (I answer correctly—Andrew Jackson.) This general led the American forces at the Battle of Thames in 1813? (I stress the fact that Thames is in Ontario, Canada, also during the War of 1812. William Henry Harrison.) This man enlisted in the army as a private, was appointed a brigadier general and fought with General Scott in capture of Mexico City—(According to the plan of the show I am to miss this question. I am to say "Ulysses S. Grant" which is wrong. The proper answer is "Franklin Pierce." This general defeated Santa Ana at the Battle of Buena Vista? (Zachary Taylor.)

Second round—"The Twenties" (I again try for 11 points since I am at zero.)

The following authors were awarded the Pulitzer prize in the twenties. Name the work for which they received this prize.

Stephen Vincent Benet ("John Brown's Body"), Edna Ferber (for her novel "So Big"), Edith Wharton (for "The Age of Innocence"), Thornton Wilder ("The Bridge of San Luis Rey").

James Snodgrass.

1957: SEPTEMBER 4
ORVAL FAUBUS TO DWIGHT EISENHOWER

Three years after the Supreme Court's historic desegregation ruling in Brown v. Board of Education, *Little Rock, Arkansas, became the national battleground for integration when nine black students attempted to enter Little Rock Central High School. Though he had not previously been considered a segregationist, Arkansas governor Orval Faubus (1910–1994) reflected the vehemence of much of his constituency when he called in the National Guard to bar the students from entering.*

Mr. President:

I was one of the soldiers of your command in World War Two. I spent 300 days of combat with an infantry division defending our country, its people and their rights on the battlefields of five nations.

The question in issue at Little Rock at this moment is not integration vs. segregation. Peaceful integration has been accomplished for some time in the University of Arkansas, state supported colleges and a number of public schools. This week peaceful integration was accomplished in three more of our largest public schools—Fort Smith, Van Buren, Ozark. It is impossible to integrate some of our schools at this time without violence. The Supreme Court recognized that conditions in each community must be considered and I have interpreted your public statements to indicate that you are in agreement with this premise.

The question now is whether or not the head of a sovereign state can exercise his constitutional powers and discretion in maintaining peace and good order within his jurisdiction, being accountable to his own conscience and to his own people.

Certain units of the National Guard have been placed on duty to preserve the peace and good order of the community. You—as a military man—know that the commander must have the authority and the discretion to take the necessary steps warranted by the situation with which he must deal.

I am reliably informed that federal authorities in Little Rock have this day been discussing plans to take into custody, by force, the head of a sovereign state. This would be in complete disregard of the constitutional guarantees of the separation and independence of the three branches of government and the rights and powers of a state. As the duly elected governor and representative of the people of Arkansas I can no more surrender these rights than you could surrender the rights of the duly elected chief executive of our nation. To do so would set a precedent that would jeopardize the rights and powers of the governor of any state.

I must follow the precedent set by you as a chief executive when you declined to have your administrative aids summoned to testify before a congressional committee.

I have strong reasons to believe that the telephone lines to the Arkansas executive mansion have been tapped—I suspect the federal agents. The situation in Little Rock and Arkansas grows more explosive by the hour. This is caused for the most part by the misunderstanding of our problems by a federal judge who decreed "immediate" integration of the public schools of Little Rock without hearing any evidence whatsoever as to the conditions now existing in this community. The situation is further aggravated by the impending unwarranted interference of federal agents. If these actions continue, or if my executive authority as governor to maintain the peace is breached, then I can no longer be responsible for the results. The injury to persons and property that would be caused—the blood that may be shed, will be on the hands of the federal government and its agents. The splendid progress we have made in Arkansas for the past few years toward meeting our problems of race relationship will have been completely and utterly destroyed. Many expressions of fairness and understanding have come from you regarding the problems of the South and of the nation. As governor of Arkansas I appeal to you to use your good offices to modify the extreme stand and stop the unwarranted interference of federal agents in this area so that we may again enjoy domestic tranquility and continue in our pursuit of ideal relations between the races.

Time is the essence of the situation with which I am confronted—may I have the assurance of your understanding and cooperation?

1957: SEPTEMBER 5
DWIGHT EISENHOWER TO ORVAL FAUBUS

Your telegram received requesting my assurance of understanding of and cooperation in the course of action you have taken on school integration recommended by the Little Rock School Board and ordered by the United States District Court pursuant to the mandate of the United States Supreme Court.

When I became President, I took an oath to support and defend the Constitution of the United States. The only assurance I can give you is that the Federal Constitution will be upheld by me by every legal means at my command.

There is no basis of fact to the statements you make in your telegram that Federal authorities have been considering taking you into custody or that telephone lines to your Executive Mansion have been tapped by any agency of the Federal Government.

At the request of Judge Davies, the Department of Justice is presently collecting facts as to interference with or failure to comply with the District Court's order. You and other state officials—as well as the National Guard which, of course, is uniformed, armed and partially sustained by the Government—will, I am sure, give full cooperation to the United States District Court.

1957: SEPTEMBER 30
THE PARENTS OF THE LITTLE ROCK
NINE TO DWIGHT EISENHOWER

After weeks of tension, the nine students entered the school on September 23. A white mob outside began a riot. The next day, Eisenhower sent in twelve hundred army paratroopers, and integration was enforced.

We, the parents of the nine colored children who have enrolled at Little Rock Central High School want you to know that your actions in safeguarding their rights have strengthened our faith in democracy.

1958: JANUARY
OLGA HUCKINS TO THE <u>BOSTON HERALD</u>

Paul Hermann Müller received the Nobel prize in 1948 for his discovery of the effectiveness of DDT in controlling the spread of insect-borne diseases. The chemical had been used in World War II, and after the war nearly eradicated malaria in more than twenty countries. It was years before the dangerous effects of the chemical became known. Olga Huckins, a former writer for the Boston Post, *was living near Cape Cod in Duxbury, Massachusetts, when she wrote this letter. Among the people influenced by it was Rachel Carson (see letter page 406), who would later credit it with having provided much of the inspiration for her celebrated* Silent Spring.

To the Editor of <u>The Herald</u>:

Mr. R. C. Codman, who wrote that he "is actively associated" with the Commonwealth of Mass. aerial spraying programs for alleged mosquito control, also says that state tests have proved that the mixture used—fuel oil with DDT—last summer over Plymouth and Barnstable Counties was entirely harmless.

These testers must have used black glasses, and the trout that did not feel the poison were super-fish.

Dr. Robert Cushman Murphy, distinguished scientist, observed after New York State sprayed Long Island in the same way, that no fish in still waters survived. All bees in a large section of the state were killed. Indeed, evidence of the havoc wrought by all air spraying of DDT is accumulating so rapidly that Mr. Codman's placid assurance becomes absurd.

The mosquito control plane flew over our small town last summer. Since we live close to the marshes, we were treated to several lethal doses as the pilot crisscrossed our place. And we consider the spraying of active poison over private land to be a serious aerial intrusion.

The "harmless" shower bath killed seven of our lovely songbirds outright. We picked up three dead bodies the next morning right by the door. They were birds that had lived close to us, trusted us, and built their nests in our trees year after year. The next day three were scattered around the bird bath. (I had emptied it and scrubbed it after the spraying but YOU CAN NEVER KILL DDT.) On the following day one robin dropped suddenly from a branch in our woods. We were too heartsick to hunt for other corpses. All of these birds died horribly, and in the same way. Their bills were gaping open, and their splayed claws were drawn up to their breasts in agony.

Mr. Codman also says that between DDT and mosquitoes, he prefers DDT. We had no choice; we have had both. All summer long, every time we went into the garden, we were attacked by the most voracious mosquitoes that had ever appeared there. But the grasshoppers, visiting bees, and other harmless insects, were all gone.

The remedy of this situation is not to double the strength of the spray and come again. It is to STOP THE SPRAYING OF POISONS FROM THE AIR everywhere until all the evidence, biological and scientific, immediate and long run, of the effects upon wild life and human beings are known.

Air spraying where it is not needed or wanted is inhuman, undemocratic, and probably unconstitutional. For those of us who stand helplessly on the tortured earth, it is intolerable.

Olga Owens Huckins
Duxbury

1958: JANUARY 4

JAMES THURBER TO ROBERT LEIFERT

James Thurber (1894–1961) joined the staff of The New Yorker *in 1927 and continued to contribute to the magazine for the rest of his life. He was the author of* My Life and Hard Times *(1933),* The Thurber Carnival *(1945), and* The Thurber Album *(1952). In most of his stories and drawings, as in this letter to a schoolboy, he gave voice to a fretful but ever wry view of life.*

West Cornwall,
Connecticut
January 4, 1958

Mr. Robert Leifert
New York City, New York

Dear Robert:

Since a hundred schoolchildren a year write me letters like yours—some writers get a thousand—the problem of what to do about such classroom "projects" has become a serious one for all of us. If a writer answered all of you he would get nothing else done. When I was a baby goat I had to do my own research on projects, and I enjoyed doing it. I never wrote an author for his autograph or photograph in my life. Photographs are for movie actors to send to girls. Tell your teacher I said so, and please send me her name. . . .

One of the things that discourage us writers is the fact that 90 percent of you children write wholly, or partly, illiterate letters, carelessly typed. You yourself write "clarr" for "class" and that's a honey, Robert, since <u>s</u> is next to <u>a</u>, and <u>r</u> is on the line above. Most schoolchildren in America would do a dedication like the following (please find the mistakes in it and write me about them):

> To Miss Effa G. Burns
> Without who's help
> this book could never
> of been finished it,
> is dedicated with
> gartitude by it's
> arthur.

Show that to your teacher and tell her to show it to her principal, and see if they can find the mistakes. . . .

Just yesterday a letter came in from a girl your age in South Carolina asking for biographical material and photograph. That is not the kind of education they have in Russia, we are told, because it's too much like a hobby or waste of time. What do you and your classmates want to be when you grow up—collectors? Then who is going to help keep the United States ahead of Russia in science, engineering, and the arts?

Please answer this letter. If you don't I'll write to another pupil.

> Sincerely yours,
> James Thurber

1958: FEBRUARY 1
RACHEL CARSON TO DOROTHY FREEMAN

Rachel Carson (1907–1964) confided her hopes for a new book to her intimate friend Dorothy Freeman (1898–1978), a fellow nature lover and a Maine neighbor. The revolutionary work would be called Silent Spring *and would be published in 1962. In exposing the dangers of pesticides, it would become not only a critically acclaimed bestseller but also the rallying point for a new environmental movement.*

About the book: I'll see if I can make any sense about it briefly. The theme remains what I have felt for several years it would be: Life and the relations of Life to the physical environment. (The older ideas of dealing just with theories of the origin of life or with the course of evolution were discarded long ago.) But I have been mentally blocked for a long time, first because I didn't know just what it was I wanted to say about Life, and also for a reason more difficult to explain. Of course everyone knows by this time that the whole world of science has been revolutionized by events of the past decade or so. I suppose my thinking began to be affected soon after atomic science was firmly established. Some of the thoughts that came were so unattractive to me that I rejected them completely, for the old ideas die hard, especially when they are emotionally as well as intellectually dear to one. It was pleasant to believe, for example, that much of Nature was forever beyond the tampering reach of man—he might level the forests and dam the streams, but the clouds and the rain and the wind were God's—the God of your ice-crystal cathedral in that beautiful passage of a recent letter of yours.

It was comforting to suppose that the stream of life would flow on through time in whatever course that God had appointed for it—without interference by one of the drops of the stream—man. And to suppose that, however the physical environment might mold Life, that Life could never assume the power to change drastically—or even destroy—the physical world.

These beliefs have almost been part of me for as long as I have thought about such things. To have them even vaguely threatened was so shocking that, as I have said, I shut my mind—refused to acknowledge what I couldn't help seeing. But that does no good, and I have now opened my eyes and my mind. I may not like what I see, but it does no good to ignore it, and it's worse than useless to go on repeating the old "eternal verities" that are no more eternal than the hills of the poets. So it seems time someone wrote of Life in the light of the truth as it now appears to us. And I think that may be the book I am to write. Oh—a brief one, darling—suggesting the new ideas not treating them exhaustively. Probably no one could; certainly I couldn't.

I still feel there is a case to be made for my old belief that as man approaches the "new heaven and the new earth"—or the space-age universe, if you will, he must do so with humility rather than arrogance. (I was pleased to notice that word in the little editorial on snow I sent you. I think I wrote you of Frank Lloyd Wright's use of it.)

And along with humility I think there is still a place for wonder. (By the way, I hope you didn't think I was serious, some weeks back, in asserting a claim to the word "wonder.")

Well, darling, that's not an outline of the book, but at least indicates the approach.

Of course, in pre-<u>Sputnik</u> days, it was easy to dismiss so much as science-fiction fantasies. Now the most farfetched schemes seem entirely possible of achievement. And man seems actually likely to take into his hands—ill-prepared as he is psychologically—many of the functions of "God."

Glad you are reading Conrad. I don't remember ever studying him formally, but of course I've read a good deal of him. Does your book include selections from <u>Mirror of the Sea</u>—which I love. See Bennett Cerf's biographical note on Galsworthy for an incidental bit on Conrad.

Rain on the roof now—maybe snow tomorrow. Had an interruption a couple of pages back to hear the announcement of the launching (?) of an American satellite. Still a maybe as I write.

Perhaps I'll put this out in the morning for the mailman who comes early Saturday. If it snows I probably wouldn't go in later.

So I'll say goodnight, my dear one, in case there's no time to say more tomorrow. Now to sleep—perhaps to dream—Guess what?

I love you
Rachel

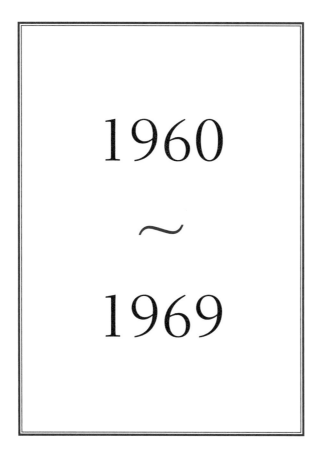

1960

~

1969

You are born into the age of worldwide revolution. You will
be thirty-one years old in the year 2000. You may well
travel to other planets. More prosaically, you have
one hell of a groovy father.

—Robin Morgan to her son
July 9, 1969

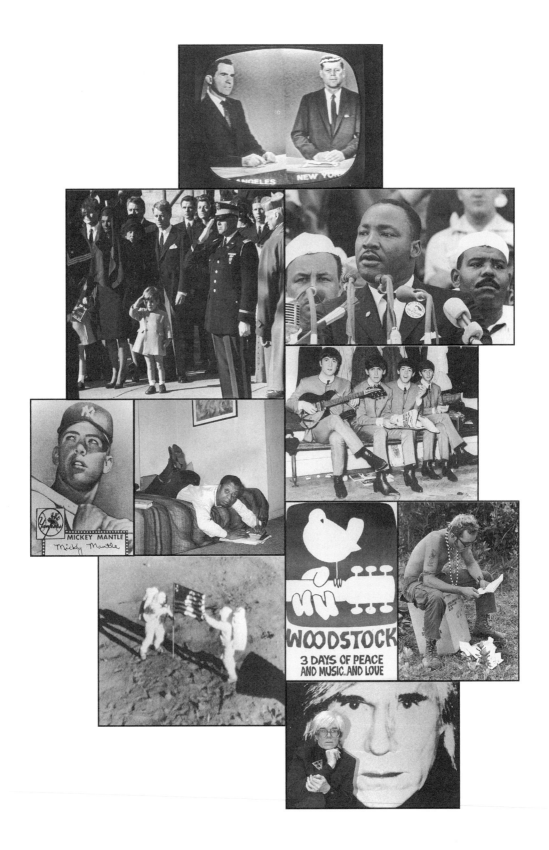

BETWEEN 1960 AND 1969 . . .

1960: The median age is 29.5 years. ★ The U.S. population is 179.3 million. ★ Bell Telephone begins to eliminate exchange names and replace them with numbers. ★ Xerox machines and felt-tip pens appear in American offices. ★ John Updike publishes *Rabbit, Run.* ★ Birth control pills are available to American women for the first time. ★ Viewers watching the televised debate between presidential candidates Richard Nixon and John Kennedy believe Kennedy has won; radio listeners give the victory to Nixon. ★ Chubby Checker introduces the Twist. **1961:** John Kennedy is inaugurated. ★ Alan Shepard becomes America's first man in space. ★ In the movie *Splendor in the Grass*, audiences can see Natalie Wood and Warren Beatty exchange the first on-screen French kiss. ★ In Cuba, the invasion at the Bay of Pigs fails, embarrassing the United States and anti-Castro forces. **1962:** New books include Ken Kesey's *One Flew Over the Cuckoo's Nest*, Joseph Heller's *Catch-22*, and Rachel Carson's *Silent Spring*. ★ Johnny Carson becomes host of *The Tonight Show*. ★ Playing for the Philadelphia Warriors, Wilt Chamberlain scores 100 points in one game. ★ President Kennedy demands that the Soviet Union withdraw its missile launching sites from Cuba. **1963:** ZIP (for Zone

Top row: Nixon-Kennedy debate; *second row, from left to right:* J.F.K., Jr., Martin Luther King, Jr.; *third row:* Mickey Mantle, James Baldwin, the Beatles; *fourth row:* the moon landing, Woodstock poster, Christmas mail in Vietnam; *bottom row:* Andy Warhol.

Improvement Plan) Codes are introduced. ★ It now costs 5 cents to send a one-ounce letter. ★ Weight Watchers is founded by Jean Neditch, a housewife from Queens, New York. ★ John Kennedy is assassinated, and Lyndon B. Johnson becomes president. **1964:** The U.S. Surgeon General issues a warning about the hazards of smoking. ★ The Beatles appear on *The Ed Sullivan Show*. ★ The Civil Rights Act becomes law. ★ GI Joe, Touch-Tone telephones, topless bathing suits, topless dancers, Pop-Tarts, and the Ford Mustang make their debuts. ★ Susan Sontag declares Tiffany lamps, *Swan Lake,* the Brown Derby restaurant, and feather boas to be "camp." **1965:** Andy Warhol's *Campbell's Tomato Soup Can* is exhibited. ★ Ralph Nader publishes *Unsafe at Any Speed*. ★ Miniskirts appear. ★ LSD is manufactured in sugar cubes. ★ Rioting breaks out in the Watts section of Los Angeles. ★ From New York to Michigan, 80,000 square miles and 30 million people are left without electricity in the biggest blackout in history. **1966:** *Star Trek*'s first episodes air. ★ In *Miranda* v. *Arizona*, the Supreme Court rules that criminal suspects must be told their rights before being questioned. ★ Jacqueline Susann's *Valley of the Dolls* is the bestselling novel of the year. ★ Pampers, the first disposable diapers, are a hit in Sacramento test markets. **1967:** Congress passes the Endangered Species Act. ★ Seeking conscientious objector status, Muhammad Ali, boxing's reigning heavyweight champion, is turned down; after refusing to be drafted, he is arrested. ★ The "Summer of Love" draws 300,000 peace marchers to New York City. ★ Seventy-seven people are killed and at least 4,000 injured during race riots in more than 100 American cities. ★ Thurgood Marshall, 59, becomes the first black Supreme Court justice. ★ Aretha Franklin is named top female vocalist of the year by *Billboard* magazine. **1968:** The Tet offensive begins. ★ President Johnson declares that he will not run for reelection. ★ Martin Luther King, Jr., is shot to death. ★ Students take over Columbia University. ★ Robert Kennedy is shot to death. ★ As police clash with protesters on the streets of Chicago, Hubert Humphrey easily defeats antiwar candidate Eugene McCarthy for the Democratic presidential nomination. ★ Jacuzzis, *60 Minutes*, and Ralph Lauren clothes are new. ★ Jacqueline Kennedy marries Aristotle Onassis. ★ Campaigning for president, Richard M. Nixon appears on *Rowan & Martin's Laugh-In* and says, "Sock it to me?" ★ Nixon is elected. **1969:** Hit songs include the Beatles' "Get Back," the Rolling Stones' "Honky Tonk Women," and the Archies' "Sugar, Sugar." ★ Senator Edward Kennedy, 36, drives off the Dyke Bridge on Chappaquiddick Island, and his passenger, brother Robert's former campaign aide Mary Jo Kopechne, drowns in the waters off Martha's Vineyard. ★ Woodstock, New York, becomes the setting for a four-day festival of peace, love, music, drugs, and mud. ★ After 148 years, *The Saturday Evening Post* publishes its last issue. ★ *Penthouse* magazine publishes its first issue. ★ Neil Armstrong walks on the moon.

Joyce Hohlwein and Pat Lamb became friends at the University of Utah and began a lasting correspondence in the summer of 1953, when they were in their early twenties. Hohlwein had grown up in Salt Lake City, Lamb in Los Angeles. Hohlwein married a German artist, Lamb a British doctor. During the week of the presidential election, Hohlwein seemed to be straddling the decades, struggling between the paradigms of the dutiful 1950s wife and the more independent woman of the 1960s.

John Kennedy defeated Richard Nixon (1913–1994) by one of the narrowest—and most questionable—margins in history.

Milwaukee
November 8, 1960

Very dear Pat,

I speak for the whole family and some number of friends in thanking you for the splendid letter of a week or so back. Hans enjoyed it as much as I, to the point of considering it a kind of document, with parts of it quite suitable for reading to an unpredicted audience. I agree. It was the most consistently fluent letter I've had from you in some time. Not only that, it was steadier, more convincing—perhaps merely more thorough.

Tonight is a very fateful one for those of us who at all consider our fortunes (literally or figuratively) tied up with America, directly or indirectly. As I should think you might assume, I am heatedly pulling for Kennedy, though at the time of the convention I felt the Democrats could go to hell for all I cared, since they would not nominate Stevenson. Now I can see, after the goopy campaign Nixon has conducted and the astonishing way its sentimentality has been swallowed, that Stevenson, being a two-time loser anyway, would not have stood a chance. As it now stands (mid-evening of election night) the race is very close. Perhaps this all seems very far from you now, but I am sure you'd be most concerned, were you here.

Wednesday

It was a long and harrowing evening with friends, watching the tight, but nonetheless dragging, race between Nixon and Kennedy, and we left with a reasonable expectancy, but no certainty of a Kennedy victory. But I just heard—at noon the following day!—his acceptance speech, and I'm grateful (it's the only word) for his victory. I feel he's a perspicacious man with both convictions and integrity. Of course he may look better than he is, but what more have we to go on? Evidently the religious issue is passé in America. We thought his wife Jackie was a real drag, being beautiful, fashionable and chic enough to invite a good deal of antagonism. But it's nice to have a really lovely woman as first lady. Imagine! She is <u>exactly</u> my age.

As you know, I am continuing to teach full-time until the baby comes in February, half-time thereafter. Grueling but pleasurable. I wish you could send me advice at this point. You are not here, you cannot know our problems, I have told you so little. But one of my major worries, being one of Hans's, if not his greatest, source of dissatisfaction with our life, is my working. To be the proper dutiful wife, I know I should quit. Yet I'm stubborn as an ox about it, resisting Hans's every mention of it with anger, insults or tears. Why this should be so, I'm not sure, partly because it's what I always wanted to do, partly because bit by bit I'm gaining sufficient prestige to allow me the literature courses that are really stimulating, partly because I feel a twelve-hour load is not a reprehensible deviation from domesticity (although I know Hans is right in that I give many, many more hours to it), partly because we need the money. But the situation is now growing to the point that my basic delight in doing it is constantly undermined by my knowledge that a rift in the harmony of our home is the price of it all. But, I wonder, <u>why</u> need it to be? I don't want to quit, but I feel I should, as a sacrifice, or an obedience to Hans. He means it well, for the sake of more peace and serenity in my life, as well as his, but I hate to give up something I am doing so well with.

To continue, as I must, in the choppy, furtive particles of time that I steal to be my own. Hans is right—there is a great deal of expense of "paying too much for things in coin of the spirit" with my routine. I can scarcely manage anything but a hodgepodge of jottings as an excuse for a letter to you. And now I have but fifteen minutes before the next class.

By the way, did <u>you</u> send me a new subscription to the <u>Times Lit. Supp.</u>? If so, a thousand gratitudes, I do enjoy it, but there was no mention of its source. A funny note: Mort Sahl, a very clever, sardonic, political comedian, said, "I hope

Kennedy doesn't slip and say it was a miracle. Somebody might get the wrong idea."

Other details of our life: Hans has advanced so beautifully far with the techniques of woodcutting and lithography. It is not the technique he has the real trouble with; his difficulty is in knowing what image to create. Boils down to the same problem I have in writing: what, really, to say? His themes are essentially religious—Saint Sebastian, Veronica, some attempts at crucifixions, Jeremiah—but they give him much trouble, and he often feels he shouldn't try that. There is much pain, much anguish involved. Quite apart from the physically grueling work of running off edition after edition by hand printing. It takes hours, hours and hours.

Like you, we both are feeling and have felt for some time the desire, almost the compulsion, to buy a home. In our case, it would be on the detestable long-drawn-out time payment system, which we're trying with tooth and nail to avoid. But we have not yet found the place, and we still regret that our desires and willingness to make purchase of an old stone farm place in France fell through, coinciding as it did with Reinhard's disease.

Yes, our boy is quite thoroughly recovered. I've no idea how many, if any, photos I've sent of him, or if you've any well-defined picture of him in your mind. As I've repeated, ad nauseam, he is beautiful. He has precious, clean little features, and eyes that are sometimes appalling in their penetration, as well as the depth of their blue. He looks as he did at two weeks, quite like a little aristocrat. And by all means the most endearing thing about him, the something which I would most have wished for had I had an order to make, would have been and did turn out to be his whimsy, his charm, his Christopher Robinish nature—a quality which over the years has made so very many people comment on him, on the fact that he was unlike most American children (if such a generality is not blithering nonsense). And it was this that made his European family lay claim to his personality, whether with determined prejudice or not is hard to say. But he is very winning. He will be going to kindergarten in January.

Reinhard shows as yet no particular talent, except the phenomenally well developed one of being a skillful diplomat and a winner of friends at all levels and ages. He has resisted painting and drawing till now, and done them very badly, but suddenly now is taking real pleasure in them both.

Physically, I am a good deal changed since last you saw me. I've probably written this long since with ill-concealed satisfaction, but it has been a continuous pleasure since summer of 1955—this pleasure in my person, which I had only had at irregular junctures before. I lost all superfluous weight with the meningitis while I was carrying Reinhard, and a nicer and happier person emerged thereafter. I cared more about everything, discovered I had a jolly good figure to work with and to dress, and that I could carry off just about any kind of clothing I had the courage to wear. Since then I have maintained my weight steadily at about 122, which is perfect for me. I have learned how to use makeup with some skill, which I resisted like poison until I was twenty-seven; I never am caught without heels, but always without a hat, and I have, with some abandon, recklessness, and great amusement and joy, purchased a really hand-some woman's wardrobe with which I am very pleased and which I'm convinced I wear well. It took me two years of marriage before I would even abandon bobby sox, except on the occasions that absolutely demanded it, and I just now am beginning to rid myself of left-over college clothes. In other words, I'm much more likely to be seen in a violet silk blouse now than in a kelly green cardigan. It's fun, really much fun, and I have a few startlingly beautiful clothes. Hans is delightfully cooperative on this score, and cares that my lingerie is as chic as my outer garb, and often comes home with some fabulous little some-thing, in exquisite taste. I've even gained quite a reputation around school and in social gatherings for my taste—hard to believe, isn't it? I still cannot drink. I eat with a good deal more attention than previously to what is good for me, and although I did smoke a lot for years, I've stopped with this pregnancy and per-haps won't go back to it. I never seem to get around to any sports of any kind.

Our social life is not so satisfying as we would like it to be. The people we see are either older, charmingly sophisticated and very involved in collecting amus-ing "art nouveau" odds and ends and doing wry or surprising things with them, and very involved in competitive entertaining (on a scale I couldn't possibly em-ulate) and drinking. Or they are the kind of average cross-section of less-than-the-best women's colleges, i.e., fairly stimulating, quite earnestly dedicated, and sort of pleasurable colleagues.

Will have to close here. Write much again soon. My thoughts are often with you.

Love,
Joyce

1961: APRIL 20
JOHN KENNEDY TO LYNDON JOHNSON

On April 12, 1961, the Soviet Union announced that Cosmonaut Yuri Gagarin had made the world's first orbital flight in the satellite Vostok I. *After a gloomy week in which the new president publicly admitted his dismay at being second to the Soviets in the space race, he sent this memo to Vice-President Lyndon B. Johnson (1908– 1973). Though the Mercury space program was already well under way (Alan Shepard would make his suborbital flight on May 5), Kennedy's message was an acknowledgment that more was needed in order to beat the Russians. On May 25, Kennedy would announce the United States' intention to land an American on the moon and return him safely to earth before the end of the decade.*

THE WHITE HOUSE
Washington

April 20, 1961
MEMORANDUM FOR VICE PRESIDENT

In accordance with our conversation I would like for you as Chairman of the Space Council to be in charge of making an overall survey of where we stand in space.

1. Do we have a chance of beating the Soviets by putting a laboratory in space, or by a trip around the moon, or by a rocket to land on the moon, or by a rocket to go to the moon and back with a man. Is there any other space program which promises dramatic results in which we could win?

2. How much additional would it cost?

3. Are we working 24 hours a day on existing programs. If not, why not? If not, will you make recommendations to me as to how work can be speeded up.

4. In building large boosters should we put our emphasis on nuclear, chemical or liquid fuel, or a combination of these three?

5. Are we making maximum effort? Are we achieving necessary results?

I have asked Jim Webb, Dr. Weisner, Secretary McNamara and other responsible officials to cooperate with you fully. I would appreciate a report on this at the earliest possible moment.

John F. Kennedy

* * *

1961: OCTOBER

ROBERT MOSES TO FELLOW SNCC MEMBERS

Founded in 1960, the Student Nonviolent Coordinating Committee (SNCC) was devoted to promoting black rights by organizing sit-in activities, and later, voter registration. Robert Moses (1935–) was a SNCC worker who taught classes in a room above a grocery store. His students were boycotting Burgland High School in McComb, Mississippi, where their schoolmates had been expelled for trying to integrate the Greyhound bus station. Moses wrote this letter after he and other jailed SNCC workers had been unable to pay their bail.

Moses would become a nationally recognized educator and head of the Algebra Project, a math literacy program.

We are smuggling this note from the drunk tank of the county jail in Magnolia, Mississippi. Twelve of us are here, sprawled out along the concrete bunker; Curtis Hayes, Hollis Watkins, Ike Lewis and Robert Talbert, four veterans of the bunker, are sitting up talking—mostly about girls; Charles McDew ("Tell the story") is curled into the concrete and the wall; Harold Robinson, Stephen Ashley, James Wells, Lee Chester Vick, Leotus Eubanks, and Ivory Diggs lay cramped on the cold bunker; I'm sitting with smuggled pen and paper, thinking a little, writing a little; Myrtis Bennett and Janie Campbell are across the way wedded to a different icy cubicle.

Later on, Hollis will lead out with a clear tenor into a freedom song, Talbert and Lewis will supply jokes, and McDew will discourse on the history of the black man and the Jew. McDew—a black by birth, a Jew by choice, and a revolutionary by necessity—has taken on the deep hates and deep loves which America and the world reserve for those who dare to stand in a strong sun and cast a sharp shadow. . . .

This is Mississippi, the middle of the iceberg. Hollis is leading off with his tenor, "Michael row the boat ashore, Alleluia; Christian brothers don't be slow, Alleluia; Mississippi's next to go, Alleluia." This is a tremor in the middle of the iceberg—from a stone that the builders rejected.

1961: DECEMBER 14

JOHN KENNEDY TO NGO DINH DIEM

The depth of JFK's commitment to South Vietnam continues to be an open question among traditional historians. Conspiracy theorists debate it vigorously, some of them taking it as an article of faith that Kennedy was assassinated by a military-industrial cabal bent on escalating a war he didn't want. Whatever Kennedy's ultimate intention, a year into his presidency he seemed to be taking seriously Diem's description of the North Vietnamese threat.

December 14, 1961

Dear Mr. President:

I have received your recent letter in which you described so cogently the dangerous condition caused by North Viet-Nam's efforts to take over your country. The situation in your embattled country is well known to me and to the American people. We have been deeply disturbed by the assault on your country. Our indignation has mounted as the deliberate savagery of the Communist program of assassination, kidnapping and wanton violence became clear.

Your letter underlines what our own information has convincingly shown— that the campaign of force and terror now being waged against your people and your Government is supported and directed from outside by the authorities at Hanoi. They have thus violated the provisions of the Geneva Accords designed to ensure peace in Viet-Nam and to which they bound themselves in 1954.

At that time, the United States, although not a party to the Accords, declared that it "would view any renewal of the aggression in violation of the agreements with grave concern and as seriously threatening international peace and security." We continue to maintain that view.

In accordance with that declaration, and in response to your request, we are prepared to help the Republic of Viet-Nam to protect its people and to preserve its independence. We shall promptly increase our assistance to your defense effort as well as help relieve the destruction of the floods which you describe. I have already given the orders to get these programs underway.

The United States, like the Republic of Viet-Nam, remains devoted to the cause of peace and our primary purpose is to help your people maintain their independence. If the Communist authorities in North Viet-Nam will stop their campaign to destroy the Republic of Viet-Nam, the measures we are taking to assist your defense efforts will no longer be necessary. We shall seek to persuade the Communists to give up their attempts of force and subversion. In any case, we are confident that the Vietnamese people will preserve their independence and gain the peace and prosperity for which they have sought so hard and so long.

*   *   *

1961: DECEMBER 29
A LOS ANGELES DOCTOR TO WHOM IT MAY CONCERN

Comedian Lenny Bruce (1925–1966) became as famous for self-destruction as he was for gathering obscenity charges with his incendiary brand of humor. Bruce, a longtime drug addict who would die of an overdose, persuaded a young orthopedic surgeon to write this letter. Bruce carried it with him everywhere.

December 29, 1961

TO WHOM IT MAY CONCERN:

Mr. Lenny Bruce of 8825 Hollywood Blvd., Los Angeles, California, has been under my professional care for the past two years for various minor orthopedic conditions. In addition, Mr. Bruce suffers from episodes of severe depression and lethargy. His response to oral amphetamine has not been particularly satisfactory, so he has been instructed in the proper use of intravenous injections of Methedrine (Metamphetamine Hydrochloride). This has given a satisfactory response.

Methedrine in ampules of 1cc. (20 mg.) together with disposable syringes, has been prescribed for intravenous use as needed.

Mr. Bruce has asked that I write this letter in order that any peace officer observing fresh needle marks on Mr. Bruce's arm may be assured that they are the result of Methedrine injections for therapeutic reasons.

Very truly yours,
[Name withheld]

1962
JAMES BALDWIN TO HIS NEPHEW

James Baldwin (1924–1987) had won his first literary acclaim with the novel Go Tell It on the Mountain *in 1953. Thereafter a novelist, essayist, and playwright, he educated Americans on the subject of race and was an eloquent voice in the civil rights struggle. This letter, clearly intended as an essay, was written to his teenage nephew James.*

An author and professor, E. Franklin Frazier headed the sociology department at Howard University.

Dear James:

I have begun this letter five times and torn it up five times. I keep seeing your face, which is also the face of your father and my brother. Like him, you are tough, dark, vulnerable, moody—with a very definite tendency to sound truculent because you want no one to think you are soft. You may be like your grandfather in this, I don't know, but certainly both you and your father resemble him very much physically. Well, he is dead, he never saw you, and he had a terrible life; he was defeated long before he died because, at the bottom of his heart, he really believed what white people said about him. This is one of the reasons that he became so holy. I am sure that your father has told you something about all that. Neither you nor your father exhibit any tendency towards holiness: you really <u>are</u> of another era, part of what happened when the Negro left the land and came into what the late E. Franklin Frazier called "the cities of destruction." You can only be destroyed by believing that you really are what the white world calls a <u>nigger</u>. I tell you this because I love you, and please don't you ever forget it.

I have known both of you all your lives, have carried your Daddy in my arms and on my shoulders, kissed and spanked him and watched him learn to walk. I don't know if you've known anybody from that far back; if you've loved anybody that long, first as an infant, then as a child, then as a man, you gain a strange perspective on time and human pain and effort. Other people cannot see what I see whenever I look into your father's face, for behind your father's face as it is today are all those other faces which were his. Let him laugh and I see a cellar your father does not remember and a house he does not remember and I hear in his present laughter his laughter as a child. Let him curse and I remember him falling down the cellar steps, and howling, and I remember, with pain, his tears, which my hand or your grandmother's so easily wiped away. But no one's hand can wipe away those tears he sheds invisibly today, which one hears in his laughter and in his speech and in his songs. I know what the world has done to my brother and how narrowly he has survived it. And I know, which is much worse, and this is the crime of which I accuse my country and my countrymen, and for which neither I nor time nor history will ever forgive them, that they have destroyed and are destroying hundreds of thousands of lives and do not know it and do not want to know it. One can be, indeed one must strive to become, tough and philosophical concerning destruction and death, for this is what most of mankind has been best at since we have heard of man. (But remember: <u>most</u> of mankind is not <u>all</u> of mankind.) But it is not permissible that the authors of devastation should also be innocent. It is the innocence which constitutes the crime.

Now, my dear namesake, these innocent and well-meaning people, your countrymen, have caused you to be born under conditions not very far removed from those described for us by Charles Dickens in the London of more than a hundred years ago. (I hear the chorus of the innocents screaming, "No! This is not true! How <u>bitter</u> you are!"—but I am writing this letter to <u>you</u>, to try to tell you something about how to handle <u>them</u>, for most of them do not yet really know that you exist. I <u>know</u> the conditions under which you were born, for I was there. Your countrymen were <u>not</u> there, and haven't made it yet. Your grandmother was also there, and no one has ever accused her of being bitter. I suggest that the innocents check with her. She isn't hard to find. Your countrymen don't know that <u>she</u> exists, either, though she has been working for them all their lives.)

Well, you were born, here you came, something like fifteen years ago; and though your father and mother and grandmother, looking about the streets through which they were carrying you, staring at the walls into which they brought you, had every reason to be heavyhearted, yet they were not. For here you were, Big James, named for me—you were a big baby, I was not—here you were: to be loved. To be loved, baby, hard, at once, and forever, to strengthen you against the loveless world. Remember that: I know how black it looks today, for you. It looked bad that day, too, yes, we were trembling. We have not stopped trembling yet, but if we had not loved each other none of us would have survived. And now you must survive because we love you, and for the sake of your children and your children's children.

This innocent country set you down in a ghetto in which, in fact, it intended that you should perish. Let me spell out precisely what I mean by that, for the heart of the matter is here, and the root of my dispute with my country. You were born where you were born and faced the future that you faced because you were black and <u>for no other reason</u>. The limits of your ambition were, thus, expected to be set forever. You were born into a society which spelled out with brutal clarity, and in as many ways as possible, that you were a worthless human being. You were not expected to aspire to excellence: you were expected to make peace with mediocrity. Wherever you have turned, James, in your short time on this earth, you have been told where you could go and what you could do (and <u>how</u> you could do it) and where you could live and whom you could marry. I know your countrymen do not agree with me about this, and I hear them saying, "You exaggerate." They do not know Harlem, and I do. So do you. Take no one's word for anything, including mine—but trust your experience. Know whence you came. If you know whence you came, there is really no limit to where you can go. The details and symbols of your life have been deliberately constructed to make you believe what white people say about you. Please try to remember that what they believe, as well as what they do and cause you to endure, does not testify to your inferiority but to their inhumanity and fear. Please try to be clear, dear James, through the storm which rages about your youthful head today, about the reality which lies behind the words <u>acceptance</u> and <u>integration</u>. There is no reason for you to try to become like white people and there is no basis whatever for their impertinent assumption that <u>they</u> must accept <u>you</u>. The really terrible thing, old buddy, is that <u>you</u> must accept <u>them</u>. And I mean that very seriously. You must accept them and accept them with love. For these innocent people have no other hope. They are, in effect, still trapped in a history which they do not understand; and until they understand it, they cannot be released from it. They have had to believe for many years, and innumerable reasons, that black men are inferior to white men. Many of them, indeed, know better, but, as you will discover, people find it very difficult to act on what they know. To act is to be committed, and to be committed is to be in danger. In this case, the danger, in the minds of most white Americans, is the loss of their identity. Try to imagine how you would feel if you woke up one morning to find the sun shining and all the stars aflame. You would be frightened because it is out of the order of nature. Any upheaval in the universe is terrifying because it so profoundly attacks one's sense of one's own reality. Well, the black man has functioned in the white man's world as a fixed star, as an immovable pillar: and as he moves out of his place, heaven and earth are shaken to their foundations. You, don't be afraid. I said that it was intended that you should perish in the ghetto, perish by never being allowed to go behind the white man's definitions, by never being allowed to spell your proper name. You have, and many of us have, defeated this intention; and, by a terrible law, a terrible paradox, those innocents who believed that your imprisonment made them safe are losing their grasp of reality. But these men are your brothers—your lost, younger brothers. And if the word <u>integration</u> means anything, that is what it means: that we, with love, shall force our brothers to see themselves as they are, to cease fleeing from reality and begin to change it. For this is your home, my friend, do not be driven from it; great men have done great things here, and will again, we can make America what America must become. It will be hard, James, but you come from sturdy, peasant stock, men who picked cotton and dammed rivers and built railroads, and, in the teeth of the most terrifying odds, achieved an unassailable and monumental dignity. You come from a long line of great poets, some of the greatest poets since Homer. One of them said, <u>The very time I thought I was lost, My dungeon shook, and my chains fell off.</u>

You know, and I know, that the country is celebrating one hundred years of freedom one hundred years too soon. We cannot be free until they are free. God bless you, James, and Godspeed.

Your uncle,
James

1962: MAY

MARION CARPENTER TO HIS SON

The seven Mercury astronauts were the elect, chosen after months of rigorous testing to represent the United States of America in the race for space. Malcolm Scott Carpenter (1925–) was thirty-seven, a former navy test pilot, and a Korean War veteran, when he became the second American (after John Glenn) to orbit the earth. On the eve of his flight, Scott's father, Marion, a chemist, wrote him this letter.

M. Scott Carpenter
PO Box 95 PALMER LAKE,
COLORADO

Dear Son,

Just a few words on the eve of your great adventure for which you have trained yourself and anticipated for so long—to let you know that we all share it with you, vicariously.

As I think I remarked to you at the outset of the space program, you are privileged to share in a pioneering project on a grand scale—in fact the grandest scale yet known to man. And I venture to predict that after all the huzzas have been uttered and the public acclaim is but a memory, you will derive the greatest satisfaction from the serene knowledge that you have discovered new truths. You can say to yourself: this I saw, this I experienced, this I know to be the truth. This experience is a precious thing; it is known to all researchers, in whatever field of endeavour, who have ventured into the unknown and have discovered new truths.

You are probably aware that I am not a particularly religious person, at least in the sense of embracing any of the numerous formal doctrines. Yet I cannot conceive of a man endowed with intellect, perceiving the ordered universe about him, the glory of the mountain top, the plumage of a tropical bird, the intricate complexity of a protein molecule, the utter and unchanging perfection of a salt crystal, who can deny the existence of some higher power. Whether he chooses to call it God or Mohammed or Buddha or Torquoise Woman or the Law of Probability matters little. I find myself in my writings frequently calling upon Mother Nature to explain things and citing Her as responsible for the order of the universe. She is a very satisfactory divinity for me. And so I shall call upon Her to watch over you and guard you and, if she so desires, share with you some of Her secrets which She is usually so ready to share with those who have high purpose.

With all my love,
Dad

1962: JULY 23
LEONARD GILBERG TO LAURIE PRITCHETT

A store owner in Albany, Georgia, Leonard Gilberg wrote to his town's police chief during the period of civil rights protests that took place in the summer of 1962. Laurie Pritchett was Albany's police chief.

Dear Chief Pritchett:

In order to inform you as to the situation business-wise for myself and other merchants with whom I have spoken, I am sure you will find the following to be true.

At least 90 to 95% of all the negro business I have enjoyed in past years has been lacking for the last 7 months due to an obvious boycott on the part of the negroes and threats and coercion toward other negroes not in sympathy with the movement to keep them from shopping downtown in Albany.

Now to top all this off, their constant harassment, sit-ins, demonstrations, marching, etc. are keeping all people both white and negro from Albany. Many customers have told me direct that they would not come to Albany from out of town due to fear of demonstrations in Albany and local people have said that they ask their wives and children to stay out of town for the same reason.

Our business is at present suffering an approximate 50% decrease due to lack of customer traffic in Albany and it is an intolerable situation. This fear of mob violence and demonstration has made our situation a dire one. Any aid you can give us in the matter will be greatly appreciated and our thanks to you for the wonderful manner in which you have handled these past events.

Very truly yours,

GILBERG'S

Leonard Gilberg

1962: OCTOBER 22
JOHN KENNEDY TO NIKITA KHRUSHCHEV

In April of 1961, Cuban exiles backed by the U.S. government attempted, unsuccessfully, to invade Cuba at the Bay of Pigs. Eighteen months after this foreign-policy fiasco, JFK received conclusive proof—in the form of aerial spy photographs—that the Soviet Union was nearing completion of nuclear missile sites in Cuba. On October 22, the president instituted a naval quarantine against Soviet ships en route to Cuba and demanded that offensive weapons systems be removed from the island. Beginning with this letter, a week of tense diplomatic exchanges ensued. In the end, the United States secretly agreed to lessen its own threat to the Soviet Union by removing fifteen Jupiter rockets that had recently become operational in Turkey. On October 28, Soviet premier Nikita Khrushchev (1894–1971) agreed to dismantle the bases, and the Cuban Missile Crisis, which had brought the world to the brink of nuclear war, came to an end.

October 22, 1962

His Excellency

Nikita S. Khrushchev

Chairman of the Council of Ministers

   of the Union of Soviet Socialist Republics

Moscow

Sir:

A copy of the statement I am making tonight concerning developments in Cuba and the reaction of my Government thereto has been handed to your Ambassador in Washington. In view of the gravity of the developments to which I refer, I want you to know immediately and accurately the position of my Government in this matter.

In our discussions and exchanges on Berlin and other international questions, the one thing that has most concerned me has been the possibility that your Government would not correctly understand the will and determination of the United States in any given situation, since I have not assumed that you or any other sane man would, in this nuclear age, deliberately plunge the world into war which it is crystal clear no country could win and which could only result in catastrophic consequences to the whole world, including the aggressor.

At our meeting in Vienna and subsequently, I expressed our readiness and desire to find, through peaceful negotiation, a solution to any and all problems that divide us. At the same time, I made clear that in view of the objectives of the ideology to which you adhere, the United States could not tolerate any action on your part which in a major way disturbed the existing over-all balance of power in the world. I stated that an attempt to force abandonment of our responsibilities and commitments in Berlin would constitute such an action and that the United States would resist with all the power at its command.

It was in order to avoid any incorrect assessment of the part of your Government with respect to Cuba that I publicly stated that if certain developments in Cuba took place, the United States would do whatever must be done to protect its own security and that of its allies.

Moreover, the Congress adopted a resolution expressing its support of this declared policy. Despite this, the rapid development of long-range missile bases and other offensive weapons systems in Cuba has proceeded. I must tell you that the United States is determined that this threat to the security of this hemisphere be removed. At the same time, I wish to point out that the action we are taking is the minimum necessary to remove the threat to the security of the nations of this hemisphere. The fact of this minimum response should not be taken as a basis, however, for any misjudgment on your part.

I hope that your Government will refrain from any action which would widen or deepen this already grave crisis and that we can agree to resume the path of peaceful negotiation.

Sincerely,
John F. Kennedy

1963: APRIL 16
MARTIN LUTHER KING, JR., TO ALABAMA CLERGYMEN

Martin Luther King, Jr., (1929–1968) was in solitary confinement, serving a sentence in a Birmingham, Alabama, jail for taking part in civil rights demonstrations, when he wrote this letter. Scrawled in the margins of a newspaper and on scraps of paper, it was ostensibly an answer to eight prominent Alabama clergymen who had urged King to cease his program of nonviolent resistance. In reality the "Letter from Birmingham Jail" would become a kind of canon for the civil rights movement.

Public Safety Commissioner Theophilus Eugene "Bull" Connor was notorious for having set attack dogs and police hoses on Birmingham protestors. He was running for mayor against Albert Boutwell, a moderate by comparison. James Meredith was the first black American to graduate from the University of Mississippi. Ross Barnett was governor of Mississippi. George Wallace was governor of Alabama.

My dear Fellow Clergymen,

While confined here in the Birmingham city jail, I came across your recent statement calling our present activities "unwise and untimely." Seldom, if ever, do I pause to answer criticism of my work and ideas. If I sought to answer all of the criticisms that cross my desk, my secretaries would be engaged in little else in the course of the day, and I would have no time for constructive work. But since I feel that you are men of genuine good will and your criticisms are sincerely set forth, I would like to answer your statement in what I hope will be patient and reasonable terms.

I think I should give the reason for my being in Birmingham, since you have been influenced by the argument of "outsiders coming in." I have the honor of serving as president of the Southern Christian Leadership Conference, an organization operating in every southern state, with headquarters in Atlanta, Georgia. We have some eighty-five affiliate organizations all across the South—one being the Alabama Christian Movement for Human Rights. Whenever necessary and possible we share staff, educational and financial resources with our affiliates. Several months ago our local affiliate here in Birmingham invited us to be on call to engage in a nonviolent direct-action program if such were deemed necessary. We readily consented and when the hour came we lived up to our promises. So I am here, along with several members of my staff, because we were invited here. I am here because I have basic organizational ties here.

Beyond this, I am in Birmingham because injustice is here. Just as the eighth century prophets left their little villages and carried their "thus saith the Lord" far beyond the boundaries of their hometowns; and just as the Apostle Paul left his little village of Tarsus and carried the gospel of Jesus Christ to practically every hamlet and city of the Graeco-Roman world, I too am compelled to carry the gospel of freedom beyond my particular hometown. Like Paul, I must constantly respond to the Macedonian call for aid.

Moreover, I am cognizant of the interrelatedness of all communities and states. I cannot sit idly by in Atlanta and not be concerned about what happens in Birmingham. Injustice anywhere is a threat to justice everywhere. We are caught in an inescapable network of mutuality, tied in a single garment of destiny. Whatever affects one directly affects all indirectly. Never again can we afford to live with the narrow, provincial "outside agitator" idea. Anyone who lives in the United States can never be considered an outsider anywhere in this country.

You deplore the demonstrations that are presently taking place in Birmingham. But I am sorry that your statement did not express a similar concern for the conditions that brought the demonstrations into being. I am sure that each of you would want to go beyond the superficial social analyst who looks merely at effects, and does not grapple with underlying causes. I would not hesitate to say that it is unfortunate that so-called demonstrations are taking place in Birmingham at this time, but I would say in more emphatic terms that it is even more unfortunate that the white power structure of this city left the Negro community with no other alternative.

In any nonviolent campaign there are four basic steps: (1) collection of the facts to determine whether injustices are alive, (2) negotiation, (3) self-purification, and (4) direct action. We have gone through all of these steps in Birmingham. There can be no gainsaying of the fact that racial injustice engulfs this community.

Birmingham is probably the most thoroughly segregated city in the United States. Its ugly record of police brutality is known in every section of this country. Its injust treatment of Negroes in the courts is a notorious reality. There have been more unsolved bombings of Negro homes and churches in Birmingham than any city in this nation. These are the hard, brutal and unbelievable facts. On the basis of these conditions Negro leaders sought to negotiate with the city fathers. But the political leaders consistently refused to engage in good faith negotiation.

Then came the opportunity last September to talk with some of the leaders of the economic community. In these negotiating sessions certain promises were made by the merchants—such as the promise to remove the humiliating racial signs from the stores. On the basis of these promises Rev. Shuttlesworth and the leaders of the Alabama Christian Movement for Human Rights agreed to call a moratorium on any type of demonstrations. As the weeks and months unfolded we realized that we were the victims of a broken promise. The signs remained. Like so many experiences of the past we were confronted with blasted hopes, and the dark shadow of a deep disappointment settled upon us.

So we had no alternative except that of preparing for direct action, whereby we would present our very bodies as a means of laying our case before the conscience of the local and national community. We were not unmindful of the difficulties involved. So we decided to go through a process of self-purification. We started having workshops on nonviolence and repeatedly asked ourselves the questions, "Are you able to accept blows without retaliating?" "Are you able to endure the ordeals of jail?" We decided to set our direct-action program around the Easter season, realizing that with the exception of Christmas, this was the largest shopping period of the year. Knowing that a strong economic withdrawal program would be the by-product of direct action, we felt that this was the best time to bring pressure on the merchants for the needed changes. Then it occurred to us that the March election was ahead and so we speedily decided to postpone action until after election day. When we discovered that Mr. Connor was in the run-off, we decided again to postpone action so that the demonstrations could not be used to cloud the issues. At this time we agreed to begin our nonviolent witness the day after the run-off.

This reveals that we did not move irresponsibly into direct action. We too wanted to see Mr. Connor defeated; so we went through postponement after postponement to aid in this community need. After this we felt that direct action could be delayed no longer.

You may well ask, "Why direct action? Why sit-ins, marches, etc.? Isn't negotiation a better path?" You are exactly right in your call for negotiation. Indeed, this is the purpose of direct action. Nonviolent direct action seeks to create such a crisis and establish such creative tension that a community that has constantly refused to negotiate is forced to confront the issue. It seeks so to dramatize the issue that it can no longer be ignored. I just referred to the creation of tension as a part of the work of the nonviolent resister. This may sound rather shocking. But I must confess that I am not afraid of the word tension. I have earnestly worked and preached against violent tension, but there is a type of constructive nonviolent tension that is necessary for growth. Just as Socrates felt that it was necessary to create a tension in the mind so that individuals could rise from the bondage of myths and half-truths to the unfettered realm of creative analysis and objective appraisal, we must see the need of having nonviolent gadflies to create the kind of tension in society that will help men to rise from the dark depths of prejudice and racism to the majestic heights of understanding and brotherhood. So the purpose of the direct action is to create a situation so crisis-packed that it will inevitably open the door to negotiation. We, therefore, concur with you in your call for negotiation. Too long has our beloved Southland been bogged down in the tragic attempt to live in monologue rather than dialogue.

One of the basic points in your statement is that our acts are untimely. Some have asked, "Why didn't you give the new administration time to act?" The only answer that I can give to this inquiry is that the new administration must be prodded about as much as the outgoing one before it acts. We will be sadly mistaken if we feel that the election of Mr. Boutwell will bring the millennium to Birmingham. While Mr. Boutwell is much more articulate and gentle than Mr. Connor, they are both segregationists, dedicated to the task of maintaining the status quo. The hope I see in Mr. Boutwell is that he will be reasonable enough to see the futility of massive resistance to desegregation. But he will not see this without pressure from the devotees of civil rights. My friends, I must say to you that we have not made a single gain in civil rights without determined legal and nonviolent pressure. History is the long and tragic story of the fact that privileged groups seldom give up their privileges voluntarily. Individuals may see the moral light and voluntarily give up their unjust posture; but as Reinhold Niebuhr has reminded us, groups are more immoral than individuals.

We know through painful experience that freedom is never voluntarily given by the oppressor; it must be demanded by the oppressed. Frankly, I have never yet engaged in a direct action movement that was "well-timed," according to the timetable of those who have not suffered unduly from the disease of segregation. For years now I have heard the word "Wait!" It rings in the ear of every Negro with a piercing familiarity. This "Wait" has almost always meant "Never." It has been a tranquilizing thalidomide, relieving the emotional stress for a moment, only to give birth to an ill-formed infant of frustration. We must come to see with the distinguished jurist of yesterday that "justice too long delayed is justice denied." We have waited for more than 340 years for our constitutional and God-given rights. The nations of Asia and Africa are moving with jetlike speed toward the goal of political independence, and we still creep at horse and buggy pace toward the gaining of a cup of coffee at a lunch counter. I guess it is easy for those who have never felt the stinging darts of segregation to say, "Wait." But when you have seen vicious mobs lynch your mothers and fathers at will and drown your sisters and brothers at whim; when you have seen hate-filled policemen curse, kick, brutalize and even kill your black brothers and sisters with impunity; when you see the vast majority of your twenty million Negro brothers smothering in an airtight cage of poverty in the midst of an affluent society; when you suddenly find your tongue twisted and your speech stammering as you seek to explain to your six-year-old daughter why she can't go to the public amusement park that has just been advertised on television, and see tears welling up in her little eyes when she is told that Funtown is closed to colored children, and see the depressing clouds of inferiority begin to form in her little mental sky, and see her begin to distort her little personality by unconsciously developing a bitterness toward white people; when you have to concoct an answer for a five-year-old son asking in agonizing pathos: "Daddy, why do white people treat colored people so mean?"; when you take a cross-country drive and find it necessary to sleep night after night in the uncomfortable corners of your automobile because no motel will accept you; when you are humiliated day in and day out by nagging signs reading "white" and "colored"; when your first name becomes "nigger" and your middle name becomes "boy" (however old you are) and your last name becomes "John," and when your wife and mother are never given the respected title "Mrs."; when you are harried by day and haunted by night by the fact that you are a Negro, living constantly at tiptoe stance never quite knowing what to expect next, and plagued with inner fears and outer resentments; when you are forever fighting a degenerating sense of "nobodiness"; then you will understand why we find it difficult to wait. There comes a time when the cup of endurance runs over, and men are no longer willing to be plunged into an abyss of injustice where they experience the blackness of corroding despair. I hope, sirs, you can understand our legitimate and unavoidable impatience.

You express a great deal of anxiety over our willingness to break laws. This is certainly a legitimate concern. Since we so diligently urge people to obey the Supreme Court's decision of 1954 outlawing segregation in the public schools, it is rather strange and paradoxical to find us consciously breaking laws. One may well ask, "How can you advocate breaking some laws and obeying others?" The answer is found in the fact that there are two types of laws: there are <u>just</u> and there are <u>unjust</u> laws. I would agree with Saint Augustine that "An unjust law is no law at all."

Now what is the difference between the two? How does one determine when a law is just or unjust? A just law is a man-made code that squares with the moral law or the law of God. An unjust law is a code that is out of harmony with the moral law. To put it in the terms of Saint Thomas Aquinas, an unjust law is a human law that is not rooted in eternal and natural law. Any law that uplifts human personality is just. Any law that degrades human personality is unjust. All segregation statutes are unjust because segregation distorts the soul and damages the personality. It gives the segregator a false sense of superiority, and the segregated a false sense of inferiority. To use the words of Martin Buber, the great Jewish philosopher, segregation substitutes an "I-it" relationship for the "I-thou" relationship, and ends up relegating persons to the status of things. So segregation is not only politically, economically and sociologically unsound, but it is morally wrong and sinful. Paul Tillich has said that sin is separation. Isn't segregation an existential expression of man's tragic separation, an expression of his awful estrangement, his terrible sinfulness? So I can urge men to disobey segregation ordinances because they are morally wrong.

Let us turn to a more concrete example of just and unjust laws. An unjust law is a code that a majority inflicts on a minority that is not binding on itself. This is difference made legal. On the other hand a just law is a code that a majority compels a minority to follow that it is willing to follow itself. This is sameness made legal.

Let me give another explanation. An unjust law is a code inflicted upon a minority which that minority had no part in enacting or creating because they did not have the unhampered right to vote. Who can say that the legislature of Alabama which set up the segregation laws was democratically elected? Throughout the state of Alabama all types of conniving methods are used to prevent Negroes from becoming registered voters and there are some counties without a single Negro registered to vote despite the fact that the Negro constitutes a majority of the population. Can any law set up in such a state be considered democratically structured?

These are just a few examples of unjust and just laws. There are some instances when a law is just on its face and unjust in its application. For instance, I was arrested Friday on a charge of parading without a permit. Now there is nothing wrong with an ordinance which requires a permit for a parade, but when the ordinance is used to preserve segregation and to deny citizens the First Amendment privilege of peaceful assembly and peaceful protest, then it becomes unjust.

I hope you can see the distinction I am trying to point out. In no sense do I advocate evading or defying the law as the rabid segregationist would do. This would lead to anarchy. One who breaks an unjust law must do it openly, lovingly (not hatefully as the white mothers did in New Orleans when they were seen on television screaming, "nigger, nigger, nigger"), and with a willingness to accept the penalty. I submit that an individual who breaks a law that conscience tells him is unjust, and willingly accepts the penalty by staying in jail to arouse the conscience of the community over its injustice, is in reality expressing the very highest respect for law.

Of course, there is nothing new about this kind of civil disobedience. It was seen sublimely in the refusal of Shadrach, Meshach and Abednego to obey the laws of Nebuchadnezzar because a higher moral law was involved. It was practiced superbly by the early Christians who were willing to face hungry lions and the excruciating pain of chopping blocks, before submitting to certain unjust laws of the Roman Empire. To a degree academic freedom is a reality today because Socrates practiced civil disobedience.

We can never forget that everything Hitler did in Germany was "legal" and everything the Hungarian freedom fighters did in Hungary was "illegal." It was "illegal" to aid and comfort a Jew in Hitler's Germany. But I am sure that if I had lived in Germany during that time I would have aided and comforted my Jewish brothers even though it was illegal. If I lived in a Communist country today where certain principles dear to the Christian faith are suppressed, I believe I would openly advocate disobeying these anti-religious laws. I must make two honest confessions to you, my Christian and Jewish brothers. First, I must confess that over the last few years I have been gravely disappointed with the white moderate. I have almost reached the regrettable conclusion that the Negro's great stumbling block in the stride toward freedom is not the White Citizen's Councilor or the Ku Klux Klanner, but the white moderate who is more devoted to "order" than to justice; who prefers a negative peace which is the absence of tension to a positive peace which is the presence of justice; who constantly says, "I agree with you in the goal you seek, but I can't agree with your methods of direct action"; who paternalistically feels that he can set the timetable for another man's freedom; who lives by the myth of time and who constantly advises the Negro to wait until a "more convenient season." Shallow understanding from people of good will is more frustrating than absolute misunderstanding from people of ill will. Lukewarm acceptance is much more bewildering than outright rejection.

I had hoped that the white moderate would understand that law and order exist for the purpose of establishing justice, and that when they fail to do this they become dangerously structured dams that block the flow of social progress. I had hoped that the white moderate would understand that the present tension of the South is merely a necessary phase of the transition from an obnoxious negative peace, where the Negro passively accepted his unjust plight, to a substance-filled positive peace, where all men will respect the dignity and worth of human personality. Actually, we who engage in nonviolent direct action are not the creators of tension. We merely bring to the surface the hidden tension that is already alive. We bring it out in the open where it can be seen and dealt with. Like a boil that can never be cured as long as it is covered up but must be opened with all its pus-flowing ugliness to the natural medicines of air and light, injustice must likewise be exposed, with all of the tension its exposing creates, to the light of human conscience and the air of national opinion before it can be cured.

In your statement you asserted that our actions, even though peaceful, must be condemned because they precipitate violence. But can this assertion be logically made? Isn't this like condemning the robbed man because his possession of money precipitated the evil act of robbery? Isn't this like condemning Socrates because his unswerving commitment to truth and his philosophical delvings precipitated the misguided popular mind to make him drink the hemlock? Isn't this like condemning Jesus because His unique God-consciousness and never-ceasing devotion to his will precipitated the evil act of crucifixion? We must come to see, as federal courts have consistently affirmed, that it is immoral to urge an individual to withdraw his efforts to gain his basic constitutional rights because the quest precipitates violence. Society must protect the robbed and punish the robber.

I had also hoped that the white moderate would reject the myth of time. I received a letter this morning from a white brother in Texas which said: "All Christians know that the colored people will receive equal rights eventually, but it is possible that you are in too great of a religious hurry. It has taken Christianity almost two thousand years to accomplish what it has. The teachings of Christ take time to come to earth." All that is said here grows out of a tragic misconception of time. It is the strangely irrational notion that there is something in the very flow of time that will inevitably cure all ills. Actually time is neutral. It can be used either destructively or constructively. I am coming to feel that the people of ill will have used time much more effectively than the people of good will. We will have to repent in this generation not merely for the vitriolic words and actions of the bad people, but for the appalling silence of the good people. We must come to see that human progress never rolls in on wheels of inevitability. It comes through the tireless efforts and persistent work of men willing to be co-workers with God, and without this hard work time itself becomes an ally of the forces of social stagnation. We must use time creatively, and forever realize that the time is always ripe to do right. Now is the time to make real the promise of democracy, and transform our pending national elegy into a creative psalm of brotherhood. Now is the time to lift our national policy from the quicksand of racial injustice to the solid rock of human dignity.

You spoke of our activity in Birmingham as extreme. At first I was rather disappointed that fellow clergymen would see my nonviolent efforts as those of the extremist. I started thinking about the fact that I stand in the middle of two op-posing forces in the Negro community. One is a force of complacency made up of Negroes who, as a result of long years of oppression, have been so completely drained of self-respect and a sense of "somebodiness" that they have adjusted to segregation, and, of a few Negroes in the middle class who, because of a degree of academic and economic security, and because at points they profit by segre-gation, have unconsciously become insensitive to the problems of the masses. The other force is one of bitterness and hatred, and comes perilously close to advocating violence. It is expressed in the various black nationalist groups that are springing up over the nation, the largest and best known being Elijah Muhammad's Muslim movement. This movement is nourished by the contem-porary frustration over the continued existence of racial discrimination. It is made up of people who have lost faith in America, who have absolutely repudi-ated Christianity, and who have concluded that the white man is an incurable "devil." I have tried to stand between these two forces, saying that we need not follow the "do-nothingism" of the complacent or the hatred and despair of the black nationalist. There is the more excellent way of love and nonviolent protest. I'm grateful to God that, through the Negro church, the dimension of nonviolence entered our struggle. If this philosophy had not emerged, I am con-vinced that by now many streets of the South would be flowing with floods of blood. And I am further convinced that if our white brothers dismiss us as "rabble-rousers" and "outside agitators" those of us who are working through the channels of nonviolent direct action and refuse to support our nonviolent ef-forts, millions of Negroes, out of frustration and despair, will seek solace and se-curity in black nationalist ideologies, a development that will lead inevitably to a frightening racial nightmare.

Oppressed people cannot remain oppressed forever. The urge for freedom will eventually come. This is what happened to the American Negro. Something within has reminded him of his birthright of freedom; something without has reminded him that he can gain it. Consciously and unconsciously, he has been swept in by what the Germans call the Zeitgeist, and with his black brothers of Africa, and his brown and yellow brothers of Asia, South America and the Caribbean, he is moving with a sense of cosmic urgency toward the promised land of racial justice. Recognizing this vital urge that has engulfed the Negro community, one should readily understand public demonstrations. The Negro has many pent-up resentments and latent frustrations. He has to get them out. So let him march sometime; let him have his prayer pilgrimages to the city hall; understand why he must have sit-ins and freedom rides. If his repressed emotions do not come out in these nonviolent ways, they will come out in ominous expressions of violence. This is not a threat; it is a fact of history. So I have not said to my people "get rid of your discontent." But I have tried to say that this normal and healthy discontent can be channelized through the creative outlet of nonviolent direct action. Now this approach is being dismissed as extremist. I must admit that I was initially disappointed in being so categorized.

But as I continued to think about the matter I gradually gained a bit of satisfaction from being considered an extremist. Was not Jesus an extremist in love—"Love your enemies, bless them that curse you, pray for them that despitefully use you." Was not Amos an extremist for justice—"Let justice roll down like waters and righteousness like a mighty stream." Was not Paul an extremist for the gospel of Jesus Christ—"I bear in my body the marks of the Lord Jesus." Was not Martin Luther an extremist—"Here I stand; I can do none other so help me God." Was not John Bunyan an extremist—"I will stay in jail to the end of my days before I make a butchery of my conscience." Was not Abraham Lincoln an extremist—"This nation cannot survive half slave and half free." Was not Thomas Jefferson an extremist—"We hold these truths to be self-evident, that all men are created equal." So the question is not whether we will be extremist but what kind of extremist will we be. Will we be extremists for hate or will we be extremists for love? Will we be extremists for the preservation of injustice—or will we be extremists for the cause of justice? In that dramatic scene on Calvary's hill, three men were crucified. We must not forget that all three were crucified for the same crime—the crime of extremism. Two were extremists for immorality, and thusly fell below their environment. The other, Jesus Christ, was an extremist for love, truth and goodness, and thereby rose above his environment. So, after all, maybe the South, the nation and the world are in dire need of creative extremists.

I had hoped that the white moderate would see this. Maybe I was too optimistic. Maybe I expected too much. I guess I should have realized that few members of a race that has oppressed another race can understand or appreciate the deep groans and passionate yearnings of those that have been oppressed and still fewer have the vision to see that injustice must be rooted out by strong, persistent and determined action. I am thankful, however, that some of our white brothers have grasped the meaning of this social revolution and committed themselves to it. They are still all too small in quantity, but they are big in quality. Some like Ralph McGill, Lillian Smith, Harry Golden and James Dabbs have written about our struggle in eloquent, prophetic and understanding terms. Others have marched with us down nameless streets of the South. They have languished in filthy roach-infested jails, suffering the abuse and brutality of angry policemen who see them as "dirty nigger-lovers." They, unlike so many of their moderate brothers and sisters, have recognized the urgency of the moment and sensed the need for powerful "action" antidotes to combat the disease of segregation.

Let me rush on to mention my other disappointment. I have been so greatly disappointed with the white church and its leadership. Of course, there are some notable exceptions. I am not unmindful of the fact that each of you has taken some significant stands on this issue. I commend you, Rev. Stallings, for your Christian stance on this past Sunday, in welcoming Negroes to your worship service on a nonsegregated basis. I commend the Catholic leaders of this state for integrating Springhill College several years ago.

But despite these notable exceptions I must honestly reiterate that I have been disappointed with the church. I do not say that as one of the negative critics who can always find something wrong with the church. I say it as a minister of the gospel, who loves the church; who was nurtured in its bosom; who has been sustained by its spiritual blessings and who will remain true to it as long as the cord of life shall lengthen.

I had the strange feeling when I was suddenly catapulted into the leadership of the bus protest in Montgomery several years ago that we would have the support of the white church. I felt that the white ministers, priests and rabbis of the South would be some of our strongest allies. Instead, some have been outright opponents, refusing to understand the freedom movement and misrepresenting its leaders; all too many others have been more cautious than courageous and have remained silent behind the anesthetizing security of the stained-glass windows.

In spite of my shattered dreams of the past, I came to Birmingham with the hope that the white religious leadership of this community would see the justice of our cause, and with deep moral concern, serve as the channel through which our just grievances would get to the power structure. I had hoped that each of you would understand. But again I have been disappointed. I have heard numerous religious leaders of the South call upon their worshippers to comply with a desegregation decision because it is the <u>law</u>, but I have longed to hear white ministers say, "Follow this decree because integration is morally <u>right</u> and the Negro is your brother." In the midst of blatant injustices inflicted upon the Negro, I have watched white churches stand on the sideline and merely mouth pious irrelevancies and sanctimonious trivialities. In the midst of a mighty struggle to rid our nation of racial and economic injustice, I have heard so many ministers say, "Those are social issues with which the gospel has no real concern," and I have watched so many churches commit themselves to a completely otherworldly religion which made a strange distinction between body and soul, the sacred and the secular.

So here we are moving toward the exit of the twentieth century with a religious community largely adjusted to the status quo, standing as a taillight behind other community agencies rather than a headlight leading men to higher levels of justice.

I have traveled the length and breadth of Alabama, Mississippi and all the other southern states. On sweltering summer days and crisp autumn mornings I have looked at her beautiful churches with their lofty spires pointing heavenward. I have beheld the impressive outlay of her massive religious education buildings. Over and over again I have found myself asking: "What kind of people worship here? Who is their God? Where were their voices when the lips of Governor Barnett dripped with words of interposition and nullification? Where were they when Governor Wallace gave the clarion call for defiance and hatred? Where were their voices of support when tired, bruised and weary Negro men and women decided to rise from the dark dungeons of complacency to the bright hills of creative protest?"

Yes, these questions are still in my mind. In deep disappointment, I have wept over the laxity of the church. But be assured that my tears have been tears of love. There can be no deep disappointment where there is not deep love. Yes, I love the church; I love her sacred walls. How could I do otherwise? I am in the rather unique position of being the son, the grandson and the great-grandson of preachers. Yes, I see the church as the body of Christ. But, oh! How we have blemished and scarred that body through social neglect and fear of being noncomformists.

There was a time when the church was very powerful. It was during that period when the early Christians rejoiced when they were deemed worthy to suffer for what they believed. In those days the church was not merely a thermometer that recorded the ideas and principles of popular opinion; it was a thermostat that transformed the mores of society. Wherever the early Christians entered a town the power structure got disturbed and immediately sought to convict them for being "disturbers of the peace" and "outside agitators." But they went on with the conviction that they were "a colony of heaven," and had to obey God rather than man. They were small in number but big in commitment. They were too God-intoxicated to be "astronomically intimidated." They brought an end to such ancient evils as infanticide and gladiatorial contest.

Things are different now. The contemporary church is often a weak, ineffectual voice with an uncertain sound. It is so often the arch-supporter of the status quo. Far from being disturbed by the presence of the church, the power structure of the average community is consoled by the church's silent and often vocal sanction of things as they are.

But the judgment of God is upon the church as never before. If the church of today does not recapture the sacrificial spirit of the early church, it will lose its authentic ring, forfeit the loyalty of millions, and be dismissed as an irrelevant social club with no meaning for the twentieth century. I am meeting young people every day whose disappointment with the church has risen to outright disgust.

Maybe again, I have been too optimistic. Is organized religion too inextricably bound to the status quo to save our nation and the world? Maybe I must turn my faith to the inner spiritual church, the church within the church, as the true ecclesia and the hope of the world. But again I am thankful to God that some noble souls from the ranks of organized religion have broken loose from the paralyzing chains of conformity and joined us as active partners in the struggle for freedom. They have left their secure congregations and walked the streets of Albany, Georgia, with us. They have gone through the highways of the South on tortuous rides for freedom. Yes, they have gone to jail with us. Some have been kicked out of their churches, and lost support of their bishops and fellow ministers. But they have gone with the faith that right defeated is stronger than evil triumphant. These men have been the leaven in the lump of the race. Their witness has been the spiritual salt that has preserved the true meaning of the gospel in these troubled times. They have carved a tunnel of hope through the dark mountain of disappointment.

I hope the church as a whole will meet the challenge of this decisive hour. But even if the church does not come to the aid of justice, I have no despair about the future. I have no fear about the outcome of our struggle in Birmingham, even if our motives are presently misunderstood. We will reach the goal of freedom in Birmingham and all over the nation, because the goal of America is freedom. Abused and scorned though we may be, our destiny is tied up with the destiny of America. Before the Pilgrims landed at Plymouth we were here. Before the pen of Jefferson etched across the pages of history the majestic words of the Declaration of Independence, we were here. For more than two centuries our foreparents labored in this country without wages; they made cotton king; and they built the homes of their masters in the midst of brutal injustice and shameful humiliation—and yet out of a bottomless vitality they continued to thrive and develop. If the inexpressible cruelties of slavery could not stop us, the opposition we now face will surely fail. We will win our freedom because the sacred heritage of our nation and the eternal will of God are embodied in our echoing demands.

I must close now. But before closing I am impelled to mention one other point in your statement that troubled me profoundly. You warmly commended the Birmingham police force for keeping "order" and "preventing violence." I don't believe you would have so warmly commended the police force if you had seen its angry violent dogs literally biting six unarmed, nonviolent Negroes. I don't believe you would so quickly commend the policemen if you would observe their ugly and inhuman treatment of Negroes here in the city jail; if you would watch them push and curse old Negro women and young Negro girls; if you would see them slap and kick old Negro men and young boys; if you will observe them, as they did on two occasions, refuse to give us food because we wanted to sing our grace together. I'm sorry that I can't join you in your praise for the police department.

It is true that they have been rather disciplined in their public handling of the demonstrators. In this sense they have been rather publicly "nonviolent." But for what purpose? To preserve the evil system of segregation. Over the last few years I have consistently preached that nonviolence demands that the means we use must be as pure as the ends we seek. So I have tried to make it clear that it is wrong to use immoral means to attain moral ends. But now I must affirm that it is just as wrong, or even more so, to use moral means to preserve immoral ends. Maybe Mr. Connor and his policemen have been rather publicly nonviolent, as Chief Pritchett was in Albany, Georgia, but they have used the moral means of nonviolence to maintain the immoral end of flagrant racial injustice. T. S. Eliot has said that there is no greater treason than to do the right deed for the wrong reason.

I wish you had commended the Negro sit-inners and demonstrators of Birmingham for their sublime courage, their willingness to suffer and their amazing discipline in the midst of the most inhuman provocation. One day the South will recognize its real heroes. They will be the James Merediths, courageously and with a majestic sense of purpose facing jeering and hostile mobs and the agonizing loneliness that characterizes the life of the pioneer. They will be old, oppressed, battered Negro women, symbolized in a seventy-two-year-old woman of Montgomery, Alabama, who rose up with a sense of dignity and with her people decided not to ride the segregated buses, and responded to one who inquired about her tiredness with ungrammatical profundity: "My feet is tired, but my soul is rested." They will be the young high school and college students, young ministers of the gospel and a host of their elders courageously and nonviolently sitting-in at lunch counters and willingly going to jail for conscience's sake. One day the South will know that when these disinherited children of God sat down at lunch counters they were in reality standing up for the best in the American dream and the most sacred values in our Judeo-Christian heritage, and thusly, carrying our whole nation back to those great wells of democracy which were dug deep by the Founding Fathers in the formulation of the Constitution and the Declaration of Independence.

Never before have I written a letter this long (or should I say a book?). I'm afraid that it is much too long to take your precious time. I can assure you that it would have been much shorter if I had been writing from a comfortable desk, but what else is there to do when you are alone for days in the dull monotony of a narrow jail cell other than write long letters, think strange thoughts, and pray long prayers?

If I have said anything in this letter that is an overstatement of the truth and is indicative of an unreasonable impatience, I beg you to forgive me. If I have said anything in this letter that is an understatement of the truth and is indicative of my having a patience that makes me patient with anything less than brotherhood, I beg God to forgive me.

I hope this letter finds you strong in the faith. I also hope that circumstances will soon make it possible for me to meet each of you, not as an integrationist or a civil rights leader, but as a fellow clergyman and a Christian brother. Let us all hope that the dark clouds of racial prejudice will soon pass away and the deep fog of misunderstanding will be lifted from our fear-drenched communities and in some not too distant tomorrow the radiant stars of love and brotherhood will shine over our great nation with all of their scintillating beauty.

Yours for the cause of Peace and Brotherhood,

Martin Luther King, Jr.

1963: NOVEMBER 26
JACQUELINE KENNEDY TO LYNDON JOHNSON

John Kennedy was assassinated in Dallas on November 22. There had never been any love lost between Kennedy and Johnson, bitter rivals during the campaign for the Democratic nomination, uneasy running mates afterward, and constitutionally as different as two politicians could be. But when it came to the grace notes in life, Jacqueline Kennedy (1929–1994) had a special gift, clearly evident in this letter written the day after her husband's funeral.

The recess was part of Caroline's kindergarten class, which would continue to meet in the White House until the Christmas break. Everett Dirksen and Mike Mansfield were U.S. senators.

November 26 Tuesday

Dear Mr. President:

Thank you for walking yesterday—behind Jack. You did not have to do that—I am sure many people forbid you to take such a risk—but you did it anyway.

Thank you for your letters to my children. What those letters will mean to them later—you can imagine. The touching thing is, they have always loved you so much, they were most moved to have a letter from you now.

And most of all Mr. President, thank you for the way you have always treated me—the way you and Lady Bird have always been to me—before, when Jack was alive, and now as President.

I think the relationship of the Presidential and Vice Presidential families could be a rather strained one. From the history I have been reading ever since I came to the White House, I gather it often was in the past.

But you were Jack's right arm—and I always thought the greatest act of a gentleman that I had seen on this earth—was how you—the Majority Leader when he came to the Senate as just another little freshman who looked up to you and took orders from you, could then serve as Vice President to a man who had served under you and been taught by you.

But more than that we were friends, all four of us. All you did for me as a friend and the happy times we had. I always thought way before the nomination that Lady Bird should be First Lady—but I don't need to tell you here what I think of her qualities—her extraordinary grace of character—her willingness to assume every burden—She assumed so many for me and I love her very much—And I love your two daughters—Lynda Bird most because I know her the best—and we first met when neither of us could get a seat to hear President Eisenhower's State of the Union message and someone found us a place on one of the steps on the aisle where we sat together. If we had known then what our relationship would be now.

It was so strange—last night I was wandering through this house—

There in the Treaty Room is your chandelier, and I had had it framed—the paper we all signed—you—Senator Dirksen and Mike Mansfield—underneath

I had written "The day the Vice President brought the East Room chandelier back from the Capitol."

Then in the library I showed Bobby the Lincoln Record Book you gave—

You see all you gave—and now you are called upon to give so much more.

Your office—you are the first President to sit in it as it looks today. Jack always wanted a red rug—and I had curtains designed for it that I thought were as dignified as they should be for a President's office—

Late last night a moving man asked me if I wanted Jack's ship pictures left on the wall for you (They were clearing the office to make room for you)—I said no because I remembered all the fun Jack had those first days hanging pictures of things he loved, setting out his collection of whales teeth etc.

But of course they are there only waiting for you to ask for them if the walls look too bare. I thought you would want to put things from Texas in it—I pictured some gleaming longhorns—I hope you put them somewhere—

It mustn't be very much help to you your first day in office—to hear children on the lawn at recess. It is just one more example of your kindness that you let them stay—I promise—they will soon be gone.

Thank you Mr. President
Respectfully
Jackie

1963: NOVEMBER 26
PAT LAMB TO JOYCE HOHLWEIN

From her temporary home in Dar es Salaam, Pat Lamb (see letter page 415) expressed to her old friend the feelings shared and suffered by many Americans.

Dar es Salaam
November 26, 1963

Dearest Joyce,

What is there to say? I cannot remember ever having grieved so continuously, so deeply, and having felt so bereft and afraid of the future at the loss of anyone as I do now, four days after this appalling and still unbelievable crime against America, against humanity, against us all.

The memorial High Requiem Mass in the cathedral here yesterday afternoon was a shattering experience. I had only begun to hold my shaking sobs and tears inside my weak body, and the Mass, which I know so well, completely unnerved me. President Nyerere was sobbing unashamedly, every woman was in tears, the cathedral was packed with every American, every diplomat, the entire cabinet and well- (or ill- ?) wishers. His loss is inestimable. I cannot see how it could happen at all. If we could do this terrible black thing, and follow it up with the violence of the next day, where is it all to lead?

Where will Johnson, either in strength or in weakness, as time will show, lead us? I have awful and grave fears for my country. You cannot imagine the impact this terrible sad thing has had on the English. We (you know how I am schizophrenic about my alliances) are deeply afraid about the future, not because, as I said, of the loss of Kennedy itself, but because of the forces of evil which caused that loss, and which may be unleashed in its train.

This beautiful intelligent brave young man, struck down in the middle of the most brilliant of careers life can offer, his lovely and devoted wife, young children—I cannot bear to think of her, though I constantly do so, in her moment of grief-stricken revelation that he was dead. There is one picture of her in the paper which arrived today clutching Bobby Kennedy by the hand, her face wiped clear of every expression but that of frozen horror, watching the coffin being taken out of that Dallas hospital where that life, which could have been the making of so much good for us all, slipped so quickly away. The blood which spatters her skirt is the blood of the dead body of all our highest hopes. I feel shame, grief, even guilt. I hate Texas, and Texans, I loathe myself even, for having at times given way in minor matters to just that sort of impulsiveness and violence which is so characteristic of America, mindless, physical, inarticulate, hating this careful, aristocratic, philosophic, patient approach to problems, but hatred is what killed him (and who knows what else?), and if anything, his death must be kept before us of his generation as the symbol of the steadfastness and courage before whatever fate may next deal us.

I went to the Soviet Embassy as usual to teach. The entire staff of the embassy was waiting for me by the reception desk. I stopped as I came in the door, wondering for a second why they were all there. Then the Ambassador, dull little Mr. Timoshenko, came forward to hug me, I burst anew into tears, the whole lot of them crowded round in one hugging mass, all of us weeping and patting each other in impotent sorrow.

I am too shocked and sad to go on. You know the rest. There is no news. We sail in eight weeks. You should have Laura's ring by now, which was taken to the States by a friend and he was to have mailed it from there last week.

> Love, and love—
> we must stand together,
> Pat

1963: DECEMBER 19
ALBERT SCHWEITZER TO ROSE KENNEDY

For a month after Kennedy's assassination, between twenty thousand and forty thousand condolence letters arrived at the White House every day. An efficiency expert was hired but resigned in futility. It took three thousand volunteers to answer the letters, and on one day alone, nine hundred thousand acknowledgments were sent out. This letter, from the renowned missionary and physician Albert Schweitzer (1875–1965), was addressed to the late president's mother.

The Moscow Agreement, signed in 1963, was the first nuclear test ban treaty, prohibiting testing in the atmosphere, in outer space, and underwater.

Mrs. Joseph P. Kennedy
200 Park Avenue
Suite 3021
New York, N.Y., U.S.A.

Dear Mrs. Kennedy:

It touched me deeply that you want for members of your family, books autographed by me. I received the books today and send them back to you on this same day.

I want to tell you about the role which your son, President Kennedy, played in my life. Einstein, the great scientist and I were great friends since we were young. When the atomic bombs commenced operating, we at once pronounced ourselves against it.

Einstein died, desperate because he protested against these horrible weapons without any success. I went on fighting. I waited year after year, if not a great political personality would sincerely occupy himself with this terrible danger for mankind.

In course of time, I became conscious that it was President Kennedy. This was a great consolation to me.

When the Moscow Treaty was published, I saw a ray of light again in the darkness. I felt prompted to congratulate your son and my congratulations touched him. I was sure that the two big powers could cooperate for freedom.

And now it happened that your son, who could have been the saviour of the world, fell a prey to a fanatic. I do not know who could have his clearsightedness, his tenacity and his authority in order to continue his great political and humanitarian work.

At present, we walk in the darkness again. Where are we going? Your son was one of the great personalities of history in the world. Millions of us mourn with you.

Yours deeply devoted,
Albert Schweitzer

Docteur Albert Schweitzer
Lambaréné, Gabon,
West Equatorial Africa
19.12.1963

1964: FEBRUARY 28

A TAXPAYER TO THE INTERNAL REVENUE SERVICE

The Sixteenth Amendment instituted a federal income tax in 1913. This letter could have been—and in many different forms has been—written at any point since then.

February 28, 1964

Dear Sir—

I am 84 and very Cranky-Fussy—

The Federal Income Tax Blanks get more complicated and hart to understand each year. I was sure I was not figuring correctly my Tax Report for those <u>over 75</u> so I went down to your office—Room 1102—& secured help from young man in Help to Taxpayers office. I was very fussy & cranky after walking & Panting for 30 minutes but he was very patient with me & laughed me out of being mad. I was ashamed of myself. I asked for help in figuring on income & credits for those over 75. He made out my report & saved me $80.00.

Thank you & this fine young employee.

Old Man

P.S. These Federal Tax reports get worse & worse each year. I can't ½ see Can't ½ figure Can ½ read instructions Can ½ write but my cussing ability is still 100%. Ha! Thank you. I am a former precinct, City, County & State Chairman of Dem. party.

1964: APRIL 9

WILLIAM REDFIELD TO ROBERT MILLS

William Redfield (1927–), who would be known to movie audiences for his roles in Fantastic Voyage, A New Leaf, *and* One Flew Over the Cuckoo's Nest, *played the part of Guildenstern in the 1964 production of* Hamlet *directed by Sir John Gielgud and starring Richard Burton. The show ran for four months in New York at the Lunt-Fontanne Theatre and for six weeks on the road, for a total of 185 performances, all sold out. The legendary actor Edwin Booth had done only 100 performances of* Hamlet, *John Barrymore 101.*

Robert Mills was a literary agent. David Belasco was an American playwright and producer who died in 1931. Hume Cronyn would win a Tony award for his portrayal of Polonius. Katharine Cornell, Ruth Gordon (see letter page 103), and Peggy Cass were actresses. Edmund Kean and William Macready were seventeenth-century actors. Nancy Berg was a model. Sam Spiegel was a major film producer. Donald Madden and George Grizzard were contemporary actors. Clement Fowler played Rosencrantz.

9 April—Thursday—
The Opening

Today is the day and tonight the night. I decided to go to the theatre this afternoon and familiarize myself with the colors. This may sound strange, but the fact is that each theatre is different, and the smallest discrepancy can throw the actor for a loop. To have "surprises" on opening night is like being accidentally shot by the starting gun. It's a discrepancy, all right, but makes it harder to win the race. As far as I am concerned, a pox on surprises.

I arrived at four p.m. Moments later, I realized that I had given the cab driver a ten-dollar bill and received thirty-five cents in change. I might as well have hired a limousine. Before passing through the stage door, I decided to get a container of coffee. As I emerged from the little diner, a rotund and red-faced man grasped me by my free hand and complimented me on my face. "You've got one of the best faces in this business, you know that? Terrific eyes. What are you doing these days?" I told him that I was in the play next door and he brightened up considerably. "With Dick Burton? Terrific guy. What a face he's got!" The man had not released my hand and I could feel the bottom of the bag which held my coffee growing damp. "Listen, pal," the man said, "I've fallen on hard times, you know, and I could use some help. I used to be the best juggler in Barnum's circus but there's not much call for that these days. I'm your biggest fan, you know that."

I gave the man a dollar because I began to feel superstitious about my misfortunes. "Give my best to Dick!" he requested, and I assured him that I would.

I entered the theatre and drank my appallingly cold coffee. As I did so, I noticed four or five police who were padding about the backstage area like so many second-story men. A police captain asked me who I was. I told him I was one of the actors. "Watch your step around here," he said gravely. "Someone has planted a bomb." I left to get some more coffee. On my way back to the theatre, a panhandler stopped me and asked me for a quarter. I reached into my pocket and found only a half dollar. I gave it to him, figuring that God would pay me back with a good performance.

After finishing my coffee, I headed straight for the set, ignoring the policemen who hunted beneath the platform for Leon Trotsky's Revenge, and I jogged up and down the staircase a few times. I also shouted a few of my lines to the empty seats out front. Some of the policemen looked up at me as though they thought me mad. As I looked down at <u>them</u>, they seemed rather mad to <u>me</u>.

I left the stage and bid my <u>adieux</u> to the cops. Once I was in the street, I remembered that there was no club soda in my dressing room. Since I knew there would be many visitors, I went to the corner grocery and bought a carton. On the way back, another panhandler accosted me and asked for a dime for a cup of coffee. "Coffee?" I said. "You want a drink is what you want or my name isn't David Belasco." The beggar's eyes blinked twice and he shifted his feet. "That's right, Dave," he said. I gave him a half dollar.

Once I had deposited my mixers next to my booze, I left the theatre again and was immediately confronted by the <u>first</u> panhandler. "Look, buddy," I said, "you already cadged half a rock out of me and you can go to hell." He did not wait to hear all of this sentence, but crossed the street as soon as my tone became ominous. I pursued him, however, and gave him another half dollar. As he glanced at the coin and back to my face, I could tell he thought me eccentric. But I knew what I was doing. I was behaving masochistically in order to guarantee an appropriate aggression when the bell for the gladiators rang.

Just before getting into a taxi for home and a nap, I called a press agent I know named Phil Leshin who is too nice a man to be a press agent, even though he is a brilliant press agent. "Phil," I said, "I've given away almost fifteen dollars trying to buy a good performance. Cab driver, panhandlers, and repeaters. What do you think?"

He told me that it wasn't over. "When you go home, there'll be a beggar in front of your house. When you leave for the theatre again, the same beggar will get another half dollar out of you. When you arrive at the stage door, the same beggar who hit you twice will hit you again. Believe me, friend, it's not over. It won't be over until eleven o'clock."

"Phil," I said, "eleven o'clock always comes."

"And so does seven."

He had me there. I went home and lay down for half an hour. I couldn't sleep but I went through the motions. I left for the theatre at six. As I bade farewell to my wife, who was tactful enough to postpone donning her finery until I had left, my five-year-old son, Adam, asked me where I was going. "I am going downtown," I replied, "to kill some bears." The boy looked at me skeptically. "Not really," he said.

He had me, too. Apparently, everyone had me. I fully expected a troop of Leshin's Beggars to accost me while I tried to hail a taxi. They didn't, though. Sometimes there is God so quickly.

The performance went moderately well and was received in a sophisticated manner by an audience too overdressed to watch <u>You Can't Take It With You</u> in comfort. For the benefit of history, I can say only that Richard Burton was vocally strong and emotionally insistent; that Hume Cronyn pleased the crowd; that many of our performers did well; and that I myself was relaxed. Since "relaxed" is one of the most confusing words in the actor's lexicon, let me add that I may merely have been paralyzed. It is said that Katharine Cornell has been all but dragged on stage for an opening night, so terrified was she; that Ruth Gordon has announced for over twenty-five years that she would never again endure an opening night; that Edmund Kean, on the occasion of his "contest" with William MacCready, had to be forced onto the stage where he proceeded to "hammer MacCready into the ground until only his head showed"; and that to be relaxed on such an occasion is to be half dead. In any case, I decided to be pleased by my "relaxation."

Afterwards, there was a gigantic party at the Rainbow Room, which has but recently become "in." I had hired a limousine for my group and we appeared, dressed to the nines, to face the professional audience, which is a good deal more professional than it is an audience. Immediately upon our entrance, my wife was asked who had made her dress. She replied, "Anne Fogarty," which was a bald-faced lie. My wife was wearing a copy of Jacques Fath by Bloomingdale's, but Anne Fogarty is a personal friend and why not let the <u>Daily News</u> print a white lie along with its black ones?

The first familiar face I saw was that of Nancy Berg, who was on the left arm of Sam Spiegel. Miss Berg said to me, "I <u>saw</u> you, Billy," and flashed her expert model's smile. Mr. Spiegel looked through me as though I were a script clerk, and the two of them passed on to respective grandeurs. I ran into Lee and Paula Strasberg. Lee looked as though he were reluctantly attending a meeting of the League of Women Voters. Paula was warm and <u>hamish</u>, which is her specialty.

She said, "I love a good actor," and I decided to accept the remark as a compliment. "I was relaxed tonight, Paula," I said, and she agreed with me. I then told both of them that I was glad to see them there and was, in a way, surprised. "Oh," said Paula gently, "we would never miss a Hamlet." Now <u>there</u> is a lady in love. Lee then spoke to me of recent Hamlets, including Donald Madden and George Grizzard.

Peggy Cass quoted Ernest Martin to me: "No direction for this show. Everyone was left to strike out on his own. Hume Cronyn got a triple." Miss Cass then added, "But <u>you</u> were good. Cool and greasy. I hated you and I think that's the way it should be."

Bob Fosse came by and asked if I could sing as well as I used to. "Better," I said, fully aware that he had not enjoyed tonight's performance. Much dancing and much drinking followed, to celebrate Shakespeare's birth year. Around 1 a.m., rumors began to circulate about the reviews. All of them were good, said the spies, and some of them sensational. A well-known actor approached me and gripped one of my shoulders. "I've got to tell you something," he said. "When we got the reports down here from Toronto, I thought you'd close out of town. I never heard such black prophecies in my life. It turns out you're the hit of the year. <u>Hello, Dolly</u> in blank verse. What do you think of that?"

"There's nothing like a hit," I said.

"Shakespeare's got it, hasn't he?"

"He certainly has."

I downed another glass of champagne as fast as possible. Clem Fowler approached me and said, "Taubman says you were good, but he doesn't mention me." I shrugged and said, "That's because of my billing. No matter what you do in the future, Clem, try to get billed above the title."

<u>Hamlet</u> has opened. Long live <u>Hamlet</u>.

William

1964: JUNE 26
MICKEY MANTLE TO BILL MOBLEY

William Mobley was six months old when he was infected with polio. He was nine years old, and the veteran of a dozen operations on a badly damaged left leg, when he received this letter. The legendary Yankee centerfielder Mickey Mantle (1931–1995) was the hero of just about every American boy in 1964, and he happened to have the same doctor as Mobley. Awed by this letter, Mobley would go on to play baseball, letter in swimming, bowl on the state high-school championship team, and spend a decade as a member of the Professional Bowlers Association of America.

New York Yankees

BUSINESS AND TICKET OFFICES   CYPRESS 3-4300

YANKEE STADIUM. BRONX. N.Y. 10451   CYPRESS 3-6000

June 26, 1964

Bill Mobley
1108 Metropolitan
Leavenworth, Kans.

Dear Bill:

It has been brought to my attention that you haven't been feeling well and that you are in "temporary drydock". Naturally, I was sorry to hear of your recent surgery and sorry, too, that a 7-day road trip prevented me from writing you sooner.

When one of my teammates gets hurt, we encourage him with this message: "hang in there, Kid". This message has a simple meaning. It means: "don't give up".

Bill, we on the Yankees, are great admirers of those who put up a game fight and I am sure that courage and determination, such as yours, will help you over the rough spots and hasten your progress.

With best wishes for a speedy and complete recovery and the hope that "good health" will be your constant companion in the years ahead.

Your friend,
Mickey Mantle

1964: JULY

RUSS MANDOR TO HIS PARENTS

Eleven-year-old Russ, who would grow up to be a successful Manhattan dentist, voiced the inner panic of a generation of sleepaway campers when he wrote this double letter home to his parents.

Dear Mom and Dad

I go swimming twice a day. I did not start lessons yet. But I'm practicing. Sorry I did not write sooner but I've been busy. I miss everyone at home. Please come soon.

Love
Russ

Dear Mom and Dad

Please come and take me home. I know how it sounds. But I miss home to much. Please Ma take me home. Robin and everyone else won't lisson to me. So please Ma take me home now. Don't ask any questions. Just come.

1964: JULY
LES JOHNSON TO HIS FAMILY

The summer of 1964—"Freedom Summer"—would remain among the most memorable in the lives of hundreds of students participating in the efforts of the SNCC to register Mississippi blacks for the vote. Volunteer Les Johnson wrote home (only these excerpts remain from his originals) the same month that President Johnson signed the Civil Rights Act of 1964.

Canvassing is very trying, you walk a little dusty street, with incredibly broken down shacks. The people sitting on porches staring away into nowhere— The sweat running down your face! Little kids half-naked in raggy clothes <u>all</u> over the place—this is what you face with your little packet of "Freedom Forms."

We don't canvass except between 4 and 7 at night because most people are in the fields in the day.

I've spent 3 hours, talking and got only <u>2</u> forms signed, other times I've gotten 10 in a hour.

We've gotten almost 2000 registered now in Clarksdale.

Unfortunately, Freedom registration is terribly remote to these people. I almost feel guilty—like I'm playing for numbers only; for you walk up to a porch, knock on a door and enter into another world. A world made up, mainly, like Pop Art. The walls are inevitably covered with a funeral hall calendar, a portrait calendar of President Kennedy, old graduation pictures. Maybe a new cheap lamp from Fred's dollar store.

You meet an afraid, but sometimes eager, curious face—one which is used to—many times over 70 years worth—saying "Yes Sir" to everything a white man says—and not really listening. You see their pain, the incredible years of suffering etched in their worn faces; and then if you convince them to sign you leave. You walk down the deteriorating steps to the dirt, to the next house—the next world and start in on your Sales pitch again, leaving behind something which has broken you a little more. Poverty in the abstract does nothing to you. When you wake up to it every morning, and come down through the streets of it, and see the same old man playing the accordian on the ground, the same man selling peaches out of a basket too heavy for his twisted body, the same children, a day older,—a day closer to those men—after this everyday, poverty is a reality that is so outrageous you have to learn to be unshocked and become jaded for the moment—or else be unable to function.

Little hands grope everyday for a nickle—it's hard to say "no" to kids who's lives are already a Hell which White America refused to care about.

These children represent a tremendous amount of energy, a talent, and value—all of which the white world says—"let this energy pitch cotton, and clean up after me, and do work I don't want to do." That energy is finally coming to the surface in Harlem and Rochester and as Mr. Baldwin has said, "if we don't find a productive channel for that energy <u>we will be destroyed by that energy</u>."

I have not been to White church since I have been here; some of the students have and have been turned away (in a non-integrated group) and the next time were treated very rudely. I am not really interested in going.

1964: AUGUST 17
FRANCIS FOX TO BRIAN EPSTEIN

The Beatles arrived in America for the first time on February 7, 1964, and the screaming crowds of lovestruck teenagers at New York's Kennedy Airport left a grave impression on airport personnel around the country. The letter below was sent to Beatles manager Brian Epstein on the eve of a Los Angeles visit. Derek Taylor, Epstein's personal assistant and the group's press agent, made sure the directions were followed. No trouble ensued.

CITY OF LOS ANGELES

DEPARTMENT OF AIRPORTS

1 WORLD WAY

LOS ANGELES, CALIFORNIA 90009

TELEPHONE 646-5252

August 17, 1964

Mr. Brian Epstein
Manager, The Beatles
5/6 Argyll
London W1, England

Delivered to Mr. Derek Taylor
        Assistant Manager of the Beatles

Dear Mr. Epstein:

Due to the dangerous conditions which have been created at airports where the Beatles have landed, the Department of Airports has held conferences with the several agencies responsible for the safety of persons, property and aircraft. Included in these meetings have been representatives of the Los Angeles Police and Fire Departments, the Federal Aviation Agency, the sponsors of the Beatles' Los Angeles appearance, and Airport Security and Operations' personnel.

We therefore advise you, as manager of the Beatles, and as a person vitally concerned with their physical welfare, as well as the safety of the Beatles' youthful fans, of the following conditions and recommendations:

(1) The Los Angeles Police Department cannot guarantee the safety of the Beatles should thousands of youngsters be urged by Beatle publicists to greet them at the airport. Only those officers who can be spared from essential duties throughout this vast city may be made available.

(2) The airport cannot permit a public airport reception here. Children have been crushed and injured at other airports when over-excited at the sight of the Beatles.

Therefore, should you elect to arrive at Los Angeles International Airport, the aircraft, be it a chartered or scheduled airline, will be directed to a restricted area to which there is no public access.

(3) We recommend that you use a charter aircraft to its best advantage for the safety of all concerned. In this area as well as in most other cities, there are numerous airports in which you can land with destination unannounced.

It is entirely within your jurisdiction to keep both the time and place of arrival unannounced in order to avoid the dangerous congregation of many thousands of children.

You might also want to consider the possibility that unsafe ground conditions brought on by uncontrolled and emotional crowds can force closure of the airport and the diversion of your aircraft.

We sincerely hope you will follow our recommendation. If you have any questions please contact this office. It is a simple procedure to arrive without fanfare. I'm quite certain fellow airport operators join with us in urging such a policy on your part.

                        Very truly yours,
                        Francis T. Fox, General Manager

1964

DONNA TO JOHN LENNON AND GEORGE HARRISON

In their wake, the "Fab Four" left, among countless others, this ever hopeful, if deeply deluded, fan.

Dear John,

Please Forward this letter to GEORGE.

I think you are WONDERFUL too.

DEAREST Darling BEATLE GEORGE

I was very disappointed when you came to the U.S.A. and didn't come to see me. You don't know what you missed. I'm really a beautiful doll. I am 5'3" tall and slender and very good looking. I would make some Beatle a very lovely wife. Since I consider you the prettiest one, I'm giving you first choice. If you decide that you will be my lucky husband, then I will know that not only are you pretty, but also very intelligent.

Every night before I go to sleep, I say, "Goodnight, Georgie. I love you. Yeah, yeah, yeah!

So think it over my love and give me your answer. If you are stupid enough to decline my offer, forward this letter to Ringo and Paul. Forget about John, he's married, you know.

I think you are the most.

All my love,
Your Donna

1964: AUGUST 25

LADY BIRD JOHNSON TO LYNDON JOHNSON

The day after the opening of the Democratic convention in Atlantic City, despite an overwhelming majority in his favor, LBJ hesitated, telling his closest advisers that he would not run. In tapes recently released by the LBJ Library, the president tells his press secretary, George Reedy: "I have a desire to unite the people, and the South is against me, and the North is against me, and the Negroes are against me, and the press doesn't really have an affection for me." It was this letter, from his wife, Lady Bird (1912–), that seemed to change his mind.

"Time" referred to the magazine, which had just published an article critical of Lady Bird.

Beloved—

You are as brave a man as Harry Truman—or FDR—or Lincoln. You can go on to find some peace, some achievement amidst all the pain. You have been strong, patient, determined beyond any words of mine to express.

I honor you for it. So does most of the country.

To step out now would be wrong for your country, and I can see nothing but a lonely waste land for your future. Your friends would be frozen in embarassed silence and your enemies jeering.

I am not afraid of Time or lies or losing money or defeat.

In the final analysis I can't carry any of the burdens you talked of—so I know it's only <u>your</u> choice. But I know you are as brave as any of the thirty-five.

I love you always

Bird

1964: NOVEMBER 20
THE FBI (ANONYMOUSLY) TO MARTIN LUTHER KING, JR.

Coretta Scott King opened the package containing this letter as well as a tape recording of her husband apparently engaging in sexual activity with a mistress. At the FBI, J. Edgar Hoover had recently been complaining that the agency hadn't been "taking the aggressive" with King; indeed, the letter below was written by FBI Assistant Director William Sullivan. Ten years later, Sullivan would tell congressional investigators looking into King's assassination that the intention had been to embarrass King and force him to resign from the Southern Christian Leadership Conference. King and his aides saw the incident more darkly, believing that the letter was meant to drive him to suicide.

KING,

In view of your low grade . . . I will not dignify your name with either a Mr. or a Reverend or a Dr. And, your last name calls to mind only the type of King such as King Henry the VIII. . . .

King, look into your heart. You know you are a complete fraud and a great liability to all of us Negroes. White people in this country have enough frauds of their own but I am sure they don't have one at this time that is anywhere near your equal. You are no clergyman and you know it. I repeat you are a colossal fraud and an evil, vicious one at that. You could not believe in God. . . . Clearly you don't believe in any personal moral principles.

King, like all frauds your end is approaching. You could have been our greatest leader. You, even at an early age have turned out to be not a leader but a dissolute, abnormal moral imbecile. We will have to depend on our older leaders like Wilkins a man of character and thank God we have others like him. But you are done. Your "honorary" degrees, your Nobel Prize (what a grim farce) and other awards will not save you. King, I repeat, you are done.

No person can overcome facts, not even a fraud like yourself. . . . I repeat—no person can argue successfully against facts. You are finished. . . . And some of them to pretend to be ministers of the Gospel. Satan could not do more. What incredible evilness. . . . King you are done.

The American public, the church organizations that have been helping—Protestant, Catholic and Jews will know you for what you are—an evil, abnormal beast. So will others who have backed you. You are done.

King, there is only one thing for you to do. You have just 34 days in which to do (this exact number has been selected for a specific reason, it has definite practical significant). You are done. There is but one way out for you. You better take it before your filthy, abnormal fraudulent self is bared to the nation.

1965

DUSTY TO A FRIEND

_____

Dusty was a marine sergeant serving in Vietnam. We were unable to learn anything more about him.

Dear Marilyn,

Before I start this letter, I want you to promise to forget it, as soon as you've read it—but I've got to talk to <u>someone</u>. Maybe, if I write about it, I'll be able to understand it a little more.

I know that I shouldn't be "unloading" my problem on you, because God knows, you don't have an answer for me; I guess nobody in this whole wide world does.

I'll be true to my nature and be very blunt, and to the point.

Yesterday I shot and killed a little 8- or 9-year-old girl, with the sweetest, most innocent little face, and the nastiest grenade in her hand, that you ever saw.

Myself and six others were walking along, when she ran out to throw that grenade at us. Of course there is always the old argument that it was us or her, but <u>what</u> in hell right did I have to kill a little child? All I can do is ask God to forgive me—I can't forgive myself.

This damned war seems so senseless at times; I can kill a man, and it doesn't bother me any more, but to kill a sweet little baby, who hasn't even learned right from wrong yet! <u>No</u> man has that right, or duty, or anything else you want to call it.

I'll be leaving here before too long, but to the last day of my life, I'll never be able to justify that. I really wonder what kind of man, or should I say animal, I've become. I know God will forgive me, but <u>I</u> have to live with myself.

I guess this isn't the kind of letter that you'd expect from a tough, hard Marine sergeant—but even we have feelings yet. Please, don't misunderstand: Right now I'm bitter, hurt, and so damned twisted up inside that I don't know what to think any more. Just bear with me, and one of these days I'll be back to myself, at least I sure hope so.

One of the things that I've always believed in was children. I love all kids. But how can I ever say that again?

I guess I've said enough for now. Thanks for "listening."

For now,
Dusty

1965: APRIL 25
TOM WOLFE TO <u>NEW YORK MAGAZINE</u>

On April 11, New York Magazine *ran a profile of* The New Yorker's *already legendary editor, William Shawn. Tom Wolfe (1931–) was the author of the article, a caustic portrait whose title ("Tiny Mummies!") conveyed both his stylistic exuberance and his irreverent viewpoint. Wolfe would soon become famous for "the New Journalism," a technique that embraced subjectivity, and eventually for such bestselling books as* The Right Stuff *and* The Bonfire of the Vanities, *in which he would continue to study status and lance the mighty. The Shawn article, one of his first, was greeted by an extraordinarily hostile array of letters to the editor. This was Wolfe's gleeful response to those responses.*

To the editor:

A lot of people are going to read the letters and wires by Richard H. Rovere, J. D. Salinger, Muriel Spark, E. B. White and Ved Mehta, five <u>New Yorker</u> writers, and compare their concepts and specific wording and say something about—you know?—funny coincidence or something like that. But that is unfair. These messages actually add up to a real <u>tribute</u> to one of <u>The New Yorker</u>'s great accomplishments of the last 13 years: an atmosphere of Total Orgthink for many writers of disparate backgrounds and temperaments. First again! But that is just an obiter dictum. What I really wish to commend these letters for is their character, in toto, as a cultural document for our times. They are evidence, I think, of another important achievement of The New Yorker. Namely, this wealthy, powerful magazine has become a Culture-totem for bourgeois culturati everywhere. Its followers—marvelous!—react just like those of any other totem group when somebody suggests that their holy buffalo knuckle may not be holy after all. They scream like weenies over a wood fire.

Best regards,
Tom Wolfe.

1965: OCTOBER

MAE BERTHA CARTER TO REPRESENTATIVES
OF THE AMERICAN FRIENDS SERVICE COMMITTEE

Mae and Matthew Carter were sharecroppers in Sunflower County, Mississippi. Their five oldest children had all attended "negro schools," which were scheduled around the dictates of the cotton season. But when state officials offered the Carters a "Freedom of Choice" form, they enrolled their eight younger children in an all-white school in Drew, Mississippi. The Carters drew jeers and worse from blacks and whites, but they were supported by the American Friends Service Committee, a Quaker group that investigated reports of intimidation and reprisals against black families. The excerpt below is from one of Mae Carter's regular updates to the AFSC. Miss Turner worked for the AFSC.

It is raining here right now. I am so tired from picking cotton. I guess I need some rest. They don't seem to smell Pearl at school anymore. What worry me so much is here on the farm the other children have to miss out of school to pick cotton. Children of eight year and younger. Their school bus be empty. Nobody doing anything about it. I go to mass meeting and the bossman found out and he was shocked. He still want slavery on the farm, because that where all the slavery is.

I am thinking about you all. How the Lord have sent you all into our home and I just want to write you. The superintendent call all the kids in to see what was happening to them. My kids are smart. They did it well. Gloria told about the bus driver saying to go on to the back after Stanley start to sit in front. My kids riding up front now. One day Pearl cried when I gave her lunch money. "Mother don't make me eat there." She told me how the kids treat her, how she left her food. I wrote the teacher. She took it to the principal. I wrote: "Dear teacher: Pearl found it hard to eat because the kids come up and put their fist in her face. Thank you."

The principal told Pearl to tell her mother, don't write no letter and send it out there. So yesterday, the superintendent ask why they wasn't eating. Pearl told him. I hope he do something about it. Deborah's teacher told her to eat and stayed there until she eat. So you see it some good people.

Oh, yes, I am glad to know Miss Marie Turner is white. It make me know some day we will all be free. Not all white is mean. We have white friend. I wish she could come to see us. But this is Mississippi, down here is the lion's den. That why we got to stand up for freedom. Nobody got anything to do with who comes to your house. I think it going to be better at the school. At least I hope so.

1965: NOVEMBER 17
KENNETH BAGBY TO HIS PARENTS

Sp-4 Kenneth W. Bagby sent this letter home to his parents in Winchester, Virginia, after the battle of the Ia Drang Valley, one of the fiercest of the entire war.

Plei-Ku, Vietnam
Nov. 17, 1965

Dear Folks,

I met a boy on the ship coming over to Vietnam. He was a good guy from the State of Missouri. He was my friend. We lived in the same tent together, went into An-Khe together, and spent most of our free time together. I got to know this boy well, and he was my best friend. His name was Dan Davis.

On Monday morning, the 15th of November, he died in my arms of two bullet wounds in the chest. He said, "Ken, I can't breathe." There was nothing I could do.

To the right of me another friend, whose last name was Balango, died of a wound in the throat. Up front Sergeant Brown, my squad leader, was hit in the chest and leg. To my left Sp-4 A. Learn was hit in the ankle.

We were crossing a field and were pinned down by automatic weapons fire from the enemy. We were pinned down for about 45 minutes before the rest of the platoon could get to us, and save the rest of us.

So went the biggest and worst battle that any American force has had in Vietnam. We outdone the Marines and Airborne by a long shot. Estimated V.C. killed, 2,000. Our casualties, I cannot give the information out. The battle took place on the Cambodian border.

In another line of attack my platoon leader Lieutenant Marm was shot in the neck right beside me, about ten feet to my right. Me and Sp-4 Ahewan took him back through the lines to the aid station.

Another situation, me, Daily, and Sergeant Riley captured two V.C. and were bringing them back through the lines when we were pinned down again, as one of them spotted a buddy and tried to signal him. I was going to kill both of them but Sergeant Riley stopped me.

Our battalion, the 1st BN 7th Cav., is completely inactive due to the killed and wounded of its men. My squad which consists of nine men, three came out, myself, Sergeant Scott, and a boy named Stidell.

Folks, by all rights I should be dead. The good Lord evidently saw fit to spare me, for some reason. I prayed, and prayed and prayed some more, the three days we were in battle.

The many men that died, I will never forget. The odor of blood and decayed bodies, I will never forget. I am all right. I will never be the same though, never, never, never. If I have to go into battle again, if I am not killed, I will come out insane. I cannot see and go through it again. I know I can't. The friends I lost and the many bodies I carried back to the helicopters to be lifted out, I will never forget.

The pen that I am writing this letter with belongs to Stash Arrows, the boy that rode up to Winchester with me, on my emergency leave. Pop, remember him. He was hit three times in the back. I don't know if he is still alive or not. I hope and pray he is. God, I hope so.

Folks, don't let these men die in vain. Appreciate what they are doing over here in Vietnam. They died protecting you all, and all the people in the United States. We just cannot have the enemy get to the folks back home. We have got to stop them here, before that happens. If it is God's will, we will do it. Tell the people back home to pray for us, as we need their prayers. . . .

We raised the American flag on the grounds. We were fighting on Tuesday, the 16th of November. It waved proudly for the Armed Forces and the people of America, as it did in so many battles won in World War II and Korea. I sat beside a tree and looked at it, and hoped I would never see the day it would be torn down and destroyed.

Folks, I am glad Eddy is not here and my son Kenny is not here. I hope they never have to see or experience the horrors of war. I will give my life to see that they don't. . . .

As always,
Your son,
Kenneth

1966: JUNE 6

JANIS JOPLIN TO HER PARENTS

At seventeen, Janis Joplin (1943–1970) left her home in Port Arthur, Texas, to hitchhike across the country. At twenty-three, she was given a bus ticket by her friends so that she could, in her own words, "go back home and straighten out, go back to college, even get married." When she headed west again soon afterward, she sent this letter of explanation to her parents. She was still with Big Brother and the Holding Company when she stunned the crowd at the 1967 Monterey Pop Festival with her uniquely haunting brand of blues. She would die of a heroin overdose just three years later. After her death, her most successful album, Pearl, *hit the top of the charts with her classic "Me and Bobby McGee."*

June 6

Mother & Dad,

With a great deal of trepidation, I bring the news. I'm in San Francisco. Now let me explain—when I got to Austin, I talked to Travis Rivers who gave me a spiel about my singing w/ a band out here. Seems Chet Helms, old friend, now is Mr. Big in S.F. Owns 3 big <u>working</u> Rock & roll bands w/ bizarre names like Captain Beefheart & his Magic Band, Big Brother & the Holding Co. etc. Well, Big Brother <u>et al</u> needs a vocalist. So I called Chet to talk to him about it. He encouraged me to come out—seems the whole city has gone rock & roll (and it has!) and assured me fame & fortune. I told him I was worried about being hung up out here w/ no way back & he agreed to furnish me w/ a bus ticket back home if I did just come & try. So I came.

Had a nice trip—camped out at night along the Rio Grande, collected rocks, etc. Now I'm staying w/ some old friends from Austin, Kit and Margo Teele—he works for Dun & Bradstreet, she for the telephone co.

I don't really know what's happening yet. Supposed to rehearse w/ the band this afternoon, after that I guess I'll know whether I want to stay & do that for awhile. Right now my position is ambivalent—I'm glad I came, nice to see the city, a few friends, but I'm not at all sold on the idea of becoming the poor man's Cher. So I guess we'll see.

I just want to tell you that I <u>am</u> trying to keep a level head about everything & not go overboard w/ enthusiasm. I'm sure you're both concerned my self-destructive streak has won out again but I'm really trying. I <u>do</u> plan on coming back to school—unless, I must admit, this turns into a good thing. Chet is a very important man out here now & he wanted <u>me</u>, specifically, to sing w/ this band.

I haven't tried yet so I can't say what I'm going to do—so far I'm safe, well-fed, and nothing has been stolen.

I suppose you could write me at this address although I don't know how long I'll be here. I expected a letter from Linda—maybe Peter—if they've arrived, please send them also. The address is c/o C.L Teele 3929 23rd St., S.F.

I'm awfully sorry to be such a disappointment to you. I understand your fears at my coming here & must admit I share them, but I really do think there's an awfully good chance I won't blow it this time. There's really nothing more I can say now. Guess I'll write more when I have more news, until then, address all criticism to the above address. And please believe that you can't possibly want for me to be a winner more than I do.

Love,
Janis

Will write a long happy & enthusiastic letter as soon as I stop feeling guilty. My love to Mike & Laura. Want to write Laura & tell her about the dances— FANTASTIC! and the clothes & people. Well, in due time.

I love you so, I'm sorry.

1966: JUNE 24
DAVID BROWN TO DARRYL ZANUCK

David Brown (1916–), producer of films including Jaws, The Verdict, Cocoon, *and* The Player, *was executive vice-president at Twentieth Century–Fox when he sent this telegram to the studio's legendary head, Darryl F. Zanuck (1902–1979). The movie* M*A*S*H *would be released in 1970, and Brown would prove entirely correct in predicting its profound antiestablishment appeal.*

Dick was Richard Zanuck, Darryl's son and Brown's partner.

Dear Darryl Dick has had submitted a very hilarious and unique book entitled "MASH". It may seem incredible that a Korean War background story would excite us but both Dick and I have now read the full galleys and we find this book better by far than "No Time Sergeants" and despite war background it is definitely not a war story. It has to do with the Mobile Army Surgical Hospital units (hence the title) in which the commanding officers were regular army medical corps but most of the surgeons working under them were civilian doctors drafted for just 18 months. Interested only in medicine some of these draftees resented Army discipline and the stresses and strains of fiendish overwork caused spectacular reactions when they were off duty. This is the story of three such surgeons at one of the MASH units. Bawdy and irreverent they became a legend—partly because of their excellent and fantastic surgical skill under unbelievable pressure but mostly because of their totally zany and mad off duty exploits. Their long suffering commanding officer would have shipped them back to the states in a flash but he had no replacements. In fact he worried most when they were quiet and well behaved for this indicated they were on the verge of breakdowns from overwork and the depressing odds against some of their patients recovery. In time the three surgeons acquire a fourth tentmate a big Negro neurosurgeon who had once been a profootball hero. In addition to building a football team around him and making a fortune betting on themselves the four doctors go through crazy and wonderful exploits that have never before been seen or read. The characters include a captain called "Trapper" who is a sensational tall thin young man carrying a complete bar in his parka another doctor named "Hawkeye" who is a complete character and a dentist who is known as "the painless Pole" and is sexually the phenomenon of the service. It is impossible to give you a full synopsis but none of the characters is stock and all of them have wives back home and are simply reacting to impossible stress. The result far from depressing or dreary is total entertainment and in todays groove because these are all anti establishment characters being themselves and defying authority while doing a terrific and courageous job. The story follows them through their tour of duty until they part in the states vowing to meet someday again although we know they probably wont. The story is loaded with sex but it is the sort of desperate comical sex obsession of isolated men thrust into unusual situations and freed from the usual restraints of society back home. Casting possibilities are great and one hilarious sequence follows another without appearing to be contrived. It is really the story of what comical and far out things happen when men are under impossible pressure. The war background is incidental and the need to show any surgery practically nil as the real story lies in the off duty happenings. Producer who brought us this is Ingo Preminger. Do not expect big best seller but do expect big and different film with some of the qualities of "Dirty Dozen" and enough visual action with war action. Read book on arrival as Dick is pushed for immediate action and may even now be too late but would like your expression and green light to see if we can make deal which will not be extraordinary financially and will naturally inform you of terms. However believe terms will be such that you would approve if we can get this project. Please telex. Affectionate regards David Brown

A leading conservative intellectual, Sidney Hook (1902–1989) had been sympathetic to the Communist movement in the early 1930s. But he came to abhor its totalitarianism and, in his teaching and writing, to reject it vigorously. When belated revelations emerged about Stalin's brutality, Hook seized the opportunity to write this letter. Corliss Lamont (1902–1995) was the considerably more left-leaning author of dozens of books of philosophy, socialism, and poetry.

July 8, 1966

Dear Corliss,

Voltaire once remarked that everyone has a natural right to be stupid, but that beyond a certain point it was a privilege that should not be abused. Your letter of June 30 replying to my attempt to reason with you has gone far beyond that point.

I did not suggest that you hang yourself. Nor did Max Eastman. He merely expressed the fear that you would do so after Khrushchev's revelations of the crimes of Stalin whom you had so zealously supported against the criticisms of John Dewey, Norman Thomas, and other democratic and socialist thinkers. Your thunderous silence as our charges against Stalin were being confirmed seemed to indicate a state of despair. That you should read this fear as a suggestion on our part is such an obvious projection of your own state of mind that it is tantamount to an acknowledgment. I predict that more revelations about Stalin's barbarities will come to light. The longer you live—and I hope you live a long time because personally I bear you no ill, objecting only to your defense of terror—the greater will be your punishment.

Nor is it true that I have defended "Johnson's war of aggression in Vietnam." I have defended the joint America–South Vietnam war of defense against the Communist North Vietnamese efforts and that of the Viet Cong agents to impose by force a Communist terror regime on the South. And although exercising the privileges of a citizen of a free society to criticize some features of American policy, I have been opposed to a withdrawal of American forces before UN supervised and guaranteed elections could be held. Otherwise this would lead to the massacre and/or enslavement of millions of South Vietnamese. Even the Buddhists are opposed to the Viet Cong!

But you cannot shed your guilt as an apologist for Stalin's terror—have you read the books the Soviets themselves have published on life under Stalin?—by making false charges about Johnson and pretending he is like Stalin. You wouldn't be alive if he were or enjoy the right under our Bill of Rights to defend the terror of the Viet Cong.

No, you don't believe that silly stuff yourself! In your heart of hearts you yourself know how deeply you committed yourself to Stalin's regime, and how lucky you are to live in a free culture that does not purge by concentration camp, frame-up trials, and death those that were proved wrong, not even those who like you betrayed its denials by pleading Stalin's cause. Bless your stars you live in the U.S. and not the U.S.S.R.! Whenever your name is mentioned, some one is sure to ask: what did he say when the Russians themselves exposed Stalin? I bet members of your own family don't mention Stalin's name for fear of embarrassing you!

1966: OCTOBER
TRUMAN CAPOTE TO 480 FRIENDS

Born in New Orleans and made famous in New York City, Truman Capote (1924–1984) was a fiction writer, journalist, frequent talk show guest, and society institution. He spent months honing the list of invitees for his famous party—technically given in honor of Washington Post *publisher Katharine Graham. The party was as renowned for those Capote invited (Frank Sinatra, Lauren Bacall, Rose Kennedy, Norman Mailer) as for those he snubbed (Carson McCullers, Kenneth Tynan, Walter Hoving) and was an event that crystallized New York society in the sixties.* Elizabeth Davis worked for Capote's agent.

In honor of Mrs. Katharine Graham
Mr. Truman Capote
REQUESTS THE PLEASURE OF YOUR COMPANY
AT A BLACK AND WHITE DANCE
ON MONDAY, THE TWENTY-EIGHTH OF NOVEMBER
AT TEN O'CLOCK
GRAND BALLROOM, THE PLAZA

R.S.V.P.   Dress
Miss Elizabeth Davis   Gentlemen: Black tie; Black mask
465 Park Avenue   Ladies: Black or White dress
New York   White mask; fan

1968: APRIL 22
MARK RUDD TO GRAYSON KIRK

The day after writing this letter, radical student leader Mark Rudd (1947–) began a protest at New York City's Columbia University in response to the school's plan to build a gym in Morningside Heights, a nearby area that was in need of low-cost housing. The protest—which also opposed university involvement in defense research—shut down the school and inspired students at other colleges throughout the country to stage similar demonstrations. Grayson Kirk (1903–1998) had been Columbia's president since 1953; he resigned in 1968, following the protests. The gym was not built.

IDA, the Institute for Defense Analyses, was a think tank with which Columbia and other universities were affiliated. CC was short for Contemporary Civilization.

> Our young people, in disturbing numbers, appear to reject all forms
> of authority, from whatever source derived, and they have taken refuge
> in a turbulent and inchoate nihilism whose sole objectives are
> destruction. I know of no time in our history when the gap between
> the generations has been wider or more potentially dangerous.
>
> —Grayson Kirk, April 12, 1968
> Charlottesville, Va.

Dear Grayson,

Your charge of nihilism is indeed ominous; for if it were true, our nihilism would bring the whole civilized world, from Columbia to Rockefeller Center, crashing down upon all our heads. Though it is not true, your charge does represent something: you call it the generation gap. I see it as a real conflict between those who run things now—you, Grayson Kirk—and those who feel oppressed by, and disgusted with, the society you rule—we, the young people.

You might want to know what is wrong with this society, since, after all, you live in a very tight self-created dream world. We can point to the war in Vietnam as an example of the unimaginable wars of aggression you are prepared to fight to maintain your control over your empire (now you've been beaten by the Vietnamese, so you call for a tactical retreat). We can point to your using us as cannon fodder to fight your war. We can point out your mansion window to the ghetto below you've helped to create through your racist University expansion policies, through your unfair labor practices, through your city government and your police. We can point to this University, your University, which trains us to be lawyers and engineers, and managers for your IBM, your Socony Mobil, your IDA, your Con Edison (or else to be scholars and teachers in more universities like this one). We can point, in short, to our own meaningless studies, our identity crises, and our revulsion with being cogs in your corporate machines as a product of and reaction to a basically sick society.

Your cry of "nihilism" represents your inability to understand our positive values. If you were ever to go into a freshman CC class you would see that we are seeking a rational basis for society. We do have a vision of the way things could be: how the tremendous resources of our economy could be used to eliminate want, how people in other countries could be free from your domination, how a university could produce knowledge for progress, not waste consumption and destruction (IDA), how men could be free to keep what they produce, to enjoy peaceful lives, to create. These are positive values, but since they mean the destruction of your order, you call them "nihilism." In the movement we are beginning to call this vision "socialism." It is a fine and honorable name, one which implies absolute opposition to your corporate capitalism and your government; it will soon be caught up by other young people who want to exert control over their own lives and their society.

You are quite right in feeling that the situation is "potentially dangerous." For if we win, we will take control of your world, your corporation, your University and attempt to mold a world in which we and other people can live as human beings. Your power is directly threatened, since we will have to destroy that power before we take over. We begin by fighting you about your support of the war in Vietnam and American imperialism—IDA and the School of International Affairs. We will fight you about your control of black people in Morningside Heights, Harlem, and the campus itself. And we will fight you about the type of mis-education you are trying to channel us through. We will have to destroy at times, even violently, in order to end your power and your system—but that is a far cry from nihilism.

Grayson, I doubt if you will understand any of this, since your fantasies have shut out the world as it really is from your thinking. Vice President Truman says the society is basically sound; you say the war in Vietnam was a well-intentioned accident. We, the young people, whom you so rightly fear, say that the society is sick and you and your capitalism are the sickness.

You call for order and respect for authority; we call for justice, freedom, and socialism.

There is only one thing left to say. It may sound nihilistic to you, since it is the opening shot in a war of liberation. I'll use the words of LeRoi Jones, whom I'm sure you don't like a whole lot: "Up against the wall, motherfucker, this is a stick-up."

Yours for freedom,

Mark

1968: APRIL 30
RENNIE DAVIS TO POTENTIAL RECRUITS

Rennie Davis (1941–) was in charge of the community organizing arm of the Students for a Democratic Society (SDS), a radical antiwar organization of the late sixties. Believing that the group could find natural allies among soldiers facing duty in Vietnam, Davis had helped establish a half-dozen coffeehouses near U.S. military bases; as this recruitment letter shows, he was hoping to set up more. The portion of the letter included here was later introduced as an exhibit at the House Committee on Un-American Activities hearings on "subversive involvement" pertaining to the August Democratic convention in Chicago. In 1969, Davis would be tried as one of the Chicago Seven.

The Wagner Act, in 1935, gave workers the right to organize as unions.

Dear——

This letter is to be shown only to those trustworthy individuals who have expressed interest in staffing one of the coffee-houses in army base parasite towns.

The coffee houses represent an attempt to work out a new way of reaching soldiers without haranguing them.

The coffee-houses come on as strictly commercial ventures—"psychedelic" painting on the windows, personality posters on the walls, flashing colored lights, folk singers, or a hi-fi playing with Judy Collins, The Mothers, etc., and outlandish prices for a cup of coffee—in which any explicit proselytizing by movement people who worked there would be inappropriate and even threatening to the coffee-houses' continued existence.

The coffee-houses are not designed to organize soldiers; they are designed to provide soldiers with a resource institution through which they can organize themselves, when they are ready. The qualities needed in coffee house staff are not those of a political activist; they are those of friend and soda-jerk. Warmth, friendliness, openness, and a willingness to listen are the qualities needed to make soldiers feel at home and unthreatened in the coffee house. The coffee houses give movement people an opportunity to make their rhetoric of fraternity real—but nothing more.

The first step in any political process is to try to find that fraction who are most ready to move. A coffee house in an Army town, amidst the bars, whorehouses, loansharks and sterile servicemen's clubs, works as a selective magnet to attract this crowd. Because of the cultural and class basis of our movement with which we are already familiar, those soldiers most likely to be turned off the army are also those most likely to be turned off the bars and whorehouses; most likely to welcome a coffee house. This ten percent of the army are those guys who, before the coffee houses, stayed in their barracks and left their weekend passes unused.

The coffee houses, therefore, by their very existence, offer soldiers an opportunity to draw support from each other simply by meeting each other in a friendly, non-military atmosphere, with open young people around who are sympathetic and willing to make an ear available to those who want to bend it. On the base, these soldiers are usually isolated from one another, lost among 30,000 other men, probably unaware of each other's existence. Just by learning that there are people of similar sensibilities, they begin to see problems as common which they had previously perceived as individual. They gain support for acts they have been contemplating; and, more important, begin to explore possibilities of common action.

This is all to say that we have undertaken a very limited, technical job that hasn't involved urging anyone to oppose the war in Vietnam. Soldiers don't have to be urged; they are the first group (for very obvious reasons) to oppose the war in their hearts. But expecting soldiers to take the enormous risks of doing something about it is unrealistic at this point; for us to ask soldiers to risk defection is, to put it kindly, arrogant.

This will be even more true, come June, when there will be a high percentage of college grads in basic training. These guys will not need to be proselytized to an anti-war position; we've been doing that for three years now and most likely, quite a bit has sunk in. What these soldiers will need, however, is a humane and familiar environment in which they can meet like minded guys and talk in a non-military atmosphere.

Let me sum up by quoting from the letter written by the originator of these coffee-houses, a former GI himself:

As movement people begin to distinguish between the unhappy conscript and the marine sgt who actually digs burning down huts with his zippo lighter, a sympathy will probably inform their attitude toward American soldiers in training. It may also become clear that the movement has long made strident and impossible demands on soldiers: Go to jail; Go into exile; Risk lifelong ostracism and unemployment; etc. Movement people may even begin to see GIs as a likely constituency. They're the same age, after all, speak the same language, like the same music. Soldiers have immediate problems that can be eased and, someday solved. They form the segment of our society that pays most heavily for the iron-heel foreign policy. . . . Finally, soldiers aren't powerless, and can change the situation if a significant fraction become articulate and willing to act on their anti-war outlook. . . . Expecting mass refusals to fight in Vietnam would be like thinking American workers could have forced through the Wagner Act in 1870. Only after soldiers have found it possible, on some level, to change their situation, might they think of pressing demands which now seem outlandish, such as the right to decline assignment to a given duty station (i.e., refuse to fight in Bolivia). The immediate changes they could fight for might include the removal of particularly sadistic NCOs from positions of authority; or doctors might demand a guaranteed 8 hours sleep for trainees at posts where meningitis is endemic . . .

We in the movement will not organize these things. But we can begin to provide a service institution for soldiers who are beginning to move on their own. Without the establishment and preservation of this institution, the movement may not be possible.

1968: AUGUST 16
ROBERT KASMIRE TO ED FRIENDLY

Rowan & Martin's Laugh-In, *an irreverent weekly comedy show, debuted in 1968, introducing audiences to such future stars as Goldie Hawn and Lily Tomlin. Along the way, it also made famous the expressions "Sock it to me" and "You bet your sweet bippy," as well as the admonition by various cameo players to "Look that* up in your *Funk and Wagnall's." As this letter to the show's producer makes clear, the NBC brass weren't always amused. Host Dan Rowan (1922–1987) later wrote to a friend: "We got around the F&W controversy to NBC's satisfaction by the simple expedient of having additional cameos taped following 'Look that* up in your *Funk and Wagnall's' saying 'That's a dictionary, you know.'"*
Robert Kasmire was vice-president for corporate information at NBC. Ed Friendly was one of the producers of *Laugh-In*.

NATIONAL BROADCASTING COMPANY, INC.

THIRTY ROCKEFELLER PLAZA, NEW YORK, NY

Robert D. Kasmire
Vice President
Corporate Information

Aug 16, 1968

Mr. Ed Friendly
George Schlatter–Ed Friendly Productions
4425 Lakeside Drive
Burbank, California 91505

Dear Ed:

I answer my mail in achronological order (look that up in your Funk and Wagnall), so this is in response to your letter of August 7.

I know my position isn't singular because when the inquisition convenes I'll be able to produce several people who agree with me. Whether it's a minority view, neither of us can say until we measure the universe we're dealing with.

Anyhow, assuming you're serious in asking me to clarify NBC's position in standing against your plan to break comedy out of references to Funk and Wagnall, I'll try to give you a serious reply.

One point of clarification is that the problem arises when the conjunction "and" drops between the names of the two gentlemen who authored the dictionary. As George Schlatter pointed out to Travie in one of the endless communiques that issues from 4425 Lakeside Drive, when you juxtapose the names of the authors, joined by "and," you get funkand wagnall, which, as George said, sounds funny. Right. It sounds funny. It sounds funny, I submit, because in actual pronunciation the funkand gets contracted to sound like funken, and at that point it comes very close in sound to a rather crude adjective, derived from the Anglo Saxon, relating to the act of coitus. I know that you and George, as students of our language, are also aware that frequently (in the better Eastern women's colleges for example) the word funken is selected by the shy and sensitive as a euphemism for the short, direct, Anglo Saxon expression, which I understand was used frequently in the Army and Navy during World War II to describe such elements as the weather, food, officers, the enemy, etc. The Australians, as a matter of fact, achieved some rather interesting and daring effects by placing the word between syllables of other words.

I can't escape the feeling that you realize this, else why would you have raised a question involving the aspiring Japanese politician Mr. Fukuda, whose name, if mispronounced, demonstrates the versatility of the adjective by changing it into a short imperative sentence.

What I am getting at is this: however innocent the intended use of the name Funk and Wagnall might be, I and others at NBC are convinced that the effect will be a double-entendre that is objectionable because of the vulgarity of the word involved. You can think of this as my personal hang-up if you wish, but I assure you that I am going to hang right here. I'm sorry you disagree, but since NBC has sole and ultimate responsibility for everything we broadcast, I believe I am taking the only position I can in this instance.

Finally, I am happy to advise you that there is no blanket prohibition against words beginning with the letters f u. There are prohibitions against some such words, but we will continue to determine these for all shows on a case-by-case basis.

I know you'll understand that I haven't yet been able to meet your request that I check off the words on the copied pages you sent me. I will get after this just as soon as possible, and I'll try to have the checked list back in your hands before "Laugh-In" begins its fourth season, and I'm certain that given the masterful touch of you and your colleagues with sharp, clean, incisive wit and humor we will all be around for that day.

With warmest regards,

Bob

1968: SEPTEMBER 20
VALERIE SOLANAS TO ANDY WARHOL

Artist, filmmaker, and provocateur Andy Warhol (1928?–1987) had already become the sovereign of Manhattan's downtown art scene when he met Valerie Solanas in the mid-sixties. Famous for attracting eccentrics to his tinfoil-lined studio, the Factory, he had initially tolerated Solanas, an aspiring playwright, feminist theoretician, and the founder and sole member of SCUM (the Society for Cutting Up Men). But on June 3, 1968, Solanas (1940–1988) shot and nearly killed Warhol. Three months later, she sent this letter to him. Years afterward, with characteristic esprit, Warhol would write: "Before I was shot, I always . . . suspected that I was watching TV instead of living life. . . . Right when I was being shot and ever since, I knew that I was watching television."

Maurice Girodias was Solanas's publisher at Olympia Press.

Valerie Solanas
F8 13608
Box 307
Beacon, N.Y. (12508)

Andy Warhol
1342 Lexington Avenue
New York, New York 10028

9-20-68

Dear Andy,

I'm writing this letter because I'm a compulsive communicator.

For the past few weeks I've been evaluating + reevaluating everything. My morale has gone way up; I no longer feel demoralized, + my attitude towards lots of things has changed. I no longer feel any hostility towards you or towards anyone else; I feel at peace with the world, + I feel, now that the Manifesto's been published + now that with all the publicity I have a chance to earn money without being dependent on men, that I'm in a much better position than I was to deal with you, Girodias + all the other vultures I encounter.

I intend to forget the past—harbor no grudges, regret no mistakes—+ begin completely anew. I also have a new attitude toward my contract situation; I made a terrible mistake signing it, but I don't intend to continue to be gotten by it; I intend to chalk it up to experience + begin anew.

I'm very happy you're alive + well, as, for all your barbarism, you're still the best person to make movies with, +, if you treat me fairly, I'd like to work with you.

Valerie

1969: FEBRUARY 5
HEINZ KOHUT TO HIS SON

Heinz Kohut (1913–1981) was one of the most prominent psychoanalytic theorists in America. In this letter to his eighteen-year-old son, Thomas, he expressed the traditional values—as well as the profound bewilderment and dismay—of a generation of American parents suffering through the sixties. Thomas would become a psychohistorian.

February 5, 1969

Dear Tom:

Yesterday's letter was written late at night when I was tired and under the direct impact of your phone call. Frankly, I have not been able to think of much else since then and have had a hard time concentrating on the work with my patients. Today we also received a communication from Oberlin College spelling out the position of the administration which, as you know, is: (1) Peaceful demonstrations and peaceful picketing are encouraged; (2) Coercive interference with the right of students to talk with armed forces representatives if they wish to do so will not be tolerated, and offenders will be expelled from the college.

I have no doubt that the college administration means what it says, and, much as it may hurt your feelings, I cannot see what else they could do. There is room for argument, of course, about the merits of the case, but the college could not survive if a group of students were permitted to take the law into their own hands and use force to make their view prevail. The point of view of the administration that the armed forces representatives simply give the students an opportunity to choose between the different services since they have to enter the service anyway might be a debatable one, but within the campus itself, it allows for a freedom of choice (i.e., students may stay away; may make propaganda about others' staying away, etc.) while coercive picketing which prevents others from entering, or sit-ins, or the like, do not allow a choice.

So much about the merits of the case which at any rate strikes me as a subtle and difficult disagreement between two sets of ethic. Beyond that, however, all that I wrote to you yesterday still stands. I am racking my brains to figure out why you have become so intolerant and so single-minded about this issue, why you have replaced thoughtfulness with absolute certainty that you are right, and that, therefore, everything goes, and why you contemplate an action that could destroy your future and all our hopes for you.

I don't know the answer. Have we failed in making clear to you what the world is really like? Always just persuading and just getting angry, but never really letting you feel the consequences? I don't think so—at any rate we could not have been otherwise, and children do learn the difference between the discipline at home and the harsh realities of life even without punitive attitudes from the side of their parents. I wondered, too, whether the thought of being a radical, an activist, etc., might not contribute at this time to your self-esteem, to defining yourself as an individual. This would be very understandable. I know how angry you get when waiters wonder about your age, and I still remember vividly my own feelings of uncertainty about myself during the analogous period of my own life. But one has to suffer through such transitional periods—they don't last forever. And hard as it seems: an honest suffering is better than a quick solution of being a revolutionary and activist. I don't mean that one should avoid a stand—but within reason. The enormous inflation of the issue by you (I cannot speak about the others whom I don't know) which might drive you to activities that could have disastrous consequences for you goes far beyond the understandable need to assert yourself against the liberal values of free speech and a democratic society ruled by laws and constitutional rights.

I would not tell you the full truth if I would hide from you how badly I feel personally. Today I reconciled my monthly account and a glance at my last check for your tuition told me that I am spending about two full months of hard work every year just in order to earn the money needed for your tuition. That I am mentioning this may sound cheap to you—but the thought adds to my feelings. It's not just the money—that is really only a symbol—but it does mean that we and you are in all this together. It's not only your hard work that's getting you through school, but also our contribution. Usually one does not think about that (and I hardly ever do, except with pleasure). But when I consider the possibility that you might risk throwing all this away in order to make one subtle point of ethics, I do get angry and upset.

For goodness sake, Gustl, don't do such a foolish thing! I wondered whether you might wish to talk things over with a psychoanalytic colleague of mine (Dr. Brian Bird in Cleveland, for example), but I don't urge you to do that at this time. If you, yourself want help with clarifying your motivations, however, let me know and I shall be glad to assist you in making an appointment with Dr. Bird. And, of course, you can arrange it on your own if you prefer.

What more can I say? Again: to hope that your angry outlook on the world which sees all authority as evil and mean will not prevail, but that you will work with increasing pleasure on learning about what goes on, deepen your understanding of the variety of experiences that life has to offer, so that you can be happy and satisfied. Mom and I don't have to tell you how much our own peace of mind and enjoyment of life will depend on that. It takes little to destroy—but that power is spurious. Please be constructive!

*   *   *

1969: FEBRUARY 16
JOSEPH VALACHI TO PETER MAAS

In September of 1963, Joseph Valachi (1903–1971) became the first member of the Mafia to testify that organized crime existed in the United States. Granted immunity for his testimony before a Senate subcommittee, Valachi introduced the country to the phrase the Cosa Nostra *("our thing") and to details of a fiercely violent, if fiercely loyal, way of life. America's fascination with the Mob was spurred to new heights by the publication, in 1968, of* The Valachi Papers, *written by Peter Maas (1929–) and initially suppressed by the FBI.*

Robert Kennedy had been attorney general when Valachi testified. Kennedy's successor, Nicholas Katzenbach, originally authorized the release of the manuscript. William Hundley was chief of the Justice Department's organized crime and racketeering division. James McShane was Chief U.S. Marshal. Marie was Valachi's close friend. The "old man" was Vito Genovese.

J.M.V.

Feb 16/69

Dear Peter;

I received your book and I thank you very much, I like what Mr Hundley and Bob Kennedy had to say. I am a Kennedy man and as you know if it were not from my experience in the underworld, knowing who was who, meaning that I knew the honesty of the Kennedys, I would have not done what I done, every man that I met in the Kennedy administration was 100% honest, the whole crew starting from the President down to you, not forgetting Mr. McShane. I am still a Kennedy man. If I have to fight the world and I were the only one I still be a Kennedy man. I talk like this because I was about the only man here and there that was a 100% for Bob Kennedy, when I came to N.Y.C. I was very encouraged, every one that I met was for Bob. I had Marie working hard for him, you can believe me. Peter, you have lots of courage only I knows how much courage you have. I wish you and your family the very best in life, you have a beautiful wife, and I call your family the beautiful people. I don't care what kind of life I lived, I have a lot of character, Dick the Agent will tell you, ask him as soon as I heard that the book was to be published I said to myself, it will kill the old man, sure money.

ATTY GENERAL Katzinback. BLESS HIM.

Joe

1969: MARCH 29

RON RIDENHOUR TO FEDERAL OFFICIALS

Ron Ridenhour (1946–1998) was a GI stationed in Vietnam when he heard about the events that came to be known as the My Lai Massacre. In all, 347 unarmed civilians had been shot on March 16, 1968, by soldiers under the command of Lieutenant William L. Calley (1943–). Calley would be convicted in 1971, sentenced to life imprisonment, then released in 1974 after a federal court overturned the verdict. It was this letter that spurred the investigation into the events at My Lai.

Medina was court-martialed and acquitted but would later admit that he had not been completely candid about the events. Ridenhour would go on to become a journalist.

Phoenix, Arizona
March 29, 1969

Gentlemen:

It was late in April, 1968 that I first heard of "Pinkville" and what allegedly happened there. I received that first report with some skepticism, but in the following months I was to hear similar stories from such a wide variety of people that it became impossible for me to disbelieve that something rather dark and bloody did indeed occur sometime in March, 1968 in a village called "Pinkville" in the Republic of Viet Nam.

The circumstances that led to my having access to the reports I'm about to relate need explanation. I was inducted in March, 1967 into the U.S. Army. After receiving various training I was assigned to the 70th Infantry Detachment (LRP), 11th Light Infantry Brigade at Schofield Barracks, Hawaii, in early October, 1967. That unit, the 70th Infantry Detachment (LRP), was disbanded a week before the 11th Brigade shipped out for Viet Nam on the 5th of December, 1967. All of the men from whom I later heard reports of the "Pinkville" incident were reassigned to "C" Company, 1st Battalion, 20th Infantry, 11th Light Infantry Brigade. I was reassigned to the aviation section of Headquarters Company 11th LIB. After we had been in Viet Nam for 3 to 4 months many of the men from the 70th Inf. Det. (LRP) began to transfer into the same unit, "E" Company, 51st Infantry (LRP).

In late April, 1968 I was awaiting orders for a transfer from HHC, 11th Brigade to Company "E," 51st Inf. (LRP), when I happened to run into Pfc "Butch" Gruver, whom I had known in Hawaii. Gruver told me he had been assigned to "C" Company 1st of the 20th until April 1st when he transferred to the unit that I was headed for. During the course of our conversation he told me the first of many reports I was to hear of "Pinkville."

"Charlie" Company 1/20 had been assigned to Task Force Barker in late February, 1968 to help conduct "search and destroy" operations on the Batangan Peninsula, Barker's area of operation. The task force was operating out of L. F. Dottie, located five or six miles north of Quang Nhai city on Viet Namese National Highway 1. Gruver said that Charlie Company had sustained casualties; primarily from mines and booby traps, almost everyday from the first day they arrived on the peninsula. One village area was particularly troublesome and seemed to be infested with booby traps and enemy soldiers. It was located about six miles northeast of Quang Nhai city at approximate coordinates B.S. 728795. It was a notorious area and the men of Task Force Barker had a special name for it: they called it "Pinkville." One morning in the latter part of March, Task Force Barker moved out from its firebase headed for "Pinkville." Its mission: destroy the trouble spot and all of its inhabitants.

When "Butch" told me this I didn't quite believe that what he was telling me was true, but he assured me that it was and went on to describe what had happened. The other two companies that made up the task force cordoned off the village so that "Charlie" Company could move through to destroy the structures and kill the inhabitants. Any villagers who ran from Charlie Company were stopped by the encircling companies. I asked "Butch" several times if all the people were killed. He said that he thought they were, men, women and children. He recalled seeing a small boy, about three or four years old, standing by the trail with a gunshot wound in one arm. The boy was clutching his wounded arm with his other hand, while blood trickled between his fingers. He was staring around himself in shock and disbelief at what he saw. "He just stood there with big eyes staring around like he didn't understand; he didn't believe what was happening. Then the captain's RTO (radio operator) put a burst of 16 (M-16 rifle) fire into him." It was so bad, Gruver said, that one of the men in his squad shot himself in the foot in order to be medivac-ed out of the area so that he would not have to participate in the slaughter. Although he had not seen it, Gruver had been told by people he considered trustworthy that one of the company's officers, 2nd Lieutenant Kally (this spelling may be incorrect) had rounded up several groups of villagers (each group consisting of a minimum of 20 persons of both sexes and all ages). According to the story, Kally then machine-gunned each group. Gruver estimated that the population of the village had been 300 to 400 people and that very few, if any, escaped.

After hearing this account I couldn't quite accept it. Somehow I just couldn't believe that not only had so many young American men participated in such an act of barbarism, but that their officers had ordered it. There were other men in the unit I was soon to be assigned to, "E" Company, 51st Infantry (LRP), who had been in Charlie Company at the time that Gruver alleged the incident at "Pinkville" had occurred. I became determined to ask them about "Pinkville" so that I might compare their accounts with Pfc Gruver's.

When I arrived at "Echo" Company, 51st Infantry (LRP) the first men I looked for were Pfc's Michael Terry and William Doherty. Both were veterans of "Charlie" Company, 1/20 and "Pinkville." Instead of contradicting "Butch" Gruver's story they corroborated it, adding some tasty tidbits of information of their own. Terry and Doherty had been in the same squad and their platoon was the third platoon of "C" Company to pass through the village. Most of the people they came to were already dead. Those that weren't were sought out and shot. The platoon left nothing alive, neither livestock nor people. Around noon the two soldiers' squads stopped to eat. "Billy and I started to get out our chow," Terry said, "but close to us was a bunch of Vietnamese in a heap, and some of them were moaning. Kally (2nd Lt. Kally) had been through before us and all of them had been shot, but many weren't dead. It was obvious that they weren't going to get any medical attention so Billy and I got up and went over to where they were. I guess we sort of finished them off." Terry went on to say that he and Doherty then returned to where their packs were and ate lunch. He estimated the size of the village to be 200 to 300 people. Doherty thought that the population of "Pinkville" had been 400 people.

If Terry, Doherty and Gruver could be believed, then not only had "Charlie" Company received orders to slaughter all the inhabitants of the village, but those orders had come from the commanding officer of Task Force Barker, or possibly even higher in the chain of command. Pfc Terry stated that when Captain Medina (Charlie Company's commanding officer Captain Ernest Medina) issued the order for the destruction of "Pinkville" he had been hesitant, as if it were something he didn't want to do but had to. Others I spoke to concurred with Terry on this.

It was June before I spoke to anyone who had something of significance to add to what I had already been told of the "Pinkville" incident. It was the end of June, 1968 when I ran into Sargent Larry La Croix at the USO in Chu Lai. La Croix had been in 2nd Lt. Kally's platoon on the day Task Force Barker swept through "Pinkville." What he told me verified the stories of the others, but he also had something new to add. He had been a witness to Kally's gunning down of at least three separate groups of villagers. "It was terrible. They were slaughtering the villagers like so many sheep." Kally's men were dragging people out of bunkers and hootches and putting them together in a group. The people in the group were men, women and children of all ages. As soon as he felt that the group was big enough, Kally ordered an M-60 (machine-gun) set up and the people killed. La Croix said that he bore witness to this procedure at least three times. The three groups were of different sizes, one of about twenty people, one of about thirty people, and one of about forty people. When the first group was put together Kally ordered Pfc Torres to man the machine-gun and open fire on the villagers that had been grouped together. This Torres did, but before everyone in the group was down he ceased fire and refused to fire again. After ordering Torres to recommence firing several times, Lieutenant Kally took over the M-60 and finished shooting the remaining villagers in that first group himself. Sargent La Croix told me that Kally didn't bother to order anyone to take the machine-gun when the other two groups of villagers were formed. He simply manned it himself and shot down all villagers in both groups.

This account of Sargent La Croix's confirmed the rumors that Gruver, Terry and Doherty had previously told me about Lieutenant Kally. It also convinced me that there was a very substantial amount of truth to the stories that all of these men had told. If I needed more convincing, I was to receive it.

It was in the middle of November, 1968 just a few weeks before I was to return to the United States for separation from the army that I talked to Pfc Michael Bernhardt. Bernhardt had served his entire year in Viet Nam in "Charlie" Company 1/20 and he too was about to go home. "Bernie" substantiated the tales told by the other men I had talked to in vivid, bloody detail and added this. "Bernie" had absolutely refused to take part in the massacre of the villagers of "Pinkville" that morning and he thought that it was rather strange that the officers of the company had not made an issue of it. But that evening "Medina (Captain Ernest Medina) came up to me ("Bernie") and told me not to do anything stupid like write my congressman" about what had happened that day. Bernhardt assured Captain Medina that he had no such thing in mind. He had nine months left in Viet Nam and felt that it was dangerous enough just fighting the acknowledged enemy.

Exactly what did, in fact, occur in the village of "Pinkville" in March, 1968 I do not know for certain, but I am convinced that it was something very black indeed. I remain irrevocably persuaded that if you and I do truly believe in the principles of justice and the equality of every man, however humble, before the law, that form the very backbone that this country is founded on, then we must press forward a widespread and public investigation of this matter with all our combined efforts. I think that it was Winston Churchill who once said "A country without a conscience is a country without a soul, and a country without a soul is a country that cannot survive." I feel that I must take some positive action on this matter. I hope that you will launch an investigation immediately and keep me informed of your progress. If you cannot, then I don't know what other course of action to take.

I have considered sending this to newspapers, magazines, and broadcasting companies, but I somehow feel that investigation and action by the Congress of the United States is the appropriate procedure, and as a conscientious citizen I have no desire to further besmirch the image of the American serviceman in the eyes of the world. I feel that this action, while probably it would promote attention, would not bring about the constructive actions that the direct actions of the Congress of the United States would.

Sincerely,
Ron Ridenhour

1969: APRIL
ANNE SEXTON TO HER DAUGHTER

Anne Sexton (1928–1974), one of the leading poets of the confessional mode and the winner of the 1967 Pulitzer prize for poetry, wrote often of her struggles as a wife, mother, and daughter beset by isolation and depression. Five years after writing this letter, she would kill herself.

Wed—2:45 p.m.

Dear Linda,

I am in the middle of a flight to St. Louis to give a reading. I was reading a <u>New Yorker</u> story that made me think of my mother and all alone in the seat I whispered to her 'I know Mother, I know.' (Found a pen!) And I thought of you—someday flying somewhere all alone and me dead perhaps and you wishing to speak to me.

And I want to speak back. (Linda, maybe it won't be flying, maybe it will be at your <u>own</u> kitchen table drinking tea some afternoon when you are 40. <u>Anytime.</u>)—I want to say back.

1st I love you.

2. You <u>never</u> let me down.

3. I know. I was there once. I <u>too</u>, was 40 and with a dead mother who I needed still. . . .

This is my message to the 40-year-old Linda. No matter what happens you were always my bobolink, my special Linda Gray. Life is not easy. It is awfully lonely. <u>I</u> know that. Now you too know it—wherever you are, Linda, talking to me. But I've had a good life—I wrote unhappy—but I lived to the hilt. You too, Linda—Live to the HILT! To the top. I love you, 40-year-old Linda, and I love what you do, what you find, what you are!—Be your own woman. Belong to those you love. Talk to my poems, and talk to your heart—I'm in both: if you need me. I lied, Linda. I did love my mother and she loved me. She never held me but I miss her, so that I have to deny I ever loved her—or she me! Silly Anne! So there!

XOXOXO
Mom

1969: APRIL 4
CESAR CHAVEZ TO E. L. BARR

Cesar Chavez (1927–1993) was a migrant worker who in 1962 began to organize California grape pickers to unionize and demand better treatment from their employers. Launching strikes, peaceful demonstrations, and nationwide boycotts of lettuce and grapes, he championed "La Causa," and later became president of the United Farm Workers. He wrote this letter to the head of the growers' league, which opposed unionization.

Good Friday 1969.

E. L. Barr, Jr., President
California Grape and Tree Fruit League
717 Market St.
San Francisco, California

Dear Mr. Barr:

I am sad to hear about your accusations in the press that our union movement and table grape boycott have been successful because we have used violence and terror tactics. If what you say is true, I have been a failure and should withdraw from the struggle; but you are left with the awesome moral responsibility, before God and man, to come forward with whatever information you have so that corrective action can begin at once. If for any reason you fail to come forth to substantiate your charges, then you must be held responsible for committing violence against us, albeit violence of the tongue. I am convinced that you as a human being did not mean what you said but rather acted hastily under pressure from the public relations firm that has been hired to try to counteract the tremendous moral force of our movement. How many times we ourselves have felt the need to lash out in anger and bitterness.

Today on Good Friday 1969 we remember the life and the sacrifice of Martin Luther King, Jr., who gave himself totally to the nonviolent struggle for peace and justice. In his "Letter from Birmingham Jail" Dr. King describes better than I could our hopes for the strike and boycott: "Injustice must be exposed, with all the tension its exposure creates, to the light of human conscience and the air of national opinion before it can be cured." For our part I admit that we have seized upon every tactic and strategy consistent with the morality of our cause to expose that injustice and thus to heighten the sensitivity of the American conscience so that farm workers will have without bloodshed their own union and the dignity of bargaining with their agribusiness employers. By lying about the nature of our movement, Mr. Barr, you are working against nonviolent social change. Unwittingly perhaps, you may unleash that other force which our union by discipline and deed, censure and education has sought to avoid, that panacean shortcut: that senseless violence which honors no color, class or neighborhood.

You must understand—I must make you understand—that our membership and the hopes and aspirations of the hundreds of thousands of the poor and dispossessed that have been raised on our account are, above all, human beings, no better and no worse than any other cross-section of human society; we are not saints because we are poor, but by the same measure neither are we immoral. We are men and women who have suffered and endured much, and not only because of our abject poverty but because we have been kept poor. The colors of our skins, the languages of our cultural and native origins, the lack of formal education, the exclusion from the democratic process, the numbers of our slain in recent wars—all these burdens generation after generation have sought to demoralize us, to break our human spirit. But God knows that we are not beasts of burden, agricultural implements or rented slaves; we are men. And mark this well, Mr. Barr, we are men locked in a death struggle against man's inhumanity to man in the industry that you represent. And this struggle itself gives meaning to our life and ennobles our dying.

As your industry has experienced, our strikers here in Delano and those who represent us throughout the world are well trained for this struggle. They have been under the gun, they have been kicked and beaten and herded by dogs, they have been cursed and ridiculed, they have been stripped and chained and jailed, they have been sprayed with the poisons used in the vineyards; but they have been taught not to lie down and die nor to flee in shame, but to resist with every ounce of human endurance and spirit. To resist not with retaliation in kind but to overcome with love and compassion, with ingenuity and creativity, with hard work and longer hours, with stamina and patient tenacity, with truth and public appeal, with friends and allies, with mobility and discipline, with politics and law, and with prayer and fasting. They were not trained in a month or even a year; after all, this new harvest season will mark our fourth full year of strike and even now we continue to plan and prepare for the years to come. Time accomplishes for the poor what money does for the rich.

This is not to pretend that we have everywhere been successful enough or that we have not made mistakes. And while we do not belittle or underestimate our adversaries—for they are the rich and the powerful and they possess the land—we are not afraid nor do we cringe from the confrontation. We welcome it! We have planned for it. We know that our cause is just, that history is a story of social revolution, and that the poor shall inherit the land.

Once again, I appeal to you as the representative of your industry and as a man. I ask you to recognize and bargain with our union before the economic pressure of the boycott and strike takes an irrevocable toll; but if not, I ask you to at least sit down with us to discuss the safeguards necessary to keep our historical struggle free of violence. I make this appeal because as one of the leaders of our nonviolent movement, I know and accept my responsibility for preventing, if possible, the destruction of human life and property. For these reasons and knowing of Gandhi's admonition that fasting is the last resort in place of the sword, during a most critical time in our movement last February 1968 I undertook a 25-day fast. I repeat to you the principle enunciated to the membership at the start of the fast: if to build our union required the deliberate taking of life, either the life of a grower or his child, or the life of a farm worker or his child, then I choose not to see the union built.

Mr. Barr, let me be painfully honest with you. You must understand these things. We advocate militant nonviolence as our means for social revolution and to achieve justice for our people, but we are not blind or deaf to the desperate and moody winds of human frustration, impatience and rage that blow among us. Gandhi himself admitted that if his only choice were cowardice or violence, he would choose violence. Men are not angels, and time and tide wait for no man. Precisely because of these powerful human emotions, we have tried to involve masses of people in their own struggle. Participation and self-determination remain the best experience of freedom, and free men instinctively prefer democratic change and even protect the rights guaranteed to seek it. Only the enslaved in despair have need of violent overthrow.

This letter does not express all that is in my heart, Mr. Barr. But if it says nothing else it says that we do not hate you or rejoice to see your industry destroyed; we hate the agribusiness system that seeks to keep us enslaved, and we shall overcome and change it not by retaliation or bloodshed but by a determined nonviolent struggle carried on by those masses of farm workers who intend to be free and human.

Sincerely yours,
Cesar E. Chavez

United Farm Workers Organizing Committee, A.F.L.–C.I.O.
Delano, California.

1969: JULY 8

EDMUND WHITE TO ANN AND ALFRED CORN

Edmund White (1940–), a leading gay writer and the author of the novels A Boy's Own Story *(1982) and* The Farewell Symphony *(1997), described the riot at New York City's Stonewall Inn to his close friends, the poet Alfred Corn (1943–) and his wife. Stonewall was one of the first major rallying points in the gay pride movement. Thirty years later, the Stonewall would be declared a national historic landmark.*

Mayor John Lindsay was running for reelection against Mario Procaccino.

Dear Ann and Alfred,

Well, the big news here is Gay Power. It's the most extraordinary thing. It all began two weeks ago on a Friday night. The cops raided the Stonewall, that mighty Bastille which you know has remained impregnable for three years, so brazen and so conspicuous that one could only surmise that the Mafia was paying off the pigs handsomely. Apparently, however, a new public official, Sergeant Smith, has taken over the Village, and he's a peculiarly diligent lawman. In any event, a mammoth paddy wagon, as big as a school bus, pulled up to the Wall and about ten cops raided the joint. The kids were all shooed into the street; soon other gay kids and straight spectators swelled the ranks to, I'd say, about a thousand people. Christopher Street was completely blocked off and the crowds swarmed from the Voice office down to the Civil War hospital.

As the Mafia owners were dragged out one by one and shoved into the wagon, the crowd would let out Bronx cheers and jeers and clapping. Someone shouted "Gay Power," others took up the cry—and then it dissolved into giggles. A few more prisoners—bartenders, hatcheck boys—a few more cheers, someone starts singing "We Shall Overcome"—and then they started camping on it. A drag queen is shoved into the wagon; she hits the cop over the head with her purse. The cop clubs her. Angry stirring in the crowd. The cops, used to the cringing and disorganization of the gay crowds, snort off. But the crowd doesn't disperse. Everyone is restless, angry, and high-spirited. No one has a slogan, no one even has an attitude, but something's brewing.

Some adorable butch hustler boy pulls up a <u>parking meter</u>, mind you, out of the pavement, and uses it as a battering ram (a few cops are still inside the Wall, locked in). The boys begin to pound at the heavy wooden double doors and windows; glass shatters all over the street. Cries of "Liberate the Bar." Bottles (from hostile straights?) rain down from the apartment windows. Cries of "We're the Pink Panthers." A mad Negro queen whirls like a dervish with a twisted piece of metal in her hand and breaks the remaining windows. The door begins to give. The cops turn a hose on the crowd (they're still within the Wall). But they can't aim it properly, and the crowd sticks. Finally the door is broken down and the kids, as though working to a prior plan, systematically dump refuse from waste cans into the Wall, squirting it with lighter fluid, and ignite it. Huge flashes of flame and billows of smoke.

Now the cops in the paddy wagon return, and two fire engines pull up. Clubs fly. The crowd retreats.

Saturday night, the pink panthers are back in full force. The cops form a flying wedge at the Greenwich Avenue end of Christopher and drive the kids down towards Sheridan Square. The panthers, however, run down Waverly, up Gay Street, and come out <u>behind</u> the cops, kicking in a chorus line, taunting, screaming. Dreary middle-class East Side queens stand around disapproving but fascinated, unable to go home, as though torn between their class loyalties, their desire to be respectable, and their longing for freedom. Sheridan Square is cordoned off by the cops. The United Cigar store closes, Riker's closes, the deli closes. No one can pass through the square; to walk up Seventh Avenue, you must detour all the way to Bleecker.

A mad left-wing group of straight kids called the Crazies is trying to organize the gay kids, pointing out that Lindsay is to blame (the Crazies want us to vote for Procaccino, or "Prosciutto," as we call him). A Crazy girl launches into a tirade against Governor Rockefeller, "Whose Empire," she cries, "Must Be De-stroyed." Straight Negro boys put their arms around me and say we're comrades (it's okay with me—in fact, great, the first camaraderie I've felt with blacks in years). Mattachine (our NAACP) hands out leaflets about "what to do if ar-rested." Some man from the Oscar Wilde bookstore hands out a leaflet describing to newcomers what's going on. I give a stump speech about the need to radicalize, how we must recognize we're part of a vast rebellion of all the re-pressed. Some jeers, some cheers. Charles Burch plans to make a plastique to hurl at cops.

Sunday night, the Stonewall, now reopened—though one room is charred and blasted, all lights are smashed, and only a few dim bulbs are burning, no hard liquor being sold—the management posts an announcement: "We appre-ciate all of you and your efforts to help, but the Stonewall believes in peace. Please end the riots. We believe in peace." Some kids, nonetheless, try to turn over a cop car. Twelve are arrested. Some straight toughs rough up some queens. The queens beat them up. Sheridan Square is again blocked off by the pigs. That same night a group of about seventy-five vigilantes in Queens chops down a wooded part of a park as vengeance against the perverts who are cruising in the bushes. "They're endangering our women and children." The Times, which has scarcely mentioned the Sheridan Square riots (a half column, very tame) is now so aroused by the conservation issue that it blasts the "vigs" for their malice toward nature.

Wednesday. The Voice runs two front-page stories on the riots, both snide, both devoted primarily to assuring readers that the authors are straight.

This last weekend, nothing much happened because it was the Fourth of July and everyone was away. Charles Burch has decided it's all a drag. When he hears that gay kids are picketing Independence Hall in Philly because they're being denied their constitutional rights, he says: "But of course, the Founding Fathers didn't intend to protect perverts and criminals." Who knows what will happen this weekend, or this week? I'll keep you posted.

Otherwise, nothing much. I've been going out with a mad boy who tried to kill me last Friday. He's very cute, and I'm sure it'd be a kick, but I think I'll take a rain check on the death scene.

Finished the first act of my play and outlined the second. My sister has a new boyfriend who's got $30 million, two doctorates, working on a third. She met him in the bughouse (shows the advantages in sending your daughter to the best bughouse in town). I'm going out to Chicago in two weeks to help her move.

I miss you both frightfully. No more fun dinners, no endless telephone conversations, no sharing of exquisite sensations, gad, it's awful.

Love,

Ed

1969: JULY 9
ROBIN MORGAN TO HER UNBORN CHILD

Feminist poet Robin Morgan (1941–) spoke to her unborn son Blake in a letter that reflected the apocalyptic vision shared by many in her generation as the sixties came to an end. Hopes for a liberated, peaceful, and creative future contended with fears of mass destruction through war, environmental disaster, political oppression, and overpopulation.

Wednesday, 9 July 1969
6:38 p.m.

Dear Blake,

I've written you no poems or letters while carrying you these past nine months, and somehow feel I can write you now only because we know, K. and I, that our labor with you has definitely begun, and so you seem finally very real, beginning your own struggle into the conscious universe.

First, I ask you to forgive us for having coalesced you via our genes from that whirling matter and energy that you were before. A planetary famine is likely within ten years; nuclear, biological, gas, and chemical warfare are all possibilities; our species is poisoning what little is left of the air, water, and soil that is our natural Edenic heritage, and it is moving out later this very month to land on (explore? contaminate?) our satellite, the moon. You are part of a population explosion which may well be alone responsible for the destruction of life on earth. Overbreed and overkill begin to be common everyday phrases.

Yet we have conceived you from our sex and love, from the blending together of our brief tissues, K. and I. I could cite excuses, some of which I believe and some of which I don't: our own egos, our curiosity about what our genes would produce, our callousness, our desire to make an ongoing revolution in our own lives, on and on. Perhaps none is the truth, or all are. Perhaps none is really relevant.

The fact is that you are now being born, a woman or a man, but mostly yourself, Blake for now (later you might want to change that name to one nobody has a right to give you but yourself), into a dimension we are all struggling to space out, to make freer, until we are ultimately free from it, into some new life or death—some meaningful way of living, or dying at least, in ecstasy.

Some people are arming themselves—for love.

Some people are refusing to bear arms—for love.

K. and I will be trying to find new ways to save ourselves and our sisters and brothers from suffering and extinction under the greedy powers of a few madmen, and you will be involved unavoidably in that struggle. But on your own terms, as soon as you know them and make them known.

We have no claims on you. We are your genetic mother and father, and beyond that, and more important, merely two people who will take the responsibility of you while you are still small and helpless, who will love you to the best of our ability, provide you with whatever tools of knowledge, skill, humor and emotional freedom seem to interest you, respect your own individuality, hope you dig us as people but hardly dare insist on that (only try to earn it)—and let go.

Of course, I already envy you. Despite the horrors that oppress people around the world, those people are rising up to fight for their freedom. You are born into the age of worldwide revolution. You will be thirty-one years old in the year 2000. You may well travel to other planets. More prosaically, you have one hell of a groovy father, which I never had, and in some ways I trust him more with you than I do myself. I know you two will have crazy beautiful fun together. I have to get my ass in gear so I can join in.

If you are a woman, you will grow up in an atmosphere—indeed, a whole Movement—for women's liberation, so that your life will be less reflective of sexual oppression than mine, more human.

If you are a man, you will also be freer; you will not need to live a form of stereotyped masculinity which is based on the oppression of the other sex.

If you are a woman, you will be free to think—unlike so many women today. If you are a man, you will be free to feel—unlike so many men today.

K. and I are trying to be humanly unisexual, or pansexual. Join us?

If any of us survive these next decades on this planet, you will live to make a society where people share and love and laugh and understand each other. If none of us survive, it won't matter, because then we'll be free. Meanwhile, we can play with each other, and create poems and colors and songs and orgasms together, and learn to fight not so much for what we believe in as for what we love.

Dear Blake, I love myself right now.

Dear Blake, I love K. so very much.

Dear Blake, I love you, even though we've not been introduced.

Dear Blake, leave my body behind you quickly. K. and I, together throughout labor and delivery, will work hard to aid you in your struggle toward light and air and independence.

Dear Blake, welcome to the universe.

Dear, dear Blake, goodbye.

R.

1969: AUGUST 17?
WOODSTOCK VOLUNTEERS TO VISITORS

It had been billed as three days of peace and music, but while Woodstock attracted the best performers of the day and the most impassioned fans, it also became something of a survival test. By the time the weekend was over, the festival had seen more than five thousand medical cases, including 797 recorded instances of drug abuse, three tracheotomies, two deaths by overdose, and one by tractor accident. Fifty additional doctors were flown in from New York City. Rain muddied the fields. There were no visible garbage cans and only six hundred portable toilets for the estimated four hundred thousand audience members (only sixty thousand had been expected). At a crucial moment, volunteers sent this note out to the participants.

SURVIVE SURVIVE SURVIVE SURVIVE SURVIVE SURVIVE

Welcome to Hip City, USA. We're now one of the largest cities in America (population 300,000 and growing all the time). We've got . . . a traffic death, 15 miscarriages and a lot of mud. This is a disaster area.

Where we go from here depends on all of us. The people who promoted this festival have been overwhelmed by their own creation. We can no longer remain passive consumers / we have to begin to fend for ourselves.

ACCESS—The highways leading to the festival site are now blocked. Cars are being turned back in an effort to clear highway 17B. The best thing you can do is to stay until the roads are cleared. If you decide to split and get stuck a team of repairmen is cruising the area and will free your car. Don't leave your vehicle.

SANITATION—Please stay off the roads. Garbage trucks need clear rights-of-way to pick up trash. Either burn your trash or dump it IN BAGS along the road (look for the stands with green bags hanging from them.) You MUST clean your area to avoid a severe health hazard.

MEDICAL—There are two major medical stations. Minor stuff (cuts, bruises) can be taken care of at the SOUTH STATION near the Hog Farm, serious injuries will be treated at the health trailer at the MAIN INTERSECTION, and drug freakouts will be tended by the Hog Farm (red armband) people at the SOUTH CAMPGROUND.

A planeload of doctors are being airlifted from New York City, and a fleet of helicopters is being gathered to drop medical supplies.

Any trained medical personnel should report to the above medical centers.

Do not take any light blue . . . acid and understand that taking strong dope at this time may make you a drag in a survival situation.

Don't run naked in the hot sun for any period of time. Water blisters are painful.

WATER—Water is scarce. Share and conserve all water. Do not drink water unless it is crystal-clear. Check with festival and Hog Farm people before using any operating mains. New mains are being readied. We will announce their location when they are made available. Black and white pipes are water pipes, don't use for walking or bridges. They break easily.

The lake is now a main source of water. Swimming will ruin the purification system—think twice before taking a dip.

FOOD—You should not be piggish about your food and water. As with medicine, festival people have promised that food will be airlifted into the area. The Hog Farm will continue to serve meals in the SOUTH AREA.

VOLUNTEERS—Go to info. stand at main intersection

GENERAL HINTS—The thing to do is survive and share. Organize your own camping area so that everyone makes it through uncomfortable times ahead. Figure out what you must do and the best ways to get it done.

PEOPLE WHO CAN HELP DISTRIBUTE THIS LEAFLET SHOULD COME TO THE MOVEMENT . . . AREA IN THE SOUTH CAMPGROUND. READ AND PASS ON

1969: DECEMBER 3

BILL CLINTON TO EUGENE HOLMES

While he was still a Rhodes Scholar, future president William Jefferson Clinton (1946–) avoided the draft by signing up for the Reserve Officers' Training Corps (ROTC) program at the University of Arkansas Law School, then persuading its director to defer his starting date. Clinton later drew the high number 311 in the draft lottery (meaning that he wouldn't be drafted), dropped his University of

Arkansas plans, and went to Yale Law School instead. This is the letter he wrote to the University of Arkansas ROTC director, Colonel Eugene J. Holmes, explaining why he had decided not to enroll in the ROTC.

The letter would be disclosed to news organizations during Clinton's 1992 campaign for the presidency.

December 3, 1969

Dear Col. Holmes,

I am sorry to be so long in writing. I know I promised to let you hear from me at least once a month, and from now on you will, but I have had to have some time to think about this first letter. Almost daily since my return to England I have thought about writing, about what I want to and ought to say.

First, I want to thank you, not just for saving me from the draft, but for being so kind and decent to me last summer, when I was as low as I have ever been. One thing which made the bond we struck in good faith somewhat palatable to me was my high regard for you personally. In retrospect, it seems that the admiration might not have been mutual had you known a little more about me, about my political beliefs and activities. At least you might have thought me more fit for the draft than for R.O.T.C.

Let me try to explain. As you know, I worked for two years in a very minor position in the Senate Foreign Relations Committee. I did it for the experience and the salary but also for the opportunity, however small, of working every day against a war I opposed and despised with a depth of feeling I had reserved solely for racism in America before Vietnam. I did not take the matter lightly but studied it carefully, and there was a time when not many people had more information about Vietnam at hand than I did.

I have written and spoken and marched against the war. One of the national organizers of the Vietnam Moratorium is a close friend of mine. After I left Arkansas last summer, I went to Washington to work in the national headquarters of the Moratorium, then to England to organize the Americans here for demonstrations Oct. 15 and Nov. 16.

Interlocked with the war is the draft issue, which I did not begin to consider separately until early 1968. For a law seminar at Georgetown I wrote a paper on the legal arguments for and against allowing, within the Selective Service System, the classification of selective conscientious objection, for those opposed to participation in a particular war, not simply to "participation in war in any form."

From my work I came to believe that the draft system itself is illegitimate. No government really rooted in limited, parliamentary democracy should have the power to make its citizens fight and kill and die in a war they may oppose, a war which even possibly may be wrong, a war which, in any case, does not involve immediately the peace and freedom of the nation.

The draft was justified in World War II because the life of the people collectively was at stake. Individuals had to fight, if the nation was to survive, for the lives of their countrymen and their way of life. Vietnam is no such case. Nor was Korea an example, where, in my opinion, certain military action was justified but the draft was not, for the reasons stated above.

Because of my opposition to the draft and the war, I am in great sympathy with those who are not willing to fight, kill, and maybe die for their country (i.e., the particular policy of a particular government) right or wrong. Two of my friends at Oxford are conscientious objectors. I wrote a letter of recommendation for one of them to his Mississippi draft board, a letter which I am more proud of than anything else I wrote at Oxford last year. One of my roommates is a draft resister who is possibly under indictment and may never be able to go home again. He is one of the bravest, best men I know. His country needs men like him more than they know. That he is considered a criminal is an obscenity.

The decision not to be a resister and the related subsequent decisions were the most difficult of my life. I decided to accept the draft in spite of my beliefs for one reason: to maintain my political viability within the system. For years I have worked to prepare myself for a political life characterized by both practical political ability and concern for rapid social progress. It is a life I still feel compelled to try to lead. I do not think our system of government is by definition corrupt, however dangerous and inadequate it has been in recent years. (The society may be corrupt, but that is not the same thing, and if that is true we are all finished anyway.)

When the draft came, despite political convictions, I was having a hard time facing the prospect of fighting a war I had been fighting against, and that is why I contacted you. R.O.T.C. was the one way left in which I could possibly, but not positively, avoid both Vietnam and resistance. Going on with my education, even coming back to England, played no part in my decision to join R.O.T.C. I am back here, and would have been at Arkansas Law School because there is nothing else I can do. In fact, I would like to have been able to take a year out perhaps to teach in a small college or work on some community action project and in the process to decide whether to attend law school or graduate school and how to begin putting what I have learned to use.

But the particulars of my personal life are not nearly as important to me as the principles involved. After I signed the R.O.T.C. letter of intent I began to wonder whether the compromise I had made with myself was not more objectionable than the draft would have been, because I had no interest in the R.O.T.C. program in itself and all I seemed to have done was to protect myself from physical harm. Also, I began to think I had deceived you, not by lies—there were none—but by failing to tell you all the things I'm writing now. I doubt that I had the mental coherence to articulate them then.

At that time, after we had made our agreement and you had sent my 1-D deferment to my draft board, the anguish and loss of my self-regard and self-confidence really set in. I hardly slept for weeks and kept going by eating compulsively and reading until exhaustion brought sleep. Finally, on Sept. 12 I stayed up all night writing a letter to the chairman of my draft board, saying basically what is in the preceding paragraph, thanking him for trying to help in a case where he really couldn't, and stating that I couldn't do the R.O.T.C. after all and would he please draft me as soon as possible.

I never mailed the letter, but I did carry it on me every day until I got on the plane to return to England. I didn't mail the letter because I didn't see, in the end, how my going in the army and maybe going to Vietnam would achieve anything except a feeling that I had punished myself and gotten what I deserved. So I came back to England to try to make something of this second year of my Rhodes scholarship.

And that is where I am now, writing to you because you have been good to me and have a right to know what I think and feel. I am writing too in the hope that my telling this one story will help you to understand more clearly how so many fine people have come to find themselves still loving their country but loathing the military, to which you and other good men have devoted years, lifetimes, of the best service you could give. To many of us, it is no longer clear what is service and what is disservice, or if it is clear, the conclusion is likely to be illegal.

Forgive the length of this letter. There was much to say. There is still a lot to be said, but it can wait. Please say hello to Col. Jones for me.

Merry Christmas.

Sincerely,

Bill Clinton

*   *   *

1969: DECEMBER 6
PETER ROEPCKE TO GAIL

Peter H. Roepcke grew up in Glendale, New York. He served in Vietnam from September of 1969 until April of 1970, when he broke his leg jumping from a helicopter. He would die of a heart attack in October of 1981.

6 Dec. '69

1230 hr.

Dear Gail:

Hi, doll. How's my girl today? I hope you are not feeling too blue. Well, we are on the move again. We got the word to pack our stuff, and we are going to Ban Me Thuot. We are not going to the village itself, but to the airfield. I think we are going to guard the airfield for a while. From what we have heard, we can get showers there and we can even get sodas or beer. Boy, we have not had anything cold to drink in a long time. It does get us mad that we have to move again. We just got our bunkers built—it took us about 1,000 sandbags to build—and now some other company is coming in and using them. That's the way it seems to be all the time. We do all the hard work and then we have to move. Well, that's the Army for you.

I remember in one of your letters you said you were surprised that I said I don't mind being here. Well in a way, that's true. Sure I want to be home with you and have all the things we dream about. But yet being here makes a man feel proud of himself—it shows him that he is a man. Do you understand? Anyone can go in the Army and sit behind a desk, but it takes a lot to do the fighting and to go through what we have to. When we go home, we can say, "Yes, I was in Vietnam. Yes, I was a line dog." To us it means you have gone to hell and have come back. This is why I don't mind being here, because we are men. . . .

Love,

Pete

1969: DECEMBER 24
CURT FLOOD TO BOWIE KUHN

Curt Flood (1938–1997) spent a dozen years as a stellar outfielder with the St. Louis Cardinals. Then he was traded to the Philadelphia Phillies, and he refused to go. This is the letter of protest he wrote to commissioner of baseball Bowie Kuhn (1926–), who promptly rejected his request to be made a free agent. Flood's case would ultimately go to the United States Supreme Court, which in 1972 ruled five to three against him. But his protest paved the way for free agency, and four years later, Minnesota Twins pitcher Bill Campbell would become the first baseball player to make his own deal.

Dear Mr. Kuhn,

After 12 years in the major leagues, I do not feel that I am a piece of property to be bought and sold irrespective of my wishes. I believe that any system that produces that result violates my basic rights as a citizen and is inconsistent with the laws of the United States and the several states.

It is my desire to play baseball in 1970 and I am capable of playing. I have received a contract from the Philadelphia club, but I believe I have the right to consider offers from other clubs before making any decisions. I, therefore, request that you make known to all the major league clubs my feelings in this matter, and advise them of my availability for the 1970 season.

Curt Flood

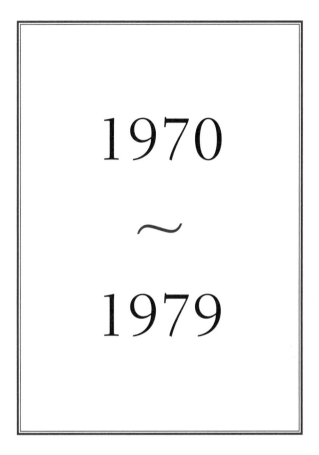

1970

~

1979

I hereby resign the office of President of the United States.

—*Richard Nixon*
August 9, 1972

BETWEEN 1970 AND 1979 . . .

1970: The top three American singles are Simon and Garfunkel's "Bridge Over Troubled Water," the Carpenters' "Close to You," and the Guess Who's "American Woman." ★ The U.S. population is 203 million. ★ The nation's women rebel against the midi skirt, asserting their independence from the fashion arbiters who have declared it chic. ★ In a century-long low, only 4.7 percent of the population, or 9.6 million, are foreign-born. ★ Coca-Cola becomes "the Real Thing." ★ The floppy disk is invented at IBM. ★ U.S. troops are sent into Cambodia. ★ Four students are killed and nine wounded by National Guardsmen at Kent State University. ★ ABC's *Monday Night Football* debuts. ★ Twenty million Americans take part in the first Earth Day. ★ An oxygen tank explodes aboard *Apollo 13*, but astronauts return safely. **1971:** Norman Lear launches *All in the Family*. ★ The voting age is lowered from 21 to 18 by ratification of the 26th Amendment. ★ It now costs eight cents to send a one-ounce letter. ★ The *New York Times* publishes the Pentagon Papers. ★ The electronic pocket calculator is developed at Texas Instruments. **1972:** Responding to increased incidents of hijacking, U.S. airlines make inspection of travelers and their bags mandatory. ★ Five men are arrested in Washington, D.C., for breaking into the national headquarters of the Democratic party

---

From left to right, top row: Kent State poster, Nixon leaving the White House; *second row:* graduation day, 1970, McDonald's arches; *third row:* Gloria Steinem, Saturn's rings, Carroll O'Connor as Archie Bunker; *bottom row:* Patricia Hearst, John Travolta.

at the Watergate apartment complex. ★ In a landslide victory, Richard Nixon and Spiro Agnew are reelected with 521 electoral votes compared to George McGovern's 17. ★ Bobby Fischer beats Boris Spassky to win the world chess title. ★ *The Joy of Sex* is published. ★ *The Waltons* and *M*A*S*H* debut on television. **1973:** The Supreme Court legalizes abortion with a seven-to-two vote in *Roe* v. *Wade*. ★ Much of the country watches as former White House legal aide John W. Dean III testifies before Senator Samuel J. Ervin, Jr.'s investigating committee about the Watergate break-in and cover-up. ★ Billie Jean King beats tennis showman Bobby Riggs 6–4, 6–3, 6–3 in a much-ballyhooed cross-gender tennis match. **1974:** Patricia Hearst is kidnapped by a radical group calling itself the Symbionese Liberation Army. ★ Nixon resigns. Leaving Washington, he says: "Others may hate you. But those who hate you don't win unless you hate them—and then you destroy yourself." ★ Gerald Ford is sworn in as president and declares: "Our long national nightmare is over." ★ Evel Knievel crashes on the banks of the Snake River Canyon after attempting to cross it on a souped-up motorcycle; his injuries are minor. ★ Streaking, the Heimlich maneuver, and *People* magazine are introduced. **1975:** The top three American singles are the Captain and Tennille's "Love Will Keep Us Together," Glen Campbell's "Rhinestone Cowboy," and Elton John's "Philadelphia Freedom." ★ Charles Manson follower Lynette "Squeaky" Fromme attempts to shoot President Ford, but her gun has been improperly loaded and she is thrown to the ground by a Secret Service agent. **1976:** As the desire for jeans and jean jackets soars, the country produces 820 million square yards of denim, nearly double the figure of only three years before. ★ Americans consume 128.5 pounds of beef per person, including more than 50 billion hamburgers, a century-long high. ★ Presidential candidate Jimmy Carter tells *Playboy*: "I've committed adultery in my heart many times." ★ Carter is elected the 39th U.S. president. ★ Writing in *New York* magazine, Tom Wolfe dubs the seventies the Me Decade. ★ Steven Jobs and Stephen Wozniak found Apple Computer.

1977: After having repeatedly demanded the death penalty for the murders of two men, Gary Gilmore is shot by a firing squad at the Utah State Prison. ★ Eighty million people, the largest TV audience in history, tune in to watch the eight installments of Alex Haley's *Roots*. ★ Top movies include *Saturday Night Fever*, *Annie Hall*, *Star Wars*, and *Close Encounters of the Third Kind*. **1978:** Americans can hear the words "The plane, boss, the plane!" every week on TV's *Fantasy Island*, and are introduced to J. R. Ewing on *Dallas*. ★ Best-sellers include James Fixx's *The Complete Book of Running* and Christina Crawford's *Mommie Dearest*. ★ After the murder of Congressman Leo J. Ryan, followers of People's Temple cult figure Jim Jones commit suicide in Jonestown, Guyana, many by drinking cyanide-laced Kool-Aid. **1979:** The average American marriage lasts 6.6 years. ★ A nuclear meltdown is avoided after an accident at Pennsylvania's Three Mile Island plant, but some radioactivity is released. ★ Long lines form at the nation's gas stations as OPEC ends its 18-month price freeze and oil prices double. ★ Consumer prices increase by 13.3 percent, the highest rate of U.S. inflation in 33 years. ★ Sony introduces the Walkman at a price of $200. ★ Jerry Falwell introduces the Moral Majority.

1970: JANUARY 2
CHARLES COLSON TO KEN COLE

By the beginning of the 1970s, a reinvigorated women's movement was gaining ground, attracting followers, and marshaling supporters for the Equal Rights Amendment. President Nixon's special counsel, Charles Colson, was not among the faithful. Ultimately, the ERA would fail to be ratified by the states.

Ken Cole was domestic counsel on the White House staff.

TO: Ken Cole
FROM: Chuck Colson
RE: National Women's Party

The National Women's Party has requested that the President allude in the State of the Union Message to the issue of equal rights for women. As you will see from the enclosed, the President has publicly supported this amendment, as has every other politician down through the years. Fortunately the good sense and ultimate wisdom of Congress has always kept this ridiculous proposal from being enacted. It is good politics to talk about this, I must admit. Could you please advise me so that I can be in touch with the National Women's Party?

1970: APRIL 6
RAY KROC TO MCDONALD'S EMPLOYEES

In 1954, Ray Kroc (1902–1984) visited a San Bernardino, California, restaurant that had set up what it called a "Speedee Service System" to prepare its hamburgers, french fries, and milk shakes. Impressed by the operation, Kroc was inspired to franchise a chain of drive-ins, promising owners Maurice and Richard McDonald one-half percent of the gross (he would later buy them out for $2.7 million). In 1955 the McDonald's Corporation's chain of restaurants was launched and, with it, the fast-food industry. By the end of the century, there would be more than twenty-five thousand McDonald's outlets around the world.

April 6, 1970

MEMO TO: All McDonald's Operators
FROM: Ray A. Kroc

May, 1970, will be the biggest month ever experienced in McDonald's history—if you are ready.

This May we have five Fridays, five Saturdays, and five Sundays—plus whatever benefit may be derived from Memorial Day, May 30, being on Saturday.

May is our first month of Daylight Savings Time, with its effect on our supper-hour business. With 15 days of May—virtually half of the month—falling on Fridays, Saturdays, and Sundays, you can see we have a great opportunity to break all records. Another important item, for those stores near college campuses, is that this is the last full month of the regular college season.

In addition, May is really the first month of nice spring weather. There is optimism in the air, and everybody looks ahead to a wonderful summer. We want to make sure that they find happiness and satisfaction at McDonald's.

Let's plan to be all spruced up by the 24th of April when Daylight Savings Time is ready to start, so we can ignite the May Day spirit. Have your patios ready and inviting, new uniforms for the crew—both men and women. Your landscaping should be in, up to date, and ready to bloom.

I urge all good McDonald's men to rally to the most exciting month in our history. Let's have everything ready for the big summer volume, but let's keep quality and cleanliness before the dollars. If we do this, we will leave competition far, far behind.

Sincerity, dedication, and integrity are the only things that will win—win and conquer all.

Ray A. Kroc

1970: MAY

AN OHIO RESIDENT TO THE PRESIDENT
OF THE KENT STATE STUDENT BODY

On April 30, President Nixon announced his decision to order United States troops into Cambodia. Though Nixon called the move a limited incursion rather than an invasion, it enraged members of the peace movement. On May 2, at Ohio's Kent State University, the ROTC building was set on fire by students. On May 4, following another demonstration, four students were killed and nine injured when twenty-eight members of the National Guard opened fire in the direction of a campus parking lot. Protests around the nation ensued. Not everyone sided with the protestors.

To the Rioters, arsonists, Killers of Decency & Sanity.

To the rioting, destructive, arsonists of college buildings window breaking goons, ROTC objectors and saddest of all that you the destructive arsonists ARE THE murderers of the four students of your college. It was your actions that are and were responsible for their deaths. Dissenting is one thing but burning and destroying and throwing missles like bottles, bricks, cement chunks etc can kill as well as bullets. <u>The National Guard did not come to Kent college on their own volition but on demand from your President of the college who called for help when the campus police were unable to stem you riotous destructive burning goons.</u> And it is you rioters who are responsible for forcing the Guard to protect their lives from your violence. Also a bullet in one of the students <u>did not come from a Guardsman's gun.</u> So their claim they WERE SHOT AT BY some or many others was factual. Shut down your colleges as tax payers want it very much. We are disgusted to pay taxes for college rioters.

> One of the many millions of
> disgusted tax payers

1970: MAY 7
GREG BAKER TO THE PRESIDENT
OF THE KENT STATE STUDENT BODY

Kent State was not an isolated incident. Ten days later, another two students would be killed by police at Mississippi's Jackson State University. Meanwhile, as the shock and fury of students around the country spread, more than seventy-five American colleges were closed for the remainder of the academic year.

ASSOCIATED STUDENTS
WESTERN WASHINGTON STATE COLLEGE

May 7, 1970

Student Body President
Kent State University
Kent, Ohio

Dear President:

Please convey the following message to your student body:

We wish to express our deepest sympathies and condolences to the people of Kent State University for the loss they have suffered. We know there is nothing we can do to relieve the sorrow you feel, but perhaps you may take some comfort in knowing that we, like so many of our brothers and sisters around the nation and the world, feel the loss as though it were our own. We the students of Western shall dedicate ourselves anew to the goals for which the four students died—an end to the genocidal American military encroachment in Southeast Asia. Do not lose courage. Do not lose heart. We can, we will, we must triumph in the end.

—Students of Western Washington State College

This message was passed in the form of a resolution at the Spring Quarter Nominating Convention on May 5, 1970. The convention was subsequently postponed for a week in view of President Nixon's move into Cambodia and the death of your classmates.

Peace,
Greg Baker
A.S. President

1970: MAY 13

RICHARD NIXON TO H. R. HALDEMAN

Richard Nixon was beset throughout his first term by protests against the Vietnam War. One month after his decision to order troops into Cambodia, he wrote this extraordinary memo to chief of staff H. R. Haldeman (1926–1993). The visit it describes was made on May 9.

Ron Ziegler was press secretary. Egil "Bud" Krogh was assistant to John Ehrlichman, who was assistant to the president for domestic affairs. Daniel Patrick Moynihan, urban affairs adviser to Nixon, would later become a U.S. senator. Leonard Garment and James Keogh were advisers to the president. Ray Price, William Safire, and Patrick Buchanan were speechwriters. "Manuel" was Manolo Sanchez, a Cuban refugee who had been chauffeur and handyman for the Nixon family since 1962 and was Nixon's valet at the White House. Walter Tkach was the president's personal physician.

May 13, 1970

TO: Bob Haldeman
FROM: The President
The attached is a memorandum of what actually took place at the Lincoln Memorial.

After you read it, I think you will share my complete frustration with regard to coverage of my activities. I realize we didn't have Ziegler at my elbow every minute or Krogh making notes. If they had been, it would have spoiled the whole thing. On the other hand, while Krogh could not hear it all—apparently his recollection was only of those matters that this memorandum clearly indicates I told the students were <u>not</u> important rather than those matters of the spirit that were important. Ziegler, of course, in his questions wanted to know what time I got up, how long I had been there, what I had for breakfast, etc., all of which were essential to the story but which were completely irrelevant as far as getting across the whole spirit and thrust of the story.

I can understand why John Ehrlichman got the idea from the news reports that I was tired and all I talked about was surfing and nonsensical things. This, of course, reflects on two points—even when I am tired I do not talk about nonsensical things and also more fundamentally, I am afraid that most of the members of our staff, to their credit, are enormously interested in material things and what we accomplish in our record, etc. etc. but that very few seem to have any interest and, therefore, have no ability to communicate on those matters that are infinitely more important—qualities of spirit, emotion, of the depth and mystery of life which this whole visit really was all about.

Perhaps it might be well for you, Ehrlichman, Moynihan—maybe Garment, Price, Keogh, Safire and Buchanan—to read this. Most of them will not really understand what I am talking about and most of them will disagree with the approach. I realize it would have made more news from the standpoint of the students for me to engage in a spirited "dialogue" with them about why we were in Cambodia, why we haven't ended the war sooner, morality of the war, etc. This kind of conversation would have been infinitely more easy for me. It would have made more news but as I evaluated the situation this was the one time this group of students—most of whom perhaps were middle class or lower middle class—most of whom were about as poor as I was when I was in college and who had driven all this long distance to Washington—this was the only time they had ever talked to a President of the United States. They will see me many times discuss these heated, angry subjects that they would hear later at the Monument and that they hear in their classrooms. Perhaps the major contribution I could make to them was to try to lift them a bit out of the miserable intellectual wasteland in which they now wander aimlessly around.

I do not write this memorandum to you critically of our staff because I think it is the best staff any President has had by far in terms of loyalty, willingness to work, etc. The only problem is that we seem to lack on the staff any one individual who really understands or appreciates what I am trying to get across in terms of what a President should mean to the people—not news, not gimmicks like rushing out to the Negro Junior College with a covey of newsreels following. All of this seems to be big stuff and I realize makes big news—perhaps it is. But on the other hand I really wonder in the long run if this is all the legacy we want to leave. If it is—then perhaps we should do our job as easily as we can—as expeditiously as we can and get out and leave the responsibilities of the government to the true materialists—the socialists, the totalitarians who talk idealism but rule ruthlessly without any regard to the individual considerations—the respect for personality that I tried to emphasize in my dialogue with the students.

As you recall, the press conference was at 10 o'clock Friday night. After the press conference I had approximately 20 calls from VIPs in addition to hundreds from others which I, of course, could not take. I completed returning my calls at approximately 2:15 in the morning. I then went to bed, slept soundly until shortly after four o'clock. When I woke up I got up and went into the Lincoln Sitting Room and was listening to an Ormandy recording with Entremont at the piano playing a Rachmaninoff album for piano and orchestra. Manuel apparently heard and came down to the Lincoln Sitting Room and asked if he could get me some coffee or hot chocolate or something else. I told him no but then as I looked out of the window and saw the small knots of students begin to gather on the grounds of the Washington Monument I asked him if he had ever been to the Lincoln Memorial at night.

He said he had not. I said, get your clothes on and we will go down to the Lincoln Memorial. I got dressed and at approximately 4:35 we left the White House and drove to the Lincoln Memorial. I have never seen the Secret Service quite so petrified with apprehension. I insisted, however, that no press be informed and that nobody in our office be informed. Apparently, they disobeyed my instructions on the latter point because Krogh, I understand, and Ron Ziegler showed up toward the end of my meeting with the students.

Manuel and I got out of the car at approximately 4:40 and walked up the steps to the Lincoln statue. I showed him the great inscription above the statue and told him that that, along with the inscription over the Tomb of the Unknown Soldier, was, in my opinion, the most moving sight in Washington, and then showed him the Gettysburg Address on the left and Lincoln's Second Inaugural on the right. Manuel was quite familiar with both. While he is a new citizen he is deeply interested in American history and reads it at every opportunity.

By this time a few small groups of students had begun to congregate in the rotunda of the Memorial. I walked over to a group of them and walked up to them and shook hands. They were not unfriendly. As a matter of fact, they seemed somewhat overawed, and, of course, quite surprised. When I first started to speak to the group there were approximately 8 in it. I asked each of them where they were from and found that over half were from upper New York State. At this point, all of them were men. There were no women. To get the conversation going I asked them how old they were, what they were studying, the usual questions. I asked how many of them had been to Washington before and found that over half the group had never been to Washington before. I told them that it was a beautiful city, that I hoped they enjoyed their visit there, that I wanted them, of course, to attend the anti-war demonstration, to listen to the speakers; that I hoped they had the time to take a tour of the city and see some of the historical monuments.

I told them that my favorite spot in all of Washington was right where we were standing—the Lincoln Memorial at night—that I had not been here at night for ten years, that I had come down here because I had awakened early after my press conference and wanted Manuel to see this wonderful sight.

Two or three of them volunteered that they had not been able to hear the press conference because they had been driving all night in order to get here. I said I was sorry they had missed it because I had tried to explain in the press conference that my goals in Vietnam were the same as theirs—to stop the killing and end the war to bring peace. Our goal was not to get into Cambodia by what we were doing but to get out of Vietnam.

They did not respond and so I took it from there by saying that I realized that most of them would not agree with my position but I hoped that they would not allow their disagreement on this issue to lead them to fail to give us a hearing on some other issues where we might agree. And also particularly I hoped that their hatred of the war, which I could well understand, would not turn into a bitter hatred of our whole system, our country and everything that it stood for. I said, I know that probably most of you think I'm an S.O.B. but I want you to know that I understand just how you feel. I recall that when I was just a little older than you, right out of law school and ready to get married, how excited I was when Chamberlain came home from Munich and made his famous statement about peace in our time. I had heard it on the radio. I had so little in those days that the prospect of going into the service was almost unbearable and I felt that the United States staying out of any kind of a conflict was worth paying any price whatever. As I pointed out too the fact that I came from a Quaker background I was as close to being a pacifist as anybody could be in those times and as a result I thought at that time that Chamberlain was the greatest man alive, and when I read Churchill's all-out criticism of Chamberlain I thought Churchill was a madman. In retrospect, I now realize I was wrong. I think now that Chamberlain was a good man but that Churchill was a wiser man and that we in the world are better off than we would be because Churchill had not only the wisdom but the courage to carry out the policies that he believed were right even though there was a time when both in England and all over the world he was extremely unpopular because of his "anti-peace" stand.

I then tried to move the conversation into areas where I could draw them out. I said that since some of them had come to Washington for the first time I hoped that while they were young that they would never miss an opportunity to travel. One of them said that he didn't know whether he could afford it, and I said I didn't think I could afford it either when I was young but my wife and I borrowed the money for a trip we took to Mexico and then one to Central America. The fact is, you must travel when you are young. If you wait until you can afford it you will be too old to enjoy it. When you're young you can enjoy it. I urged them to start with the United States. I said there was so much to see in this country. I told them that as they went West, that I particularly thought they should go to places like Santa Fe, New Mexico, and see American Indians. I pointed out that I knew that on their campuses that the major subject of concern was the Negro problem. I said this was altogether as it should be because of the degradation of slavery that had been imposed upon the Negroes and it would be impossible for us to do everything that we should do to right that wrong, but I pointed out that what we have done with the American Indians was in its way just as bad. We had taken a proud and independent race and virtually destroyed them, and that we had to find ways to bring them back into decent lives in this country.

I said along the same lines that they would find in California that the Mexican-Americans were even from an economic standpoint worse off than the Negroes. I said that in both cases we needed to open channels of communication to Indians, to Mexicans as well as to Negroes, and I hoped that they would do so.

At that time a girl joined the group and since I had been discussing California I asked if anybody there was from California. She spoke up and said she was from Los Altos and I said that was one of my favorite towns in Northern California and I hoped it was as beautiful as I remembered it. She did not respond.

In trying to draw her out, I told the rest of the group that when they went to California that they would see there what massive strides we could take to deal with the problem of the environment which I knew they were all interested in. I said that right below where I live in California there was the greatest surfing beach in the world, that it was completely denied to the public due to the fact that it was Marine Corps property, and that I had taken steps to release some of this property to the public for a public beach so that the terribly overcrowded beaches further north could be unburdened, and so that the people could have a chance to enjoy the natural beauty which was there. I said that one of the thrusts of our whole quality of life environmental program was to take our Government property and put it to better uses and not simply to continue to use it for military or other purposes because it had been used for that way from time immemorial.

Most of them seemed to nod in agreement when I made this point.

I then spoke of how I hoped that they would have the opportunity to know not only the United States but the whole world. I said most people will tell you to go to Europe. I said Europe was fine, but it's really an older version of America. It is worth seeing but the place that I felt they would particularly enjoy visiting would be Asia. I told them my great hopes that during my Administration, and certainly during their lifetime, that the great mainland of China would be opened up so that we could know the 700 million people who live in China who are one of the most remarkable people on earth.

Most of them seemed to nod in agreement when I made this point.

I then went on to say, however, that they should not overlook when they were in Asia the people of India. I said the people in India are terribly poor, but they have a history and philosophical background and a mystique which they should try to understand.

I also touched lightly on places like Malaysia. One of them mentioned that we had a Peace Corps in Malaysia and I said, that's right, we have them in several of these countries wherever they will allow it.

I then moved on to the Soviet Union. Then one of them asked me what Moscow was like, and I said gray. It's very important if you go to Russia, of course, to see it because of the historical and governmental operations that are there, but if you really want to know Russia, its exciting variety and history, you must go to Leningrad. I said that in Russia Leningrad was really a more interesting place to visit, that the people were really more outgoing there since they were not so much under control and domination of the central government.

I also said that in terms of beautiful cities they would find Prague and

Warsaw of much more architectural beauty than Moscow. I made this point because I was speaking directly to one of the students who said he was a student
of architecture. In fact, there were two who said they were studying architecture and I thought that they would be interested in knowing about [words miss-
ing] but the most important point I made about Russia was that as you went
across the country, that they should go to places like Novosibirsk, a raw, new
city in the heart of Siberia, and Samarkand in Asian Russia where the people
were Asians rather than Russians.

One of them asked whether it would be possible to get a visa to such cities,
and I said I was sure they could and if any of them took a trip to Russia and
wanted to contact my office I would help out.

This seemed to get a little chuckle from them.

I then moved back to the problem and my thrust then of what really mattered
in the world was people rather than cities and air and water and all the other
things that were material. I said, for example, Haiti of all the countries I have
visited in Latin America is probably the poorest with Bolivia slightly poorer, but
that the Haitians, as I recalled from 1955, while they were poor had a dignity
and a grace which was very moving, that I always had wanted to return, not because there was anything in Haiti worth seeing in terms of cities or good food,
etc., but because the people had such character.

I then made this same point again with regard to the people I had seen in
Asia and India and returned again to the United States where I again emphasized the importance of their not becoming alienated from the people of this
country, its great variety.

I expressed distress that on the college campuses the blacks and whites,
while they now go to school together, have less contact with each other than
they had when they weren't going to school together on some of our major campuses. This seemed to get through, although none of them had much to say and
none of them responded specifically.

By this time the group around me had begun to get considerably larger. I
would say that the original group of approximately 8 to 10 had now become perhaps 30 and some of those who seemed to be more leader types and older began
to take part in the conversation.

One spoke up and said, "I hope you realize that we are willing to die for what
we believe in."

I said I certainly realize that. Do you realize that many of us when we were
your age were also willing to die for what we believed in and were willing to do
so today. The point is that we were trying to build a world in which you will not

have to die for what you believe in, in which you are able to live for. I put in one brief comment with regard to the point I had made in the press conference that while we had great differences with the Russians we had to find a way to limit nuclear arms and I had hoped that we could make some progress in that direction. They seemed to have very little interest in that subject. Perhaps it was because we moved through so fast and perhaps because they were overawed by the whole incident.

Then another spoke up and said, we are not interested in what Prague looks like. We are interested in what kind of life we build in the United States.

I said the whole purpose of my discussing Prague and other places was not to discuss the city but the people. For the next 25 years the world is going to get much smaller. We are going to be living in all parts of the world and it is vitally important that you know and appreciate and understand people everyplace, wherever they are, and particularly understand the people in your own country.

I said I know that the great emphasis that is currently being put on the environment—the necessity to have clean air, clean water, clean streets—that, as you know, we have a very bold program going further than any program has ever gone before to deal with some of these subjects, but I want to leave just one thought with you, that cleaning up the air and the water and the streets is not going to solve the deepest problems that concern us all. Those are material problems. They must be solved. They are terribly important. We must have clean air and clean water. We must make the country more beautiful and remove the ugly blotches that our modern society has put on the face of the earth. But you must remember that something that is completely clean can also be completely sterile and without spirit. What we all must think about is why we are here. What are those elements of the spirit which really matter. And, here again, I returned to my theme of thinking about people rather than about places and about things. I said candidly and honestly that I didn't have the answer, but I knew that young people today were searching as I was searching 40 years ago for an answer to this problem. I just wanted to be sure that all of them realized that ending the war and cleaning up the streets and the air and the water was not going to solve spiritual hunger which all of us have and which, of course, has been the great mystery of life from the beginning of time.

The last 20 minutes of the conversation Manuel made mention to me a couple of times that I had a telephone call in the car. I, of course, smiled and said, let it wait. I realized that the Secret Service were becoming more and more concerned as they saw the crowd begin to mount and probably feared that some of the more active leaders would get word of my visit and descend upon us. By this time the dawn was upon us, the first rays of the sun began to show and they began to climb up over the Washington Monument and I said I had to go and shook hands with those nearest to me and walked down the steps.

A bearded fellow from Detroit was taking a picture as I began to get in the car. I asked him if he wouldn't like to get in the picture. He stepped over with me and I said, look, I'll have the President's doctor take the picture, and Tkach took the picture. He seemed to be quite delighted—it was, in fact, the broadest smile that I saw on the entire visit. As I left him I said, I came back to the theme I had made up above, and I knew he had come a long way for this event and I knew, too, that he and his colleagues were terribly frustrated and angry about our policy and opposed to it. I said, I just hope your opposition doesn't turn into a blind hatred of the country. But remember this is a great country with all of its faults. I said, if you have any doubt about it go down to the passport office and you won't see many people lining up to get out of the country. Abroad, you will see a number lining up to get in.

He smiled and took it all in good humor. We shook hands, I got into the car and drove away. From there I asked the driver to take us up to the Capitol. Manuel had never been in the Capitol before—I took him for a tour of the House side, the Senate side, the Rotunda where I told him the services for President Eisenhower and Senator Dirksen had been conducted.

Finally, we found a fellow by the name of Frazer who said he had come to the Congress the same year I did in 1947 as a page boy for Charlie Halleck. Frazer had the morning shift and opened the House Chamber to us. We walked in with the Secret Service men, Tkach—I had Manuel go up and sit in the Speaker's Chair. We all clapped as he got into the chair.

When we left we tried to find some place to see if we could have breakfast down there and, of course, nothing was available. Several of the Negro women who do the cleaning came up to speak to me. Three of them had known me when I was there as Vice President. One of them asked me to sign her Bible. I told her that it made me very proud to sign her Bible and I was glad to see that she carried it with her but that the trouble is that most of us these days didn't read it enough. She said, I read it all the time. After I signed her Bible she went down and brought up two or three others who were working on the cleaning detail for signing of pictures and other odds and ends that they had for their children, grandchildren, etc.

We then left the Capitol and went down to the Mayflower restaurant. I hadn't been in a public restaurant in Washington since becoming President except, of course, on official functions. They were all delighted to see us and I had corned beef hash and poached egg for the first time in five years, and at the conclusion signed autographs for everybody in the restaurant. I found, incidentally, almost without exception, individually the waitresses were for what I had said, what we were doing in Cambodia. As we drove away from the restaurant, eight to ten of the waitresses all stood at the door, outside on the street, and waved goodbye.

1970: DECEMBER 20?
ELVIS PRESLEY TO RICHARD NIXON

One of the most bizarre encounters of Nixon's presidency was planned and recorded in this series of memos. Elvis Presley (1935–1977) was in the Las Vegas stage of his legendary singing career when he wrote the initial letter.
The gift turned out to be a commemorative World War II Colt .45 pistol.

Dear Mr. President:

First, I would like to introduce myself. I am Elvis Presley and admire you and Have Great Respect for your office. I talked to Vice President Agnew in Palm Springs 3 weeks ago and expressed my concern for our country. The Drug Culture, the Hippie Elements, the S.D.S, Black Panthers, etc do <u>not</u> consider me as their enemy or as they call it the Establishment. <u>I call it America and</u> I Love it. Sir I can and will be of any service that I can to help the country out. I have no concerns or motives other than helping the Country out. So I wish not to be given a title or an appointed position, I can and will do more good if I were made a Federal Agent at Large, and I will help out by doing it my way through my communications with people of all ages. First and Foremost I am an entertainer but all I need is the Federal credentials. I am on this Plane with Sen. George Murphy and we have been discussing the problems that our Country is faced with.

Sir I am Staying at the Washington Hotel Room 505–506–507. I have 2 men who work with me by the name of Jerry Schilling and Sonny West. I am registered under the name of Jon Burrows. I will be here for as long as it takes to get the credentials of a Federal Agent. I have done an in depth study of Drug Abuse and Communist Brainwashing Techniques and I am right in the middle of the whole thing, where I can and will do the most good.

I am Glad to help just so long as it is kept very Private. You can have your staff or whomever call me anytime today tonight or tomorrow. I was nominated this coming year one of America's Ten Most Outstanding Young Men. That will be in

January 18 in my home town of Memphis, Tenn. I am sending you the short autobiography about myself so you can better understand this approach. I would love to meet you just to say hello if you're not too Busy.

Respectfully

Elvis Presley

P.S. I believe that you Sir were one of the Top Ten Outstanding Men of America also.

I have a personal gift for you also which I would like to present to you and you can accept it or I will keep it for you until you can take it.

1970: DECEMBER 21
DWIGHT CHAPIN TO H. R. HALDEMAN

The first order of business at the meeting between Nixon and Presley was the taking of photographs. Then the singer showed the president various badges he had received from police departments. Nixon and Presley talked about the singer's ability to reach young people. Presley told Nixon how much he supported him, and before he left, hugged him.

Dwight L. Chapin (1940–) was Nixon's appointments secretary. Next to Chapin's last line, about meeting young people, Haldeman scrawled: "You must be kidding." But he put his "H" beside the approval line at the end of the memo.

December 21, 1970

MEMORANDUM FOR: Mr. H. R. Haldeman
FROM: Dwight L. Chapin
SUBJECT: Elvis Presley

Attached you will find a letter to the President from Elvis Presley. As you are aware, Presley showed up here this morning and has requested an appointment with the President. He states that he knows the President is very busy, but he would just like to say hello and present the President with a gift.

As you are well aware, Presley was voted one of the ten outstanding young men for next year and this was based upon his work in the field of drugs. The thrust of Presley's letter is that he wants to become a "Federal agent at large" to work against the drug problem by communicating with people of all ages. He says that he is not a member of the establishment and that drug culture types, the hippie elements, the SDS, and the Black Panthers are people with whom he can communicate since he is not part of the establishment.

I suggest that we do the following:

This morning Bud Krogh will have Mr. Presley in and talk to him about drugs and about what Presley can do. Bud will also check to see if there is some kind of an honorary agent at large or credential of some sort that we can provide for Presley. After Bud has met with Presley, it is recommended that we have Bud bring Presley in during the Open Hour to meet briefly with the President. You know that several people have mentioned over the past few months that Presley is very pro the President. He wants to keep everything private and I think we should honor his request.

I have talked to Bud Krogh about this whole matter, and we both think that it would be wrong to push Presley off on the Vice President since it will take very little of the President's time and it can be extremely beneficial for the President to build some rapport with Presley.

In addition, if the President wants to meet with some bright young people outside of the Government, Presley might be a perfect one to start with.

Approve Presley coming in at end of Open Hour _____
Disapprove _____

1971: FEBRUARY 9
H. R. HALDEMAN TO ALEXANDER BUTTERFIELD

Alexander Butterfield (1926–) was an assistant to H. R. Haldeman and would later be famous for revealing the taping system that Nixon used in the White House and that contributed to his downfall. The Henry in this memo was Henry Kissinger (1923–), then assistant for national security affairs and later secretary of state.

TO: Alex Butterfield
FROM: H. R. Haldeman

In seating at State Dinners, the President feels that Henry should not always be put next to the most glamorous woman present. He should be put by an intelligent and interesting dinner partner and we should shift from the practice of putting him by the best looking one. It's starting to cause unfavorable talk that serves no useful purpose.

*   *   *

1971: JUNE 1

A. M. ROSENTHAL TO ARTHUR OCHS SULZBERGER
AND JAMES RESTON

———————————

Twelve days after New York Times *executive editor A. M. Rosenthal (1922–) sent this memo, the* Times *would begin publication of the Pentagon Papers, a confidential and highly damaging report on U.S. involvement in Vietnam from 1945 to 1968. For the first time in the nation's history the Justice Department, citing national security considerations, was granted a court injunction against further publication. But on June 30, the Supreme Court overturned the decision, and the series continued to run.*

Arthur Ochs Sulzberger was publisher of the *Times*. Pulitzer prize–winner James Reston (1909–1995) was at the time a vice-president of the newspaper. Neil Sheehan was the lead reporter on the stories; other members of the reporting team were Hedrick (Rick) Smith, Fox Butterfield, and E. W. Kenworthy. Congressman Paul (Pete) McCloskey was an antiwar Republican. Walt Rostow, as National Security assistant to President Johnson, had been a key architect of the U.S. military buildup in Vietnam.

CONFIDENTIAL
MEMORANDUM for: Mr. Sulzberger   from A. M. ROSENTHAL
                     Mr. Reston

I believe we are now in a position to give the Publisher sufficient information on which to base a decision.

I am submitting this material for two purposes:

(1) In case this story breaks elsewhere, we would be in a position to publish the bulk of the story quickly. What I am giving you is the guts of it.

This would be our plan for publication in case the story broke elsewhere:

A piece by Rick Smith explaining the origins and import of the Pentagon study. Several pages will be inserted in this story giving some of the highlights of the total material. This is in hand.

This will be published on the first day. Also to be published on the first day is the first half of Neil Sheehan's piece dealing with the most important aspects of the material—the events leading up to the Tonkin Gulf.

The next day we would publish the second half of the Tonkin Gulf story by Sheehan. This whole story is in hand.

The third day we would publish Sheehan's piece dealing with the events leading to the bombing of North Vietnam and continuing through the beginning of the land war in Asia.

This piece is not yet in hand but should be available early next week. The Publisher will see this.

It is important for us to publish the Sheehan material early in the series because this is the material that we believe is in the hands of McCloskey and others. If we did it all chronologically, we would not get to Sheehan until the fifth or sixth day and by that time, the story might be busted by others.

The fourth day we will start with the beginning chronologically—Fox Butterfield's piece on the Geneva Accords and up through the early 1950's. This is in hand.

The fifth day we will publish Rick Smith's piece on the Kennedy administration from 1961–1963. This will be in hand Thursday and the Publisher will see it.

The sixth day we will publish Rick Smith's piece on the Diem coup. This is in hand.

Also in hand are pieces to be published subsequently on Rostow by Kenworthy and another piece by Butterworth on the roots of the insurgency.

Each day we will also publish textual documentation.

In hand to be submitted to the Publisher is the documentation of all the stories listed above. Also to be submitted to the Publisher is the textual documentation we would publish with the total series.

(2) We are now in a position, I believe, where the Publisher can make the decision not only in connection with the possibility of the material being published elsewhere first but in relation to the fundamental decision as to whether we should publish if there is no substantive leak, when we have the remaining few pieces in hand and the total series is ready to go.

We all believe that the remaining few pieces will not affect this basic decision, particularly since all the documentation that we will print with them is now available to the Publisher. If I believed that the few pieces not yet in hand in any way could affect the basic decision on whether or not to publish, I would not be submitting any. We have the total documentation, to repeat, and most of the stories. The remaining stories do not present any other legal, ethical or journalistic problems that are not inherent in the material now being submitted to the Publisher.

If we wait until all these pieces are in, we could not submit them to the Publisher until after he returned from Europe. I wish to make it clear that if we thought these remaining pieces could substantively affect the crucial decision on publication, I would wait.

If an affirmative decision is made on the basis of this material, we will not only be in a position to publish in case of an emergency but we will also be able to proceed with printing the entire series as soon as possible even if there is no leak.

I believe that even if the material is not exposed elsewhere, we should print the series as soon as physically possible.

As you will see, the whole series follows some rather decided philosophical and journalistic ground rules.

What we are presenting is the Pentagon version of the war and its origins. What our reporters have contributed is the essential task of selecting the essence of 7,000 single-spaced pages of Pentagon analysis and documentation and presented it in a sequential and logical manner.

This is not The New York Times history, I emphasize, but The New York Times's report on the Pentagon's history—and this is what makes it far different and far more significant, in my opinion, than previously published material.

A.M.R.

1972: FEBRUARY 17
"PAUL MORRISON" TO WILLIAM LOEB

The letter below helped undo the political hopes of Maine senator Edmund Muskie (1914–1996). In February of 1972, he was a leading candidate for the Democratic nomination for president when the right-wing Manchester Union-Leader *printed this letter, as well as a brutal editorial by William Loeb (1905–1981). Defending himself in New Hampshire on February 26, Muskie called Loeb a "gutless coward" and appeared to weep in referring to another item, which the* Union-Leader *had run about his wife. In truth, the infamous "Canuck letter" was one of the many "dirty tricks" for which the administration would soon become known (the* Washington Post *named the administration's Ken Clawson as the author; he denied the charge). And though Muskie later claimed that what had appeared to be tears was really melting snow, the image of the tearful candidate would irreparably damage his campaign.*

Canucks *is a derogatory term for Franco-Americans.*

Feb 17, 1972
Deerfield Beach
Fla.

Mr Loeb
Manchester Guardian
Manchester
New Hampshire

Dear Mr Loeb—

I saw you on TV the other night and my friends father gets your newspaper. We went to Ft Lauderdale to meet Sen Muskie—we were right beside him at Seed house when one of the men asked him what did he know about blacks and the problems with them—he didn't have any in Maine—a man with the senator said No, not blacks but we have <u>CANNOCKS</u>

What did he mean? We asked—Mr Muskie laughed, and said come to New England and see. Could you ~~right~~ write me the answer. Or print it in your paper—my friend gets it from you—

Thank you
Paul Morrison
Deerfield Beach
Fla. 33064

1972: AUGUST 1
PAT TO HER PARENTS

Pat came from a small town in Ohio, where both her parents worked for the government. She attended college in the early 1970s. Her letter below, as well as her parents' reply on page 528, reflects the way the gulf between generations continued to grow as young people embarked on a sexual revolution that left many of their parents confused, angry, and disappointed.

1 August 1972

Dear Mom and Dad,

. . . I'm not moving back home after I graduate. There is really nothing for me there (aside from being with the family). I am contented, happy, and settled down in a place where I don't mind living. What would you rather have: me as a mature adult, handling my own affairs and making my own decisions . . . or me as a "child" depending on you for everything? I want to be able to handle my own financial matters after I graduate. It is time for me to stop accepting money from you and start supporting myself. I don't want to limit my world to one thing or one place or one set of ideals.

My roommate is moving out at the end of this term. There is a possibility that Tony will move in. We have talked about it and it seems like the logical thing to do since we might as well be living together anyway. I hope you have realized by now that I am not a little girl any more. I firmly believe we have made the right decision and so does Tony. We are happy together and we have much to learn and gain, and much to experience by doing this. Also, if I am living with a man I will feel safer living in an area where rapes and robberies are a common occurrence.

I assume you think that living together is morally wrong as opposed to marriage which is morally "right". I feel that two people can be just as close and happy living together, and they do not need a marriage contract to make theirs a "legal" partnership. If marriage is a form of "security", then I don't want that form of security. Security alone is not a valid reason for two people to be together. This is what I believe and I want you to be able to accept it and be aware that this is what I really am.

Much love,
your daughter, Pat

1972: AUGUST 7
ANNIE MOORE TO HER SISTER AND BROTHER-IN-LAW

In 1978, 913 followers of the Reverend Jim Jones would die—some by gunshot wound, others by drinking cyanide-laced Kool-Aid—in a mass suicide at the People's Temple compound in Jonestown, Guyana. Annie Moore, Jones's personal nurse, was believed to be the last to die (see letter page 552). When she first joined the People's Temple in 1972, she was eighteen years old and trying, in this letter, to explain her decision. Carolyn was Annie and Becky's older sister. She would die at Jonestown, too, along with her young son Kimo.

August 7, 1972

Dear Becky and Pat,

Well, I have finally made up my mind for good I think and I am not going to stay permanently with you. It was hard for me to make that decision since I have been looking forward to it for almost a year. I hope you won't be angry at me for not coming to stay and I hope that you won't think that I don't love you. Maybe you'll be relieved.

The reason is because (and you'll probably groan) I am going to maybe live with Carolyn or in one of her church dorms. I visited her and her church a week or so ago and I am convinced that it is a good place to be. (Even better than D.C. I guess.) I get along with you guys better than I get along with Carolyn but I think her church really has something to offer. It seems like most of the people who go there, stay. Well, now I know why. Her church or Jim Jones has and knows more secrets about the world than any other group or person. Also their church is socialist in the real sense (the kind of society Jesus was talking about). I thought I may be dumping the real regular world by joining with them, but I think there is little alone that I can do.

So that's my decision. I was also convinced about Jim Jones' power and his "words of wisdom" when I saw him pull incurable cancers out of peoples' throats. I've never heard of any faith healer who could do that (let alone any doctor). So as you can imagine, Mom and Dad are really bugged by my decision because they think that Carolyn's church is a real weirdo church. I must admit that I think it's pretty weird. But the reason people are afraid of it and ridicule it is because they don't understand it, and because they are skeptics. So if I hadn't of gone to visit Carolyn I would still be coming to Washington and although I was really looking forward to being in Washington, I'm glad that I will be involved with Peoples Temple. You probably think that I am brainwashed and stuff, but I think I am a sensible person and no one can tell me what to do. I decide for myself.

I think another reason why Mom and Dad are bugged is because they think I'll be like Carolyn and cut all ties with my family and friends which I have tried to convince them that I won't do. Carolyn kind of went overboard and I don't think I'm the kind that would. Well, enough talk of this. Now you know what I have decided. I hope you will still like me and not think I have deserted you. And I hope you will treat me the same and not like some mentally ill person from Peoples Temple. So I'll see you when Mom and Dad and I come and I hope I haven't caused you any trouble like moving around in the house and stuff.

Love,
Annie

*   *   *

The bewildered rebukes of her parents notwithstanding, Pat (see letter page 525) did move in with Tony.

Sharon was Pat's sister. A family snapshot was enclosed.

8 August 1972

Dear Pat,

I don't know what reaction you expected from us after reading your Air Mail letter to us this week. Naturally we are disappointed at your apparent lack of appreciation and respect for us, as well as respect for yourself. We did the best we could for both our girls, and expected to see you graduate, as did Sharon, knowing where you were going and with both feet on the ground. As it is, you seem to be in a confused state, changing your major for the third time and not knowing exactly what you want or where you are going.

When you gave us the snow job several months ago, convincing us that you wanted to move from the dorm into an apartment, even though we had a few misgivings as to the advisability of it, our trust and confidence in you overruled our doubts and we gave our consent. At that time you seemed to be acting with mature judgement with goals firmly set. We are now convinced that you weren't as prepared as we thought you were to handle the outside world.

You always prided yourself on dating fellows who respected you. What happened along the way that you can no longer demand such respect? Aren't you able to look ahead and visualize what may be in store for you in two, five, or ten years? When this fellow has finished with you and moves on to someone else, and when you meet THE ONE you will want to spend the rest of your life with, will he want to settle for secondhand, used merchandise?

No Pat, we didn't expect you to move here after graduation. You had wanted to go to grad school, and we had made plans to see you thru after your graduation. We wanted to give you every opportunity to fit yourself for self-support. If you are willing to throw all this away, there is nothing we can do about it since you are now an adult and must make your own decisions. If you believe Tony is THE ONE in your life, then he will be willing to wait for you to attain your goals. You have your whole life ahead of you and one more year or less shouldn't make any difference.

Naturally we are disappointed that you do not want to spend your quarter break with us, but you know what is best so far as your studies are concerned. We do want you to be able to retain your good grades and graduate when you planned, and hope that you will reconsider what you proposed in your letter so that we will want to put you through this last quarter. Of course you realize that would be impossible if you should go through with it.

How about Tony's sweet mother, the one who mailed the violin to you? Are you a girl whom he would like to take home to meet his mother? Would she condone such an arrangement? Is he considering her feelings? I'm leaving the remainder to be said by your daddy.

Your loving

Mom

P.S. Whatever will I do with the pretty blue print corduroy bedspread I have just made for you?

Honey, anytime you want to come home for a visit, your room will be waiting for you. Your husband, if and when you get one, will also be welcome. Here is a picture of the happy family that once was.

Pat, as you can well understand from what your mother has written, you know we do not condone your proposal to shack up with Tony. You stated in your letter that you wanted to be independent and make your own decisions. We have let you do just that. However, if you decide to go through with your proposal, God pity you. Here are some of my proposals:

1. Be sure and get some insurance.
2. Get acquainted with income tax rules and regulations.
3. Don't expect any more financial assistance from us.
4. Straighten up and fly right. You will be all the better off if you do.

If you are going to live with a man I will expect him to support you. I pray that you will give this matter some serious thought. Let us know your decision so we can know where we stand financially.

Daddy

1972: NOVEMBER 3
KATHARINE GRAHAM TO JOHN EHRLICHMAN

After the suicide of her husband, Philip, in 1963, Katharine Graham (1917–) succeeded him as publisher of the Washington Post *and* Newsweek. *Often called the most powerful woman in America, she presided over the* Post's *coverage of Watergate by Bob Woodward and Carl Bernstein, even while most of Washington was decrying the newspaper's handling of the story. As the news and rumors continued to appear, Graham sent this letter to one of Watergate's main players.*

At the time, Robert Dole was chairman of the Republican National Committee. He would later become Senate majority leader and make three unsuccessful bids for the presidency.

November 3, 1972

Dear John:

A short while back you threw me a message over the fence, and I genuinely appreciated it. Here is a message I want to send you.

Among the charges that have been flying over the past few weeks, many have disturbed me for the general misunderstanding they suggest of the Post's purposes in printing the stories we do. But none has disturbed me more than an allegation Senator Dole made the other day. It was that the Post's point of view on certain substantive issues was explained by me as proceeding from the simple fact that I "hate" the President.

There are so many things wrong with this "anecdote," that one hardly knows where to begin in correcting them. But I would begin with the fact that I cannot imagine that the episode ever took place at all or that I ever expressed such a childish and mindless sentiment—since it is one that I do not feel.

I want you to know that. And I also want you to know that the fiction doesn't stop there. For the story suggests, as well, that somehow editorial positions on public issues are taken and decisions on news made on the basis of the publisher's personal feelings and tastes. This is not true, even when the sentiments attributed to me—unlike this alleged and unworthy "hate" for the President—may be real.

What appears in the Post is not a reflection of my personal feelings. And by the same token, I would add that my continuing and genuine pride in the paper's performance over the past few months—the period that seems to be at issue—does not proceed from some sense that it has gratified my personal whim. It proceeds from my belief that the editors and reporters have fulfilled the highest standards of professional duty and responsibility.

On this I know we disagree. I am writing this note because I think we have enough such areas of sharp and honest disagreement between us not to need a harmful and destructive overlay of personal animosity that I, for one, don't feel and don't wish to see perpetuated by misquotation! (My turn, it seems.)

Best regards to you and Jean,

[Katharine Graham]

1972: NOVEMBER 15

NORMAN LEAR TO LEROY ELLIOTT

His armchair would end up in the Smithsonian Institution, and Archie Bunker—as brilliantly portrayed by Carroll O'Connor—would end up in the American lexicon, along with the terms "Meathead," "Dingbat," and "Stifle yourself." But when All in the Family *debuted on TV in January of 1971, it was an unlikely hit. With a mixture of malapropisms and roving bigotry, Bunker brought taboo topics into America's living rooms, challenging political and social assumptions. The show ran for seven years, spawned spin-offs including* The Jeffersons *and* Maude, *and changed the television industry forever. It also made a liberal hero of its producer, Norman Lear (1922–), who in the letter below offered an answer to a clergyman who had found the show profane as well as profound.*

November 15, 1972

Rev. Leroy F. Elliott
First Baptist Church
608 Evangeline Drive
Ville Platte, Louisiana

Dear Reverend Elliott:

I want to thank you for taking the time to write even though you have an important complaint. It is wonderful to hear from thoughtful viewers who have the passion to make their feelings known. Thank you too for the kind things you have to say about our shows. It is much easier to thank you for that than it is to answer your complaint—but I would like to take the harder road.

In writing our shows we do not intend to be "crude, blasphemous, irreverent to be relevant or funny" . . . We are crude, blasphemous and irreverent (in your view) only because we believe that the people we are writing about are real and that they would say what we have them say in the situation we depict. There is no way I can prove this point to you—but despite your aversion to certain bits of language on these shows, the characters would not come off with the same degree of validity were such language missing, and consequently your enjoyment of the programs would suffer.

I believe in God, and a poll of our writers and directors indicates that believers in the deity are predominant here. We also believe that Maude Findlay and

Archie Bunker—and certainly Edith Bunker—believe in God too. But you and I know that many God-believing and God-fearing people spend the better part of their lives Goddamning this and that and the other thing.

If you did not cringe too much at the expletive above, perhaps you will realize that the point I wished to make could not be made without it. That is the way we feel about the characters in our shows.

You said in your letter that I have publicly stated that my prime interest is making money. I have never uttered such a foolish statement. If it were true that my prime interest was making money, you would not find so many of all of our shows dealing with subjects such as Nixon and McGovern, Abortion laws, Marijuana laws, etc., etc., etc., which for re-run purposes in future years threaten to be dated. Our prime interest is to entertain and to do that with a view toward the real world we are living in, the things people are talking about and the attitudes they hold in their hearts.

It was a joy answering your letter because I loved receiving it so very much. Thank you for caring.

Sincerely,
Norman Lear

1972: NOVEMBER 30
ALAN BRUDNO TO HIS WIFE

Air Force Major Edward Alan Brudno was shot down over North Vietnam in October of 1965. He remained there as a prisoner of war for seven and a half years. On June 3, 1973, four months after his release and a day before his thirty-third birthday, he would kill himself.

30 November 1972

Merry Xmas, my darling—indeed, for me, a very merry Xmas this year. Merry for all the blessings I've re-discovered, for all the hopes & dreams I've repossessed. My values have changed over these many long years; future plans have come & gone, and, from time to time, I've faltered. But my new values, my new dreams, will bear delicious fruit—I assure you—for they've matured well these past months. I've searched very carefully for lasting happiness—for what life really means to me—and I've found it. I've found it in a family & a home—the dream home we'll soon build together. I've found it in the beautiful New England that I loved so well—that I miss so much. But most of all, Debby, I've found it in <u>you</u>. And I've searched for a realistic career worthy of my talents—fascinating &

challenging. And I've found that, too—in scientific research. Everything—even school, now—is calling me back to Boston, to Franny, to a fulfilling & rewarding life. On top of all that, I'll add a pipe-dream or two—But my old ambitions have ceased to be a prime factor in my life—only the frosting on my cake.—Life will begin in Hawaii, Debby, no matter how or when I return—we <u>must</u> start there! Begin now arranging for the most perfect three weeks there possible. Let's spend most of it on two of the outer islands—first, in the privacy of a simple beach cottage, with all services provided, then at a plush resort hotel. Honolulu will be last, & we'll return to San Francisco by luxury liner. Reunion with Bob next—then home for six weeks: to see the family, to find the perfect homesite, to begin our house plans, & to prepare for our flings abroad (including shopping trips to Denmark & Sweden for furniture & accessories).—I dream every day, my darling, of that magic moment when at last we will meet: There, at ebb tide, I'll find you standing at the water's edge—your back to me. As I approach with pounding heart, I'll whisper your name, & you'll turn. Few people have known, or will ever know, the incomparable joy we will share then. And there as we stand, face to face, hand in hand, and we gaze into glistening eyes—at last we'll find peace. And til time should ever cease, for us there'll be no more goodbyes.

<u>Alan</u>

1972: DECEMBER 6
PATRICIA LOUD TO A WNET OFFICIAL

An American Family was a first-of-its-kind television show. During the course of seven months, the Loud family (Patricia, Bill, and their five children) had allowed producer Craig Gilbert and a television crew to follow them around, documenting their highs and lows—most famously the breakup of Pat and Bill's marriage and the sexual realizations of their gay son, Lance. The result, which was shown on PBS in twelve segments, set off national debates about the nature of the American family, television, and reality. Margaret Mead called the series the most significant event in human thought since the invention of the novel. For her part, as she made clear in this letter to a public-television official, Pat Loud insisted that she and her family had been betrayed.

December 6, 1972

DEAR "ONE WNET OFFICIAL WHO HAS SEEN ONLY THE FIRST TWO EPISODES":

It is part of my job to clip the Washington <u>Post</u>, and today I picked up the mail, went to the office, and looked over the paper. The enclosed article generates this letter.

It is one thing to be sniped at by people who don't know you, or with whom you have no commingling of interests. It is quite another to stick your head furtively over the trenches, only to be shot at from the rear. You remind me of the Congressman who visits Saigon for three days of revelry, and returns to Washington, a <u>bona fide</u> authority on Southeast Asia. Yet you have a certain power—you can preprogram the viewpoints of many who will watch this series and I know you are too misinformed to take this job upon yourself.

You say we are "<u>damned attractive people who have come a long way, and don't know why.</u>" I don't understand that kind of talk. Come a long way from where? Toward what? Could it be that you judge us by your own flagging standards? If so, I can assure you that your standards are not mine, and therefore are not valid in the comparison.

"<u>Lots of times they travel and you get the feeling that it's so they don't have to think.</u>" Now, this statement offends me so deeply (coming from someone who is supposed to be friendly) that I just am not going to answer it. I suggest that you ask one of us why we traveled so much that summer before you go around making such insulting statements about us—statements that can only obfuscate some very real issues.

As for the rest of it, like the show opening on an "<u>Esquire-like Christmas</u>"—it was New Year's Eve. We always decorate our house for the holidays. Don't you? My children love it. Don't yours? Is that bad? You speak of people not communicating. I can assure you, you have communicated to me. This letter is my attempt to communicate to you, since words seem to be the only means of communication with which you are familiar. I feel compelled to say that I fervently hope that you will not busy yourself with this series anymore. You have already done us irredeemable harm. You do not understand us, and yet you have taken it upon yourself to stereotype us through a prejudgment funneled through your own experience, or what you <u>want</u> to see. Repeat—you have done us enough harm. I plead with you to say no more—to disassociate yourself from the series. I feel like asking, "So what's your problem?" but I really don't want to hear that. Please allow such people as will watch this series to make up their own minds. You have been unfair to us. You have dealt with us as if we were objects, not humans. I resent it. You could look at all three hundred hours of that film, and I would still say, "If you want to know about us, <u>ask us</u>." It is not all there, I assure you.

When we entered into this thing with Craig Gilbert there was nothing in the contract that said, "Abandon hope all ye who enter here." That contract is also yours. Don't shoot at us from the rear anymore, or we must fight back. I want you to understand; I expect a written answer to this letter.

Sincerely,

Patricia Loud

1973: JUNE
CLAUDIA HELLER TO MS. MAGAZINE

Founded by Gloria Steinem (1934–), Ms. *magazine began publication in 1972 and was a cornerstone of the new women's movement, reflecting and responding to the increasingly ardent feelings of women seeking new opportunities at home and in the workplace.*

My husband says I used to be a bitch once a month but, since I subscribed to <u>Ms.</u>, now I'm a bitch twice a month.

Claudia N. Heller

Los Angeles, California

1973: OCTOBER 20
ELLIOT RICHARDSON TO RICHARD NIXON

At the height of the Watergate scandal, Special Prosecutor Archibald Cox (1912–) subpoenaed Nixon's secret tapes concerning the Watergate break-in and apparent cover-up. Nixon refused to hand the tapes over, citing national security concerns. Then U.S. District Court Judge John Sirica (1904–1992) ordered the president to comply, and the U.S. Court of Appeals upheld that order in October. Nixon next suggested that he deliver edited summaries of the tapes instead. When Cox refused, Nixon attempted to fire him. The result was the drama of the "Saturday Night Massacre," in which Cox would be sacked, but not before the top two Justice Department officials resigned rather than agreeing to fire him.

October 20, 1973

The President

The White House

Dear Mr. President:

It is with deep regret that I have been obliged to conclude that circumstances leave me no alternative to the submission of my resignation as Attorney General of the United States.

At the time you appointed me, you gave me the authority to name a special prosecutor if I should consider it appropriate. A few days before my confirmation hearing began, I announced that I would, if confirmed, "appoint a special prosecutor and give him all the independence, authority, and staff support needed to carry out the tasks entrusted to him." I added, "Although he will be in the Department of Justice and report to me—and only to me—he will be aware that his ultimate accountability is to the American people."

At many points throughout the nomination hearings, I reaffirmed my intention to assure the independence of the special prosecutor, and in my statement of his duties and responsibilities, I specified that he would have "full authority" for "determining whether or not to contest the assertion of 'Executive Privilege' or any other testimonial privilege." And while the special prosecutor can be removed from office for "extraordinary improprieties," I also pledged that "The Attorney General will not countermand or interfere with the Special Prosecutor's decisions or actions."

While I fully respect the reasons that have led you to conclude that the Special Prosecutor must be discharged, I trust that you understand that I could not in the light of these firm and repeated commitments carry out your direction that this be done. In the circumstances, therefore, I feel that I have no choice but to resign.

In leaving your Administration, I take with me lasting gratitude for the opportunities you have given me to serve under your leadership in a number of important posts. It has been a privilege to share in your efforts to make the structure of world peace more stable and the structure of our own government more responsive. I believe profoundly in the rightness and importance of those efforts, and I trust that they will meet with increasing success in the remaining years of your Presidency.

Respectfully,
Elliot L. Richardson

1973: OCTOBER 20
WILLIAM RUCKELSHAUS TO RICHARD NIXON

William D. Ruckelshaus (1932–) was deputy attorney general.

Dear Mr. President,

It is with deep regret that I tender my resignation. During your Administration, you have honored me with four appointments—first in the Justice Department's Civil Division, then as administrator of the Environmental Protection

Agency, next as acting director of the Federal Bureau of Investigation, and finally as Deputy Attorney General. I have found the challenge of working in the high levels of American Government an unforgettable and rewarding experience.

I shall always be grateful for your having given me the opportunity to serve the American people in this fashion.

I am, of course, sorry that my conscience will not permit me to carry out your instruction to discharge Archibald Cox. My disagreement with that action at this time is too fundamental to permit me to act otherwise.

I wish you every success during the remainder of your Administration.

Respectfully,

William D. Ruckelshaus

1973: OCTOBER 20
ROBERT BORK TO ARCHIBALD COX

Robert Bork (1927–) was solicitor general when the resignations of Richardson and Ruckelshaus made him acting attorney general. In that position, he fired Cox. Years later, as a federal judge, Bork would come into public view again when Ronald Reagan nominated him for the Supreme Court and a rancorous political fight about the depths of Bork's conservatism denied him the post.

October 20, 1973

Dear Mr. Cox:

As provided by Title 28, Section 508(b) of the United States Code and Title 28, Section 0.132(a) of the Code of Federal Regulations, I have today assumed the duties of Acting Attorney General.

In that capacity I am, as instructed by the President, discharging you, effective at once, from your position as Special Prosecutor, Watergate Special Prosecution Force.

Very truly yours,

ROBERT H. BORK

Acting Attorney General

Honorable Archibald Cox
Special Prosecutor
Watergate Special Prosecution Force
1425 K Street, N.W.
Washington, D.C.

1974: FEBRUARY 4
SYMBIONESE LIBERATION ARMY
TO ITS WESTERN REGIONAL UNIT

---

*Granddaughter of the publishing magnate, Patricia Hearst (1954–) was an art
student with no great political passions when she was kidnapped by the radical left-
wing Symbionese Liberation Army in accordance with the directions of the following "warrant." Apparently brainwashed, Hearst was held for a ransom of $2 million
worth of food and supplies intended for minority communities. When her parents
paid the ransom, they received a tape-recorded message saying, "I have chosen to
stay and fight." Eventually, as "Tania," Hearst would espouse the SLA's views, going
so far as to join in the holdup of a San Francisco bank.*

Despite attorney F. Lee Bailey's defense at trial, Hearst would be sentenced to seven years in
prison for armed robbery. After serving twenty-two months, she would have her sentence commuted by President Jimmy Carter.

SYMBIONESE LIBERATION ARMY
<u>Western Regional Adult Unit</u>
February 4, 1974

Communiqué #3   WARRANT ORDER:
SUBJECT: Prisoners of War   Arrest and protective
TARGET: Patricia Campbell Hearst   custody and, if
         Daughter of Randolph Hearst   resistance, execution
         Corporate enemy of the people

On the above-stated date, combat elements of the United Federation Forces
of the Symbionese Liberation Army armed with cyanide-loaded weapons served
an arrest warrant upon Patricia Campbell Hearst.

It is the order of this court that the subject be arrested by combat units and
removed to a protective area of safety and only upon completion of this condition to notify Unit #4 to give communication of this action.

It is the directive of this court that during this action ONLY, no civilian elements be harmed if possible, and that warning shots be given. However, if any
citizens attempt to aid the authorities or interfere with the implementation of
this order, they shall be executed immediately.

This court hereby notifies the public and directs all combat units in the future to shoot to kill any civilian who attempts to witness or interfere with any
operation conducted by the peoples' forces against the fascist state.

Should any attempt be made by authorities to rescue the prisoner, or to arrest or harm any S.L.A. elements, the prisoner is to be executed.

The prisoner is to be maintained in adequate physical and mental condition, and unharmed as long as these conditions are adhered to. Protective custody shall be composed of combat and medical units, to safeguard both the prisoner and her health.

All communications from this court MUST be published in full, in all newspapers, and all other forms of the media. Failure to do so will endanger the safety of the prisoner. Further communications will follow.

S.L.A.

DEATH TO THE FASCIST INSECT

THAT PREYS UPON THE LIFE OF

THE PEOPLE

1974: AUGUST 6

JULIE NIXON EISENHOWER TO RICHARD NIXON

Nixon's younger daughter, Julie (1948–), left this note for her father a few nights before he resigned. Nixon later wrote that if anything could have changed his mind, it would have been this.

Dear Daddy— I love you. Whatever you do I will support. I am very proud of you.

Please wait a week or even ten days before you make this decision. Go through the fire just a little bit longer. You are so strong!

I love you,

Julie

Millions support you.

1974: AUGUST 9

RICHARD NIXON TO HENRY KISSINGER

Gerald Ford (1913–) became president at 11:35 A.M., as soon as Kissinger initialed this letter. Nixon was at that moment en route—aboard Air Force One for the last time—to his home in California.

THE WHITE HOUSE
Washington

August 9, 1974

Dear Mr. Secretary:

I hereby resign the office of President of the United States.

Sincerely,

Richard Nixon

The Honorable Henry A. Kissinger
The Secretary of State
Washington, D.C. 20520

1974: OCTOBER

JAN TO HER MOTHER

Jan was eighteen years old when she wrote this letter to her mother. Abortion had been legalized by Roe v. Wade *the year before.*

October 1974

Dear Mom,

Health-wise I'm OK but I've been through some unfortunate experiences as of late. Day before I left for my New York visit I went to the doctor for a check-up. He examined me and told me I was 6 weeks pregnant. I was shocked. He offered to give me an abortion that day but I knew I had to prepare myself emotionally and I also wanted to continue with my New York trip.

My first thoughts were that I could never have an abortion, but the more I thought it over and the more Al and I discussed it I realized it was the only thing I could do.

The day of the abortion Al and I went to the clinic at 10 a.m. I saw a counselor; we discussed my feelings and she felt my decision was carefully thought over and one I believed in. She also explained the actual procedure: dilation, suction and then a scraping of the womb.

I can only feel fortunate that I live in a time when abortion is legal and I did not have to suffer through an unwanted pregnancy or find means of an illegal, unsafe abortion. The other women there—one 35, one 50, one 15; all making an important decision about their lives.

I was pretty calm about it. The counselor was there with me as well as a doctor and a nurse. I was given a local anesthetic but I swear I never knew such physical pain existed. I thought I would die or leap off the table (they said my cramping was much worse than usual). But when it was over so was the pain.

Immediately after, they led me into a small room where Al was allowed to come sit with me. It was then I cried and I haven't cried since. The feeling was mostly of relief—the pain was gone but most of all the pregnancy.

I knew from the start that I would tell you, but I waited till now to give you the reassurance that I'm alright. I'm too close to you not to tell you. I guess I still fear that I'm the little girl that will be punished. I just want to be understood. I know you will feel sad but don't feel disappointed. Just understand.

The night after the abortion I had a dream. I dreamt that I was walking down a street in New York. A young boy, 16 or so, offered me a ride. We drove and drove all the way to Mississippi and gradually he became younger until he was about 8 years old. He lived in a big house by a lake. Then Al was in the dream—we were telling the boy we wanted to make love with him to show him how much we loved him. Then his mother came home and we left. To me, that symbolized our love for the child even though we had to leave it behind and realizing that it had found another place.

Please write me of your feelings. I'm glad that I felt I could write you of this. I will see you and talk to you soon.

Much love,
Jan

1974: NOVEMBER

HER MOTHER TO JAN

November 1974

Dearest Daughter,

Your adolescent years have provided us with the usual tense moments that all parents must associate with "growing-up". Your wailing despair with hair and figure. Your ups and downs with "first-lover" and the gradual moving away from the once close companionship that you shared with your father.

As you know the "new sexuality" was not hard for me to accept. I think I was relieved to know that we were now living in an era that allowed a young woman to explore her sexual curiosity without the shame of feeling <u>ruined</u> or the necessity of having to "marry the boy". You are not a promiscuous girl and when you did lose your virginity we discussed it thoroughly along with the responsibilities it entailed.

I think my only real days of despair came when you entered into this "live-in" relationship with Al. It was neither the "live-in" that bothered me nor the fact that he is almost twice your age but the knowledge that he is a deeply <u>disturbed</u> person. I was afraid for you.

During the week-end that dad and I spent with the two of you, we were so shaken by his violent mood-swings. On our long drive home the silence was broken only by my tears and dad's laments of disbelief.

Now I have before me the letter telling of your recent abortion. It's difficult to explain how very saddened I am—not by the loss of a grandchild but by the necessity to deny some spark of human potential, its existence. I, who would not knowingly step on an ant, do understand how you have done what you <u>had</u> to do. At eighteen, with your life before you, you are not ready for a child nor are you ready for marriage to its father. This unfortunate "flying Dutchman" who drifts from coast to coast, crashing with friends until they can no longer abide his temper could provide neither emotional nor financial support for a "family".

I think my real sorrow stems from the fact that you had to undergo this traumatic experience. That you had to make this decision, endure the physical pain and mental anguish; the knowing loss. And finally that I should, somehow, have "been there" to comfort, to hold you in my arms and tell you (although we would both know, deep inside that it wasn't) that everything was all right—

With my love,
Dorothy

1975: JANUARY 23
J. F. HIND TO C. A. TUCKER

This memo was written by an official in the market research department of R. J. Reynolds, the second-largest tobacco company in the United States. Addressed to the vice-president of marketing and stamped SECRET, *it laid out a strategy that would eventually produce the cartoon figure Joe Camel, attract untold teenage smokers, and become one piece of evidence in the tobacco litigation of the 1990s.*

January 23, 1975

<u>Mr. C. A. Tucker</u>:
Our attached recommendation to expand nationally the successfully tested "Meet the Turk" ad campaign and new Marlboro-type blend is another step to meet our marketing objective: To increase our young adult franchise. To ensure

increased and longer-term growth for CAMEL FILTER, the brand must increase its share penetration among the 14–24 age group which have a new set of more liberal values and which represent tomorrow's cigarette business.

Presently, almost two-thirds of the CAMEL FILTER business is among smokers over 35 years of age, more than twice that for Marlboro. While "Meet the Turk" is designed to shift the brand's age profile to the younger age group, this won't come over night. Patience, persistence, and consistency will be needed. There may even be temporarily a softness in CAMEL FILTER's growth rate as some of the older, more conservative CAMEL FILTER smokers are turned off by the campaign and younger, more liberal smokers begin to come into the brand's franchise. Test market results suggest, though, that this risk is small.

The current media spending level will be maintained since test market shipments indicate no significant short-term volume gains from increased spending. Other competitive brands, such as VANTAGE, Newport, and Virginia Slims with sharply directed advertising have demonstrated significant growth rates attainable with CAMEL FILTER's media spending level. We would prefer, as we did for VANTAGE, to demonstrate an increased growth rate with this campaign/blend and then give consideration to asking for extra monies.

Jim

1975: MARCH 6
LEONARD MATLOVICH TO THE SECRETARY OF THE AIR FORCE

Leonard Matlovich (1943–1988) was a U.S. Air Force sergeant and a Vietnam veteran who had been decorated with the Bronze Star and a Purple Heart. In this letter, he declared his homosexuality, provoking his expulsion from the armed forces (which came the same year) and paving the way for a landmark case in which the U.S. Court of Appeals declared his expulsion illegal. (Matlovich later settled out of court.) Providing a visual milestone for the young gay-rights movement, his photograph ran on the cover of Time *magazine above the words "I Am a Homosexual." He would die of AIDS, having continued to champion the cause of gay rights. His headstone reads: "When I was in the military, they gave me a medal for killing two men, and a discharge for loving one."*

March 6, 1975

TO: The Secretary of the Air Force

THRU: Captain Dennis M. Collins

        4510th Support Sq. (T.A.C.)

        Lt. Col. Charles R. Ritchie

        Commander

        4510th Support Sq. (T.A.C.)

        Commander

        Tactical Air Command

FROM: T/Sgt Leonard Matlovich, 463-76-2847

1. After some years of uncertainty, I have arrived at the conclusion that my sexual preferences are homosexual as opposed to heterosexual. I have also concluded that my sexual preferences will in no way interfere with my Air Force duties, as my preferences are now open. It is therefore requested that those provisions in AFM 39-12 relating to the discharge of homosexuals be waived in my case.

2. I will decline to answer specific questions concerning the functioning of my sex life, for AFM 39-12 as currently in effect could subject me to a less than fully honorable discharge. However, I will be glad to answer any questions concerning my personal life if reasons are given detailing how the questions relate to specific fitness and security concerns rather than the generally unconstitutional provisions of AFM 39-12 relating to the discharge of homosexuals. If more specific criteria other than the notion that homosexuals are morally unqualified for service in the Air Force can be shown as basis for questioning, I will answer the appropriate questions.

3. Before any specific questions are addressed to me about this matter my attorney, David F. Addlestone, 1346 Connecticut Avenue N.W., Suite 604, Washington, D.C. 20036, requests that he be notified.

4. In sum, I consider myself to be a homosexual and fully qualified for further military service. My almost twelve years of unblemished service supports this position.

                               Leonard Matlovich

                               T/Sgt, USAF

                               463-76-2847

1976: FEBRUARY 3

BILL GATES TO COMPUTER HOBBYISTS

The Altair was the first personal computer, and William Henry Gates III (1955–) was one of the first people who knew what to do with it. Teaming up with high-school friend Paul Allen (1953–) in 1975, Gates developed a version of the computer language BASIC that could run on the Altair. The same year, he dropped out of Harvard and with Allen founded Micro-soft (then hyphenated) to develop operating systems and applications software. His argument in this letter—that software had value—would of course prevail, and he would become the wealthiest man in the world, with an approximate worth in 1999 of $90 billion.

MITS, or Micro Instrumentation and Telemetry Systems, was a model-airplane radio-control company that developed the Altair. Monte Davidoff, a fellow student at Harvard, contributed some of the math routines to BASIC.

AN OPEN LETTER TO HOBBYISTS

To me, the most critical thing in the hobby market right now is the lack of good software courses, books, and software itself. Without good software and an owner who understands programming, a hobby computer is wasted. Will quality software be written for the hobby market?

Almost a year ago, Paul Allen and myself, expecting the hobby market to expand, hired Monte Davidoff and developed Altair BASIC. Though the initial work took only two months, the three of us have spent most of the last year documenting, improving, and adding features to BASIC. Now we have 4K, 8K, EXTENDED, ROM and DISK BASIC. The value of the computer time we have used exceeds $40,000.

The feedback we have gotten from the hundreds of people who say they are using BASIC has all been positive. Two surprising things are apparent, however: 1) Most of these "users" never bought BASIC (less than 10% of all Altair owners have bought BASIC), and 2) The amount of royalties we have received from sales to hobbyists makes the time spent on Altair BASIC worth less than $2 an hour.

Why is this? As the majority of hobbyists must be aware, most of you steal your software. Hardware must be paid for, but software is something to share. Who cares if the people who worked on it get paid?

Is this fair? One thing you don't do by stealing software is get back at MITS for some problem you may have had. MITS doesn't make money selling software. The royalty paid to us, the manual, the tape, and the overhead make it a break-even operation. One thing you do do is prevent good software from being written. Who can afford to do professional work for nothing? What hobbyist can put 3-man years into programming, finding all bugs, documenting his product and distribute for free? The fact is, no one besides us has invested a lot of money in hobby software. We have written 6800 BASIC, and are writing 8080 APL and 6800 APL, but there is very little incentive to make this software available to hobbyists.

Most directly, the thing you do is theft.

What about the guys who resell Altair BASIC, aren't they making money on hobby software? Yes, but those who have been reported to us may lose in the end. They are the ones who give hobbyists a bad name and should be kicked out of any club meeting they show up at.

I would appreciate letters from any who wants to pay up, or has a suggestion or comment. Nothing would please me more than being able to hire ten programmers and deluge the hobby market with good software.

> Bill Gates
> General Partner
> Micro-Soft
> 1180 Avarado SE, #114
> Albuquerque, NM 87108

1976: DECEMBER 29
GARY GILMORE TO "THOSE WHO OPPOSE"

Gary Gilmore (1941–1977) offered no defense during his trial for the 1976 murders of two Utah residents. When the jury found him guilty, he did not attempt to appeal the verdict. And when faced with the choice between being hanged and being shot, he calmly declared: "I prefer to be shot." Opponents of the death penalty began to protest, but Gilmore—with a mercurial combination of apparent sincerity and apparent scorn—kept challenging the state of Utah to do its job. After two unsuccessful suicide attempts, and despite a circus of press and legal attention, Gilmore would become, on January 17, 1977, the first person in ten years to be executed in America. Shirley Pedler was executive director of the American Civil Liberties Union in Utah.

An open letter from Gary Gilmore to all and any who still seek to oppose by whatever means my death by legal execution. Particularly: ACLU, NAACP legal defense fund, sundry assorted lawyers for cowardly condemned criminals.

I invite you to finally butt out of my life. Butt out of my death.

It does not concern you.

The lawyers for other condemned men: What right have you to impose your particular wants or attitudes on my life? Certainly you have no legal right.

And of course you have no moral right. Your claim is that your clients may be affected by my execution.

That's balderdash. A hollow shallow argument. Your clients are staying alive (and living in fear) by the merits of their own appeals. My case has nothing to do with the cases of any other condemned persons.

Frankly I'm amazed that your clients choose to live in the abject fear that haunts and surrounds their meagre existense.

Why not accept? I mean, if you're dumb enough to get yourself sentenced to death in the first place why cry about it?

Why not simply accept graciously and quietly? That's all I'm trying to do.

To my mind you don't kill or torture or maim somebody and then start snivelling because you were dumb enough to get caught and the going gets rough.

That's the way I look at it.

But you other condemned fellas can do your own thing any way you want. Appeal forever. Good luck. It's of no concern to me how you choose to lead your lives.

And my life is of no concern to you.

Shirley Pedler, Gees, baby, lay off. I wouldn't dare to be so presumptuous as to presume I could impose any unwanted thing on your life. Incidentally, Shirley, I once, couple years ago, asked your outfit for legal aid. I was refused. I had been transferred for disciplinary reasons from Oregon State Prison to Marion Federal Pen, Illinois. I had not been given a hearing prior to my transfer. The transfer was illegal. I asked ACLU for help and was refused. Get out of my life Shirley.

NAACP-LDF: I'm a white man. Don't want no uncle tom blacks buttin in on my life. Your contention is that if I am executed then a whole bunch of black dudes will be executed. Well that's so apparently stupid I won't even argue with that kind of silly illogic.

But you know as well as I do that they'll kill a white man these days a lot quicker than they'll kill a black man.

Y'all ain't really disadvantaged lak ya used to be.

Capital punishment is a thing that has been around since before recorded history.

The death penalty is in actuality a thing that comes and goes. Gets voted out then gets voted back in.

I'm not a proponent of it. Neither am I exactly against it.

I do believe it will always be a part of mankind.

There are people in the world so evil that their lives are forfeit by the nature of their beings, manifested in dark acts against other men they warrant execution.

But there are always "civil activists" clamoring to keep such people alive. Why?

Personally I was given a sentence that I did not seek. But when I got it I took it serious and accepted it. It was the death sentence.

I would have taken any other sentence equally as serious and accepted it too.

An eye for an eye—a life for a life. I got to admit I find that truely fair. Obviously just. By virtue of its logical form.

I've been asked about atonement. It was a personal question. To me atonement and religious beliefs are personal private things. But maybe I better say what I feel about atonement.

I'm willing.

I know what I did. I know how unreasonable how wrong it was. How evil.

I know the awful effect it had on the lives of two families.

I'm willing to pay ultimately.

Let me.

As for those of you who would question my sanity, well, I question yours.

from my heart
Gary Gilmore

1977: MARCH 5
NAN BISHOP TO CLARE BOWMAN

Nan Bishop and Clare Bowman met in 1966, when, along with their friend Sarah Hamilton, they roomed together in Benefit, Indiana, while taking college drama classes. A three-way correspondence was rekindled in 1977, when all of their marriages were falling apart. Like vast numbers of American wives, the three women found themselves trying to reconcile the expectations they had had in the fifties with the realities they met in the seventies.

Nan would divorce her husband soon after writing this letter.

Rocking and writing by
the kitchen stove

Dear lovely vibrant Clare,

Duncan slapped me and Justin around last night and I am still upset today. I do not like violence. I'm a Cream of Wheat person. I'm afraid. My eyes feel heavy and puffy. I am crying inside but can't cry real tears. Monday evening Duncan came in the door drunk, just as Sarah phoned me. He yelled in my ear and tried to grab the phone away. I told Sarah all was okay, because when Duncan is drunk it's best never to say anything negative. He was angry that I was even talking to Sarah, so I hung up right away. He cursed and yelled at me, then sat down to eat.

The food was cold and Duncan got uncontrollably angry. He threw the food against the wall and pushed me out of the room. I called a neighbor who came over and stood with his hands in his pockets and watched Duncan throw me on the floor, slap my face five or six times, and pull my hair (some actually continued to fall out all evening). I threatened to call the police. The neighbor told Duncan he could come over to his house and have coffee. Duncan said he wouldn't, so I said Justin and I had better go for a ride and Duncan let us go. We went to a girl friend's house overnight. When I got back today Duncan wasn't home. I imagined him out doing more drinking, or buying a gun to kill us or something. Finally he came home—after spending the night in jail for driving while intoxicated. His license was revoked, he was fined, and must go to driver's rehabilitation classes. He says he will never drink again! (We went through same thing a few years ago when he lost his license on a DWI charge when he totaled his Fiat.) I see a lawyer Friday—not sure if it will be for temporary or permanent separation.

Sometimes I feel I am horrid for not wanting to try to "work things out," but I just want to get away from him. I feel I've failed the marriage counselor. I feel I am being closed-minded, unliberal, prejudiced, almost "fanatical," which I don't want to be. I want to be a loving, warm, sympathetic, compassionate, passionate person.

My neck aches, I am so tense. I am so happy to be writing to you and Sarah. I love your letters and (is this awful?) I love that Clare got her divorce because she wanted to and for no other reason. It gives me support. I need support through role models at this point, perhaps I always have. But I am also searching for the core of me from which, with confidence, will emanate all the secondary me's—mother, lover, worker, player.

Justin is running around the couch and getting Caruso to chase him. Caruso jumps on the couch and stands on the top. Justin was "sick" today till about noon, then suddenly got "well."

Love,
Nan

1977: APRIL 17

SON OF SAM TO JOSEPH BORRELLI

Between July of 1976 and August of 1977, a host of New York detectives struggled to find the gunman—and the motive—behind the series of seemingly random shootings that left six people dead, seven injured, and many citizens terrified. The first true lead came when this letter to a Queens police detective was found at one of the crime scenes. In it, David Berkowitz, calling himself the "Son of Sam," declared that he was being ordered to kill by his father. When he came to trial in 1977, he would plead insanity and explain that his "father" had actually been a neighbor's dog. Found sane, he was convicted of murder and sentenced to 365 years in prison.

Dear Captain Joseph Borrelli,

I am deeply hurt by your calling me a wemon hater. I am not. But I am a monster. I am the "Son of Sam." I am a little "brat."

When Father Sam gets drunk he gets mean. He beats his family. Sometimes he ties me up to the back of the house. Other times he locks me in the garage. Sam loves to drink blood.

"Go out and kill," commands Father Sam.

Behind our house some rest. Mostly young—raped and slaughtered—their blood drained—just bones now.

Papa Sam keeps me locked in the attic, too. I can't get out but I look out the attic window and watch the world go by. I feel like an outsider. I am on a different wavelength then everybody else—programmed too kill.

However, to stop me you must kill me. Attention all police: Shoot me first—shoot to kill or else. Keep out of my way or you will die!

Papa Sam is old now. He needs some blood to preserve his youth. He has had too many heart attacks. Too many heart attacks. "Ugh, me hoot it urts sonny boy."

I miss my pretty princess most of all. She's resting in our ladies house. But I'll she her soon.

I am the "monster"—"Bellzebub"—the "Chubby Behemouth."

I love to hunt. Prowling the streets looking for fair game—tasty meat. The wemon of Queens are z prettyist of all. I must be the water they drink. I live for the hunt—my life. Blood for Papa.

Mr. Borrelli, Sir, I don't want to kill anymore no sir, no more but I must, "Honour thy Father." I want to make love to the world. I love people. I don't belong on earth. Return me to yahoos. To the people of Queens, I love you. And I want to wish all of you a happy Easter. May God bless you in this life and in the next. And for now I say goodbye and goodnight.

Police: Let me haunt you with these words:

I'll be back!

I'll be back!

To be interrpreted as—bang, bang, bang, bang, bang—ugh!!

Your in murder

Mr. Monster

1977: JUNE 16
JIMMY CARTER TO THE COSMOS

Jimmy Carter (1924–), thirty-ninth U.S. president, sent this letter into the cosmos aboard the space probe Voyager. Along with it went a gold-plated phonograph record featuring music and greetings in fifty-five languages, as well as the sounds of animals, volcanoes, rain, laughter, and a mother's kiss.

THE WHITE HOUSE

June 16, 1977

This Voyager spacecraft was constructed by the United States of America. We are a community of 240 million human beings among the more than 4 billion who inhabit the planet Earth. We human beings are still divided into nation states, but these states are rapidly becoming a single global civilization.

We cast this message into the cosmos. It is likely to survive a billion years into our future, when our civilization is profoundly altered and the surface of the Earth may be vastly changed.

Of the 200 billion stars in the Milky Way galaxy some—perhaps many—may have inhabited planets and spacefaring civilizations. If one such civilization intercepts Voyager and can understand these recorded contents, here is our message:

This is a present from a small distant world, a token of our sounds, our science, our images, our music, our thoughts and our feelings. We are attempting to survive our time so we may live into yours.

We hope someday, having solved the problems we face, to join a community of galactic civilizations. This record represents our hope and our determination, and our good will in a vast and awesome universe.

Jimmy Carter

President

United States of America

1978: NOVEMBER 18
ANNIE MOORE

On November 14, California congressman Leo Ryan arrived in Guyana along with aides, reporters, and some relatives of Jim Jones's followers. Four days later, as Ryan and his group prepared to leave—along with fourteen cult defectors—Jones ordered them killed. Ryan and four others were assassinated; the rest survived, and Jones feared they would bring reprisals. His exhortations to mass suicide followed. This note, written by Jones's personal nurse, Annie Moore (see letter page 526), was found next to her body.

I am 24 years of age right now and don't expect to live through the end of this book.

I thought I should at least make some attempt to let the world know what Jim Jones and the People's Temple is—OR WAS—all about.

It seems that some people and perhaps the majority of people would like to destroy the best thing that ever happened to the 1,200 or so of us who have followed Jim.

I am at a point right now so embittered against the world that I don't know why I am writing this. Someone who finds it will believe I am crazy or believe in the barbed wire that does NOT exist in Jonestown.

It seems that everything good that happens to the world is under constant attack. When I write this, I can expect some mentally deranged fascist person to find it and decide it should be thrown in the trash before anyone gets a chance to hear the truth—which is what I am now writing about.

Where can I begin—JONESTOWN—the most peaceful, loving community that ever existed, JIM JONES—the one who made this paradise possible— much to the contrary of the lies stated about Jim Jones being a power-hungry, sadistic mean person who thought he was God—of all things.

I want you who read this to know Jim was the most honest, loving, caring, concerned person whom I ever met and knew. His love for animals—each creature, poisonous snakes, tarantulas. None of them ever bit him because he was such a gentle person. He knew how mean the world was and he took any and every stray animal and took care of each one.

His love for humans was insurmountable and it was many of those whom he put his love and trust in that left him and spit in his face. Teresa Buford, Debbie Blakey—they both wanted sex from him which he was too ill to give. Why should he have to give them sex?—And Tim and Grace Stoen—also include them. I should know.

I have spent these last few months taking care of Jim's health. However, it was difficult to take care of anything for him. He always would do for himself.

His hatred of racism, sexism, elitism, and mainly classism, is what prompted him to make a new world for the people—a paradise in the jungle. The children loved it. So did everyone else.

There were no ugly, mean policemen wanting to beat our heads in, no more racist tears from whites and others who thought they were better. No one was made fun of for their appearance—something no one had control over.

Meanness and making fun were not allowed. Maybe this is why all the lies were started. Besides this fact, no one was allowed to live higher than anyone else. The United States allowed criticism. The problem being this and not all the side tracks of black power, woman power, Indian power, gay power.

Jim Jones showed us all this—that we could live together with our differences, that we are all the same human beings. Luckily, we are more fortunate than the starving babies of Ethiopia, than the starving babies in the United States.

What a beautiful place this was. The children loved the jungle, learned about animals and plants. There were no cars to run over them; no child-molesters to molest them; nobody to hurt them. They were the freest, most intelligent children I had ever known.

Seniors had dignity. They had whatever they wanted—a plot of land for a garden. Seniors were treated with respect—something they never had in the United States. A rare few were sick, and when they were, they were given the best medical care. . . .

We died because you would not let us live in peace.

Annie Moore

1979: APRIL 22
KENNETH TYNAN TO JOHNNY CARSON

It would be another thirteen years before Johnny Carson (1925–) would actually leave The Tonight Show *entirely—and in doing so earn a front-page story in the* New York Times. *But having begun his domination of late-night television in 1962, Carson, at the time this letter was written, was responsible for an audience of more than seventeen million, and some 17 percent of NBC's profits. On hearing a rumor that Carson was planning to retire, the erudite British drama critic Kenneth Tynan (1927–1980) felt compelled to dispatch this plea.*

1500 Stone Canyon Road
Bel Air
April 22, 1979

Dear John,

What follows is sheer impertinence on my part; all I can say in its defence is that it is well-meant. When I read in the paper that you might be quitting <u>The Tonight Show</u> in the fall, I felt a twinge of quite definite grief, and suddenly realized how much it meant to me, when contemplating a trip to this country, to reflect that whatever else might have dried up or degenerated, one sparkling fountainhead of pleasure would still remain—Carson at 11:30. Here at least was something I couldn't get anywhere else in the world. I cannot tell you how many bad days you have saved, and good days you have improved, by simply being there on Channel 4, doing what nobody else can do anything like as well.

And now I hear talk of Specials. Dear John, <u>all</u> your shows are Specials. I hear, too, that you are bored. Was Dickens bored after writing novels for seventeen years? Did Matisse burn his brushes after seventeen years' daubing? Did you never hear the great remark of the painter Delacroix: "Talent does whatever it wants to do: genius only what it can do"? What other TV format would give you the freedom to improvise, to take off and fly, to plunge into the unpredictable? Carson script-bound would be Carson strait-jacketed. We all know you are like a great dish that combines all your flavours. It resembles the pressed duck at the Tour d'Argent in Paris: the recipe hasn't changed in my lifetime, yet it tastes as inimitably fresh every time I order it.

Was it unadventurous for Astaire to stick to tap-dancing instead of venturing into ballet? On the contrary: it was brave, and it was what made him (and will keep him forever) a classic. Similarly, I honour Cary Grant for never having played <u>Macbeth</u> and Muhammad Ali for keeping out of the Wimbledon championships.

I wouldn't insult you by supposing that you haven't thought along these lines yourself. I'm sure you are convinced that there is a new Carson ready to emerge from the old and stagger us all once again. And your track record is such that you may well be right. But I beseech you—as Oliver Cromwell said on a famous occasion—to consider in the bowels of Christ whether ye may not be wrong. (I may have misquoted Cromwell but I hope ye get my drift.)

No need for a reply. This is an impulse letter that I simply had to get off my chest. In terms of entertainment, to lose Carson would be like erasing a star from the flag.

Yours sincerely,
Kenneth Tynan

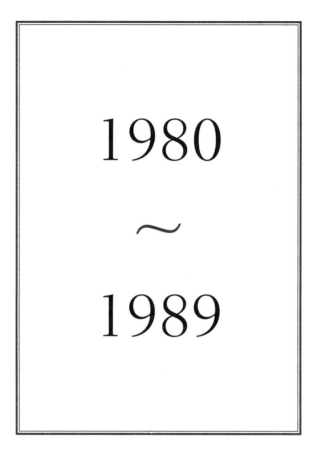

1980

~

1989

Since we have had intimate sexual contact where sperm
has passed between us, I feel it only fair to tell you
that I have just found out I have AIDS.

—*Rock Hudson to former sexual partners*
June 1984

BETWEEN 1980 AND 1989 . . .

1980: Sixty percent of working Americans travel 45 minutes or more to work each day. ★ The U.S. population is 226,000,000. ★ Ted Turner launches CNN, the first network in the world to broadcast news 24 hours a day. ★ Mount St. Helens in the state of Washington erupts, spraying volcanic ash 60,000 feet into the air, killing 60 people, countless animals, and destroying ten million trees. ★ *The Official Preppy Handbook* is published. ★ Popular films include *Ordinary People*, *The Elephant Man*, and *Coal Miner's Daughter*. ★ 3M introduces Post-it Notes. ★ Protesting the December 1979 Soviet invasion of Afghanistan, the United States boycotts the Moscow summer Olympics. ★ After a suspenseful summer and fall, 88 million television viewers find out that J. R. Ewing was shot by his wife's younger sister. ★ Ronald Reagan is elected president. ★ John Lennon is killed by Mark David Chapman. **1981:** The Iranian hostages are released after 444 days in captivity. ★ MTV, Pac-Man, and the IBM PC debut. ★ Reagan and three others are shot by John Hinckley, Jr. ★ The 15,000-member air traffic controllers' union goes on strike; within a week, Reagan has fired a majority of them. ★ Jane Fonda releases *Jane Fonda's Workout Book* and videotape, and Americans first hear the phrase "feel

---

From left to right, top row: Michael Jackson, *Jane Fonda's Workout Book*; Jimmy Swaggart; *second row:* the *Challenger,* Ronald Reagan, the Vietnam War Memorial; *third row:* Michael Milken, Donald Trump, Rock Hudson; *bottom row:* the baby boom's baby boom.

the burn." ★ After 19 years as America's top anchorman, Walter Cronkite goes off the air. ★ Sandra Day O'Connor becomes the first woman on the Supreme Court. **1982:** John Updike wins the Pulitzer prize, the National Book Critics Circle Award, and the American Book Award for *Rabbit Is Rich*. ★ Reagan asks for deep cuts in domestic programs and increases in military spending. ★ The Gannett Company launches *USA Today*, a national daily newspaper printed in color. ★ Michael Jackson releases *Thriller*, which will sell 30 million copies in two years, becoming the best-selling album to date. **1983:** Nancy Reagan introduces the antidrug slogan "Just Say No." ★ Costing $3,000 apiece, plus $150 a month for service, the first cellular phones in America become available to Chicago motorists. ★ The stock market soars, while the percentage of Americans living in poverty reaches a 19-year high. ★ Championing a "rainbow coalition" of minorities, Jesse Jackson announces his presidential candidacy. **1984:** Popular films include *Amadeus*, *Birdy*, *Beverly Hills Cop*, and *The Terminator*. ★ Nude photographs of Miss America Vanessa Williams are published in *Penthouse*, and she relinquishes her crown. ★ Apple introduces the Macintosh. ★ The new board game Trivial Pursuit posts sales of $777 million. ★ *The Cosby Show* debuts on television. **1985:** Rock Hudson dies of AIDS. ★ The government estimates that at least a quarter of a million Americans are homeless. ★ For the first time since 1914, the United States has become a debtor nation. ★ Found liable for undermining Pennzoil's bid for Getty Oil, Texaco is ordered by a jury to pay $10.53 billion to Pennzoil in a record-setting case. ★ R. J. Reynolds acquires Nabisco. **1986:** The space shuttle *Challenger* explodes 73 seconds after liftoff, killing all seven astronauts aboard. ★ Johnson & Johnson destroys 31 million Tylenols when seven people die after taking cyanide-laced capsules. ★ Nintendo introduces its video games and posts sales of $300 million. **1987:** Nintendo posts sales of $830 million. ★ Half of all American TV owners have sets connected by cable. ★ Shearson Lehman Brothers traders tack up a sign saying "To the lifeboats!" as the Dow

Jones Industrial Average drops 36 percent. ★ Tom Wolfe publishes *The Bonfire of the Vanities*. **1988:** On television, evangelist Jimmy Swaggart confesses to his congregation that he has visited a prostitute and sobs: "I have sinned against you, and I beg your forgiveness." ★ George Bush is elected president. ★ *Roseanne* debuts. ★ More than a million fax machines are sold. **1989:** $6 billion in damage and an estimated 90 deaths are caused by a San Francisco earthquake. ★ The *Exxon Valdez* hits a reef and spills 240,000 barrels of oil into Alaska's Prince William Sound. ★ Michael Milken is indicted on 98 counts of conspiracy, stock manipulation, racketeering, and securities fraud. ★ Hotel doyenne Leona Helmsley is convicted on 33 counts of income tax evasion and tax fraud. ★ PTL minister Jim Bakker is convicted of 24 counts of fraud and conspiracy. ★ Real estate tycoon Donald Trump buys the Eastern Airlines shuttle and renames it the Trump Shuttle.

1980: FEBRUARY 22
JUDY NAPIER TO JIMMY CARTER

Soviet troops invaded Afghanistan in December of 1979, and in protest, President Carter first organized economic sanctions, then led fifty-nine other nations in a boycott of the Moscow summer Olympics. Though many American athletes voiced their support for the boycott, there were other citizens, including the wife of weight lifter Jim Napier, who felt profoundly disappointed. Carter, however, stayed firm in his resolve, and the American athletes did not compete in Moscow.

PRESIDENT CARTER
WHITE HOUSE
WASHINGTON DC 20500

MY HUSBAND HAS TRAINED FOR 8 YEARS IN A GARAGE TO MAKE U.S. WEIGHT LIFTING TEAM IN MOSCOW. WE HAVE SACRIFICED OUR TIME, ENERGY, PERSONAL INCOME AND EMOTIONS TO HAVE THIS DREAM COME TRUE. HE IS NOT ALONE. THERE ARE THOUSANDS OF OTHER ATH-LETES LIKE HIM. PLEASE RECONSIDER YOUR BOYCOTT. WE ARE NOT POLITICIANS. THE DIFFERENCES BETWEEN COUNTRIES SHOULD NOT BE MANIFESTED IN ATHLETICS. OUR SACRIFICES HAVE BEEN MANY. WE COUNT TOO.

JUDY NAPIER

1980: APRIL 26
JIMMY CARTER TO CONGRESS

On November 4, 1979, hundreds of militant followers of the Ayatollah Ruhollah Khomeini (1900?–1989) seized the United States embassy in Iran and took its sixty-six occupants hostage. The initial demand: that the Shah, who was in New York City for cancer treatment, be returned to Iran to stand trial for alleged crimes of torture and murder. Despite numerous diplomatic attempts by Carter, as well as the freezing of Iranian oil imports and assets, the hostages remained in captivity. Then came the fatal rescue described in this letter.

Letter to the Speaker of the House and the President Pro Tempore
of the Senate Reporting on the Operation

April 26, 1980

Because of my desire that Congress be informed on this matter and consistent with the reporting provisions of the War Powers Resolution of 1973 (Public Law 93-148), I submit this report.

On April 24, 1980, elements of the United States Armed Forces under my direction commenced the positioning stage of a rescue operation which was designed, if the subsequent stages had been executed, to effect the rescue of the American hostages who have been held captive in Iran since November 4, 1979, in clear violation of international law and the norms of civilized conduct among nations. The subsequent phases of the operation were not executed. Instead, for the reasons described below, all these elements were withdrawn from Iran and no hostilities occurred.

The sole objective of the operation that actually occurred was to position the rescue team for the subsequent effort to withdraw the American hostages. The rescue team was under my overall command and control and required my approval before executing the subsequent phases of the operation designed to effect the rescue itself. No such approval was requested or given because, as described below, the mission was aborted.

Beginning approximately 10:30 AM EST on April 24, six U.S. C-130 transport aircraft and eight RH-53 helicopters entered Iran airspace. Their crews were not equipped for combat. Some of the C-130 aircraft carried a force of approximately 90 members of the rescue team equipped for combat, plus various support personnel.

From approximately 2 to 4 PM EST the six transports and six of the eight helicopters landed at a remote desert site in Iran approximately 200 miles from Tehran where they disembarked the rescue team, commenced refueling operations and began to prepare for the subsequent phases.

During the flight to the remote desert site, two of the eight helicopters developed operating difficulties. One was forced to return to the carrier Nimitz; the second was forced to land in the desert, but its crew was taken aboard another of the helicopters and proceeded on to the landing site. Of the six helicopters which landed at the remote desert site, one developed a serious hydraulic problem and was unable to continue with the mission. The operational plans called for a minimum of six helicopters in good operational condition able to proceed from the desert site. Eight helicopters had been included in the force to provide sufficient redundancy without imposing excessive strains on the refueling and exit requirements of the operation. When the number of helicopters available to continue dropped to five, it was determined that the operation could not proceed as planned. Therefore, on the recommendation of the force commander and my military advisers, I decided to cancel the mission and ordered the United States Armed Forces involved to return from Iran.

During the process of withdrawal, one of the helicopters accidentally collided with one of the C-130 aircraft, which was preparing to take off, resulting in the death of eight personnel and the injury of several others. At this point, the decision was made to load all surviving personnel aboard the remaining C-130 aircraft and to abandon the remaining helicopters at the landing site. Altogether, the United States Armed Forces remained on the ground for a total of approximately three hours. The five remaining aircraft took off about 5:45 PM EST and departed from Iran airspace without further incident at about 8:00 PM EST on April 24. No United States Armed Forces remain in Iran.

The remote desert area was selected to conceal this phase of the mission from discovery. At no time during the temporary presence of United States Armed Forces in Iran did they encounter Iranian forces of any type. We believe, in fact, that no Iranian military forces were in the desert area, and that the Iranian forces were unaware of the presence of United States Armed Forces until after their departure from Iran. As planned, no hostilities occurred during this phase of the mission—the only phase that was executed.

At one point during the period in which United States Armed Forces elements were on the ground at the desert landing site a bus containing forty-four Iranian civilians happened to pass along a nearby road. The bus was stopped and then disabled. Its occupants were detained by United States Armed Forces until their departure, and then released unharmed. One truck closely followed by a second vehicle also passed by while United States Armed Forces elements were on the ground. These elements stopped the truck by a shot into its headlights. The driver ran to the second vehicle which then escaped across the desert. Neither of these incidents affected the subsequent decision to terminate the mission.

Our rescue team knew, and I knew, that the operation was certain to be dangerous. We were all convinced that if and when the rescue phase of the operation had been commenced, it had an excellent chance of success. They were all volunteers; they were all highly trained. I met with their leaders before they went on this operation. They knew then what hopes of mine and of all Americans they carried with them. I share with the nation the highest respect and appreciation for the ability and bravery of all who participated in the mission.

To the families of those who died and who were injured, I have expressed the admiration I feel for the courage of their loved ones and the sorrow that I feel personally for their sacrifice.

The mission on which they were embarked was a humanitarian mission. It was not directed against Iran. It was not directed against the people of Iran. It caused no Iranian casualties.

This operation was ordered and conducted pursuant to the President's powers under the Constitution as Chief Executive and as Commander-in-Chief of the United States Armed Forces, expressly recognized in Section 8(d)(1) of the War Powers Resolution. In carrying out this operation, the United States was acting wholly within its right, in accordance with Article 51 of the United Nations Charter, to protect and rescue its citizens where the government of the territory in which they are located is unable or unwilling to protect them.

Sincerely,
Jimmy Carter

1980: MAY 27
CHERYL TAYLOR TO DIXY LEE RAY

After several ominous months of earthquakes, minor eruptions, and dramatic changes in its appearance, Mount St. Helens in southwestern Washington State erupted on May 18, 1980. Ice falls, avalanches, landslides, magma flow, and blasts of gas, ash, and stone followed. The volcano killed more than sixty people and caused $2.7 billion in damage. The blasts devastated approximately two hundred square miles of forestland and spread debris as far away as seventeen miles. While the dust was literally still settling, one despairing resident sent this letter to Washington's governor, Dixy Lee Ray (1914–1994).

The town of Randle was located to the northeast of the volcano in Lewis County; Longview was to the west. CETA, standing for Comprehensive Employment and Training Act, was a government-funded job-training program. More than a billion dollars would be appropriated by Congress for disaster relief.

May 27, 1980

Dear Governor Ray:

I just watched your television adress about disaster relief. I heard about the CETA people in Eastern Washington working on ash clean up, the center in Longview where people can receive financial help, and the help the farmers are going to receive. What I didn't hear was any help for the logging industry in eastern Lewis County, mainly the Randle, Packwood area.

We have no logging industry anymore. Even if the USDA forest service would let people in the woods you can't run heavy equipment in this ash. Who knows when the ash is going to be gone—I don't.

My husband owns a small automobile repair business in Randle. We have had people calling us to repair their cars, the only trouble is—they have no money to pay us. They have no jobs. We don't have money to repair their cars for nothing.

Oh, yes, the national guard you mentioned is sitting down at white pass high school. They are really helping us here in the valley. Why can't they help with the ash clean up? We are unincorporated towns here with no facilities for clean up. People that are retired around here can't even get out to the grocery story. How can we get to Longview to receive food stamps???

People that can afford it are moving away or sending their children away to relatives. The last month my family's income has been $319.00—I can't afford to send my children anywhere. They will have to stay and breathe this silicone in the air.

This is just a small part of the problem. Many people here have worse problems than I. Just because we don't own huge wheat ranches or have had our property wiped out by mud doesn't mean that our lives aren't threatened. Come see for yourself. Come talk to the people in this valley and see why we are so bitter and desperate.

> Sincerely,
> Cheryl Taylor
> Bx. 24
> Randle, Wash.
> Eastern Lewis Co.

1980: OCTOBER 20
RONALD REAGAN TO ROBERT POLI

Reagan was deep into his campaign for the presidency when he wrote this letter to the head of the Professional Air Traffic Controllers Organization. Less than a year later, in August of 1981, demanding a four-day workweek and increased pay, PATCO would strike, and Reagan, setting a tough tone for his new presidency, would fire all but two thousand of the group's members.

October 20, 1980

Robert E. Poli, President
Professional Air Traffic Controllers Organization
444 Capitol Street
Washington, D. C.

Dear Mr. Poli:

I have been thoroughly briefed by members of my staff as to the deplorable state of our nation's air traffic control system. They have told me that too few people working unreasonable hours with obsolete equipment has placed the nation's air travellers in unwarranted danger. In an area so clearly related to public safety the Carter administration has failed to act responsibly.

You can rest assured that if I am elected President, I will take whatever steps are necessary to provide our air traffic controllers with the most modern equipment available and to adjust staff levels and work days so that they are commensurate with achieving a maximum degree of public safety.

As in all other areas of the federal government where the President has the power of appointment, I fully intend to appoint highly qualified individuals who can work harmoniously with the Congress and the employees of the government agencies they oversee.

I pledge to you that my administration will work very closely with you to bring about a spirit of cooperation between the President and the air traffic controllers. Such harmony can and must exist if we are to restore the people's confidence in their government.

Sincerely,
Ronald Reagan

901 South Highland Street, Arlington, Virginia 22204
Paid for by Reagan-Bush Committee
United States Senator Paul Laxalt, Chairman. Roy Buchanan, Treasurer.

*   *   *

1981: MARCH 30
JOHN HINCKLEY, JR., TO JODIE FOSTER

Jodie Foster (1962–), in 1981 an eighteen-year-old movie actress and college stu-
dent, later a director and Oscar-winning star, had been for some time the inexplica-
ble obsession in the life of John Hinckley, Jr. (1955–). On March 30, Hinckley
wrote this letter to Foster, then went to Washington's Hilton Hotel, where he emerged
from a crowd and began shooting. The newly inaugurated Ronald Reagan, who had
just addressed a labor convention, was shot in the chest. A Secret Service agent and
policeman were also wounded, and press secretary James Brady was shot in the
head. On June 21, 1982, Hinckley would be found not guilty by reason of insanity.

Dear Jodie,

There is a definite possibility that I will be killed in my attempt to get Reagan. It is for this very reason that I am writing you this letter now.

As you well know by now, I love you very much. The past seven months I have left you dozens of poems, letters and messages in the faint hope you would develop an interest in me.

Although we talked on the phone a couple of times, I never had the nerve to simply approach you and introduce myself. Besides my shyness, I honestly did not wish to bother you. I know the many messages left at your door and in your mail-box were a nuisance, but I felt it was the most painless way for me to express my love to you.

I feel very good about the fact that you at least know my name and how I feel about you. And by hanging around your dormitory I've come to realize that I'm the topic of more than a little conversation, however full of ridicule it may be. At least you know that I'll always love you.

Jodie, I would abandon this idea of getting Reagan in a second if I could only win your heart and live out the rest of my life with you, whether it be in total obscurity or whatever. I will admit to you that the reason I'm going ahead with this attempt now is because I just cannot wait any longer to impress you. I've got to do something now to make you understand in no uncertain terms that I am doing all of this for your sake. By sacrificing my freedom and possibly my life I hope to change your mind about me. This letter is being written an hour before I leave for the Hilton Hotel.

Jodie, I'm asking you to please look into your heart and at least give me the chance with this historical deed to gain your respect and love.

I love you forever.

John Hinckley

1981: AUGUST 13
JERRY FALWELL TO AMERICANS

Jerry Falwell (1933–) founded a Baptist church in Lynchburg, Virginia, in 1956, and his enormously popular television show, Old-Time Gospel Hour, *soon followed. By 1979, when he started Moral Majority, Inc., Falwell was using his popularity as a preacher—in addition to considerable volumes of direct mail—to further a conservative political agenda. Falwell would be vocal in his support of Ronald Reagan, school prayer, and strong defense spending, and unbending in his attacks on the Equal Rights Amendment, abortion, and homosexuality.*

PLEASE READ THIS LETTER BEFORE OPENING THE SEALED ENVELOPE I'VE ENCLOSED.

August 13, 1981

Dear Friend,

I refuse to stop speaking out against the sin of homosexuality.

With God as my witness, I pledge that I will continue to expose the sin of homosexuality to the people of this nation. I believe that the massive homosexual revolution is always a symptom of a nation coming under the judgement of God.

Romans 1:24–28, Paul clearly condemns the sin of homosexuality. In verse 28, when a nation refuses to listen to God's standard of morality, the Bible declares, "God gave them over to a reprobate mind."

Recently, 250,000 homosexuals marched in the streets of San Francisco. Several weeks ago, 75,000 more were marching in the streets of Los Angeles. The homosexuals are on the march in this country.

Please remember, homosexuals do not reproduce! They recruit!

And many of them are out after my children and your children.

This is one major reason why we must keep the Old-Time Gospel Hour alive! The Old-Time Gospel Hour is one of the few major ministries in America crying out against militant homosexuals. . . .

So don't delay! Let me hear from you immediately! I will be anxiously awaiting your reply.

In Christ,
Jerry Falwell

P.S. Let me repeat, a massive homosexual revolution can bring the judgement of God upon this nation. Our children must not be recruited into a profane lifestyle.

1981: NOVEMBER 30

THE SISTER OF A VIETNAM VETERAN TO AN ANTIWAR GROUP

Introduced in the 1940s, Agent Orange was a herbicide that, by defoliating trees and shrubs, was intended to take away an enemy's crucial cover. It wasn't used widely until the Vietnam War, when an estimated nineteen million gallons were sprayed into the jungles of South Vietnam. But Agent Orange (named for the orange band on the drums in which the chemical mixture was stored) turned out to contain TCDD, the contaminant dioxin, whose apparent effects—including cancer—were still being experienced years after the war ended. In 1984, American veterans would reach a $180 million out-of-court settlement with seven chemical companies in a class-action suit.

November 30, 1981

In the late 60s, my brother Keith was drafted and sent to Vietnam. I was marginally involved in the anti-war movement; my father had put a large peace sign out on our front yard. Both he and I urged Keith to go to Canada; my mother was unsure what she thought he should do. He was timid and hesitant to disobey government orders; in any case, he felt that, although he didn't believe the war was just, that he had a duty to his country. Nineteen-year-olds often feel that way; I'm sure that's why they draft kids. He went to Vietnam and, with tremendous luck, was kept in the typing pool for the whole year he was there—an interesting irony: he knew how to type because that was what the commercial program at high school had offered him. The only time he was ever in danger was when his sergeant, drunk, mistook him for a "viet cong" and nearly shot him.

I was doubly relieved that he wasn't in battle. I didn't want my kid brother getting killed, and I didn't want him killing anyone else—especially in a totally unjustified war. And I didn't want him going through life with the kind of trauma I knew he'd face if he killed anyone. When he came back he married the girl-next-door—literally—and got a job with the post office. A few years later they had a daughter. His life was as happy and unhappy as most people's, but whatever problems he faced, it never occurred to any of us that he would ever have to worry about Vietnam again. Even when I started reading about Agent Orange, I never thought it would affect my brother.

Two years ago, at Christmas time, he had a case of bronchitis that wouldn't go away. His wife got worried and talked him into getting a chest X-ray. We found out, early on New Year's Eve, that the "bronchitis" was a huge tumor pressing against his lung, that he had lymphoma. Soon after his cancer was diagnosed, he started wondering about Agent Orange. He got in contact with a local vets group in New York and found out that the area he was in in Vietnam had indeed been sprayed with Agent Orange. And he found out that lymphoma is one of the forms of cancer associated with dioxin, the carcinogenic toxin used in Agent Orange.

My brother lived for two years going through a number of chemotherapy treatments, refusing to be defeated when each treatment in turn proved a failure. At my urging he even began work with a psychic healer.

At one point, I wrote a poem about his cancer and Agent Orange, and gave it to him. I asked if he'd mind my reading it at an anti-draft rally. He was very pleased: never politically active himself, he was glad that I was—and he liked to think that the poem might keep some other young man from going to the next war, to face whatever the government might do to its own soldiers.

Keith died this past September. It was a peaceful and beautiful death, but it was a death that should never have been.

When you've been in the army, the army pays for your funeral, so Keith was buried in a military cemetery. They had a flag on his coffin and they played "Taps," and some honcho in uniform rattled off some garbage about how Keith had nobly served his country. He didn't say anything about how nobly Keith's country had served him—poisoning him with dioxin and then turning down his claim when he tried to get compensation for what they had done to him.

What they did to my brother they did to thousands of other American soldiers who went to Vietnam because they bought all that crap about duty and honor and serving your country. And they did it to God knows how many Vietnamese. How many Vietnamese are going through what Keith went through? How many Vietnamese families are going through what my family and I are going through? And what "harmless" little chemicals are they planning to use in the next war, against innocent civilians and indigenous soldiers defending their country against our troops—and against those troops themselves, the naive boys who really believe their government gives a damn about them?

1982

A SOAP OPERA FAN TO THE <u>GUIDING LIGHT</u> PRODUCERS

First aired on radio, The Guiding Light *made the transition to television in 1952 and went on to become the longest-running series in television history, offering a classic soap opera stew of passion, greed, redemption, misfortune, and rampant villainy. By 1982, the soap opera's audience had grown to more than ten million, and as this letter from one of its devoted viewers attests, not all of them were entirely clear on the line between reality and fantasy.*

Gentlemen:

Here I am actually "hooked" on a program, to the extent of not even accepting an invitation if it means not being able to see my program! In fact, I buy everything but the diapers that are advertised!

The reason I am writing is to tell you how I feel about some of your cast.

The little lady that plays Nola Reardon is a darling, beautiful child—and certainly should go places. While she plays a difficult part, she actually makes you live the story with her.

Puhlease—don't let her do any more damage. Tell your writers to let her mend her ways.

Bad girls do, you know, and find happy solutions in their lives.

This weekend past was a very hectic one—so realistic for me, that I had to take extra heart pills to calm down (I'm a heart patient) when I thought Nola was going to wreck Kelly's life. Your writers were great on that issue—except I doubt if Bea would have, in reality, gone to Kelly. In my mind, Kelly would have asked the doctor how long Nola was pregnant, and found out that way. Nola needs her mother now. Kelly sounded like a nut when he spoke to the doctor—not like a medical student.

I love him, he's like my son. He didn't follow thru.

The story is great—I love it and the actors and actresses are wonderful.

> Sincerely,
>
> [Anonymous]

1983: APRIL 15

A PENNSYLVANIA RESIDENT TO
THE BLOOMSBURG PRESS ENTERPRISE

Since 1970, when President Nixon organized a confusion of local, state, and federal agencies into the Environmental Protection Agency, recycling had been considered a logical approach to America's problem of solid waste disposal. It was not until the early 1980s, however, that the procedure began to become mandatory. In one Pennsylvania town, the newly passed recycling ordinance—the first in the state—was met with exasperation by at least one local resident.

Please allow me to comment on the law adopted by the Bloomsburg Town Council concerning the new mandatory recycling.

I have never participated in the volunteer recycling program. After getting up at 5:30 a.m. to get my husband to work and my children to school by 7:30 a.m., I then put in eight hours on my feet at my job.

When I come home at night and open a jar of spaghetti sauce for supper, side dish of a jar of instant coffee, I'm in no mood to stand at the sink washing these jars and peeling off labels. I believe that piece of glass became my property when I purchased it from the store and I'll do with it as I please. I use my empty jars to throw away such things as grease, coffee grounds and leftovers.

When the town council supplies me with a dishwasher, several garbage cans, twine, extra garbage bags or cartons, pays me for my time, and lowers my monthly garbage bill, then I'll be glad to give them my recyclables.

Figure this out: Two days in jail for drunk driving; 30 days in jail for a garbage violation! I think this new law needs to be recycled.

I don't drink, but I'll probably see you in jail!

E. S.

1983: SEPTEMBER 3
HARRY KUHIMEYER, JR., TO MCMARTIN PRESCHOOL PARENTS

This letter, sent to parents of children in the McMartin Preschool in Manhattan Beach, California, provoked a frenzy. Seven adults connected to the preschool were eventually accused of molesting more than three hundred children and forcing many of them to engage in rituals ranging from naked games and animal mutilation to infanticide and the drinking of blood. Widely publicized, the subsequent trial became the longest in U.S. history, spanning three years and costing California a record $15 million. No convictions were obtained. Like the reports of satanic ritual abuse that would follow in the eighties and nineties, the McMartin accusations seem to have been the products of suggestive questioning and mass hysteria.
Ray Buckey was the twenty-five-year-old son of the school's director and grandson of its founder, Virginia McMartin.

Dear Parent,

This department is conducting a criminal investigation involving child molestation (288 P.C.). Ray Buckey, an employee of Virginia McMartin's Preschool was arrested September 7, 1983, by this department. The following procedure is obviously an unpleasant one, but to protect the rights of your children as well as the rights of the accused, this inquiry is necessary for a complete investigation. Records indicate that your child has been or is currently a student at the preschool. We are asking your assistance in this continuing investigation. Please question your child to see if he or she has been a witness to any crime or if he or she has been a victim. Our investigation indicates that possible criminal acts include oral sex, fondling of genitals, buttocks, or chest area, and sodomy, possibly committed under the pretense of taking the child's temperature. Also, photos may have been taken of children without their clothing. Any information from your child regarding having ever observed Ray Buckey to leave a classroom alone with a child during a nap period or if they have ever observed Ray Buckey tie up a child is important. Please complete the enclosed information form and return it to this department in the enclosed stamped envelope as soon as possible. We will contact you if circumstances dictate same. We ask you to keep this information strictly confidential because of the nature of the charges and the highly emotional effect it could have on our community. Please do not discuss this investigation with anyone outside your immediate family. Do not contact or discuss this investigation with Raymond Buckey or any member of the accused defendant's family or employees connected with the McMartin Preschool. THERE IS NO EVIDENCE TO INDICATE THAT THE MANAGEMENT OF VIRGINIA McMARTIN'S PRESCHOOL HAD ANY KNOWLEDGE OF THIS SITUATION AND NO DETRIMENTAL INFORMATION CONCERNING THE OPERATION OF THE SCHOOL HAS BEEN DISCOVERED DURING THIS INVESTIGATION FOR ANY CRIMINAL ACT. Your prompt attention to this matter and reply no later than September 16, 1983, will be appreciated.

> Harry L. Kuhimeyer, Jr.
> Chief of Police
> John Wenner, Captain

1983: WINTER
MARVA COSNER TO RONALD REAGAN

On April 18, sixty-three people were killed and the U.S. embassy in Beirut, Lebanon, was leveled by a suicidal member of the fundamentalist Islamic Jihad. On October 23, a truck carrying twenty-five hundred pounds of TNT was driven into the U.S. Marines headquarters. Two hundred forty-one marines, most of them sleeping, were killed in the blast, which President Reagan later deemed "a vicious, cowardly, and ruthless" attack. Among the victims was a lieutenant corporal named David Cosner, whose mother wrote this letter to the president some months later.

Dear President Reagan:

I am the mother of L/Cpl David Cosner, killed recently in Lebanon.

I want to thank you for your kind letter sharing our grief. I know this was hard for you to do since you think everyone is blaming you for this tragedy. I was very angry at everyone, including you. I was not ready to give David up and I felt it was not <u>our</u> country he was keeping peace for.

As the 23rd of Oct. dragged on, I was constantly reminded that I had asked God to watch over him. I knew if he was safe, God was giving him strength to help his fallen buddies but, if he was dead, I also knew he would be at peace in God's arms. This turmoil continued until 9 p.m. The blessed peace and comfort came, telling me he was in his Heavenly Home.

I really believe it was simply David's destiny to have been there.

He was an excellent Marine and therefore had the <u>choice</u> of any base in the world. He chose to stay at Camp Lejeune knowing he was going to Lebanon.

He was not sent nor did he have to go. This is why I am telling you this so you will know that David did indeed give his most precious gift to America, very unselfishly, and some good must come of this tragedy.

He left us a beautiful 2½ year old granddaughter, Leanna, and wonderful memories from the 22 years we shared.

I am so proud to be David's mother and I know in time I will get the hugs from him that are denied me now.

I have asked our wonderful town to stand behind you, our chosen leader, so our enemies will know we are strong. One Nation, Under God.

I pray that God will give you the strength to make the right decisions and keep you safe in His protective arms.

Sincerely,
Marva Cosner

1983: DECEMBER
JOHN JOHNSON TO HIS PARENTS

John Johnson, a management consultant, was thirty-one years old when he wrote this letter.

Dear Mom & Dad,

This letter has been a long time coming. There have been many times when I wanted to tell you, but held back. So, today's the day. You may not be surprised, because you've always known something about me is different. Mom, you called it "special." The fact is I'm gay.

That was ever hard to write—I'm sure it was hard to read. But now the secret's out—I don't have to hide it anymore—or pretend with you that I'm somebody else. That's always been hard. I've felt so lonely and distant around you—like a stranger—because I couldn't tell you the truth. Mom, you said that when I was younger, I changed—became more reserved, quieter, distant. It was because I knew I was different from everyone else—Doug and David, the kids at school. I didn't know how, but I knew I was. And it scared me. I remember the nights crying alone in my room and not knowing how to tell anybody. When my fear got so bad I couldn't stand it, I asked you to send me to a psychiatrist. I had suspicions then that I might be gay. When you asked me why I was going (Dad, you also said, "You don't like boys, do you?") I felt I had to come up with another reason. I just didn't want you to be disappointed in me.

I've tried just about everything to deal with being gay. I've dated girls, almost got married, went to psychiatrists, tried to drink it away, tried to move away from it. But the fact is I'm gay and that's what I am.

In 1979 I knew I couldn't go on pretending. I knew that I needed to get away and try to find out who I <u>really</u> was—not worry about if it was good or bad, right or wrong, acceptable or unacceptable. I just <u>had</u> to find out what was the truth about me. That's when I decided to apply for jobs outside the state.

I wish I could tell you of all the miracles that have happened for me since I moved here. I know without a doubt that God led me here because he loved me. I feel better about myself than I have <u>ever</u> felt in my life. I have more <u>real</u> friends than ever before. Money, self confidence, respect, my home, a bright outlook for the future, and yes, a wonderful lover, Tom. I hope you can be happy for me—I am.

The most important thing for you to know is that my being gay is not your fault. <u>Please</u> don't blame yourselves. I know right now you're asking, "Where did we go wrong?" <u>You didn't</u> go wrong. You both are terrific parents. I've had the strength of character to deal with what could have been a problem. I've turned it into an asset—I got that strength of character from you. You gave me the tools to deal with the greatest test I've been given. Thank you—I love you both so much. I am extremely happy and thankful about the way things turned out.

I also know what kind of pictures come to people's heads when they hear the words "gay" or "homosexual." Society has brainwashed us to think of the <u>worst</u>. When the images of sub-human animals come to your mind—just remember me—I've got high moral standards, am ambitious, am a Christian, <u>and</u> I'm gay. This will be confusing for you at first. So, I'm sending you a book in a few days that will help to give you more reliable information about gay people. I hope you will read it.

Again, I am <u>proud</u> to be who I am. God doesn't make junk and he was especially good to me.

I'm going to write Doug and David today also, so you should be getting letters on the same day. As far as who you can tell, that's up to you. I don't mind if Nita and Patsy know. The only one I want to keep it from now is my employer. I don't trust them to be very understanding. That's why I'm looking for another job.

The reason why I decided to tell you now is because of Christmas. I promised myself I'm never going home again a stranger. That's too painful and I feel like a liar. My plan is to stay in Minnesota this year with Tom and his family. It took his family awhile to accept him, but once they found out he wasn't a monster and that he was happy, they got closer than ever. That's my dream. Take as long as you need to get used to this news. Just remember, I haven't changed— you just know more about me now. I'm still the same great kid.

You should get this letter by Wednesday or Thursday, and the book by Monday. I will be back in town (I'm going to Florida to relax) by Tuesday the 13th.

I love you now more than I ever have before. However you feel about me is O.K. Just don't punish yourselves over this. Believe me it's not that big a deal after you get over the shock. At least that's the way it's been for me.

Love,
John

1984: JANUARY 18

A READER TO ANN LANDERS

The best-known advice columnists in the country were twins born seventeen minutes apart and named Esther Pauline Friedman and Pauline Esther Friedman. In 1955 Esther became Ann Landers, with a column in the Chicago Sun-Times; *Pauline followed three months later as Dear Abby in the* San Francisco Chronicle. *By the mid-1980s, both columnists were still going strong, even as readers were adding to questions of etiquette and romance some very modern problems—like cocaine.*

Dear Ann Landers:

I'm 34, living with the guy who fathered my nine-year-old son. We've been together 10 years. He is a good father and a nice person.

There's one problem—he uses cocaine and is a free-baser. I worry that he might burn down the place. All his money goes for the white stuff. He never answers the phone, steals money from me left and right and is a wonderful liar. And I've been supporting him.

I love him dearly and know things could be like they once were if he could get off the coke. I have asked him to call a drug-abuse hotline or go to a center where he can get help. He says he doesn't have a problem and can quit anytime he wants to.

I am not asking him to quit cold turkey. If he could just cut down, I'm sure he could lick it. I am—

> Open For Suggestions In
> Beantown

1984: JANUARY
ANN LANDERS TO "BEANTOWN"

Dear Beantown: I fail to see how a "nice person" can be a liar, a thief and a free-loader. A coke junkie who refuses to admit he has a problem is hopeless. My advice is for you, not him. Unload the guy before he destroys your life.

1984: MARCH 16
CALVIN TRILLIN TO DOMINIQUE RICHARD

The 1980s saw the revival of a glamorous—if ever more crowded—Manhattan. Even famous people, when trying to buy an apartment, had to grovel before the city's co-op boards. John Gregory Dunne (1932–) and Joan Didion (1934–) had been celebrated for their works of fiction (including Play It as It Lays *by Didion), nonfiction (including* Vegas *by Dunne), and screenplays (including* The Panic in Needle Park *by both). But when they decided to move east from Los Angeles, they suspected that they would need some solid references. They turned to their friend, the longtime* New Yorker *contributor Calvin Trillin (1935–), who offered the co-op board the epistolary equivalent of screaming "Fire" in a crowded theater.*

The letter was never delivered to the board, though a purported copy was sent to Dunne and Didion.

March 16, 1984

Ms. Dominique Richard
Alice F. Mason, Ltd.
30 East 60th Street
New York, N.Y. 10022

Dear Ms. Richard:

This is in answer to your inquiry of March 12 concerning Mr. and Mrs. John Gregory Dunne.

I have known both Mr. and Mrs. Dunne for more than twenty years, and I can say that they would make a splendid addition to any co-operative apartment building. As you may have learned by now from neighbors of Mr. and Mrs. Dunne in Brentwood, the role played by Mr. Dunne's temper in the incidents there was greatly exaggerated in the press.

I have known the Dunne's daughter, Quintana, since her infancy, and I can assure you that she is an attractive and responsible young woman who is working hard day and night on the gruelling practice schedule necessary for anyone who aspires to be a successful punk-rock drummer. The dog that injured the UPS delivery man is hers.

In the event that you have been concerned about the presence of the male nurse who is retained to escort Mr. Dunne home on evenings out, I would like to put your mind at rest. The male nurse in question is remarkably skilled at keeping control without making a fuss. I understand that, by a happy coincidence, he is related to your doorman, Mr. O'Leary, as is Mr. Dunne.

Mrs. Dunne is not Jewish.

Yours sincerely,
Calvin Trillin

1984: JUNE
ROCK HUDSON TO FIVE FORMER SEXUAL PARTNERS

The first cases of AIDS in the United States had been reported in 1981, but no event so brought the disease into the consciousness of the American press and public as the announcement, in July of 1985, that former screen idol Rock Hudson had the disease. Hudson (1925–1985), who would leave a quarter of a million dollars to AIDS research, sent out the following letter on the same day that he learned of his illness.

Hi

This note shall remain anonymous for obvious reasons.

Since we have had intimate sexual contact where sperm has passed between us, I feel it only fair to tell you that I have just found out I have AIDS.

I am most sorry to tell you this.

I suggest you have tests made to make sure you're ok.

Most sincerely

1984: JUNE 11
THÉRÈSE DONATH TO VIRGINIA GREENE

Thérèse Donath met Virginia Greene at a Monterey, California, writing group in 1980. At the time, Donath had been divorced for six years, following a twenty-six-year marriage; she had three grown children. Greene, the mother of four, had been in her third marriage for more than a decade. In 1984, she moved with her husband Bob from Pacific Grove to northeastern California, and the two women began a correspondence in which they exchanged both the problems and the reassurances of many middle-aged women in the 1980s. But just months after this letter was written, Greene would commit suicide.

P.G. was Pacific Grove. MPC was Monterey Peninsula College. The chicken stamp had adorned a previous letter.

Pacific Grove
Monday, June 11, 1984

Dear Virginia,

The boys (yours and mine) hung up yesterday before I had the chance for a few last words with you. Like "We'll leave P.G. about 7:30 a.m. or 8:00 and with a lunch-stop someplace (other than Jack-In-The-Box) we should be up your way about 1:00 p.m."

Don't you think we'll make it by one o'clock with me as navigator? THAT (being navigator) is my greatest feat since I stopped burning pork chops. (HIM-SELF said, "If I dropped one of those chops on my foot, the chop would survive but my foot would break!") Now I know why I hated cooking for him.

My navigating ability <u>has</u> improved since I took the dyslexia class at MPC. Those crazy non-word alphabet games must have helped—now I can read a map and navigate from point A to B, but not yet from A to Z. My former inability to map-read was another imperfection that drove HIMSELF crazy. I feel navigator-confident now despite the fact that last week, on our return from Calistoga, I navigated us right to the spot where Bianco was suppose to be, but wasn't. The Bermuda Triangle has a sister called the Bianco Triangle. Before we turned off Route 1 to hunt for Bianco, I'd asked a native for directions and he'd replied, "Look quick or you'll miss it!" I looked quick, slow, sideways, and up and down, and still we missed Bianco. The excursion produced some breathtaking ocean views and a gang of prisoners road-working. (I thought that went out with the Depression!) The side-trip also produced two extra hours of driving. Unlike HIMSELF, Jeff is patient and a good sport and THAT is a refreshing change from my former driving partner. I wanted to see Bianco ever since I'd heard it was a hidden place for literary types—boy was it hidden!

Jeff says the whole country is homogenized, and I agree. I've traveled north, south, east, west and Jack-In-The-Box jumps out everywhere. (Jock-In-The-Box once jumped out at me from a newspaper ad—sometimes dyslexia can be fun!) Jeff says he hates the commercialization of America, and yet when we pass a Denny's or Jack's or a "golden arch" he says, "Shall we stop?" HE CAN EAT ANYTHING! When hunger demanded a lunch-stop, I persisted in walking three blocks in two directions to avoid Jack's, but there was no other restaurant. I settled for fries and a malt—even Jack can't screw that up. Where are the hamburger stands of my youth?

I still cherish the memory of an old railroad-car-diner in Hammond, Indiana. HIMSELF, the kids, and I looked forward each week to Saturday night's short-order-fry before the movies. The grease hung in clouds as you entered, but oh those sweet fries tasted better than homemade. The two or three waitress/cooks looked like over-age prostitutes, always a little too heavy, much too late for bleach, lipstick curled up and over their lips. Their grease-spattered, once-upon-a-time white aprons wrinkled across their wide hips as they squished the grease to the back of the grill with a spatula and applied a pre-shaped meat (I hoped) patty to the front.

I could hear the sputter and sizzle of the burgers and watch those minimum-wage-women work off their buns as they laid the burger-buns on the back-burner. The meat turned dark and crisp, the waitress/cook assembled bun, patty, tomatoes, lettuce, pickles, and we soaked on the mustard provided on the counter. That old-fashioned burger reminded me of my childhood on the boardwalk in Venice, California. The nickle-play miniature juke-box on the counter still played the same old records that played in Venice, I swear. "Pennies from Heaven," the first song I remember as a child, always got my nickel.

When Mark (my eldest) thought he was too old for the Saturday night tradition, he still frequented the establishment with one of his long-haired friends. Occasionally we'd bump into him at the boxcar-diner and he'd give me a hug and kiss, HIS long hair criss-crossing my forehead as he kissed me. The still socially-conscious waitress would look distressed, as if she still remembered him as clean and snot-nosed, not clean and long-haired.

Now Mark's hair and beard are trimmed, and he calls to inquire about my health. Now he's thirty-five and it's difficult to realize that not-so-long-ago I still looked up to men that age. In my single days—I feel married, or at least connected now—I worked my way through men ten, fifteen, or twenty years younger than myself. How grand it is to be with Jeff who is even older than I, though not by much. Yesterday, Jeff put on a Vaughn Monroe record and we could BOTH smile in remembrance.

My lifestyles seem to keep pace with the societal changes in America, sociologically speaking. In the fifties my life was the model of "togetherness," my mother's heart bled through the turbulent sixties, and in the seventies I was a devoted practitioner of serial monogamy. I tried on a man like a new dress—each man represented a new lifestyle. If I survive the eighties, who knows what changes the country and I will undergo.

This morning I arrived home from my weekend at Jeff's and as usual my untended house felt cold (do I leave my warmth at his house?). The apartment looked messed and in need of TLC. I don't understand. I leave my apartment on Friday or Saturday with everything orderly, even the dishwasher emptied, and then on Monday morning I return and drag in me and my bag of clean laundry (I launder at Jeff's rather than play the slot machines in the basement that are euphemistically called washer and dryer), and return to the car for another load. I climb the steps, carrying a paper bag filled with empty plastic containers that were filled with home cooking when I left for the weekend, and gently hold on to my weekly surprise gift. This week Jeff presented me with a conch shell, which I mispronounced as "CUNTsh," and I wasn't trying to be funny, only my mis-wired dyslectic brain makes me mispronounce the simplest of words.

The shell is softly, smoothly pink inside its opening, and it is a splendid addition to my collection. I stick my finger inside the shell and touch the pink smoothness and wonder if my mispronunciation is that far off after all.

So there I sat looking at piles of small messes, laundry to be put away, paper bags to unpack, and I plucked my eyebrows rather than attack the debris. I finally forced myself up from my chair when I heard the mailman. I ran down the stairs (thank God, they're inside my apartment, and not outside, or I wouldn't be able to leave my litter until I had the strength to carry up the next load) and back up with your grand letter in hand. I muse and amuse myself with your four pages of visual prose that take me deep into your gold country. I sit here reading your letter and answering immediately rather than doing my endless Monday morning clean and tidy chores. Like you, I want to sit at my typewriter while all the mundane requirements for daily life just wait until I fill the creative hole in me that demands attention.

A weekend at Jeff's, cooking, talking, reading, talking, listening, crying, laughing and I want to be at my typewriter, not writing the article that's due, but writing my thoughts and feelings to you. When I type I never know what my intuition will produce through my fingers and brain, and what I write becomes a delightful surprise. Expressing my first thought betrays my mother's admonishment to "think before you speak," and I love it! So down guilt, down "shoulds," down downs, and up, up and away, for today at least. I believe the moon must be full at last, so my mood is light again. I swear, living near the water, the moon tugs on my watered body in a stronger way, and my TIDE turns (pun intended!).

You say I write in an organized fashion. Ha, today I skitter from subject to subject, maybe I'm moon-looney. I could see the moon last night through Jeff's sparkling windows, so this morning I called the window-washer to clean the year-long smudges from my windows. It's been a long time since my Romeo-window-washer scaled the walls to my living room. I just can't afford the honor of his presence more often. For months now I could barely see my smidgen of ocean through the begrimed and scabbed glass. "Why bother?" I'd ask myself. "I'll be moving soon." Then I thought, "Bother, I'd better," life being hung by a strand of hair so-to-speak. I'd better bother and enjoy this wee view while I can. Who knows what's coming next.

In the middle of the last paragraph the phone rang: my Yvonne contact informed me that Yvonne Champlin wants to know why she hasn't heard from me. So I called MS. Champlin, whined about my surgery, and promised that a copy of the article would be mailed to her by Friday. (Hope I haven't blown it again by allowing the interviewee to read before I turn in copy to the editor.) Now I GOTTA write the article. I sat back down at the typewriter, wrote one word and the phone rang again. (It must be a conspiracy—as soon as we sit down to write, the natives get restless!)

My second caller wanted to make a palm-reading appointment as a gift for her friend who is driving here from Santa Cruz. She said she remembered reading my palm-reading column in <u>Community Spirit</u>. God, that was three years ago! Now I charge $40 for a forty-five-minute reading. That sure beats the hell out of the $2 readings at the amusement park. That summer I spent as a gypsy-palm-reader (you should have heard my fake jewels clang as I bent over a palm!) I averaged a $100 a day, so you know how many palms I read. I'm really amazed by that call. Last year, when I worked nine-to-five, and longer, for someone else, I rarely had a request for a palm-reading; and now that I'm a struggling free-lancer again and money is a problem, I receive frequent calls for my "psychic skills." I don't know why I fret and worry about money. Money always seems to flow to me when I need it. Now IF I averaged four readings a week, I'd be able to support my writing habit and never have to go straight again. You know the strange jobs I've created since I left my lady-of-the-manor period. I read palms at "The Club" in my gypsy get-up, and I wore a long blond wig as a fairy god mother and told children's stories at the Del Monte Shopping Center. I thought my conservative mother would be shocked, but she surprised me by telling me SHE read tea leaves as a girl—but of course, "not professionally." Hummm, maybe my Hungarian blood <u>was</u> infected by the gypsies.

This letter has been too interrupted to continue and I'll be seeing you soon. Whee! I can't wait! So this will be all for today.

Love you,

Therese

Oops, I almost forgot, Jeff wants to take us all out for dinner on Sunday night. We don't want our writer-friend to spend all of our visit in the kitchen. So please, pick out your newest favorite eating establishment. They're probably all "new" with your move. Right?

I love your chicken stamp, and you. See you soonest.

1984: AUGUST 2
HENRY CABOT LODGE, JR., TO CORLISS LAMONT

Henry Cabot Lodge (1902–1985) served as a Republican senator from Massachu-setts and as the United States representative to the United Nations before becoming ambassador to South Vietnam in the mid-sixties. Corliss Lamont (see letter page 468) had been a college classmate of Lodge, and in 1965 had written him a letter asking him to admit that he was wrong in supporting U.S. intervention in Vietnam. It took nearly two decades, but Lodge finally sent this reply. He would die six months later.

Dear Corliss,

Regarding your open letter of November 1, 1965, concerning me: You were right. We were wrong and we failed. I should have resigned sooner.

Thank you for your most interesting book <u>Yes to Life</u> which I am reading with avidity.

Best wishes always.
Cabot

1984: OCTOBER
LEE ATWATER TO THE REAGAN CAMPAIGN

One of the most flamboyant political figures of the late twentieth century, strategist Lee Atwater (1951–1991) was young, tough, and confident when he wrote this memo to the Reagan campaign about an upcoming debate between the president and Walter Mondale (1928–). Famous for his take-no-prisoners tactics, as well as for his good-old-boy blues guitar, Atwater helped secure Reagan a 1984 reelection landslide, helped George Bush (1924–) win four years later, and became, in 1989, chairman of the Republican party. In 1990, Atwater would be diagnosed with a fatal brain tumor. He would spend his remaining months experiencing a religious conversion and offering apologies to those he felt he had wronged.

George Shultz, Caspar Weinberger, Jeane Kirkpatrick, Robert McFarlane, William Clark, Brent Scowcroft, and Donald Rumsfeld were all high-level members of the Reagan administration. John Tower was a Republican senator from Texas. Geraldine Ferraro was running for vice-president on the Democratic ticket. Former Budget Director Bert Lance, Speaker of the House Thomas "Tip" O'Neill, and former presidential candidate George McGovern were all considered Democratic liabilities by the Republicans. The "270 strategy" refers to the number of electoral votes needed to elect the president. GOTV stands for "get out the vote."

IF WE LOSE THE KANSAS CITY DEBATE

1. Don't claim victory, but deny that we lost.
   Expectations for the President were low following Louisville. However many gaffes he made, however inarticulate he seemed in that pressure cooker, however "off" he was that night, he still succeeded in laying out the fundamentals of his vision of America—prouder, stronger, better.

2. The SWAT team
   Shultz, Weinberger, Kirkpatrick, McFarlane, and Clark will have to get out there immediately to defend the Administration.
   We should go all out to round up Kissinger, Scowcroft, Rumsfeld, Tower, etc. to help in this task. We should not hesitate to violate protocols by enlisting top Pentagon brass to help.

3. Create a fog machine

If it's clear that the President did badly, then it's our job to obscure the result.

The single most important mission of the fog machine will be to shift the emphasis to Mondale, and to drive up his negative rating.

4. Paid media counter-offensive

We can't depend on free media or surrogates to carry our message. We will need both, of course, but our main counterthrust in the wake of the debate should be paid media.

The paid media counter-offensive would have three key elements:

—A five minute spot by Gerald Ford (see #5, below)

—A five minute spot using Robert Dole (see #5, below)

—A half hour speech by the President (see #7, below)

5. Ford and Dole spots

If the Great Communicator loses the debate, then for the purposes of the campaign, he is no longer the Great Communicator. We will be in a situation similar to '76, when the Republican incumbent was a nice guy with a good record, who unfortunately could not get his message out to the American people. So the incumbent, Jerry Ford, was defeated, and we got Jimmy Carter.

Who better to warn the American people against being swayed by words than Ford himself? Robert Dole, if he were willing, could help make the same case. Each man could do a five minute spot for us.

Ford would tell the American people that he lost the debates in 1976, and he lost the presidency to Jimmy Carter. But the American people lost a lot more. They lost four years to malaise, inflation, and the shame of Iran. Let's not forget what happened under Jimmy Carter and Walter Mondale. Let's not let that crew get control of the White House again and lead us back down that same road! Don't find out the hard way what four years of liberal Democratic politics would do to your paycheck, your job, your security, and your future.

Dole could amplify these same points, and perhaps focus more on the false notion that a debate with Walter Mondale means anything in terms of the future of the country.

In 1981, Dole could say, while Ronald Reagan was bringing down inflation and averting economic catastrophe, Walter Mondale was "reeducating" himself and doing a lot of talking.

In 1982, Ronald Reagan was engineering the economic recovery. Walter Mondale was making a fortune as a Washington lawyer and doing a lot of talking.

In 1983, Ronald Reagan was rolling back communism in Grenada, and Walter Mondale was doing a lot of talking.

In 1984, Ronald Reagan was leading America back to greatness, and Walter Mondale was doing a lot of talking.

The choice of 1984 is between results and words. Walter Mondale wants you to base your decision as to who will lead this country for the next four years on the basis of 90 (or 180) minutes of television. He wants you to forget the last four years for America and the previous four years of disaster. That's 180 minutes of television versus 8 years of history.

Don't make the same mistake twice. Don't let the words of Mondale fool you. If you want to bring back the policies and results of Carter, bring back Mondale.

6. Other points to make about debates

—The capacity to endure a 90 minute TV debate has nothing to do with the capacity to govern the Nation. Debates don't measure effectiveness, judgment, shrewdness, innovation, or other qualities that bring about results.

—TV debates are artificially contrived "pressure cookers" which do not coincide with the actual pressures that confront a president.

—Debates can be and frequently are misleading and deceptive: winning a debate often depends more upon an effective "cheap shot" than anything else. A sitting president is a sitting duck for such tactics.

—Polished oratory is more frequently used to hide or disguise the facts than it is to reveal them. A good juror can and should, for example, "tune out" a slick lawyer's rehearsed advocacy in favor of an unpolished, but credible, witness's testimony.

—There is something fundamentally degrading about the entire process.

—Most, if not all, civilized nations manage to select their leaders without subjecting them to this bizarre ritual.

—The debates seem to have become a forum for the press to display its arrogance and to exert their control over the nation's leaders. One is reminded, for example, of the spectacle of Barbara Walters thanking the President of the United States for being so "obedient" in Louisville.

—Many of the world's greatest visionaries and leaders would not hold up well in a TV debate. This does not diminish Lech Walesa, Andrei Sakharov, etc.

—In the foreign policy debate in particular, there was a lot that the President could not talk about.

—The election will be on November 6, not on October 21. Don't let anyone deprive you of your right to vote and determine the course of the nation for the next four years.

There is of course an irony in the above counter-strategy. The media will notice that for the first time we are minimizing the importance of words and television; but they will just have to understand, along with the voters, that Ronald Reagan takes the presidency and his incumbency seriously, and he is not going to take time out from his job as leader of the free world to polish his lines the way Mondale did.

7. Reagan speech

Although we can use Ford and Dole and perhaps others to knock down the importance of debates, only the President can demonstrate to the American people that he is in full command. A half-hour address, dealing with all aspects of his presidency—domestic and foreign policy, leadership, and plans for the future, would be enormously helpful in putting the debates behind us.

8. Bush activities

If things go badly in Kansas City, then the Vice President's relative importance to the ticket goes way up. As we all know, he kicked Ferraro's ass in Philadelphia.

Since the age issue is sure to resurface in the aftermath of a disappointing performance on the 21st, the image of an active, aggressive, youthful Vice President will be reassuring to the American people.

9. "The Reagan-Bush Team"

We will need all the help we can get. There will be GOP governors and senators and congressmen who will be stronger in their states or districts than the President. They can help by cutting paid media spots, in addition to surrogate activity.

By developing the "team" concept, we emphasize that the voters aren't just choosing between Ronald Reagan and Walter Mondale, but between the good people associated with Reagan and the bad people associated with Mondale. This is tricky, but it fits into our strategy of driving up Mondale's negative rating.

10. The all-out assault on Mondale

We won't be able to worry much about charges of "desperation." We will have to clobber Mondale on the following, plus anything else we can think of:
—Waltergate
—Delegate committees
—Ferraro
—Income tax discrepancies

—Patsy for the Soviets

—Pal of Jesse Jackson, Teddy Kennedy, Bert Lance, Tip O'Neill, and George McGovern

—Associates with known alumni of the Carter administration

This last point focuses on the contrast between the "Reagan-Bush team" and the "Mondale-Carter" team.

11. Polarization and the 270 strategy

We'd like to win the country, but we only have to win a little over half of it. Indeed, given the vagaries of the electoral college, we can win with a minority of the popular vote.

Therefore we shouldn't hesitate to polarize, play the South against the North, the West against the East, and so on.

12. Countertheme #1: We Will Still Win

The debates don't matter, because the American people know that results are what count. Reagan is "the real thing."

The debates don't matter, because our organization (4 million registered voters, 13 million GOTV phone calls, 14 million pieces of mail), will carry the day.

The debates don't matter, because we have a lock on the electoral college. (I'm not sure how much it helps to put this out, but it may persuade a few journalists that we are still in the ball game.)

13. Countertheme #2: Reagan-Ike parallels

They used to say that Eisenhower "couldn't talk his way out of a paper bag." Yet he led America through 8 years of peace, progress, and prosperity, in spite of a heart attack, ileitis, etc. The RR-Truman parallelism will in any case have to go.

14. Countertheme #3: Media Bias

Everyone knows that the Big Media, especially the networks, have been out to get Ronald Reagan since day one. Recount how the polls as to who won and who lost in Louisville were relatively even, until the media did its hatchet job on the President. Cite the Michael J. Robinson study that shows network coverage of the President is 13:1 negative.

Ford could recall that the same thing happened to him in '76—people didn't "learn" that he "lost" the San Francisco "Poland" debate until days after the event itself.

15. Countertheme #4: Reagan the Crisis Manager

From the Suez Crisis in '56 to "peace is at hand" in '72, incumbents always look their best while decisively handling a crisis.

We should certainly consider a trip to Grenada on 10/25, the first anniversary of the liberation.

1984: DECEMBER 27

AN ANTIABORTION ACTIVIST TO THE <u>PENSACOLA NEWS</u>

The Supreme Court's legalization of abortion in 1973 galvanized the antiabortion movement. Some activitists, claiming a religious justification, advocated violence to deter what they viewed as baby-killing. On Christmas morning, 1984, pipe bombs exploded at a Pensacola, Florida, abortion clinic and at the offices of two doctors who performed the procedure. This letter was printed in the Pensacola News *two days later. The following year, the National Abortion Federation would record 224 acts of violence against abortion clinics nationwide. In separate incidents in 1993 and 1994, two abortion doctors would be slain in Pensacola.*

Dear Editor:

So you want to know who bombed the 3 abortion clinics, huh?

I did.

Let me tell you why.

When I was stationed here in the waves, before I got married, I got pregnant. Everyone had told me that a fetus was just a little shapeless blob anyway, so I got an abortion. I was almost 6 months pregnant by then.

Later, after it was too late, a friend gave me some literature one day showing how the baby developed at different stages. I never realized that at that stage, a fetus is so much a baby that some of them have been born at that point and lived!

Well, you cannot imagine what that did to me, knowing that I had not just "had an unwanted intra-uterine growth "removed," but had KILLED MY BABY! It just about ruined my life. Even today, several years later, I lay awake at nights sometimes crying about it.

So maybe you can understand my reason for doing what I did.

It was not because of religious fanaticism . . . I don't even go to church.

It was because I have seen for myself what the psychological effects of an abortion can do to a woman, and I didn't want what happened to me to happen to anyone else.

I did not act alone. And if these clinics reopen, we will see that they are closed again.

Some will say that it is wrong to use violent means to put an end to the killing. Well, we used a lot of violence in World War II to stop the killing of the Jews.

It is a well-established principle of justice that force, even deadly force, is justified in order to save innocent lives if necessary. So, I do not feel that I have done anything wrong.

We will stop the slaughter of the innocents. We WILL put an end to the murder of babies. And we WILL prevent any more lives from being ruined.

Signed,
A Woman Who Knew What She Was Doing

1985: APRIL
A CUSTOMER TO COCA-COLA

By 1985, Americans were drinking an average of more than thirty-five gallons of soft drinks a year per capita, and although Coca-Cola was still the clear leader in the "cola wars," its top brass was hoping that New Coke, with its sweeter formula, would lure younger converts from Pepsi while keeping loyal Coke drinkers. The product was a resounding failure.

Dear Sir:

Changing Coke is like God making the grass purple or putting toes on our ears or teeth on our knees.

1985: APRIL
ANOTHER CUSTOMER TO COCA-COLA

My littele sisther is cring because coke changed and she sayed that shed is not going to stop cring every day unitl you chang back. . . . I am geting tryer of hearing her now if you don't chang I'll sue evne if I'm just 11.

1985: APRIL 21
ROGER ENRICO TO PEPSI BOTTLERS

If the new Coke failed to thrill Coke's customers, it was a huge hit with Pepsi chairman Roger Enrico (1944–).

To all Pepsi Bottlers and
Pepsi-Cola Company personnel:

It gives me great pleasure to offer each of you my heartiest congratulations. After 87 years of going at it eyeball to eyeball, the other guy just blinked.

Coca-Cola is withdrawing their product from the marketplace, and is refor-mulating brand Coke to be "more like Pepsi." Too bad Ripley's not around . . . he could have had a field day with this one.

There is no question the long-term market success of Pepsi has forced this move.

Everyone knows when something is right it doesn't need changing.

Maybe they finally realized what most of us have known for years . . . Pepsi tastes better than Coke.

Well, people in trouble tend to do desperate things . . . and we'll have to keep our eye on them.

But for now, I say victory is sweet, and we have earned a celebration. We're going to declare a holiday on Friday.

Enjoy!

> Best Regards,
> Roger Enrico
> President, Chief Executive
> Officer
> Pepsi-Cola USA

1985: MAY 5
LYNNE SIPIORA TO BARBARA SHULGOLD

Lynne Sipiora was in the waiting room of her gynecologist's office when she read a letter to the editor by Barbara Shulgold in Resolve, *a national newsletter for infer-tile people. Shulgold had recently tried the fertility drug Pergonal for the second time and had again failed to become pregnant. Sipiora, who was just embarking on her own quest for fertility, wrote to Shulgold, and Shulgold responded. Like many women facing ever more sophisticated and complex reproductive technologies, Shulgold and Sipiora would find a bond in their shared pursuit of motherhood.*

May 5, 1985

Barbara,

Wonderful to receive your second letter—it arrived on the same day that I had a lengthy consult with my infertility specialist, so I suppose fate is <u>some-times</u> on my side. I have not yet started Pergonal and probably will not for at least three more cycles. First I have to get rid of an infection I recently con-tracted, and then my doctor is insisting upon a <u>second</u> laparoscopy. She has an excellent reputation but is rather conservative in her approach. Though I'm anxious to get started, I'm also kind of relieved to be able to put it off for a while. Frankly, at this point I have no idea how I'll manage Pergonal. As you know, the Pergonal treatment requires going to the doctor for endless blood tests and ultrasounds during the first seven to twelve days of each menstrual cycle. My job requires me to travel, and my daily schedule is very unpredictable. I explained all of this to my doctor, and she said, "It's your choice." And so, once again I find myself angry! My career has been my salvation through all of this, and yet now I'm told rather plainly to choose between maintaining my career or risking it for a long shot on a baby. Actually there is no choice—I will opt for the latter and somehow or another work out the schedule—but <u>damn</u> it's just not fair!

Funny, but I knew you'd understand when I attempted to define the other me. I think I did it more for myself because I have to keep remembering that there <u>is</u> another me! Infertility <u>is</u> all consuming!

Re: adoption. Do you have any idea when you may get a baby? I am not opposed to the idea at all—but have been scared by a variety of stories on the unavailability of babies. Is this true? Are you going through an agency? How long have you been told you must wait? As usual, I have so many questions . . .

Know that I'll be thinking of you as your neighbor's baby arrives on the scene. I face a similar situation. My husband has a nine-year-old daughter from a previous marriage. She is a sweet kid and we get along well—but she is <u>not</u> mine. Ann is with us every other weekend, and sometimes just looking at her is difficult. I find myself consumed with jealousy that my husband was able to have a child with another woman, but not with me! From time to time she asks very normal questions about when she was born, and when Ken tells the story of the trip to the hospital, etc., I really cannot bear it! I had not intended to get into yet <u>another</u> of my problems, but somehow I think you'll understand.

You're right—the statistics on Pergonal are encouraging, but like you, I am cautious. Ovulation <u>and</u> cervical mucus are a problem for me—the ultimate double whammy! While I await Pergonal, I continue to take 100 milligrams of Clomid a day for five days per month, and I continue to hope. Despite many, many disappointments, I continue to feel symptoms of pregnancy—every month—right up to the day my period arrives. Crazy, I know.

I've tried to take your advice about being good to myself and it does help. I also talk to no one (except Ken) about my problem—I think that helps me keep it in perspective. Also, I could not stand the monthly requests for progress reports. I did speak to my mother once, who only said, "Oh well you're a career woman, not the maternal type anyway." Needless to say, we've not discussed it again. I think that's why writing to you has become very important—not only do I feel free to say exactly what I feel but, wonder upon wonder, you know what I'm talking about. Yes, Barbara, there just are not many people who can intelligently talk cervical mucus and the luteal phase—pity to be so uninformed! The last line of your recent letter confirmed what I've always believed—I do <u>deserve</u> a baby. I know you do too. I will anxiously await all the details of your soon-to-arrive "preciousness," because I feel confident that when that baby is in your arms you'll be able to put all of this aside. I hope I, too, have such a happy ending. I also hope I end up half as well adjusted as you are!

Keep in touch. My thoughts are with you.

Lynne

P.S. I <u>hate</u> Mother's Day!

1985: MAY 22

A TIPSTER TO MERRILL LYNCH OFFICIALS

This unsigned letter landed on the desk of Merrill Lynch's compliance department vice-president, Richard Drew, on May 25. Its arrival set off an inquiry that would eventually produce a full Securities and Exchange Commission investigation of insider trading on Wall Street. Within a year, alleged ringleader Dennis Levine would plead guilty to felony charges, and his cooperation with investigators would help bring down the firm of Drexel Burnham Lambert, along with Ivan Boesky, Michael Milken, and other erstwhile idols of what came to be known as the Decade of Greed.

Hofer (his name was misspelled in the note) and Zubillaga were fired by Merrill Lynch but did not face civil or criminal charges.

May 22, 1985

Dear Sir: please be informed that two of your executives from the Caracas office are trading with inside information.A copie with description of ther trades so far has been submitet to the S.E.C. by separate mail.As is mantion on that letter if us customers do not benefit from their knoledg, we wonder who surveils the trades done by account executives.Upon you investigating to the last consequecies   we will provide with the names of the insider on their owne hand writing.

executives max hoffer 14899052

carlos zubillaga 14899073

mr frank granados might like to
have a copie

1985: SEPTEMBER 18
JOSEPH JAMAIL TO JOHN JEFFERS

At the height of the corporate-takeover boom of the 1980s, just as Pennzoil was about to merge with Getty Oil, Texaco swept Getty away with a higher offer. The deal, as set forth at trial by folksy lawyer Joe Jamail (1925–), looked sleazy to a Texas jury. On November 19, it would award an unprecedented $10.53 billion to Pennzoil (Texaco would later settle for $3 billion). Midtrial, with the jury apparently in his thrall, Jamail passed this exuberant note to cocounsel John Jeffers.

JJ,
I'm beginning to like this fucking case.

—JJ

1985: NOVEMBER 28
RONALD REAGAN TO MIKHAIL GORBACHEV

In March of 1983, Ronald Reagan had declared the Soviet Union an "evil empire" and proposed the high-tech Strategic Defense Initiative (nicknamed "Star Wars") to protect the United States from nuclear attack. In 1985, when a comparatively accessible Mikhail Gorbachev (1931–) became the USSR's new Communist party leader, Reagan leapt at the chance for a new beginning. With perestroika *(restructuring) and* glasnost *(openness) the watchwords of Gorbachev's reform movement, the U.S. and Soviet Union inched closer to one another after decades of mutual antipathy.*

Dear General Secretary Gorbachev:

Now that we are both home and facing the task of leading our countries into a more constructive relationship with each other, I wanted to waste no time in giving you some of my initial thoughts on our meetings. Though I will be sending shortly, in a more formal and official manner, a more detailed commentary on our discussions, there are some things I would like to convey very personally and very privately.

First, I want you to know that I found our meetings of great value. We had agreed to speak frankly, and we did. As a result, I came away from the meeting with a better understanding of your attitudes. I hope you also understand mine a little better. Obviously there are many things on which we disagree and we disagree very fundamentally. But, if I understand you correctly, you, too, are determined to take steps to see that our nations manage their relationship in a peaceful fashion. If this is the case, then this is one point on which we are in total agreement—and it is after all the most fundamental one of all.

As for our substantial differences, let me offer a thought or two of my own.

Regarding strategic defense and its relation to the reduction of offensive nuclear weapons, I was struck by your conviction that the American program is somehow designed to secure a strategic advantage or even to permit a first strike capability. I also noted your concern that research and testing in the area could be a cover for developing and placing offensive weapons in space.

As I told you, neither of these concerns is warranted. But I can understand, as you explained so eloquently, that there are matters that cannot be taken on faith. Both of us must cope with what the other side is doing and judge these implications for the security of our own country. I do not ask you to take my assurances on faith.

However, the truth is that the United States has no intention of using its strategic defense program to gain any advantage and there is no development under way to create space-based weapons.

Our goal is to eliminate any possibility of a first strike from either side. This being the case, we should be able to find a way, in practical terms, to relieve the concerns you have expressed.

For example, could our negotiators, when they resume work in January, discuss frankly and specifically what sort of future development each of us would find threatening? Neither of us, it seems, wants to see offensive weapons, particularly weapons of mass destruction, deployed in space. Should we not attempt to define what sort of systems have that potential and then try to find verifiable ways to prevent their development?

And can't our negotiators deal more frankly and openly with the question of how to eliminate a first strike potential on both sides? Your military now has an advantage in this area—a three to one advantage in warheads that can destroy hardened targets with little warning. That is obviously alarming to us and explains many of the efforts we are making in our modernization program. You may feel perhaps that the U.S. has some advantage in other categories. If so, let's insist that our negotiators face up to these issues and find a way to improve the security of both countries by agreeing on appropriately balanced reductions. If you are as sincere as I am in not seeking to secure or preserve one-sided advantages, we will find a solution to these problems.

Regarding another key issue we discussed, that of regional conflicts, I can assure you that the United States does not believe that the Soviet Union is the cause of all the world's ills. We do believe, however, that your country has exploited and worsened local tensions and conflicts by militarizing them and, indeed, intervening directly and indirectly in struggles arising out of local causes. While we both will doubtless continue to support our friends, we must find a way to do so without use of armed force. This is the crux of the point I tried to make.

One of the most significant steps in lowering tensions in the world—and tensions in U.S.-Soviet relations—would be a decision on your part to withdraw your forces from Afghanistan. I gave careful attention to your comments on this issue at Geneva and am encouraged by your statement that you feel political reconciliation is possible.

I want you to know that I am prepared to cooperate in any reasonable way to facilitate such a withdrawal and that I understand that it must be done in a manner which does not damage Soviet security. During our meetings, I mentioned one idea which I thought might be helpful and I will welcome any further suggestions you may have.

These are only two of the key issues on our current agenda. I will soon send some thoughts on others. I believe that we should act promptly to build the momentum our meeting initiated.

In Geneva I found our private sessions particularly useful. Both of us have advisers and assistants, but, you know, in the final analysis, the responsibility to preserve peace and increase cooperation is ours. Our people look to us for leadership and nobody can provide it if we don't. But we won't be very effective leaders unless we can rise above the specific but secondary concerns that preoccupy our respective bureaucracies and give our governments a strong push in the right direction.

So what I want to say finally is that we should make the most of the time before we meet again to find some specific and significant steps that would give meaning to our commitment to peace and arms reductions. Why not set a goal—privately, just between the two of us—to find a practical way to solve critical issues—the two I have mentioned—by the time we meet in Washington?

Please convey regards from Nancy and me to Mrs. Gorbachev. We genuinely enjoyed meeting you in Geneva and are already looking forward to showing you something of our country next year.

Sincerely yours,
Ronald Reagan
November 28, 1985

1986

CHER TO CHUCK

Designed by American architect Maya Lin and built in 1982, the Vietnam War Memorial was inscribed with the names of the more than fifty-eight thousand Americans killed or missing in action during the war. The Wall, as it has come to be known, provided a place of pilgrimage for veterans and survivors, many of whom— like the anonymous author of this letter—left tokens of their love.

Dearest Chuck,

This is the first time I've written you since April, 1970. But I know you wouldn't think it silly. I've written a lot of poems from my heartache of being without you. I wish that you weren't shipped out on that early flight. We would have been married before you left. Not seeing you after made it hard for me to believe. I looked for you in the face of every young man. I thought about having your baby and making love to you. We really were ripped off of the most beautiful things in life.

They told me you didn't die right away. God I hope you didn't suffer too badly. It's not fair. They didn't know how gentle you were, how precious. I wonder if I'll see you in heaven. I dream occasionally. They say you then know of my love. Remember the letter you wrote? When you said you were fighting a war you didn't understand? It seemed no one really understood. We were only 19 then babe and here I am, 16 years later, still wondering. I went to the cemetery once in California where they buried you. I hope you saw me. This is all very hard for me. Even now I still have the ring you gave me and all the poems and pictures. I have a special friend now who understands all of this. He listens to the story of how we met and all the crazy things we did. He knows how much I love you even now. It's the only thing that did not die or end. God be with you Chuck. I'll always dream of you.

Love,
Cher

1986: FEBRUARY 10

BARBARA SHULGOLD TO LYNNE SIPIORA

It probably would have been impossible for Barbara Shulgold to believe, as she wrote this painful letter, that both she and Sipiora (see letter page 591) would, indeed, eventually become mothers. Of the four children they would have, three would be adopted; the fourth would be the product of Sipiora's successful in vitro fertilization. Throughout their shared ordeals, the women continued to write letters and speak on the phone but never met in person.

February 10, 1986

Dear Lynne,

It's taken two tall glasses of wine in the middle of the afternoon to help me get up the courage to write this to you. I came extremely close to calling you the other night, but figured you didn't need to hear my voice for the first time in a state of wild hysteria. Anyhow, you are the only person who is going to get this—all of this—in writing. If you feel the need, now is a good time for a glass of wine.

By now you have received our mourning note, which has apparently crossed with a note you sent me. I have not opened it and will not until we have a baby. There is just so much pain a body can take, and warm congratulations from you, after all we have been through together, would be too much.

Our precious baby was with us five days before the birth mother changed her mind. Five days was just long enough for BOTH of us to realize that a new life is indeed as breathtakingly, achingly wonderful as we had dreamed. We fell in love, could not keep our eyes or hands off her, and even loved the exhaustion of the 3:00 a.m. feedings. She was an easy baby, which of course makes our pain harder to bear. She would quiet instantly when we held her, and we held and cuddled and loved her all the time. We took rolls of pictures (I am afraid I sent you one with the birth announcement). We called everyone and told everyone, and I took a child-rearing leave, and my class sent me congratulations—tinged with sadness, as they did not know I was leaving—and the faculty (also kept totally in the dark) called endlessly with congratulations and—well, you get the picture. The most beautiful week of our lives was followed by the worst. Everyone has been extraordinarily wonderful, as they always are when someone dies (and this is as close to a death as I can imagine). The women in my adoption group have been super: fixing us meals, holding our hands, notifying all our friends, offering country homes for a getaway—you name it. They were here when the baby was taken away, and they held me and cried with us. I am so grateful. TIME OUT FOR A GODDAM KLEENEX.

So, they say, this happens about 5 to 10 percent of the time, particularly when the mother has no family support system (Nancy had tons), when she doesn't bond with the adoptive parents (we spent hours and hours and hours with her), when she is young (Nancy is thirty), or when she has no children of her own (she has a son). Big deal statistics. I don't think she was conning us; I think she was just one of those people who are not introspective and do not genuinely know their own minds until it is too late. I feel betrayed, raped, empty, and enraged.

Part of me worries about you and Melissa, a woman in my school district who keeps approaching and avoiding the idea of adoption, saying, "I'll believe it works when I see you holding your baby." I fear this has set her back a few steps.

And YOU: I know how strange and risky and expensive everything I have been writing to you about these many months has sounded. I know how badly you want to give birth to your own baby, but think about adoption "just in case." I hope it makes a hell of a lot of difference to you to know that here, in the midst of this hellish pain, albeit numbed a bit by alcohol, I am far more certain than ever that I will <u>NEVER NEVER</u> give up my search for a baby. This pain is worth it: I will be a mother. So will you.

As to Rich: He underwent the most amazing transformation. At first he was so scared to care for her that he almost threw up. Then the nurse came to give us parenting lessons, told us we were doing just fine and were the kind of people who would make great parents, showed us a few tricks, and left. And from then on there was no stopping him. HE became the expert on diapering techniques, burping, poop analysis—you name it. I took dozens of photos (gone now) of him kissing and cuddling her and just touching her cheek. SHIT, he really went for her hook, line, and sinker.

The night they took her, I watched him cry for the first time in the nine years I have known him. And he wept and wept and wept. I have awakened in the middle of the night to hear him crying. The difference is now he says, "Now I understand what you have been fighting for all these years. I will not rest until we have another baby, and it must be a newborn: they are nature's greatest creation." Well, I coulda told him. But, better late than never.

So, what now? Well, as the book title goes: first you cry. I am crying a lot, sleeping a lot, watching a lot of TV, and having a little too much wine. Also, ignoring the telephone and letting the machine take the condolence messages. Can't take it. I am retreating for a week, going back to my therapist who got me through the infertility crisis (I went to see her the morning after, and she cried more than I did; I was the one screaming—really screaming—in rage). I don't think I will be able to go back and face the class and the hundreds of kids at my school who know me and will ask what happened to my baby and the faculty . . . so, I am not going back. It may be a mistake, but I am going to look for temporary work <u>away</u> from children: working in a little store, or as a secretary or something. I need a break.

Needless to add, this is probably the worst time financially for me not to be working. The adoption cost us $3,500, and we just don't have an equivalent sum to start again. Our wonderful lawyer is beginning a campaign to try to get the money back, but since Nancy doesn't really have money or a job, I am hoping a guilt trip or two on her mother (a college professor, for God's sake) will get her to reimburse us. I will stop at nothing to get the money back, including taking her to court, although I am as yet unsure if the agreement was legally binding. But my rage is real, and I have no intention of just giving up. THAT is impossible.

Ellen Roseman, upon whom all our hopes are now placed, assures us we are at the top of her list. I would not be surprised if we have a baby in three months. She is marvelous. She has had all sorts of former clients who have gone through the same heartbreak call us. All but one have babies now and were so comforting. Sometimes I think I would be a basket case were it not for the Resolve/adoption group/Ellen Roseman networks.

You will be here in early March, yes? Spending time with you in person has now become an important future event for me. I guess, friend, there will be time for the two of us to talk uninterrupted by a baby's squalls, dammit. I do look forward to it, believe me.

My therapist says she admires me for enduring what I have endured, says that she sees me as a strong woman and that I will survive. You know, even now I can see that she is right. But, dammit, I would like to be weak for a while, and I would like to be a mother.

I know, I feel, how you hurt for me, Lynne. And it is a comfort.

Love,
Barbara

1986: MARCH 21
DREXEL BURNHAM LAMBERT TO IVAN BOESKY

When regulators closed in on Michael Milken (1946–), defenders argued that he had at most skirted some technical securities regulations in using high-risk, high-yield "junk bonds" to finance corporate deals. But the SEC and prosecutors insisted that Milken, who earned as much as $550 million in one year, had conspired with confessed Wall Street transgressor Ivan Boesky (1937–) in a series of complicated frauds. Prosecutors viewed this 1986 invoice as their smoking gun: It showed, they claimed, that Boesky was paying Milken for his help in illegal deals.

DREXEL BURNHAM LAMBERT

March 21, 1986

Mr. Ivan F. Boesky
Ivan F. Boesky Corporation
450 Fifth Avenue
25th Floor
New York, NY 10019

FOR PROFESSIONAL SERVICES

FOR CONSULTING SERVICES AS AGREED UPON ON MARCH 21, 1986
$5,300,000.00

PLEASE SEND REMITTANCE TO THE ATTENTION OF THE CORPORATE FI-
NANCE DEPARTMENT

1986: JULY 28
JOSEPH KERWIN TO RICHARD TRULY

*One of the most horrifying images of the century was the televised explosion of
the* Challenger *space shuttle on January 28, 1986. While there would be little debate about what caused the explosion—a faulty set of O-rings sealing the rocket's
boosters—what lingered was the awful question of precisely when and how the
seven astronauts on board had died.*

Joseph P. Kerwin was a biomedical specialist from the Johnson Space Center in Houston. Rear
Admiral Richard H. Truly had flown on previous *Challenger* missions.

RADM Richard H. Truly
Associate Administrator for Space Flight
NASA Headquarters
Code M
Washington, DC 20546

Dear Admiral Truly:

The search for wreckage of the Challenger crew cabin has been completed.
A team of engineers and scientists has analyzed the wreckage and all other
available evidence in an attempt to determine the cause of death of the Challenger crew. This letter is to report to you on the results of this effort. The

findings are inconclusive. The impact of the crew compartment with the ocean surface was so violent that evidence of damage occurring in the seconds which followed the explosion was masked. Our final conclusions are:

- the cause of death of the Challenger astronauts cannot be positively determined;
- the forces to which the crew were exposed during Orbiter breakup were probably not sufficient to cause death or serious injury; and
- the crew possibly, but not certainly, lost consciousness in the seconds following Orbiter breakup due to in-flight loss of crew module pressure.

Our inspection and analyses revealed certain facts which support the above conclusions, and these are related below: The forces on the Orbiter at breakup were probably too low to cause death or serious injury to the crew but were sufficient to separate the crew compartment from the forward fuselage, cargo bay, nose cone, and forward reaction control compartment. The forces applied to the Orbiter to cause such destruction clearly exceed its design limits. The data available to estimate the magnitude and direction of these forces included ground photographs and measurements from onboard accelerometers, which were lost two-tenths of a second after vehicle breakup.

Two independent assessments of these data produced very similar estimates. The largest acceleration pulse occurred as the Orbiter forward fuselage separated and was rapidly pushed away from the external tank. It then pitched nose-down and was decelerated rapidly by aerodynamic forces. There are uncertainties in our analysis; the actual breakup is not visible on photographs because the Orbiter was hidden by the gaseous cloud surrounding the external tank. The range of most probable maximum accelerations is from 12 to 20 G's in the vertical axis. These accelerations were quite brief. In two seconds, they were below four G's; in less than ten seconds, the crew compartment was essentially in free fall. Medical analysis indicates that these accelerations are survivable, and that the probability of major injury to crew members is low.

After vehicle breakup, the crew compartment continued its upward trajectory, peaking at an altitude of 65,000 feet approximately 25 seconds after breakup. It then descended striking the ocean surface about two minutes and forty-five seconds after breakup at a velocity of about 207 miles per hour. The forces imposed by this impact approximated 200 G's, far in excess of the structural limits of the crew compartment or crew survivability levels.

The separation of the crew compartment deprived the crew of Orbiter-supplied oxygen, except for a few seconds supply in the lines. Each crew member's helmet was also connected to a personal egress air pack (PEAP) containing an emergency supply of breathing air (not oxygen) for ground egress emergencies, which must be manually activated to be available. Four PEAP's were recovered, and there is evidence that three had been activated. The non-activated PEAP was identified as the Commander's, one of the others as the Pilot's, and the remaining ones could not be associated with any crew member. The evidence indicates that the PEAP's were not activated due to water impact.

It is possible, but not certain, that the crew lost consciousness due to an in-flight loss of crew module pressure. Data to support this is:

- The accident happened at 48,000 feet, and the crew cabin was at that altitude or higher for almost a minute. At that altitude, without an oxygen supply, loss of cabin pressure would have caused rapid loss of consciousness and it would not have been regained before water impact.
- PEAP activation could have been an instinctive response to unexpected loss of cabin pressure.
- If a leak developed in the crew compartment as a result of structural damage during or after breakup (even if the PEAP's had been activated), the breathing air available would not have prevented rapid loss of consciousness.
- The crew seats and restraint harnesses showed patterns of failure which demonstrates that all the seats were in place and occupied at water impact with all harnesses locked. This would likely be the case had rapid loss of consciousness occurred, but it does not constitute proof.

Much of our effort was expended attempting to determine whether a loss of cabin pressure occurred. We examined the wreckage carefully, including the crew module attach points to the fuselage, the crew seats, the pressure shell, the flight deck and middeck floors, and feedthroughs for electrical and plumbing connections. The windows were examined and fragments of glass analyzed chemically and microscopically. Some items of equipment stowed in lockers showed damage that might have occurred due to decompression; we experimentally decompressed similar items without conclusive results.

Impact damage to the windows was so extreme that the presence or absence of in-flight breakage could not be determined. The estimated breakup forces would not in themselves have broken the windows. A broken window due to flying debris remains a possibility; there was a piece of debris imbedded in the frame between two of the forward windows. We could not positively identify the origin of the debris or establish whether the event occurred in flight or at water impact. The same statement is true of the other crew compartment structure. Impact damage was so severe that no positive evidence for or against in-flight pressure loss could be found.

    Finally, the skilled and dedicated efforts of the team from the Armed Forces Institute of Pathology, and their expert consultants, could not determine whether in-flight lack of oxygen occurred, nor could they determine the cause of death.

Joseph P. Kerwin

1986: SEPTEMBER 25
OLIVER NORTH TO JOHN POINDEXTER

In 1984, Congress passed the Boland Amendment, banning U.S. aid to the right-wing Contra rebels in Communist Nicaragua. But in 1986, it was discovered that Oliver North, a National Security Council aide, had been using profits from the illegal sale of missiles to Iran to lead a covert Contra supply operation. The unraveling of its cover is detailed in the White House memo below, sent (in an early form of e-mail) to North's boss, National Security advisor John Poindexter. The fallout from the "Iran-Contra Affair" was considerable: North would receive a felony conviction (later overturned on a technicality), Poindexter would resign, and numerous administration officials would be implicated. For his part, President Reagan would claim not to remember if he had ever approved the sales to Iran.

Elliott Abrams was assistant secretary of state for inter-American affairs. "Dick" was Richard Secord, the National Security Council contractor for the operation. Alan Fiers was head of the CIA task force on Central America. Oscar Arias was the Costa Rican president.

09/25/86 11:23:45

To: NSJMP   —CPUA
***Reply to note of 9/13/86 12:01
NOTE FROM: OLIVER NORTH
Subject: Public Affairs Campaign on Central America

    Elliott Abrams has just called from New York, followed by an urgent call from Fiers. Last night Costa Rican Interior Minister Garion held a press conference in San Jose and announced that Costa Rican authorities had discovered a secret airstrip in Costa Rica that was over a mile long and which had been built and used by a Co. called Udall Services for supporting the Contras. In the press conference the minister named one of Dick's agents (Olmstead) as the man who set up the field as a "training base for U.S. military advisors." Damage assessment: Udall Resources, Inc., S.A. is a proprietary of Project Democracy. It will cease to exist by noon today. There are no USG fingerprints on any of the operation and Olmstead is not the name of the agent—Olmstead does not exist.

We have moved all Udall resources ($48K) to another account in Panama, where Udall maintained an answering service and cover office. The office is now gone as are all files and paperwork. The bottomline is that Arias has now seriously violated the understanding we have had with his administration since shortly after his inaugeral. Elliott has said that he and the Secretary want to cancel the Arias visit with the President and replace him with Cerrezo. They are due to meet with Arias at 1145. I strongly urge that you concur with the Secretary's recommendation. Arias has screwed us badly—and we should not give him what he so obviously wants.

1987
LISA CONKLIN TO THE TOOTH FAIRY

Lisa Conklin was an eight-year-old living in Wichita, Kansas, when she wrote this note.

Dear Tooth Fairy:
Loosing teeth is fun! Once I had about four teeth loose! Now they are all out. I have one loose tooth now. I am really trying to take care of my teeth. I try to remember to floss my teeth. You must be ritch to give all the children mony. When you were little, and lost teeth, who was the tooth farry then? Dose your dentest know that you are the tooth farry? We have tons of dentle floss. When you were in school, did you tell yur teacher that you were the tooth farry?
Love,
Lisa

1987: AUGUST 2
JOAN QUIGLEY TO RONALD REAGAN

For seven years—until chief of staff Donald Regan revealed the association in his 1988 memoirs—First Lady Nancy Reagan (1921–) was frequently advised by an astrologer named Joan Quigley. Once unveiled, Quigley claimed that she had dictated the timing of almost all of the president's press conferences, as well as his speeches, debates, trips, and announcements. Nancy Reagan, while disputing the extent of Quigley's influence, would nonetheless concede that she had sought the astrologer's advice, especially in the wake of the Hinckley shooting. "While I was never certain that Joan's astrological advice was helping to protect Ronnie," she would write in her memoir, "the fact is that nothing like March 30 ever happened again."

Dear Ronnie,

With the exception of Washington, America's most outstanding presidents have been Aquarians. Lincoln, Roosevelt and Reagan. They occupy a very special place in their people's hearts but they have had their problems as well. It is said, "A great man, great problems."

It is also said that the only lasting evil a bad experience can do to anyone is to warp their judgment. This has not happened to you. You have borne up nobly during a period when your astrological transits could be likened to the adverse weather conditions that threaten to destroy a farmer's carefully planted crops. But you, the farmer unaltered by adversity, will come through your trials intact, and mindful of the rich harvests of past years, will surpass past successes. . . .

You have remained firm and balanced as your personal good aspects indicate and have gone about your business with a smile and now, having passed the test by so doing, you will emerge triumphant.

Already you have in place three brilliant strategies: the missiles in Europe, the development of SDI and the strong military.

It is my conviction that of the American presidents, Lincoln and Reagan will go down in world history as the very greatest. Both have Jupiter rulers. Lincoln's in Pisces, gave him the problem of slavery. Your ruler in Scorpio gave you the problem of war. And as Lincoln abolished slavery, you, Ronald Reagan, will bring peace to the world. Your vision will be vindicated, your role in history unparalleled.

As your astrologer, your steadfastness and courage, your true spiritual strength did not surprise me. They are only what I expected.

With admiration,

Joan

❊   ❊   ❊

RUSSELL STONE TO A SON OR DAUGHTER

The Dalkon Shield was an intrauterine device introduced by A. H. Robins in 1971 with the goal of providing a safe and effective alternative to other forms of contraception. Millions of American women are estimated to have used it. Eventually revealed as a disaster, the device was linked to eighteen deaths, thousands of infections and miscarriages, and untold cases of infertility. In 1985, Robins filed for bankruptcy in the wake of 325,000 lawsuits. Three years later, the husband of one of the IUD's former users wrote this letter.

A. H. Robins denied that the Dalkon Shield was defective or that it was any more dangerous than other intrauterine devices.

May 5, 1988

Dear Son or Daughter,

I write this letter to you because I don't know what else to do. You never existed. You were never born. You never even had a chance to be born because of a mistake your mother and I made a long time ago.

Back in 1970, when your mother and I were married, we had already decided to hold off having children until we felt we could give them the best life possible, so your mother and I agreed together to use a birth control device. We chose the Dalkon Shield IUD. That was a mistake! One that we have both paid for very dearly.

You see, my son or daughter, the Dalkon Shield was a device that was both unsafe and, in some cases, deadly. We didn't know that. The inventor (Dr. Hugh Davis) and the manufacturer (A. H. Robins) did. But they didn't tell anyone! So your mother had it in her body for almost 7 years, thinking it was okay. But it wasn't.

On December 19, 1977, at about 11 p.m., the doctor at the hospital told me and your mom that if he didn't operate right away that night and give your mother a complete hysterectomy, she would die! The infection that the IUD had caused to happen in so many other women had happened in your mom. What could we do? What could your mother do? What could I do? We agreed to the operation.

About four and one-half hours later, the doctor came down the hall (all sweaty and very, very tired) to the waiting room where I was and told me it was done. "Your wife is in recovery," he said. It was done. All your mother's eggs had been removed. She would never have a child or be a mother. I would never be a father. You would never be born.

Sometimes I feel such a hate in my heart because of these people. Sometimes I want to hurt them as much as they hurt us. But what good would that do? You still wouldn't be here. I ask myself: What kind of a world do I live in? That people would hurt other people this way just for money? I get no answer. It is known now, by a lot of people and the supposed justice system, how evil these people are and what they did and then tried in every deceitful way to cover up. Yet still the battle rages to make them pay. At least in a monetary way. But I don't think they really know or believe just how bad they are. And I don't think they'll ever really pay.

But in the meanwhile, you were never born and you are not here. No Little League games. No Sunday outings. No shared plastic model building times. No pretty new dress. No first kiss. No high school. No marriage. No grandchildren. No nothing.

Sometimes at work the other men talk about their kids. About how this one is good in swimming class or that one did something funny in front of everybody. Or how this one is changing jobs. Or that one is good with tools or something. I have to just sit and listen and take it. Sometimes it really hurts, but I just take it.

It's not that I just want a child so I can show him off. If it were only that. I helped raise a couple of brothers so I know what a pain in the butt kids can be sometime. I know there are bad times with kids just like everything else. But sometimes when I hear them talking at work, or I see a baby diaper ad on television or I see a kid walking with their parents, I think of a little pair of arms. A little pair of arms around my neck. A little voice saying DADDY! What I would give for that!

How little those people who have that know. A little pair of arms around my neck and the little voice that says <u>daddy</u>.

They say you usually feel better when you get something off your chest. I guess that's what this letter was supposed to do. But I don't feel any better. I feel the same way as when I started . . . empty.

Your father who never was nor will be,
Russell M. Stone

*   *   *

By the mid-1990s, Jerry Seinfeld (1955–) would top the television ratings charts, and his show's comedic portrait of modern manners and urban drift would help change NBC's fortunes—and Americans' vernacular. But in 1988, though he had appeared on The Tonight Show *and in comedy clubs, Seinfeld was still mostly a gleam in the eye of his agent, George Shapiro. This seemingly innocuous letter led to a meeting, a pilot, and, in 1990, the launching of the famous "show about nothing."* Along with Larry David and Howard West, Shapiro would become one of the show's executive producers.

August 31, 1988

Mr. Brandon Tartikoff
Mr. Warren Littlefield
Mr. Perry Simon
C/O NBC
3000 W. Alameda Avenue
Burbank, CA 91523

RE: JERRY SEINFELD

Dear Brandon, Warren & Perry:

Call me a crazy guy, but I feel that Jerry Seinfeld will soon be doing a series on NBC, and I thought you'd like to see this article from the current issue of People Magazine.

Jerry will be appearing in concert in New York City at Town Hall on Saturday, September 10. If any of you will be in New York at that time I'll be happy to arrange tickets for you and your guests.

Warmest regards,

Sincerely,
George Shapiro

*   *   *

---

*With this letter, New York senator Alfonse D'Amato (1937–) and North Carolina
senator Jesse Helms (1921–) launched their part of a high-profile campaign against
the National Endowment for the Arts. On the same day this letter was read into
the Congressional Record, D'Amato ripped up—and threw to the Senate floor—a
copy of* Piss Christ, *an Andres Serrano photograph that showed a plastic crucifix
submerged in the artist's urine. The senator's outrage was based on the fact that
something he considered so abhorrent had been funded by tax dollars. "The Senator
from New York is absolutely correct in his indignation," declared Senator Helms. "I
do not know Mr. Andres Serrano, and I hope I never meet him. Because he is not an
artist, he is a jerk."*
Hugh Southern (1932–) was deputy chairman for programs at the National Endowment for
the Arts from 1982 to 1989.

U.S. Senate, Washington, DC, May 18, 1989
Mr. Hugh Southern, Acting Chairman,
National Endowment for the Arts, Washington, DC.

Dear Mr. Southern: We recently learned of the Endowment's support for a so-
called "work of art" by Andres Serrano entitled "Piss Christ." We write to express
our outrage and to suggest in the strongest terms that the procedures used by
the Endowment to award and support artists be reformed.

The piece in question is a large and vivid photograph of Christ on a crucifix,
submerged in the artist's urine. This work is shocking, abhorrent and completely undeserving of any recognition whatsoever. Millions of taxpayers are
rightfully incensed that their hard-earned dollars were used to honor and support Serrano's work.

There is a clear flaw in the procedures used to select art and artists deserving of taxpayers' support. That fact is evidenced by the Serrano work itself.
Moreover, after the artist was selected and honored for his "contributions" to
the field of art, his work was exhibited at government expense and with the im-
primatur of the Endowment.

This matter does not involve freedom of artistic expression—it does involve
the question whether American taxpayers should be forced to support such
trash.

And finally, simply because the Endowment and the Southeastern Center for Contemporary Art (SECCA) did not have a direct hand in choosing Serrano's work, does not absolve either of responsibility. The fact that both the Endowment and the SECCA with taxpayer dollars promoted this work as part of the Awards in Visual Arts exhibition, is reason enough to be outraged.

We urge the Endowment to comprehensively review its procedures and determine what steps will be taken to prevent such abuses from recurring in the future.

We await your response.

Sincerely,

Alfonse D'Amato, Bob Kerrey, Warren R. Rudman, Rudy Boschwitz, Dennis DeConcini, Pete Wilson, Bob Dole, Chuck Grassley, James A. McClure, John Heinz, Wendell Ford, Howell Heflin, Harry Reid, Richard Shelby, John W. Warner, Larry Pressler, Conrad Burns, Tom Harkin, Trent Lott, Jesse Helms, John McCain, Arlen Specter, Steve Symms.

1989: JUNE 28
BOBBY LAZEAR TO HIS PARENTS

By 1989, AIDS had been contracted by nearly two hundred thousand North Americans. Among them was Bobby Lazear, a bartender and aspiring actor who lived in New Orleans. Ever mindful of his parents' feelings, he waited until nearly the end to tell them of his illness. A month before his death, at the age of thirty-one, he warned them that this letter would be coming and that they should read it together.

Dear Folks,

I don't relish this and am sure it is not something you wish to dwell on either but—full steam ahead.

Basically, I see two concerns that I must address; in both of these it will be my requests that will become your assurance, I trust.

1. Disposal of my personal property. I would like what little I may have to be passed on to George. This applies, of course, only to my personal assets now. To the question of family assets; in the unlikely event of your prior deaths those assets should most assuredly remain in the family. That you can cover in your wills.

There may be some things of mine that you would like, such as G.Ma Allen's silver spoons. We can try to settle these things before I die but if that does not work out I'm sure you & George will have no problems.

2. Disposal of my person. This makes me think of what a strange and varied path I have taken through religion.

First, I want to be cremated. I made a few inquiries and it would be much cheaper to have that done here rather than shipping my body to New England. This, of course, is up to you. If at all possible I would like to be put under the choke cherry tree behind the house with no marker. However, if that is not feasible or agreeable to you simply anywhere on Cuttyhunk.

While I view a ceremony centered on a casket, open or closed, as rather barbaric and an unnecessary expense I do understand the need for some sort of communal experience where family and friends may share their grief and give each other support. However you would choose to do this is fine with me, after all I won't be there, so whatever will ease you through my passing is what is right.

Your loving Son,
Bobby

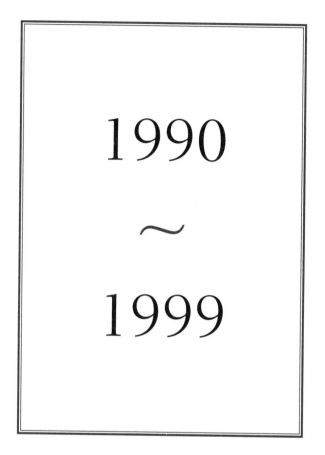

1990

~

1999

Talk to your husband about your wants and needs and try
to put some energy back into your marriage. Perhaps you
and your husband could begin to E-mail each other as
a way of reviving your communication process.

—*Dr. Shirley Glass to an on-line correspondent*
June 1999

BETWEEN 1990 AND 1999 . . .

1990: Number of civilians working for the federal government: 3,508,463. ★ The U.S. population is 248,718,291. ★ Popular films include *Dances With Wolves, Ghost,* and *Goodfellas.* **1991:** A 25-year-old unarmed black motorist named Rodney King is severely beaten by Los Angeles police, and the event is captured on videotape. ★ Law professor Anita Hill accuses Supreme Court nominee Clarence Thomas of sexual harassment. Thomas is confirmed by a 52 to 48 Senate vote. ★ America goes to war in the Persian Gulf. ★ There are 24,700 victims of homicide in the nation, an all-time high. ★ Magic Johnson tests positive for the virus that causes AIDS and announces his retirement from professional basketball. **1992:** The four white Los Angeles police officers accused of beating Rodney King are acquitted; riots break out. ★ Sixty percent of Americans participate in some exercise program; 56 percent garden; half will attend an amusement park at least once this year. ★ William Jefferson Clinton is elected president. **1993:** Muslim fundamentalists protesting United States policy in the Middle East plant a bomb in New York City's World Trade Center that kills five people, injures hundreds, and traps thousands in the two skyscrapers. ★ A standoff between the FBI and a religious sect known as the Branch Davidians ends in fire and the death of everyone

---

From left to right, top row: Magic Johnson, Lee Atwater and George Bush; *second row:* Oprah Winfrey, *Titanic; third row:* Lyle and Erik Menendez, Mike Tyson; *fourth row:* Jerry Seinfeld, Bill Clinton and Al Gore, Monica Lewinsky; *bottom row:* gay marriage.

inside the Waco, Texas, compound. **1994:** A boy born this year can expect to live to be 72, a girl to be 79. ★ In an incident of so-called road rage, a Massachusetts deacon shoots a medical technician to death with a crossbow. ★ Olympic hopeful Nancy Kerrigan is clubbed on the knee by friends of rival skater Tonya Harding. ★ A quarter of Americans 18 years old and over smoke. ★ Americans buy 830 million hardcover books. ★ Former football star O. J. Simpson is arrested and charged with the murder of his ex-wife, Nicole Brown Simpson, and her friend Ronald Goldman. ★ Fifty-seven people are killed and $15 billion of damage is caused by a huge Los Angeles earthquake. **1995:** A dark blue elephant Beanie Baby named Peanut sells for five dollars. ★ Forty-one million Americans have no health insurance. ★ O. J. Simpson is acquitted. ★ Twenty-five million Americans golf. ★ A federal building in Oklahoma City is bombed, and 168 people, including 15 children, die. **1996:** Television talk-show host Oprah Winfrey launches the Oprah Book Club, making instant best-sellers of all her selections. ★ Doctors have success controlling the AIDS virus with treatments that involve new combinations of drugs. ★ For the fifth year in a row, the Ford Taurus is the country's top-selling passenger car, domestic or foreign. ★ President Clinton is elected to a second term. **1997:** World chess champion Garry Kasparov loses to IBM's Deep Blue computer. ★ Thirty-nine members of the religious cult Heaven's Gate are found dead in their California compound, their leader having explained that after their deaths they would be picked up by a spaceship trailing the Hale-Bopp comet. ★ During a heavyweight championship bout in Las Vegas, boxer Mike Tyson bites off a piece of rival Evander Holyfield's ear. ★ Tobacco companies agree to a $368 billion settlement of smokers' litigation claims. **1998:** Congress rejects the tobacco deal. ★ Country singer Garth Brooks becomes the all-time best-selling solo recording artist, with 81 million albums sold. ★ The dark blue elephant Beanie Baby named Peanut (now "retired" by manufacturer Ty) sells to collectors for more than $5,000. ★ *Titanic* becomes the highest-grossing film of all time, the first movie to earn more than $1 billion at the box office worldwide. ★ Seventy-six million viewers tune in to watch the final episode of the sitcom *Seinfeld*. ★ Mark McGwire and Sammy Sosa both break Roger Maris's home-run record. ★ Speaking forcefully and shaking his finger, President Clinton denies having had "sexual relations" with former White House intern Monica Lewinsky, whom he calls "that woman." ★ Despite a global economic crisis, the United States experiences low inflation rates and the longest bull market in history. ★ President Clinton admits to having had an "improper" relationship with Monica Lewinsky. ★ Former professional wrestler Jesse "The Body" Ventura is elected governor of Minnesota. ★ More than a third of all Americans over 16 use the Internet. ★ Clinton becomes the second president in U.S. history to be impeached. **1999:** Michael Jordan retires from professional basketball. ★ Assisted-suicide doctor Jack Kevorkian is convicted of second-degree murder. ★ U.S. warplanes lead NATO air strikes on Serbia in an effort to stem the violence against ethnic Albanians in Kosovo. ★ Twelve students and a teacher are killed when two classmates attack a Colorado high school, then kill themselves. ★ The Dow Jones Industrial Average tops 11,000. ★ Serbian forces withdraw from Kosovo as NATO peacekeepers move in. ★ John F. Kennedy, Jr., dies in a plane crash. ★ It costs 33 cents to send a one-ounce letter.

LETY MARTINEZ GONZALEZ TO ARGELIA GONZALEZ MORALES

Nearly two million illegal immigrants from Mexico were living in the United States in 1990. Some had overstayed their temporary visas. Others, like Lety Martinez Gonzalez, had never had legal approval to enter the country but had hired guides, known as coyotes, to help them make the perilous border crossing. The U.S. Border Patrol estimated that it apprehended fewer than half of those who tried to slip into the country illegally. Though anti-immigration laws became even tougher in the 1990s, immigration advocates continued to offer evidence that the new arrivals were helping, not hurting, the economy.

The original text of this letter was in Spanish. *Aguas negras* means "sewage"; *migras* are immigration agents.

June 4, 1990
Argelia Gonzalez Morales
Oaxaca, Oaxaca, Mexico

Argelia, Jaime, Nancy, Grandma,

What's up? How are you all? I hope all's well at the house because I'm feeling very sad here, since never in my life did I come to think that I'd have to go through so many, many things in order to be here. Before anything, I want to tell you that I didn't cry very much when I said goodbye to all of you; well I made myself be brave since the stewardess informed us that we would be flying in the plane that transported Pope John Paul II, as you'll see, my plane was blessed and I felt very good knowing this. Thirty-five minutes later we arrived in Mexico City and we confirmed the flight and we waited for them to announce our flight, but first we ate a sandwich and a soda. When they announced it we boarded the plane; I got the window and I'll tell you that feels really beautiful. They gave Gaby another seat, since they don't allow there to be children near the window. Then they announced that they would give us headphones to listen to music or watch a movie, shortly after they passed them out they served the meal, really delicious by the way, and they ran the movie, likewise very entertaining.

We arrived in Tijuana. The airport's ugly, we had the luck to pass through without them inspecting our bags or anything. On the way out we bought a ticket for the bus that would take us to the Alaska motel. When we arrived Gaby left me outside with the boy, Tijuana's horrible, it has nothing but pure slums at night, but I'll tell you that Wilfrido arrived for the boy while we were renting a room. When it struck 11 at night they directed us to a disguised diner, well in reality it was a cantina, from there we talked with the person who was going to take me across. But he told me to wait until the next day since everything was very rushed at that moment, from there we went back to the coffee shop and a dwarf arrived who told us to wait, but we didn't like his looks and so we went back to the hotel, passing all the while through the so-called "Zona Roja," everything is corrupt, and us making ourselves be brave, well there are many men in the street and women too, but you know which ones, don't you? We slept at the hotel and the next day the man called, telling us not to move from the hotel and that he'd arrive at 2 in the afternoon, he arrived and told us that at 9 at night he'd come by for us again to take us to the diner. In that time we ate something and slept, at 9 the man arrived, he took us and gave orders to his workers, we were waiting until 10 when the guys who would cross us over arrived, and they gave us orders that we all go out in pairs. I went with the dwarf, and Gaby with another guy who would cross with us. I'll make you a sketch below of the immense trip we took.

1. We left from here and walked these 5 blocks.
2. We crossed the Boulevard.
3. Wire Fence.
4. We travelled along the fence, walking.
5. We entered here. 1 block. Borde. This whole part of El Borde has lights and searchlights.
6. This is a bridge where we bought plastic bags to cross the aguas negras.
7. This is a sandy area.
8. All this is like 6 blocks.
9. Here we crossed a large puddle of aguas negras.
10. This is the street where those of the migra constantly pass by.
11. This that I mark over with the pen is a pit where you have to cross practically on all fours.

12. And these things like trees are pure shrubs.
13. Gaby fell in the aguas negras.
14. Police car.
15. Dirt road. Here we had to throw ourselves down so they wouldn't grab us. And when the car passed we were off to the races.
16. This was all running, to the point I couldn't bear my legs anymore.
17. Here we jumped into the gully because the migra saw us there and told us to stop.
18. When we jumped I fell because someone grabbed me and it was a fat potbellied guy. I got myself up thanks to another guy who urged me on.
19. Here we left to enter this fucking country.
20. We walked up this street. Now we were supposedly on the other side.
21. This now is the U.S., one block.
22. Here they put us into some of their cars to go to San Diego.

I want to clarify that on the map where I put a Y we ran back and forth like 4 times since the guy, I don't know if it was his nerves but he couldn't find the way out, until we ran into another coyote who came up behind us, he was the one who told him, and we passed through an immensity of bushes, we had to jump treetrunks, aguas negras, it was all very different from what I had seen, or what they had told me, Gaby says I was very brave, since she was going to die of nerves, well don't believe it. If I'm here it's because I believe in God and because in those moments I asked the Virgin of Guadalupe, Juguila and the Virgin of Solitude, and above all my son counted a lot to me. But now I'm here, with pains and scratches, bruises and to finish the grind off with this monster in my throat. But I'm here. I arrived yesterday in the early morning at like 5 in the morning. Now by way of an anecdote, when we jumped into the gully the dwarf was grabbed by the migra, since when we fell he couldn't get up because of the shortness of his legs, and when we ran I would have liked to take him in my arms, well it drives you to despair that his little legs wouldn't give enough to run. Well though you won't believe this, I've never run so fast, now I laugh but in those moments I didn't feel my saliva, the blows, nothing, everything was worse than in the movies. I believe that we traveled like 7 to 10 kilometers, but in short I won't cross like this again, seriously, listen, follow the arrows that I put down here for you and read what I tell you in each one of them.

What follows is for you Arge, the foregoing, yes, read it to everyone.

Anyway, moving on to another thing, today Silvia arrives, I hope she arrives well. Tell me how my baby has been, you took him to the doctor yesterday, what did he tell you about his feet, his weight, his height, or what did he tell you in general, how is he? Tell me with whom he's been sleeping, if he's eaten well. I miss him very much. And Papa, how is he, what did he say? And Nancy, how did Nancy feel? And grandma, how is she? Because I feel like a fool, what's more I feel all fucked-up, yesterday we went to the doctor because the boy's vomiting and he's super-pink, since I think the day he stayed with Rosa they didn't look after him very well, but in short Wester is better now, Gaby too. I already told Everardo what you recommended that I tell him, and he told me that he already talked with Papa, Everardo now has a car, cassette recorder, television, not to mention the fact that yesterday Guicho himself bought a VW Caribe for 150 dollars that's way better than the white Caribe my boy's godfather has. Listen, speaking of him, what happened, I won't say any more about that, because I'm willing to clarify everything, listen, what will he say that I came? Who knows? I didn't write the letter to Hilda yet, anyway now I say goodbye, tomorrow I'll begin my other letter. Answer me soon. Greetings to all, I'll keep you informed.

Kisses for my baby. Take care of him.

Warmly,
Lety

1990: JULY 10
DR. JACK KEVORKIAN TO DR. GARY SLOAN

In 1989, retired Michigan pathologist Jack Kevorkian (1928–) developed the Mercitron, a machine that enabled a terminally ill person to inject himself or herself with a lethal dose of drugs. Dubbed Dr. Death, Kevorkian went on to assist in the suicides of more than 130 sick patients while becoming the most visible symbol of the burgeoning "right to die" movement. In and out of court throughout the nineties, he would be convicted of second-degree murder in 1999, after he let 60 Minutes videotape his role in a mercy killing.

Gary Sloan was a forty-three-year-old dentist who had sought Kevorkian's help while a court injunction against the doctor's activities was pending in Michigan. Sloan, who suffered from colon cancer, would use a device similar to the Mercitron to kill himself in Los Angeles in March of 1991.

The enclosed diagram will give you a general idea of how my device is constructed. There are several ways that details of the internal structure can be worked out satisfactorily. All it takes are a couple of solenoids and switches, a timer, and a couple of small valves (the latter can be those tiny plastic slides that come with the tubing on an I.V. sets). I'm sure you could put it all together yourself, especially if helped by a friend who is good with his hands or is an engineer. As you told me, you yourself could obtain the drugs.

Another option might be to make arrangements to come to Michigan if and when the court injunction against me is lifted. It is preferable to do the procedure in a private home or office of a friend or relative of yours who lives in Michigan (if that is possible and can be arranged). In all likelihood there will be some action on the injunction in 4–6 weeks at most, which you should hear about through news reports. If it is lifted, and if you are interested, I could notify you so that you could begin making necessary arrangements.

Best wishes,
Jack Kevorkian, M.D.

1990: SEPTEMBER 4
ISAIAH ZELDIN TO KIMBA WOOD

In 1989, Michael Milken, who had pioneered the use of junk bonds to finance corporate deals, was indicted by a federal grand jury on ninety-eight counts of violating federal securities and racketeering laws. After steadfastly maintaining his innocence, he reluctantly pleaded guilty to six felony charges on April 24, 1990. Before he was sentenced to ten years (he ultimately served two, as well as paying more than a billion dollars in fines to the government), dozens of colleagues and friends, including his rabbi, pleaded with Judge Kimba Wood for leniency.

September 4, 1990

The Honorable Kimba M. Wood
United States District Judge
United States Court House
Foley Square, 40 Centre Street
New York, New York 10007

Dear Judge Wood:

I am writing this letter on behalf of Michael Milken, whose family joined Stephen S. Wise Temple eleven years ago.

I first met Michael when his father passed away shortly after the family affiliated with my congregation, and I was called upon to officiate at the funeral. In the intervening years I was also the officiant at Mike's oldest son Greg's Bar Mitzvah and his middle child Lance's Bar Mitzvah. During these years I have personally come to know Michael's wife Lori, his daughter Bari, his mother Ferne, and all the members of his extended family. The above is by way of explaining that my relationship with Michael and his family has been long and deep.

Most important, in the last four years I have been pastor and religious counsellor to Michael in his anguish and struggles to confront the charges levied against him. I have been with him as he went from denial of culpability to where he could truly repent his violations and sincerely regret his failure to meticulously observe the rules and regulations that govern his industry.

Others have no doubt written to you about Michael's genius in business and charitableness in hosts of causes.

Permit me to tell you of some of Michael's humaneness. Michael has a protective quality about him that leads him to care about the personal well-being of everyone whose life he touches. Perhaps it was the same protectiveness that misled him to guarantee for his clients financial gain beyond the regulations.

But please consider the obverse contribution of protectiveness and the good that comes to fellow humans when someone develops this quality.

Case in point is when my wife of 40 years was diagnosed five years ago as having bone cancer. Michael's solicitousness for her and for me during the past five years has been phenomenal. During that entire year of chemo-therapy and the subsequent series of operations when her right knee and bone up to the femur were removed and replaced by a 5-pound piece of steel prosthesis, Michael, though engulfed with his own problems, was constantly solicitous, helped us look for cures and solutions, and suffered with us the tortures of hell as we together fought for the life of my dear wife. Thanks to God she is still alive and well, though we constantly face x-ray examinations and doctors' visits to guard against recurrence of that dreadful disease.

About three years ago, our youngest son and father of three children was diagnosed as having multiple sclerosis. Once again, Michael's concern and empathy, all the time while being pressured with his own problems, have helped our family cope with this debilitating though not life-threatening disease.

During the above-cited personal cries in my own family's life, I have regularly served as clergyman and pastor to Michael. The first half-hour of our sessions together were about the Zeldin family, and the last hour to hour-and-a-half were about Michael and the Milken family.

I am convinced that Michael would not knowingly harm any human being. I have been with him as he agonized over the accusations levelled against him. His intent always was to help the disadvantaged, to contribute of his wisdom and substance towards the ameliorization of difficult social conditions. What he did to help struggling industries, he also did for social and human causes. He is gifted in his ability to find solutions to personal, institutional and governmental problems.

To incarcerate such a sensitive and caring human being would, in my way of thinking, serve no useful purpose. His punishment to date has been severe enough. He can no longer use his acumen in the securities industry. He has brought opprobrium and suffering upon his family. And this proud man has been humiliated by the barbs of the press, so that wherever he goes he is pointed to as an admitted violator of the law.

Permit me to cite a Biblical passage in furtherance of my plea for leniency in Michael Milken's case, since I know that he has already paid dearly for his mistakes. In the Book of Jonah we are taught that the Almighty Himself forgave the people of Nineveh and did not destroy the city for "God saw their works, that they turned from their evil way". I pray that you will find it in your heart to be lenient with Michael, since he is a true penitent.

Were he to be given community service, his sensitivity and empathy would redound to the benefit of whatever persons and institutions he would be asked to serve. And American justice would also be served, for he has already paid dearly for his wrongdoings.

If there is anything in addition to the above that I can inform you about without violating clergy-congregant confidentiality, please do not hesitate to call upon me. I would be happy to come to New York to meet with you, if that would help in the final disposition of this case.

Sincerely yours,
Rabbi Isaiah Zeldin

1990: SEPTEMBER 17
THE HOLY CHURCH OF THE WHITE FIGHTING
MACHINE OF THE CROSS TO MORRIS DEES

Morris Dees, Jr. (1937–), founder of the Southern Poverty Law Center in Montgomery, Alabama, pioneered the use of civil lawsuits to weaken white supremacist groups by decimating their bank accounts. This letter arrived as Dees was preparing to go to trial against avowed racist Tom Metzger for allegedly inciting skinheads to *murder an Ethiopian immigrant. The letter's source, though unknown to Dees, was a group clearly sympathetic to Metzger and his organization, the White Aryan Resistance. On October 22, Dees would win a $12.5 million award on behalf of the victim's family, and Metzger's home would indeed be sold to help pay the damages.* Civil rights activist Al Sharpton was based in New York City.

Morris,

Are you trying to steal Tom Metzger's house? Shame, shame. There could be very bad things happen to you, if you carry out this exercise in futility. You are taking on too much, Morris baby, you are messing (or trying to) mess with white power. Nobody messes with white power. You go against nature, if you mess with white power. We want you to drop all of the charges, in the lawsuit in Portland, and step messing with Tommy. We don't want to have to do anything bad to you, Morris, even if you are the lowest form of scum whitey goyim alive, it would hurt us badly if we had to take you out. Think about it. We will give you plenty of time to stop your nonsense. You can't stop white men from trying to save the race in Amerika. You would do better to stop guys like Sharpton from going into the white mans neighborhood, in jew york. Wise up, buddy, there are a whole bunch of real serious people out here watching you, boy. The time has come for you to back right off from Tommy and his family, we don't want to hurt anybody. The time is real ripe, right now, Morris, you haven't dealt with us. We're real bad, honey, we hurt, bone breaking is not our forte, but when we hurt, we hurt real bad, honey, get it? Take all the crap away on this one, baby, because Tommy didn't have anything to do with all of that directly, you know it, and we know it, so times ready to cease and desist, honey. You are causing us to spend all of the funds it has taken us so long to get, for the movement, so your sin is real bad, honey, and its not fair to us, or to the race. We don't want to hurt you man. Stop all the nonsense right now, baby, ok? We know of many white men in the general movement that want you real bad, baby, and we've been holding back. We are giving you a chance, man, Stop the business now, dig? You haven't thought out your moves too good, man, you didn't realize just who you were messing with, so this is the warning, now is the time to back off. Drop the suit. You have until December. Hey dude. We don't want you that bad, ok? Don't make us. Tom didn't write this, but he is not your concern any longer.

THE HOLY CHURCH OF THE WHITE FIGHTING
MACHINE OF THE CROSS

*   *   *

1990: DECEMBER 31

GEORGE BUSH TO HIS CHILDREN

Bruised and restless from nearly ten years of war with Iran, Iraqi dictator Saddam Hussein invaded and annexed his oil-rich neighbor Kuwait in August of 1990. By the winter, as a United Nations deadline for Saddam's withdrawal approached, the peacekeeping operation Desert Shield gave way to plans for the offensive Desert Storm, and President George Bush (1924–) sat down alone to type this letter to his children.

Dorothy's children, Sam and Ellie, had not gone to Maryland for Christmas.

Dear George, Jeb, Neil, Marvin, Doro.

I am writing this letter on the last day of 1990.

First, I can't begin to tell you how great it was to have you here at Camp David. I loved the games (the Marines are still smarting over their 1 and 2 record). I loved Christmas Day, marred only by the absence of Sam and Ellie. I loved the movies—some of 'em—I loved the laughs. Most of all, I loved seeing you together. We are a family blessed; and this Christmas simply reinforced all that.

I hope I didn't seem moody. I tried not to.

When I came into this job I vowed that I would never ring my hands and talk about "the loneliest job in the world" or ring my hands about "the pressures or the trials".

Having said that, I <u>have</u> been concerned about what lies ahead. There is no "loneliness" though because I am backed by a first rate team of knowledgeable and committed people. No President has been more blessed in this regard.

I have thought long and hard about what might have to be done. As I write this letter at Year's end, there is still some hope that Iraq's dictator will pull out of Kuwait. I vary on this—Sometimes I think he might, at others I think he simply is too unrealistic—too ignorant of what he might face. I have the peace of mind that comes from knowing that we have tried hard for peace. We have gone to the UN; we have formed an historic coalition; there have been diplomatic initiatives from country after country. And so, here we are a scant 16 days from a very important date—the date set by the UN for his total compliance with all UN resolutions including getting out of Kuwait—totally.

I guess what I want you to know as a father is this:

Every Human life is precious. When the question is asked "How many lives are you willing to sacrifice"—it tears at my heart. The answer, of course, is none—none at all. We have waited to give sanctions a chance, we have moved a tremendous force so as to reduce the risk to every American soldier if force has to be used, but the question of loss of life still lingers and plagues the heart. My mind goes back to history:

How many lives might have been saved if appeasement had given way to force earlier on in the late '30's or earliest '40's? How many Jews might have been spared the gas chambers, or how many Polish patriots might be alive today? I look at todays crisis as "good" vs. "evil" . . . yes, it is that clear.

I know my stance must cause you a little grief from time to time; and this hurts me; but here at "years-end" I just wanted you to know that I feel:

—every human life is precious . . . the little Iraqi kids' too.

—Principle must be adhered to—Saddam cannot profit in any way at all from his aggression and from his brutalizing the people of Kuwait.

—and sometimes in life you have to act as you think best—you can't compromise, you can't give in . . . even if your critics are loud and numerous.

So, dear kids—batten down the hatches

Senator Inouye of Hawaii told me: "Mr. President, do what you have to do. If it is quick and successful everyone can take the credit. If it is drawn out, then be prepared for some in Congress to file impeachment papers against you" . . . that's what he said, and he's 100% correct.

And so I shall say a few more prayers, mainly for our kids in the Gulf, and I shall do what must be done, and I shall be strengthened every day by our family love which lifts me up every single day of my life. I am the luckiest Dad in the whole wide world.

I love you, Happy New Year and may God Bless every one of you and all in your family.

Devotedly,
Dad

1991: FEBRUARY 22
RHONDA CORNUM TO HER MOTHER

Roughly thirty-five thousand American women served in the Gulf War. Among them was Rhonda Cornum, an army major, flight surgeon, wife, and mother. She wrote this letter home five days before the helicopter she was flying in was shot down during a search-and-rescue mission. Captured by Iraqis and held for eight days as a POW, she would, despite broken arms and dislocated knees, be molested by a guard, interrogated, and denied medical care. But she would survive her grueling experience to return home.

Dear Mother:

I have gotten several letters from you lately (Thank you, by the way!), and I have been debating about what to write. I could lie, and say I am safe in a nice quiet medical job somewhere, but A) I don't lie, and haven't for twenty years; and B) I'd rather you know what I'm really thinking and feeling about being here.

Five days ago I was (I think) the first American female service member to fly into Iraq, get out of my aircraft, be a part of taking the first prisoners of war that the 101st took, and fly back out with these guys in my helicopter. No, I wasn't scared. It was in fact the most exciting thing since sex I've done. No, this is not a particularly romantic war, but going into combat is the real reason people stay in the army. It isn't the money because I could not possibly make as little as I do if I was a civilian. It isn't the lifestyle, because I haven't lived like this since Freeville, New York. But it is in some ways—it is a personal test to see if you have the "right stuff." And let's admit it—that's me. I seem to gravitate to doing things that are difficult just because I crave challenge. And the army likes me for it! And I like, no, I love what I do. It was like being a surgery intern at Walter Reed. That is the most difficult internship offered by the army—and I liked it!

I feel what I'm doing here is important, and I am very proud to be doing it. My family (husband and daughter) are happy with me. . . . So go to the library or something—but it doesn't help me focus on what I need to do here to worry about you worrying about me!

I love you; I'm glad you are doing well. Please, just laugh at some of my stories, be proud of me doing my patriotic thing, fly your flag. Sure, we've got body bags—I'm even considering using one as an outside liner for my sleeping bag, warm and dry!

Love always,
Rambo Rhonda (it's a joke)

1991: MAY 5

GEORGE PAPCUN TO JEFFREY KAYE

In March of 1991, a twenty-five-year-old black motorist named Rodney King was brutally beaten, clubbed, and kicked by four white Los Angeles police officers who later claimed that King had resisted arrest. The incident, which happened to be captured by an onlooker on videotape, crystallized a feeling among many citizens that police, especially in Los Angeles, were racist and corrupt, and that race relations hadn't improved much since the tumultuous sixties. Nightly news programs all over the country aired the images relentlessly. Two months later, a local TV station became interested in the sounds on the tape as well and solicited the assistance of an expert. In 1992, an all-white jury would acquit the officers, setting off a series of riots in Los Angeles that would last three days and be responsible for fifty-one deaths.

Dear Mr. Kaye:

I have received from you via Federal Express a video cassette tape recording labeled "M/C P8 SPCL 'Rodney King' 4-24-91" followed by what appear to be the initials "K.S." In accordance with your request, I have enhanced the acoustic part of the recording by attenuating ambient noise (which appears to be the noise of a helicopter) that interferes with the intelligibility of the recording, and attempted to discern what was being said in the recording.

I have listened to the recording with appropriate equipment that transduces the full range of audio frequencies relevant to understanding the speech in this recording. I have also listened to the recording under various conditions of parametric filtering. Consequently, I can report to you the following words shouted by men in the distance:

12:53:04:

Voice 1: "Nigger, hands behind your back!"

12:53:09

Voice 2: "Hands behind your back!"

12:53:13

(Voice 2:) "Behind your back!"

I am prepared to explain in detail the technical characteristics of the playback and filtering methods I used, and to testify under oath as to the conclusions I have reached.

Enclosed you will find a copy of the video cassette recording with the soundtrack enhanced under three of the filtering conditions I used in my assessment of the recording.

I make the representations contained in this letter solely as a private citizen, and not as a representative of the United States Government or the University of California.

Under separate cover I will send a curriculum vita listing my technical qualifications in this area of expertise. Please do not hesitate to contact me if I can answer any questions or furnish any additional information.

Sincerely yours,
George Papcun, Ph.D.

1991: AUGUST 5
CARLA GORRELL TO SHELLIE BOWERS

In an early test of the legal right of homosexuals to marry, Craig Dean and Patrick Gill claimed that the city of Washington, D.C., had discriminated against them by refusing to grant them a marriage license. While the lawsuit was pending, Presbyterian minister Carla Gorrell (1944–) wrote this letter to the judge, Shellie Bowers. Gorrell had herself performed—and been challenged within her church for performing—what she called "holy union ceremonies" for same-sex couples. Dean and Gill would lose the case in 1992, with Judge Bowers writing that the nature of marriage was that "the parties thereto be a male and a female."

Honorable Shellie Bowers
Superior Court of the District of Columbia

August 5, 1991

Dear Judge Bowers,

I write to support the appeal by Craig Dean and Patrick Gill for their right to a marriage license. I am an ordained Minister of Word and Sacrament in the Presbyterian Church (USA) and a Parish Associate at Westminster Presbyterian Church in Southwest D.C. I am licensed to perform marriages in the District of Columbia and the state of Virginia.

I was ordained to specialized ministry to people with AIDS in 1988. As Executive Director of Foods & Friends, which provides home-delivered meals to people with AIDS, I have the privilege of working with the gay and lesbian community. This ministry has given me the opportunity to know hundreds of gay people and their families. I have experienced their hospitality, shared their joys, and heard their concerns. I know the positive contributions gay and lesbian people are making to the wider community. And I see them living their daily lives with courage, caring, and moral integrity.

I receive occasional requests to perform a religious ceremony for gay men or lesbians who have made a commitment to live together as life-partners. The first of these requests led me to study the meaning of gay and lesbian unions as they relate to the Bible, Reformed theology, and our denomination's constitution. In this search I have found no prohibition against a religious ceremony to bless the solemn decision by gay couples to take vows to enter into a faithful, covenant relationship. These long-term relationships function like a marriage between a man and a woman, except that the partners were born with an orientation to love and to bond with a member of their own sex.

Condemnation of homosexuality has been based on a literal interpretation of a few texts from the Bible, which have a particular historical context. It took long experience and self-examination for the church to confess that it has used Scripture to perpetuate the injustices of racism, sexism, and anti-semitism. Today, a growing number of clergy from mainline denominations throughout the country agree that new knowledge about the etiology of human sexuality and modern Biblical scholarship makes it impossible to perpetuate discrimination based on old interpretations of Biblical texts.

Unfortunately, homophobia in the church and society is a barrier to changing public opinion. The question is, When will our civil and religious systems take the lead to overcome unreasoned prejudice, as was necessary in earlier movements for African-American and women's rights?

Enclosed is a collection of background papers developed to educate the church on this issue. I strongly urge the District of Columbia to acknowledge the civil right of gay and lesbian couples to the benefits and responsibilities of marriage that are granted to heterosexual couples.

Respectfully,

Reverend Carla B. Gorrell

1991: DECEMBER 29
JAMES BAKER III TO MIKHAIL GORBACHEV

James A. Baker III (1930–) served President Reagan as chief of staff and secretary of the treasury. He served President Bush as campaign manager and chief of staff, and was secretary of state when he answered a Christmas letter from Mikhail Gorbachev (1931–), the last Communist leader of the Soviet Union.

Dear Mikhail:

Your heartfelt Christmas day letter is appreciated more than I can say. Working with you and President Bush during these momentous times has been a privileged experience that I will never forget.

What you have accomplished since 1985 is nothing short of remarkable. You took an ossified system that was crushing the people with its weight, and through sheer personal courage, vision, and will, lifted it off them, allowing them the freedom to think and act for themselves. This in itself was an extraordinary act—an act of revolutionary importance that launched a transformation no one could have imagined would come so peacefully.

On the world stage, your actions were equally revolutionary. You saw the folly in superpower competition and in the isolation of your country from the rest of the world. Your speech to the United Nations in 1988 ushered in a new era in world politics. With every step you took, you asked the United States to join you to help build a new world. We were ready to do so and to build a new partnership between our nations as well. And we did that in a remarkable way—in Afghanistan, Central America, Cambodia, Namibia, the Persian Gulf and the Middle East. In addition, we cooperated not just to control arms, but to eliminate them, and to bring the risk of nuclear war to its lowest point since such arms were invented.

Most importantly, together we saw the map of Europe transformed—peacefully and democratically. We saw Germany united and the people of Central and Eastern Europe set free to determine their own future. And as I have said on many occasions, none of this would have happened without your leadership. Your place in history will forever be secure.

Working with you was a real pleasure for me. One of the things I appreciate most was that your word was your bond. And by that personal bond, your working with President Bush transformed the superpower competition of old. Indeed, we did engage in a sort of competition—a competition in trust and partnership, not arms. The world is eternally grateful for that—and I am grateful for the opportunity to have joined with you and President Bush in making the world a better place for our children and grandchildren. Susan and I are touched by the kind words in your letter, and she joins me in sending you and Raisa our warmest personal regards and best wishes.

> With respect,
> James A. Baker III

*   *   *

1992: APRIL 27
MANDY GRUNWALD AND FRANK GREER
TO THE CLINTON CAMPAIGN

A team of professional political consultants, memorialized in the movie The War Room, *played a significant role in engineering Bill Clinton's 1992 presidential victory. Among them was media strategist Mandy Grunwald (1957–), who came up with an approach that took full advantage of the growing reach of cable TV and other popular-culture forums. Most memorably, that tactic would land Clinton on* The Arsenio Hall Show, *where he bantered with the popular host and gamely played the saxophone. Ensuing radio and TV appearances on forums far from the staid evening news would help change the rules of campaigning as they helped Clinton attract attention. This memo was written by Grunwald on behalf of the Clinton media consulting firm of Greer, Margolis, Mitchell, and Grunwald.*

In January of 1992, Gennifer Flowers claimed to have had a twelve-year affair with Clinton. Mandy Grunwald is Lisa Grunwald's sister.

MEMORANDUM

To: Clinton Campaign
From: Mandy and Frank
Date: April 27, 1992
RE: FREE MEDIA SCHEDULING

We have spoken generally about the need to do pop-culture shows like Johnny Carson, but we have yet to lay out a plan to do this sort of thing, or to incorporate local radio talk shows into our schedule in any concerted way.

What are we waiting for?

We know from research that Bill Clinton's life story has a big impact on people. We know that learning about the fights he's taken on (education reform, welfare reform, dead-beat dads etc.) tells people a lot about his personal convictions. We know that moments of passions, personal reflection and humor do more for us than any six-second sound bite on the network news or for that matter any thirty-second television spot.

In tandem with our high road, serious speech effort, we ought to design a parallel track of pop culture national and local media efforts.

We must also coordinate this effort with a free media plan for Hillary. Which magazine should appear during the convention with Bill, Hillary and Chelsea on the cover? LIFE? Parade? We need to decide now.

This period leading up to the convention is CRITICAL for this kind of positive information. If we don't fill in the blanks now, we'll never get to it after the Republican Convention. That means time is pressing. Given the lead times for magazines and some TV programs, we have to move immediately.

I suggest a free media meeting (or call) as soon as possible to consider how to rethink scheduling to incorporate these opportunities and to consider some of the following kinds of ideas.

1. Which TV journalist should we invite to Arkansas for a tour with Bill of his childhood haunts etc.? Barbara Walters? Jane Pauley?

2. If Carson is booked, should Bill do Letterman? Arsenio? The new Jay Leno? All three?

3. What about Larry King, Oprah Winfrey, Sally Jessy Raphael? Who would allow a focus on his childhood/accomplishments etc. without 1000 Gennifer Flowers questions?

4. What about national radio programs? Rush Limbaugh?

5. There's a Don Imus in every market in America, and a serious call-in political/talk radio show. Can we make a commitment that every day in every city we go to, we book Bill on those kinds of radio programs.

I understand that many people will say these kinds of things are "Un-Presidential." Bull. This is how people get information. These are forums for more personal and varied looks at Bill and Hillary and Chelsea.

Obviously, it would be better to be using these forums when the overall message of the campaign has been sharpened so that Bill's biography could be put in a more strategic context. But I'm not sure we have the luxury of waiting until that process is complete.

At least, let's get together and discuss these media options, so that decisions are not just made on an ad-hoc basis.

1992: MAY 4
MARY FISHER TO HER SONS

As AIDS spread, victims like Mary Fisher (1948–)—white, wealthy, and female—became some of its newest casualties. With her gripping speech to the 1992 Republican National Convention and her subsequent founding of the Family AIDS Network, Fisher attempted to educate an often biased, often indifferent public about the disease. Fisher's two sons, Max and Zack, were five and three when Fisher wrote them this letter. Their father, from whom Fisher had contracted the disease, would die of AIDS in 1993.

Dear Max and Zack,

You're sleeping now at last . . .

Some days I think this nighttime peace will never come. I love my days with you. Your reliable smile was the only thing that lit up this frantic house today, Max. And, Zachary, I sometimes think that if I had half your energy and persistence, I'd accomplish miracles in minutes. But loving my days with you as I do, I have a motherly confession to make—I love the hour you fall asleep as well.

It's a delicious time. A quiet time. For those few minutes, I will not hear the word I love most: "Mom!" I just visited your rooms to pull the covers over each of you and thought how blessed I am, not only to have you, but to have you asleep.

Often at this time of night I write in your journals, the ones I've been keeping for each of you since you were born. You see, it wasn't enough to just record your first haircuts, steps and words. I wanted you to know how I felt about those monumental moments as well as what I fear most.

You're children and I'm an adult but by the time you read this letter, you'll be adults too—and I'll no longer be the young mother I am now. So you could know, as an adult, who your Mom is—I've kept your journals.

I've not said much in your journals about "being positive," about the swirl of publicity and confusion and the weariness that has accompanied our last year. Usually by this time of night I've had all of that I can stand. I want to return to being a Mom or an artist or a friend. I'm tired of being "The AIDS Person." I want to be me for a little while.

Tomorrow I must leave you again for another trip to visit with important people about important things. It's all very, very important. And I wish I were with you—because you, Max and Zack, are the most important to me.

People will ask me questions about AIDS. And I will answer the questions again, as I've answered them a hundred times before. But what I would really like to say is based on something small and simple . . . us.

I'm eager to go out in the world with the message that "If Mary Fisher can get AIDS, so can you." I'll happily donate time to the causes that could enable me to attend your high school graduation.

But I'm also eager to stay home. Because I'm keenly aware, in ways I never imagined, of the consequences this illness has had, is having, and will have on our family. We have, all of us, now discovered what hundreds of thousands of American families discovered before us: AIDS does more than kill bodies. It destroys families.

The single hardest day of my life was not the day I heard my test results.

Stunning as that was—standing at LaGuardia airport with you two playing nearby, getting the news from an apologetic stranger—more difficult by far was the day I needed to tell your grandfather the truth about AIDS in his family. I did not fear my dying from the disease at that moment. I feared how he might live with the truth. It took me weeks to come to grips with the reality. I kept saying to myself, "This isn't possible. This can't be real." It took me months to move from shock to anger to hurt to grief to surrender and acceptance—and only recently, to effective action.

Once I had accepted the truth, I expected everyone else would accept it too. I was totally unprepared for the reality that everyone who loved me would go through every stage I'd gone through.

If they were shocked and angry, I assumed they were angry with me, because I had this dread disease. I hadn't even known I was at risk. But when they faced prejudice and stigma because of my condition, I felt guilty, as if I had done something wrong.

What I know today, Max and Zack, is more than I knew a year ago. Your grandparents, your uncles and aunts and our extended family of relatives and friends, they have rallied around us with affection and commitment as quickly as they were able. Much as I needed to endure the process, they, too, wrestled with their own griefs, confronted their own feelings of anger and shame, and moved again to tighten the bands of unconditional love that hold us together as a family.

If I have not told you so before, let me say it to you plainly now. Max and Zack, I not only love you wildly, I need you. I need my family. I need you and everyone else more now than I ever have before. And sometimes when I look too far in the future, I realize how much I will need you then.

But when fear becomes a poison, threatening to rob us of the joy we had rolling on the floor, tickling each other and laughing today, the antidote is us, our family. So long as we have family—you and I—all of us will go on.

Tonight when I tucked each of you into bed, I said to you what you've heard me say every night of your lives. Since the moment you came from my body, Max, and the hour you were placed in my arms, Zachary, I have known that I would, one day, need to give you up.

And so, each night, I rehearse for the day when I must give you over. That is why as I reach for the day's last kiss and hug, you always hear me say the same four words,

"Sleep with the angels . . ."

Love,
Mom

1992: SEPTEMBER 24
MAGIC JOHNSON TO GEORGE BUSH

In November of 1991, Earvin "Magic" Johnson (1959–), one of the most revered and talented athletes in history, stunned the country by announcing that he was retiring from the Los Angeles Lakers because he had tested positive for HIV, the virus that causes AIDS. Days later, President Bush appointed Johnson to a fifteen-member bipartisan AIDS commission. Within a year, however, Johnson wrote this letter, having become frustrated with what he perceived as the administration's continuing lack of support.

Dear Mr. President:

I am writing to advise you of the decision which I have made regarding serving on the National Commission on AIDS.

I am grateful to have had the opportunity to serve on the commission because it has given me the chance to learn so much about AIDS and what must be done to fight it. My fellow commissioners are a wonderful group of caring and dedicated people who have worked hard and effectively to develop a bipartisan consensus and plan of action this country should follow in the fight against AIDS.

As I think you know, along with all of my fellow commission members I have been increasingly frustrated by the lack of support, and even the opposition, of your Administration to our recommendations—recommendations which have an urgent priority and for which there is a broad consensus in the medical and AIDS communities.

Your kind words to me aside, your Administration has not done what it could and should to address a situation which, day by day, poses an increasing danger to the well being of millions of Americans, and which threatens to cast an even wider pall across our nation. AIDS is a crisis of monumental proportions, and it cannot be fought with lip service and photo opportunities.

I cannot in good conscience continue to serve on a commission whose important work is so utterly ignored by your Administration.

Mr. President, when we met in January I gave you a letter in which I expressed my hope that you would become more actively involved in the fight against AIDS. No matter how good the team may be, I said, it won't win the championship without the owner fully in the game. I am disappointed that you have dropped the ball, and that your Administration is not doing everything that it must to fight this disease.

I am sorry to have to write this letter, but I am afraid that there is little that will be accomplished in the next four months. Accordingly, I have regretfully decided to resign your appointment to the National Commission on AIDS.

Sincerely,

Earvin Johnson, Jr.

1993: FEBRUARY 5
LYLE MENENDEZ TO TRACY BAKER

In 1990, Lyle and Erik Menendez were arrested for the shotgun murders of their parents, Kitty and José. In a televised trial that stretched on for months and was zealously covered by the media, the brothers claimed that although they had killed their parents, they should not be found guilty of murder. Their reasoning was that years of sexual and psychological abuse had impaired their judgment and caused them to act out of fear for their lives. Tracy Baker (her name was misspelled by Lyle) was a friend who would testify to much of what Lyle described in this letter to her. The second page of his letter is missing.

The Menendezes' first trial would end in a hung jury, their second in convictions. Their sentence would be life in prison without parole.

LAW OFFICES   Feb 5

Ms. Baker

Alright Traci this is the information we discussed on the phone about visiting Erik. Im going to get right to the point because after you read this and feel youve absorbed it, I want you to throw it away. Do that right away so you dont forget. Maybe you can take some notes in your own hand writing. OK well basically there are two incidents. They may seem strange and irrelevent to my case but I assure you they will be very helpful. Youll just have to trust me on it. Later on I can explain why but for now Ill just lay them out. I have given alot of thought to this and I really feel that you can do it however just let me know if youd rather not. Alright the first incident is as follows. You were at my Beverly Hills house about to eat dinner with me, my parents and my brother. Ed wasnt there. We will decide later around what date this incident occurred. It was a weekend however. (I hate writing in pen) You and I had spent the day together. Mrs. Menendez had cooked dinner and it was served in the dining room. Everyone was seated except Mrs. Menendez. She was still bringing this and that in from the kitchen . . . next to me with your back to the . . . seated at the head of the table to my left. Erik was seated accross from us. Behind Mr Menendez were the doors that open to the foyer. All the food was on the table. There was lots of it but you don't remember what the food was. Anyway all of a sudden Mr Menendez said in a stern voice to Mrs. Menendez who was standing behind you, "what did you do to the food?!" There was a long silence or at least it seemed long and then Mr Menendez shoved his plate forward, knocking over some stuff. He got up and said something like "go out and wait for me by the car boys, we're going out to eat." Then I got up immediately and said "come on Traci" and we both walked out into the foyer. Erik walked out too. You got your purse and jacket. We walked outside and stood in front of the big mercedes. Erik and I were discussing something, whispering. You were just kind of standing there confused and embarassed. Then Mr Menendez came storming out of the house. He seemed upset. Either Erik or I (you cant remember which) said to him "What's the matter Dad, you think she tried something?" As Mr Menendez was getting into the front seat he said, "I don't know, but I dont trust her today." We all got in the car, you and I in the back seats and we drove in silence listening to some radio station. We made a right coming out of our house but youre unsure the way we went after that. Anyway we ended up parking somewhere and eating at Hamburger Hamlet. It was a big one. We all ate dinner talking about various things. Mr Menendez was charming. He paid the bill. We drove back home. You and I stayed out front and kissed for a long time. You didnt feel you should ask about what had happened earlier. You then left in your car. It wasn't that late. You never saw Mrs Menendez. (It had just gotten dark when we left for Hamburger Hamlet.) You drove home still confused about what had happened in the dining room, although it seemed obvious Mr Menendez thought Mrs Menendez did something to the food. You were dying to ask me what it was all about but you just couldn't. OK, thats the first incident. You really dont need to know anymore detail than Ive provided here. It was a long time ago. It would be strange if you remember things too well. However you do remember the statements I mentioned above very well—who said what to whom. You dont remember the unimportant conversations like what was said at Hamburger Hamlet ect. The best answer to any question you dont know the answer to is, "I dont remember." Its obvious why you remember certain things and certain statements. It was scarey and confusing . . .

*   *   *

1993: APRIL 14

DAVID KORESH TO DICK DEGUERIN

The Branch Davidian sect settled near Waco, Texas, in 1935 and at one point at-
tracted as many as fourteen hundred followers. By 1990 the group, now consisting
of roughly a hundred believers, was under the sway of David Koresh (1959–1993),
a cult leader with an apocalyptic vision. Tipped off that the group's compound was
bristling with weapons, federal agents launched an unsuccessful raid on Febru-
ary 28, then backed off and surrounded the premises. Negotiations were prolonged
and enigmatic. Forty-six days later, Koresh sent his lawyer this letter, which was in-
terpreted by the FBI as one more delaying tactic. After another five days, the agents
would close in again, and Koresh and more than seventy others would die in a fire
apparently set from within.
The seals to which Koresh referred appear in the book of Revelation. Jim Tabor and Phil
Arnold were both biblical scholars.

As far as our progress is concerned, here's where we stand.

I related two messages from God to the FBI, one of which concerned present
danger to people here in Waco. I was shown a fault line running through Lake
Waco area. Many people here in Waco know that we are a good people, and
yet they have shown the same resentful spirit of indifference to our warnings
of love.

I am presently being permitted to document in structured form the decoded
messages of the seven seals. Upon the completion of this task, I will be freed of
my waiting period. I hope to finish this as soon as possible and stand before man
and answer any and all questions regarding my activities.

This written revelation of the seven seals will not be sold, but is to be available to all who wish to know the truth.

The four angels of Revelation, Chapter 7, are here now ready to punish foolish mankind. But the writing of these seals will cause the winds of God's wrath
to be held back a little longer.

I have been praying for so long for this opportunity to put the seals in written form.

Speaking the truth seems to have very little effect on man. I have shown that
as soon as I am given over to the hands of man, I will be made a spectacle of and
people will not be concerned about the truth of God, but just the bizarrity of me
in the flesh.

I want the people of this generation to be saved. I am working night and day to complete my final work of writing out these seals. I thank my father. He has finally granted me this chance to do this.

It will bring new light and hope for many and they won't have to deal with me the person. The earthquake in Waco is not to be taken lightly. It will probably be the thing needed to shake some sense into the people.

Remember, the warning came first and I fear that the FBI is going to suppress this information. It may be left up to you.

I will demand the first manuscript of the seals be given to you. Many scholars and religious leaders will wish to have copies for review. I will keep a copy with me.

As soon as I can see that people like Jim Tabor and Phil Arnold have a copy, I will come out and then you can do your thing with this beast.

I hope to keep in touch with you through letters. We are standing on the threshold of great events. The seven seals in written form are the most sacred information ever.

1993: JULY?
VINCENT FOSTER

Like Bill Clinton (1946–), Vincent Foster (1945–1993) had been born in Hope, Arkansas. He was one of Bill and Hillary Clinton's oldest friends and had been one of Hillary's law partners at the Rose Law Firm in Little Rock. In the Clinton administration, Foster became White House deputy counsel, providing legal advice on a number of controversial matters, including the Clintons' failed Whitewater land deal. On July 26, six days after Foster was found dead in a Virginia park, this note— torn into pieces—would be discovered in his briefcase. Like other evidence with potential links to Whitewater, Foster's death would be minutely examined by independent counsels Robert Fiske and Kenneth Starr, both of whom would conclude that it had been a suicide. Yet conspiracy theorists, on and off the Internet (where this letter was widely circulated), continued to argue otherwise.

"AG" is short for attorney general. Kaki Hockersmith was an Arkansas-based decorator who was working with Hillary Clinton on a White House renovation. "HRC" stood for Hillary Rodham Clinton, and "WSJ" for *Wall Street Journal*. Travel office references involve allegations of mismanagement and misuse of funds by the staff of the White House travel office.

I made mistakes from ignorance, inexperience and overwork

I did not knowingly violate any law or standard of conduct

No one in the White House, to my knowledge, violated any law or standard of conduct, including any action in the travel office. There was no intent to benefit any individual or specific group

The FBI lied in their report to the AG

The press is covering up the illegal benefits they received from the travel staff

The GOP has lied and misrepresented its knowledge and role and covered up a prior investigation

The Ushers Office plotted to have excessive costs incurred, taking advantage of Kaki and HRC

The public will never believe the innocence of the Clintons and their loyal staff

The WSJ editors lie without consequence

I was not meant for the job or the spotlight of public life in Washington. Here ruining people is considered sport.

1994

"DAVID RHODES" TO "FRIENDS"

Pyramid schemes, in which tiers of early investors are paid off with capital gathered from larger tiers of later investors, had been around since at least 1920, when Charles Ponzi's fraudulent investment scheme was uncovered. There was nothing new about chain letters either, but the Internet gave new life to both nuisances. Throughout the 1990s, "David Rhodes" letters would clutter the in-boxes of cyberspace. It is unlikely that it will ever be known who the person or people behind "David Rhodes" were—or how many people would be duped into this and other get-rich-quick Internet schemes.

Ten names and addresses followed the instructions.

Dear Friends,

My name is David Rhodes. In September 1988 my car was repossessed and the bill collectors were hounding me like you wouldn't believe. I was laid off and my unemployment checks had run out. The only escape I had from the pressure of failure was my computer and my modem. I longed to turn my advocation into my vocation. This January 1989 my family and I went on a ten day cruise to the tropics. I bought a Lincoln Town Car for CASH in February 1989.

I am currently building a home on the West Coast of Florida with a private pool, boat slip, and a beutiful view of the bay from my breakfast room table and patio. I will never have to work again. Today I am rich! I have earned over $400,000.00 (Four Hundred Thousand Dollars) to date and will become a millionaire within 4 or 5 months. Anyone can do the same. This money making program works perfectly every time, 100% of the time. I have NEVER failed to earn $50,000.00 or more whenever I wanted. Best of all you never have to leave home except to go to your mailbox or post office.

In October 1988, I recieved a letter in the mail telling me how I could earn $50,000.00 or more whenever I wanted. I was naturally very skeptical and threw the letter on the desk next to my computer. It's funny though, when you are desperate, backed into a corner, your mind does crazy things. I spent a frustrating day looking through the want ads for a job with a future. The pickings were sparse at best. That night I tried to unwind by booting up my computer and calling several bulletin boards. I read several of the message posts and then glanced at the letter next to the computer. All at once it came to me, I now had the key to my dreams. I realized with the power of the computer I could expand and enhance this money making formula into the most unbelievable cash flow generator that has ever been created. I substituted the computer bulletin boards in place of the post office and electronically did by computer what others were doing 100% by mail. Now only a few letters are mailed manually. Most of the hard work is speedily downloaded to other bulletin boards throughout the world. If you believe that someday you deserve that lucky break that you have waited for all your life, simply follow the easy instructions below. Your dreams will come true.

Sincerely yours,
Dave Rhodes

INSTRUCTIONS

Follow these instructions EXACTLY, and in 20 to 60 days you will have recieved well over $50,000.00 cash, all yours. This program has remained successful because of the HONESTY and INTEGRITY of the participants. Please continue its success by carefully ADHERING TO THE INSTRUCTIONS.

Welcome to the world of Mail Order! This little business is a little different than most mail order houses. Your product is not solid and tangible, but rather a service. You are in the business of developing Mailing Lists. Many large corporations are happy to pay big bucks for quality lists. (The money made from the mailing lists is secondary to the income which is made from people like yourself requesting that they be included in that list.)

1) IMMEDIATELY mail $1.00 to the first 5 (five) names listed below starting at number 1 through number 5. Send CASH only please (total investment $5.00). Enclose a note with each letter stating: "Please add my name to your mailing list." For other countries the equvielent amount may be sent, e.g. in

Hong Kong send HK$10 as this is the lowest denomination note. (This is a legitimate service that you are requesting and you are paying $1.00 for this service).

2) REMOVE the name that appears number 1 on the list. Move the other 9 names up on position. (Number 2 will become number 1 and number 3 will become number 2, etc.)

3) Post the new letter with your name in the number 10 position into 10 (ten) seperate bulletin boards in the message base or to the file section. Call the file, MAKE.MONEY.FAST.

4) Within 60 days you will recieve over $50,000.00 in CASH. Keep a copy of this file for yourself so that you can use it again and again whenever you need money. As soon as you mail out these letters you are automatically in the mail order business and people are sending you $1.00 to be placed on your mailing list. This list can than be rented to a list broker that can be found in the Yellow Pages for additional income on a regular basis. The list will become more valuable as it grows in size. This is a service. This is perfectly legal. If you have any doubts, refer to Title 18, Sec. 1302 & 1341 of the postal lottery laws.

NOTE: Make sure you retain EVERY Name and Address sent to you, either on computer or hard copy, but do not discard the names and notes they send you. This is PROOF that you are truly providing a service and should the IRS or some other Government Agency question you, you can provide them with this proof!

Remember as each post is downloaded and the instructions carefully followed, five members will be reimbursed for their participation as a List Developer with one dollar each. Your name will move up the list geometrically so that when your name reaches the number five position you will be receiving thousands of dollars in cash!

1994: JUNE 17

O. J. SIMPSON TO WHOM IT MAY CONCERN

The most visible "trial of the century"—that of the People v. *Orenthal James Simpson—was a media circus that ultimately served more as a referendum on race relations, spousal abuse, DNA evidence, and police ethics than as an exploration of the events of June 12, 1994. Until that day, Simpson (1947–) had been best known as a football hero, actor, and product pitchman. But on that night, Simpson's ex-wife Nicole Brown Simpson and her friend Ronald Goldman were savagely murdered, and police suspected Simpson. Five days later, as police followed Simpson*

down the Los Angeles freeway in a mesmerizing slow-speed, televised chase, Simp-
son's friend Robert Kardashian read this apparent suicide letter to the press.

A. C. Cowlings, one of Simpson's best friends, drove Simpson's white Ford Bronco during the chase. Marguerite was Simpson's first wife, and Paula Barbieri his girlfriend. Simpson would be found not guilty in his criminal trial, but liable for the murders in a later civil case.

To Whom It May Concern:

First, everyone understand I had nothing to do with Nicole's murder. I loved her, always have, and always will. If we had a problem, it's because I loved her so much. Recently we came to the understanding that for now we were not right for each other, at least for now. Despite our love we were different and that's why we mutually agreed to go our separate ways.

It was tough splitting for a second time, but we both knew it was for the best. Inside, I had no doubt that in the future we would be close friends, or more. Unlike what has been written in the press, Nicole and I had a great relationship for most of our lives together. Like all long-term relationships, we had a few downs and ups.

I took the heat New Year's 1989 because that's what I was supposed to do. I did not plead no contest for any other reason but to protect our privacy. I was advised it would end the press hype.

I don't want to belabor knocking the press, but I can't believe what is being said. Most of it is totally made up. I know you have a job to do, but as a last wish please, please, please leave my children in peace. Their lives will be tough enough.

I want to send my love and thanks to all my friends. I'm sorry I can't name every one of you. Especially A. C.—man, thanks for being in my life. The support and friendship I received from so many—Wayne Hughes, Louis Marks, Frank Olson, Mark Packer, Bender, Bobby Kardashian—I wish we had spent more time together in recent years. My golfing buddies—Hoss, Alan Austin, Mike, Craig, Denver, Wyler, Sandy, Jay, Donnie—thanks for the fun.

All my teammates over the years: Reggie, you were the soul of my pro career, Ahmad, I never stopped being proud of you. Marcus, you've got a great lady in Catherine, don't mess it up. Bobby Chandler, thanks for always being there. Skip and Cathy, I love you guys—without you I never would have made it through this far. Marguerite, thanks for the early years—we had some fun. Paula—what can I say? You are special. I'm sorry we're not going to have our chance. God brought you to me, I now see. As I leave, you'll be in my thoughts.

I think of my life and feel I've done most of the right things. So why do I end up like this? I can't go on. No matter what the outcome, people will look and point. I can't take that. I can't subject my children to that. This way they can move on and go on with their lives. Please, if I've done anything worthwhile with my life, let my kids live in peace from you, the press.

I've had a good life. I'm proud of how I lived. My mama taught me to do unto others—I treated people the way I wanted to be treated. I've always tried to be up and helpful. So why is this happening? I'm sorry for the Goldman family. I know how much it hurts.

Nicole and I had a good life together. All this press talk about a rocky relationship is no more than what every long-term relationship experiences. All her friends will confirm that I have been totally loving and understanding of what she's been going through. At times I have felt like a battered husband or boyfriend. But I loved her, make that clear to everyone. And I would take whatever it took to make it work.

Don't feel sorry for me. I've had a great life, great friends. Please think of the real O. J. and not this lost person. Thanks for making my life special. I hope I helped yours.

Peace and love,

O. J.

1994: NOVEMBER 5
RONALD REAGAN TO AMERICANS

Approximately four million Americans had Alzheimer's disease in 1994, and, with the aging of the baby boomers, the number was expected to grow as high as twenty million by 2050. Ronald Reagan was eighty-three years old and almost six years out of office when he released this handwritten letter, an effort to bring attention to the illness. For several years afterward he would continue to venture from his Bel Air, California, home to shake hands with well-wishers at the Reagan Library, though it was said that the only person he recognized consistently was his wife, Nancy.

My Fellow Americans,

I have recently been told that I am one of the millions of Americans who will be afflicted with Alzheimer's Disease.

Upon learning this news, Nancy and I had to decide whether as private citizens we would keep this a private matter or whether we would make this news known in a public way.

In the past Nancy suffered from breast cancer and I had my cancer surgeries.

We found through our open disclosure we were able to raise public awareness. We were happy that as a result many more people underwent testing.

They were treated in early stages and able to return to normal, healthy lives.

So now, we feel it is important to share it with you. In opening our hearts, we hope this might promote greater awareness of this condition. Perhaps it will encourage a clearer understanding of the individuals and families who are affected by it.

At the moment I feel just fine. I intend to live the remainder of the years God gives me on this earth doing the things I have always done. I will continue to share life's journey with my beloved Nancy and my family. I plan to enjoy the great outdoors and stay in touch with my friends and supporters.

Unfortunately, as Alzheimer's Disease progresses, the family often bears a heavy burden. I only wish there was some way I could spare Nancy from this painful experience. When the time comes I am confident that with your help she will face it with faith and courage.

In closing let me thank you, the American people, for giving me the great honor of allowing me to serve as your President. When the Lord calls me home, whenever that may be, I will leave with the greatest love for this country of ours and eternal optimism for its future.

I now begin the journey that will lead me into the sunset of my life. I know that for America there will always be a bright dawn ahead.

Thank you, my friends. May God always bless you.

Sincerely,

Ronald Reagan

1995: JANUARY 27
MICHAEL OKUDA TO A <u>STAR TREK</u> FAN

The series debuted in September of 1966, received poor ratings, ran for only three seasons, and spawned an industry that three decades later was prospering. The original Star Trek, created by Gene Roddenberry (1921–1991), featured a crew of intergalactic travelers whose every iteration was studied by its most devoted fans. With the advent of the Internet, a medium perfectly suited to the techno-literate Trekkies, came electronic trivia questions like "What writer of the Star Trek episode 'The Lights of Zetar' is better known as the creator of a famous children's puppet?" (Answer: Shari Lewis.) What came, too, were on-line letters like the following, written by Michael Okuda, a technical adviser and scenic artist for Star Trek films and se-

ries. It was accompanied by pages of fans' interpretations, mathematical calculations, charts, and graphs.

The new series included *Star Trek: The Next Generation* (ST:TNG), which first aired in 1987, and *Star Trek: Voyager*, debuting in 1995.

Date: Fri, Jan 27, 1995 02:09 AM EST
From: MOkuda
Subj: Re: Star Trek Warp
To: Yar of Spit

The warp factors we've used in ST:TNG were computed in an arbitrary way to fit some specific characteristics we needed.

First, the speed for any given warp factor had to be greater than it was in the original <u>Star Trek</u> series. This was primarily to satisfy fan expectations.

Second, the new warp speeds couldn't be TOO much faster, or it would be possible for the ship to cross the galaxy in a fairly brief time. (In a way, maintaining this restriction made Voyager's story situation possible. If we hadn't done this, Voyager could have gotten home too quickly.)

We used an exponent of (I think) 3.33 or 3.33333 . . . for warp factors less than 9.

Between 9 and 10, I gradually increased the exponent so that it approached infinity as the warp factor approached 10. Lacking knowledge of calculus, I just drew what looked to me to be a credible curve on graph paper, then pulled the points from there. I think I re-created the curve fairly accurately in the <u>Star Trek: The Next Generation Technical Manual</u>.

Hope this helps.
Mike

1995: FEBRUARY 10
TIM MCVEIGH TO GWENN STRIDER

In 1992, at Ruby Ridge, Idaho, white separatist Randy Weaver's wife and son were shot to death by federal agents. This use of force, followed by the incident at Waco, were proof to a group of right-wing partisans that the United States government had become repressively brutal. Timothy McVeigh (1968–) was among this group. Approximately two months after he sent this letter to a friend and exactly two years after the Waco fire, the Alfred P. Murrah Federal Building in Oklahoma City was destroyed by a bomb. The explosion injured more than five hundred people and killed one hundred sixty-eight, including fifteen children. Evidence would quickly lead to McVeigh, who would be convicted of murder in June of 1997 and sentenced to death by lethal injection.

Lon Horiuchi, an FBI sniper, shot Weaver's wife, Vicki, while she was holding her baby daughter.

10 February 1995

Gwenn,

Kevin hurt his back, eh?

As far as the main context of your letter, I really don't know what to tell you, except write your representative in Congress—they represent the people and they listen to them (Yea, right!)

No, really, let me try to explain—I was in the educational literature dissemination (desert wind is wreaking havoc on my already scratchy writing) field for quite some time. I was preaching and "passing out" before anyone had ever heard the words "patriot" and "militia."

—Just got out of the wind—

"Onward and upward," I passed on that legacy about a ½ year ago. I believe the "new blood" needs to start somewhere; and I have certain other "militant" talents that are short in supply and greatly demanded. So I gave all my informational paperwork to the "new guys" and no longer have any to give. What I can send you, is my own personal copies; ones that are just gathering dust, and a newsletter I recently received.

If you are willing to write letters, I could pass your name on to someone; but let there be no doubt, with the letters I have in mind, the literature that would be forwarded to you for copying; etc., you would probably make a list. (Currently, there are over 300,000 names on the Cray Supercomputer in Brussels, Belgium, of "possible and suspected subversives and terrorists" in the U.S., all ranked in order of threat). Letters would be of an "on notice" nature, like the ones many people (myself included) wrote to Lon Horiuchi (The FBI sniper who blew Vicki Weaver's head off), saying in effect: "What goes around comes around . . ."

Hey, that's just the truth, and if we're scared away from writing the truth because we're afraid of winding up on a list, then we've lost already. "To sin by silence when they protest makes Cowards of men."—Abe L.

If the founding fathers had been scared of a "list," we'd still be under the tyrannical rule of the crown.

They knew, without a doubt, that by signing the Declaration of Independence, they would be sentenced to death, for high treason against the crown. But they realized something was more important than their sole or collective lives—the cause of liberty.

Hell, you only live once, and I know you know it's better to burn out, than . . . rot away in some nursing home. My philosophy is the same—in only a short 1–2 years, my body will slowly start giving away—first maybe knee pains, or back pains, or whatever, but I won't be "peaked" any more. Might as well do some good while I can be 100% effective!

Sorry I can't be of more help, but most of the people sent my way these days are of the direct-action type, and my whole mindset has shifted, from intellectual to . . . animal (Rip the bastards heads off and shit down their necks! and I'll show you how with a simple pocket knife . . . etc.)

So take your time, read all the enclosed paperwork, and maybe pass it on to other interested parties. If you want to go on a propaganda mailing list, let me know.

> See ya,
> The Desert Rat

1995: APRIL 20
"FC" TO THE <u>NEW YORK TIMES</u>

Ted Kaczynski (1942–) was a Harvard graduate; he had taught math at the University of California, Berkeley; he was living in a ten-by-twelve-foot Montana cabin, abhorring a world he felt had been ruined by technology and industry. For seventeen years, Kaczynski had managed to conceal these facts while sending letter bombs that killed three recipients and wounded twenty-three others. Known only as the Unabomber (the un *for universities, the* a *for airlines, both among his early targets), he finally offered the* New York Times *and the* Washington Post *the deal explained in this letter. With financial help from the* Times *and at the urging of the FBI and the attorney general, the* Post *would publish Kaczynski's thirty-five-thousand-word anarchist manifesto in September. Recognizing themes expounded in letters he had received, Ted's brother David would take his suspicions to the FBI in February. Ted would be arrested in April of 1996, and would plead guilty in January of 1998 to avoid the death penalty.*

FC, standing for "Freedom Club," was in reality a group of one. The tanker *Exxon Valdez* had hit a reef in Prince William Sound in March of 1989, spilling eleven million gallons of oil and killing hundreds of thousands of birds and fish.

[Passage deleted at the request of the F.B.I.]

This is a message from the terrorist group FC.

We blew up Thomas Mosser last December because he was a Burston-Marsteller executive. Among other misdeeds, Burston-Marsteller helped Exxon clean up its public image after the Exxon Valdez incident. But we attacked Burston-Marsteller less for its specific misdeeds than on general principles. Burston-Marsteller is about the biggest organization in the public relations field. This means that its business is the development of techniques for manipulating people's attitudes. It was for this more than for its actions in specific cases that we sent a bomb to an executive of this company.

Some news reports have made the misleading statement that we have been attacking universities or scholars. We have nothing against universities or scholars as such. All the university people whom we have attacked have been specialists in technical fields. (We consider certain areas of applied psychology, such as behavior modification, to be technical fields.) We would not want anyone to think that we have any desire to hurt professors who study archaeology, history, literature or harmless stuff like that. The people we are out to get are the scientists and engineers, especially in critical fields like computers and genetics. As for the bomb planted in the Business School of the U. of Utah, that was a botched operation. We won't say how or why it was botched because we don't want to give the FBI any clues. No one was hurt by that bomb.

In our previous letter to you we called ourselves anarchists. Since "anarchist" is a vague word that has been applied to a variety of attitudes, further explanation is needed. We call ourselves anarchists because we would like, ideally, to break down all society into very small, completely autonomous units. Regrettably, we don't see any clear road to this goal, so we leave it to the indefinite future. Our more immediate goal, which we think may be attainable some time during the next several decades, is the destruction of the worldwide industrial system. Through our bombing we hope to promote social instability in industrial society, propagate anti-industrial ideas and give encouragement to those who hate the industrial system.

The FBI has tried to portray these bombings as the work of an isolated nut. We won't waste our time arguing about whether we are nuts, but we certainly are not isolated. For security reasons we won't reveal the number of members of our group, but anyone who will read the anarchist and radical environmentalist journals will see that opposition to the industrial-technological system is widespread and growing.

Why do we announce our goals only now, through we made our first bomb some seventeen years ago? Our early bombs were too ineffectual to attract much public attention or give encouragement to those who hate the system. We found by experience that gunpowder bombs, if small enough to be carried inconspicuously, were too feeble to do much damage, so we took a couple of years off to do some experimenting. We learned how to make pipe bombs that were powerful enough, and we used these in a couple of successful bombings as well as in some unsuccessful ones.

[Passage deleted at the request of the F.B.I.]

Since we no longer have to confine the explosive in a pipe, we are now free of limitations on the size and shape of our bombs. We are pretty sure we know how to increase the power of our explosives and reduce the number of batteries needed to set them off. And, as we've just indicated, we think we now have more effective fragmentation material. So we expect to be able to pack deadly bombs into ever smaller, lighter and more harmless looking packages. On the other hand, we believe we will be able to make bombs much bigger than any we've made before. With a briefcase-full or a suitcase-full of explosives, we should be able to blow out the walls of substantial buildings.

Clearly we are in a position to do a great deal of damage. And it doesn't appear that the FBI is going to catch us any time soon. The FBI is a joke.

The people who are pushing all this growth and progress garbage deserve to be severely punished. But our goal is less to punish them than to propagate ideas. Anyhow we are getting tired of making bombs. It's no fun having to spend all your evenings and weekends preparing dangerous mixtures, filing trigger mechanisms out of scraps of metal or searching the sierras for a place isolated enough to test a bomb. So we offer a bargain.

We have a long article, between 29,000 and 37,000 words, that we want to have published. If you can get it published according to our requirements we will permanently desist from terrorist activities. It must be published in The New York Times, Time or Newsweek, or in some other widely read, nationally distributed periodical. Because of its length we suppose it will have to be serialized. Alternatively, it can be published as a small book, but the book must be well publicized and made available at a moderate price in bookstores nationwide and in at least some places abroad. Whoever agrees to publish the material will have exclusive rights to reproduce it for a period of six months and will be welcome to any profits they may make from it. After six months from the first appearance of the article or book it must become public property, so that anyone can reproduce or publish it. (If material is serialized, first instalment becomes public property six months after appearance of first instalment, second instalment, etc.) We must have the right to publish in the New York Times, Time or Newsweek, each year for three years after the appearance of our article or book, three thousand words expanding or clarifying our material or rebutting criticisms of it.

The article will not explicitly advocate violence. There will be an unavoidable implication that we favor violence to the extent that it may be necessary, since we advocate eliminating industrial society and we ourselves have been using violence to that end. But the article will not advocate violence explicitly, nor will it propose the overthrow of the United States Government, nor will it contain obscenity or anything else that you would be likely to regard as unacceptable for publication.

How do you know that we will keep our promise to desist from terrorism if our conditions are met? It will be to our advantage to keep our promise. We want to win acceptance for certain ideas. If we break our promise people will lose respect for us and so will be less likely to accept the ideas.

Our offer to desist from terrorism is subject to three qualifications. First: Our promise to desist will not take effect until all parts of our article or book have appeared in print. Second: If the authorities should succeed in tracking us down and an attempt is made to arrest any of us, or even to question us in connection with the bombings, we reserve the right to use violence. Third: We distinguish between terrorism and sabotage. By terrorism we mean actions motivated by a desire to influence the development of a society and intended to cause injury or death to human beings. By sabotage we mean similarly motivated actions intended to destroy property without injuring human beings. The promise we offer is to desist from terrorism. We reserve the right to engage in sabotage.

It may be just as well that failure of our early bombs discouraged us from making any public statements at that time. We were very young then and our thinking was crude. Over the years we have given as much attention to the development of our ideas as to the development of bombs, and we now have something serious to say. And we feel that just now the time is ripe for the presentation of anti-industrial ideas.

Please see to it that the answer to our offer is well publicized in the media so that we won't miss it. Be sure to tell us where and how our material will be published and how long it will take to appear in print once we have sent in the manuscript. If the answer is satisfactory, we will finish typing the manuscript and send it to you. If the answer is unsatisfactory, we will start building our next bomb.

We encourage you to print this letter.

FC

[Passage deleted at the request of the F.B.I.]

1995: JUNE 5

PATSY CLARKE TO JESSE HELMS

The letter below was written by the widow of a former consultant to Jesse Helms (1921–), the conservative North Carolina senator. Helms, who had first been elected to the Senate in 1972, was a powerful and visible advocate of school prayer and a strong national defense, and a fierce opponent of forced busing, abortion, and homosexual rights.

Raleigh, North Carolina
June 5, 1995

Dear Jesse,

This is a letter I have wanted to write for a long time. I do it now because its time has come.

When my husband (and your strong friend), Harry Clarke, died in a plane crash at the Asheville airport on March 9, 1987, you called me in the night. You told me of your sorrow at our loss and of what Harry had meant to you as a friend. You placed your praise for him and his principles in the Congressional Record. You sent me the flag flown over the capitol in his memory. You did all of these things and I am grateful.

Harry and I had another son, Mark. He was almost the image of his father, though much taller. He was blessed with great charm and intelligence and we loved him. He was gay. On March 9, 1994, exactly seven years to the day that his father died, Mark followed him—a victim of AIDS. I sat by his bed, held his dear hand and sang through that long last night the baby song that I had sung to all of our children. "Rock-a-bye and don't you cry, rock-a-bye little Mark. I'll buy you a pretty gold horse to ride all around your pasture . . ."

A few days before he died, Mark said these words: "This disease is not beating me. When I draw my last breath I will have defeated this disease—and I will be free." I watched him take his last breath and claim his freedom. He was 31.

As I write these words I re-live the most difficult time of my life. The tears will smudge this if I don't take care. No matter, I will type so it is legible. My reason for writing to you is not to plead for funds, although I'd like to ask your support for AIDS research; it is not to ask you to accept a lifestyle which is abhorrent to you; it is rather to ask you not to pass judgement on other human beings as "deserving what they get." No one deserves that. AIDS is not a disgrace, it is a TRAGEDY. Nor is homosexuality a disgrace; we so-called normal people make it a tragedy because of our own lack of understanding.

Mark gave me a great gift. A quote returns to me from long ago: "I have no lamp to light my feet save the lamp of experience . . ." I think Patrick Henry said it. Mark's life and death have illuminated my own and I am grateful for him.

So, that's what this letter is about, and I hope I have written it well. I wish you had known Mark. His life was so much more eloquent than any words which I might put on paper. I ask you to share his memory with me in compassion.

Gratefully,
Patsy M. Clarke

1995: JUNE 19
JESSE HELMS TO PATSY CLARKE

After receiving Senator Helms's response, Patsy Clarke would found MAJIC—Mothers Against Jesse In Congress—to work against his reelection.

Washington, D.C.
June 19, 1995

Dear Patsy,

I hope you will forgive my first-naming you. Having known Harry as I did and having read your poignant letter, I just don't feel like being formal in this response.

I know that Mark's death was devastating to you. As for homosexuality, The Bible judges it, I do not. I do take the position that there must be some reasonableness in allocation of federal funds for research, treatment, etc. There is no justification for AIDS funding far exceeding that for other killer diseases such as cancer, heart trouble, etc.

And, by the way, the news media have engaged in their usual careless selves by reporting that I am "holding up" the authorizing legislation that includes AIDS funding. One of the homosexual activists sent out a totally erroneous press release (and he knew what he was saying was not true) hoping to cause me problems. He failed. I did file a "notify" request because I have two or three amendments that I intend to offer to restore balance to the spending of taxpayers' money for research and treatment of various diseases.

I understand the militant homosexuals and they understand me. They climbed onto the roof of Dot's and my home and hoisted a giant canvas condom.

As for Mark, I wish he had not played Russian roulette with his sexual activity. He obviously had a great deal to offer to the uplifting of his generation. He did not live to do all of the wonderful things that he might otherwise have done.

I have sympathy for him—and for you. But there is no escaping the reality of what happened.

I wish you well always.

Jesse H.

1995: NOVEMBER

REBECCA MARTIN TO THE JOSEPHINE COUNTY COURIER

Though dissatisfaction with public education had been a frequent theme of the twentieth century, the chorus of disapproval grew louder in the nineties. With reading skills and standardized-test scores declining, peer pressure intense, and discipline often lax, parents sought alternatives. One approach, especially among social conservatives, was to persuade the government to issue vouchers enabling parents to choose private schools over public ones. Another approach was home schooling. By 1995, parents of more than six hundred thousand children had chosen—for religious, moral, or educational reasons—to teach their children at home. An explanation for that choice was offered in this letter from a thirteen-year-old girl living in Grants Pass, Oregon.

I am a seventh grader at Fleming Middle School. I transferred from a private school about three months before the end of the school year.

I expected a school where I could go and learn something, but I got a big surprise. Everyone was nice at first, but after a few weeks, I quickly found out that everything is not always as it seems.

First of all, the education level there is very low. My math work is similar to work I did in fifth grade, yet no one moved me to a more challenging class. I feel that I have fallen behind tremendously in the level of work that I was doing at private school.

The teaching methods are counter-productive to the way that I am used to learning. We are frequently asked to pick what we want to learn, then are sometimes expected to teach ourselves. A teacher's aide is sometimes supposed to help us, but often they just talk and disturb our work. The noise level gets out of control a lot, which makes it hard to study or to get any of our work done.

One of my teachers is frequently late or absent due to "site-council" meetings. My class is so used to having a substitute, it is a shock to see our teacher back in class.

Group learning is used in all of my classes. It does not work because the smart kid in the group ends up doing all the work while the rest of the kids sit around and talk. When the work is finished, the kids who sat around and talked snatch up the paper like hungry wolves. Group learning also means that the individual student loses control over the quality of the work that she will be graded on.

In English class, we are reading and performing "Driving Miss Daisy." My group decided to call it "Driving Over Miss Daisy." In their version, Miss Daisy goes to bars, gets drunk, smokes and plays poker. The "Piggly-Wiggly" store is a bar in their version. When Miss Daisy's chauffeur gets sick of her, he runs her over. I totally disagree with this because it adulterates the original play. But, to go against my group would make me "uncool." Our teacher has allowed this version as a "variation," and my group will be performing it the way they want.

Most kids use filthy language at school. The "F" word is the word that is used the most. Students who are heard using bad language are barely disciplined at all. Students also write filthy words in notes and on school property. Some students have pictures of barely-dressed women in their lockers, and one boy has his locker "wallpapered" with condoms. Feminine hygiene products can be found laying around by the locker rooms and on the nature trail.

I experienced sexual harassment every day. Both male and female students behave and speak very suggestively. Not only is this tolerated, it is expected in order to be "cool." Both male and female students grab each other in inappropriate places on their bodies. Sex is talked about all the time, and in nasty ways, such as "household pets and family members you might have had sex with." If a person has any values or morals at all, they are considered a "geek."

Some students spend time out of class to get counseling. They never seem to have to make up their work. We are asked all the time, "How are you feeling?" I am tired of all the self-evaluation and self-esteem building. My personal life is my business, and if I want to talk about something, I'll talk to God or my parents. I would rather talk to people who know me and love me than teachers or students that I am unfamiliar with. I have been made to feel stupid for telling my mom what's going on in my life. According to some of the students, that's not a good thing to do.

I tried to think of anything good about my experience at Fleming Middle School. I did like some of my teachers, but overall, I feel very disappointed. I would rather do real schoolwork than the unchallenging things we are asked to do. I feel a little confused because there didn't seem to be a clear line between right and wrong: everything got all lumped together.

I am looking forward to being home schooled next year.

1995: DECEMBER 18, 6:49 P.M.
A THIRTY-NINE-YEAR-OLD WOMAN
TO HER ON-LINE CORRESPONDENT

With the advent of the Internet came the on-line romance—and the on-line breakup. The letter writers preferred to remain anonymous.

DATE: MON, DEC 18, 1995 6:49 PM EDT
FROM: ———
SUBJECT: INTO THE DANCE WITH COURAGE
TO: ———

Hey there, my friend. I hope all is going well for you.

Where to start? I know you knew that eventually we would come to the place of parting ways. My husband and I are doing intensive counseling in hopes of coming to terms with some of the difficulties in our marriage. Because honesty is key in the process, I can't lie about the "extracurricular" feelings which make escape much too easy for me. To give our marriage an honest shot, I have to be focused to know what I need to do for myself. Now is the time for me to put play aside and get into the trenches with life. It takes a lot for me to write this letter. It feels like giving up a part of myself.

And *oh* that playfulness. Thank you, thank you for it. Our affair of the soul has opened my heart a little wider and allowed me to become myself a little more. Here is the depth and length we spoke of. No wonder flirtation and sexuality were so much a part of this process . . . the essential and mysterious stuff of life itself.

I've had to be so tough for so much of my life. I allowed myself to surrender here . . . to you I thought for awhile, but in truth, I was opening and accepting a deeper part of myself. What a gift you have given me. I will always remember the best parts of this time with you. Now I have to find out what I do with my *real* life.

I will miss you. Have a good marriage; loving is so important to this experience of being human. Continue to write from your soul so you can always touch the souls of others. I believe the most valuable gifts we give come from our most vulnerable places. Ultimately, it comes back. I have never, ever disbelieved my heart. I just couldn't. So I'll choose to think of us as soulfully connected. Somewhere. Out there.

Be well. Be happy. Most of all, to thine own self be true.

Always,

[Anonymous]

1996: MARCH 31, 2:50 A.M.
COMPUSERVE TO ROBERT RICHE

In 1996, novelist Robert Riche, author of Poppy & Me, *became one of millions of Americans who attempted to enter cyberspace via the World Wide Web. The next five letters represent the e-mail correspondence that followed.*

Welcome to CompuServe. You've joined over two million members around the world who count on our more than 2,000 products and services for the latest information, the best entertainment, and quality service.

To help you get started, we've created the New Member Welcome Center. This is where you can pick up helpful tips, learn how to find our services that match your interest, and get an idea of what we have to offer.

To help us improve our service to you, you can provide us with valuable feedback. Your opinions are important to us!

Once again, welcome to the information service you won't outgrow.

1996: APRIL 1, 1:52 P.M.
ROBERT RICHE TO COMPUSERVE

Thank you for your welcome message of 3/31/96 2:50 a.m. Despite having followed software installation instructions carefully (I think), I have been unable to access the Internet. When I click on the Internet icon I get an ERROR MESSAGE that says simply, "Already installed." I know that (I think). What next?

Thank you for any help.

1996: APRIL 3, 3:29 A.M.
COMPUSERVE TO ROBERT RICHE

Thank you for your feedback reply. I understand that you are writing to inquire about accessing the World Wide Web.

There are many different ways to access the World Wide Web, and the Internet. There are a few suggestions that I can offer to help you. The first suggestion is that if you are a PC user, you GO: NETLAUNCHER. This command will take you to a place, online, where you may download the necessary program for "Web surfing."

If you are using a terminal emulation program you can get more Internet information by typing GO INTERNET at any (!) prompt. If you are using the Information Manager, you may use the GO command, which is accessed through the SERVICES pull down menu, in the initial screen. Selecting the GO command will bring a prompt to enter a topic. Enter INTERNET at this prompt. At this point, you will see a screen entitled INTERNET. Then you may want to select INTERNET FORUMS, where you may post questions, and see other members' questions answered, or you may want to select INTERNET Q & A, for frequently asked questions, and answers about the Internet.

I hope that this information is helpful to you. Should you have any further questions, comments, or concerns please contact us again.

1996: APRIL 4, 2:37 A.M.
ROBERT RICHE TO COMPUSERVE

Thank you for the feedback reply with instructions. I am having a little bit of trouble following you. I think I lost you at the beginning of the third paragraph, referring to the "terminal emulation program." I am not sure whether I am using a terminal emulation program, or not. In fact, I have no idea. I think I am using a computer, with an internal modem.

Thanks again for your time.

1996: APRIL 4, 7:01 P.M.
COMPUSERVE TO ROBERT RICHE

This Feedback message is concerning the problem that you encountered accessing the Internet with a Winsock connection. I have addressed this below.

This is usually the result of a settings problem in the Session Settings.

However, it may also be related to a problem with the location of the Winsock.DLL files.

First, delete the CIS.INI file located in the C:\CSERVE\directory. You will need to know all of your Session Setting information, including your password. Once you have deleted this file, enter all of the Session Settings information in the Information Manager.

If your baud rate is set to 19200, try changing it to 14400. If the baud rate is set to 14400 try changing to 19200. If you are connecting at 28800 bps, try 38400 and 57600 baud rate settings. In addition, make sure that the system.ini file has the default comm.drv=comm.drv. if you see anything different in the [boot] section of the system.ini, such a comm.drv=fax.drv, replace it with the default setting.

If these suggestions do not work, copy the \CSERVE\CID\WINSOCK.DLL to the \CSERVE\WINCIM\, and \CSERVE\MOSAIC\ directories. This should allow the application to access Winsock without interfering in other Internet applications on you system. If this does not work, try reinstalling WinCIM.

Thank you for using Feedback! Please let us know if you need further assistance.

1996: APRIL 6
ROBERT RICHE TO COMPUSERVE

_____

Thank you all for being so patient with me, and so helpful. I have decided to use the radio for weather reports, <u>The Wall Street Journal</u> for stock market reports, <u>The New York Times</u> for news reports, the telephone for my "chats," my travel agent for travel reservations, the movie and television media for entertainment, and the town library (fortunately, only a short stroll from my house) for reference materials. I also plan a trip into New York City soon to visit the Metropolitan Museum of Art to view some of their paintings.

Please cancel my subscription, and do accept my best wishes.

1996: APRIL 19
MARY TO HER SON'S ADOPTIVE PARENTS

_____

Eighteen years after putting her son up for adoption, a mother wrote this letter to the couple who had raised him.

April 19, 1996

To John's Mom and Dad,

First, let me apologize for the delay of this letter. It's been nearly a year since I received that plain, brown envelope in the mail from the adoption agency, containing your wonderful letters and pictures of John. I can't tell you how much both the letters and pictures mean to me. When I first saw the pictures, I cried with joy . . . the long wait to know my son's first name and what he looks like was finally over! It has given me a peace of mind I have been searching for, for a long, long time. I can't tell you how grateful I am, along with my family. My mom and my siblings all were overjoyed to finally see what their birthgrandson/birthnephew looks like, to hear how well he is doing, and to hear what wonderful parents he has.

I think about John and your family every day, and hope you are doing well. With John's 18th birthday and graduation from high school drawing near, I have been thinking about him a lot, and wondering what his plans are for after high school. I'm sure he has been or will be accepted at a fine university. My mom and dad were the only ones in their generation to get college degrees in our family, and all five of their children have college degrees. Two of my sisters have advanced degrees. Education is very important to us, as I'm sure it is to you. I'm glad to hear John is doing so well in school. What is his intended major? . . .

There hasn't been any change in my family's health history over the past year. I was wondering if you would like me to try to contact John's birthfather and ask him to provide an updated medical history. I don't know if he ever provided one at the time of John's birth. I'm sure that you and John would like to have John's complete and current medical history.

Please tell John congratulations on his upcoming graduation, and that I'm always available to answer any questions he may have. Your family is always in my heart, and never far from my thoughts. Take good care of each other, as you have been. I'm so glad you were chosen to be John's parents.

Love,
Mary

1996: DECEMBER

S.B.T.C. TO JOHN RAMSEY

A six-year-old who had recently been named Little Miss Christmas in a local beauty pageant, JonBenét Ramsey was found dead in the basement of her family's Boulder, Colorado, mansion the day after Christmas. News reports revealed that she had been beaten and strangled, that sexual abuse was suspected, and—in the first of many glimpses into the freakish world of children's beauty competitions—that her baby teeth had been capped. The letter below, found on the floor near the Ramseys' kitchen, was one of the few pieces of evidence in a crime that was as noted for its ghastliness as it was for the seemingly odd behavior of the victim's parents, John and Patsy, who initially refused to speak to police. As of this writing, the crime was unsolved, and "S.B.T.C." remained an obscure acronym.

Mr. Ramsey,

Listen carefully! We are a group of individuals that represent a small foreign faction. We respect your bussiness but not the country that it serves. At this time we have your daughter in our posession. She is safe and unharmed and if you want her to see 1997, you must follow our instructions to the letter.

You will withdraw $118,000.00 from your account. $100,000 will be in $100 bills and the remaining $18,000 in $20 bills. Make sure that you bring an adequate size attache to the bank. When you get home you will put the money in a brown paper bag. I will call you between 8 and 10 am tomorrow to instruct you on delivery. The delivery will be exhausting so I advise you to be rested. If we monitor you getting the money early, we might call you early to arrange an earlier delivery of the money and hence a earlier pick-up of your daughter.

Any deviation of my instructions will result in the immediate execution of your daughter. You will also be denied her remains for proper burial. The two gentlemen watching over your daughter do not particularly like you so I advise you not to provoke them. Speaking to anyone about your situation, such as Police, F.B.I., etc., will result in your daughter being beheaded. If we catch you talking to a stray dog, she dies. If you alert bank authorities, she dies. If the money is in any way marked or tampered with, she dies. You will be scanned for electronic devices and if any are found, she dies. You can try to deceive us but be warned that we are familiar with law enforcement countermeasures and tactics. You stand a 99% chance of killing your daughter if you try to out smart us. Follow our instructions and you stand a 100% chance of getting her back. You and your family are under constant scrutiny as well as the authorities. Don't try to grow a brain John. You are not the only fat cat around so don't think that killing will be difficult. Don't underestimate us John. Use that good southern common sense of yours. It is up to you now John!

Victory!

S.B.T.C.

1997: MAY

AN <u>ELLEN</u> VIEWER TO HER MOTHER

In April of 1997, comedian Ellen DeGeneres announced first her own and then her sitcom character's homosexuality on the network show Ellen. *Huge numbers of viewers tuned in to watch the "coming-out episode," conservative groups protested, gay rights groups cheered—and one young woman wrote the following letter to her mother.*

May 1997

Dear Mom,

With all the Ellen stuff that's been happening lately, I figured that this would be a good time to tell you that I'm attracted to women too. The main reason I haven't told you is because I was afraid that you would treat me differently. You and —— are the two people I love the most, and I've been worried that you wouldn't love me anymore if I told you.

This whole thing seems SO ridiculous because I have no idea who the heck decided that being gay is a bad thing in the first place! I don't even think it's a big deal at all! And I certainly don't think it's a bad thing. When two humans love each other, no matter what gender the two of them are, why should it be wrong? It shouldn't matter who we love—all that matters is that we love! I wish more people would realize this.

One of the reasons Ellen's coming out was so amazing for me is because it's the first time a t.v. character depicted my own feelings and experiences about this "issue." It doesn't surprise me that so many gay/bisexual people grow up thinking they are "abnormal" or "wrong." I mean, how many gay or lesbian characters have there been in t.v. and in movies? We've been brainwashed into thinking that the only valid (and "normal") relationships are heterosexual ones.

I totally understand that this will probably freak you out—especially because we've all been taught that being attracted to the same sex is a "bad" thing. I really have no expectations about how you will react. Most families (and friends) have trouble accepting this news, especially when it is their own daughter, son, sister, or brother. I bet that most families try to deny/ignore it—hoping they will change (that it's "just a phase," etc.). I can imagine the kinds of feelings that you might have about this, and I don't want you to think that you "shouldn't" have any negative feelings or thoughts, etc. Know that however you react or feel will not change how I feel about you.

It's SO hard to describe, but I've often said that it's as though my heart (emotion) doesn't "activate" with men the way it does when I am with a woman. As Ellen described, that "click" just doesn't occur. A lot of people think that the "reason" people are gay is because they have had bad experiences with the opposite sex, or because they had a bad childhood. But it's not like being with men is some horrible experience for me—because it is not like that at all. I have lots of fun with them. I feel comfortable with men, enjoy their company, etc. It's just that when I am in a relationship with a man, there is always a sense that something is missing. I enjoy being with women so much more. I can relate to them on a much deeper level, and can therefore really love and care about them. Being able to feel such deep love and connection with another person, whatever their gender (or race, ethnicity, etc.) is such a wonderful thing. It makes me really sad (and angry) that we've been taught the complete opposite, and I know that if I continue to hide who I am out of fear of what other people will think, I will only be contributing to the false (and harmful) belief that being gay or bisexual is wrong or bad. And I don't want to do that. That's pretty much why I'm telling you this.

I thought that writing you a letter would be easier—I've always been able to express myself better in writing anyway.

I love and miss you!!

xoxox

1997: JULY 28

DR. JONATHAN LAPOOK TO A HEALTH PLAN ADMINISTRATOR

In his State of the Union message on January 25, 1994, President Clinton brandished a pen and said he would veto any health-reform bill that failed to "guarantee every American private health insurance." But Clinton's elaborate plan to provide universal health care was soon overwhelmed by opposition. In its place flourished a private-sector initiative to slash health costs and generate profits through so-called managed care. Insurers and health maintenance organizations (HMOs) were typically making decisions about patients that traditionally had been the sole province of physicians. Doctors like New York City gastroenterologist Jonathan LaPook didn't always take kindly to the changes.

In a later reply to the patient in February of 1998, the health plan reiterated its position on nonreimbursement for the drug. The names are changed to protect privacy.

July 28, 1997

Dear Ms. Jones,

I am a board certified internist and gastroenterologist and assistant professor at Columbia-Presbyterian Medical Center. I am writing you in the hope that you can assist my patient, Mrs. Smith, who is covered by your drug plan and who has been paying for Prilosec "out of pocket" for the last several years.

I called you 9/12/96 and left a message with Ann (you were at a meeting). My call was not returned so I called again 10/25/96 and spoke to Mary Frank (you were not there) and was told that Ms. Johnson would call me. My call was not returned so I called again 10/28/96 (you were not there). I was told by Ann to write a letter to Ms. Johnson with details of Mrs. Smith's situation. I wrote a detailed letter on October 29, 1996 and faxed it to Ms. Johnson. I included copies of past upper endoscopic exams (8/1/94 and 5/14/96), including pathology reports. I am enclosing a copy of my letter of 10/29/96.

You sent Mrs. Smith a form letter dated 11/14/96, stating "your diagnosis is not one of the F.D.A.'s Approved indications for prolonged usage". No copy was sent to me. When Mrs. Smith returned to my office 4/15/97, she informed me that she was still paying for the Prilosec herself. I called Ms. Johnson while Mrs. Smith was in the office. First I was told that Ms. Johnson was not in. I explained the situation to Ms. Betty Hart and soon Ms. Johnson got on the phone.

I asked Ms. Johnson why I never received a reply from Ms. Jones. She told me that "we respond to our members, not to the doctor". Ms. Johnson was belligerent and uncooperative from the onset of our conversation. Initially she told me that I had never sent her my 10/29/96 fax, then looked further and said I had sent the fax but that she only received page #2 of the pathology report. I asked to speak to the medical consultant who reviewed the case and she replied that she was "not at liberty to tell you the name of the medical consultant".

I told Ms. Johnson that "a plan should cover the medications which a patient needs", to which she replied (direct quote), "what it should and what it does is two different things". At the end of the conversation I asked her to have the medical consultant call me "as soon as possible".

Over three months later, I am still waiting for a call from your medical consultant.

Mrs. Smith continues to REQUIRE Prilosec (and Propulsid) treatment for chronic acid reflux disease which has been associated with potentially premalignant (adenomatous) changes on biopsy. Her disease has been unresponsive to other medications, including Pepcid 40 milligrams twice daily.

I remain extremely anxious to talk to your medical consultant about the situation. Since my repeated requests for an explanation have been ignored since 10/96, I feel that Mrs. Smith not only should receive coverage for her Prilosec but that she should be reimbursed for her "out of pocket" Prilosec expenses retroactive to at least 10/96.

I eagerly await your timely response.

Sincerely,

Jonathan LaPook, M.D.

1997: NOVEMBER 12

MONICA LEWINSKY TO BILL CLINTON

In 1998, Bill Clinton would become only the second president in U.S. history to be impeached by the House of Representatives. Many Democrats would blame a rabid right wing—and Independent Counsel Kenneth Starr—for their zealous efforts to dig up any dirt on the president. But the proximate cause for the impeachment was Clinton's relationship with a White House intern named Monica Lewinsky (1973–)—or, more specifically, the way in which he denied that the relationship had been sexual. Before the scandal ended, the American public would be awash in the intimate details of the affair, including those disclosed in this letter, which Lewinsky sent by courier when she was feeling frustrated by the president's evident loss of interest.

Handsome:

I asked you three weeks ago to please be sensitive to what I am going through right now and to keep in contact with me, and yet I'm still left writing notes in vain. I am not a moron. I know that what is going on in the world takes precedence, but I don't think what I have asked you for is unreasonable. I can't help but to have hurt feelings when I sent you a note last week and this week, and you still haven't seen me or called me.

I thought if I took away your burden of having to try to place me in the WH you would open yourself up to me again; I missed that more than anything. It was awful when I saw you for your birthday in August. You were so distant that I missed you as I was holding you in my arms.

You have functions tonight, tomorrow night and then you leave on Friday afternoon. Yesterday was the best window of opportunity to see me and you didn't. I'm left wondering why. I am begging you to please be nice to me and understanding until I leave. This is so hard for me. I am trying to deal with so much emotionally, and I have nobody to talk to about it. I need you right now not as president, but as a man. PLEASE be my friend.

Betty said that you come back from your dinner tomorrow somewhere between 8:30 and 9:00. For my sake, can we make an arrangement that I will be waiting for you when you get back, and we can visit just for a little while. It's really not that difficult . . . yes or no?

1997: NOVEMBER 13
JAMES KALLSTROM TO
THE FAMILIES OF TWA FLIGHT 800 VICTIMS

On July 17, 1996, TWA Flight 800 exploded off the coast of Long Island, New York, killing all 230 people on board. A former marine platoon leader in Vietnam, FBI Assistant Director James Kallstrom vowed to track down the "coward" who had destroyed the Paris-bound 747. But more than a year later, after leading a dogged, closely watched investigation, Kallstrom expressed a more resigned view of the tragedy in his letter to the families of those killed in the explosion.

By the end of 1997, Kallstrom would close the investigation, having found no evidence of foul play.

In early summer, I wrote to you stating that the FBI had entered what could be the last phase of the criminal investigation into the TWA Flight 800 tragedy and that I would communicate to you as soon as we were in a position to reach a conclusion and prior to any release going to the public in general. We are now in that position.

As you all know, the FBI's investigation into this tragedy has been one of the most far-reaching, thorough, exhaustive and expensive ever conducted by this agency. The FBI and the law enforcement team interviewed more than 7,000 individuals, conducted extensive forensic testing, engaged in extensive and unprecedented research and analysis and accomplished the largest aircraft reconstruction mock-up in commercial aviation history.

Our agents have worked in a team effort with the National Transportation Safety Board, as well as numerous federal, state, and local law enforcement agencies and in close collaboration with all the members of the United States intelligence community, pursuing every theory with equal vigor, including conspiracy theories, such as "friendly fire" that gained media prominence at various times over the past sixteen months.

While I am totally confident that these conspiracy theories have no factual basis, I realize that those who want to believe that a conspiracy exists or sadly, seek to profit from promoting such theories will seldom admit they are mistaken. In sum, every lead has been covered, all possible avenues of investigation exhaustively explored and every resource of the United States government has been brought to bear in this investigation. In my 28 years of FBI service, I have never encountered such exceptional interagency cooperation at every level.

As I have stated repeatedly since the beginning of this investigation, we have been dedicated to conducting the most thorough, complete, finest investigative effort that the FBI can produce with the sole goal of determining with a high degree of certainty, if there is any evidence that the TWA Flight 800 catastrophe was the result of a criminal act, including a missile, or a bomb, and if so, to bring those responsible to justice. Having conducted just such an investigation, I must report to you, and in the near future will be reporting to the public that our investigation has found absolutely no evidence to cause us to believe that the TWA Flight 800 tragedy was the result of a criminal act.

For the future, we will maintain a presence to preserve the evidence, continue our liaison with the NTSB's investigators and provide whatever support and assistance we can to NTSB's efforts. In the event that any new information is developed that warrants FBI scrutiny, we are prepared to immediately undertake whatever additional investigation that may be necessary.

In closing, I, personally and on behalf of all the men and women of the law enforcement team, want to thank each of you for your support and patience throughout this tragic ordeal. Your dignity, strength, and support have inspired us throughout this investigation. We will be ever mindful of your loss and our prayers will always be with you. You have my warm personal regards and thanks for your understanding.

> Sincerely,
> James K. Kallstrom
> Assistant Director in Charge

1997: NOVEMBER 20
PATTY TO A COCAINE ANONYMOUS NEWSGROUP

In addition to its chat rooms, where participants could "talk" in real time, the Internet provided virtual space for posting messages to ongoing "newsgroups," where people with common interests could exchange information or ideas. The newsgroup was a particularly useful forum for self-help programs, where participants could offer one another support, encouragement, and confessions. Patty, a crack addict who lived in a Pennsylvania town that had no Cocaine Anonymous, attended local Alcoholics Anonymous meetings and relied on an addiction newsgroup. She sent this letter to her on-line confidantes while she was trying to stay clean after a relapse.

Subject: Keep Coming Back
Hi Everyone,

My name is Patty and I am an addict/alcoholic. I have not written to share in awhile. I went into detox the last 2 weeks in June. I was clean for 26 days. Then I thought that I could handle smoking crack once in a while. Well people that did not work. Crack took me over 10 fold. Before I was only spending $50–$75 a day. When I started back up I went to spending $150 to $200 a day. I went on a binge and spent $2000 in 3 days staying up not sleeping.

That was when I hit bottom. I signed myself into a detox. Was there for 6 days because of a bone disease also. I did not want to go to a rehab but I did because the doctor said that he could fix it that I could get the operation I needed on my neck as soon as I checked in. (If I stayed on the streets I couldn't get the operation for 3 weeks.) I was fighting the people at rehab saying that I did not belong here. Within 3 days I had a revalation that I did need help and also WANTED help.

So I have been just listening to all of you because I had a relapse. I thought that I was like 3 strikes and your out, and I felt like a hypocrite for sharing.

I relapsed, have chronic pain, and I own a bar. But the people at Stepping Stones made me feel worth it to clean up and make something of myself. I felt that people didn't care and wouldn't help because I was a crackhead. I was wrong they did care.

I am probably boring you with all this but I finally felt that I could share again and thank you for listening. And remember:

Keep coming back.
It works if you if you work it.
AND
Work it cause your worth it!!!
You people mean the world to me.

> Thanks
> Patty

1998: APRIL 15
MARILYN KAY MERCER TO THE
WILDWOOD HEALTH CARE CENTER

Marilyn Kay Mercer was among nearly sixty Medicaid recipients evicted from an Indianapolis nursing home in January of 1998, after its owner, Vencor, a large hospital and nursing-home chain, concluded that it could maximize profits by catering to wealthier patients. The move reflected the increased commercialism of patient care in the nineties. In this instance, the company ended up thinking better of its initiative, and in the wake of press reports, inviting the residents back and agreeing to pay for their costs. A sixty-two-year-old stroke victim, Mercer had relocated and wasn't planning to return. Instead, she sent this invoice. The clowns she refers to comprised a cherished collection.

TO WHOM IT MAY CONCERN;
ITEMIZED BILL FOR MOVING EXPENSES FOR MARILYN KAY MERCER

PHONE BILL	$47.00
GAS TO LOOK FOR A PLACE	$14.40
GAS TO MOVE	$43.20
LUNCH FOR FIVE PEOPLE	$20.00
TOTAL EXPENSES =	$124.60

ITEMS MOVED
2 WHEELCHAIRS
1 ELECTRIC BED
1 T.V.
378 CLOWNS
1 CLOWN CABINET
MANY BOXES OF CRAFTS
CLOTHES

YOU CANNOT PUT A PRICE ON INCONVENIENCE. YOUR DISCRIMINATION AGAINST THE MIDDLE CLASS AND THE POOR PUT OUR HEALTH AND WELFARE ON THE LINE

MARILYN KAY MERCER

*   *   *

1998: AUGUST 17

AN FBI EXAMINER TO THE FBI

Rumors of a semen-stained blue dress had accompanied the talk about Monica Lewinsky from the beginning of the case. But the question everyone was asking on late-night talk shows and at office watercoolers was who would actually stash such a dress away instead of sending it out to be cleaned. The answer was Monica Lewinsky (see letter page 668), and the dress proved to be the turning point in the Clinton sex scandal. At the end of July, Lewinsky handed it over to Kenneth Starr. On August 3, Clinton provided a blood sample. The same day this memo was written, the president admitted for the first time that he had misled the public about his relationship with the former intern.

According to the numbers at the bottom of the memo, the genetic markers matching the president's DNA were characteristic of one in 7.87 trillion Caucasians.

FEDERAL BUREAU OF INVESTIGATION

WASHINGTON, D.C. 20535

Report of Examination

Unit: DNA Analysis 1

FBI File No.: 29D—0IC-LR-35063

Date: 08/17/98

Lab No.:   980730002 S BO

980803100 S BO

Results of Examinations:

Deoxyribonucleic acid (DNA) profiles for the genetic loci D2S44, D17S79, D1S7, D4S139, D10S28, D5S110 and D7S467 were developed from HaeIII-digested high molecular weight DNA extracted from specimens K39 and Q3243-1 (a semen stain removed from specimen Q3243). Based on the results of these seven genetic loci, specimen K39 (CLINTON) is the source of the DNA obtained from specimen Q3243-1, to a reasonable degree of scientific certainty.

No DNA-RFLP examinations were conducted on specimen Q3243-2 (a semen stain removed from specimen Q3243).

BLACK—1,440,000,000,000

CAUC—7,870,000,000,000

SEH—3,140,000,000,000

SWH—943,000,000,000

1998: DECEMBER
MIGUEL REYES TO SANTA CLAUS

Using their own money to send toys, clothing, and food to the needy, New York City postal workers first began answering children's letters to Santa Claus during the Depression. That informal effort evolved into Operation Santa, which by 1998 was intercepting two hundred thousand letters bound for the North Pole, and with the help of volunteers, granting the wishes of many thousands of children. The letters, arriving in greater numbers every year and in cities nationwide, were painful reminders of the depths of deprivation amid the country's riches.

Dear Santa Claus,

My name is Miguel Reyes and I am 12 years old. I am doing good in school with most of my grades in the 90's. I attend a special High School program at Bx. High School of Science, and my grades are good in there, too. I hardly have enough time to play with the few toys I have.

Also, my father doesn't live with me and my mom lives off of Public Assistance. The money she gets is spent completely on paying the bills except for a few dollars that are saved.

I only want a <u>real</u> Christmas for a change. All that I am asking for is not that much. I just want my family to have something this Christmas that will make it a pleasurable one.

Thanking you immensely,

Miguel Reyes

P.S. I have 1 brother and 1 sister. I love them very much and would do anything to get them a Christmas gift.

Thank you.

1999: JANUARY 16
WILLIAM SUMMERS TO HENRY HYDE

Representative Henry Hyde of Illinois was the leader of the congressional effort to impeach Clinton, and, in the Senate, to remove him from office. In the course of an impassioned closing argument, Hyde read this letter, written by a Chicago third-grader. On February 12, the Senate would vote against dismissing the president. A Gallup Poll taken immediately afterward would show Clinton's job-approval rating at a robust 68 percent—higher than before the allegations involving Lewinsky had first surfaced more than a year earlier.

Dear Congressman Hyde:

My name is William Preston Summers. How are you doing? I am a third grader in room 504 at Chase Elementary School in Chicago.

I am writing this letter because I have something to tell you. I have thought of a punishment for the President of the United States of America. The punishment should be that he should write a 100-word essay by hand.

I have to write an essay when I lie. It is bad to lie because it just gets you in more trouble. I hate getting in trouble. It's just like the boy who cried "wolf" and the wolf ate the boy.

It is important to tell the truth. I like to tell the truth because it gets you in less trouble. If you do not tell the truth, people do not believe you.

It is important to believe the President because he is a important person. If you cannot believe the President, who can you believe? If you have no one to believe in, then how do you run your life?

I do not believe the President tells the truth any more right now. After he writes the essay and tells the truth, I will believe him again.

William Summers

1999: JUNE 30

"CONFUSED AND CHARMED" TO AN ON-LINE THERAPIST

As the century drew to a close, the letter-writing form had certainly been altered . . .

Dear Dr. Glass,

I met a very interesting man online a couple of weeks ago, and have talked to him on the phone several times as well. He is enchanting, charming, and everything I could possibly want. The trouble is that I'm already married and all the way across the country from Mr. Wonderful. I really think I love this new man, but what can I do?

*   *   *

. . . but even in an electronic age, the pleasure of writing letters—and the need to do so—clearly remained.

Dear Confused and Charmed:

Your "Mr. Wonderful" may be somebody else's philandering husband. Internet relationships create a romantic mystique because you can create exciting fantasies about the other person. Add a little dose of secrecy, emotional intimacy, and sexual innuendos, and you've got a full blown emotional affair. It is easy to be charming when you are not dealing with the everyday irritations of leaking roofs and noisy kids. The love which you feel for this man is based on romantic idealization, whereas your marriage is based on reality. Furthermore, stable long-term relationships are seldom as exciting as Stage 1 relationships. What does your on-line search for companionship and romance indicate about your marriage? Talk to your husband about your wants and needs and try to put some energy back into your marriage. Perhaps you and your husband could begin to Email each other as a way of reviving your communication process.

Reflectfully yours,
Dr. Shirley Glass

Sources and Permissions

Allen, Fred. Letter to Earl Wilson. 1947[?]. In *Fred Allen's Letters*, ed. Joe McCarthy, pp. 38–39. Garden City, N.Y.: Doubleday, 1965. Copyright © 1965 by Fred Allen. Reprinted by permission of the William Morris Agency on behalf of the author.

Anthony, Susan B. Letter to Elizabeth Cady Stanton. October, 1902. In *The Elizabeth Cady Stanton–Susan B. Anthony Reader: Correspondence, Writings, Speeches*, ed. Ellen Carol DuBois, pp. 298–99. Boston: Northeastern University Press, 1992.

Antiabortion activist. Letter to the *Pensacola Journal*. December 27, 1984. In *Abortion: A Reader*, ed. Lloyd Steffen, pp. 447–48. Cleveland, Ohio: Pilgrim Press, 1996. Reprinted by permission of the *Pensacola News Journal*.

Army doctor. Letter to a colleague. September 29, 1918. In "A Letter from Camp Devens, Massachusetts," Influenza 1918, *The American Experience*. On-line at http:newshour.com/wgbh/pages/amex/influenza/sfeature/devens.html. February 2, 1999.

Atwater, Lee. Memo to the Reagan campaign. October, 1984. In Peter Goldman and Tony Fuller, *The Quest for the Presidency 1984*, pp. 434–38. New York: Bantam Books, 1985.

Bagby, Kenneth. Letter to his parents. November 17, 1965. In *Letters from Vietnam*, ed. Bill Adler, pp. 28–30. New York: Dutton, 1967.

Baker, Greg. Letter to Kent State student body president. May 8, 1970. In "Letter, Associated Students, Western Washington," Lynda Lyke Papers—Folder 5, May 4 Collection, Kent State University. On-line at http://www.library.kent.edu/exhibts/4may95/lyke/lasw.html. April 21, 1999.

Baker, James, III. Letter to Mikhail Gorbachev. December 29, 1991. Printed by permission of James A. Baker III.

Baldwin, James. Letter to his nephew. 1962. In James Baldwin, *The Fire Next Time*, pp. 17–24. New York: Dial Press, 1963. This letter originally appeared in *The Progressive* as "My Dungeon Shook," © 1962 by James Baldwin. Copyright renewed. Reprinted by permission of the James Baldwin estate.

Bando, J. F. Letter to Franklin Roosevelt. March 13, 1933. In item ND4, file unit 200B, National Archives. On-line at http://monitor.nara.gov:80/cgi-bin/starfinder/26904/standard. text. April 14, 1999.

Barrow, Clyde. Letter to Henry Ford. April 10, 1934. In Ford Industrial Archives, Dearborn, Mich.

Bernard, Jessie. Letter to her unborn child. May 4, 1941. In *Self-Portrait of a Family: Letters by Jessie, Dorothy Lee, Claude, and David Bernard*. Boston: Beacon Press, 1978. Copyright © 1978 by Jessie Bernard. Reprinted by permission of the publisher.

Bierly, Ken. Memo to Raymond Bell. July 21, 1953. In Victor S. Navasky, *Naming Names*, pp. 93–94. New York: Viking, 1980.

"Bintel Brief" editor. Letter to "The Newborn." 1906. In *A Bintel Brief: Sixty Years of Letters from the Lower East Side to the* Jewish Daily Forward, ed. Isaac Metzker, pp. 54–55. 1971. Reprint, New York: Schocken Books, 1991.

Bishop, Nan. Letter to Clare Bowman. March 5, 1977. In Nan Bishop, Sarah Hamilton, and Clare Bowman, *Nan, Sarah & Clare: Letters Between Friends*, pp. 65–67. New York: Avon, 1980. Reprinted by permission of Nan Bishop.

Bork, Robert. Letter to Archibald Cox. October 20, 1973. In *Historic Documents*, pp. 877–78. Washington, D.C.: Congressional Quarterly, 1973.

Borowsky, Zipporah. Letter to her family. November 29, 1948. In Zipporah Porath, *Letters from Jerusalem: 1947–1948*, pp. 227–29. Jerusalem: Association of Americans and Canadians in Israel, 1987. Reprinted by permission of Zipporah Porath.

Brainerd, John. Letter to Harold Pender. April 26, 1943. In the Herman H. Goldstine Collection, Hampshire College Archives, Amherst, Mass.

Breen, Joseph. Memo to Jack Warner. May 21, 1942. In Casablanca Story File, Warner Bros. Archives, Production Code Administration files, Margaret Herrick Library, Academy of Motion Picture Arts and Sciences, Beverly Hills, Calif.

Breen, William. Letter to his wife. May 18, 1927. In records relating to seized vessels, 1926–35, file for *Carrie L. Hirtle*, entry 291, Records of the United States Coast Guard, Record Group 26; National Archives, Washington, D.C.

Brewster, O. C. Letter to Harry Truman. May 24, 1945. In Vertical File, Atomic Energy–Ethical Aspects (Yale University Material), Harry S Truman Library, Independence, Mo.

Briggs, Dr. L. Vernon. Letter to Dr. Owen Copp. December 22, 1910. In L. Vernon Briggs, *Occupation as a Substitute for Restraint in the Treatment of the Mentally Ill: A History of the Passage of Two Bills Through the Massachusetts Legislature*, pp. 59–60. Boston: Wright and Potter, 1923.

Brooklyn worker. Letter to Frances Perkins. March 29, 1935. In Records of Secretaries, Records of the Department of Labor, Record Group 174; National Archives, Washington, D.C.

Brown, Bertrand. Letter to Charles Dillingham. December 3, 1919. In Charles B. Dillingham Papers, Manuscripts and Archives Division, New York Public Library.

Brown, David. Telegram to Darryl Zanuck. June 24, 1966. In David Brown, *Let Me Entertain You,* pp. 92–93. New York: Morrow, 1990. Reprinted by permission of David Brown.

Brown, Grace. Letter to Chester Gillette. July 5, 1906. In Craig Brandon, *Murder in the Adirondacks: 'An American Tragedy' Revisited,* pp. 108–109. Utica, N.Y.: North Country Books, 1986.

Brudno, Alan. Letter to his wife. November 30, 1972. In *Dear America: Letters Home from Vietnam,* ed. Bernard Edelman for the New York Vietnam Veterans Memorial Commission, p. 268. 1985. Reprint, New York: Pocket Books, 1988. Letter reprinted by permission of Deborah C. Brudno.

Bush, George. Letter to his children. December 31, 1990. Printed by permission of President George Bush.

Butler, Morris. Letter to the *New York Times.* March 26, 1911. In Gus Tyler, *Look for the Union Label: A History of the International Ladies' Garment Workers' Union,* p. 92. Armonk, N.Y.: M. E. Sharpe, 1995.

Butler, Smedley. Letter to his parents. October 5, 1918. In Smedley Butler, *The Letters of a Leatherneck, 1898–1931,* ed. Anne Cipriano Venzon, pp. 205–208. New York: Praeger, 1992. Reprinted by permission of the estate of Smedley D. Butler.

Butt, Archibald. Letter to his sister. February, 1909. In *The Letters of Archie Butt,* ed. Lawrence F. Abbott, pp. 332–33. Garden City, N.Y.: Doubleday, Page and Company, 1924.

Butters, Harry. Letter to his parents. September, 1915. In *"The Good Soldier": A Selection of Soldiers' Letters, 1914–1918,* ed. N. P. Dawson, pp. 84–86. New York: Macmillan, 1918.

Cabot, Elizabeth. Letter to her husband. October 16, 1901. In *Letters of Elizabeth Cabot, Vol. II,* pp. 345–46. Boston: Rockwell and Churchill Press, privately printed, 1905.

Calkins, Earnest Elmo. Letter to the *New York Times.* October 29, 1929. In "Was Loss Paper or Real? One Feels that Results of Market Break Have Been Overstated." *New York Times,* vol. 79, no. 26,213, October 31, 1929, p. 24.

Capote, Truman. Invitation to 480 friends. October, 1966. In "A Night to Remember." *Vanity Fair,* July, 1996, p. 122.

Captain of *The Howorth.* Letter to Mrs. Orville Raines. April 7, 1945. In *Good Night Officially: The Pacific War Letters of a Destroyer Sailor, The Letters of Yeoman James Orvill Raines,* ed. William M. McBride, p. 278. Boulder, Colo.: Westview Press, 1994. Copyright © 1994 by Westview Press. Reprinted by permission of the publisher.

Carnegie, Andrew. Note to Henry Phipps, Jr. March 10[?], 1901. In Burton J. Hendrick, *The Life of Andrew Carnegie: Volume II,* p. 140. Garden City, N.Y.: Doubleday, Doran and Company, 1932.

————. Letter to J. S. Billings. March 12, 1901. Printed by permission of the Carnegie Corporation of New York.

Carpenter, Marion. Letter to his son. May, 1962. In *Letters of a Nation: A Collection of Extraordinary American Letters*, ed. Andrew Carroll, pp. 46–47. New York: Kodansha International, 1997. Reprinted by permission of Howard Benedict, Astronaut Scholarship Foundation.

Carson, Rachel. Letter to Dorothy Freeman. February 1, 1958. In *Always, Rachel: The Letters of Rachel Carson and Dorothy Freeman, 1952–1964*, ed. Martha Freeman, pp. 248–49. Boston: Beacon Press, 1995. Carson letters copyright © 1995 by Roger Allen Christie. Freeman letters, other text, and compilation copyright © 1995 by Martha Freeman. Reprinted by permission of the publisher and by Frances Collin, trustee.

Carter, Jimmy. Letter to the cosmos. June 16, 1977. In *Letters in American History: Words to Remember, 1770 to the Present*, ed. H. Jack Lang, p. 88. New York: Harmony Books, 1982.

————. Letter to Congress. April 26, 1980. In Primal Scream, the Library of Criminal Justice. On-line at http://www.ieway.com/~csukbr/juslib1/iran2.html. August 16, 1998.

Carter, Mae Bertha. Letter to Representatives of the American Friends Service Committee. October, 1965. In Constance Curry, *Silver Rights*, pp. 134–35. Chapel Hill, N.C.: Algonquin Books of Chapel Hill, 1995. Copyright © 1995 by Constance Curry. Reprinted by permission of Algonquin Books of Chapel Hill, a division of Workman Publishing.

Carver, George Washington. Letter to a student. January 9, 1922. In *George Washington Carver in His Own Words*, ed. Gary R. Kremer, p. 85. Columbia, Mo.: University of Missouri Press, 1987. From the Tuskegee University Archives, reel 6, frame 1000 of the George Washington Carver Papers. Reprinted by permission of Tuskegee University.

Chapin, Dwight. Memo to H. R. Haldeman. December 21, 1970. In "When Nixon Met Elvis," The Exhibit Hall, National Archives and Records Administration. On-line at http://www.nara.gov/exhall/nixonelvis/chapin.jpg. June 25, 1998.

Chaplin, Charlie. Letter to his brother. August, 1913. In David Robinson, *Chaplin: His Life and Art,* pp. 97–98. New York: McGraw-Hill, 1985. Copyright © 1999 by Roy Export Company Establishment. All rights reserved.

Chase, Myrna [Anna Hunt Davis]. Letter to a medical secretary. 1951. In Anna Hunt Davis, *Letters to a Doctor's Secretary,* pp. 3–6. Rutherford, N.J.: Medical Economics, 1952.

Chavez, Cesar. Letter to E. L. Barr. April 4, 1969. In "Manifesto from a Friend: Letter from Delano," *Christian Century,* vol. 86, no. 17, April 23, 1969, pp. 539–40. Reprinted by permission of the Cesar E. Chavez Foundation.

Cher. Letter to Chuck. 1986. In Laura Palmer, *Shrapnel in the Heart: Letters and Remembrances from the Vietnam Veterans Memorial,* p. 50. New York: Random House, 1987.

Clarke, Patsy. Letter to Jesse Helms. June 5, 1995. In "Dear Jesse," Letters Magazine. On-line at http://www.signature.pair.com/letters/October96/Jesse.html. September 12, 1998. Reprinted by permission of Patsy M. Clarke.

Clarke Sales Company manager. Letter to James M. Joyce. October 14, 1908. In corporate records of Talon, Inc., Crawford County Historical Society, Meadville, Pa. Printed by permission of the Society.

Clinton, Bill. Letter to Eugene Holmes. December 3, 1969. In "A Letter by Clinton on His Draft Deferment: 'A War I Opposed and Despised' " *New York Times,* vol. 141, no. 48,875, February 13, 1992, p. A25.

Cohen, Gus. Letter to his girlfriend. April 18, 1912. In the Titanic Historical Society, Indian Orchard, Mass. Printed by permission of Edward S. Kamuda for the Society.

Coke Customer #1. Letter to Coca-Cola. April, 1985. In Thomas Oliver, *The Real Coke, the Real Story,* p. 155. New York: Random House, 1986.

Coke Customer #2. Letter to Coca-Cola. April, 1985. In Mark Pendergrast, *For God, Country, and Coca-Cola: The Unauthorized History of the Great American Soft Drink and the Company That Makes It,* p. 363. New York: Scribner's, 1993.

Collins, Frederick. Letter to his family. April 24, 1906. In "Eyewitness Account of Frederick H. Collins," Eyewitness Accounts, The Great 1906 Earthquake and Fire, Museum of the City of San Francisco. On-line at http://www.sfmuseum.org/1906/ew11.html. April 12, 1999. Reprinted by permission of Frederick Collins's grandnephews, David Hill and Donald Hill.

Collins, Joseph. Letter to a patient. April 23, 1908. In Joseph Collins, *Letters to a Neurologist to Which Are Appended Brief Replies Purporting to Set Forth Concisely the Nature of the Ailments Therein Described, with Remarks on Their Appropriate Treatment,* pp. 99–103. New York: William Wood, 1908.

Colson, Charles. Memo to Ken Cole. January 2, 1970. In *From the President: Richard Nixon's Secret Files,* ed. Bruce Oudes, p. 85. New York: Harper and Row, 1989.

Comiskey, Charles. Telegram to Swede Risberg, Fred McMullin, Joe Jackson, Ed Cicotte, Happy Felsch, Buck Weaver, Chick Gandil, and Lefty Williams. September 28, 1920. In Eliot Asinof, *Eight Men Out: The Black Sox and the 1919 World Series,* p. 179. Evanston, Ill.: Holtzman Press, 1963.

CompuServe. Three e-mails to Robert Riche. March 31, April 3, April 4, 1996. In Robert Riche, "How an Internet Wannabe Became an I-Really-Don't-Wannabe," *New York Times,* vol. 146, no. 50,586, October 20, 1996, Section 4, p. 7. Reprinted by permission of Robert Riche.

"Confused and Charmed." Letter to an on-line therapist. June 1999. In Online Love, Online Relationships, Dr. Shirley Glass@keyword:electra. Printed by permission of Oxygen Media.

Conklin, Lisa. Letter to the Tooth Fairy. October, 1987. In *Letters to the Tooth Fairy.* Wichita: The Wichita, Kansas, District Dental Society, 1987. Reprinted by permission of Lisa Conklin.

Corey, Elizabeth. Letter to her mother. December 8, 1909. In Elizabeth Corey, *Bachelor Bess: The Homesteading Letters of Elizabeth Corey, 1909–1919,* ed. Philip L. Gerber, pp. 55–58. Iowa City: University of Iowa Press, 1990. Copyright © 1990 by University of Iowa Press. Reprinted by permission of the publisher.

Cornum, Rhonda. Letter to her mother. February 22, 1991. In Rhonda Cornum as told to Peter Copeland, *She Went to War: The Rhonda Cornum Story,* pp. 133–34. Novato, Calif.: Presidio Press, 1992. Reprinted by permission of the publisher.

Cosner, Marva. Letter to Ronald Reagan. Winter, 1983. In Ronald Reagan, *An American Life,* p. 460. New York: Simon & Schuster, 1990. Copyright © 1990 by Ronald W. Reagan. Reprinted by permission of the publisher.

Cowley, Samuel. Memo to J. Edgar Hoover. July 24, 1934. In "John Dillinger," Gangster Era, Federal Bureau of Investigation Freedom of Information Act Electronic Reading Room. On-line at http://www.fbi.gov/foipa/dillnger.htm. August 9, 1998.

Crayton, H. W. Letter to the parents of Raymond Hoback. July 9, 1944. In *Lines of Battle: Letters from American Servicemen 1941–1945*, ed. Annette Tapert, pp. 165–66. New York: Times Books, 1987. Reprinted by permission of Lucille H. Boggess.

Cullen, Michael. Letter to the president of Kroger. 1930. In Richard S. Tedlow, *New and Improved: The Story of Mass Marketing in America,* pp. 381–84. New York: Basic Books, 1990. Reprinted by permission of the King Kullen Grocery Company.

D'Amato, Alfonse, et al. Letter to Hugh Southern. May 18, 1989. In *The Congressional Record,* Senate, May 18, 1989, pp. 5594–95. On-line at http://thomas.loc.gov./home/r101query. html. August, 1998.

Darrow, Clarence. Letter to the *Chicago Tribune.* July, 1923. In "Darrow Asks W. J. Bryan to Answer These," *Chicago Daily Tribune,* vol. 82, no. 159, July 4, 1923, p. 1.

Daugherty, Harry. Letter to George Wharton Pepper. February 21, 1924. In Harry M. Daugherty, *The Inside Story of the Harding Tragedy,* pp. 284–86. New York: Churchill, 1932.

Davis, Rennie. Letter to potential recruits. April 30, 1968. In U.S. House Committee on Un-American Activities, *Subversive Involvement in Disruption of 1968 Democratic Party National Convention, Part 2: Hearings Before the Committee on Un-American Activities,* 90th Cong., 2nd sess., pp. 2667–68. December 2 and 3, 1968.

Day, Jesse. Application to Oregon's secretary of state. August 1, 1916. In "The Prohibition Years: Bootleggers and Imagination," Oregon State Archives. On-line at http://arcweb.sos. or.gov/50th/prohibition1/nothing.jpg. April 13, 1999.

De Kooning, Elaine. Letter to William Theo Brown. 1952. In William Theo Brown Papers, Reel, 1095; Archives of American Art, Smithsonian Institution, Washington, D.C. Printed by permission of the estate of Elaine De Kooning.

Detroit Club. Invitation to members. April, 1917. In Philip P. Mason, *Rumrunning and the Roaring Twenties: Prohibition on the Michigan-Ontario Waterway,* p. 32. Detroit: Wayne State University Press, 1995.

Diamond, Fred. Letter to his parents. April 13, 1945. In the U.S. Holocaust Museum, Washington, D.C. Printed by permission of Fred Diamond and courtesy of the Museum.

Dickens, Marion. Letter to the Federal Writers' Project. July 6, 1936. In Textual Records, Negro studies, Records of the Federal Writers' Project, Records of the Work Projects Administration, Record Group 69; National Archives, Washington, D.C.

Donath, Thérèse. Letter to Virginia Greene. June 11, 1984. In Thérèse Donath and Virginia Greene, *Before I Die: A Creative Legacy,* pp. 63–68. Buffalo, N.Y.: Prometheus Books, 1989. From *Before I Die,* Copyright © 1989. Reprinted by permission of the publisher.

Donna. Letter to John Lennon and George Harrison. 1964. In Derek Taylor, *Fifty Years Adrift,* ed. George Harrison, p. 204. Guildford, Surrey, England: Genesis Publications Limited in association with Hedley New Zealand and Hedley Australia, 1984.

Draper, George. Letter to Franklin Roosevelt. August 29, 1934. In Franklin D. Roosevelt Library, Hyde Park, N.Y.

Dreier, Mary. Letter to Victor Berger. March 1, 1912. In William Cahn, *Lawrence, 1912: The Bread and Roses Strike,* p. 23. New York: Pilgrim Press, 1980.

Dreiser, Theodore. Letter to Yvette Szekely. April 3, 1930. In Yvette Szekely Eastman, *Dearest Wilding: A Memoir, with Love Letters from Theodore Dreiser,* pp. 120–21. Philadelphia: University of Pennsylvania Press, 1995. Reprinted by permission of the Department of Special Collections, University of Pennsylvania Library.

Drexel Burnham Lambert. Memo to Ivan Boesky. March 21, 1986. In James Stewart, *Den of Thieves,* following p. 62. New York: Simon & Schuster, 1991.

Du Bois, W.E.B. Letter to Vernealia Fareira. January 7, 1905. In *A Documentary History of the Negro People in the United States, Volume 2: From the Reconstruction to the Founding of the N.A.A.C.P.,* ed. Herbert Aptheker, p. 864. New York: Carol Publishing Group, Citadel Press, 1992.

———. Letter to Woodrow Wilson. October 10, 1916. In *The Correspondence of W.E.B. Du Bois,* vol. 1, *Selections, 1877–1934,* ed. Herbert Aptheker, pp. 217–18. Amherst: University of Massachusetts Press, 1973. Copyright © 1973 by the University of Massachusetts Press. Reprinted by permission of the publisher.

Dusty. Letter to a friend. 1965[?]. In *Letters from Viet Nam,* ed. Glenn Munson, pp. 126–27. New York: Parallax Publishing, 1966.

Earhart, Amelia. Letter to George Palmer Putnam. February 7, 1931. In *Letters From Amelia: 1901–1937,* ed. Jean L. Backus, pp. 104–105. Boston: Beacon Press, 1982. Copyright © 1982 by Jean L. Backus. Reprinted by permission of the publisher.

Edison, Thomas. Letter to William Feather. September 16, 1919. In *Letters in American History: Words to Remember, 1770 to the Present,* ed. H. Jack Lang, pp. 81–82. New York: Harmony Books, 1982.

Einstein, Albert. Letter to Franklin Roosevelt. August 2, 1939. In *The Faber Book of Letters,* ed. Felix Pryor, pp. 282–84. London: Faber and Faber, 1988.

Eisenhower, Dwight. Letter to Mamie Eisenhower. October 30, 1942. In Dwight D. Eisenhower, *Letters to Mamie,* ed. John S. D. Eisenhower, pp. 50–52. Garden City, N.Y.: Doubleday, 1978. Reprinted by permission of John S. D. Eisenhower.

———. Letter to Clyde Miller. June 10, 1953. In item LTRCM, file unit D52JU53(2), series DDEDIARY, collection EPRES, Dwight D. Eisenhower Library, Abilene, Kans.

————. Letter to Ngo Dinh Diem. October 23, 1954. In "U.S. Aid to Viet-Nam," *State Department Bulletin,* vol. 31, no. 803, pub. 5667, November 15, 1954, pp. 735–36.

————. Telegram to Governor Orval Faubus. September 5, 1957. In *The Eisenhower Administration, 1953–1961: A Documentary History,* ed. Robert L. Branyan and Lawrence H. Larsen, pp. 1122–23. New York: Random House, 1971.

Eisenhower, Julie Nixon. Note to Richard Nixon. August 6?, 1974. In Stephen E. Ambrose, *Nixon,* vol. 3, *Ruin and Recovery, 1973–1990,* pp. 420–21. New York: Simon & Schuster, 1991. Reprinted by permission of Julie Nixon Eisenhower.

Elder, O. J. Letter to Columbus Pittman. January 14, 1909. In Arthur J. Cramp, M.D., *Nostrums and Quackery: Articles on the Nostrum Evil, Quackery and Allied Matters Affecting the Public Health; Reprinted, With or Without Modifications, from The Journal of the American Medical Association, Volume II,* p. 693. Chicago: Press of American Medical Association, 1921.

Ellen viewer. Letter to her mother. May, 1997. In "The whole thing seems SO ridiculous," Letters Magazine. On-line at http://www.signature.pair.com/letters/julyaug97/mom2.html. September 12, 1998.

Enrico, Roger. Letter to bottlers. August 21, 1985. In *The New York Times,* vol. 84, no. 46,388, April 23, 1985, p. D7. Reprinted by permission of Pepsico.

Eringa, Ulbe. Letter to his sister and brother-in-law. November 10, 1904. In Brian W. Beltman, *Dutch Farmer in the Missouri Valley: The Life and Letters of Ulbe Eringa, 1866–1950,* pp. 113–14. Urbana: University of Illinois Press, 1996. Copyright © 1996 by the Board of Trustees of the University of Illinois. Reprinted by permission of Brian W. Beltman and the University of Illinois Press.

Expectant mother. Letter to Eleanor Roosevelt. January 2, 1935. In Robert S. McElvaine, *Down & Out in the Great Depression: Letters from the Forgotten Man,* pp. 62–63. Chapel Hill: University of North Carolina Press, 1983. Copyright © 1983 by University of North Carolina Press. Reprinted by permission of the publisher.

Faithfull, Starr. Letter to a former boyfriend. June 4, 1931. In Jonathan Goodman, *Postmortem: The Correspondence of Murder,* pp. 129–30. New York: St. Martin's Press, 1972.

Falen, Gus. Letter to Eddie Hoffman. September 6, 1942. In *Letters Home,* ed. Mina Curtiss, pp. 10–11. Boston: Little, Brown and Company, 1944. Reprinted by permission of the Falen family.

Falwell, Jerry. Letter to Americans. August 13, 1981. In Perry Deane Young, *God's Bullies: Native Reflections on Preachers and Politics,* p. 307. New York: Holt, Rinehart and Winston, 1982.

Faubus, Orval. Telegram to Dwight Eisenhower. September 4, 1957. In *The Eisenhower Administration, 1953–1961: A Documentary History,* ed. Robert L. Branyan and Lawrence H. Larsen, pp. 1120–22. New York: Random House, 1971.

Faulkner, William. Letter to his mother. January, 1925. In *Thinking of Home: William Faulkner's Letters to His Mother and Father, 1918–1925,* ed. James G. Watson, pp. 178–79. New York: Norton, 1992. Reprinted by permission of the publisher.

———. Letter to Malcolm Franklin. July 4, 1943. In *Selected Letters of William Faulkner*, ed. Joseph Blotner, pp. 175–76. New York: Random House, 1977. Copyright © 1977 by Jill Faulkner Summers. Reprinted by permission of Random House.

FBI [anonymously]. Letter to Martin Luther King, Jr. November 20, 1964. In David J. Garrow, *The FBI and Martin Luther King, Jr.: From "Solo" to Memphis*, pp. 125–26. New York: Norton, 1981.

FBI examiner. Memo to the FBI. August 17, 1998. In *The Starr Report: The Evidence*, ed. Phil Kuntz, p. 592. New York: Pocket Books, 1998.

FBI Dallas. Memo to J. Edgar Hoover. July 8, 1947. In "Unusual Phenomena," Federal Bureau of Investigation Freedom of Information Act Electronic Reading Room. On-line at http://www.fbi.gov/foipa/unusual.htm. August 9, 1998.

FC [Ted Kaczynski]. Letter to the *New York Times*. April 20, 1995. In "Excerpts from Letter by 'Terrorist Group' FC, Which Says It Sent Bombs," *New York Times*, vol. 144, no. 50,043, April 26, 1995, p. A16.

Fifield, Arthur. Letter to Gertrude Stein. April 19, 1912. In *The Flowers of Friendship: Letters Written to Gertrude Stein*, ed. Donald Gallup, p. 58. New York: Knopf, 1953. Reprinted by permission of the Yale Collection of American Literature, Beinecke Rare Book and Manuscript Library, Yale University.

Fisher, Irving. Letter to his wife. January 2, 1904. In Irving Norton Fisher, *My Father, Irving Fisher*, pp. 87–88. New York: Comet Press Books, 1956. Reprinted by permission of George W. Fisher.

Fisher, Irving Norton. Letter to his father. November 14, 1929. In Irving Fisher Papers, Manuscripts and Archives, Yale University Library, New Haven, Conn. Printed by permission of George W. Fisher.

Fisher, Mary. Letter to her sons. May, 1992. In Mary Fisher, *Sleep with the Angels: A Mother Challenges AIDS*, pp. 20–23. Wakefield, R.I.: Moyer Bell, 1994. Reprinted by permission of the Family AIDS Network.

Fitzgerald, F. Scott. Letter to Zelda Fitzgerald. Summer, 1930. In *F. Scott Fitzgerald: A Life in Letters*, ed. Matthew J. Bruccoli, p. 198. New York: Scribner's, 1994. Reprinted by permission of Scribner, a division of Simon & Schuster; copyright © 1994 by the trustees under agreement dated July 3, 1975, created by Frances Scott Fitzgerald Smith; and by permission of Harold Ober Associates Incorporated; copyright © 1980 by Frances Scott Fitzgerald Smith.

Flood, Curt. Letter to Bowie Kuhn. December 24, 1969. In Marvin Miller, *A Whole Different Ball Game: The Sport and Business of Baseball*, pp. 190–91. Secaucus, N.J.: Carol Publishing Group, 1991. Reprinted by permission of Marvin J. Miller.

Ford Motor Company. Two letters to Marianne Moore. October 19, 1955, and November 8, 1956. In Marianne Moore and David Wallace, *Letters from and to the Ford Motor Company*, unpag. New York: Pierpont Morgan Library, 1958. Reprinted by permission of the Library.

Former flapper. Letter to Nancy Brown. September 6, 1923. In *Dear Nancy: The Pattern of American Life Revealed in Letters*, ed. Annie Louise Brown Leslie, pp. 20–22. Chicago: The Detroit News, 1933.

Foster, Vincent. Suicide note. July 1993. In "Inside Beltway, 'Ruining People Is Considered Sport,'" *Salt Lake Tribune*, August 11, 1993, Nation–World, p. A3.

Fox, Francis. Letter to Brian Epstein. August 17, 1964. In Derek Taylor, *Fifty Years Adrift,* ed. George Harrison, pp. 196–97. Guildford, Surrey, England: Genesis Publications Limited in association with Hedley New Zealand and Hedley Australia, 1984.

Foxworth, P. E. Memo to J. Edgar Hoover. May 6, 1937. In "The Hindenburg Disaster," Gangster Era, Federal Bureau of Investigation Freedom of Information Act Electronic Reading Room. On-line at http://www.fbi.gov/foipa/hindburg.htm. August 9, 1998.

Frank, Leo. Letter to Adolph Ochs. November 20, 1914. In Richard F. Shepard, *The Paper's Papers: A Reporter's Journey Through the Archives of the "New York Times,"* pp. 198–99. New York: Random House, 1996. Reprinted by permission of Catherine J. Smithline on behalf of the family of Leo M. Frank.

Franklin, W. Letter to the Keeley Institute. December 3, 1913. In Peter H. Odegard, *Pressure Politics: The Story of the Anti-Saloon League,* p. 57. New York: Columbia University Press, 1928.

Frost, Robert. Letter to Susan Hayes Ward. February 10, 1912. In Robert Frost, *Selected Letters,* ed. Lawrance Thompson, pp. 45–46. New York: Holt, Rinehart and Winston, 1964. Copyright © 1964 by Lawrance Thompson, 1992 by Janet A. Thompson, Copyright © 1964 by Holt, Rinehart and Winston, Inc. Reprinted by permission of Henry Holt and Co., the estate of Robert Frost, and Jonathan Cape, Random House, UK.

Gates, Bill. Letter to computer hobbyists. February, 1973. In "An Open Letter to Hobbyists," *Computer Notes,* February 3, 1976, p. 4. Reprinted by permission of Microsoft.

Gates, Percival. Letter to his father. November 4, 1918. In *An American Pilot in the Skies of France: The Diaries and Letters of Lt. Percival T. Gates, 1917–1918*, ed. David K. Vaughan, p. 171. Dayton, Ohio: Wright State University Press, 1992. Reprinted by permission of the Owls Head Transportation Museum, Owls Head, Me.

Gilberg, Leonard. Letter to Laurie Pritchett. July 23, 1961. In *The Eyes on the Prize Civil Rights Reader: Documents, Speeches, and Firsthand Accounts from the Black Freedom Struggle, 1954–1990*, ed. Clayborne Carson et al., p. 146. New York: Viking, 1991.

Giles, Henry. Letter to Janice Holt. February 12, 1945. In *Hello, Janice: The Wartime Letters of Henry Giles,* ed. Dianne Watkins, pp. 166–67. Lexington: University Press of Kentucky, 1992. Reprinted by permission of the Department of Special Collections, Library of Western Kentucky University.

Gilmore, Gary. Letter to "Those Who Oppose." December 29, 1976. In "Gilmore Issues an Open Letter," *Provo Herald,* Provo, Utah. Wednesday, December 29, 1976, p. 2.

Glass, Dr. Shirley. Letter to "Confused and Charmed." June 1999. In Online Love, Online Relationships, Dr. Shirley Glass@keyword:electra. Printed by permission of Oxygen Media.

Gobitas, Billy. Letter to the Minersville School District Board. November 5, 1935. In Library of Congress, *American Treasures in the Library of Congress: Memory, Reason, Imagination,* p. 81. New York: H. N. Abrams, in association with the Library of Congress, 1997. Reprinted by permission of Lillian Gobitas Klose.

Gold, Mary. Letter to her sister. May 8, 1929. In *Holding On: A Woman and Farm, Shenandoah Valley, 1920's–1930's—Letters of Mary Gold,* ed. Mary N. Woodrich, pp. 62–65. Chagrin Falls, Ohio: Treehouse Press, c. 1985. Reprinted by permission of Mary N. Woodrich.

Gonzalez, Lety Martinez. Letter to Argelia Gonzalez Morales. June 4, 1990. In *Between the Lines: Letters Between Undocumented Mexican and Central American Immigrants and Their Families and Friends,* ed. and trans., Larry Siems, pp. 3–7. Hopewell, N.J.: Ecco Press, 1992. Copyright © 1992 by Larry Siems. Reprinted by permission of the publisher.

Gordon, Ruth. Letter to her parents. December 22, 1915. In *Theatrical Letters: 400 Years of Correspondence Between Celebrated Actors, Actresses, Playwrights, Their Families, Friends, Lovers, Admirers, Enemies, Producers, Managers and Others,* ed. Bill Homewood, pp. 187–88. London: Marginalia Press, 1995. From *My Side* by Ruth Gordon, copyright © by the TFT Corporation 1976. Reprinted by permission of the Corporation.

Gorrell, Carla. Letter to Shellie Bowers. August 5, 1991. Printed by permission of Carla Gorrell.

Graham, Billy. Telegram to Harry Truman. June 25, 1950. In Billy Graham, *Just As I Am: The Autobiography of Billy Graham,* p. xvii. San Francisco: HarperSanFrancisco, Zondervan, 1997. Copyright © 1997 by Billy Graham Evangelistic Association. Reprinted by permission of HarperCollins Publishers.

Graham, Katharine. Letter to John Ehrlichman. November 3, 1972. Printed by permission of Katharine Graham.

Grunwald, Mandy and Frank Greer. Memo to the Clinton campaign. April 27, 1992. In Peter Goldman et al., *Quest for the Presidency 1992,* pp. 665–66. College Station: Texas A&M University Press, 1994. Reprinted by permission of Mandy Grunwald.

Grzegorcky, Johnny. Letter to Barbara Clegg. October 29, 1950. In "A Letter from the Front," 5th Cavalry Regiment, Korean War Project. On-line at http://www.koreanwar.org/html/units/family/clegg/htm. April 19, 1999. Reprinted by permission of Ted Barker, the Korean War Project, Dallas, Tex.

Hadden, Briton. Letter to his mother. February 7, 1922. In the Time, Inc. Archives, New York. Printed by permission of Crowell Hadden.

Haldeman, H. R. Memo to Alexander Butterfield. February 9, 1971. In *From the President: Richard Nixon's Secret Files,* ed. Bruce Oudes, p. 215. New York: Harper and Row, 1989.

Hall, E. G. Letter to the *New York Times*. June 30, 1947. In *Talking Back to The New York Times: Letters to the Editor, 1851–1971*, ed. Kalman Seigel, p. 186. New York: Quadrangle Books, 1972. Copyright © 1972 by Kalman Seigel. Reprinted by permission of Quadrangle Books, published by Times Books, a division of Random House.

Hall, Prescott. Letter to whom it may concern. March 21, 1910. In Box 1, Correspondence, US 10583.9.8–US 10587.43, Houghton Library, Harvard University, Cambridge, Mass.

Harris, Joel Chandler. Letter to his son. April 5, 1900. In *Dearest Chums and Partners: Joel Chandler Harris's Letters to His Children, A Domestic Biography*, ed. Hugh T. Keenan, pp. 350–52. Athens: University of Georgia Press, 1993.

Hauptmann, Bruno. Ransom note to Charles Lindbergh. March 4, 1932. In Jim Fisher, *The Lindbergh Case*, pp. 32–33. New Brunswick, N.J.: Rutgers University Press, 1987.

Haywood, William. Letter to John Reed. September 1, 1918. In John Reed Collection, BMS Am 1091 (482). Houghton Library, Harvard University, Cambridge, Mass.

Hearst, William Randolph. Letter to Herbert Hoover. November 14, 1929. In "Hearst Asks Hoover to Reassure Public: In Open Letter, He Also Calls for Stimulating 'Legitimate' Federal Reserve Activities," *New York Times*, vol. 79, no. 26,228, November 15, 1929, p. 3.

———. Memo to editors. 1933. In *Selections from the Writings and Speeches of William Randolph Hearst*, pp. 329–32. San Francisco: privately printed, 1948.

Hefner, Hugh. Letter to newsstand wholesalers. June 13, 1953. In Russell Miller, *Bunny: The Real Story of Playboy*, p. 39. London: Michael Joseph, 1984. Reprinted by permission of *Playboy* magazine. Copyright © 1953, 1998 by Playboy. All rights reserved.

Heller, Claudia. Letter to *Ms.* June, 1973. In *Letters to Ms.: 1972–1987*, ed. Mary Thom, p. 27. New York: Henry Holt, 1987. Reprinted by permission of the Ms. Foundation for Education and Communication.

Hellman, Lillian. Letter to John Wood. May 19, 1952. In Lillian Hellman, *Scoundrel Time*, pp. 92–94. Boston: Little, Brown and Company, 1976.

Helms, Jesse. Letter to Patsy Clarke. June 19, 1995. In "Dear Jesse," Letters Magazine. On-line at http://www.signature.pair.com/letters/October96/Jesse.html. September 12, 1998.

Hemingway, Ernest. Letter to F. Scott Fitzgerald. July 1, 1925. In Matthew J. Bruccoli, *Fitzgerald and Hemingway: A Dangerous Friendship*, pp. 28–29. New York: Carroll & Graf Publishers, 1994. Copyright © 1999 by the Ernest Hemingway Foundation and © Hemingway Foreign Rights Trust. Reprinted by permission.

Henderson, Caroline. Letter to Evelyn. June 30, 1935. In "Letters from the Dust Bowl," *The Atlantic Monthly*, vol. 157, May, 1936, pp. 540–43.

Hendon, Robert. Memo to Clyde Tolson. June 30, 1942. In *From the Secret Files of J. Edgar Hoover*, ed. Athan G. Theoharis, pp. 349–50. Chicago: Ivan R. Dee, 1991.

Herrick, Howard. Telegram to J. J. McAuliff. May 11, 1918. In File 10A-A1, Records of the Committee on Public Information, Record Group 63; National Archives, Washington, D.C.

Hinckley, John, Jr. Letter to Jodie Foster. March 30, 1981. In Jack Hinckley and Jo Ann Hinckley, with Elizabeth Sherrill, *Breaking Points*, pp. 168–69. Grand Rapids, Mich.: Chosen Books, 1985.

Hind, J. F. Memo to C. A. Tucker. January 23, 1975. In "Meet the Turk," Tobacco and Teenagers, Archive, The Smoking Gun. On-line at http://www.thesmokinggun.com/tobacco/tucker1.html. April 21, 1999.

Hiss, Alger. Telegram to J. Parnell Thomas. August 3, 1948. In John Chabot Smith, *Alger Hiss: The True Story*, p. 160. New York: Holt, Rinehart and Winston, 1976.

Hohlwein, Joyce. Letter to Pat Lamb. November 8, 1969. In Patricia Frazer Lamb and Kathryn Joyce Hohlwein, *Touchstones: Letters Between Two Women, 1953–1964*, pp. 199–202. New York: Harper and Row, 1983.

Holy Church of the White Fighting Machine of the Cross. Letter to Morris Dees. September 17, 1990. In papers of Morris Dees, Montgomery, Ala.

Hook, Sidney. Letter to Corliss Lamont. July 8, 1966. In *Letters of Sidney Hook: Democracy, Communism, and the Cold War*, ed. Edward S. Shapiro, pp. 289–90. Armonk, N.Y.: M.E. Sharpe, 1995. Reprinted by permission of the publisher.

Hoover, J. Edgar. Memo to Communications Section. January 14, 1949. In *In Re Alger Hiss: Petition for a Writ of Error Coram Nobis*, ed. Edith Tiger, p. 339. New York: Hill and Wang, 1979.

Hope, Bob. Telegram to Harry Truman. November 3, 1948. Printed by permission of Hope Enterprises.

Horiuchi, Shizuko. Letter to Henriette Von Blon. May 24, 1942. In the Hoover Institution, Stanford University, Stanford, Calif. Printed by permission of Shizuko Horiuchi.

Houdini, Harry. Letter to C. Howard Watson. February 1, 1913. In "The American Variety Stage: Vaudeville and Popular Entertainment, 1870–1920," Library of Congress. On-line at http://memory.loc.gov/ammem/vshtml/vshome.html; (h) varshoud hs013. April 13, 1999.

House, Edward. Three cablegrams to Woodrow Wilson. November 10, 1918. In *The Intimate Papers of Colonel House*, vol. 4, *The Ending of the War*, arr. as a narrative by Charles Seymour, pp. 141–43. St. Clair Shores, Mich.: Scholarly Press, 1971.

Howells, William Dean. Letter to Charles Eliot Norton. April 6, 1903. In *Life in Letters of William Dean Howells, Volume Two*, ed. Mildred Howells, pp. 170–72. New York: Russell and Russell, 1968. Reprinted by permission of Scribner, a division of Simon & Schuster.

Huckins, Olga. Letter to the editor of the *Boston Herald*. January, 1958. In Paul Brooks, *The House of Life: Rachel Carson at Work*, pp. 231–32. Boston: Houghton Mifflin, 1972.

Hudson, Rock. Letter to five former sexual partners. June, 1984. In Rock Hudson and Sara Davidson, *Rock Hudson: His Story*, p. 252. New York: Morrow, 1986. Reprinted courtesy of Mark Miller and George Nader and by permission of Wallace Sheft and the Rock Hudson AIDS Research Foundation.

Huff, William Henry. Telegram to Hugh White. August 31, 1955. In Sanford Wexler, *The Civil Rights Movement: An Eyewitness History*, p. 62. New York: Facts on File, 1993.

Humphries, E. J. Telegram to Jeannie Cornell. October 27, 1934. In Lynching File, Series 278, Florida State Archives, Tallahassee, Fla.

Jamail, Joseph. Note to John Jeffers. September 18, 1985. In Thomas Petzinger, Jr., *Oil & Honor: The Texaco-Pennzoil Wars*, p. 347. New York: Putnam, 1987. Reprinted by permission of Joseph Jamail.

James, Henry. Letter to Henry Adams. March 21, 1914. In *The Correspondence of Henry James and Henry Adams, 1877–1914*, ed. George Monteiro, pp. 88–89. Baton Rouge: Louisiana State University Press, 1992. Reprinted by permission of Bay James, literary executor for the James family.

Jan. Letter to her mother. October, 1974. In *Between Ourselves: Letters Between Mothers and Daughters, 1750–1982*, ed. Karen Payne, pp. 70–71. Boston: Houghton Mifflin, 1983. Reprinted by permission of Karen Payne.

Jan's mother. Letter to her daughter. November, 1974. In *Between Ourselves: Letters Between Mothers and Daughters, 1750–1982*, ed. Karen Payne, pp. 71–72. Boston: Houghton Mifflin, 1983. Reprinted by permission of Karen Payne.

Johnson, John [pseud.]. Letter to his parents. December, 1983. In *Breaking Silence: Coming Out Letters*, pp. 9–11. New York: Xanthus Press, 1995.

Johnson, Lady Bird. Letter to Lyndon Johnson. August 25, 1964. In August 1964, President's Decision to Run in 1964, Family Correspondence, Lyndon B. Johnson Library and Museum, Austin, Texas. Printed by permission of Lady Bird Johnson.

Johnson, Les. Letter to his family. July[?], 1964. In Sandra Hard Papers, State Historical Society of Wisconsin, Madison.

Johnson, Magic. Letter to George Bush. September 24, 1992. In *Historic Documents*, p. 893. Washington, D.C.: Congressional Quarterly, 1992.

Johnson, Nunnally. Letter to Thornton Delehanty. January 26, 1954. In *The Letters of Nunnally Johnson*, ed. Dorris Johnson and Ellen Leventhal, pp. 111–13. New York: Knopf, 1981. Copyright © 1981 by Dorris Johnson. Reprinted by permission of the publisher and Dorris Johnson.

Jones, Mary Harris "Mother." Letter to James Peabody. March 26, 1904. In *Mother Jones Speaks: Collected Writings and Speeches*, ed. Philip S. Foner, p. 557. New York: Monad Press, 1983. Copyright © 1983 by Philip S. Foner. Reprinted by permission of Pathfinder Press.

Joplin, Janis. Letter to her parents. June 6, 1966. In the Rock and Roll Hall of Fame and Museum, Cleveland, Ohio. Copyright © 1992 Fantality Corp. All rights reserved. Printed by permission of Laura Joplin.

Kallstrom, James. Letter to the families of TWA Flight 800 victims. November 13, 1997. In "Text of FBI Letter to TWA Flight 800 Families," U.S. News Story Page, CNN Interactive. On-line at http://cnn.com/US/9711/13/fbi.letter/index.html. September, 1998.

Kansas mother. Letter to the Children's Bureau. January 13, 1928. In file 4-4-1-3, Children's Bureau Records, Record Group 102; National Archives, Washington, D.C.

Kasmire, Robert. Letter to Ed Friendly. August 16, 1968. In Dan Rowan and John D. MacDonald, *A Friendship: The Letters of Dan Rowan and John D. MacDonald, 1967–1974*, pp. 65–67. New York: Knopf, 1986. Letter copyright © National Broadcasting Company, Inc. All rights reserved. Reprinted by permission of NBC.

Keller, Helen. Letter to Alexander Woollcott. November 1, 1935. In Papers of Helen Adams Keller, bMS Am 1449 (878), Houghton Library, Harvard University, Cambridge, Mass. Copyright © 1935. Printed by permission of the American Foundation for the Blind, New York, N.Y.

Kelly, George "Machine Gun." Letter to Charles Urschel. September 19, 1933. In Rick Mattix, "Machine Gun Kelly," *Oklahombres Journal*, vol IV, no. 1, Fall 1992. On-line at http://www.oklahombres.org/kelly.htm. February 25, 1999.

Kennedy, Jacqueline. Letter to Lyndon Johnson. November 26, 1963. In Merle Miller, *Lyndon: An Oral Biography*, pp. 335–36. New York: Putnam, 1980.

Kennedy, John. Message to the town of Rendova. August 3, 1943. In "PT 109," John F. Kennedy Ready Reference Information. On-line at http://www.cs.umb.edu/jfklibrary/jfkmisc.htm#PT109. March 14, 1999.

———. Memo to Lyndon Johnson. April 20, 1961. In Dr. John Logsdon, "Major Space Policy Issues," Issues in NASA Program and Project Management. On-line at http://www.hq.nasa.gov/test/office/codef/codeft/docs/issues10/inppm10b.htm. March 23, 1999.

———. Letter to Ngo Dinh Diem. December 14, 1961. In "President Responds to Request From Viet-Nam for U.S. Aid," *The Department of State Bulletin*, vol. 46, no. 1175, pub. 7319, January 1, 1962, p. 13.

———. Letter to Nikita Khrushchev. October 22, 1962. In *JFK Wants to Know: Memos from the President's Office, 1961–1963*, ed. Edward Claflin, pp. 205–206. New York: Morrow, 1991.

Kerouac, Jack. Letter to John Clellon Holmes. October 12, 1952. In *Jack Kerouac: Selected Letters, 1940–1956*, ed. Ann Charters, pp. 380–82. New York: Viking, 1995. Copyright © 1995 by John Sampas, Literary Representative. Reprinted by permission of Sterling Lord Literistic, Inc.

Kerwin, Joseph. Memo to Richard Truly. July 28, 1986. In "NASA Historical Reference Collection," History Office, NASA Headquarters, Washington, D.C. On-line at http://www.hq.nasa.gov/office/pao/History/kerwin.html. July 30, 1998.

Kevorkian, Jack. Letter to Dr. Gary Sloan. July 10, 1990. In Joan M. Brovins and Thomas Oehmke, *Dr. Death: Dr. Jack Kevorkian's RX*, p. 41. Hollywood, Fla.: Lifetime Books, 1993.

King, Martin Luther, Jr. Letter to Alabama clergymen. April 16, 1963. In *A Testament of Hope: The Essential Writings of Martin Luther King, Jr.*, ed. James M. Washington, pp. 289–302. San Francisco: Harper and Row, 1986. Copyright © 1963 by Martin Luther King, Jr. Copyright renewed 1991 by Coretta Scott King. Reprinted by arrangement with the heirs to the estate of Martin Luther King, Jr., c/o Writers House Inc. as agent for the proprietor.

Kinsey, Alfred. Letter to Albert Ellis. May 6, 1948. In the Kinsey Institute for Research in Sex, Gender, and Reproduction, Bloomington, Ind. Printed by permission of the Institute.

Kirstein, Lincoln. Letter to A. Everett Austin. July 16, 1933. In Francis Mason, *I Remember Balanchine: Recollections of the Ballet Master by Those Who Knew Him*, pp. 115–19. New York: Doubleday, 1991. Writing by Lincoln Kirstein copyright © 1933, 1999 by the New York Public Library (Astor, Lenox and Tilden Foundations). Reprinted by permission of Nicholas Jenkins, literary executor of the Lincoln Kirstein papers and copyrights.

Kohut, Heinz. Letter to his son. February 5, 1969. In *The Curve of Life: The Correspondence of Heinz Kohut, 1923–1981*, ed. Geoffrey Cocks, pp. 226–27. Chicago: University of Chicago Press, 1994. Copyright © 1994 by the University of Chicago. Reprinted by permission of the publisher and Thomas A. Kohut.

Koresh, David. Letter to Dick DeGuerin. April 14, 1993. In "Koresh's Letter to his Lawyer," *Forth Worth Star-Telegram*, April 15, 1993, p. 2.

Kroc, Ray. Memo to McDonald's operators. April 6, 1970. In Archives of the McDonald's Corporation, Oak Brook, Ill. Printed by permission of the McDonald's Corporation.

Kuhimeyer, Harry, Jr. Letter to McMartin Preschool parents. September 3, 1983. In Paul Eberle and Shirley Eberle, *The Abuse of Innocence: The McMartin Preschool Trial*, pp. 18–19. Buffalo, N.Y.: Prometheus Books, 1993.

Kuhn, Walt. Letter to Walter Pach. December 12, 1912. In Reel D72, 397, the Archives of American Art. Printed by permission of James T. Phillips.

Kurowsky, Agnes von. Letter to Ernest Hemingway. March 7, 1919. In *Hemingway in Love and War: The Lost Diary of Agnes von Kurowsky, Her Letters, and Correspondence of Ernest Hemingway*, ed. Henry Serrano Villard and James Nagel, pp. 163–64. Boston: Northeastern University Press, 1989. Copyright © by Henry Serrano Villard and James Nagel. Reprinted by permission of the publisher.

Laitinen, Gertrude. Letter to Eugene V. Debs. January 20, 1921. In *Letters of Eugene V. Debs*, vol. 3, *1919–1926*, ed. J. Robert Constantine, p. 183. Urbana: University of Illinois Press, 1990. Reprinted by permission of the Debs Collection, Indiana State University Library.

Lamb, Pat. Letter to Joyce Hohlwein. November 26, 1963. In Patricia Frazer Lamb and Kathryn Joyce Hohlwein, *Touchstones: Letters Between Two Women, 1953–1964*, pp. 303–304. New York: Harper and Row, 1983.

Landers, Ann. Letter to "Beantown." January, 1984. In "She should trust intuition," Ann Landers, *Denver Post*, vol. 92, no. 170, January 19, 1984, p. 7B. Reprinted by permission of Ann Landers and Creators Syndicate.

LaPook, Dr. Jonathan. Letter to a health plan administrator. July 28, 1997. Printed by permission of Dr. Jonathan LaPook.

Lazear, Bobby. Letter to his parents. June 28, 1989. Printed by permission of Rebecca Lazear Okrent.

Leahy, William. Memo to the Joint Chiefs of Staff. June 14, 1945. In Bruce Lee, *Marching Orders: The Untold Story of World War II*, p. 571. New York: Crown Publishers, 1995.

Lear, Norman. Letter to Leroy Elliott. November 15, 1972. Printed by permission of Norman Lear.

Levitt and Sons. Letter to a prospective buyer. August 8, 1949. In Lynne Matarrese, *The History of Levittown, New York: 50th Anniversary Edition*, Appendix. New York: Levittown Historical Society, 1997. Reprinted by permission of the Society.

Lewinsky, Monica. Letter to Bill Clinton. November 12, 1997. In *The Starr Report: The Evidence*, ed. Phil Kuntz, p. 430. New York: Pocket Books, 1998.

Lodge, Henry Cabot, Jr. Letter to Corliss Lamont. August 2, 1984. In *"Dear Corliss": Letters from Eminent Persons*, ed. Corliss Lamont, p. 131. Buffalo, N.Y.: Prometheus Books, 1990. Reprinted by permission of Beth K. Lamont and the Half-Moon Foundation.

Long, Huey. Letter to Charles Stair. August 28, 1924. In Louisiana Political Museum and Hall of Fame, Winnfield, La.

Long, Perrin. Letter to the Surgeon, NATOUSA. August 16, 1943. In Martin Blumenson, *The Patton Papers: 1940–1945*, pp. 330–32. Boston: Houghton Mifflin, 1974.

Los Angeles doctor. Letter to whom it may concern. December 29, 1961, In Albert Goldman, *Ladies and Gentlemen, Lenny Bruce!!*, p.11. New York: Random House, 1974.

Loud, Patricia. Letter to a WNET official. December 6, 1972. In Pat Loud with Nora Johnson, *Pat Loud: A Woman's Story*, pp. 140–42. New York: Coward, McCann and Geoghegan, 1974. Reprinted by permission of Patricia Loud.

Maass, Meta. Letter to her parents. May 14, 1945. Printed by permission of Henry Grunwald.

MacLeish, Kenneth. Letter to his fiancée. December 4, 1917. In *The Price of Honor: The World War One Letters of Naval Aviator Kenneth MacLeish*, ed. Geoffrey L. Rossano, pp. 54–55. Annapolis, Md.: Naval Institute Press, 1991. Copyright © 1991 by the U.S. Naval Institute, Annapolis, Md. Reprinted by permission of the publisher.

McVeigh, Timothy. Letter to Gwenn Strider. 1995. In "May 8, 1997-Morning," Oklahoma City Bombing: The Trials. On-line at http://archive.abcnews.go.com/sections/us/oklahoma/am_transcripts0508.html. March 18, 1999.

McWilliams, Carey. Letter to Louis Adamic. October 3, 1937. In Vicki L. Ruiz, *Cannery Women, Cannery Lives: Mexican Women, Unionization, and the California Food Processing Industry, 1930–1950*, pp. 135–36. Albuquerque, N.M.: University of New Mexico Press, 1987. Reprinted by permission of the University of California, Los Angeles.

Mandor, Russ. Letter to his parents. July, 1964. Printed by permission of Dr. Russ. B. Mandor.

Mantle, Mickey. Letter to Bill Mobley. June 26, 1964. Printed by permission of the estate of Mickey Mantle.

Marianne [Jane Burr]. Letter to Lorna. September, 1907. In Jane Burr, *Letters of a Dakota Divorcee*, pp. 9–17. Boston: Roxburgh Publishing, 1909.

Markel, Lester. Memo to Arthur Hays Sulzberger. December 18, 1941. In Richard F. Shepard, *The Paper's Papers: A Reporter's Journey Through the Archives of the* New York Times, pp. 117–18. New York: Times Books, 1996. Copyright © 1941 by the *New York Times*. Reprinted by permission of the *New York Times*.

Marshall, George. Letter to Herby Funston. February 2, 1944. In *The Papers of George Catlett Marshall*, vol. 4: *Aggressive and Determined Leadership*, ed. Larry I. Bland and Sharon R. Ritenour, p. 261. Baltimore, Md.: Johns Hopkins University Press, 1996.

Martin, Rebecca. Letter to the *Josephine County Courier*. November, 1995. In Rebecca Martin, "The 'new' education in Oregon Schools?" Salem News. On-line at http://www.ncn.com/~snews/pages/9511/orgnobe.htm. January 15, 1999.

Marx, Groucho. Three letters to the Warner brothers. 1946. In Groucho Marx, *The Groucho Letters: Letters from and to Groucho Marx*, pp. 14–18. New York: Simon & Schuster, 1967. Copyright © 1967 by Groucho Marx. Reprinted by permission of Simon & Schuster and by Penguin Putnam.

Mary. Letter to her son's parents. April 19, 1996. In "Adoption," Letters Magazine. On-line at http://www.sipu.com/letters/archive/adoption.html. September 12, 1998.

Masters, Edgar Lee. Letter to Edwin Reese. July 27, 1925. In the Edgar Lee Masters Papers, Illinois State Historical Society, Springfield, Ill. Reprinted by permission of Hilary Masters.

Matlovich, Leonard. Letter to the Secretary of the Air Force. March 6, 1975. In Number 88-1, Leonard Matlovich Papers, Gay and Lesbian Historical Society of Northern California, San Francisco. Printed by permission of the Society.

Mattingly, Lawrence. Note to C. W. Herrick. 1930. In Laurence Bergreen, *Capone: The Man and the Era*, p. 451. New York: Simon & Schuster, 1994.

Mencken, H. L. Letter to Raymond Pearl. July 14[?], 1925. In *The New Mencken Letters*, ed. Carl Bode, pp. 187–88. New York: Dial Press, 1977. Reprinted by permission of the Enoch Pratt Free Library, Baltimore, Md., in accordance with the terms of the will of H. L. Mencken.

Menendez, Lyle. Letter to Tracy Baker. February 5, 1993. In Lyle Menendez as told to Norma Novelli, with Mike Walker, *The Private Diary of Lyle Menendez: In His Own Words*, ed. Judith Spreckles, pp. 180–81. Beverly Hills, Calif.: Dove Books, 1995.

Mercer, Marilyn. Letter to the Wildwood Health Care Center. April 15, 1998. Printed by permission of Marilyn Mercer.

Meyers, Irving. Letter to Ira Marion. September 14, 1951. In Irving Meyers Correspondence, 1949–1954, Radio Writers Guild Papers, New York Performing Arts Library, N.Y. Printed by permission of Irving Meyers.

Mitchell, Margaret. Letter to Joseph Henry Jackson. June 1, 1936. In *Margaret Mitchell's* Gone With the Wind *Letters: 1936–1949*, ed. Richard Harwell, pp. 12–13. 1976. Reprint, New York: Collier Books, 1986. Reprinted by permission of the literary estate of Margaret Mitchell.

Moore, Annie. Letter to her sister and brother-in-law. August 7, 1972. In Rebecca Moore, *The Jonestown Letters: Correspondence of the Moore Family, 1970–1985*, pp. 76–78. Lewiston, N.Y.: Edwin Mellen Press, Studies in American Religion, vol 23, 1986. Reprinted by permission of Rebecca Moore.

———. Suicide note. November 18, 1978. In Rebecca Moore, *The Jonestown Letters: Correspondence of the Moore Family, 1970–1985*, pp. 284–86. Lewiston, N.Y.: Edwin Mellen Press, Studies in American Religion, vol. 23, 1986. Reprinted by permission of Rebecca Moore.

Moore, Marianne. Three letters to the Ford Motor Company. November 19, November 28, December 8, 1955. In Marianne Moore and David Wallace, *Letters from and to the Ford Motor Company*, unpag. New York: Pierpont Morgan Library, 1958. Reprinted by permission of Marianne Craig Moore, literary executor for the estate of Marianne Moore. All rights reserved.

Morgan, Robin. Letter to her unborn child, July 9, 1969. In Robin Morgan, *Going Too Far: The Personal Chronicles of a Feminist*, pp. 52–54. Copyright © 1977 by Robin Morgan. Reprinted by permission of the Edite Kroll Literary Agency.

Morrison, Paul [pseud.]. Letter to William Loeb. February 17, 1972. In Jules Witcover, "William Loeb and the New Hampshire Primary: A Question of Ethics," *Columbia Journalism Review*, May/June, 1972, p. 16.

Moses, Robert. Note to fellow SNCC members. October, 1961. In *Nonviolence in America: A Documentary History*, ed. Staughton Lynd and Alice Lynd, pp. 246–47. Maryknoll, N.Y.: Orbis Books, 1995. Reprinted by permission of Robert Parris Moses.

Mother of two. Letter to Margaret Sanger. August, 1922. In "Appeals from Mothers," *The Birth Control Review*, vol. 6, no. 8, August, 1922, p. 151.

Napier, Judy. Letter to Jimmy Carter. February 22, 1980. In "Olympics, Cables, Important," Jimmy Carter Library, Atlanta, Ga.

Nixon, Richard. Memo to H. R. Haldeman. May 13, 1970. In *From the President: Richard Nixon's Secret Files*, ed. Bruce Oudes, pp. 127–34. New York: Harper and Row, 1989.

———. Letter to Henry Kissinger. August 9, 1974. In "American Originals," The Exhibit Hall, National Archives and Records Administration. On-line at http://www.nara.gov/exhall/originals/nixon.html. June 28, 1998.

North, Oliver. Memo to John Poindexter. September 25, 1986. In *White House E-mail: The Top Secret Computer Messages the Reagan/Bush White House Tried to Destroy*, ed. Tom Blanton, p. 99. New York: New Press, 1995.

Ohio resident. Postcard to Kent State student body president. May, 1970. In "Postcard, 'Hold Kent Rioters for Death,' " Lynda Lyke Papers—Folder 5, May 4 Collection, Kent State University. On-line at http://www.library.kent.edu/exhibts/4may95/lyke/priot.html. April 21, 1999.

O'Keeffe, Georgia. Letter to Henry McBride. July, 1931. In National Gallery of Art, *Georgia O'Keeffe, 1887–1986*, exhibition catalogue, pp. 192–93. New York Graphic Society Books, 1987. Copyright © 1999 The Georgia O'Keeffe Foundation/Artists Rights Society (ARS), New York. Reprinted by permission of ARS.

Okuda, Mike. Letter to *Star Trek* fan. January 27, 1995. In "Mini-FAQ: Warp Velocities," On-line at http://www.bham.net/users/jbishop/warp.html. August, 1998. Printed by permission of the author and the author's agents, Scovil Chichak Galen Literary Agency.

Otisville Sanatorium. Notice to patients. 1914. In Mark Caldwell, *The Last Crusade: The War on Consumption 1862–1954*, p. 98. New York: Atheneum, 1988.

Page, Walter Hines. Letter to his son. December 20, 1914. In Burton J. Hendrick, *The Life and Letters of Walter Hines Page,* vol. I, pp. 353–56. Garden City, N.Y.: Doubleday, Page and Company, 1922.

Papcun, George. Letter to Jeffrey Kaye. May 5, 1991. In Tom Owens and Rod Browning, *Lying Eyes: The Truth Behind the Corruption and Brutality of the LAPD and the Beating of Rodney King*, p. 98. New York: Thunder's Mouth Press, 1994. Reprinted by permission of George Papcun.

Parents of Little Rock Nine. Telegram to Dwight Eisenhower. September 30, 1957. In Sanford Wexler, *The Civil Rights Movement: An Eyewitness History*, p. 105. New York: Facts on File, 1993.

Parker, Dorothy. Letter to Gerald Murphy. 1936[?]. In Dorothy (Rothschild) Parker Letters, bMS AM 1449 (1279), Houghton Library, Harvard University, Cambridge, Mass. Copyright © 1999 the National Association for the Advancement of Colored People. Printed by permission of the NAACP.

———. Letter to Alexander Woollcott. September 2, 1942. In Dorothy (Rothschild) Parker Letters, bMS Am 1449 (1278), Houghton Library, Harvard University, Cambridge, Mass. Copyright © 1999 the National Association for the Advancement of Colored People. Printed by permission of the NAACP.

Pat. Letter to her parents. August 1, 1972. In *Between Ourselves: Letters Between Mothers and Daughters, 1750–1982*, ed. Karen Payne, pp. 32–33. Boston: Houghton Mifflin, 1983. Reprinted by permission of Karen Payne.

Pat's parents. Letter to their daughter. August 8, 1972. In *Between Ourselves: Letters Between Mothers and Daughters, 1750–1982*, ed. Karen Payne, pp. 33–34. Boston: Houghton Mifflin, 1983. Reprinted by permission of Karen Payne.

Patient. Letter to Dr. Joseph Collins. April 16, 1908. In Joseph Collins, *Letters to a Neurologist to Which Are Appended Brief Replies Purporting to Set Forth Concisely the Nature of the Ailments Therein Described, with Remarks on Their Appropriate Treatment*, pp. 93–99. New York: William Wood, 1908.

Patton, George, Jr. Letter to Dwight Eisenhower. October 1, 1940. In Martin Blumenson, *The Patton Papers: 1940–1945*, p. 15. Boston: Houghton Mifflin, 1974. Copyright © 1974 by Martin Blumenson. Reprinted by permission of the publisher and by Blanche C. Gregory. All rights reserved.

Patty. Letter to Internet newsgroup. November 20, 1997. Printed by permission of Patty.

Peary, Robert. Telegraph to the world. September 6, 1909. In "Peary, Robert Edwin," Compton's Encyclopedia Online v. 2.0, 1997.

Pennsylvania resident. Letter to the Bloomsburg *Press Enterprise*. April 15, 1983. In *Letters to the Editor: Two Hundred Years in the Life of an American Town*, ed. Gerard Stropnicky et al., pp. 59–60. New York: Simon & Schuster, Touchstone, 1998.

Pepper, George Wharton. Letter to Harry Daugherty. February 20, 1924. In Harry M. Daugherty, *The Inside Story of the Harding Tragedy*, pp. 283–84. New York: Churchill, 1932.

Perkins, Maxwell. Letter to a reader. August 28, 1928. In *Editor to Author: The Letters of Maxwell Perkins*, ed. John Hall Wheelock, pp. 58–60. Dunwoody, Ga.: Norman S. Berg, 1977. Copyright © 1950 by Scribner's, renewed 1978 by John Hall Wheelock. Reprinted by permission of Scribner, a division of Simon & Schuster.

Peters, Agnes Maxwell. Letter to Dr. Fredric Wertham. September 7, 1948. In James Gilbert, *A Cycle of Outrage: America's Reaction to the Juvenile Delinquent in the 1950s*, p. 105. New York: Oxford University Press, 1986. Reprinted by permission of James B. Gilbert.

Picotte, Susan La Flesche. Letter to Francis Leupp. November 15, 1907. In Omaha Agency file number 90863-07-162, Records of the Bureau of Indian Affairs, Record Group 75; National Archives, Washington, D.C.

Plaisier, Aart. Letter to his cousin. May 1, 1910. In *Dutch American Voices: Letters from the United States, 1850–1930*, ed. Herbert J. Brinks, pp. 323–24. Ithaca, N.Y.: Cornell University Press, 1995. Reprinted by permission of Herbert J. Brinks.

Poulton, Jack. Letter to his wife. August 13, 1945. In *A Better Legend: From the World War II Letters of Jack and Jane Poulton*, ed. Jane Weaver Poulton, pp. 241–42. Charlottesville: University Press of Virginia, 1993. Reprinted by permission of the publisher.

Poulton, Jane. Letter to her husband. August 11, 1945. In *A Better Legend: From the World War II Letters of Jack and Jane Poulton*, ed. Jane Weaver Poulton, p. 240. Charlottesville, Va.: University Press of Virginia, 1993. Reprinted by permission of the publisher.

Presley, Elvis. Letter to Richard Nixon. December 20?, 1970. In "When Nixon Met Elvis," the Exhibit Hall, National Archives and Records Administration. On-line at http://www.nara.gov/exhall/nixonelvis/letter1.jpg. June 25, 1998.

Price, G. W. Letter to fellow Klansmen. July 6, 1922. In "G. W. Price," Ku Klux Klan, Realm of California Records, 1922–1947, California State University Northridge, University Library. On-line at http://www.csun.edu/~vfoao0cq/images_kkk/kkkframe.htm. April 12, 1999.

Quigley, Joan. Letter to Ronald Reagan. August 2, 1987. In Joan Quigley, *"What Does Joan Say?": My Seven Years as White House Astrologer to Nancy and Ronald Reagan*, pp. 167–68. New York: Carol Publishing Group, Birch Lane Press Book, 1990. Copyright © 1990 by Joan Quigley. Reprinted by permission of the publisher.

Rand, Ayn. Letter to Frank Lloyd Wright. May 14, 1944. In *The Letters of Ayn Rand*, ed. Michael S. Berliner, pp. 112–14. New York: Dutton, 1995. Copyright © 1995 by the estate of Ayn Rand, introduction copyright © 1995 by Leonard Peikoff. Reprinted by permission of Dutton, a division of Penguin Putnam.

Reader. Letter to Ann Landers. January, 1984. In Ann Landers, "She should trust intuition," *Denver Post*, vol. 92, no. 170, January 19, 1984, p. 7B.

Reader. Letter to the Bintel Brief editor. 1906. In *A Bintel Brief: Sixty Years of Letters from the Lower East Side to the Jewish Daily Forward*, ed. Isaac Metzker, p. 55. 1971. Reprint, New York: Schocken Book, 1991.

Reader. Letter to the *Women's Home Companion*. March, 1926. In *Second to None: A Documentary History of American Women*, vol. 2, *From 1865 to the Present*, ed. Ruth Barnes Moynihan, Cynthia Russett, and Laurie Crumpacker, pp. 153–54. Lincoln: University of Nebraska Press, 1993.

Reagan, Ronald. Letter to Robert Poli. October 20, 1980. In "Reagan Letter to PATCO," the NATCA Voice, National Air Traffic Controllers Association. On-line at http://www.natcavoice.org/natca/f/reaganl.htm. April 17, 1999.

———. Letter to Mikhail Gorbachev. November 28, 1985. In Ronald Reagan, *An American Life*, pp. 642–45. New York: Simon & Schuster, 1990.

———. Letter to Americans. November 6, 1994. In *Historic Documents*, p. 500. Washington, D.C.: Congressional Quarterly, 1994.

Redfield, William. Letter to Robert Mills. April 9, 1964. In William Redfield, *Letters from an Actor*, pp. 227–31. New York: Viking, 1966. Reprinted by permission of the estate of William Redfield.

Reed, John. Letter to Lincoln Steffens. June 29, 1918. In Special MS Collections—Steffens, Columbia University Libraries, New York.

Reed, Walter. Letter to his wife. December 9, 1900. In Albert Truby, *Memoir of Walter Reed: The Yellow Fever Episode*, pp. 159–60. New York: Harper and Brothers, Paul B. Hoeber, Medical Book Department, 1943.

Reyes, Miguel. Letter to Santa Claus. December, 1998. Printed by permission of Nancy Reyes.

Rhodes, David [pseud.]. Letter to "Friends." 1994. Online. (Spam.)

Richardson, Elliot. Letter to Richard Nixon. October 20, 1973. In *Historic Documents*, pp. 875–76. Washington, D.C.: Congressional Quarterly, 1973.

Riche, Robert. Three letters to CompuServe. April 1, April 4, April 5, 1995. In Robert Riche, "How an Internet Wannabe Became an I-Really-Don't-Wannabe," *New York Times,* vol. 146, no. 50,586, October 20, 1996, Section 4, p. 7. Reprinted by permission of Robert Riche.

Rickey, Branch. Letter to the Pittsburgh Pirates. June 15, 1954. In"Miscellany," Words and Deeds in American History, American Memory Collection, Library of Congess, On-line at http://memory.loc.gov/cgi-bin/query/r?ammem/mcc:@field (DOCID+@lit (mcc/044)). April 16, 1999. Printed by permission.

Ridenhour, Ron. Letter to the United States Army. March 29, 1969. In William Peers, *The My Lai Inquiry,* pp. 4–7. New York: Norton, 1979. Reprinted by permission of Mary E. Howell on behalf of Ron Ridenhour's mother, brother, and sister.

Robinson, Jo Ann. Letter to W. A. Gayle. May 21, 1954. In *The Montgomery Bus Boycott and the Women Who Started It: The Memoir of Jo Ann Gibson Robinson*, ed. David J. Garrow, p. viii. Knoxville: University of Tennessee Press, 1987.

Rockefeller, John D. Letter to John D. Rockefeller, Jr. September 12, 1918. In *"Dear Father"/"Dear Son": Correspondence of John D. Rockefeller and John D. Rockefeller, Jr.,* ed. Joseph W. Ernest, pp. 86–87. New York: Fordham University Press in cooperation with the Rockefeller Archive Center, North Tarrytown, N.Y., 1994. Reprinted by permission of the Center.

Rockefeller, John D., Jr. Letter to John D. Rockefeller. August 1, 1918. In *"Dear Father"/"Dear Son": Correspondence of John D. Rockefeller and John D. Rockefeller, Jr.,* ed. Joseph W. Ernest, pp. 85–86. New York: Fordham University Press in cooperation with the Rockefeller Archive Center, North Tarrytown, N.Y, 1994. Reprinted by permission of the Center.

Roepcke, Peter. Letter to his girlfriend. December 6, 1969. In *Dear America: Letters Home From Vietnam,* ed. Bernard Edelman for the New York Vietnam Veterans Memorial Commission, p. 129. 1985. Reprint, New York: Pocket Books, 1988. Reprinted by permission of Bernard Edelman.

Roosevelt, Eleanor. Letter to Mrs. Henry Robert, Jr. February 28, 1939. In Papers of Eleanor Roosevelt, Franklin D. Roosevelt Library, Hyde Park, N.Y.

Roosevelt, Franklin. Letter to George Draper. September 6, 1934. In Franklin D. Roosevelt Library, Hyde Park, N.Y.

———. Letter to Margaret Suckley. September 30, 1935. In *Closest Companion: The Unknown Story of the Intimate Friendship between Franklin Roosevelt and Margaret Suckley,* ed. Geoffrey C. Ward, pp. 41–42. Boston: Houghton Mifflin, 1995.

———. Telegram to Hirohito. December 6, 1941. In Leonard Baker, *Roosevelt and Pearl Harbor,* pp. 299–301. New York: Macmillan, 1970.

————. Letter to the president of the United States in 1956. December 17, 1941. In *Letters in American History: Words to Remember, 1770 to the Present*, ed. H. Jack Lang, p. 88. New York: Harmony Books, 1982.

————. Letter to Kenesaw Mountain Landis. January 15, 1942. In the National Baseball Hall of Fame, Cooperstown, N.Y.

————. Letter to J. Robert Oppenheimer. June 29, 1943. In "Presidential Items," Words and Deeds in American History, American Memory Collection, Library of Congress. On-line at http://memory.loc.gov/cgi-bin/query/r?ammem/mcc:@field (DOCID+@lit (mcc/083)). April 13, 1999.

Roosevelt, Theodore. Letter to Henry Cabot Lodge. September 23, 1901. In Theodore Roosevelt, *Letters,* Volume 3–4: *The Square Deal, 1901–1905,* ed. Elting E. Morison, p. 150. Cambridge, Mass.: Harvard University Press, 1951.

————. Letter to his son. November 19, 1905. In *Letters to Kermit from Theodore Roosevelt, 1902–1908,* ed. Will Irwin, pp. 123–25. New York: Scribner's, 1946. Copyright © 1946 by Charles Scribner's Sons. Reprinted by permission of the Theodore Roosevelt Association and by Scribner, a division of Simon & Schuster.

Rosenberg, Ethel. Letter to her sons. June 19, 1953. In *The Rosenberg Letters: A Complete Edition of the Prison Correspondence of Julius and Ethel Rosenberg,* ed. Michael Meeropol, pp. 702–703. New York: Garland, 1994. Reprinted by permission of Michael and Robert Meeropol.

Rosenthal, A. M. Memo to Arthur Ochs Sulzberger and James Reston. June 1, 1971. In Richard F. Shepard, *The Paper's Papers: A Reporter's Journey Through the Archives of the New York Times,* pp. 190–91. New York: Random House, Times Books, 1996. Copyright © 1996 by the *New York Times,* Reprinted by permission of the *New York Times.*

Ruckelshaus, William. Letter to Richard Nixon. October 20, 1973. In *Historic Documents,* p. 876. Washington, D.C.: Congressional Quarterly, 1973.

Rudd, Mark. Letter to Grayson Kirk. April 22, 1968. In Jerry L. Avorn, *Up Against the Ivy Wall: A History of the Columbia Crisis,* pp. 25–27. New York: Atheneum, 1969. Copyright © 1968 by Members of the Board Associates. Reprinted by permission of Scribner, a Division of Simon & Schuster.

Salk, Jonas. Letter to Eleanor Roosevelt. March 26, 1955. Copyright © by the 1998 Jonas Salk Trust. Printed by permission of the family of Dr. Jonas Salk.

Samuelson, Alexander. Application to the United States Patent Office. August 18, 1915. In "American Culture: Coca-Cola," Georgia Stories: History On-line at http://www.peachstar.gatech.edu/ga_stories/topics/058t/058cite/058016p.htm. March 11, 1999.

Sarnoff, David. Memo to O.D. Young. January 31, 1922. In the David Sarnoff Library, Princeton, N.J. Printed by permission of the David Sarnoff Library.

S.B.T.C. [pseud.]. Letter to John Ramsey. December, 1996. In Ann Louise Bardach, "Missing Innocence," *Vanity Fair,* October, 1997, pp. 322–78.

Scherer, Jacob. Letter to Dr. C. D. Spivak. October 12, 1904. In the Beck Archives of Rocky Mountain Jewish History, Center for Judaic Studies and Special Collections, Penrose Library, University of Denver. Printed by permission of the Center.

Schweitzer, Albert. Letter to Rose Kennedy. December 19, 1963. In *A Tribute to John F. Kennedy*, ed. Pierre Salinger and Sander Vanocur, pp. 68–69. Chicago: Encyclopædia Britannica, 1964. Reprinted by permission of Rhena Schweitzer Miller.

Seago, Rubye. Letter to Richard Long. December 7, 1941. In *Since You Went Away: World War II Letters from American Women on the Home Front,* ed. Judy Barrett Litoff and David C. Smith, p. 9. New York: Oxford University Press, 1991. Copyright © by Judy Barrett Litoff and David C. Smith. Reprinted by permission of the publisher.

Secor, Lella. Letter to her mother. May 15, 1916. In *Lella Secor: A Diary in Letters, 1915– 1922,* ed. Barbara Moench Florence, pp. 69–74. New York: Burt Franklin and Company, 1978. From the papers of Lella Secor Florence, Swarthmore College Peace Collection.

Sellers, Helen. Letter to Jackson Pollock. August 8, 1949. In Jackson Pollock Papers, Archives of American Art, Washington, D.C.

Selznick, David. Letter to Will Hays. October 20, 1939. In *Memo from David O. Selznick,* ed. Ruby Behlmer, pp. 221–23. New York: Viking, 1972. Reprinted by permission of the Harry Ransom Humanities Research Center, University of Texas at Austin.

Sexton, Anne. Letter to her daughter. April, 1969. In *Anne Sexton: A Self-Portrait in Letters*, ed. Linda Sexton and Lois Ames, p. 424. Boston: Houghton Mifflin, 1977. Copyright © 1976 by Linda Gray Sexton. Reprinted by permission of Sterling Lord Literistic.

Shapiro, George. Letter to Brandon Tartikoff, Warren Littlefield, and Perry Simon. August 31, 1988. Printed by permission of Shapiro/West and Associates, Beverly Hills, Calif.

Shaw, George Bernard. Telegram to the Theatre Guild. December, 1923. In *Barbed Wires*, ed. Joyce Denebrink, unpag. New York: Simon & Schuster, Monocle Periodicals, 1965. Reprinted by permission of the Society of Authors on behalf of the Bernard Shaw estate.

Shulgold, Barbara. Letter to Lynne Sipiora. February 10, 1986. In Barbara Shulgold and Lynne Sipiora, *Dear Barbara, Dear Lynne: The True Story of Two Women in Search of Motherhood,* pp. 49–51. Reading, Mass.: Addison-Wesley, 1992. Copyright © 1992 by Barbara Shulgold and Lynne Sipiora. Reprinted by permission of Perseus Books Publishers, a member of Perseus Books, L.L.C.

Shurbet, Joanna. Letter to Jonas Salk. April 13, 1955. Printed by permission of the family of Dr. Jonas Salk.

Simpson, O. J. Letter to whom it may concern. June 17, 1994. In "Simpson Murder Case: June 17, 1994. Text of Simpson's Letter to the Public," *Los Angeles Times,* June 18, 1994, pt. A, p. 6.

Sipiora, Lynne. Letter to Barbara Shulgold. May 5, 1985. In Barbara Shulgold and Lynne Sipiora, *Dear Barbara, Dear Lynne: The True Story of Two Women in Search of Motherhood,* pp. 8–10. Reading, Mass.: Addison-Wesley, 1992. Copyright © 1992 by Barbara Shulgold and

Lynne Sipiora. Reprinted by permission of Perseus Books Publishers, a member of Perseus Books, L.L.C.

Sister of a Vietnam veteran. Letter to an antiwar group. November 30, 1981. In "Agent Orange Letter," Vietnam Veterans Against the War Anti-Imperialist. On-line at http://www.oz.net/~vvawai/sw/sw32/agentorange.html. March 5, 1999.

Snodgrass, James. Letter to whom it may concern. May 11, 1957. In Kent Anderson, *Television Fraud: The History and Implications of the Quiz Show Scandals,* pp. 205–206. Westport, Conn.: Greenwood Press, 1978.

Soap opera fan. Letter to the *Guiding Light* producers. 1982. In Michael James Intintoli, *Taking Soaps Seriously: The World of* Guiding Light, pp. 208–209. New York: Praeger, 1984.

Solanas, Valerie. Letter to Andy Warhol. September 20, 1968. In the Andy Warhol Museum Archives Study Center, Pittsburgh, Pa. Printed by permission of Judith Martinez.

Son of Sam [David Berkowitz]. Letter to Joseph Borrelli. April 17, 1977. In Marilyn Bardsley, "Son of Sam: The Letter," Library of Criminal Justice. On-line at http://www.crimelibrary.com/serial/son/sonmain.htm. January 30, 1999.

Southern migrant. Letter to the *Chicago Defender.* April 20, 1917. In *Up South: Stories, Studies, and Letters of This Century's African-American Migrations,* ed. Malaika Adero, pp. 137–38. New York: New Press, 1993.

Spach, Allen. Letter to his father. February, 1943. In *Lines of Battle: Letters from American Servicemen, 1941–1945,* ed. Annette Tapert, pp. 71–74. New York: Times Books, 1987. Reprinted by permission of Curtis Allen Spach.

Spencer, Karl. Letter to his mother. June, 1918. In *The American Reader, from Columbus to Today; Being a Compilation or Collection of the Personal Narratives, Relations and Journals Concerning the Society, Economy, Politics, Life and Times of Our Great and Many-tongued Nation, by Those Who Were There,* ed. Paul M. Angle, pp. 500–503. New York: Rand McNally and Company, 1958.

Steffens, Lincoln. Letter to John Reed. June 17, 1918. In Lincoln Steffens Collection, BMS Am 1091 (854), Houghton Library, Harvard University, Cambridge, Mass. Reprinted by permission of Pete Steffens.

Steinbeck, John. Letter to Elizabeth Otis. March 7, 1938. In *Steinbeck: A Life in Letters,* ed. Elaine Steinbeck and Robert Wallsten, pp. 161–62. New York: Viking, 1975. Copyright © 1952 by John Steinbeck, © 1969 by the Estate of John Steinbeck, © 1975 by Elaine A. Steinbeck and Robert Wallsten. Reprinted by permission of Viking Penguin, a division of Penguin Putnam, and by permission of McIntosh & Otis.

Stevens, Wallace. Letter to Elsie Moll. March 21, 1907. In *Letters of Wallace Stevens,* ed. Holly Stevens, pp. 97–98. New York: Knopf, 1966. Copyright © 1966 by Holly Stevens. Reprinted by permission of Alfred A. Knopf and by Faber and Faber.

Stimson, Henry. Cable to Harry Truman. August 6, 1945. In Harry S Truman, *Memoirs,* vol. 1, *Year of Decisions,* p. 421. Garden City, N.Y.: Doubleday, 1955.

———. Letter to Harry Truman. April 24, 1945. In Harry S Truman, *Memoirs,* vol. 1, *Year of Decisions,* p. 421. Garden City, N.Y.: Doubleday, 1955.

Stone, Russell. Letter to a son or daughter. May 5, 1988. In Karen M. Hicks, *Surviving the Dalkon Shield IUD: Women v. The Pharmaceutical Industry,* pp. 171–72. New York: Teachers College Press, 1994. Reprinted by permission of the publisher.

Suckley, Margaret. Letter to Franklin Roosevelt. October 1, 1935. In *Closest Companion: The Unknown Story of the Intimate Friendship Between Franklin Roosevelt and Margaret Suckley,* ed. Geoffrey C. Ward, pp. 42–43. Boston: Houghton Mifflin, 1995. Copyright © 1995 by Wilderstein Preservation. Reprinted by permission of the publisher. All rights reserved.

Suffragette. Valentine to William Pou. February 14, 1916. In Judith Papachristou, *Women Together: A History in Documents of the Women's Movement in the United States,* p. 177. New York: Knopf, 1976.

Summers, William. Letter to Henry Hyde. January 16, 1999. In "In Closing, the Words of a Child," *New York Times,* vol. 148, no. 51,405, January 17, 1999, p. 27.

Surgeon General. Notice to whom it may concern. 1916. In Naomi Rogers, *Dirt and Disease: Polio before FDR,* p. 37. New Brunswick, N.J.: Rutgers University Press, 1992.

Symbionese Liberation Army. Letter to Western Regional Unit. February 4, 1974. In Marilyn Baker and Sally Brompton, *Exclusive! The Inside Story of Patricia Hearst and the SLA,* pp. 58–59. New York: Macmillan, 1974.

Taxpayer. Letter to the Internal Revenue Service. February 28, 1964. In *Dear Internal Revenue: Funniest Letters from Taxpayers,* ed. Bill Adler, p. 51. Garden City, N.Y.: Doubleday, 1966. Reprinted by permission of the publisher.

Taylor, Cheryl. Letter to Dixy Lee Ray. May 27, 1980. In Archives and Records Management Division, Office of the Secretary of State, Olympia, Wash.

Taylor, Dorothea. Letter to her brother. December 7, 1941. In Mary Dewhurst Miles Papers, Illinois State Historical Library, Springfield, Ill. Printed by permission of the Library.

Terrell, Mary Church. Letter to the *Washington Post.* May 14, 1949. In Gerda Lerner, *Black Women in White America: A Documentary History,* pp. 547–50. New York: Vintage Books, 1992.

Texan. Letter to Pattillo Higgins. September 15, 1902. In the Pattillo Higgins Collection, Texas Energy Museum, Beaumont, Tex. Printed by permission of the Museum.

Thayer, William Roscoe. Letter to Theodore Roosevelt. October 17, 1901. In *The Letters of William Roscoe Thayer,* ed. Charles Downer Hazen, pp. 106–108. Boston: Houghton Mifflin, 1926.

———. Letter to Margaret Foster. May 11, 1915. In William Roscoe Thayer Papers, bMS Am 1081 (2009), Houghton Library, Harvard University, Cambridge, Mass.

Theatre Guild. Telegram to George Bernard Shaw. December, 1923. In *Barbed Wires,* ed. Joyce Denebrink, unpag. New York: Simon & Schuster, Monocle Periodicals, 1965. Reprinted by permission of the Theatre Guild.

Thirty-nine-year-old woman. Letter to an online correspondent. December 18, 1995. In "Parting ways," Letters Magazine. Online at http://www.sipu.com/letters/mayjune97/m.html. September 12, 1998.

Thurber, James. Letter to Robert Leifert. January 4, 1958. In *Selected Letters of James Thurber*, ed. Helen Thurber and Edward Weeks, pp. 205–206. Boston: Little, Brown and Company, 1980. Copyright © 1958 by James Thurber. Copyright © renewed 1986 by Rosemary A. Thurber. Reprinted by permission of Sarah Feider on behalf of Rosemary A. Thurber.

Tipster. Note to a Merrill Lynch official. May 22, 1985. In James Stewart, *Den of Thieves*, following p. 62. New York: Simon & Schuster, 1991.

Towne, Harry. Letter to his mother. March 19, 1945. In *Lines of Battle: Letters from American Servicemen, 1941–1945*, ed. Annette Tapert, pp. 243–44. New York: Times Books, 1987. Reprinted by permission of Harry Towne.

Train conductor. Letter to the *Ladies' Home Journal*. December 23, 1922. In *The Uncertain World of Normalcy: The 1920s*, ed. Paul A. Carter, pp. 151–52. New York: Pitman Publishing Corporation, Jerome S. Ozer, 1971.

"Travelers." Note to Jackie Robinson. May 22, 1951. In Jules Tygiel, *Baseball's Great Experiment: Jackie Robinson and His Legacy*, p. 10 of photographs. New York: Oxford University Press, 1983.

Trillin, Calvin. Letter to Dominique Richard. March 16, 1984. Printed by permission of Calvin Trillin.

Truman, Harry. Letter to his mother and sister. May 8, 1945. In *Letters to Mother: An Anthology*, ed. Charles Van Doren, pp. 305–306. Great Neck, N.Y.: Channel Press, 1959.

———. Note to Henry Stimson. July 31, 1945. In David McCullough, *Truman*, p. 448, and photo, between pp. 288 and 289. New York: Simon & Schuster, 1992.

———. Letter to Paul Hume. December 6, 1950. In David McCullough, *Truman*, p. 829. New York: Simon & Schuster, 1992.

Trumbo, Dalton. Letter to a motion picture associate. December 30, 1947. In *Additional Dialogue: Letters of Dalton Trumbo, 1942–1962* ed. Helen Manfull, pp. 68–69. New York: M. Evans, 1970. Reprinted by permission of Cleo Trumbo.

Tumulty, Joseph. Note to W.E.B. Du Bois. October 17, 1916. In *The Correspondence of W.E.B. Du Bois*, vol. 1, *Selections, 1877–1934*, ed. Herbert Aptheker, pp. 218–19. Amherst: University of Massachusetts Press, 1973.

Twain, Mark. Letter to Edward Dimmitt. July 19, 1901. In *Mark Twain's Letters, Volume II*, ed. Albert Bigelow Paine, pp. 708–709. New York: Harper and Brothers, 1917.

———. Letter to the president of New York's Western Union. Summer, 1902. In *Mark Twain's Letters, Volume II*, ed. Albert Bigelow Paine, pp. 722–26. New York: Harper and Brothers, 1917.

Tyler, Elizabeth Stearns. Letter to Miss R. November 7, 1918. In *Letters of Elizabeth Stearns Tyler*, pp. 26–28. Norwood, Mass.: Plimpton Press, privately printed, 1920.

Tynan, Kenneth. Letter to Johnny Carson. April 22, 1979. In *Theatrical Letters: 400 Years of Correspondence Between Celebrated Actors, Actresses, Playwrights, Their Families, Friends, Lovers, Admirers, Enemies, Producers, Managers and Others*, ed. Bill Homewood, pp. 246–47. London: Marginalia Press, 1995. From *Kenneth Tynan: Letters*, edited by Kathleen Tynan. Copyright © 1998 by the estate of Kenneth Tynan. Reprinted by permission of Random House.

Underwood, Walter. Letter to Frank Knox. February 18, 1942. In House Committee Investigating National Defense Migration, *Hearings Before the Select Committee Investigating National Defense Migration Pursuant to H. Res. 113*, 77th Cong., 1st sess., p. 11318. Washington, D.C.: U.S. Government Printing Office, 1942.

Unemployed worker. Letter to Franklin Roosevelt. July 31, 1934. In Robert S. McElvaine, *Down & Out in the Great Depression: Letters from the Forgotten Man,* pp. 84–85. Chapel Hill: University of North Carolina Press, 1983. Copyright © 1983 by the University of North Carolina Press. Reprinted by permission of the publisher.

Unwed mother. Letter to Valeria Parker. June 23, 1938. In Folder 11:1, Florence Crittenton Collection, Social Welfare History Archives, University of Minnesota-Twin Cities. Printed by permission of the University.

Valachi, Joseph. Letter to Peter Maas. February 16, 1969. In the Joseph Valachi Papers, John Fitzgerald Kennedy Library, Boston, Mass.

Van Doren, Carl. Letter to his mother. April 1, 1909. In *Letters to Mother: An Anthology*, ed. Charles Van Doren, pp. 156–57. New York: Channel Press, 1959. Reprinted by permission of Barbara Van Doren Klaw. All rights reserved.

Van Vechten, Carl. Letter to Theodore Dreiser. January 19, 1923. In *Letters of Carl Van Vechten*, ed. Bruce Kellner, p. 48. New Haven: Yale University Press, 1987. Reprinted by permission of the estate of Carl Van Vechten.

Vanzetti, Bartolomeo. Letter to Dante Sacco. August 21, 1927. In Marion D. Frankfurter and Gardner Jackson, *Letters of Sacco and Vanzetti*, pp. 431–32. New York: Viking, 1928. Copyright © 1928, renewed © 1955 by the Viking Press. Reprinted by permission of Viking Penguin, a division of Penguin Books USA Inc.

Wainwright, Jonathan. Letter to Franklin Roosevelt. May 6, 1942. In *General Wainwright's Story: The Account of Four Years of Humiliating Defeat, Surrender, and Captivity*, ed. Robert Considine, pp. 122–23. Garden City, N.Y.: Doubleday, 1946.

Ward, Robert. Letter to his mother. December 1, 1950. In *Letters in American History: Words to Remember, 1770 to the Present*, ed. H. Jack Lang, pp 105–106. New York: Harmony Books, 1982.

Washington, Booker T. Letter to the *Birmingham Age-Herald*. February 27, 1904. In "A Protest Against the Burning and Lynching of Negroes," African American Perspectives: Pamphlets from the Daniel A. P. Murray Collection, Library of Congress. On-line at http://lcweb2.loc. gov/cgi-bin/query/D?aap:8:/temp/~ammem_kplj::;E449 .D16 vol. 20, no. 6. April 12, 1999.

Watson, James. Letter to Max Delbrück. March 12, 1953. In California Institute of Technology Archives, Pasadena, Calif. Reprinted by permission of James Watson.

Westbrook, Daisy. Letter to Louise Madella. July 19, 1917. In *Journal of the Illinois State Historical Society*, pp. 328–30. Springfield: Illinois State Historical Society, 1972. Reprinted by permission of the Society.

Wharton, Edith. Letter to W. Morton Fullerton. Winter, 1910. In *The Letters of Edith Wharton*, ed. R.W.B. Lewis and Nancy Lewis, pp. 197–99. New York: Scribner's, 1988. Reprinted by permission of the estate of Edith Wharton and the Watkins/Loomis Agency.

White, E. B. Memo to William Shawn. July 9, 1944. In *Letters of E. B. White*, ed. Dorothy Lobrano Guth, pp. 262–63. New York: Harper and Row, 1976. Copyright © 1976 by E. B. White. Reprinted by permission of HarperCollins Publishers.

White, Edmund. Letter to Ann and Alfred Corn. July 8, 1969. In *The Violet Quill Reader: The Emergence of Gay Writing After Stonewall*, ed. David Bergman, pp. 1–4. New York: St. Martin's Press, 1994. Reprinted by permission of Edmund White.

White, Hugh. Telegram to the NAACP. August 31, 1955. In Sanford Wexler, *The Civil Rights Movement: An Eyewitness History*, p. 62. New York: Facts on File, 1993.

White, Walter. Telegram to David Sholtz. October 26, 1934. In Lynching File, Series 278, Florida State Archives, Tallahassee, Fla.

White, William Allen. Letter to Gabriel Wells. February 26, 1927. In *Selected Letters of William Allen White, 1899–1943*, ed. Walter Johnson, pp. 266–67. New York: Henry Holt and Company, 1947. Reprinted by permission of Barbara White Walker.

Wilder, Laura Ingalls. Letter to her husband. September 21, 1915. In *West From Home: Letters of Laura Ingalls Wilder to Almanzo Wilder, San Francisco, 1915*, ed. Roger Leo MacBride, pp. 59–63. New York: Harper and Row, 1974. Copyright © 1974 by Roger Leo MacBride. Reprinted by permission of HarperCollins Publishers.

Williams, William Carlos. Letter to his son. March 13, 1935. In *Selected Letters of William Carols Williams*, ed. John C. Thirlwall, pp. 153–55. 1957. Reprint, New York: New Directions, 1984. Copyright © 1957 by William Carlos Williams. Reprinted by permission of the publisher.

Wilson, Woodrow. Letter to Edith Galt. August 26, 1915. In *A President in Love: The Courtship Letters of Woodrow Wilson and Edith Bolling Galt*, ed. Edwin Tribble, pp. 160–61. Boston: Houghton Mifflin, 1981.

Winslow, Rose. Notes to her husband and friends. December, 1917. In *Nonviolence in America: A Documentary History*, ed. Staughton Lynd and Alice Lynd, pp. 87–89. Maryknoll, N.Y.: Orbis Books, 1995.

Winter, Paul. Letter to Alfred Smith. December 23, 1927. In "New York's Culture and Society," *Uniquely New York: A Virtual Exhibit*, New York State Archives and Records Administration. On-line at http://unix6.nysed.gov/virtual/exhibit/culture-klanlet.jpg. April 14, 1999.

Wolfe, Thomas. Letter to Maxwell Perkins. August 12, 1938. In *Editor to Author: The Letters of Maxwell E. Perkins*, ed. John Hall Wheelock, p. 141. Dunwoody, Ga.: Norman S. Berg, 1977. Copyright © 1950 by Charles Scribner's Sons, renewed 1978 by John Hall Wheelock. Reprinted by permission of Scribner, a division of Simon & Schuster.

Wolfe, Tom. Letter to the editor of *New York*. April 25, 1965. In "Aftermath: Tom Wolfe on The New Yorker," *New York: The Sunday Herald Tribune Magazine*, April 25, 1965, p. 22. Reprinted by permission of Tom Wolfe.

Woodstock volunteers. Notice to visitors. August 17?, 1969. In "Woodstock Miscellaneous," *1969 Woodstock Festival & Concert*. On-line at http://www.woodstock69.com/woodstock_misc.htm. August, 1998.

Woollcott, Alexander. Letter to Paul Harper. November 22, 1935. In *The Letters of Alexander Woollcott*, ed. Beatrice Kaufman and Joseph Hennessey, pp. 152–55. New York: Viking, 1944. Copyright © 1944 by the Viking Press. Reprinted by permission of Viking Penguin, a division of Penguin Putnam.

————. Letter to Walt Disney. January 12, 1942. In *The Letters of Alexander Woollcott*, ed. Beatrice Kaufman and Joseph Hennessey, pp. 292–93. New York: Viking, 1944. Copyright © 1944 by the Viking Press. Reprinted by permission of Viking Penguin, a division of Penguin Putnam.

Wright, Frank Lloyd. Letter to Edgar Kaufmann. August 30, 1936. In *Letters to Clients: Frank Lloyd Wright*, ed. Bruce Brooks Pfeiffer, pp. 98–99. Fresno: The Press at California State University, 1986. The letters of Frank Lloyd Wright are copyright © 1998 by the Frank Lloyd Wright Foundation. Reprinted by permission of the Foundation.

Wright, Orville. Telegram to his father. December 17, 1903. In "Selected Documents Celebrating the Manuscript Division's First 100 Years," *Words and Deeds in American History*, American Memory Collection, Library of Congress. On-line at http://memory.loc.gov/cgi-bin/query/r?ammem/mcc:@field(DOCID+@lit(mcc/061)).

Yale student. Letter to Carry Nation. October, 1902. In Herbert Asbury, *Carry Nation*, p. 267. New York: Knopf, 1929.

Zeldin, Isaiah. Letter to Kimba Wood. September 4, 1990. In *United States of America v. Michael R. Milken*, U.S. District Court, Southern District of New York, Number SS 89 Cr. 41, Appendix A. 1990.

Zimmermann, Arthur. Telegram to Johann von Bernstorff. January 19, 1917. In *Documents of American History*, ed. Henry Steele Commager, p. 128. New York: Meredith Corporation, 1973.

A good-faith effort has been made to secure the permission to reprint all of the letters in this book. In a small number of instances, particularly with letters from the early part of this century, we have been unable to locate the copyright holder despite our efforts. In such instances, the copyright holders are welcome to contact us through our publisher, and we will be glad to include the proper copyright information in all future editions of the book. If any copyright holders have been accidentally overlooked, we offer our sincere apologies.

ADDITIONAL SOURCES

This list includes reference works that we consulted for the chapter openings, as well as books in which we found partial versions of, or references to, some letters that we later found in more complete forms.

Allen, Everett S. *The Black Ships: Rumrunners of Prohibition.* Boston: Little, Brown and Company, 1965.

Clark, Cindy Dell. *Flights of Fancy, Leaps of Faith: Children's Myths in Contemporary America.* Chicago: University of Chicago Press, 1995.

Culbert, David. *Film and Propaganda in America: A Documentary History,* Vol. II, *World War I,* ed. Richad Wood. New York: Greenwood Press, 1990.

Daniel, Clifton, ed. *Chronicle of America.* New York: DK Publishing. 1997.

Davidson, Cathy N., ed. *The Book of Love: Writers and Their Love Letters.* New York: Pocket Books, 1992.

Desmond, Kevin. *A Timetable of Inventions and Discoveries: From Pre-History to the Present Day.* New York: M. Evans, 1986.

Encyclopædia Britannica Online.

Eskridge, William N., Jr. *The Case for Same-Sex Marriage: From Sexual Liberty to Civilized Commitment.* New York: Free Press, 1996.

Ferrell, Robert H., ed. *The Twentieth Century: An Almanac.* New York: World Almanac Publications, 1985.

Friedel, Robert. *Zipper: An Exploration in Novelty.* New York: Norton, 1994.

Glennon, Lorraine, ed. *Our Times: The Illustrated History of the 20th Century.* Atlanta: Turner Publishing, 1995.

Gould, Tony. *A Summer Plague: Polio and Its Survivors.* New Haven: Yale University Press, 1995.

Knappman, Edward W., ed. *Great American Trials: From Salem Witchcraft to Rodney King.* Detriot: Gale Research, Visible Ink Press, 1994.

Ladd-Taylor, Molly, ed. *Raising a Baby the Government Way: Mothers' Letters to the Children's Bureau, 1915–1932.* New Brunswick, N.J.: Rutgers University Press, 1986.

Levine, Bruce, et. al., eds. *Who Built America? Working People and the Nation's Economy, Politics, Culture, and Society,* vol. 2. New York: Pantheon, 1989.

Maas, Peter. *The Valachi Papers.* New York: Putnam, Bantam Books, 1968.

Markowitz, Gerald and David Rosner. *"Slaves of the Depression": Workers' Letters About Life on the Job.* Ithaca, N.Y.: Cornell University Press, 1987.

McGovern, James R. *Anatomy of a Lynching: The Killing of Claude Neal.* Baton Rouge: Louisiana State University Press, 1982.

New York Public Library. *American History Desk Reference.* New York: Macmillan, Stonesong Press, 1997.

Olby, Robert C. *The Path to the Double Helix.* Seattle: University of Washington Press, 1974.

Parsons, Nicholas. *A Letter Does Not Blush: A Collection of the Most Moving, Entertaining and Remarkable Letters in History.* London: Buchan and Enright, 1984.

Rothman, Sheila M. *Living in the Shadow of Death: Tuberculosis and the Social Experience of Illness in American History.* New York: BasicBooks, 1994.

Salzman, Jack, ed. *The Cambridge Handbook of American Literature.* Cambridge, England: Cambridge University Press, 1986.

Schuster, M. Lincoln, ed. *A Treasury of the World's Great Letters.* New York: Simon & Schuster, 1968.

Sherr, Lynn. *Failure Is Impossible: Susan B. Anthony in Her Own Words.* New York: Times Books, 1995.

Steffens, Lincoln. *The Letters of Lincoln Steffens,* Volume 1, *1899–1919,* ed. Ella Winter. 1938. Reprint, Westport, Conn.: Greenwood Press, 1974.

Stevens, Doris. *Jailed for Freedom.* Troutdale, Ore: NewSage Press, 1995.

Trager, James. *The People's Chronology.* Henry Holt and Company. 1994. Microsoft Works and Bookshelf, '94. CD-ROM.

Urdang, Laurence, ed. *The Timetables of American History.* 1981. Reprint, New York: Simon & Schuster, Touchstone, 1996.

Valentine, Alan, ed. *Fathers to Sons: Advice Without Consent.* Norman: University of Oklahoma Press, 1963.

Vernoff, Edward, and Rima Shore. *The International Dictionary of 20th Century Biography.* New York: New American Library, 1987.

Photo Credits

1900–1909:

1. First Flight, Kitty Hawk, North Carolina, December 17, 1903. Photograph by John T. Daniels. Courtesy of the Library of Congress (LC).

2. The Palace Theatre nickelodeon, Washington, D.C., ca. 1900. Photograph by a *Washington Post* staff photographer. LC.

3. Little Orphan Annie in a Pittsburgh institution, 1909. Photograph by Lewis Hine. LC.

4. Carry Nation. Drawing courtesy of UPI/Corbis-Bettmann. (UPI.)

5. Evelyn Nesbit. Photograph courtesy of UPI.

6. Theodore Roosevelt on Glacier Point, Yosemite Valley, California, 1904. LC.

7. Mark Twain. Photograph by Alvin F. Bradley, Sr. LC.

8. A frontier wife gathering buffalo chips on the plains. UPI.

9. Immigrants at Ellis Island. "There Is the Land of Freedom," ca. 1900. UPI.

10. Patent-medicine advertisement. "Tired Nervous Mothers." From Arthur J. Cramp, M.D., *Nostrums and Quackery: Articles on the Nostrum Evil, Quackery and Allied Matters Affecting the Public Health; Reprinted, With or Without Modifications, from The Journal of the American Medical Association, Volume II.* Chicago: Press of American Medical Association, 1921, p. 161.

1910–1919:

11. *The Birth of a Nation* film poster. LC.

12. Woodrow Wilson delivering his inaugural address, 1917. Photograph by Leven C. Handy. LC.

13. W.E.B. Du Bois, 1915. UPI.

14. John Reed. Photograph by Pirie MacDonald. LC.

15. Night attack with phosphorous bomb, Goudrecourt, France, August 15, 1918. Photograph by J. J. Marshall. U.S.A. Signal Corps. LC.

16. War poster. "Wake Up, America." LC.

17. Suffragists marching to the Capitol, April 7, 1913. Photograph by W. R. Ross. LC.

18. Harry Houdini preparing to submerge. LC.

19. Laura Ingalls Wilder. UPI.

20. The *Titanic* leaving Queenstown, England, 1912. UPI.

1920–1929:

21. Prohibition tombstone. LC.

22. George Washington Carver with a student in his Tuskegee Institute laboratory. UPI.

23. Charlie Chaplin and Jackie Coogan in *The Kid*, 1920. LC.

24. Sacco and Vanzetti. LC.

25. F. Scott and Zelda Fitzgerald, ca. 1923. Photograph by Alfred Cheney Johnston. UPI.

26. Amelia Earhart, 1920. UPI.

27. Bathing beauties. LC.

28. Margaret Sanger. UPI.

29. The stock market crash. James N. Rosenberg lithograph. "October 29—*DIES IRAE*." LC.

30. An early radio. LC.

1930–1939:

31. An apple seller's sign during the Depression. UPI.

32. Social Security poster. "A monthly check to you." Poster by C. Newman. LC.

33. Margaret Mitchell. Photograph by William F. Warnecke. LC.

34. Albert Einstein, 1931. UPI.

35. The Dust Bowl. Farmer and sons walking in the face of a dust storm, Cimarron County, Oklahoma, April 1936. Photograph by Arthur Rothstein. LC.

36. The *Hindenburg* in flames, May 6, 1937. UPI.

37. Al Capone's mug shot, Miami Police Department, 1930. UPI.

38. George Balanchine. Photograph by Henri Cartier-Bresson. Magnum Photos.

39. The New York World's Fair, 1939. Photograph by Alice Mumford Culin. LC.

1940–1949:

40. December 8, 1941, headline, *New York World-Telegram,* UPI.

41. Ben Shahn FDR poster. "Our Friend—National Citizens Political Action Committee." LC.

42. The Marx brothers in *A Night in Casablanca,* 1946. UPI.

43. Coast Guardsman Robert O'Connell writes home to Grosse Pointe, Michigan, on the eve of D day. UPI.

44. Thomas Hart Benton war poster. "Back Him Up! Buy War Bonds." LC.

45. Clyde Tolson and J. Edgar Hoover. UPI.

46. Nagasaki, August 1945. UPI.

47. Dumbo. From the film by Walt Disney. © Walt Disney/LGC.

48. Levittown, Long Island. UPI.

49. ENIAC. UPI.

1950–1959:

50. Campaign buttons. UPI.

51. Map of Korea. G. Braundorf. LC.

52. Elvis Presley on RCA Victor record jacket, 1956. LC.

53. Joseph McCarthy. Senate Historical Office. LC.

54. Marilyn Monroe. UPI.

55. Polio poster by Herbert Matter. LC.

56. Model of DNA molecule. UPI.

57. Jack Kerouac, ca. 1958. UPI.

58. The Edsel, 1958. UPI.

59. Howdy Doody. UPI.

1960–1969:

60. Nixon-Kennedy debate, 1960. LC.

61. John F. Kennedy, Jr., St. Matthew's Cathedral, Washington, D.C., November 25, 1963. UPI.

62. Martin Luther King, Jr., delivers his "I Have a Dream" speech at the March on Washington, August 28, 1963. UPI.

63. Mickey Mantle baseball card. UPI.

64. James Baldwin, January 1963. UPI.

65. The Beatles, November 1963. UPI.

66. The moon landing, July 20, 1969. UPI.

67. "Woodstock." Poster by Arnold Skolnick. LC.

68. Sgt. John Autenrieth of Valparaiso, Indiana, reads Christmas mail at Chu Lai, South Vietnam. Photograph by Ian Wilson. UPI.

69. Andy Warhol with a self-portrait. UPI.

1970–1979:

70. Kent State poster. "Avenge" LC.

71. Richard Nixon leaving the White House, August 9, 1974. UPI.

72. Graduation day at the University of Massachusetts, Amherst, May 1970. UPI.

73. McDonald's arches. UPI.

74. Gloria Steinem, 1972. UPI.

75. Saturn's rings. Photograph courtesy of NASA.

76. Carroll O' Connor as Archie Bunker in *All in the Family*. UPI.

77. Patricia Hearst in the Symbionese Liberation Army, 1974. UPI.

78. John Travolta in *Saturday Night Fever*, 1978. UPI.

1980–1989:

79. Michael Jackson, 1987. UPI.

80. *Jane Fonda's Workout Book,* Simon & Schuster, 1981.

81. Jimmy Swaggart repents on television, 1988. UPI.

82. The *Challenger* explodes. January 28, 1986. NASA.

83. Ronald Reagan being fitted with a microphone, 1980. UPI.

84. The Vietnam War Memorial, Washington, D.C. Photograph by Erich Hartmann. Courtesy of Magnum.

85. Michael Milken, 1989. UPI.

86. Donald Trump with his model of Television City, New York, 1985. UPI.

87. Rock Hudson in *All That Heaven Allows*. LC.

88. The baby boom's baby boom. Editors' collection.

1990–1999:

89. Magic Johnson, 1985. UPI.

90. Lee Atwater and George Bush, 1990. Photograph by Cliff Owen. UPI.

91. Oprah Winfrey, 1991. UPI.

92. *Titanic,* 1998. Leonardo DiCaprio and Kate Winslet in Paramount Pictures/Courtesy Neal Peters Collection.

93. Lyle and Erik Menendez on trial for murder, 1991. UPI.

94. Mike Tyson. Photograph by Charlie Blagdon. UPI.

95. Jerry Seinfeld receives an honorary doctorate from Queens College, New York, 1994. UPI.

96. Bill Clinton and Al Gore in Little Rock, Arkansas, 1992. UPI.

97. Monica Lewinsky. UPI.

98. Gay marriage. Reuters/Blake Sell/Archive Photos

Acknowledgments

For help in suggesting and/or locating letters, we'd like to offer our enthusiastic thanks to Dr. Jeanne Abrams at the University of Denver Center for Judaic Studies; John Austin at the Illinois State Historical Society; Dan Barber; Mary Bogen at the William Allen White Library; Andrew Carroll; Susan Dayall at the Harold F. Johnson Library Center, Hampshire College; John Gregory Dunne; Polly Dwyer at the Levittown Historical Society; Chuck Eberling at the McDonald's Corporation; Shelley Erwin at the California Institute of Technology; Darleen Flaherty at the Ford Industrial Archives; Martin Flumenbaum; Margaret Harter at the Kinsey Institute; Alix Freedman; David Friend; Judy Goodstein at the CalTech Institute Archives; Louise Grunwald; John Helyar; Bill Hooper at the Time, Inc. archives; Patricia Hopkins at the Archives and Records Management Division, Office of the Secretary of State, Olympia, Washington; Suzanne Huff at the City of Provo, Utah, Library; David Klassen at the Social Welfare History Archives, University of Minnesota; Edward Kamuda at the Titanic Historical Society; Aaron Kornblum at the U.S. Holocaust Memorial Museum Archives; Dr. Jonathan LaPook; Roger Launius at NASA; Carol Leadenham at the Hoover Institution, Stanford University; Kate Lear; Nancy Lyon at the Yale University Library archives; Peter Maas; Alex Magoun at the Sarnoff Corporation; Sean McCandless at the Crawford County Historical Society; Jim McGrath at the office of George Bush; Harold Miller at the State Historical Society of Wisconsin; Michael Moss; Susan Moldow; Albert Nason at the Jimmy Carter Library; Becky Okrent; Scot Paltrow; Darrell Salk; E. Cheryle Schnirring at the Illinois State Historical Library; Tony Seaton at the Orange County Cocaine Anonymous; Linda Seelke at the Lyndon Baines Johnson Library and Museum; Greg Shaw at the Microsoft Corporation; Lynn Sherr; Evelyn Small in the office of Katharine Graham; D. Ryan Smith at the

Texas Energy Museum; Raymond Teichman at the Franklin D. Roosevelt Library; Rosemary Wells at the Tooth Fairy Museum; Tim Wilson at the San Francisco Public Library; Matt Wrbican at the Andy Warhol Museum; Rebecca Zisch at the Rock and Roll Hall of Fame and Museum; and the Grunwalds, Adlers, and Coopers.

Adam Bialow did a tireless and truly inspired job in helping us secure the rights. Chris Jerome brought insight, speed, and humor to the job of copyediting. Working with photo editor Vincent Virga was a gift: both an education and a joy. Maya Gurantz offered much-needed last-minute research, and Fred Courtright much-needed last-minute contract work. Rachel Silverman, through her imaginative and energetic efforts, found some of the best letters in the book. And Donna Ash offered invaluable assistance, sometimes by helping with the book directly, sometimes by keeping our children busy, always by adding cheer to our home.

In addition to all these people, we would like to thank Suzie Bolotin, Betsy Carter, Lee Eisenberg, Dan Okrent, and Michael Solomon for reading parts of the book in various stages and offering their wisdom and friendship.

Liz Darhansoff and Kathy Robbins, whom we are so lucky to have as our agents, combined forces to represent us on this book. We will always remember the afternoon we used four telephones to talk about the prospects for the book. Our respect for their shared and separate talents grew deeper during this project, which we hadn't thought possible.

Finally, and most important, Susan Kamil understood this book, and eagerly wanted us to do it, from the moment she first heard about it. We will be lastingly grateful for her generosity, her patience, and her transcendent enthusiasm.

Index